Controversies in Globalization

Controversies in Globalization

CONTENDING APPROACHES TO INTERNATIONAL RELATIONS

EDITED BY

Peter M. Haas, John A. Hird, and Beth McBratney

University of Massachusetts, Amherst

CQ PRESS

A Division of SAGE
Washington, D.C.

CQ Press
2300 N Street, NW, Suite 800
Washington, DC 20037

Phone: 202-729-1900; toll-free, 1-866-4CQ-PRESS (1-866-427-7737)

Web: www.cqpress.com

Cover design: Kimberly Glyder
Composition: Auburn Associates, Inc.

⊚ The paper used in this publication exceeds the requirements of the American National Standard for Information Sciences—Permanence of Paper for Printed Library Materials, ANSI Z39.48-1992.

Printed and bound in the United States of America

13   12   11   10   09   1   2   3   4   5

Library of Congress Cataloging-in-Publication Data

Controversies in globalization : contending approaches to international relations / edited by Peter Haas, John Hird, and Beth McBratney.
        p. cm.
    ISBN 978-0-87289-505-8 (alk. paper)
    1. Globalization.   I. Haas, Peter M.   II. Hird, John A.   III. McBratney, Beth.
IV. Title.

    JZ1318.C6577 2009
    327—dc22

                                                                          2009003337

CONTENTS

CONTRIBUTORS

ABOUT THE EDITORS

Peter M. Haas is professor at the University of Massachusetts, Amherst. He is a member of the editorial boards of *Journal of European Public Policy; Global Environmental Politics;* and the MIT Press series on *Politics, Science, and the Environment.* Haas's books include *Emerging Forces in Environmental Governance* (with Norichika Kanie, 2004); *The International Environment in the New Global Economy* (with Edward Elgar, 2003); *Knowledge, Power, and International Policy Coordination* (1997); *Institutions for the Earth* (with Robert O. Keohane and Marc A. Levy, 1993); and *Saving the Mediterranean* (1990).

John A. Hird is professor of political science and department chair at the University of Massachusetts, Amherst. He has served at the Brookings Institution and on the President's Council of Economic Advisers. He is the first recipient of the Mills Award from the Policy Studies Organization for an outstanding contributor to policy studies under age 35. His books include *Power, Knowledge, and Politics: Policy Analysis in the States* (2005); *Controversies in American Public Policy* (with Michael A. Reese and Matthew Shilvock, 2003); and *Superfund: The Political Economy of Environmental Risk* (1994).

Beth McBratney holds a master's degree in public policy and administration and a bachelor's degree in history from the University of Massachusetts, Amherst. Her principal interest is the impact of globalization on policy and international development. She currently lives in Switzerland and is chief administrator for a charitable foundation focused on development and social issues in Russia.

ABOUT THE CONTRIBUTORS

Kenneth Anderson is professor of law at Washington College of Law, American University, and a fellow of the Hoover Institution at Stanford University. He was formerly general counsel to the Open Society Institute and was founding director of the Human Rights Watch Arms Division. He has written widely in scholarly and policy journals, is a member of the editorial board of the *Journal of Terrorism and Political Violence*, and was legal editor of *Crimes of War* (1999).

Kwame Anthony Appiah is Laurance S. Rockefeller University Professor of Philosophy at the Center for Human Values at Princeton University. His books include two monographs in the philosophy of language, as well as *In My Father's House: Africa in the Philosophy of Culture* (1992), *Color Conscious: The Political Morality of Race* (with Amy Gutmann, 1996), and *Cosmopolitanism: Ethics in a World of Strangers* (2006). He has also edited or coedited many books, including *Africana: The Encyclopedia of the African and African-American Experience* (with Henry Louis Gates Jr., 1996). His most recent book is *Experiments in Ethics* (2008).

Scott Atran is director of research in anthropology at the National Center for Scientific Research in Paris, Presidential Scholar in Sociology at John Jay College of Criminal Justice in New York City, and visiting professor of psychology and public policy at the University of Michigan. Atran's broadly interdisciplinary scientific studies have been featured around the world in science publications, such as *Science, Nature, Proceedings of the National Academy of Sciences USA,* and *Brain and Behavioral Sciences,* as well as in the popular press, including feature stories on BBC television and radio, NPR, the *Wall Street Journal, Newsweek* and the *New York Times Magazine.* His books include *Cognitive Foundations of Natural History: Towards an Anthropology of Science* (1990), *In Gods We Trust: The Evolutionary Landscape of Religion* (2002), *The Native Mind and the Cultural Construction of Nature* (with Douglas Edin, 2008), and *Talking to the Enemy* (forthcoming).

George B.N. Ayittey, a native of Ghana, is Distinguished Economist at American University and president of the Free Africa Foundation. He was nominated for the Africa Prize for Leadership by *The Times of London,* was a National Fellow at the Hoover Institution, Stanford University, and a Bradley Scholar at the Heritage Foundation. In 1993 he started the Free Africa Foundation to serve as a catalyst for reform in Africa. An internationally renowned authority on Africa, Ayittey has written several books, including *Africa Betrayed* (1992), which won the H. L. Mencken Award for "Best Book for 1992." His latest book is *Africa Unchained* (2005). A frequent contributor to the *Wall Street Journal* and the *Los Angeles Times,* he has written numerous book chapters and articles on Africa. He has also appeared on several radio talk shows and television programs and has testified before many U.S. congressional committees.

Ruth Greenspan Bell is a senior fellow in the Climate & Energy program at World Resources Institute. Previously, she was a senior adviser to the Assistant Secretary of State for Oceans and International Environmental and Scientific Affairs, and held various domestic management positions in the U.S. EPA's

Office of General Counsel. Bell's publications address policy and environmental audiences (articles in *Foreign Affairs, Issues in Science and Technology, Environment,* and *Harvard International Review,* among them) with the view to impact policy and to seek innovative solutions. Bell is a member of several boards, including the Environmental Alliance, 2020Vision, the Mountain Institute, and the Alumni Board of University of California (Boalt Hall) School of Law, and a long-standing member of the Council on Foreign Relations.

Nancy Birdsall is the founding president of the Center for Global Development. Previously, she served for three years as senior associate and director of the Economic Reform Project at the Carnegie Endowment for International Peace, where her work focused on issues of globalization and inequality, as well as on the reform of the international financial institutions. From 1993 to 1998, Birdsall was executive vice president of the Inter-American Development Bank. Prior to that, she spent fourteen years in research, policy, and management positions at the World Bank, most recently as director of the Policy Research Department. Birdsall is the author, coauthor, or editor of more than a dozen books and over 100 articles in scholarly journals and monographs, published in English and Spanish. Shorter pieces of her writing have appeared in dozens of U.S. and Latin American newspapers and periodicals. She holds a PhD in economics from Yale University.

Simon Chesterman is Global Professor and director of the New York University School of Law Singapore Programme, and an associate professor of law at the National University of Singapore Faculty of Law. His books include *Law and Practice of the United Nations* (with Thomas M. Franck and David M. Malone, 2008); *From Mercenaries to Market: The Rise and Regulation of Private Military Companies* (editor, with Chia Lehnardt, 2007); *Secretary or General? The UN Secretary-General in World Politics* (editor, 2007); *You, The People: The United Nations, Transitional Administration, and State-Building* (2004); and *Just War or Just Peace? Humanitarian Intervention and International Law* (2001).

Isobel Coleman is senior fellow for U.S. foreign policy at the Council on Foreign Relations and director of its Women and Foreign Policy program. Her areas of expertise include economic and political development in the Middle East, regional gender issues, educational reform, and microfinance. In 2006 she coauthored (with A. Lawrence Chickering, P. Edward Haley, and Emily Vargas-Baron) *Strategic Foreign Assistance: Civil Society in International Security.* Her forthcoming book, *Paradise Beneath Her Feet: Women and Reform in the Middle*

East, will be published in 2009. Prior to joining the Council, Coleman was CEO of a health care services company and a partner with McKinsey & Co. in New York. She was formerly a research fellow at the Brookings Institution and an adjunct professor at American University, where she taught political economy. A Marshall Scholar, she holds a DPhil and an MPhil in international relations from Oxford University and a BA in public policy and East Asian studies from Princeton University.

David Dollar has been World Bank country director for China and Mongolia, based in Beijing, since July 2004. He speaks and writes frequently on economic, environmental, and social issues in China. Prior to moving to China, Dollar spent eight years in the research department of the World Bank. He was the World Bank country economist for Vietnam from 1989 to 1995, a period of intense reform and structural adjustment. Before joining the Bank, Dollar taught in the economics department at University of California, Los Angeles (UCLA) and spent the spring semester of 1986 on a Ford Foundation program teaching economics at the Chinese Academy of Social Sciences in Beijing. He has a PhD in economics from NYU and a BA in Chinese language and history from Dartmouth College. He has published a wide range of studies on issues of globalization, trade and growth, investment climate, and growth and poverty.

Jack Donnelly is the Andrew Mellon Professor at the Joseph Korbel School of International Studies, University of Denver. The author of three books and over sixty articles and book chapters on the theory and practice of human rights, including *Universal Human Rights in Theory and Practice* (2nd ed., 2003), he is best known for his work on the concept of human rights, cultural relativism, development and human rights, international human rights regimes, and human rights and foreign policy. He has also published in the area of international relations theory, including *Realism and International Relations* (2000). He is currently working on two major projects: a book on politics in Homeric Greece—a prelude to a planned study of ancient Greek international society—and a series of articles leading to a book on rethinking the nature of structural theory in international relations.

Christopher Flavin is president of the Worldwatch Institute, an international research organization that focuses on innovative solutions to global environmental problems. Flavin is a leading voice on the potential for new energy options and strategies to replace fossil fuels, thereby increasing energy security and avoiding dangerous climate change. He is coauthor of three books on energy, including *Power Surge: Guide to the Coming Energy Revolution* (with

Nicholas Lenssen, 1994), which anticipated many of the changes now underway in world energy markets. Flavin is a founding member of the board of
directors of the Business Council for Sustainable Energy and serves as a board
member of the Climate Institute. He is on the advisory boards of the American
Council on Renewable Energy and the Environmental and Energy Study
Institute. He is also a member of the Greentech Innovation Network, an initiative of the venture capital firm, Kleiner Perkins Caufield & Byers.

Francis Fukuyama is the Bernard L. Schwartz Professor of International Political Economy at the Paul H. Nitze School of Advanced International
Studies (SAIS) of Johns Hopkins University, and the director of its
International Development Program. He is also chairman of the editorial
board of *The American Interest*. His book, *The End of History and the Last Man*
(1992), has appeared in over twenty foreign editions and made the best-seller
lists in the United States, France, Japan, and Chile; it has been awarded the *Los
Angeles Times*'s Book Critics Award in the Current Interest category, as well as
the Premio Capri for the Italian edition. Fukuyama is the author of several
other books, including *State-Building: Governance and World Order in the 21st
Century* (2004), *America at the Crossroads: Democracy, Power, and the
Neoconservative Legacy* (2006), and *Falling Behind: Explaining the Development
Gap between Latin America and the United States* (2008).

Laurie Garrett is senior fellow for global health at the Council on Foreign
Relations in New York. She is the only writer ever to have been awarded all
three of the Big "Ps" of journalism: the Peabody, the Polk, and the Pulitzer.
Garrett is also author of the best-selling book, *The Coming Plague: Newly
Emerging Diseases in a World Out of Balance* (1994) and *Betrayal of Trust: The
Collapse of Global Public Health* (2001). At the Council on Foreign Relations,
Garrett has written several reports and articles including: *HIV and National
Security: Where Are the Links? A Council Report* (2005); "The Next Pandemic?"
(*Foreign Affairs*, July–August 2005); "The Lessons of HIV/AIDS" (*Foreign Af-
fairs*, July–August 2005); and "The Challenge of Global Health" (*Foreign
Affairs*, January–February 2007). A member of the National Association of
Science Writers, Garrett served as the organization's president during the mid-
1990s. She serves on the advisory boards for the Noguchi Prize, the François-
Xavier Bagnoud Center for Health and Human Rights, and the Health Worker
Global Policy Advisory Group.

Marlies Glasius is a lecturer in international relations at the School for
Social and Behavioural Sciences at the University of Amsterdam and a visiting

fellow at the Centre for the Study of Global Governance, London School of Economics and Political Science. She is the author of *The International Criminal Court: A Global Civil Society Achievement* (2006) and a founding editor of the *Global Civil Society Yearbook.*

Indur M. Goklany has worked with the U.S. Department of the Interior, federal and state government, think tanks, and the private sector for over thirty years. He has been involved with the Intergovernmental Panel on Climate Change and was part of the U.S. team that negotiated the UN Framework Convention on Climate Change. He was chief of the Technical Assessment Division of the National Commission on Air Quality and managed the emissions-trading program in the Environmental Protection Agency before it became the vogue. He was also the first Julian Simon Fellow at the Property and Environment Research Center, a visiting fellow at the American Enterprise Institute, and the winner of the Julian Simon Prize and Award in 2007. He is the author of, among other books, *The Precautionary Principle: A Critical Appraisal of Environmental Risk Assessment* (2001) and *The Improving State of the World: Why We're Living Longer, Healthier, More Comfortable Lives on a Cleaner Planet* (2007).

John D. Graham is dean of the Indiana University School of Public and Environmental Affairs. He is the author of seven books and 200 articles on health, safety, and environmental issues. Graham founded and led the Harvard Center for Risk Analysis from 1990 to 2001; during that time, he was elected president of the Society for Risk Analysis, an international membership organization of 2,400 scientists and engineers. Graham reached out to risk analysts in Europe, China, Japan, and Australia as he helped to organize the first World Congress on Risk Analysis (Brussels, 2000). From 2001 to 2006, he served as the Senate-confirmed administrator of the Office of Information and Regulatory Affairs, White House Office of Management and Budget. From March 2006 to July 2008, he was dean of the Frederick Pardee RAND Graduate School in Santa Monica, California.

Marcia Greenberg is adjunct professor of law at the Cornell Law School, where she teaches courses on international perspectives on law and social change as well as international women's rights. She received her JD from Northwestern University School of Law and a master's of law and diplomacy from the Fletcher School of Law and Diplomacy at Tufts University. Her law-related work has included litigation on labor and employment cases, and human rights work for the Reebok Corporation and the Robert F. Kennedy Center for Human Rights. For more than a decade, she has focused on gender mainstreaming in relation to democracy programs, post-conflict reconstruction, community development, youth development, and food security. She has worked with women's groups in Eastern Europe on the five-year review of the Beijing Platform for Action, undertaken gender assessments of U.S. programs in Eastern Europe and Africa, and evaluated gender mainstreaming for the United Nations Development Programme and the World Food Programme.

Mark Heywood is executive director of the AIDS Law Project (ALP) and an executive member of the Treatment Action Campaign (TAC); he has worked for the ALP since 1994 and was one of the founders of the TAC. He is an editor of *HIV/AIDS and the Law: Resource Manual* (3rd ed., 2003), as well as a coeditor of *Health and Democracy: A Guide to Health, Law and Policy in Post-apartheid South Africa* (2007) and *The National Health Act, a Guide* (2008). He has published more than 100 articles on legal, ethical, and human rights questions linked to HIV/AIDS and health.

James F. Hollifield is professor and director of the Tower Center for Political Studies at Southern Methodist University. He is a member of the Council on Foreign Relations; has worked as a consultant on trade, migration, and development for the UN, the World Bank, and OECD; and has published widely on these issues, including *Immigrants, Markets, and States* (1992), *L'immigration et l'État Nation* (1997), *Controlling Immigration* (2nd ed., 2004), *Migration Theory: Talking Across Disciplines* (2nd ed., 2008), and *International Political Economy: History, Theory, and Policy* (forthcoming).

Michael Lynch is president of Strategic Energy and Economic Research. He has combined bachelor of science and master's degrees in political science from the Massachusetts Institute of Technology (MIT), and he has performed a variety of studies related to international energy matters, including forecasting of the world oil market, energy and security, and corporate strategy in the energy industries, as well as analysis of oil and gas supply. He is a former Chief Energy Economist at DRI-WEFA, Inc., a leading economic consulting firm, and a past-president and senior fellow of the United States Association for Energy Economics. His publications have appeared in eight languages, and he serves on several editorial boards, including those of the journals *Energy Policy* and *Geopolitics of Energy*.

Edward D. Mansfield is Hum Rosen Professor of Political Science and director of the Christopher H. Browne Center for International Politics at the University of Pennsylvania. His research focuses on international security and international political economy. He is the author of *Power, Trade, and War* (1994) and the coauthor of *Electing to Fight: Why Emerging Democracies Go to War* (with Jack Snyder, 2005). He has edited ten books and has published over seventy articles in various journals and books. The recipient of the 2000 Karl W. Deutsch Award in International Relations and Peace Research, Mansfield has been a National Fellow at the Hoover Institution. He is coeditor of the University of Michigan Press Series on international political economy and an associate editor of the journal *International Organization.*

Philip Martin is a labor economist in the Department of Agricultural and Resource Economics at the University of California, Davis (UCD). After graduating from the University of Wisconsin–Madison, he worked at the Brookings Institution and the White House on labor and immigration issues. He has worked for the World Bank, IMF, and UN agencies such as the ILO and UNDP in countries around the world, and is the author of numerous articles and books on labor and immigration issues. Martin's research focuses on farm labor and rural poverty, labor migration and economic development, and immigration policy and guest worker issues; he has testified before Congress and state and local agencies numerous times on these issues. Martin is the editor of *Migration News* and *Rural Migration News,* and he received UCD's Distinguished Public Service award in 1994.

Michael McFaul was named senior director for Russian affairs at the National Security Council in 2009. Previously, he served as the director of the Center on Democracy, Development, and Rule of Law at Freeman Spogli Institute for International Studies at Stanford University and as the Peter and Helen Bing Senior Fellow at the Hoover Institution, where he codirected the Iran Democracy Project. He is the author of several books and monographs, most recently, *The Democratic Imperative: Why and How the United States Should Support Democratic Development around the World* (2009). McFaul's current research interests include democracy promotion, comparative democratization, and the relationship between political and economic reform in the postcommunist world.

John Mueller holds the Woody Hayes Chair of National Security Studies, Mershon Center, and is professor of political science at Ohio State University, where he teaches courses in international relations. His most recent book, *Overblown* (2006), deals with exaggerations of national security threats, particularly terrorism. Among his other books are *The Remnants of War* (2004), *Retreat from Doomsday* (1996), and *War, Presidents and Public Opinion* (1973).

Sarah Olmstead is a doctoral fellow in policy analysis at the Pardee RAND Graduate School (PRGS), where she studies issues related to energy and the environment. Prior to coming to PRGS, she was at the Science and Human Rights Program of the American Association for the Advancement of Science, where she worked on such diverse topics as using geospatial technologies to identify large-scale human rights violations; using social and economic indicators and budget analysis to examine governments' fulfillment of rights under national international conventions; and assessing the effectiveness of transitional justice mechanisms. She has an master's degree in physics from the University of Minnesota and a bachelor's degree in physics from Harvey Mudd College. Olmstead also worked at the Los Alamos Neutron Science Center, with the Parliamentary Monitoring Group and the Black Sash in South Africa, and in the Dominican Republic with the Movimiento de Mujeres Dominico-Haitiana.

Jeffrey Sachs is director of The Earth Institute, Quetelet Professor of Sustainable Development, and professor of health policy and management at the Earth Institute at Columbia University. He is also Special Advisor to UN Secretary-General Ban Ki-moon. From 2002 to 2006, he was director of the UN Millennium Project and Special Advisor to UN Secretary-General Kofi Annan on the Millennium Development Goals. Sachs is also president and cofounder of Millennium Promise Alliance, a nonprofit organization aimed at ending extreme global poverty. For more than twenty years, Sachs has been in the forefront of the challenges of economic development, poverty alleviation, and enlightened globalization, promoting policies to help all parts of the world to benefit from expanding economic opportunities and well-being. He is the author of hundreds of scholarly articles and many books, including the *New York Times* best-sellers *Common Wealth: Economics for a Crowded Planet* (2008) and *The End of Poverty* (2005).

Scott D. Sagan is professor of political science at Stanford University and codirector of Stanford's Center for International Security and Cooperation. He has served as a special assistant to the director of the Organization of the Joint Chiefs of Staff in the Pentagon and as a consultant to the Office of the Secretary of Defense, the National Intelligence Council, Sandia National Laboratory, and Los Alamos National Laboratory. He has authored a number of books, including *Moving Targets: Nuclear Strategy and National Security* (1989) and *The Limits of Safety: Organizations, Accidents, and Nuclear Weapons* (1993), winner of the American Political Science Association's award for best book in science, technology, and environmental studies. Sagan was the recipient of Stanford University's 1996 Hoagland Prize for Undergraduate Teaching and the 1998

Dean's Award for Distinguished Teaching. He cofounded (with Steven Stedman) Stanford's Interschool Honors Program in International Security Studies in 2000.

Kammerle Schneider is assistant director of the Global Health Program at the Council on Foreign Relations in New York. Previously she was a Refugee/ Internally Displaced Persons Program officer for the USAID-funded Extending Service Delivery Project, where she managed the agency's activities to extend reproductive health and family-planning services to refugees and displaced persons. Prior to this experience, she held successive internships at Americans for UNFPA (United Nations Population Fund) and the International Centre for Migration and Health in Geneva. She served as a Peace Corps volunteer in Guatemala from 2001 until 2003. Schneider holds a master of international affairs with a concentration in Health and Development from Columbia University, and a BA from the University of Washington.

Todd S. Sechser is assistant professor of politics at the University of Virginia. His publications include articles about nuclear weapons safety, civil-military relations, and European-American relations, and he is currently writing a book about the effectiveness of coercive threats. Sechser holds a PhD in political science from Stanford University and a BA in economics, political science, and international relations from Drake University.

Jack Snyder is the Robert and Renée Belfer Professor of International Relations in the political science department and the Saltzman Institute of War and Peace Studies at Columbia University. His books include *Electing to Fight: Why Emerging Democracies Go to War* (with Edward D. Mansfield, 2005); *From Voting to Violence: Democratization and Nationalist Conflict* (2000); and *Myths of Empire: Domestic Politics and International Ambition* (1991). His articles have appeared in *Foreign Affairs, Foreign Policy*, and academic journals. He is a fellow of the American Academy of Arts and Sciences.

Elsa Stamatopoulou is chief of the Secretariat of the UN Permanent Forum on Indigenous Issues. She has worked for more than twenty years in the human rights field at the UN, publishing and lecturing extensively. In recent years, a major focus of her efforts has been on integrating indigenous peoples' issues and human rights in development and peace processes, as well as development with culture. She is the founder and member of human rights and other NGOs and has been recognized by various awards. She obtained her law degree from the University of Athens Law School and entered the Athens Bar Association.

She did her master's studies in the administration of criminal justice at Northeastern University in Boston, and her doctoral studies in political science with specialization in international law at the University Institute of Graduate International Studies, University of Geneva, as well as additional graduate training at the University of Vienna. In 2007 she published *Cultural Rights in International Law.*

Samuel Thernstrom is resident fellow at the American Enterprise Institute (AEI) for Public Policy in Washington, D.C., where he is the codirector of a program exploring the policy implications of geoengineering. Prior to coming to AEI in 2003, Thernstrom served as director of communications for the White House Council on Environmental Quality. Previously, he was a speechwriter for New York governor George E. Pataki, a press secretary for the New York State Department of Environmental Conservation, and chief speechwriter at the U.S. Department of Labor. Thernstrom is a frequent guest on radio and television, commenting on climate policy for National Public Radio, BBC News, ABC News, CNN, Fox News, and *The NewsHour with Jim Lehrer* on PBS. He was educated at Harvard University.

Kate Vyborny was a program coordinator for Nancy Birdsall, president of the Center for Global Development. She was previously a junior fellow for trade, equity, and development at the Carnegie Endowment for International Peace. She is currently a Rhodes Scholar and a graduate student in economics at the University of Oxford.

Robert H. Wade is professor of political economy at the London School of Economics and Political Science, and winner of the Leontief Prize in Economics for 2008. His research and writing have taken him from Italy to South Korea (*Irrigation and Agricultural Politics in South Korea*, 1982), India (*Village Republics*, 1988, 2007), East Asia more generally (*Governing the Market*, 1990, 2004), the World Bank ("Greening the Bank", in *The World Bank*, vol. 2, ed. D. Kapur et al., 1997), the world economy and global governance ("Globalization, Growth, Poverty, Inequality, Resentment and Imperialism," in *Global Political Economy*, ed. J. Ravenhill, 2008), and financial crises ("Financial Regime Change?" *New Left Review*, September–October 2008).

Josh A. Weddle is a second-year law student at Stanford Law School. Previously, he researched nuclear proliferation in Iran and South Asia while serving as assistant to director Scott D. Sagan at Stanford's Center for International Security and Cooperation. In 2004, he graduated with highest honors in political science and mathematics from the University of Georgia, where he focused on nuclear nonproliferation studies.

L. Alan Winters is professor of economics at the University of Sussex. He is a research fellow and former program director of the Centre for Economic Policy Research in London and fellow of the Institute for the Study of Labor in Munich. From 2004 to 2007, he was director of the Development Research Group of the World Bank, where he had previously been division chief and research manager (1994–1999) and economist (1983–1985). He has been editor of the *World Bank Economic Review* and associate editor of the *Economic Journal*, and currently he is editor of *The World Trade Review*. He has also advised, inter alia, the Organization for Economic Cooperation and Development, the UK Department for International Development, the Commonwealth Secretariat, the European Commission, the European Parliament, the United Nations Conference on Trade and Development, the World Trade Organization, and the Inter-American Development Bank.

PREFACE

Globalization is variously viewed as the solution to national economic problems, the scourge of the developing world, the source of job dislocations and economic stratification in the wealthy West, the means to more interesting culture and food, the path to lower consumer prices, and just about anything else reflecting the increasingly international character of society, politics, and economics. It is said—theoretically and with a touch of hyperbole—that a butterfly's movements can bring about a hurricane half a world away. While this metaphor exaggerates the extent of life's global interconnections, it is clear that they are a prominent feature of the lives of the world's citizens and environment. How we understand, adapt, and act toward trends in globalization will condition the impacts they have on the world's human and natural environment. Because the term *globalization* is both vague and ubiquitous, it offers a convenient catchall for what we like and dislike about the past and future integration of our economies, politics, and cultures.

There are plenty of books on globalization, and yet we believe that an important gap remains because many fail to fully appreciate the various dimensions of and perspectives on the subject. This gap derives in part from the polemical nature of much that has been written about globalization, and in part from the simplistic assertions and beliefs that too often prevail as a result. This book seeks to acknowledge that the most important issues involving globalization—whether they involve trade, security, the environment, the role of women in development, or a host of other crucial matters—are best understood and addressed by recognizing the different perspectives (or discourses) through which they are viewed. We seek to illuminate *some* of these perspectives here, and we hope that the recognition that reasonable people can and do disagree on important matters will spur our readers to seek additional views, both complementary and competing, than just those elucidated here.

It is no secret that many view globalization warily: a BBC worldwide poll showed that half of respondents believed that economic globalization and trade were growing too quickly, while only a third felt that such growth was moving too slowly. In G7 countries, fully 57 percent said that globalization was moving too quickly. Nonetheless, according to the Pew Global Attitudes survey, vast majorities of the world's population believe that trade is beneficial, and even multinational corporations are generally viewed favorably. According to the Pew poll, free markets are widely accepted in much of the world, although Americans and Western Europeans are less receptive to globalization than they were five years ago, particularly in the United States, Italy, France, and Great Britain.

Interestingly, the generally supportive view of economic globalization does not translate to immigration, which many worldwide believe should be restricted. For example, fully three-quarters of U.S. respondents—as well as 87 percent of Italians, 89 percent of South Africans, and large percentages elsewhere—support further restrictions and controls on immigration. Of forty-seven countries surveyed, in only three (South Korea, the Palestinian territories, and Japan) did a majority of the public favor more immigration, while majorities in all forty-seven had favorable views of international trade. (The United States had the least support for free trade among these countries, with just 59 percent.) Thus, even in polls conducted prior to the economic deterioration that became apparent in late 2008, the world's citizens clearly had mixed views on how far and in which directions globalization should go.

We hope that this book will be of interest to students, as well as to a more general audience of readers who seek to expand their understanding of globalization by examining the opposing perspectives of scholars and practitioners engaged in thoughtful debate.

HOW THE BOOK IS ORGANIZED

This book is geared to courses in international relations, world or global politics, and other topics that cover globalization more generally. The controversies format is intended to highlight important issues involved in contemporary globalization and to expose readers to the intellectual underpinning of the debates. Instructors should remind students that for each controversy, these are but two of the possible perspectives. Students should be encouraged to read further to understand other views and to begin to develop their own.

The book is organized around a series of fifteen issues that we believe are among the most important in the globalization debate. For each general topic, we provide a brief introductory overview and some frames of reference, as well as a few discussion questions that are intended to stimulate dialogue in class. Each chapter then offers original articles crafted by some of the world's leading scholars in response to a question that highlights a specific issue. Through these articles, we seek to promote the recognition that debates about globalization are not simply about self-interest but involve the clash of values and ideas.

Students should remain aware of several points about this book's depiction of globalization. First, although each chapter's controversy is treated separately, there are important relationships between these controversies that instructors should explore and discuss in class. For example, what is the relationship between globalization's impacts on economic growth and democracy, or on the role of women in society? Second, we have isolated fifteen topics that we believe are central to an understanding of globalization, but instructors and students may choose to concentrate instead on their interconnections—such as the relationship of immigration to national security or economic growth—as well as on other areas not covered in this volume. Finally, and perhaps most importantly, there are many other perspectives on globalization to be explored and developed. The two perspectives presented in each chapter here should be only the beginning of an exploration of alternative views that extends far beyond this book. The glossary at the end of the book defines many of the more technical terms and deciphers acronyms presented throughout.

ACKNOWLEDGMENTS

We are indebted to many for their help in developing this book. We would like to thank our families for indulging our curious pursuit of the meaning of globalization. This book emerged, in part, from the ongoing hiring initiative on contemporary political change in the University of Massachusetts, Amherst, Department of Political Science, which is organized around cross-field themes: global forces; governance and institutions; and democracy, participation, and citizenship. We continue to benefit from the lively intellectual atmosphere in the department. We would like to thank the editors and staff at CQ Press, who have been a joy to work with, and, in particular, Charisse Kiino for helping us to bring this book to fruition. Allyson Rudolph, Katharine Miller, and Allison McKay were everything we could ask for in helping to move the book through production. We received valuable feedback from Charli Carpenter (of UMass, Amherst), Craig Murphy (of Wellesley College), and two reviewers enlisted by CQ Press: Michael Colaresi, of the University of Colorado, and Faten Ghosn, of the University of Arizona. We also had superb research assistance along the way from Rachel Jackson and Sorin Dan. We would like to thank for their financial support the Dean of the College of Social and Behavioral Sciences as well as the Center for Public Policy and Administration at UMass, Amherst. Finally, the Dirty Truth in Northampton, Massachusetts, served as an excellent venue for hashing out many of the ideas in this volume, sustaining our efforts with great food and an outstanding beer selection that reflects one of the benefits of a globalized world.

UNDERSTANDING GLOBALIZATION

We have witnessed three economic transformations in the
past century. First came the Industrial Revolution, then the
technology revolution, then our modern era of globalization.

UN Secretary-General Ban Ki-moon,
Washington Post, December 3, 2007

Globalization is a reality, not a choice or a policy. But how we respond
to it is a matter of choice and of policy.

Richard N. Haass, director, Office of the Policy Planning Staff,
"Remarks to the National Defense University," September 21, 2001

Globalization has become the political lodestone of contemporary international relations. Political positions and political identities are defined in
light of their orientation to it. Yet definitions of globalization abound, and the
consequences of globalization are deeply contested—as are the available techniques for altering the distribution of its costs and benefits. At the heart of
globalization is an array of multiple transboundary forces and processes that
reduce national control over what happens within national boundaries and
enable a set of new political actors to project social, economic, and political
influence over long distances. Globalization includes a host of problems or
issues that do not respect national boundaries—they are, as some have written,
"problems without passports." Since national governments remain the primary
legal authorities at the international and national levels, this transnational
impact represents a considerable challenge to governance and to the international political system.

It is no wonder that globalization is controversial. The term itself is subject
to multiple interpretations, as well as measurements, chronologies, and explanations. As a result, any fixed definition of globalization remains elusive, and
the multiple definitions that exist tend to highlight whatever features its proponents (or opponents) want to emphasize. Contending understandings of
international relations provide alternative interpretations of the consequences
of globalization, and, indeed, of the desirability and even the possibility of
effectively guiding such an unwieldy set of global forces. The consequences of
globalization are also significant. Just as Charles Lindblom defined politics as a
matter of who gets what, when, how, and why, globalization forces influence
the systematic distribution of who gets what, when, how, and why.

Thus, groups that are inconvenienced by some set of social, cultural, economic, or political setbacks now have a vocabulary and a frame for assigning meaning and blame to their misfortune: globalization did it. Yet, because it is so widely contested a term, who and what one reads on globalization can color its meaning for those seeking to understand their own experiences, and how to change them. Thus, "globalization" may become a proxy for opposition to the Iraq War, for xenophobia, for worries about one's own job security, for fears of cultural hegemony, or for fears about the ecological health of the planet.

In order to frame the debate on this elusive topic, we review here, first, the core elements of globalization; next, the history of globalization; then, some contending perspectives on globalization; and, finally, the various implications or effects of globalization on citizens' lives and on the major political processes that influence citizens' lives worldwide. In this introduction we focus on the sets of forces that characterize globalization, rather than presuming the effects to which those forces may contribute or be associated, such as the end of space and spatial divisions as meaningful categories in international politics (see Held and McGrew 1999; Scholte 2000; and Rosenau 2003). We do, however, discuss some of the possible effects of globalization itself, from alternative perspectives.

WHAT'S NEW ABOUT GLOBALIZATION?

Scholars dispute the origins of globalization. Some historians claim that aspects of globalization have been present always—or at least since the Industrial Revolution. International economic interdependence was high from the 1880s through World War I, during which period, proportions of national reliance on foreign sources of trade for markets, and capital markets for investment, were similar to current levels. Migration flows were significant—indeed, the American transcontinental railroads would not have been built without the cheap labor of Chinese immigrants.

So what is new about globalization? Observers in the late nineteenth and early twentieth centuries painted a similar picture, reflecting unprecedented volumes of international commerce—trade, financial exchanges—and flows of people. Indeed, the most extreme drops in the cost of transportation and communication occurred in the late nineteenth century. Pandemics were also global—the influenza epidemic of 1918 killed millions of people across Europe and the United States. Possibly, it was only the incomplete global nature of telecommunications that impaired our understanding of widespread health conditions in the developing world.

John Maynard Keynes wrote in 1919:

> The inhabitant of London could order by telephone, sipping his morning tea in bed, the various products of the whole earth, in such quantity as he might see fit, and reasonably expect their early delivery upon his doorstep: he could at the same moment and by the same means adventure his wealth in the natural resources and new enterprises of any quarter of the world, and share, without exertion or even trouble, in their prospective fruits and advantages; or he could decide to couple the security of his fortunes with the good faith of the townspeople of any substantial municipality in any continent that fancy or information might recommend. He could secure forthwith, if he wished it, cheap and comfortable means of transit to any country or climate without passport or other formality, could dispatch his servant to the neighboring office of a bank for such supply of the precious metals as might seem convenient, and could proceed abroad to foreign quarters, without knowledge of their religion, language, or customs, being coined wealth [*sic*] upon his person, and would consider himself greatly aggrieved and much surprised at the least interference. But, most important of all, he regarded this state of affairs as normal, certain, and permanent, except in the direction of further improvement, and any deviation from it as aberrant, scandalous, and avoidable. (quoted in Frieden 2006, 28)

The possible effects of globalization during this early period were depicted in hyperbolic terms, similar to those employed in the contemporary era. Norman Angell argued that high levels of economic interdependence would lead to the end of war, because the cost of severing valued economic ties would simply be too great. As with many of the grandiloquent claims for the effects of globalization in the current era, these projections were proved painfully false by the outbreak of World Wars I and II.

Still, there are several new key developments in the current era of globalization. The spread of political actors—in numbers and types—is new. Foreign investment has shifted from portfolio to equity investment and, more recently, to global production lines. The increasingly universal acceptance of democratic and liberal values appears to be another distinguishing feature of our contemporary era of globalization. Environmental globalization is also increasingly important: global resource depredation and ecosystem collapse may be irreversible.

The most important aspect of contemporary globalization may be the pace of individual globalization processes—what we have amounts to a synchronicity of acceleration (Crutzen 2002; Schellnhuber and Crutzen et al. 2004). Whereas, in the past, globalization was primarily economic and demographic, over the past forty years the scope of global forces has increased to include environmental and political globalization. Although rates of technological change themselves may not have changed, the speed of globalization has accelerated, making the elapsed time between a decision taken in one part of the world and its effects elsewhere far shorter than it has been in the past.

With synchronicity has come a transformation in the nature of international relations. As the world has become more complex and uncertain, surprises such as the recent pace of climate change and the 2008 global financial melt-down are more likely to occur frequently. New forms of threats to national security have also received attention.

Thomas Pickering, a U.S. diplomat, identified three major foreign threats to U.S. security: financial crisis, accidental nuclear exchange, and environmental dangers. None are geographic, but all are global functional threats. Ernesto Zedillo, a former president of Mexico, concurs, listing the following prospects as potentially destabilizing threats from globalization: financial crises triggered by persistent U.S. balance-of-payments imbalances; tariff wars; public health pandemics; nuclear exchanges; and climate change (Zedillo 2008, 10–11).

Another aspect of acceleration is the declining longevity of power concen-trations internationally. The Roman Empire lasted roughly five hundred years, and the Ottoman Empire nearly seven hundred years. Spain, France, and England each prevailed as superpowers for periods between one hundred and one hundred and fifty years. U.S. dominance lasted perhaps sixty years. To the extent that the United States was deemed "imperial" following the collapse of the Soviet Union in 1991, the American empire had to be one of the shortest on record, having dissipated by 2004, when its imperial overstretch in Iraq undermined its ability to claim legitimacy for its efforts to lead the interna-tional community (Brzezinski 2007, 3).

There is a "chicken or the egg" dimension to understanding that globaliza-tion is driven both by physical forces such as technology and trade (which reduce the costs of long-distance transactions and make them more attractive to citizens in individual countries) and by social forces (which create and rein-force the physical forces themselves). Groups that benefit from economic globalization—such as those that specialize in the production of tradable goods (agricultural or manufactured) and foreign investment—become polit-ical supporters of globalization and seek to promote policies that will cement its forces in place. For example, lower flying costs spur greater international air travel by the general public, which in turn creates political and cultural demands for its continuation. Similarly, lower costs of trade stimulate more trade and also create coalitions in participating nations in support of addi-tional trade.

Globalization is most commonly experienced through a variety of more tan-gible social pressures. Among the many international forces commonly identi-fied as the drivers of globalization are these:

- Technological innovation

- Economic interdependence/expansion

- Demographic dispersion

- Political diversification

- Environmental degradation/concern

- Ideational convergence (aspirations and doctrines of management)

TECHNOLOGICAL INNOVATION

At its heart, globalization occurs by means of advancing technology. Starting with the Industrial Revolution, developments in communication and transportation greatly facilitated contact and commerce over long distances, while the use of fossil fuels allowed for far greater industrial productivity. Transport over long distances was eased by the invention of the steamship, the building of railroads, the opening of canals (Suez in 1869, Panama in 1914), and the introduction of refrigeration (which allowed more products to travel long distances, such as beef exported from Argentina to England and the United States). Communications advances included the telegraph (whose reach was greatly extended in 1850 by the first Atlantic cable linking the United States and England) and the telephone; by the 1870s, both technologies had spread broadly. The historian Tim Blanning estimates that until the late nineteenth century, most information and goods flowed at the pace of walking on rutted tracks—perhaps 2 to 2.5 miles per hour—while horse livery might go as fast as 20 mph. Today, goods travel greater distances and far faster, and the pace of information flows is nearly instantaneous in much of the world.

Technological change continued apace throughout the twentieth century, as containerization, airplanes, fiber optics, and satellite telecommunications further drove down the cost of long-distance transport and communication. The average cost of freight and port charges fell from $90 per ton in 1920 to roughly $25 in 1980 and $30 in 1990. The cost of a three-minute telephone call between London and New York fell from $250 in 1930 to $31 in 1970 to $3 in 1990 (in real, inflation-adjusted, terms)—the precipitous rate of reduction contributing to a doubling of phone traffic between 1988 and 1993.

The pace of innovation and dissemination of new technologies has accelerated as new generations of technologies are brought online. It took thirty-eight years from the inception of radio to its adoption by 50 million users, but similar transitions required only sixteen years for the personal computer, thirteen

GLOBALIZATION IN ACTION
CULTURE-CROSSING MUSIC AND FOOD

Globalization, as popularized in the mass media and scholarly press since the late twentieth century, has come to refer to the integration of international trade. The intended exchange of goods is invariably accompanied by integration of cultural elements as well. In music, this exchange has resulted in hybrid forms and ensembles. It is not rare in contemporary music to hear an electric sitar featured on a Brazilian pop record, or raga rhythms employed by a jazz composer. As these eclectic ensembles and compositional approaches evolve, their development is accompanied by controversy between the adherents of purism and those who advocate cultural mixing as an inevitable and desirable part of artistic advancement. Does such integration diminish the purity of the traditional musical cultures that gave birth to the current generation of hybrids?

However, while the concept of globalization may be a modern one when used in a purely economic context, the concept of culture accompanying the international exchange of goods is as old as the human urge to travel. Eleventh-century trouvères brought North African musical influences with them to France and Spain, and ancient trade routes likewise encircled the Sahara desert for centuries, leaving an enduring cultural legacy, as well as the intended (though arguably more temporary) economic one. And what well-known musical form could be said to have more cross-cultural roots than the blues? Taken in this larger context of human history, was Duke Ellington's 1966 "Far East Suite" (or its subsequent remake by Anthony Brown employing indigenous Asian instruments) really a product of a different impulse?

In addition to hybrid forms of music, globalization has spawned entirely new cuisines. The proximity of peoples triggered by migration has given rise to a variety of fusion cuisines now popular in the United States and Europe, including French-Asian, pan-Asian, and Cuban-Chinese restaurants and dishes. Consequently, a diverse array of fresh and processed international foods are now available in Western supermarkets, expanding the parameters of the American diet and creating more jobs in agriculture in the developing world.

An interesting related phenomenon is the spread of American fast-food restaurants to foreign countries, where they have had to adjust their menus and presentations to accommodate local tastes and cultures. For instance, KFC tried to expand to India, but found the Hindu market resistant to chicken cooked in lard; ultimately, the Colonel learned to serve curries. Similarly, McDonalds alters its condiments and offerings to reflect local tastes. Despite such efforts to adapt to foreign markets, there remains widespread concern, in terms of health, economics, and cultural identity, about the spread of American fast food worldwide.

Source: Andrew W. Jaffe, Lyell B. Clay Artist-in-Residence in Jazz and Director of Jazz Performance, Williams College.

years for television, and four years for the World Wide Web. In real terms, the cost per mile of air passenger travel today is less than one-tenth the amount required in the mid-1920s. In each case, the upshot of these forces was to create new proximities: people were in closer contact with another—physically through travel, and symbolically through access to each other's goods, music, Internet sites, and movies.

But such technical forces are not the only driving forces behind globalization, which is reinforced as well by social institutions that governments have created to accelerate globalization and to stimulate technological change. For instance, the gold standard in the nineteenth century and the Bretton Woods set of international institutions in the twentieth century greatly accelerated the spread of economic globalization, by providing incentives for firms to conduct business across long distances. Similar institutional support encouraged the flow of people, although to a lesser extent.

EXPANDED ECONOMIC INTERDEPENDENCE

Economic globalization involves growing interdependence among national economies across various forms of commercial exchange: trade, finance and investment, and flows of people.

Trade

National economies have become increasingly reliant on one another. Volumes of international trade have grown dramatically since World War II, at nearly three times the rate of national economic growth, on average. Figure 1 shows this increase in international trade contrasted with growth in gross domestic product (GDP). Tariffs also dropped during this period, showing the intent of governments to reduce barriers to trade.

Trade has grown across the board as a share of GDP. Consequently, individual countries are increasingly reliant on other countries to purchase their goods, thus providing the demand for goods that stimulates jobs and economic growth. Figure 2 shows the increasing share that trade has played in the U.S. economy. The United States is more subject to foreign influence than it was in the past, but is still less vulnerable than are most other countries. By the late 1990s, commerce with other countries accounted for nearly 25 percent of U.S. national income (measured as GNP). By international standards, this is a relatively low reliance on other countries, thus insulating the United States to some extent from decisions taken abroad. On the other hand, the share of foreign influence over the U.S. economy has grown dramatically since World War II,

Figure 1

Growth in Real World Exports and GDP after World War II

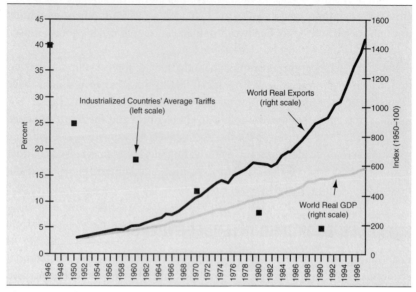

Source: Joseph Grieco. "The International Political Economy since World War II," prepared for the CIAO Curriculum Case Study Project, October 2000, exhibit 1.
Note: The squares denote industrialized countries' average tariffs (left scale). Tariff reduction is part of trade liberalization, promoting growth in exports.

reducing the ability of U.S. politicians to make decisions independently of their colleagues abroad. Economic policies made by U.S. trading partners may influence the demand for U.S. products, as well as employment in the related sectors of the U.S. economy. Conversely, because the impact of trade on the United States is still relatively low, its leaders may feel freer than those of other countries to use instruments of trade policy (such as tariffs, quotas, embargoes, and subsidies).

The nature of international trade and production has changed over the past five decades. A vast proportion of what is recorded as trade is actually intrafirm transfers, between affiliates within a corporation. For example, General Motors may import computer technology for its automobiles from Southeast Asia into Mexico, for assembly there before selling the finished product in the United States. Beyond such internal transfers, much of the sale of goods between countries consists of partnerships and supply chains, wherein a company sells a partially finished product or component to a foreign company with which it has a long-standing contractual relationship. Consequently, trade may actually

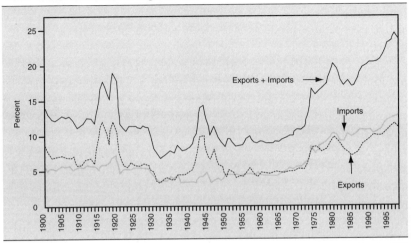

Figure 2

U.S. Trade as a Percentage of GNP

Source: Joseph Grieco. "The International Political Economy since World War II," prepared for the CIAO Curriculum Case Study Project, October 2000, exhibit 2.

be a set of international relationships, in which the partners have long-standing commitments to one another and learn about markets and production from one another.

Considered in this light, trade is a social relationship that can contribute to forms of social learning, as well as to simple commercial exchange. As we will see in the substantive chapters of this volume, different interpretations are available as well. Such supply chains can be seen as exploitative, when those at the bottom end have no choice but to continually cut costs, trim their labor force, reduce wages, and otherwise make sacrifices to keep their partners happy. This negative view of supply chains has been termed the "Wal-Mart Effect" (Fishman 2006).

Investment

Another aspect of economic globalization is the growing ability of countries to borrow abroad. Since banking deregulation in the 1960s—and especially since 1995—capital flows worldwide have grown dramatically. The International Monetary Fund (IMF) records that gross global capital flows rose from $1.5 trillion in 1995 (about 3 percent of world GDP) to $12 trillion in 2005 (15 percent of world GDP).[1] Capital flows encompass foreign investment by companies, as well as public and private purchases of government securities. To a large extent, the United States has been able to sustain government deficits by selling its debt and treasury bonds to other governments, sovereign wealth funds, and private firms. By 1994 capital inflows accounted for about 9 percent of U.S. gross national product (GNP)—well above the historical average, as can be seen in figure 3.

More generally, firms and governments have been able to pay for fixed capital formation (basically the money to pay for building infrastructure) by means of borrowing abroad. Infrastructure, because it includes the physical apparatus for production and transportation—airports, railroads, highways, power plants, mobile phone networks, electricity grids, and fiber optic cables—is key to long-term sustainable development. Worldwide, direct foreign investment (DFI) as a percentage of gross fixed capital formation (GFCF) grew from a little over 2 percent in 1980 to over 7 percent by 1997, for all geographic regions. GFCF is the total of construction, so the share of imported capital to pay for all construction projects provides an insight into how foreign firms' investment decisions can influence broader infrastructure development in other countries.

Figure 3

Direct Foreign Investment: Inflows and Outflows by Region

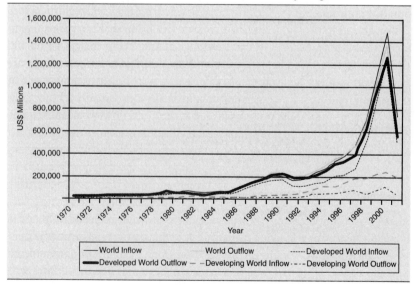

Source: Joseph Grieco. "The International Political Economy since World War II," prepared for the CIAO Curriculum Case Study Project, October 2000, exhibit 5.

GLOBALIZATION IN ACTION

CAMPAIGNING FOR THE ENVIRONMENT ON THE GLOBAL STAGE

The diffusion of global media and institutions allows nongovernmental organizations (NGOs) to deftly apply political pressure and effect change, especially in the environmental realm. In 1995 Shell Oil decided to dispose of the aged *Brent Spar* oil-storage buoy on the seabed of the North Sea. Greenpeace International believed that this decision was environmentally destructive, and that disposal was better done on land. Unable to secure any political influence over Shell in England, where the government supported Shell's decision, Greenpeace quickly shifted the target of its campaign and launched a consumer boycott against Shell Oil in Germany, where the company had a substantial market share and consumers were environmentally aware. Fearful of losing significant profits in Germany, Shell reversed its position within weeks and chose to dispose of the *Brent Spar* onshore, where it was soon being dismantled. A few years later, the governments of nations in the northern Atlantic region imposed a ban on seabed disposal of oil platforms in the North Sea. By leveraging its international presence and refocusing its campaign in Germany, Greenpeace International effectively swayed both a global corporation and an international regulating body to achieve its environmental goal.

When NGOs are unable to exercise direct influence in one locale, they can apply their influence in other venues and over other political actors who may be able to influence their target. Political scientists Katharine Sikkink and Margaret Keck have dubbed this tactic the "boomerang effect." One example is the effort in the late 1980s by the U.S.-based Environmental Defense Fund (EDF) to reverse policies of the Brazilian government that were encouraging rapid deforestation of the Amazonian rain forest, often with loans from the World Bank. Unable to gain any direct political purchase within Brazil, the EDF instead successfully lobbied the U.S. Congress to threaten to withhold U.S. contributions to World Bank–funded projects that had environmentally destructive effects.

In turn, the World Bank adopted a number of internal reforms to make its own lending practices more environmentally friendly, including withholding money that had been targeted for the construction of a key road project in Brazil's program for opening up the Amazon to economic development. Thus, like Greenpeace's boycott of Shell Oil, EDF's strategy took advantage of the interrelatedness of institutions on the global stage, following a serpentine route in influencing a previously unresponsive government and thus accomplishing policy change.

Source: Bruce Rich, *Mortgaging the Earth* (Boston: Beacon Press, 1995).

Internationally, DFI has grown from around US$100 billion in 1970 to US$1.5 trillion in 2000, followed by a dip and growth back by 2007 (see figure 3). A booming Chinese economy is increasingly attracting DFI. But DFI is no longer exclusively the purview of the industrialized countries. Tata Industries, India's largest manufacturing company (and one of the world's largest), is, according to its executive director, "surfing the tsunami of globalization." Over the past seven years, Tata spent US$18 billion buying thirty-seven companies in other countries.

DEMOGRAPHIC DISPERSION

Many patterns of social movement contribute to globalization. Larger numbers of people are mobile across national borders than ever before. Total tourist flows worldwide have risen from around 180 million in 1970 to 650 million in 1999.

Immigration is a major factor contributing to globalization. The decade 1990–1999 saw the largest number of people (some 10 million) moving internationally, exceeding the previous highest-migration decade—8 million people between 1900 and 1909—by about 25 percent. Most migrants move in order to search for better employment opportunities, and the majority of them come to live in the United States, as is seen in figure 4.

Migrants also transform the identity of the country that welcomes them. Figure 5 indicates the high percentages of foreign-born residents (not all are citizens) in the populations of many countries.

Refugees, who move for political reasons, tend to concentrate in far fewer places, because they are placed in refugee camps, and so lack the ability to travel freely. Some 11.4 million refugees were forced to leave their home countries in 2007, up from 9.9 million in 2006. Some 26 million were displaced within their own countries. Overall, some 37.4 million people are involuntarily uprooted from their place of origin.

Increased flows of people increase the ease of transmission of communicable diseases. In part because of the increase in numbers of business travelers worldwide, diseases can be easily and rapidly transmitted through human contact and in the air of airplanes. Concerns about the rapid spread of Severe Acute Respiratory Syndrome (SARS) from Asia in 2003 led to the introduction of significant limits on travel, which reduced the rate of economic growth in the region for 2004. China, fearing the bad publicity that might follow from reporting on SARS, then suppressed its published data, making it more difficult for the international public health community to contain the disease. Advances in transportation thus mean that new diseases can spread worldwide

Figure 4

Number of Migrants per Country

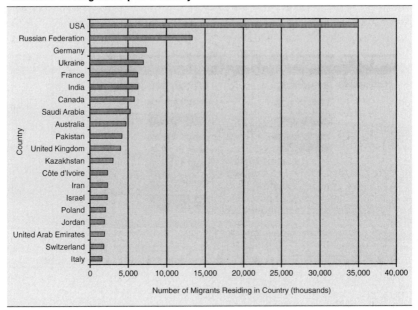

Number of Migrants Residing in Country (thousands)

Source: Global Policy Forum, "Countries Hosting Largest Number of Migrants, 2000." For the chart: http://www.globalpolicy.org/globaliz/charts/migtotalcount.htm; for the table: http://www.globalpolicy.org/globaliz/charts/migtotalcounttable.htm.

much more rapidly, when in the past they would have been contained geographically.

POLITICAL DIVERSIFICATION

The core political actor in international affairs remains the nation state. Only nation states are allowed to be members of the United Nations or to make foreign policy with respect to other governments. Nation states enjoy the legal convention of national sovereignty, which gives them the right to make policy within their own territory and to represent that territory to other nation states.

The number of nation states has grown nearly geometrically since 1900, and particularly since the decolonization movement of the 1950s and 1960s. In 1900 there were fewer than 25 independent states, a number that had grown to over 190 by 2008. The United Nations had an original membership of 51 states in 1945; it included 192 members by 2008. With the independence of former colonies throughout the Third World, the political balance within the United

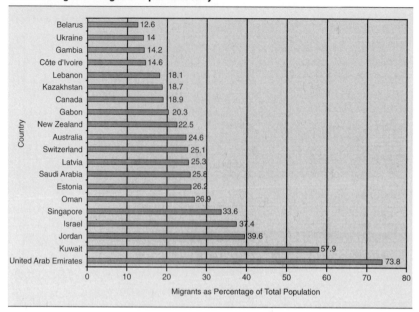

Figure 5

Percentage of Migrants per Country

Source: Gobal Policy Forum, "Countries with Largest Percentage of Migrants, 2000." For the chart: http://www.globalpolicy.org/globaliz/charts/migpercount.htm; for the table: http://www.globalpolicy.org/globalizx/charts/migpercounttable.htm.

Nations shifted: there are now more developing country members than industrialized country members.

The number of international organizations has also grown dramatically. In 1900 there were roughly 50 international organizations, according to the *Yearbook of International Organizations.*[2] By 2005 there were over 250, although the number had fallen since 1985 with the elimination of many alliances and organizations left over from the Cold War era. The functional focus of international organizations has also expanded dramatically, growing from their original military and diplomatic roles to address human rights, food, public health, environment, and economic issues.

Accompanying the spread of functional international organizations— bodies responsible for administering or coordinating policies in a specific functional domain such as public health, economic relations, food supply, environmental quality, and so on—has come growth in international law. Two trends are remarkable in this area: over 90 percent of the multilateral treaties negotiated since 1648 have been concluded since 1951, and the post–World

War II years have seen a dramatic increase in attention paid to economic and environmental concerns, at the expense of the more traditional political/diplomatic and military focus of international law (Chasek 1995).

Nongovernmental organizations (NGOs) grew at a similarly exponential pace over the twentieth century. Whereas there were only 176 NGOs worldwide in 1909, by 1951 there were 832; the number had increased to 3,318 by 1968, to 9,521 by 1978, and to 40,306 by 1997. NGOs work with social movements to educate populations, and to hold governments and private firms accountable for their commitments. They often coordinate strategies and campaigns in multiple countries, and others work as gadflies, publicizing various aspects of globalization.

Multinational corporations (MNCs)—also called transnational corporations (TNCs)—have also become important global actors. Firms first started siting production facilities in multiple countries, run from headquarters that were typically located in the United States or the United Kingdom, in the late nineteenth century. Previously, companies had been involved in long-distance trade of raw materials, but few had owned or had joint ownership over factories abroad. Thus foreign investment by MNCs came to provide the technological and skill-based foundation for global economic development. The UN and other sources estimate the current number of MNCs at about 60,000 parent firms, which direct the operations of some 500,000 affiliates around the world. Figure 6 depicts the global distribution of MNCs in 1997. As it shows, the majority of MNCs are headquartered in the industrialized world—what is known as the "triad" of the United States, Europe, and Japan.

When the revenues of the largest MNCs are compared to the national income of states, the singular economic power of MNCs becomes evident. Figure 7 contrasts some of the largest MNCs and states, contrasting countries' annual GNP with annual corporate earnings.

Scientific networks have also proliferated. Loose organizations of scientists who are experts in various aspects of global concern have become increasingly important in the governance of globalization as collective rules are developed to deal with aspects of globalization. As political actors find the need to cope with the increasingly complex and technical aspects of globalization, they look to professionals—engineers, scientists, economists—both in their own countries and abroad.

Many groups of political actors or stakeholders organize themselves through issue-specific policy networks. Groups drawn from many sets of actors who share a common interest in a specific issue meet regularly to identify interests and develop common policies to deal with globalization.

One of the most important political actors of the twentieth century, of course, was the United States. To some extent, globalization has consisted of

Figure 6

Corporations and Foreign Affiliates

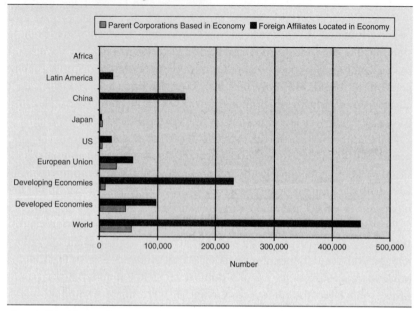

Source: United Nations Conference on Trade and Development (UNCTAD), "World Investment Review, 1997," www.unctad.org.en/docs/wir97ove.en.pdf.

the projection of the U.S. military presence worldwide, by means of military bases and foreign deployments. Just since the end of the Cold War, U.S. military operations have occurred in the following locales:

- Panama (1989)

- Colombia (military advisers, 1989)

- Iraq (1991)

- Somalia (1992)

- Haiti (1994)

- Bosnia (1995)

- Kosovo (1999)

- Afghanistan (2001)

- Iraq (2003)

Figure 7

The World's Largest Corporations and the GDP of Selected Countries, 2007

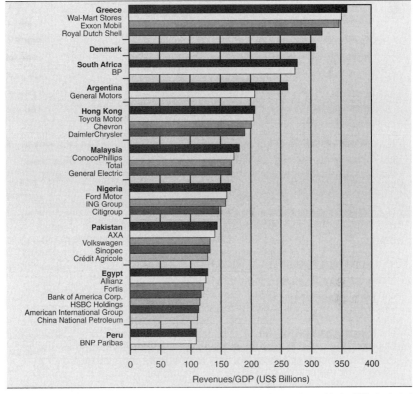

Source: Global Policy Forum, "Comparison of the World's Largest Corporations with the GDP of selected Countries, 2007" (data from *Forbes* magazine and the World Bank), http://www.globalpolicy.org/socecon/tncs/tables/gdpcompare2007.htm.

Changes in military technology have increased the ability of nonstate actors to deploy force at long distances. Before the twentieth century, for instance, terrorists tended to operate locally, but two sets of global forces have since contributed to the globalization of security concerns. One has to do with the emergence of new groups—criminals and political terrorists—with antipathy toward the West and a wish to apply force against their enemy. The spread of such formal political networks facilitates the diffusion of military technology, as seen by the sale of nuclear weapon technology by the Pakistan-based A.G. Khan in the 1990s. Second, the spread of biological and chemical weapons, as well as the dispersion of "loose-nukes" after the end of the Cold War, have

GLOBALIZATION IN ACTION
THE WORLDWIDE MARKETPLACE

Especially since the rise of the Internet, globalization has greatly facilitated consumers' access to inexpensive items from abroad by virtually bringing together consumers and sellers who would not otherwise interact in person. One of this book's authors recalls two personal experiences that capture this phenomenon.

Shortly after 9/11, he made plans to fly out of his local airport, and, unheeding the new security rule, brought with him his favorite Swiss Army knife—which was then seized at the airport. Upon returning from his trip, he tried to replace the knife but discovered that sale of his preferred model had been discontinued in the United States. Using the online service eBay, however, he was able to purchase that model from a vendor in Poland, new, for about 40 percent of what he'd paid for the confiscated knife.

Some years later, he was looking for a birthday present for his son, who liked Peruvian music. While searching online, he found a professional model of a Peruvian panpipe (a "semi-toyo") that was available from a vendor in Bolivia. The panpipe was made by hand and shipped to the United States within a month. Third World artisans are able to make a living selling goods internationally, as well as having their cultures recognized and supported through such small-scale, personal international trade.

While the Internet allows information to travel instantaneously and at nearly zero cost, in some instances the cost of shipping goods impedes further globalization. For example, in 2008 Tesla Motors, the California-based electric car maker, planned to manufacture 1,000-pound battery packs in Thailand, ship them to the United Kingdom for installation, and then import the nearly-assembled cars to the United States. But the shipping costs were found to be prohibitive, forcing the company to manufacture the batteries in California. While an integrated global economy contributes to the bulk of the goods we consume, from the coffee we drink to the cars we drive, globalization still faces obstacles—such as high oil prices—that may hinder its continued spread.

Source: Larry Rother, "Shipping Costs Start to Crimp Globalization," *New York Times*, August 3, 2008.

given terrorists access to more lethal weapons, which they can more easily deploy against far-away populations and deliver either by airplane or ship.

ENVIRONMENTAL DEGRADATION (AND CONCERN)

Globalization has given rise to a whole new class of environmental threats. Humanity has always influenced the natural environment in which it lived. But since the nineteenth century, modern industrial societies have generated contaminants that have the potential to degrade the global ecosystems on which human survival depends. The shift to fossil fuels during the Industrial Revolution led to widespread emissions of carbon dioxide and sulfur dioxide, contributing respectively to global warming and acid rain. As countries have emulated the economic model of England and the early industrializers, the ecological footprint of the world's population is growing increasingly heavy. And estimates of per capita consumption at current rates suggest that satisfying the material needs of the world's aspiring consumers would require four or five Earths.

Other dimensions of globalization have generated and augmented environmental threats around the world. Because of the reliance on national sovereignty as the organizing political principle for global governance, accumulated wastes concentrate in parts of the world that are beyond the political jurisdiction of the world's authorities: "tragedies of the commons" occur in the atmosphere, in open oceans, and in tropical rainforests. Concern about global environmental threats was initially sparked in the late 1960s, when residues of the pesticide DDT were discovered in Antarctica, far from its original application. Most of the world's fisheries are overused because there is no effective enforcement of fishery quotas on the open oceans. Acid rain and the 1986 Chernobyl nuclear disaster made it clear that environmental destruction does not stop at national boundaries.

Long-distance trade contributes to environmental degradation and loss of biodiversity. For instance, tropical hardwoods are pillaged in Malaysia, Burma, and Brazil, in order to supply furniture for consumers in the West. Low stumpage fees charged to the forestry companies by the government increase the incentive to overcut the forests.

Also, long-distance trade often physically interferes with local ecosystems. Invasive species are transmitted by freighters, introducing them to parts of the world where there are no natural predators and so they proliferate. For example, the Black Sea fisheries have collapsed due to the new presence of jellyfish, while underwater exhaust vents from nuclear power plants on the Great Lakes are being clogged by the profusion of various species of nonnative mussels.

Many of the human stresses on the global environment began with the Industrial Revolution, but they have accelerated unabated since the 1950s. World production of sulphur dioxide and carbon dioxide, pesticide use, toxic-waste emissions, production of synthetic chemicals, and numbers of vehicles all continue to grow, causing potentially devastating effects on the integrity of global ecosystems (Kates et al. 1990; Ponting 1993; Speth 2008).

Globalization, and the attendant concentration of production and employment in cities, has led to worldwide urbanization. Over 50 percent of the world's population now lives in cities, rather than in the countryside (see figure 8). Consequently, basic commodities must be transported to where people live, requiring greater consumption of energy for their transport and emissions of greenhouse gases.

IDEATIONAL CONVERGENCE

At the global level, a number of ideas or beliefs inform popular and elite attitudes about the world—affecting both legitimate aspirations and calculations about who is likely to be viewed favorably as an ally and to whom resources should be extended on favorable terms.

Many ideas have competed historically for dominance, at least in terms of hemispheric scale. From the fifteenth through the seventeenth centuries, Spanish Catholicism competed with the British Reformation for the hearts and minds of people in Europe and Latin America. The consequences of this ideational struggle, Weber argued, were the consolidation of the cultural institutions that located the Industrial Revolution and early economic innovation and development in the United Kingdom and Protestant Europe.

Figure 8

Percentages of Population Living in Cities, 1970–2015

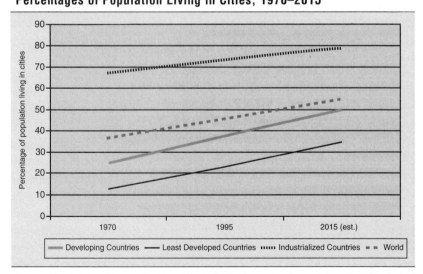

Source: Global Policy Forum, "Growing Urbanization," *Human Development Report 1998*; chart at http://www.globalpolicy.org/globaliz/charts/urbaniz2.htm; table at http://www.globalpolicy.org/globaliz/charts/urbaniz1.htm.

More recently, some other ideas have attracted almost universal acclaim. By the 1980s, most economists had agreed on a loose set of principles about how states should manage their economies, dubbed the Washington Consensus. Such a blueprint, often administered by the International Monetary Fund (IMF) but widely endorsed by international cohorts of economists, laid out a common set of policy guidelines, primarily for developing-country governments:

- Fiscal discipline by the state
- Tax reform
- Financial liberalization
- Unified and competitive exchange rates
- Trade liberalization
- Openness to foreign direct investment
- Privatization
- Deregulation
- Secure property rights

This list was never meant to be universally applied, or categorical. By the turn of the new century, as the importance of national and international institutions was increasingly recognized, Harvard economist Dani Rodrik (2001, 51) notes that the original list had been augmented to include these further guidelines:

- Legal/political reform
- Regulatory institutions
- Anti-corruption regulations
- Labor market flexibility
- WTO agreements
- Financial codes and standards
- "Prudent" capital-account opening
- Non-intermediate exchange rate regimes
- Social safety nets
- Independent central banks and targeting inflation
- Targeted poverty reduction[3]

Governments have embraced a core set of aspirational goals to be pursued by the international community. The eight Millennium Development Goals (MDGs) adopted by the UN General Assembly in 2000 call for fighting poverty, improving gender equality, improving public health, and environmental protection.[4] The MDGs, which set specific targets that are to be reached by 2015 from a 2000 baseline, are discussed at greater length by Jeffrey Sachs in chapter 3 of this book.

- Halve the proportion of people living on less than a dollar a day

- Ensure that all children complete primary school

- Educate boys and girls equally

- Reduce the mortality rate among children under five by two-thirds

- Reduce the maternal mortality rate by three-quarters

- Halt and begin to reverse the spread of HIV/AIDs, malaria, and other major diseases

- Halve the proportion of people without access to safe water and sanitation

- Increase aid and improve governance

By 2008 good progress had been made on achieving these goals in all areas other than Africa.

New economic development doctrines have also been gaining currency. The idea of sustainable development and belief in the inseparable nature of economic development, democracy, peace, and environmental quality have become solidly entrenched on the international agenda since it is was first popularized in the 1987 *Our Common Future* report by the World Commission on Sustainable Development. Decision makers worldwide are increasingly recognizing the complexity of the global policy environment—and the need to heed the connections between policy domains when making choices (Clark and Munn 1986; Haq 1995).

Democracy has gained currency as an idea about how to politically organize domestic society. In 1850 there were, at best, three democracies in the world—the United States, the United Kingdom, and France. One of the biggest surges in democratization occurred in the 1990s, and by 1998, about 45 percent of the world's countries could be regarded as democratic, according to standard basic political science measures of democracy (Huntington 1991; Simmons et al. 2006, 913). World public opinion polls administered in 2008 by Gallup and by WorldPublicOpinion.org confirmed that, on average, 85 percent of respondents across the world agreed that "the will of the people should be the basis

GLOBALIZATION IN ACTION
THE NEW FACE OF OUTSOURCING

One feature of globalization is the increased ease of outsourcing—subcontracting services to a third party, which often involves moving jobs overseas. Idaho-based Nighthawk Radiology hires radiologists in India to interpret x-rays for hospitals in the United States and elsewhere. X-rays are sent via the Internet from U.S. laboratories to Indian laboratories for interpretation. The Indian doctors' findings are promptly relayed back to the United States and other countries using the service. Given the scarcity of medical specialists in the United States and the relatively low wages of Indian workers, such practices bring down U.S. medical costs while creating technical infrastructure in India, and, because of the time zone differences involved, may even speed the interpretation of medical tests.

Outsourcing was once thought to involve the U.S. and Western European countries sending jobs to India and other economically-developing nations. But in some cases, outsourcing itself is being outsourced. Infosys, the Indian technological giant based in Mysore, trains thousands of workers from dozens of countries in six-month stints, and then sends them overseas to work in its overseas operations. Indian technology companies are opening offices in Uruguay, Mexico, Canada, Portugal, Romania, Thailand, China, and parts of the United States. In one office alone, more than a dozen languages are spoken.

As an Infosys vice-president puts it, in the new world of outsourcing, the effort is "to take the work from any part of the world and do it in any part of the world." In one example, a U.S. bank wanted to market to Hispanic customers, so it contracted with a Monterrey, Mexico, office of Infosys to provide the services. This new form of outsourcing supports rising Indian wages and currency, as well as increased competition from other up-and-coming countries, such as China, Morocco, and Mexico, on the ever-changing terrain of the global economy.

Source: Anand Giridharadas, "Outsourcing Works, So India Is Exporting Jobs," *New York Times*, September 25, 2007.

for the authority of government" and stated that they favored democratic governance in their country, even if many expressed discontent with the way that such democracy might operate in practice (Gilani 2008, 15–20). At a deeper level, globalization itself has been gaining currency as a shared belief in how the world should be organized (Biersteker 2000). While many people worldwide report, in response to surveys, that they favor increased trade liberalization between countries, they are concerned about the possible negative side-effects of globalization, such as threats to their culture, damage to the environment, and challenges posed by immigration (Knowlton 2007).

GLOBALIZATION'S EFFECTS

In this section we review some of the major claims about the effects of globalization. Who benefits? Who suffers? In large part, these debates presume that globalization itself is responsible for many of the outcomes that are to be either celebrated or lamented. But far more research is needed to tease out the interaction between global forces and the role played by domestic factors and policy choices in the effects that are so widely discussed.

Much progress in the quality of individual livelihood has been documented over the past fifty years. Infant mortality has fallen, and life expectancy has increased for most of the world. Only some countries in Eastern Europe, Central Asia, and sub-Saharan Africa have failed to see these improvements (World Bank 2004, 10–11, 22–23). But to what extent are these observed differences attributable to globalization itself? That is, in the absence of globalization, would things be any different, or might these changes actually be due to one or more other factors? A long-standing puzzle that captures this question is the differential development trajectory of South Korea and Ghana: Ghana is rich in natural resources, and South Korea lacks them. In the 1950s Ghana's per capita GDP was higher, yet today South Korea is no longer a Third World country, while conditions have not significantly changed in Ghana.

Another factor to be considered in this debate is to what extent the benefits of globalization are regionally concentrated. The IMF reports that annual average GDP growth in sub-Saharan Africa has lagged behind world rates since the 1970s. The much discussed "digital divide"—reflecting unequal access to computers and the Internet—is another instance of how many of the benefits of globalization have accrued to the countries of the North (the industrialized countries in North America, Australia, New Zealand, Japan, and Western Europe).

Figures 9 and 10 demonstrate the unequal distribution of income. Figure 9 presents income per head as a percentage of the North, indicating a decline outside of Asia—in this table, primarily Japan, Malaysia, Thailand, Taiwan, Singapore, and Hong Kong—and China since 1950. Figure 10 shows regional percentages of world GDP over time: the world's richest countries (the G8, consisting of the United States, the United Kingdom, France, Canada, Italy, Germany, Russia, and Japan) controlled 30 percent of world GDP in 1820, 55 percent in 1975, and around 45 percent in 2004.

In the early 1970s, Harvard economist Richard Cooper realized that economics textbooks had to be rewritten to accommodate globalization. Economic management could no longer occur in isolation of what was going on in other countries. Indeed, the role of foreign trade for such countries as the United States, which historically has remained relatively insulated from the

Figure 9

Income per Head as Percentage of the North, 1950–2001

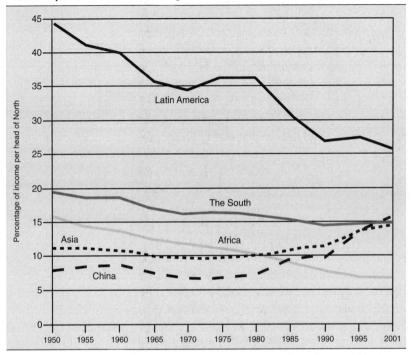

Source: Global Policy Forum, http://www.globalpolicy.org/socecon/inequal/income/tables/income perhead.htm.
Note: The North includes North America, Australia, New Zealand, Japan, and Western Europe.

world economy, has been growing—making it (and other vulnerable countries) increasingly sensitive to economic turmoil from abroad. For instance, a recession in a major trading partner would reduce demand for U.S. goods. As Cooper argued originally, central bank policies must be coordinated, or unilateral efforts at economic management will be counterproductive.

Many economists suggest that globalization should lead to convergence of economic conditions across countries. However, Benjamin Cohen finds that exchange rates have not yet fully converged. Geoffrey Garrett shows that left-leaning governments are able to preserve higher labor standards and stronger social support policies in the face of global pressures. Peter Katzenstein demonstrates that small, politically liberal social democracies are able to work with labor and quickly adjust to international economic conditions without facing extensive domestic economic cuts.

Figure 10

Percentage of World GDP by Region, 1820–2004

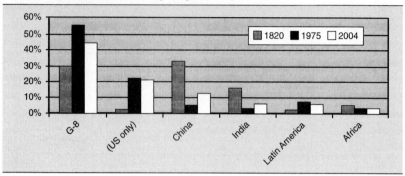

Source: Global Policy Forum, http://www.globalpolicy.org/socecon/inequal/income/tables/income perhead.htm.
Note: The North includes North America, Australia, New Zealand, Japan, and Western Europe.

One of the most widely contested aspects of economic globalization involves economic equality. Does globalization accentuate or reduce economic inequalities between and within countries? The evidence is mixed, and much depends on the chosen tools of statistical interpretation.

The World Bank estimates that economic inequality between countries has decreased since 1950, although economic inequality within countries has increased during that period. However, there are a variety of ways of calculating economic inequality within countries. One common technique is to look at the percentage or numbers of the population living on less than $1 or $2 per day. The percentage of people living in poverty appears to have fallen between 1970 and 1998, although different analysts offer widely diverging estimates of the number of people in absolute poverty. Much of the change has to do with the growing size of the Chinese middle class, which has elevated between 250 and 400 million people out of absolute poverty.

Until the 1970s, economic growth rates in the industrialized countries far exceeded that of the developing world, leading to a deep divide in GDP per capita figures worldwide. However, over the past twenty-five years or so, the so-called Asian Tigers have outpaced the West. Despite a 1997 setback from the financial meltdowns in Southeast Asia, Taiwan, South Korea, Singapore, Thailand, Malaysia, and China have had exceptionally high rates of economic growth, nearly doubling that of the West from 1973 to 2001 (Maddison 2007, 337, 379–382).

Another way of estimating inequality within countries is by looking at the ratio of incomes of the richest fifth of the population to the incomes of the poorest fifth. Estimates of wealth rather than income would be a better indicator of such inequality, but rich people have to disclose only their income for tax purposes, some assets are difficult to value, and cross-national estimates of individual wealth are difficult to come by. Worldwide, income inequality grew much worse from 1960 to 2000. The UNDP Human Development Index reports that the ratio of income of the richest to that of the poorest fifth of the world's population spread from 30 percent to nearly 75 percent over that period.[5]

Power Shifts

The nature and distribution of political influence is also changing as a consequence (or a cause) of globalization. Many analysts either observe or predict profound changes in the nature of diplomacy and international relations.

National sovereignty, the bedrock of international relations, is being transformed. Diplomats and international lawyers have regarded states as the paramount legal authorities in international politics since the Treaty of Westphalia in 1648. States are responsible for formulating foreign policy; only representatives of states may legally commit their countries to any obligations at international meetings (one of the first actions that newly independent countries take is to seek recognition by the United Nations); and national governments are the notional authorities responsible for maintaining control (security and economic prosperity) within their national boundaries.

The influence of new political actors is posing increasing challenges to the state's national sovereignty. Exercising control domestically is virtually impossible without close consultation with MNCs and NGOs. Economic and environmental conditions are often the consequence of decisions taken by firms and individuals, not by the state. Foreign policy is increasingly subject to direct influence by MNCs, NGOs, scientists, and even international organizations.

This diffusion of power makes it ever more difficult for states to impose policies. Effective policy implementation requires consensus, and states must feel that their interests are represented if they are to willingly accept meaningful international obligations and enforce them at home. Legitimacy is thus based on process for small powers (were they heard and able to participate?), recourse to broader underlying principles by leaders, and representation (for an increasing number of nonstate actors). There is a paradox here about participatory legitimacy, though, as nonstate actors require some measure of participation if they are to consider an international decision to be legitimate, whereas traditional state actors may base their assessment of legitimacy on whether the states were able to dominate the process and so ensure that the principle of sovereignty persists.

States face a dilemma in justifying their policies. Domestically, they must demonstrate that the policies they support represent the interests of their population. In the international arena though, they have to justify their positions against those of many other actors, whose interests may not be regarded as legitimate in the eyes of domestic constituencies. Consider the difficulties that the United States encounters at the United Nations: although the UN does not enjoy widespread legitimacy, at least in the U.S. Congress, Europeans and other international partners regard decisions taken outside the UN as highly suspect. Ulrich Beck, a German sociologist, writes that "globalization denotes the processes through which sovereign nation states are criss-crossed and undermined by transnational actors" (Beck 1992, 11).

The conduct of diplomacy is changing with globalization as well. Many more political partners must be consulted when formulating policies. It was striking that Colin Powell, then the U.S. secretary of state, would greet by name not just journalists, as was the practice of his predecessors, but also NGO representatives at meetings.

The nature of diplomacy is also changing. With the growth of new political issues, and the increased salience of perceived legitimacy based both on the articulation of domestic interests and the process by which policies are created, the tools of diplomacy have to be modified. Pure force is no longer the solution to most problems—and it may often be counterproductive. Joseph Nye, a Harvard political scientist with an acute foreign policy eye, has written persuasively of the need for "soft power": leading by example, and relying on multilateralism and close consultation with other political actors worldwide. In terms of the tools of statecraft, soft power emerges from the attractiveness of a country's culture, and from consistency between its policies and uniformly accepted norms, such as democracy and human rights (Nye 2002, 127; Brzezinski 2007).

As table 1 indicates, there are multiple measures of power and of a country's ability to project influence at a great distance. The United States still enjoys preeminence in terms of the size of its economy, nuclear warheads, and aircraft carriers—and, thus, its ability to quickly project airpower abroad. While other countries may have large traditional militaries, they lack the capacity to project military force at a great distance, and the size of their economies still do not measure up that of the United States.

Still, the ability to exercise economic leverage over other countries—one of the major sources of diplomatic statecraft—may be shifting away from the United States to China and India. A forecast of GDP in 2020 in terms of purchasing power parity (a measure of how much can be bought with a particular currency) has China first at approximately US$30 trillion, the United States

Table 1

Measures of Power and Ability to Project Influence at a Great Distance, 2005–2007

	Population (% of total, 2005)	GDP (% of world) 2006	Armed forces 2007	Nuclear warheads 2007	Aircraft carriers
USA	4.6	27.5	1.5 million	5163	12
China	20.2	5.5	2.3 million	400	0
France	0.9	4.6	.3 million	350	2
India	17.4	1.8	1.3 million	50	1
Russia	2.2	2.0	1.0 million	5830	1
UK	0.9	4.9	.2 million	No data	3
Germany	1.3	6.0	No data	No data	0

Source: *The Economist,* June 30, 2007, 29–30.

second at slightly less, and India third at around US$12 trillion. By 2050, China may have a GDP of US$(2006)75 trillion, with the United States and India tied at $40 trillion.[6]

Shifting Political Identities

As exposure to the rest of the world grows and people become more mobile, identity shifts occur as well. In Europe, public opinion polls reveal that an increasing number of citizens regard themselves as European, rather than (or in addition to) being citizens of a particular country. Diasporic communities often associate themselves with their country of origin, where they may hope to retire and where many of their relatives continue to reside. In addition to the economic remittances they send back to their country of origin—which in some instances accounts for a significant proportion of the national income of the country of origin (Philippines, Pakistan, Egypt)—migrants acquire new attitudes, for good and ill.

Many political consequences are associated with globalization as well. Many critics express concern about the "Americanization" of the world—a homogenization of culture that is a consequence of the dissemination of American styles and values (through the deliberate exercise of soft power) and the spread of U.S. multinationals. Smaller languages become extinct. Traditional lifestyles are endangered. And other cultures feel swamped by the American juggernaut, leading to protectionism (as promoted by the French film industry) or political backlash (as embodied in Moslem fundamentalism).

It is possible that this view of the overarching power of U.S. mass culture to project its cultural shadow abroad, unchallenged, is overdrawn. Indigenous cultures are robust. One example is beer. There was long a concern that the large breweries were generating a uniformly boring product that was overwhelming the market; similar arguments were made about coffee. Yet, currently, the United States is awash in microbreweries offering innovative and distinctive flavors of beer, while local coffee roasters and cafés compete with Dunkin' Donuts and Starbucks.

The United States also projects a disproportionately large ecological footprint. If other countries fully emulate the American consumer model, the globe will suffer. Estimates from 2003 indicated that satisfying the demands of one American required 9.6 hectares (about 2.5 acres) while individuals in Europe required 4.2 hectares; those in the Middle East and Central Asia, 2.2 hectares; Latin America, 2.0 hectares; Asia Pacific, 1.3 hectares; and those in Africa, 1.1 hectares (Burman 2007, 16–17). In the aggregate, satisfying individuals worldwide at the American level of consumption (or even less) will deplete the world's total resource base and deplete its ecosystemic foundations. The global projection of U.S. consumer habits through movies and advertising reinforces these pressures.

Complexity of Decision Making

The growing agenda of political participants makes the entire enterprise of diplomacy and international relations more complex than ever before (La Porte 1975; Simon 1981; Jervis 1997; Perrow 1999).

More political actors mean that there are simply more possible political connections to track. The number of binary connections follows from the simple formula $n^*(n-1)/2$. For instance: a world of 81 states requires 2,140 embassies and foreign ministry desks simply to maintain bilateral ties; a world of 167 states requires 7,762 embassies and foreign ministry desks. While most governments find shortcuts to deal with such complexity, such as regional representation and bargaining through blocs, the proliferation of other actors makes things even messier.

Many issues on the international agenda are poorly understood, or are interconnected with other issues in ways that are often not fully recognized. Some contemporary analysts refer to these global issues as "networked problems." They make it much more difficult for decision makers to accurately understand their own interests (as well as others' interests), or to identify clear policies that may be widely acceptable. Decision makers operate under conditions of uncertainty—

they are subject to frequent unanticipated consequences, surprises, and crises, as the interconnection between issues transmits policy effects geographically and functionally. Consequently, states increasingly value political actors who may promise to attenuate such uncertainty by clarifying the nature of the international system, helping actors to identify their interests, and helping to establish useful policies and the likely consequences of alternate policies.

An example of unanticipated consequences is U.S. reliance on biofuel substitutes for petroleum. The U.S. government has encouraged its farmers to convert agricultural crops to corn, in order to generate feedstocks for substitute energy sources. Yet the effect of this policy has been to drive up the price of grain, while producing a fuel that may require more energy to produce than it generates. (Brazilian ethanol comes from sugar beets rather than corn, and thus requires far less energy inputs to produce it). Consequently, the United States, by trying to protect national security, contributes to food scarcity and to energy inefficiency. Policies that may make good political sense for the American Midwest generate policy effects that are globally detrimental.

This new global policy environment creates the need for new approaches to policymaking. Organization theorist Donald Chisholm notes that "central coordinating schemes work well when the task environment is known and unchanging, and can be treated as a closed system" (cited in Scott 1998, 82). Globalization challenges all these assumptions about the policy environment. Effective responses to globalization call for international cooperation and governance—including agreement on common rules, norms, participatory arrangements, and enforcement provisions.

PERSPECTIVES ON GLOBALIZATION

A variety of clear perspectives on globalization have been identified. David Held and Anthony McGrew (2007) find three general normative orientations and six analytic or policy views, while James Rosenau (2003, 78) has five views on multilevel governance and democracy, and Jan Aart Scholte (2000) has four.

For our purposes, there are five dominant perspectives on globalization, as shown in table 2. Each perspective, or worldview, varies in how the key political driving forces are defined, who are identified as the principal actors, what is the assessment of costs and benefits to the majority of the world's population, and what specific policy agenda is recommended to better steer globalization forces. Each perspective has its proponents, whose publications (provided in the bibliography at the end of this chapter) can be read in order to follow the perspective in greater detail.

Table 2

Dominant Perspectives on Globalization

	Political Realism	Market Liberalism	Skepticism/ Political Liberalism	Radicalism	Transforma- tionalism/ Cosmopoli- tanism
Key proponents	Kissinger, Brzezinski, Rice	Friedman, Wolf	Krugman, Rodrik, Stiglitz, Keohane, Nye, Slaughter	Bello, Khor, Klein, Roy, Shiva	Ruggie, Held, Castells, Giddens, Sikkink, Khagram
Key actors	States	MNCs	All	MNCs	Nonstate actors
Major forces	Military, economic	Economic	Military, economic, cultural	Markets, culture	Networks
General assessment	Mixed	Positive	Mixed	Overwhelmingly negative	Hopeful
Guidance techniques	Reassertion of strong state leadership	Market liberal- ization, rule of law	Multilateralism	Constant challenges, regional cooperation, national self- reliance, citizen mobi- lization	Network formation

Political Realism: L'État Eternel

Political realism is a long-standing perspective on international relations that emphasizes the key role of the nation-state in international politics. According to realists such as Henry Kissinger, Condoleezza Rice, Brent Scowcroft, Zbigniew Brzezinski, Robert Kagan, and Richard Haass, global forces operate according to the wishes of powerful states. All states are obsessed with protecting their national security and wealth, and all states construct international rules and allow international flows of goods, people, and ideas within these parameters. Globalization, according to this perspective, is largely an artifact of British hegemony in the nineteenth century and U.S. hegemony in the twentieth century. The dominant political powers—the hegemons—set the rules by which their own interests can be served through global actions.

Realists thus take a highly pragmatic view of globalization. For them, globalization is not a seamless whole but rather a set of highly controlled and dis-

GLOBALIZATION IN ACTION

GLOBAL CRIME

Globalization makes corporate crime possible on a large scale. Two recent examples can be found in the scandals involving financier Bernard L. Madoff and the German firm Siemens. Madoff is the con artist who swindled $50 billion from investors by constructing a "Ponzi scheme"—in effect, gathering funds from new investors to pay off current ones. To be successful, one needs many potential investors, but even the world was not big enough to handle Madoff's enterprise, which was called the world's first global Ponzi scheme. Starting with an "exclusive" set of friends and clients in New York and in Florida, Madoff expanded his scope to Europe and eventually starting hawking his products in China and elsewhere in Asia. But feeding such a large number of investors requires attracting ever more new investors, which cannot go on forever, even in a globalized world. However, such a scheme now can grow larger and last longer because the con artist's reach is vastly extended through globalization.

A second example of the global scale of corruption is the recent multibillion-dollar fine charged to the German engineering conglomerate, Siemens, by agencies of the U.S. and German governments. Reportedly, Siemens ran a bribery operation on the scale of $30 to $40 million per year, paying off government officials and companies in Russia, Argentina, China, and around the world.

Bribery is hardly new, yet Siemens' operations were brazen and transparent, setting up "cash desks" where employees could fill suitcases with up to one million euros in cash for the purpose of bribing foreign officials to grant them telecommunications contracts. Moreover, Siemens claimed tax deductions for these bribes—called "useful expenditures"—which was legal in Germany until 1999. From 2001 through 2007, Siemens paid foreign officials over $800 million to help them win contracts. On December 15, 2008, Siemens pleaded guilty in U.S. court and agreed to pay fines of $800 million in the United States and $540 million in Germany.

Globalization, it seems, fosters both multinational trade and multinational graft.

Sources: "Madoff Scheme Kept Rippling Outward, Across Borders," *New York Times*, December 19, 2008; "At Siemens, Bribery Was Just a Line Item," *New York Times*, December 20, 2008; and "Bavarian Baksheesh," *The Economist*, December 20, 2008, 112.

crete sets of activities. Realists believe that certain forces of globalization are allowed to proliferate, such as international trade liberalization, because it is seen in the United States as benefiting the U.S. economy. Conversely, other forces of globalization—such as migration—are suppressed if they are seen to undermine long-term U.S. interests.

Too much globalization, from a realist perspective, is a bad thing, because it erodes the power of dominant players. A wider balance of power internationally is seen as detrimental to political order at the international level, because there is no clear source of leadership or enforcement for collective commitments. Deeper influence of nonstate actors further undermines the ability of dominant states to provide the clear leadership on which systemic order relies.

However, many realists realize that some aspects of globalization may be moving beyond simple control by powerful states. This is a terrifying prospect, as it raises doubts about the stability of the international system and the political calculus that they have held to be universal and eternal.

Market Liberalism: Swords into Stock Shares

Market liberals believe that free markets provide universal benefits. All good liberal values go together: free trade reinforces democratization and human prosperity, as well as the rule of law, human rights, and the welfare of women. Market liberals—most notably economist Milton Friedman and the journalist Thomas Friedman (no relation)—advance the long-standing argument for capitalism that if human competitive urges are channeled into commerce, there will be less violence, and individuals everywhere will press for a strong respect for the rule of law and transparent democratic principles so that they can be confident in making contracts and engaging in long-distance commerce. They believe that if economic markets are allowed to prevail in most areas of human endeavor, then MNCs will spread their operations worldwide, providing employment, prosperity, and Western values.

Globalization, for market liberals, is a decidedly good thing that is to be embraced and promoted in almost all forms since it expands the reach of free markets. However, market liberals would still advocate the use of force against groups that violently challenge globalization, such as political regimes or non-state actors that could interfere with the easy flow of energy supplies.

Skepticism: Accentuate the Positive and Adjust the Negative

Political liberals tend to be skeptical about globalization. They see much to like about its creative possibilities—such as the potential for mutual economic benefit, and for political identity formation beyond the nation-state (thus serving as a bulwark against nationalism and warfare)–but they are concerned about globalization's potential for forging connections between opponents of liberal ideals and generating backlash against the forces that may be beneficial.

Liberals are aware of possible contradictions in the short term between democracy-building in new states and other goals, such as peace and economic vitality. Political scientist Ronald Parris argues that economic growth in many emerging economies may be best accomplished by deferring democratization. Others have noted that supporting democratization, particularly in the Middle East, may entail supporting political parties that oppose the West.

Basically, despite their skepticism, liberals believe in the potential for what the economist Jagdish Bhagwati calls "globalization with a human face" (Bhagwati 2008). They believe that states can and should intervene to temper the excesses of globalization, such as widespread financial crises or environmental degradation. Environmental regulations and labor standards should be adopted to counter the tendencies toward a race to the bottom from pure, market-based globalization.

Liberals are also aware of the possibility that globalization may foster a backlash that undermines any potential gains. Thus they seek to promote globalization cautiously, in domains that are least likely to galvanize opposition, to offer carefully qualified defenses of globalizing forces, and to educate people about their benefits, hoping to diffuse challenges based on emotional response to radical change.

Radicalism: Challenge the Dominant Paradigm

Radicals believe that globalization is primarily a set of economic and social forces that consolidate political control in the hands of northern multinational corporations (Bello 2004; Cavanagh 1995; Ling and Khor 2001; Roy 2001; Shiva 2005). They are outraged by the unequal distribution of benefits from globalization. Since the demonstrations against the World Trade Organization (WTO) in Seattle in 1999, many radical critiques have been launched that seek to document growing inequities—claiming, or instance, that during the period of highest global engagement in the United States, the share of total income accruing to the wealthiest 1 percent of Americans grew from about 7.5 percent throughout the 1970s to nearly 18 percent in 2006.[7]

Globalization, in this view, is merely imperialism by another name, for it has the effect of projecting unsustainable and inappropriate modes of production to the majority of the world, by facilitating free trade, foreign investment, and exposure to foreign mass-consumption culture. The resulting economic integration brings with it a race to the bottom: lowered labor standards, environmental degradation, exacerbated economic inequality, and the consolidation of political power in the hands of a plutocratic few. Radicals advocate a constant campaign of challenging globalization through public demonstrations and public education. They support viable alternatives to globalization such as national self-reliance, more radical forms of democratic participation at all levels of governance, and greater cooperation among countries and groups in the global South.

Cosmopolitan Transformationalism: Jazz and Constant Improvisation

Globalization has given rise to a distinctive new set of perspectives that are associated with cosmopolitanism at the international level. These authors, such as Kenneth Kwame Appiah (whose essay on culture and diversity is included here) and British sociologist David Held, believe in the transformative potential of globalization, the salient feature of which, from their perspective, is the proliferation of networks of new political actors. These networks, driven by rapid technological innovation, facilitate the prompt flow of information between major state and nonstate actors. According to the adherents of this perspective, globalization may be seen metaphorically as jazz, full of improvisation and change, unlike the more bombastic military marches of the realists or the carefully orchestrated classical symphonies of the liberals. These globalized networks create the potential for widespread learning, as well as decentralized mechanisms of oversight and information that can facilitate international cooperation.

Cosmopolitans recognize the geographic and regional disparities that may inhibit the spread of these networks. China and Russia still actively suppress nonstate claimants to political legitimacy. Still, many cosmopolitans believe that there is a great potential for inducing political change in such staunch statist opponents through opening up global channels to China and Russia and promoting civil society within those countries. Elsewhere, endemic poverty can be a serious limit to the spread of virtual networks, and economic policies and foreign aid may provide the infrastructure from which networks may continue to grow in Latin America and Africa.

CONCLUSION

Globalization is a contested concept. Views differ on the prospects it presents for humanity. The essays in this volume seek to span some of the perspectives on globalization, presenting arguments about the degree to which its positive potential may be realized. At a high level of abstraction one could ask, to what extent does globalization further the development and transmission of new useful new ideas for better policy? To what extent does it consolidate ossified political structures that inhibit progress? To what extent is political change possible to promote reform and change?

The essays and debates that follow in this volume focus less abstractly on applied policy debates that are associated with globalization. Authors engage one another on questions of what interventions are politically and technically likely to improve basic human conditions under conditions of globalization: how and when can human rights be promoted, poverty alleviated, ecological sustainability assured, and individuals protected from threats of violence?

Discussion Questions

1. How can actors deal with the uncertainty created by globalization?
2. What does globalization mean for identity?
3. Should globalization be made more equitable? How can the distribution of benefits from globalization be made more egalitarian?
4. Which features of globalization appear to be most important? Why?

trade liberalization and economic growth

Does Trade Liberalization Contribute to Economic Prosperity?

YES: David Dollar, *The World Bank*

NO: Robert H. Wade, *London School of Economics*

The economic underpinnings of arguments for freer trade (trade liberalization) stem from the belief that the voluntary exchange of goods and services between individuals increases the well-being of both the buyer and the seller. This belief, which has served as the foundation of modern economics since Adam Smith wrote *The Wealth of Nations* in 1776, was originally a highly subversive idea: that not only would trade liberalization lead to mutual benefits, but also, increased trade and interconnections would contribute to international peace. Writ large, the argument goes that the accumulation of individual voluntary economic exchanges benefits nations as a whole, for the benefits of exchange aggregate and transcend political boundaries.

While it is well understood that rapidly increasing communications technologies have facilitated nearly instantaneous long-distance exchanges involving many more actors (whether news or financial markets) than in the past, at a more prosaic level, so, too, have reduced transportation costs facilitated international trade. Thus, the costs of trade—both financial and temporal—have been significantly reduced, thereby facilitating trade's rapid expansion. Coupled with neoclassical economic thinking and, in particular, the notion of "comparative advantage"—that more specialization and trade expands economic growth even for nations facing absolute trade disadvantages compared with more productive counterparts—the reduced costs of trade should directly translate to more trade and, therefore, to more aggregate prosperity. While the theory is well-understood, the question is whether trade liberalization has led empirically to greater prosperity.

Yet it is also clear to some observers that the stylized version of free trade championed by many—the "win-win" promise of free exchange—fails to live up to the realities of international trade. Global institutions that have been pushing trade liberalization, such as the World Bank and the World Trade Organization (WTO), have been buffeted by political protest as a result. While chapter 2 takes up the impact of trade on inequality, the initial consideration here is the impact of trade on overall economic prosperity. While the vast majority of economists believe that free trade promotes aggregate economic expansion, the policy choices required typically involve not binary choices between trade and no-trade but, instead, more complex decisions over expansion or contraction of relatively modest tariffs and export subsidies and who is likely to benefit in the short term from trade liberalization.

Aside from aggregate trade levels, an important policy issue involves the "trade deficit" (total exports minus imports) for any particular nation. For many years, the United States enjoyed positive trade balances—meaning that it exported a greater value of goods than it imported. However, beginning with the sudden onset of elevated petroleum prices in the late 1970s, the nation began running trade deficits, and it has done so ever since. Recent increases in oil prices have exacerbated the situation, to the point that, by mid-2008, trade deficits were hovering around $60 billion per month, or over $700 billion annually, despite a relatively weak dollar (which favors U.S. exports by enabling foreign buyers to purchase U.S. products with relatively inexpensive dollars). The political and economic concern is that consistent and increasing trade imbalances mean that the U.S. economy is, in effect, borrowing from the rest of the world to sustain its current consumption. Figure 1 shows the value of U.S. imports and exports since 1960, while Figure 2 portrays the difference between them—exports minus imports—thus reflecting the recent large and growing trade deficits.

Trade is, of course, more than a product of economics; it involves overt political and policy considerations as well. A general, global political preference for market liberalization, as well as efforts by the WTO, have had the effect of reducing import duties and other "barriers to trade" worldwide. The General Agreement on Tariffs and Trade (GATT) of 1947, along with other subsequent treaties, has reduced tariffs around the world. Many argue that reducing tariffs and diminishing other barriers to trade have increased levels of economic growth. While trade barriers tend to be lower in the wealthier nations of the Organization of Economic Cooperation and Development (OECD), the costs of trade have been reduced overall by lowering both economic and political costs. Figures 3 and 4 detail the broad reduction in import duties from 1989 to 2004. In addition, increased transportation costs—particularly the cost

Figure 1

U.S. Exports and Imports in Goods and Services, 1960–2006

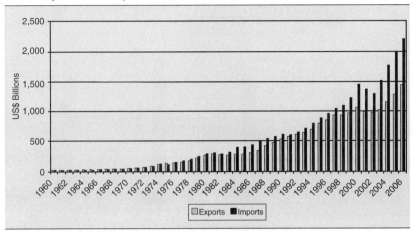

Source: U.S. Department of Commerce, Bureau of Economic Analysis, http://www.bea.gov/index.htm.

of the petroleum that fuels most transportation—may affect overall levels of international trade.

The question raised here—whether tariff reductions and other trade liberalization policies contribute to economic prosperity—inevitably leads to discussion of whether these measures are preferable to some kind of industrial or

Figure 2

U.S. Trade Balance, 1960–2006

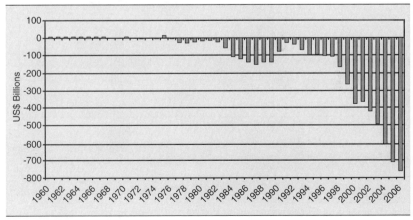

Source: U.S. Department of Commerce, Bureau of Economic Analysis, http://www.bea.gov/index.htm.

4

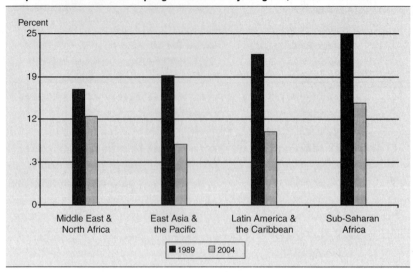

Figure 3

Import Duties in Developing Countries by Region, 1989 and 2004

Percent

(Bar chart with y-axis marked 0, .3, 12, 19, 25. X-axis categories: Middle East & North Africa, East Asia & the Pacific, Latin America & the Caribbean, Sub-Saharan Africa. Legend: ■ 1989, □ 2004)

Source: United Nations Development Programme, *Human Development Report 2005* (New York: Oxford University Press, 2005), 116.

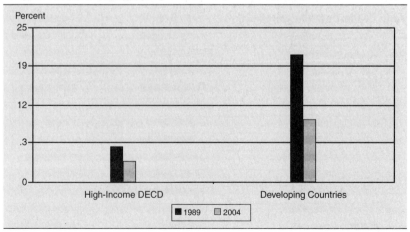

Figure 4

Import Duties in Developing Countries, 1989 and 2004

Percent

(Bar chart with y-axis marked 0, .3, 12, 19, 25. X-axis categories: High-Income DECD, Developing Countries. Legend: ■ 1989, □ 2004)

Source: United Nations Development Programme, *Human Development Report 2005* (New York: Oxford University Press, 2005), 116.

strategic trade policy (such as export subsidies or tariffs on imported goods) that is intended to benefit domestic firms. Contemporary trade theory casts doubt on the simple notion that more trade equals more prosperity, in part because of increasing returns to scale (that is, the cost per unit produced decreases as more of it is produced), which suggests that free markets may lead to dominance by one or a few producers. Also, the benefits from expanded trade may not be evenly distributed within societies. For example, if sugar tariffs were reduced in the United States, domestic producers would be hurt while foreign producers would gain—as would U.S. taxpayers and consumers, who would pay slightly reduced prices for sugar. Thus, even if aggregate prosperity increases, the benefits may be highly concentrated in the firms or sectors that are most competitive internationally and the costs imposed on those least internationally competitive. Furthermore, the empirical evidence linking trade and prosperity is mixed. For all the rhetoric surrounding economists' belief that free trade leads to greater prosperity, there are also other means of addressing problems associated with trade liberalization, such as economic assistance and retraining programs for workers who lose jobs as a result of the heightened competition.

The following two articles detail opposing viewpoints by two prominent economists: David Dollar and Robert Wade. Wade favors a nuanced approach to international trade policy rather than grand "free trade agreements," while Dollar argues that trade liberalization explains the economic resurgence of several developing economies.

Discussion Questions

1. Trade liberalization has made the world economy more highly integrated than ever before. Are there risks to such a highly integrated global economy? What are they? Do the benefits outweigh the risks?
2. Global trade liberalization has reduced tariffs and barriers to trade. One impact of this is that it has made it cheaper to import many goods. As a result, the United States has run a trade deficit for the past three decades. What are the risks of running a trade deficit instead of a trade surplus? What are the benefits?
3. China has emerged as one of the largest economies in the world, but its integration into the global economy and its move toward trade liberalization have not occurred without controversy or concern. What have the concerns been about, and who has expressed them? Consider such issues as jobs, quality standards of goods, foreign

policy, democratization, and human rights. Are these concerns valid? Why or why not?

4. Is trade liberalization good for all countries? Why or why not? In what situations would a country reject liberalization as a trade policy?

5. What evidence does David Dollar cite to link trade liberalization and economic prosperity? Is his evidence convincing?

6. Robert Wade argues that trade liberalization is not a necessary condition for economic growth. What evidence does he use to argue his point? What would Dollar say in regard to Wade's claims? Who do you think is right?

YES: David Dollar, *World Bank Country Director, China and Mongolia*[1]

Trade liberalization is one of the controversial issues in the debates about the benefits and costs of globalization. There is no doubt that trade liberalization increases economic prosperity. Trade enables a country to sell more of the things it produces relatively efficiently and to purchase in return things that it produces not at all or less efficiently. The notion that this exchange is a "win-win" situation for both countries involved was developed as the theory of comparative advantage by David Ricardo. These benefits, however, are "static" in the sense that they represent a one-time increase in real income, rather than leading to continual increases in income (that is, economic growth).

A more interesting and controversial question is whether in general there are "dynamic" benefits to trade liberalization that lead to faster growth and hence much larger cumulative benefits. To address this question, it is useful to begin with what one would expect from economic theory. As Paul Romer (1986) has suggested, traditional theories about growth and differences in income levels among countries focused on accumulation and the "object gap" between poor countries and rich ones:

> To keep track of the wide range of explanations that are offered for persistent poverty in developing nations, it helps to keep two extreme views in mind. The first is based on an object gap: Nations are poor because they lack valuable objects like factories, roads, and raw materials. The second view invokes an idea gap: Nations are poor because their citizens do not have access to the ideas that are used in industrial nations to generate economic value. ...
>
> Each gap imparts a distinctive thrust to the analysis of development policy. The notion of an object gap highlights saving and accumulation. The notion of an idea gap directs attention to the patterns of interaction and communication between a developing country and the rest of the world.

If the preferred way to grow income is just to increase the number of factories and workplaces, then it does not matter if this increase is accomplished in a closed environment or a state-dominated environment. That model was followed in the extreme by China and the Soviet Union, and, to a lesser extent, by most developing countries, which followed import-substituting industrialization strategies throughout the 1960s and 1970s. It was the disappointing results from this development approach that led to new thinking both from policymakers in developing countries and from economists studying growth.

Romer was one of the pioneers of the new growth theory that put more emphasis on how innovation occurs and is spread and on the role of technological advance in improving the standard of living. According to this theory, trade liberalization—by allowing specialization, economies of scale, and purchase of the latest equipment and technology—can potentially help to overcome the "idea gap" that separates poor and rich nations. The straightforward approach, then, is to write down a growth model in which access to a large world market will accelerate growth, at least for some period of time. The debate over whether trade liberalization actually leads to faster growth is not going to be settled by theory, however, for this is inherently an empirical question.

In order to shed light on this question, we need to briefly review the history of trade liberalization, noting that the developed countries of Western Europe, North America, and Japan went through a postwar period of multilateral trade liberalization, while developing nations mostly sat on the sidelines. Starting around 1978, however, more and more developing economies chose to undertake unilateral trade liberalization. At about the same time, the aggregate growth rate of the developing world accelerated, and the world entered a remarkable period of poverty reduction.

Next, we will need to consider whether or not one can make a convincing empirical link from trade liberalization to faster growth. Case studies, cross-country statistical evidence, and micro evidence from firms all support the view that trade liberalization accelerates growth in an underdeveloped economy.

GROWING INTEGRATION BETWEEN NORTH AND SOUTH

Global economic integration has been going on for a long time; in that sense, globalization is nothing new. What is new in this most recent wave of globalization is the way in which developing countries are integrating with rich countries. As in previous waves of integration, this change is driven partly by technological advances in transport and communications, and partly by deliberate policy changes.

The first great era of modern globalization ran from about 1870 to 1914, spurred by the development of steam shipping and by an Anglo-French trade agreement. In this period, the world reached levels of economic integration comparable in many ways to those of today. Global integration took a big step backward, however, during the period of the two world wars and the Great Depression. Some discussions of globalization today assume that it is inevitable, but this painful episode is a powerful reminder that restrictive policies can halt and reverse integration. By the end of this dark era, both trade and foreign asset ownership were back down nearly to their levels of 1870—the protectionist period had undone fifty years of integration.

In the period from the end of World War II to about 1980, the industrial countries restored much of the integration that had existed among them. They negotiated a series of mutual trade liberalizations under the auspices of the General Agreement on Tariffs and Trade (GATT). In this second wave of modern globalization, many developing countries chose to sit on the sidelines. Most developing countries in Asia, Africa, and Latin America followed import-substituting industrialization strategies—that is, they kept their levels of import protection far higher than those in the industrial countries in order to encourage domestic production of manufactures, and they usually restricted foreign investment by multinational firms as well in order to encourage the growth of domestic firms. While limiting direct investment, quite a few developing countries turned to the practice of international bank borrowing that was expanding in the 1970s and thereby took on significant amounts of foreign debt.

The most recent wave of globalization began in 1978 with the initiation of China's economic reform and opening to the outside world. China's opening coincided roughly with the second oil shock, which contributed to external debt crises throughout Latin America and elsewhere in the developing world. In a growing number of countries—from Mexico to Brazil to India to sub-Saharan Africa—political and intellectual leaders began to fundamentally rethink their development strategies. What is distinctive, then, about this latest wave of globalization is that the majority of the developing world (measured in terms of population) has shifted from an inward-focused strategy to a more outward-oriented one.

Some measure of this policy trend can be seen in average import tariff rates for the developing world. Average tariffs have declined sharply in South Asia, Latin America, and East Asia—mostly the result of decisions to unilaterally liberalize trade—while in Africa and the Middle East there has been much less tariff-cutting (see Figure 1). These reported average tariffs, however, capture only a small amount of what is happening with trade policy.

Often the most pernicious impediments are nontariff barriers: quotas, licensing schemes, restrictions on purchasing foreign exchange for imports. In China's case, reducing such nontariff impediments starting in 1979 led to a dramatic surge in trade (see Figure 2). Whereas in 1978 external trade had been monopolized by a single government ministry, in the following year China began to shift to a policy of "free trade." (That phrase refers to a situation in which trade is not monopolized by the government, but rather is permitted to private firms and citizens as well.) The specific measures adopted in China included allowing a growing number of firms, including private ones, to trade directly and opening a foreign exchange market to facilitate this trade.

The immediate result of this altered strategy can be seen in the huge increases in trade integration of developing countries over the last two decades

Figure 1

Average Unweighted Tariff Rates by Region, 1980–1998

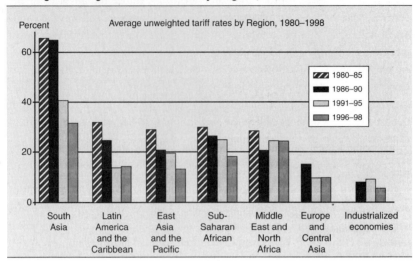

Source: Berg, Andrew and Anne Krueger, 2003. "Trade, Growth, and Poverty: A Selective Survey." IMF Working Paper, WP/03/30, p. 16.

Figure 2

Trade Reforms and Trade Volumes, China 1978–2000

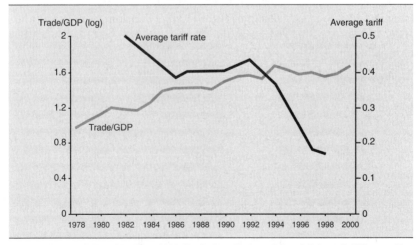

Source: Dollar, David and Aart Kraay. 2003. "Institutions, Trade, and Growth," *Journal of Monetary Economics* 50 (133–162), p. 151.

of the twentieth century. China's ratio of trade to national income more than doubled in that period, and countries such as Mexico, Bangladesh, Thailand, and India saw large increases as well (see Figure 3). It was also the case, however, that quite a few developing countries traded less of their income over those two decades. Some of these countries engaged in relatively little formal trade liberalization, while in others, such as Kenya, formal trade liberalization was not complemented by efforts to improve customs and ports, with the result that the country traded less of its income in 1997 than it had done twenty years before.

The change was reflected not just in the *amount*, but also in the *nature of what was traded*. Prior to 1980, nearly 80 percent of developing countries' merchandise exports were primary products—the stereotype of poor countries exporting tin or bananas had a large element of truth. The big increase in merchandise exports over the next two decades, however, consisted of manufactured products, so that, by the century's end, 80 percent of merchandise exports from the low-income countries of the South were manufactures (see Figure 4). Garments from Bangladesh, refrigerators from Mexico, computer peripherals from Thailand, CD players from China—this had become the modern face of developing country exports. Service exports from the developing world had also increased enormously, both traditional services such as

Change in Trade/GDP, 1977–1997 (selected countries)

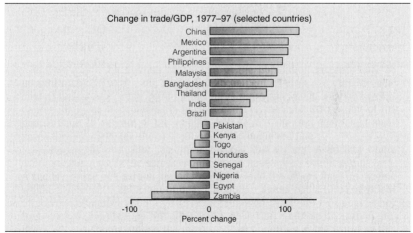

Source: Dollar, David. 2004. "Globalization, Poverty, and Inequality since 1980." World Bank Policy Research Working Paper, No. 3333, p. 7.

Figure 4

Developing Country Exports, 1965–1998

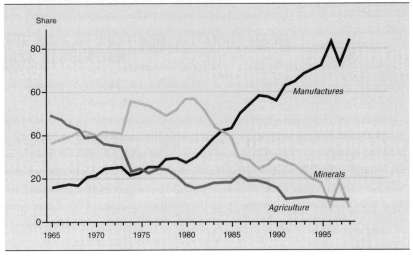

Source: Dollar, David. 2004. "Globalization, Poverty, and Inequality since 1980." World Bank Policy Research Working Paper, No. 3333, p. 8.

tourism and more distinctively modern ones, such as software from Bangalore, India.

At the same time as trade was being liberalized, the aggregate growth rate of the developing world was accelerating. We have reasonably good data on economic growth going back to 1960 for about one hundred countries, which make up the vast majority of the world's population, summarized in the Penn World Tables. If you aggregate all of the industrial countries (members of the Organization for Economic Cooperation and Development [OECD]) and all of the developing countries for which there are data back to 1960, you find that, in general, rich country growth rates declined until the end of the century, while growth of the developing world accelerated (see Figure 5). In particular, in the 1960s growth of OECD countries was about twice as fast as that of developing countries. This was a period in which the OECD countries were benefiting from mutual trade liberalization while developing countries largely chose to follow inward-oriented strategies. The rich country growth then gradually decelerated from about 4 percent per capita in the 1960s to 1.7 percent in the 1990s. The latter figure is close to the long-term historical growth rate of the OECD countries.

In the 1960s and continuing into the 1970s, the growth rate of developing countries in the aggregate was well below that of rich countries—a paradox whose origin has been long debated in the economics profession. The slower

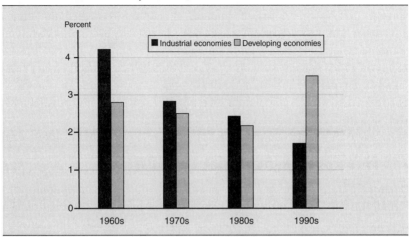

Figure 5

Growth Rates of Per Capita GDP, 1960s–1990s

Source: Dollar, David. 2004. "Globalization, Poverty, and Inequality since 1980." World Bank Policy Research Working Paper, No. 3333, p. 13.

growth of backward economies in that period appeared to contradict the dominant neoclassical growth theory, which suggested that, other things being equal, poor countries should grow faster. This expected pattern finally emerged in the 1990s, when per capita growth in developing countries reached about 3.5 percent, more than twice the rate of rich countries. Since 2000, developing country growth has been even faster.

Poverty reduction in low-income countries is very closely related to the GDP growth rate. Hence, the accelerated growth of low-income countries has led to unprecedented poverty reduction. (By *poverty,* we mean subsisting below some absolute threshold. In global discussions, one often sees reference to an international poverty line of $1 per day, calculated at purchasing power parity.) Shenhua Chen and Martin Ravallion (2004) have used household survey data to estimate the number of individuals classified as poor worldwide based on the $1 poverty line, back to 1981. They find that the incidence of extreme poverty (consuming less than $1 per day) was basically cut in half over a twenty-year period, from 40.3 percent of the developing world's population in 1981 to 21.3 percent in 2001. In 1981 extreme poverty was concentrated in East and South Asia, and these were the regions that grew especially well over the next two decades, dramatically reducing extreme poverty.

Poverty incidence has been gradually declining throughout modern history, but in general population growth has outstripped the decline in incidence, so that the total number of poor people was actually rising. Even in the 1960–1980 period, which was reasonably good for developing countries, the number of poor continued to rise (see Figure 6).[2] What is really striking about the two decades that followed—indeed, it was unprecedented in human history—is that the number of extreme poor declined by 375 million, while at the same time the world's population rose by 1.6 billion. While this overall decline in global poverty is encouraging, it should be noted that there has been very different performance across regions. While East and South Asia grew well and reduced poverty, sub-Saharan Africa had negative growth between 1981 and 2001 and a rise in poverty.

THE LINK FROM INTEGRATION TO GROWTH

Developing countries became more integrated with the global economy over the last two decades of the twentieth century, while growth and poverty reduction accelerated. A natural question to ask is whether there was a link between these two phenomena. In other words, could countries such as Bangladesh, China, India, and Vietnam have grown as rapidly as they did, had they remained as closed to foreign trade and investment as they were in 1980? This

Figure 6

World Poverty, 1820–2001

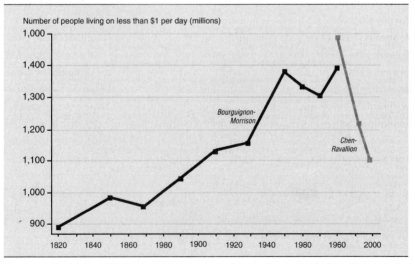

Source: Dollar, David. 2004. "Globalization, Poverty, and Inequality since 1980." World Bank Policy Research Working Paper, No. 3333, p. 18.

is not the kind of question that can be answered with scientific certainty, but there are several different types of evidence that we can bring to bear on it.

First, a large number of case studies show how this process can work in particular countries. Among the countries that were very poor in 1980, China, India, Vietnam, and Uganda provide an interesting range of examples.

China

China's initial reforms in the late 1970s focused on the agricultural sector and emphasized strengthening property rights, liberalizing prices, and creating internal markets. As indicated in Figure 2, liberalizing foreign trade and investment was also part of the initial reform program and played an increasingly important role in growth as the 1980s proceeded.

The role of international linkages is described in a case study by Richard Eckaus (1997):

> After the success of the Communist revolution and the founding of the People's Republic of China, the nation's international economic policies were dominated for at least thirty years by the goal of self-reliance. ... China's foreign trade began to expand rapidly as the turmoil created by the Cultural Revolution dissipated and new leaders came to power. Though it was not done without controversy, the argument that opening of the economy to foreign trade was necessary to obtain new capital equipment and new technology was made official policy.

At the same time, Eckaus notes, international transactions outside the state planning system were growing. Enterprises created by foreign investors were exempted from the foreign trade planning and control mechanisms, and substantial amounts of other types of trade, particularly that between township and village enterprises and private firms, were made relatively free. "The expansion of China's participation in international trade since the beginning of the reform movement in 1978 has been one of the most remarkable features of its remarkable transformation," says Eckaus. "While GNP was growing at 9 percent from 1978 to 1994, exports grew at about 14 percent and imports at an average of 13 percent per year."

India

India pursued an inward-oriented strategy into the 1980s and got disappointing results in terms of growth and poverty reduction. Jagdish Bhagwati (1992) crisply defines the main problems and failures of the strategy:

> I would divide them into three major groups: extensive bureaucratic controls over production, investment and trade; inward-looking trade and foreign investment policies; and a substantial public sector, going well beyond the conventional confines of public utilities and infrastructure.
>
> The former two adversely affected the private sector's efficiency. The last, with the inefficient functioning of public sector enterprises, impaired additionally the public sector enterprises' contribution to the economy. Together, the three sets of policy decisions broadly set strict limits to what India could get out of its investment.

Under this policy regime, India's growth in the 1960s (1.4% per annum) and the 1970s (–0.3%) was disappointing. The country's economic performance improved during the 1980s, but this surge was fueled by deficit spending and borrowing from abroad that was unsustainable. In fact, the spending spree led to a fiscal and balance of payments crisis that brought a new, reform government to power in 1991. Key aspects of its program of reform were an initial devaluation of the rupee and subsequent market determination of its exchange rate, abolition of import licensing (with some important exceptions), convertibility of the rupee on current account; reduction in the number of tariff lines as well as tariff rates, and an easing of entry requirements for direct foreign investment.

In general, India has gotten good results from its reform program, as per capita income growth remained above 4 percent per annum in the 1990s and then accelerated to around 6 percent after 2000. This pattern reinforces the conclusion that growth and poverty reduction have been particularly strong in states that have made the most progress in liberalizing their economies.

Vietnam

Another interesting case is Vietnam—a country that went from basket-case status in the mid-1980s to that of a dynamic exporter and darling of international investors twenty years later. In a case study of that startling turn-around, Dollar and Ljunggren (1997) reflect on its proximate causes:

> That Vietnam was able to grow throughout its adjustment period can be attributed to the fact that the economy was being increasingly opened to the international market. As part of its overall effort to stabilize the economy, the government unified its various controlled exchange rates in 1989 and devalued the unified rate to the level prevailing in the parallel market. This was tantamount to a 73 percent *real* devaluation; combined with relaxed administrative procedures for imports and exports, this sharply increased the profitability of exporting.

According to these authors' analysis, this policy produced strong incentives for export throughout most of the 1989–1994 period, during which real export growth averaged more than 25 percent per annum. Exports—mainly of rice at first, but later of a wide range of exports, including processed primary products (for example, rubber, cashews, and coffee), labor-intensive manufactures, and tourist services—were a leading sector spurring the expansion of the economy.

While the country's current account deficit declined from more than 10 percent of GDP in 1988 to zero in 1992, Vietnam's export growth was sufficient to ensure that imports could continue to grow, rather than being cut back, as might have been expected. Noting that investment increased sharply between 1988 and 1992, while foreign aid [from the Soviet Union] was drying up, Dollar and Ljunggren explain: "In response to stabilization, strengthened property rights, and greater openness to foreign trade, domestic savings increased by twenty percentage points of GDP, from negative levels in the mid-1980s to 16 percent of GDP in 1992."

Uganda

Uganda was one of the most successful reformers in Africa during this recent wave of globalization, and its experience has interesting parallels with Vietnam's. It, too, was a country that was quite isolated economically and politically in the early 1980s.

According to Paul Collier and Ritva Reinikka (2001, 30–39), trade liberalization was central to Uganda's structural reform program:

> During the 1970s, export taxation and quantitative restrictions on imports characterized trade policy in Uganda. Exports were taxed, directly and implicitly at very high rates. All exports except for coffee collapsed under this taxation.
>
> Part of the export taxation was achieved through overvaluation of the exchange rate, which was propelled by intense foreign exchange rationing, but mitigated by an active illegal market. Manufacturing based on import substitution collapsed along with the export sector as a result of shortages, volatility, and rationing of import licenses and foreign exchange.

The NRM government that came to power in 1986 thus inherited a trade regime that included extensive nontariff barriers, biased government purchasing, and high export taxes, coupled with considerable smuggling. The nontariff barriers were gradually removed after the introduction in 1991 of automatic licensing under an import certification scheme. During the latter half of the

1990s, the government implemented a major tariff reduction program, and, as a result, "by 1999 the tariff system had been substantially rationalized and liberalized, which gave Uganda one of the lowest tariff structures in Africa." The maximum tariff was set at 15 percent on consumer goods, zero for capital goods, and 7 percent for intermediate imports.

Collier and Reinikka summarize the results of this reform effort:

> The country's average real GDP growth rate was 6.3 percent per year over the entire recovery period (1986–1999) and 6.9 percent in the 1990s. The liberalization of trade has had a marked effect on export performance. In the 1990s export volumes grew (at constant prices) at an annualized rate of 15 percent, and import volumes grew at 13 percent. The value of non-coffee exports increased fivefold between 1992 and 1999.

CONCLUSION

These cases provide persuasive evidence that openness to foreign trade and investment—coupled with complementary reforms—can lead to faster growth in developing countries. All of them also illustrate the earlier failure of import-substitution strategies based on protecting the domestic market. However, individual cases always beg the question, how general are these results? Does the typical developing country that liberalizes foreign trade and investment get good results?

Cross-country statistical analysis is useful for looking at the general patterns in the data, and such studies generally find a correlation between trade and growth. As reflected in the case studies reviewed above, some developing countries have had large increases in trade integration (measured as the ratio of trade to national income), while others have had small increases or even declines. In general, the countries that have had large increases in trade integration have also seen accelerations in growth. This relationship between trade and growth persists after controlling for reverse causality from growth to trade and for changes in other institutions and policies (Dollar and Kraay 2002).

A third type of evidence about integration and growth comes from firm-level studies and links us back to Paul Romer's theories about trade liberalization and innovation, quoted earlier. Developing countries often have large productivity dispersion across firms making similar things: high productivity and low productivity firms coexist, and in small markets there is often insufficient competition to spur innovation. A consistent finding of firm-level studies is that openness leads to lower productivity dispersion—the less efficient, high-cost producers exit the market as prices fall. While the destruction and creation of new firms is a normal part of a well-functioning economy, attention is too often paid only to the destruction of firms, missing half of the picture. In a more open economy, there are more firm start-ups, a prime source of jobs and productivity growth. The higher turnover of firms is thus an important source of the dynamic benefit of openness. In general, dying firms have falling productivity, and new ones tend to increase productivity.

While these studies shed some light on why open economies are more innovative and dynamic, they also remind us why integration is controversial. There will be more dislocation in an open, dynamic economy, as some firms close and others start up. If workers have good social protection and opportunities for developing new skills, everyone can benefit. But without such policies, there can be some big losers.

The economic historians Peter Lindert and Jeffrey Williamson (2001, 29–30) make a nice point about the different pieces of evidence linking integration to growth: "The doubts that one can retain about each individual study threaten to block our view of the overall forest of evidence. Even though no one study can establish that openness to trade has unambiguously helped the representative Third World economy, the preponderance of evidence supports this conclusion." Going on to note the "empty set" of "countries that chose to be less open to trade and factor flows in the 1990s than in the 1960s and rose in the global living-standard ranks at the same time," they conclude: "As far as we can tell, there are no anti-global victories to report for the postwar Third World. We infer that this is because freer trade stimulates growth in Third World economies today, regardless of its effects before 1940."

NO: Robert H. Wade, *London School of Economics and Political Science*

There is nothing that economists agree about more than the virtues of free or almost-free trade.[1] Nicholas Stern, former chief economist at the World Bank, declared in 2008, "95 percent of the arguments for protection are rubbish, and the other 5 percent don't work in practice."[2] Jagdish Bhagwati, a distinguished trade economist, claimed that belief in the superiority of the free or near-free trade strategy over the "import substitution" strategy is all but universal among economists, "insofar as any kind of consensus can ever be found in our tribe."[3] A survey of economists' opinions elicited responses to twenty-seven propositions about the economy from about 1,000 economists in five industrialized countries, in terms of "generally agree," "agree with provisos," and "generally disagree." Of the twenty-seven, "tariffs and import controls lower economic welfare" elicited the most agreement. Fifty-seven percent of the whole sample—including 79 percent of the American economists (though only 27 percent of the French economists)—"generally agreed" with it.[4]

Economists typically deploy words such as *protectionism* and *protectionist* as automatic negatives. To seek to persuade by ensuring that the phenomenon cannot be described without simultaneously being given a normative evaluation is a standard rhetorical technique, but it makes for bad science. Phrases such as "price distortion" and "financial repression" show the same tactic deployed to the same end—to load the scales in favor of free markets.

This free trade consensus has justified the World Bank's emphasis on trade liberalization as not just one policy reform among many but as the queen of reforms. Its Structural Adjustment Loans over the 1980s and 1990s carried more trade liberalization conditions than those in any other policy domain.[5]

To see how these ideas shape country policy today, take the case of Mongolia. The government that took power as communism ended in 1991 swung to the noncommunist extreme and embarked on fast, unstrategic economic liberalization. It was hailed as a star pupil of the Washington Consensus. But the industrial sector collapsed, urban unemployment soared, people retreated into pastoralism, pastoral yields collapsed, and social indicators fell (having been high relative to per capita income in the bad old communist days).[6]

However, the government did want to retain one primitive industrial policy: a tax on the export of unprocessed wool (an instrument the English government had used to develop the wool industry in competition with already-established competitors on the Continent in the fifteenth century). The Asia Development Bank offered the government a big loan (roughly $200 million)—on condition that the government drop the export tax. The government obliged, removed the export tax, and Mongolia's wool came to be processed in China and Italy. Good for China and Italy, bad for Mongolia—which continues to struggle with high unemployment, overpopulation in the pastoral economy, and a large current account deficit. Mongolia's experience illustrates that the alternative to an "inefficient" industrial sector, measured in world market prices, may be not an "efficient" one, but none.

Fast forward to 2002, when a German Development Bank mission arrived in Ulan Bator to help with the country's World Trade Organization (WTO) accession. The mission discussed Mongolia's situation with the World Bank country director and floated the idea of restoring an export tax on unprocessed wool. The World Bank country director put his foot down, declaring, "That would be going backwards. We don't want the government to intervene in the economy. We want the government to stick to free trade."[7] In the Mongolia story, we see the Asian Development Bank, the World Bank, and the postcommunist Mongolian government giving a high priority to free trade policy, as if there were no sensible alternative.

The idea that trade has almost magical developmental effects is frequently reiterated from authoritative positions in the international development community, as in World Bank president Paul Wolfowitz's declaration that, "It is trade that will allow poor countries to generate growth. ... It is trade that has helped 400 million Chinese escape poverty in the past 20 years and the same can happen elsewhere." Fudging the important distinction between "trade policy" and "trade quantities and values," such statements assume that freer trade policy reliably generates more trade and that more trade reliably improves indicators of economic development.

In the same vein, most commentators in the West agree that the early 2007 collapse of the WTO's Doha Round trade negotiations—aimed at intensifying the Uruguay Round's multilateral liberalization of trade and investment (while retaining tough protection of intellectual property)—was a bad thing for everyone except some special interest groups. They paint a post-Doha scenario of crumbling multilateral trade arrangements, proliferating bilateral or regional trade agreements ("stumbling blocks" rather than "building blocks"), and trade quarrels seemingly immune to the WTO's Dispute Settlement Mechanism. They also say that developing countries are the big losers, because various aid-for-trade and trade facilitation measures written into Doha will be suspended while agricultural support in the United States, the European Union, and Japan will continue, making it more difficult for developing countries both to sustain their own agriculture in the face of cheap food imports and to export agricultural products to the developed countries' markets—and thus assuming that they should specialize more in agriculture, their "comparative advantage."

The larger normative vision is of a "globalized" world where national borders have little economic significance, except perhaps to restrain labor migration. As Martin Wolf of the *Financial Times* says, "It cannot make sense to fragment the world economy more than it already is but *rather to make the world economy work as if it were the United States*"—that is, with national borders having no more economic significance than the borders between U.S. states.[8]

Yet one need look no further than the Latin America–China comparison to see that something is amiss with the free trade consensus. Twenty years ago, Latin America was the champion liberalizer, while China not only retained high barriers to trade and foreign investment and capital flows but also allowed its government to continue to steer the economy. Latin America was expected to ascend to the First World while China would languish in the Third World.

Twenty years on, however, China is the great success story; it is now a major world economic power, and many fewer of its people are living in poverty. Latin America, meanwhile, experienced an export boom, from $100 billion in 1981 to $750 billion in 2007. But the export boom was in primary products; Latin America's growth now depends heavily on China's; the industrial sector has been eroded; and its poverty headcount (number of people living on less than $2-a-day) soared from 140 million in 1980 to 210 million in 2005.

This essay will argue that both theoretical developments and new empirical evidence call for a rethinking of the free trade consensus. Indeed, it shows that the consensus does not hold among the subset of economists working directly on trade and trade policy. Economists-in-general, political leaders, business leaders, and concerned citizens should pay attention to the shifting ground of theory and evidence, taking a questioning approach to the claim that trade liberalization is a necessary condition for economic progress and even more so to the claim that it is an almost sufficient condition for economic progress.

But these days trade is not the only highly contentious international economic issue; so, too, are foreign investment and intellectual property rights, because international business in the West is increasingly interested in investing in foreign locations, as distinct from producing at home and exporting. The main governance body for multilateral trade and investment, the WTO, has some strongly antidevelopmental features, and reform efforts should focus on removing these features while protecting what is valuable—notably the Dispute Settlement Mechanism.

GIVENS AND NOT GIVENS

To clear the ground, here are some propositions that can be taken as given.

- Some trade is better than no trade (but no one champions autarky, not even Kim Jong Il of North Korea).

- Trade can expand markets, lower costs, intensify competition, disseminate knowledge of tastes and technology, and raise productivity.

- Countries that have sustained fast growth have experienced a rising share of trade in GDP.

- In these cases, the broad direction of change in trade barriers has been downward.

- Very high average tariffs (say 50 percent +) and large variations in effective tariffs between one sector and another reflecting not national strategy but inertia or interest-group pressures constitute a "bad" trade regime. As between this bad regime and free trade, free trade wins hands down.

But this last is a phony choice. The policy question generally is, "Should the government now give high priority to *further and across-the-board* trade liberalization?" as distinct from all the other things that compete for the government's attention. Part of the answer should rest on the answer to the question, "Is trade liberalization reliably associated with subsequent higher growth and lower poverty?"

Here are some further propositions that are more controversial.

- The claims for large growth benefits from trade liberalization tend to be based on computable general equilibrium (CGE) models. These models typically rest on implausible assumptions that bias the benefits upward, notably the assumption that full employment persists through the liberalization (so no account is taken of lost output due to higher unemployment). Moreover, the models typically ignore distributional effects.

- Prior trade policy liberalization is not sufficient for subsequent higher trade/GDP or for subsequent higher GDP growth rates, as seen from the number of cases where trade liberalization has not had these effects.

- Case study evidence suggests that trade protection *can* be good for economic growth and diversification of production. The case study evidence includes the historical experience of now developed countries, almost all of which used substantial protection during their industrialization. (This is not to say that trade protection is *generally* good for growth and diversification, still less to say, "more trade protection is better.")

- The effects of a given level of trade protection depend on how it is designed and how long it has been in place. They depend, for example, on whether protection is granted unconditionally or against performance requirements of protected industries or firms.

- Trade liberalization has diminishing returns. When average tariffs are 10 percent, a 10 percent cut has smaller effects than when average tariffs start at 40 percent.

- The effects of trade liberalization depend on how fast it is done and how soon after the establishment of new industries. Gradual trade liberalization is likely to have more benign effects than fast liberalization, and liberalization after learning-by-doing has occurred has more benign effects than liberalization concurrent with the establishment of new activities.

- The effects of trade liberalization depend heavily on the production and demand characteristics of the goods and services whose production is stimulated and those whose production is curbed. A trade liberalization that stimulates the production of goods and services with increasing returns and high income elasticity of demand and curbs the production of those with decreasing returns and low income elasticity of demand—possibly as a result of complementary industrial policies—will have better results than one that does the opposite.

- The effects of "bad" trade regimes on growth and poverty may come from a second set of causes that produce both the bad regime and the slow growth. The "bad" trade regime may be more a *symptom* of growth-inhibiting features than a direct cause, in the sense that a strong trade liberalization of even a "bad" regime (let alone one closer to average) may not bring improvements in overall performance on its own and may even make things worse. See the case of Mongolia, above, and country A, below.

- China's rise to be the workshop of the world for labor-intensive manufactures poses a development headache for the rest of the developing world, including Latin America and sub-Saharan Africa. It is deeply irresponsible for Western development organizations such as the World Bank to advocate trade liberalization and export-orientation country-by-country, on the assumption of "other things held constant in the rest of the world." Without special measures of industrial policy, existing and incipient manufacturing activity is likely to be knocked out by the China factor.

Before coming back to these complexities, let us rehearse the standard argument.[9]

FREE TRADE THEORY

If the residents of London and Manchester both gain by trading, why not equally the residents of England and Portugal? What difference does a national border make? If two autarchic economies start trading with each other, both will gain as each moves to specialize in its "comparative advantage." Therefore, according to free trade theory, trade is good and more trade is better. If an economy currently has tariffs or restrictions on imports, it can almost always gain (improve efficiency) by lowering or removing them, regardless of starting level, even if other countries maintain protection. In the words of a *Financial Times* editorial, "The case for trade liberalisation is simple: it is not wise to throw rocks into your own harbours. Liberalisation has run aground [in the failure of the Doha Round of trade negotiations] because its defenders have failed to make that simple argument."[10] Another homely analogy is often deployed to make the same case: if the bicycle does not keep moving forward, it will topple over. (Only a noncyclist could believe this!)

The core proposition of this popular theory is that fully employed resources will be utilized more efficiently in the absence of barriers to trade. It assumes that fuller exposure to international competition does not cause higher unemployment, so the efficiency gains from lifting trade barriers are not measured against the various kinds of costs associated with higher unemployment. Where, as is common in developing countries, the economy's main problem is failure to fully utilize its resources rather than failure to direct them into the most efficient uses, this assumption is deeply problematic.

The principle of comparative advantage, formalized by David Ricardo in the early nineteenth century, forms the theoretical foundation of free trade theory. This principle states that even if one country could produce all goods more cheaply than other countries, it would benefit—in the sense of experiencing a one-time increase in total consumption in the move from no trade to free trade—by specializing in the production and export of its relatively cheapest good (the good in which it has a comparative advantage) while importing the rest of its consumption bundle. Should each country do the same, the whole world would gain. What is more, rising trade tends to narrow income and price differentials among countries—such as the present 350:1 ratio of American to Ethiopian average incomes, or 50:1 when average incomes are adjusted to take account of differences in the purchasing power of the two currencies—even as production structures become more divergent. Capital flows to where labor is cheaper, and knowledge and new technologies flow in the same direction. If economic activities are characterized by diminishing returns (as is assumed), economic activity and incomes become spread across space more evenly as trade and capital mobility grow.

Evidence for Free Trade

An impressive amount of evidence seems to support this argument. Since the late 1960s, a dozen major studies have examined the impact of trade regimes on economic growth, income distribution, poverty, and other development indicators.[11] These studies confirm that free or almost-free trade produces the best economic results (with some small exceptions), and that countries with freer, less distorted trade regimes have better development performance than countries with less open, more distorted ones. In the words of one such study, "The best evidence available shows…the current wave of globalization, which started around 1980, has actually promoted economic equality and reduced poverty."[12]

The implications of this finding go well beyond trade policy. Import tariffs and import controls are only a subset of the ways in which governments try to alter the composition of economic activity. The neoclassical mainstream theorist believes that most such interventions are a mistake—not just one mistake among many, but a mistake so big as to constitute one of the main reasons for the slow progress of most developing countries. As a cause of poor development performance, bad government intervention dwarfs other domestic factors such as lack of natural resources and "inherent" market failures (those not caused by government), and also external factors such as falling terms of trade, volatility in exchange rates between the major currencies, and rich country trade regimes rigged against exports from developing countries.[13] The free market argument is derived from classical liberalism, which sees "the state" as artificial and "the market" as natural, and the two in fundamental tension.

The proposition that real-world states are even more imperfect than real-world markets has not been subject to testing in any direct way, but the many studies of trade policy do constitute the most systematic testing of propositions derived from it. Through their support for free (or always freer) trade, they also support the meta-belief that imperfect markets are generally better than imperfect states, and therefore that states should, by and large, be shrunk. And so these studies of trade regimes also support the allergy in neoclassical economics toward anything called "industrial policy," which involves the state protecting or giving preferential resources to certain sectors, such as infant industry protection.[14]

New Trade Theory

However, the foundational ideas of free trade advocates—the line of theory associated with Smith-Ricardo-Heckscher-Ohlin-Samuelson—deal with the static efficiency gains from trade, as in the reallocation of *existing* resources due to the switch from no-trade to trade, causing a one-time increase in the level of GDP per capita. This is quite separate from the proposition that a rise in the trade-to-GDP ratio causes higher *growth* rates (faster expansion of available resources), and also from the separate proposition that trade policy liberalization (cutting tariffs and nontariff barriers) causes higher growth rates.

Also, the foundational ideas assume that international trade is inter-industry trade (English cloth in exchange for Portuguese wine, for example); they assume a "representative" producer of each product and hence no variety in firms; they assume that the free international market will "automatically" shunt every national economy into its comparative advantage specialization by the same "invisible hand" mechanism that operates in the domestic economy;

they assume that countries have no spatial structure between them or within them—no clustering or agglomeration; and above all, they assume that diminishing returns to economic activities prevail over increasing returns. On this wobbly pyramid of assumptions and factoids economists' confidence in free trade is based.

In the mid- to late 1980s, "the deep slumber of a decided opinion" (to use J. S. Mill's phrase) suddenly stirred to life. A number of younger economists—including Paul Krugman, Elhanan Helpman, Gene Grossman, and Paul Romer—tried to develop theory capable of explaining two glaring facts not explainable by standard theory:

1. very large spatial disparities in income and wealth persist over decades and centuries, even within well-functioning market economies (northern and southern Italy, for example), and still more between countries at different levels of development that are engaged in international trade; and

2. most trade is of the kind that earlier trade theory assumed away: intra-industry trade (Italian shoes to India, Indian shoes to Italy).[15]

The resulting stream of literature came to be known as "new trade theory." It incorporated more "realistic" assumptions, such as imperfect competition, increasing returns to scale, and knowledge spillovers from innovating firms to follower firms; and it allowed for different products (grain, apparel, machine tools) having different intensities of these characteristics and so having different potential for further growth and diversification.

New New Trade Theory

New trade theory retained the earlier assumption of no differences between firms—the assumption of a "representative" firm. By the early 2000s, however, large-scale data on firm-level participation in international trade became available, making it clear that differences among firms matter for understanding international trade. Most firms, even in traded-goods sectors such as manufacturing, agriculture, and mining, do not export: in the United States in 2000, only 15 percent of firms in these sectors exported. Also, among exporting firms, exports are highly concentrated: the top 10 percent of U.S. exporting firms account for 96 percent of aggregate U.S. exports. These stylized facts about firm differences prompted a new wave of literature—known, clunkily, as "new new trade theory"—that was developed by Marc Melitz, Stephen Redding, Richard Baldwin, and others.[16]

The policy implications of this theoretical upheaval have hardly begun to be developed, but it is clear that they seriously complicate the old verities. Still, even those who have done most to develop the new theories—and to show theoretical mechanisms by which countries might gain from managed trade—tend to lean back toward free trade as the best *practical* policy, as in Paul Krugman's dictum, "Free trade rules are best for a world whose politics are as imperfect as its markets." [17] They justify the retreat to free trade by reference to the danger that more strategic policy would be "hijacked" by special interests. Yet they make no analysis of this claim, in contrast to the sophistication they bring to the arguments against free trade. As for the operational economists in organizations such as the World Bank, they don't pay much attention to the new theory. They have strong career incentives to prescribe with certainty—"I know what country X should do even before I get out of the airplane"—and they can be more certain if they believe in a single broad policy package for all countries, whether Mongolia, Sri Lanka, or Brazil. The commitment of operational economists to this orthodoxy limits the diffusion of the new ideas, because the World Bank has a strong "cowbell" effect, a disproportionate weight in shaping others' beliefs about what is true or not true.

Theories of Increasing Returns, Multiple Equilibria, and Spatial Structure

The most profound challenge to the theory of comparative advantage comes from beyond the new and newer trade theories—from a broader, less trade-specific economics of "multiple equilibria" and spatial structure, which sometimes goes under the name of "new economic geography." [18] Ralph Gomery, William Baumol, Paul Krugman, Anthony Venables, Dani Rodrik, and Anthony Thirlwall are leading thinkers in this stream. [19]

The empirical starting point for this theoretical approach is the finding that the location of a given industry in one country or another is often not a matter of comparative advantage but of accident and path-dependence. There is no reason of comparative advantage to explain why Switzerland has long dominated the watch industry, why Taiwan now dominates the production of laptops (but not their branding), why Pakistan specializes in soccer balls and Bangladesh specializes in hats rather than the other way around, or why Liechtenstein's big companies specialize in, respectively, power tools, microwave meals, and false teeth. [20] It turns out that industries have different "retainability" scores, in the sense that some industries, once established, are sheltered from the blast of full competition and can earn "super-normal" returns, because would-be competitors find it difficult to break in.

The new stream of theory shows how, in a world of increasing returns (rather than constant or diminishing, as in standard models), the existing market equilibrium may not be optimal. The existing allocation of industries across countries is (a) fragile and (b) not necessarily "globally" optimal (globally in the sense of better than any feasible alternative, not in the geographical sense). But the market lacks a mechanism for getting to a global optimum. The theory suggests that trade liberalization would not necessarily shunt the economy into a more desirable position than it could have reached with more activist trade and industrial policy, contrary to Ricardian trade theory. The theory of comparative advantage, being concerned with how an economy can best exploit its *present* stock of resources, cannot tackle the trade-off between acting today to maximize short-term efficiency and acting today to accelerate the economy's shift of tomorrow's comparative advantage into higher value-added, higher return products.[21]

One of the key analytical mechanisms is the link from spatial proximity to productivity, a link which is generally characterized by increasing returns ("proximity promotes productivity"). Denser spatial configurations of economic activity—more firms and more skilled people in the same space—promote productivity more than looser ones, up to some point of diminishing returns due to congestion and other costs. This kind of market "externality" underlies the importance of clustered networks of supporting industries for the growth of any one industry.

For example, U.S. military procurement is a giant industrial policy protecting whole chains of high-tech supplier industries in the United States under the justification of "national security," which allows the U.S. government to give protection to firms producing in the United States while demanding that other countries give up protecting their own.[22] The U.S. government paid for 50–70 percent of total R&D expenditures in the United States from the 1950s to the mid-1990s, mostly under cover of the defense umbrella. But the opposite tendencies are also in evidence. As Boeing switches component suppliers to China, U.S.-based component suppliers stop producing in the United States; U.S. supply networks fragment, causing knock-on costs to other industries; and Chinese firms buy U.S. component-making technology, the better to supply companies such as Boeing from China.

INDUSTRIAL POLICY AND INTER-STATE COMPETITION

The "new economic geography" theory suggests a new rationale for "infant industry protection," a long-but-grudgingly accepted partial exception to the prescription of free trade. In conventional trade theory, the infant industry exception is presumed to apply—if at all—only to newly-industrializing countries trying to lay down basic industries. But multiple equilibria theory suggests that the continuous technological evolution of the world economy means that parts of many industries are "infants" at any one time, even in the most technologically advanced economies. The task of governments, even in advanced economies, is to capture "high retainability" industries for their jurisdiction, using trade and other industrial policy instruments—even at the cost of short-term inefficiency. The new thinking suggests how strategic industrial policy (including trade as well as technology and education policy) can help in securing the economy's place in higher-potential industries with higher "retainability" scores. But as a general rule, the intervention should be temporary so that the market eventually supports the better equilibrium unaided. Of course, all governments—not just that of the United States—try to disguise what they are doing, so as to get others to do what they *say*: "we must all embrace free trade." The strategy could be called "optimal obfuscation."

In these terms we can make sense of the observed intense rivalry between nations as they jockey for industrial advantage—a far cry from the harmonious world of comparative advantage theory (whose assumption of mutual interests rather than conflicting interests is one of its strongest selling points for the international development community). Developed nations are silently implementing mercantilist industrial policy not mainly with trade instruments such as tariffs, but with more subtle, less noticeable behind-the-border instruments such as anti-dumping legislation, anti-trust, rules of origin, health standards, and especially government procurement; and, as suggested earlier, they often invoke national security to justify support that cannot be concealed. This internation rivalry helps to explain why the business school myth of multinational corporations as free-floating, cosmopolitan entities owing allegiance to nowhere is just that—a myth. State support tends to be geared toward high-tech firms regarded as "nationals" of the same state: the United States channels its support more toward American firms than to foreign firms operating within its borders, as do the other two centers, Europe and Japan-China.

In these terms we can also make sense of the difficult-to-deny motive behind the Doha trade talks agenda, which was devised almost entirely in service of U.S. and EU interests—to "hold back" developing countries from advancing into industrial and service areas now dominated by the developed countries.[23] For the theory shows that productivity growth in the less-productive trading partners of an advanced country is not necessarily in the interests of the advanced country—such growth in China and Vietnam is not necessarily in the interests of the United States. Paul Samuelson recently developed an argument along these lines, showing that as China, for example, catches up in the production of goods that had been produced in the United States (whether through outsourcing or through domestic innovation), U.S. export prices fall, worsening the U.S. terms of trade. The United States still benefits from trade, relative to "no trade," but less so than before.[24]

However, all this new thinking remains within the tradition of trade theory insofar as it assumes away unemployment, financial instability, and trade deficits. When these noticeable effects are factored in, the case for strategic industrial and trade policy—for not letting the market work freely—becomes even stronger. The objective of strategic policy is to enable resources to be combined and employed in a national economy when those resources would not be employed—or would be employed less productively—if the economy were fully exposed to efficiency criteria derived from world market prices. Its corollary objective is that this assistance be delivered in such a way that learning-by-doing takes place, so that after a time the strategic policy support can be redirected to other resource combinations. (See country B, below.)

OLD EVIDENCE REVISITED

In short, new and newer theory no longer support the old truth about free trade being, with only partial exceptions, best in theory. The case for free trade has been further undermined by (a) exposure of the serious defects in the major studies referred to earlier which purport to find that freer trade is better in the real world, (b) new evidence on structural changes during development, and (c) evidence from the development trajectories of the pre– and post–Second World War industrializers.

Constraints on space prevent more than a bald summary. It turns out that the impressive support for giving a high priority to further trade liberalization is not impressive when the methods, data, and conclusions are subject to unbiased scrutiny. For example, following a large-scale review of the existing literature on the relationships between trade liberalization, growth, inequality, and poverty, a set of economists concludes that "the results are weak: we find no robust evidence that inequality, or indeed growth, are determinants of cross-country variations in poverty. ... [A]ny claims regarding growth and poverty or trade liberalization (even globalization) and poverty should be interpreted with extreme caution."[25]

Meanwhile, an independent panel of economists tasked with evaluating World Bank research on development policies said of the big cross-country studies allegedly showing that free market policies are best:

> We see a serious failure in the checks and balances within the system that
> has led the Bank to repeatedly trumpet these early empirical results with-

out recognizing their fragile and tentative nature. ... Once the evidence is chosen selectively without supporting argument, and empirical skepticism selectively suspended, the credibility and utility of the Bank's research is threatened.[26]

New Cross-Country Evidence

Not only does the existing evidence adduced in support of free trade, or further trade liberalization as a policy priority, turn out to be weak, but also, new empirical findings contradict the conventional view. For example, Dani Rodrik, Ricardo Hausmann, and Lant Pritchett find that spells of accelerated (national) growth often occur spontaneously, without preceding "reforms," or only marginal ones, whether in trade or anything else. They identify more than eighty episodes since 1950 in which a country's growth rate increased by at least 2 percentage points for at least seven years—almost all of them without preceding liberalization or opening.[27]

Again, we now have good evidence that the dominant process in development is not increasing specialization in line with comparative advantage (rising Gini coefficient of sectoral shares in production), but *diversification* of production and employment.[28] Not just the familiar diversification from agriculture to manufacturing and on to services, but also diversification within manufacturing. As poor countries get richer, sectoral production and employment within manufacturing become more diversified among sectors. Diversification dominates specialization right up to a per capita level at the lower end of the "old" OECD countries (such as Portugal in the early 1990s)—above which, specialization dominates diversification. And as suggested by the Gomery-Baumol-Krugman-Venables work, the pattern of diversification in each country seems to have a large element of arbitrariness or randomness, in the sense that it reflects "self-discovery" of export opportunities and cost structures by a small number of entrepreneurs whom others then copy.

The evidence confirms the intuition that a central process of development is mastery over an expanding range of activities, rather than specialization in "what one does best today." Since diversification is central, the question becomes whether "the market" can be relied on to promote diversification—learning to master an expanding range of activities—sufficient to sustain catch-up growth; and if not, what the state can do to accelerate the process. The market may encourage diversification into "nearby" products (those with similar inputs) but with much the same value added. Diversification to more distant products with increasing returns and higher income elasticity of demand, and higher potential for further diversification (from radios to steel, in the

Korean case) may well require a push from the state. This kind of state push into products distant from present ones (requiring the supply of new private and public inputs) might be called "leading the market." Diversification to products in between "nearby" and "distant" might entail the state's "following the market"—helping to support private entrepreneurs to do (some of) what they would want to do anyway.[29]

Historical Evidence

Finally, the historical evidence from development trajectories gives little support for the proposition that trade liberalization reliably generates higher economic growth and lower poverty. Almost all the now developed countries used substantial trade protection during their rapid development stage. Britain was one of the most protectionist of countries for three hundred years until it attained industrial superiority in the mid-nineteenth century and started to champion free trade for all (except for its own colonies, of course).[30] In 1820 Britain's average tariff on manufactured imports was between 45 and 55 percent, compared to tariff levels ranging between 6 and 20 percent in Western Europe; yet British manufacturing came out on top. The United States was "the mother country and bastion of modern protectionism" during the nineteenth and first half of the twentieth centuries, in the words of economic historian Paul Bairoch.[31] At the end of the nineteenth century, when U.S. per capita income (adjusted for purchasing power) was about equal to that of the average of developing countries today, its industrial tariffs averaged close to 50 percent, compared to levels around 10 percent in developing countries today. At the same time it was also the world's fastest growing economy, rapidly ascending to No. 1.

The newly industrialized East Asian countries (Japan, Taiwan, South Korea) managed their trade as part of a larger industrial policy for the best part of forty years, such that industries to be nurtured to international competitiveness initially received substantial protection that was conditional on performance—especially on movement toward international prices and quality standards; as they became internationally competitive, protection was scaled back—as it was also scaled back if they continued not to be competitive. Hence, at any one time, the East Asian countries showed fairly high dispersion of effective protection rates across industrial sectors, quite contrary to the "low dispersion" prescription of neoclassical trade policy.[32] Of course, some of the supported industries "failed," in the sense of not becoming internationally competitive. But as Thomas Watson, the founder of IBM, is reputed to have said, "If you want to be more successful, increase your failure rate."

The East Asian countries provide concrete examples of how protection can be combined with competition, of how "inward orientation" can be combined with "export orientation." It takes fundamentalist liberal faith to argue that these countries, which have demonstrated the fastest development in history (recent China aside), would have done *even better* had they practiced free market economics.[33] As for China, it maintained average tariffs of more than 30 percent for decades up to the mid-1990s, when it was already growing and diversifying very fast. Recall the contrast in development performance between China and Latin America made earlier.

Many economists, however, dismiss the historical evidence on grounds that the causality is always unclear. Maybe the United States or Korea did grow fast with protection, they say, but they could have grown still faster with less protection. These traditionalists prefer to rely on computable general equilibrium (CGE) models, with clearly spelled-out assumptions and clear lines of causality—which tend to support the claim that trade liberalization produces big gains in national income. But the big gains generally appear only when the models make very unrealistic assumptions, such as the notion that employment is unaffected by cuts in tariffs. So the temptation is for the analyst to work backward from the desired gains to the selection of appropriate assumptions and coefficients. In the end, the trade debate goes on and on because protagonists use two different ontologies, or beliefs about what kind of evidence counts, which may be roughly summarized as "history" versus "mathematics."

OPTIMAL TRADE POLICY

No one argues that a strongly inward-oriented trade regime—with high, uniform and unconditional import protection plus export taxes—is better than a liberal trade regime. The point is that trade liberalization has been oversold, and does not deserve the priority it receives in the international development community.[34] Further openness is not always in every country's national interest, and a prescription of freer trade and freer investment (through the WTO or through bilateral trade agreements) is not generally in the global interest—though it is in the collective *advanced country* interest, given that such global rules make it more difficult for developing countries to diversify and upgrade into more technologically sophisticated products other than as subcontractors of advanced country firms. That is, the prescription supports the collective "primacy" project of the United States, European Union, and Japan, to keep other countries and firms asymmetrically dependent on them.[35]

To clinch the point, consider two countries, A and B.[36] A is a member of the WTO; it undertook comprehensive trade liberalization in 1994–1995 (cutting tariffs to a maximum of 15 percent and removing all quantitative restrictions); and it has implemented far-reaching liberalization within the domestic economy, including privatization, foreign ownership of national companies, full repatriation of profits, and the like. It is next door to North America. B is not a member of the WTO; it has maintained quantitative restrictions and tariffs of 30–50 percent; much of its trade is through state firms and import monopolies, and foreign ownership of national companies is restricted. It is far from North America and Europe.

Orthodox thinking would identify A as the likely success story. In fact, A is Haiti, which has had dismal economic performance, while B is Vietnam, which has grown at more than 8 percent a year since the mid-1980s, with sharply reduced poverty, and which has rapidly but strategically integrated with the world economy, its high trade barriers notwithstanding.

Now consider country C. In 2003 the country came under the "provisional" administration of the U.S. government after the United States and allies replaced the previous regime. The U.S. administration passed several detailed new economic laws, including almost free trade, privatization of public enterprises, full foreign ownership of domestic companies, full repatriation of profits, and foreign ownership of national banks; and it declared that these arrangements should be impossible to reverse by an incoming national government. In effect, the U.S. administration was trying to lock in arrangements of the country A kind. Country C is Iraq.

Trade policy will be an even more controversial subject going forward than it has been in the recent past, especially because of China. First, the ability of China's manufacturing agglomerations to produce a wide range of manufactured goods at 50 percent of the cost of other producers poses the acute question of how manufacturing can flourish elsewhere. (At this point, Chinese door makers are even able to ship doors to landlocked Mali and outcompete local carpenters.) Increased specialization in (diminishing returns) commodities and raw materials is bad news for the people of Africa and Latin America, and bad news for the prospects of a wider diffusion of the material benefits of growth. It is a recipe for specialization in poverty, except for those lucky enough to produce commodities with high income elasticity of demand (such as fish from Iceland). Getting the "proximity-productivity" dynamic to work in these economies has to involve some kinds of protection, even though not only the West but now also China will insist otherwise.

Second, trade policy will also be involved in the West's strategy for curbing China's ability to develop its own world-beating firms. The West is anxious that China not be allowed to follow Japan and Korea with their Toyotas and Samsungs; rather, Chinese firms should be accommodated as junior partners to Western firms or wiped out. Getting China to lift restrictions on trade, foreign investment and capital flows, and eschew a "developmental state"—in other words, getting China to behave "responsibly"—is a key part of the strategy.[37]

The policy implications of this argument—at both national (developing country) and multilateral level—are anything but straightforward. Within broad limits, beyond which everyone would agree that a policy is crazy, there is no one-policy-fits-all for strategic trade policy akin to the universal free trade policy of neoclassical economics. Like other powerful policy instruments, trade protection can be used well and it can be used badly. The fact that it has often been used badly does not mean that it cannot be used well, and the gains from using it well are high compared to possible substitute instruments, such as targeted subsidies, which tend to be more difficult for developing country states to implement. Sensible policy prescription starts here.

The next step is to discard the neoclassical distinction between "inward oriented" trade regimes and "outward oriented" ones, or at least to qualify it to recognize that a given trade regime—such as Japan's in 1950–1980, South Korea's in 1955–1990—can be both, in the sense of including policy-based incentives for both import substitution and export promotion but in different sectors at any one time.

Then one has to recognize that import substitution is the mother of most (not all) new exports, for the good reason that learning to produce for the domestic market—given that the demand already exists—is easier than producing for export sales. Further, import substitution policies do not necessarily give rise to cozy monopolies. Protection and competition can go together, even though, historically, protection has often been designed in such a way that it does cut competition, whether intentionally or not. Protection can coexist not only with domestic competition, but also with (buffered) international competition. For example, governments can use the price and quality gap between domestic and internationally-available versions of the same product to calibrate protection—as in, "you have two years to bring your price and quality to within X percent of the imported price, and you can get access to several kinds of publicly-supported facilities in order to do so; but after two years we will phase out the protection."[38]

Finally, one has to see trade policy as a subset of a larger strategic development policy designed to build on increasing returns and the proximity-productivity mechanism, rather than seeing trade policy as the queen and industrial policy as a pawn. As suggested earlier, both new theory and new evidence suggest that a low and uniform level of trade restrictions and tariffs is neither a necessary nor a sufficient condition for a successful growth strategy.

On the other hand, rising trade/GDP and foreign investment/GDP are indeed likely outcomes of a successful growth strategy, and if these ratios are prevented from rising—perhaps by advanced countries' rigging their trade regimes against upgraded exports from developing countries—the strategy may not remain successful.

For neoclassical economists brought up to believe the classic liberal postulate of "natural" markets vs. "artificial" government, this line of argument is upsetting. For others, the challenge is to develop guidelines for strategic trade policy which correspond with empirical evidence from the successful developing countries, which have some foundation in theoretical mechanisms, and which are not wide open to hijacking by vested interests. Then they have to translate these guidelines into revisions of WTO treaties, World Bank prescriptions, U.S. and EU preferential trade agreements, and other components of the Western primacy project.

CONCLUSION

"Does trade liberalization promote economic progress?" is the wrong question. Successful countries have used both protection and liberalization, often simultaneously in different sectors, and their protected sectors have changed over time. Protection is a powerful policy instrument, which—like any powerful policy instrument—can be used well or used badly. At least in its policy documents, though not always in its on-the-ground operational advice, even the World Bank has softened its earlier belief in free trade as optimal for all countries.[39]

The Doha trade round, now on life-support, constitutes a bad deal for developing countries, because it requires them to make big cuts in tariffs on both agricultural and industrial products in return for advanced countries' cuts in agricultural support. In response to the blockage in multilateral negotiations, advanced countries are falling over themselves to negotiate bilateral and regional trade agreements. Though deplored by many champions of free trade, the growth of spaghetti-ball inconsistencies of trade rules via these preferential trade agreements may be the best hope for generating commitment to a new round of multilateral negotiations once Doha fails.

In any new round, foreign direct investment and knowledge protectionism (aka intellectual property rights) will loom large, because international business is keenly interested in clearer rules and stronger enforcement. But developing countries will then be in a stronger position to resist—and especially to resist WTO insistence on the principle of nondiscrimination or "national treatment" (foreign firms must be treated no worse than domestic firms), which makes it difficult for the developing countries to nurture domestic firms. Yet, ironically, the ground may be beginning to shift on the West's preference for strict national treatment and strong knowledge protectionism, because far-sighted Western firms are already calculating that in twenty years' time, when Chinese firms have established operations in the West and taken out clutches of patents and copyrights, they themselves will need some flexibility to discriminate against Chinese firms. China, on the other hand, is now familiar with the multilateral game and supportive of the WTO, even to the point of no longer regarding the U.S. threat of taking it before the Dispute Settlement Mechanism as equivalent to sailing a warship along the Chinese coast.

Going forward, we should give up on the ambition of reaching another Big Trade and Investment Deal that all must sign. Progress is more likely to be made by asking, "What are the ten key challenges that 'the world' must act on in the next ten years, and what changes should be made to the multilateral (and bilateral/regional) trade regime to address them?" Only closed-minded neo-classical economists who mistake policy means for economic ends—or who support the western primacy project—would say that the answer includes, "More across-the-board trade liberalization in order to move the global political economic order further towards one in which sovereign states have no more ability to influence flows of goods, services, or capital across their borders than the states of the United States."

2

trade and equality

Does Free Trade Promote Economic Equality?

YES: L. Alan Winters, *University of Sussex*

NO: Kate Vyborny and Nancy Birdsall,
Center for Global Development

Chapter 1 addressed the issue of whether trade liberalization promotes economic prosperity. This chapter tackles an even knottier problem—the effects of trade on economic equality—both because the impacts of international trade are difficult to assess and because definitions of equality vary significantly. When you imagine a society of economic equality, what do you consider? That every individual earns approximately the same income? That basic needs are met for everyone? (And, what is a "need"?) That every individual has access to conditions (such as education) that would enable her to earn a living? Among the many competing definitions of what "economic equality" might mean, the Millennium Development Goal targets (discussed in chapter 3) are one means of setting minimum international goals for equality.

Layered on top of the conceptual issues entailed in defining economic equality is the problem of choosing the unit of analysis along which to gauge its extent within a given context. For example, if (in)equality is to be measured internationally, using states as units of analysis, the process will involve taking the mean income (or some other aggregate statistic) for a given country and comparing that statistic cross-nationally. Another form of inequality can be measured at the intra-national level: how much income inequality exists within nations? Yet another means of measuring inequality focuses on the purely individual level, without respect to national boundaries. Of course, each of these varying levels of analysis will provide different perspectives on how equal or unequal economic *outcomes* are without regard to how people attained their income or how it compares with that of others in the society.

In measuring economic inequalities, a common measure is the Gini coefficient, which represents the ratio of the cumulative share of individuals (represented on the horizontal axis in Figure 1) to their cumulative share of income (the vertical axis). A society with an equal distribution of income will be represented as the 45-degree line connecting endpoints of the two axes, while societies with more unequal distributions will be represented with steeply-sloped curved lines. The larger the Gini coefficient—the ratio of shaded area in the figure compared with the entire triangle—the more unequal the distribution of economic outcomes.

There are multiple ways of measuring Gini coefficients, and the results vary depending on whether they are aggregated at the individual, national, or international levels. Measured this way, the Gini coefficient of world income inequality increased between 1970 and 2000, as represented in Figure 2. And income disparities are particularly pronounced in some nations, such as those in the developing countries of Latin America and Africa (see Figure 3). Another factor complicating these calculations is whether equality is measured before or after any governmental transfer payments, such as public welfare, pension payments, subsidized or public education and housing, and so on. Needless to say, those who wish to make a political point can choose among competing statistics to support their views.

Figure 1

The Gini Coefficient

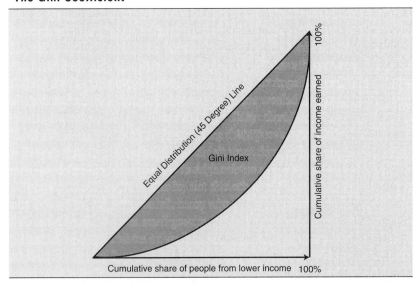

Figure 2

Gini Coefficient of World Income Inequality, 1970–2000

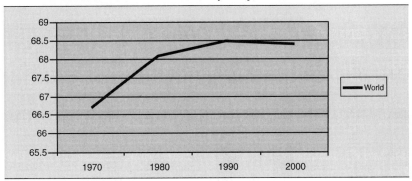

Source: Y. Dikhanov, "Trends in Global Income Distribution, 1970–2000 and Scenarios for 2015," United Nations Development Programme, New York, 2005, 37–43.

This chapter questions the impact of trade on economic inequality. At one level, it is natural to think that trade is advantageous to wealthier nations that are able to capitalize on more educated populations and superior technologies. But these advantages in trade expand income gaps cross-nationally, while intra-nationally widening gaps between high- and low-skilled workers. On the other hand, trade brings economic possibilities to workers globally and helps to lower prices for all. What to some is "free trade" is viewed by others as exploitative when the economic exchange occurs between vastly unequal actors. Because trade produces not just exchanges of finished products but also changes in *where* goods are produced, tensions arise involving manufacturing facilities owned by multinational corporations in developing nations, particularly those characterized by substandard labor practices. Yet, despite conditions that many in the West would abhor, even some social liberals — such as *New York Times* columnist Nicholas Kristof[1]—view the possibilities of jobs at "sweatshops" as a net improvement in living conditions.

The mobility of both goods and means of production contributes to a complicated relationship between trade and immigration, which also complicates policy responses. For example, policies that would restrict immigration may serve to increase pressures to send manufacturing facilities overseas, and vice versa. This effect, in turn, complicates domestic political responses to "outsourcing" and immigration policy. Those actors (such as organized labor) who favor policies to "protect" U.S. workers thus face a trade-off between wanting to restrict immigration (for fear of losing jobs to immigrants) and encouraging outsourcing.

Figure 3

Gini Coefficient of Income Inequality by Region, 1970–2000

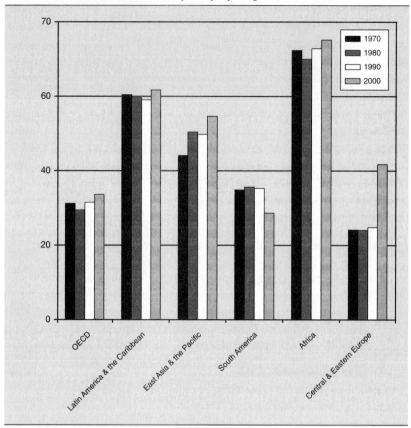

Source: Y. Dikhanov, "Trends in Global Income Distribution, 1970–2000 and Scenarios for 2015," United Nations Development Programme, New York, 2005, 37–43.

Trade policy is also influenced in important ways by domestic political constituencies—perhaps none so strong and enduring as the political sway held by farmers in wealthy nations. Subsidized farmers in the United States, the European Union, Japan, and elsewhere produce and sell crops at below market rates at the expense of farmers (or prospective farmers) in some developing nations that could compete were it not for these agricultural subsidies, export controls, tariffs, and so on. And yet, as Figure 4 indicates, agricultural support has grown in the developed nations in recent years.

The impact of trade on economic equality is one of the most politically potent and economically compelling issues raised by globalization. Owing to

Figure 4

Support to Agriculture in High-Income Countries, 1986–1988 and 2004

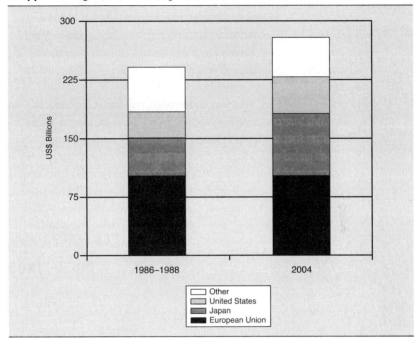

Source: United Nations Development Programme, *Human Development Report 2005* (New York: Oxford University Press, 2005), 129.

the complexities involved, the two articles that follow are not diametrically opposed in their views on this issue but nonetheless represent different perspectives on the likely impacts of free trade. Kate Vyborny and Nancy Birdsall argue that trade tends to increase inequalities, while Alan Winters suggests that overall inequalities will be dampened by freer trade.

Discussion Questions

1. How do you measure "equality"—by income? By standard of living? And between whom do you measure it—between countries? Between individuals within a country? Between all individuals in the world? What is most fair?

2. Is economic equality a desirable goal? An achievable goal? Why or why not? Aside from moral reasons, why is equality important?

3. Opponents of globalization and free trade often cite the poor working conditions and low wages of "sweatshops" and factories set up

in developing nations by wealthy multinational companies as evidence that free trade does not promote equality. Proponents of free trade say that the jobs and wages provided at these factories are better than the local alternatives, allowing those workers achieve a higher standard of living. Which argument do you agree with? Why?

4. What challenges does Alan Winters cite before considering whether free trade promotes economic equality? How does he address these challenges?

5. How do Kate Vyborny and Nancy Birdsall propose to address the inequality brought on by trade liberalization? What specific policies do they recommend? Do you agree with their policy proposals?

YES: L. Alan Winters, *University of Sussex and Centre for Economic Policy Research*

Unfortunately, the question "Does free trade promote economic equality?" doesn't admit an easy answer. It depends on what you mean by "economic equality" and by "free trade"—and even then it depends on the specific circumstances of the case. I will argue that free trade is likely to promote equality overall, but that there are clearly some senses and circumstances in which it may not do so. A closely related question that, indeed, is sometimes confused with the title question, is "Does freeing international trade reduce poverty?" I have done a good deal of research on the latter question over the past decade and, while explicitly recognizing the existence of exceptions, I would answer, "Almost always yes." [1]

GROUND CLEARING

So what do we mean by "economic inequality"? There are many significant dimensions to inequality and poverty—such as access to power, cultural fulfillment, freedom from violence—but I shall focus just on the economic variables of real income and consumption. The latter typically tracks very closely with wealth, however, so I will not even deal with wealth explicitly. When I deal with poverty, I will refer to people with incomes below the (very low) poverty line that is often fixed, for international comparisons, at $1 a day per head at 1985 international prices.

The principal question in regard to inequality is "Between whom?" There are three obvious alternatives: between countries, between individuals (or households) within a country, and between all the individuals in the world. The last of these alternatives combines elements of the first two, allowing, so far as the data permit, for the fact that some Indians are richer than some Americans, but there is no simple mathematical formula for the combination.

The definitive discussion and measurement of these different concepts is the brilliant book by Branko Milanovic (2005a), which shows that about 80 percent of world income inequality is due to differences in mean income between countries, while only about 20 percent is due to differences within countries. The former statistic has increased significantly since around 1980, and the latter a little; overall inequality has also increased a little, but not dramatically. [2]

The remaining concept to define is "free trade." Strictly, there is no such thing—all trade costs effort to conduct—but we could imagine international trade free from all interferences by government. Even this limited sort of freedom is relatively rare, however: many imports pay no tariff but still face inspection for, say, conformity to local safety standards. Hence we need to be rather pragmatic about the definition and hold to a notion of trade that is *relatively* free from official frictions and conducted with *relatively* efficient logistics and physical infrastructure. Precise measurement of the degree of trade friction poses serious challenges (as we shall see), although we can often identify changes in the "freedom of trade"—that is, trade liberalizations—easily enough.

TRADE AND INTER-COUNTRY INEQUALITY

Trade liberalization may affect inter-country inequality in two ways: either all countries free their trade but the consequences for national income per head differ by country, or only some countries do so, which will affect distribution even if all economies respond to liberalization the same way. Remember that inequality will be reduced if the poor experience strong growth relative to the rich. If all countries achieve the same growth rate, inequality—which is almost always measured as a relative magnitude—will be unchanged.[3]

Obviously, the experience of different countries will vary in detail, but some scholars have argued in theory that trade between rich and poor countries systematically benefits the rich countries and harms the poor ones (see Winters 2008 for a brief account). There is no hard evidence at all to support this theory. Over any given period, some countries will do relatively badly, by definition, and will get relatively poorer, but this outcome is not systematically related to their initial levels of income or their economic structures. In fact, the evidence suggests that, once we make allowance for the fact that policies are generally better in rich than in poor countries, poorer countries tend to grow a bit faster—that is, they catch up, reducing inequality, albeit slowly. As examples, think of Botswana, Chile, Korea, and Mauritius, which have all grown from very low levels of income and have all opened up their economies pretty strongly, too.

To make the discussion more concrete and more policy-relevant, let us narrow the question a little. Suppose that we have a set of rich and largely open economies—those of the OECD—which show steady growth: will developing countries improve their chances of catching up with them by opening up their economies strongly? That is, does openness boost developing countries' incomes?[4]

Economic theory offers many reasons to expect a country's own trade liberalization to stimulate its economic growth, at least for a period:

- specializing in goods for which world prices exceed those that would be available at home

- reaping economies of scale

- improving performance in the face of new competition, and

- benefiting from better inputs and technologies available from abroad

None of these effects is guaranteed, though, so whether trade does stimulate developing countries' incomes is ultimately an empirical matter. Over the 1990s, several highly visible global cross-country studies argued that openness is good for income levels, but at the decade's end, these studies were subjected to a searching criticism and reworking by Francisco Rodriguez and Dani Rodrik (2001). These authors showed that the earlier studies' measures of openness were not appropriate to the theories they propounded, that their results were sensitive to particular but extraneous features of the data, and that the econometric methods they used failed adequately to identify causation running from trade liberalization to growth. Rodriguez and Rodrik also found it hard to replicate some of the results reported in the literature, raising some concern about their accuracy.

The difficulty of establishing an empirical link between liberal trade and income arises from at least four sources (Winters 2004). First, apart from extreme cases such as North Korea (closed) or Hong Kong (open), it is difficult to measure a country's trade stance accurately: for example, tariffs need to be aggregated across goods, quantitative restrictions assessed and then aggregated, and the levels of predictability and enforcement of trade policies measured. Second, causation is difficult to establish, for actual openness, which is usually measured by the ratio of international trade to national income, is almost certainly the result of growth as well as a possible cause of it. But there is also concern that even policy-based measures, such as average tariffs, could face the same problem, because growing countries might be more willing to liberalize. There are technical fixes for this analytical problem, but they leave at least some doubt.

The third challenge is that, while liberal trade policies are likely to be somewhat beneficial under any circumstances (because they enlarge the set of opportunities for economic agents), a lasting effect almost certainly requires combination with other good policies and sound institutions as well. This necessary combination makes it difficult to isolate the individual effects of trade reform—indeed, it raises the question of whether it is even worth trying to do so if policies always come in packages. It also raises the issue of "which other policies"—that is, when is trade liberalization most effective? This situation becomes even more complex if, fourth, openness could *cause* improvements in other policies and institutions. For example, countries with simple, open trade regimes appear to be less corrupt, and open economies have less inflation. Both outcomes could be associated with higher incomes.

Since 2001, further work has re-established to most economists' satisfaction that openness does generally enhance income—at least conditionally. Researchers have worked hard to establish causation by isolating those parts of international trade that are genuinely not caused by income (such as economic size and distance between trading partners) and asking if they, in turn, cause higher incomes; it turns out that they do (see Noguer and Siscart 2005). Researchers have also determined that at least a minimal degree of labor market flexibility, firm entry flexibility, financial access, and human capital investment are appropriate complementary policies if liberalization is to have strong effects (Chang, Kaltani, and Loayza 2005).

Further scrutiny of the connection between openness and income examines possible causal links between openness and growth separately. Many studies associate openness with faster accumulation (that is, investment) and have observed that policies that hinder investment will reduce the benefits of trade liberalization. A second key linkage is between openness and productivity. Everyone agrees that improved productivity is necessary for sustained economic growth and development, and that it is the only secure basis for higher incomes at the level of the individual worker. The evidence from country, sectoral, and firm-level studies suggests very strongly that opening up international trade stimulates productivity. Part of the way in which it does so is by allowing more efficient (exporting) firms to grow faster than less efficient ones, and allowing import competition to pick off weaker domestic firms. Such rationalization effects may lead to short-term poverty concerns, for failing firms can easily harm their workers and owners. But equally clearly, long-term progress requires adaptation and adjustment, so that higher productivity can become the norm and generate higher incomes throughout a sector. One such case is the Chilean experience—in which firms were allowed to disappear during the trade liberalizations of the 1970s and 1980s, and the economy eventually emerged much stronger and richer.

Despite the econometric difficulties of establishing beyond all doubt that openness enhances income, the weight of experience and evidence seems to lean strongly in that direction. Thus, by boosting growth among countries, trade liberalization can narrow the gap between wealthy, industrialized nations and poor, developing ones—an important component of global inequality. Liberalizers have to undertake other reforms as well, but to a fair extent we know what these are: for example, reasonably flexible labor markets, capital markets, and corporate regulations that allow new firms to emerge, and decent port facilities and administration to allow goods to get in and out.

Moreover, even the critics (Rodriguez and Rodrik 2001) concede that there is no coherent evidence that openness adversely affects income. One might think of parallels with the debate on smoking. There was a long period during which the weight of evidence was sufficient to convince most rational people that smoking was harmful to health, although proof conclusive by either scientific or judicial standards had not been achieved. And during this period, just as in today's openness and growth debate, the hold-outs often cited specific counterexamples as if they overturned the general presumption.

TRADE AND INTRA-COUNTRY INEQUALITY

Let us now turn to whether international trade raises or lowers inequality within countries—and the related question of whether it causes or cures poverty. The baseline facts are that liberalizing international trade certainly affects people's incomes, that it can affect overall inequality either way, that there is a *little* evidence that it widens inequality in poor countries, and that, although it can drive some individuals into poverty, it tends to reduce poverty overall. I shall consider the arguments in two steps. First, as we have seen, trade liberalization tends to increase growth, so we need to ask how growth affects inequality. Second, we can move inside the aggregates to ask how trade affects individual incomes and then infer poverty/inequality effects from this perspective.

Economists have long argued that economic growth tends, overall, to reduce poverty (see Fields 1989). David Dollar and Aart Kraay (2002) recently quantified this assertion by relating the mean income of the poor—the bottom 20 percent of the income distribution—to overall mean income plus some of the additional variables that economists associate with influencing the rate of economic growth and that are often argued to affect the distribution of income. Among these variables, they found that, while inflation appeared to have an adverse effect on the poor on top of its growth-reducing effects, factors such as government consumption, the rule of law, democracy, social expenditure, primary school enrollment, and two measures of openness had no effects other than their effects on economic growth. While there were some instances in which growth was associated with rising poverty, Dollar and Kray's results suggest that, on average, these instances were balanced by those in which growth disproportionately benefited the poor.

An overview of the growth and inequality literature by Martin Ravallion (2001) reviews the data and their shortcomings and reminds us that even if rich and poor receive proportionately equal increases in income, the rich still receive several times more absolutely. Ravallion also discusses the role of initial income inequalities in determining the effect of growth on the number of poor—the concept known as "poverty-elasticity." The greater the inequality, the lower is the share of aggregate growth that accrues to the poor and, hence, the smaller the number of those who are likely to be pulled out of poverty by any given growth increment.[5] Ravallion concludes that all these aggregate approaches to poverty lose information by ignoring differences between individuals: one needs, as the title of his article suggests, to look beyond the averages. If this advice is important for estimating the effects of growth on poverty and inequality, it is doubly so for estimating the effects of trade and trade reform, for these effects will typically be far less evenly spread over individuals, sectors, or regions than will "regular" growth.

Two more recent contributions shed further light on the issue. First, Kraay (2006) revisits the Dollar and Kraay exercise with better data and methods, but finds the basic results unchanged. For longer periods—above, say, six or seven years—by far the largest determinant of whether a country has reduced poverty is whether it has grown. Changes in income distribution do occur, but they account for only about 6 to 8 times less of the change in poverty than does growth.

Second, Milanovic (2005b) uses a similar dataset to explore the effects of growth and openness on the whole of the distribution of income by looking at the share of total income accruing to individuals with incomes in each decile of the distribution, allowing the openness effect to vary with the level of average income. He finds that, for poorer countries (below around $8,000 per annum at international prices), openness is unequalizing—that is, higher incomes grow by more than lower ones—presumably because the richer members of society are better placed or better equipped to take advantage of the opportunities it offers. Above the ($8,000 yearly) threshold, openness is apparently equalizing, perhaps because its ability to curb market power is more important where incomes are higher.

The conclusion from all this scholarly analysis is that there is not much evidence that growth worsens inequality, even when it is caused by openness, although one study has suggested that it might do so in low-income economies. There is no evidence that growth or, in the long run, openness, is bad for the poor. Figure 1 offers a useful summary view. It reflects growth and inequality over 117 periods since 1970 for which we have reasonably good and comparable household surveys for two years for the same developing country; about 70 countries are covered, so some countries contribute more than one period to this exercise. When income is rising, there is no clear tendency in inequality (see the righthand column); when income falls (see the lefthand column), there is some tendency for

Figure 1

Growth, Inequality, and Poverty

		What is happening to average household income between the surveys?	
		Falling	Rising
What is happening to relative inequality?*	Rising	**16% of spells** Poverty is *rising* at a median rate of 14.3% per year	**30% of spells** Poverty is *falling* at a median rate of 1.3% per year
	Falling	**26% of spells** Poverty is *rising* at a median rate of 1.7% per year	**27% of spells** Poverty is *falling* at a median rate of 9.6% per year

Source: Martin Ravallion, "Globalization and Poor People: The Debate and Evidence," Max Corden Lecture, University of Melbourne, 2005.

inequality to do so, too. Notice, however, the entries on poverty: where incomes rise, poverty falls (on average) and vice versa.

INTRA-COUNTRY INEQUALITY: THE DIRECT EFFECTS ON HOUSEHOLDS

Finally, let us turn to the direct effects of trade liberalization on households. After all, even if inequality/poverty doesn't change in aggregate, there may be a great deal of what economists call "churning," whereby households change places in the income distribution. Treating the household as the basic unit for which income is defined, household fortunes depend on how the price changes generated by liberalization affect their consumption and sources of income. I distinguish three channels of causation: the prices of goods and services, the market for labor, and the role of the taxation and government expenditure.

Taxation

The role of taxation and government expenditure is important but not sophisticated analytically. Critics of trade liberalization frequently argue that it reduces government revenue. The share of total revenue provided by trade taxes is higher for poorer countries than for rich ones, so this is potentially a major issue at low levels of economic development. But, in fact, there is no simple link between trade reform and tariff revenue. In many cases, as tariff rates are reduced, total collections actually increase because, at lower rates of tax, fewer exemptions are sought or granted, it is less worthwhile to engage in tax evasion, and the volume of trade—the tax base—increases.

Of course, as the tariff rate falls to zero, tariff revenue must also eventually fall to zero—a zero tax raises zero revenue no matter how large the tax base. But whether the revenue loss affects services for the poor is essentially a political decision, albeit one constrained by a country's administrative capacity, and so, too, is the choice of alternative taxes to replace revenue losses. That is, there is no law of physics requiring that losses of government revenue must hurt the poor—that is a decision taken by governments, which often prefer to hit the poor rather than other constituencies.

Prices and Markets

A more interesting link is that between trade policy and the prices of the goods that poor households consume and produce. The bulk of the world's poor are self-employed in either low-level agriculture or the informal sector of the economy.[6] Thus their incomes are directly affected by price changes induced by international trade. An increase in the price of something that the household sells (labor, good, or service) increases its real income, while a decrease reduces it. Equally important, prices also matter to households as consumers, just as they do to individuals who earn wages, salaries, or rents.

Whether trade-policy changes on the border get transmitted into price changes for poor or nearly-poor households depends on factors such as transport costs and other costs of distribution, the structure of markets, and domestic taxes and regulations. Some impediments, such as transport costs, are unavoidable, although they may be increased by policy decisions such as the levying of fuel taxes or provision of inadequate infrastructure. But some other impediments represent direct economic inefficiency, such as permitting marketing monopsonies (where there is only one buyer for a product or service) or monopolies (only one seller).

Price transmission is likely to be particularly ineffective for poor people living in remote rural areas, possibly preventing families from making market transactions almost completely. Such isolation saves the poor from any negative shocks emanating from the international economy, but it also prevents them from experiencing positive shocks or the secular benefits from openness that were the subject of the previous section. Their problem is too little globalization, not too much. Thus the policy conclusion of most of this literature is that governments should pursue complementary reforms such as enhanced infrastructure or human capital accumulation to try to connect poor households to the market and thence to the border, while at the same time remaining aware of the possible adverse consequences for subsets of these newly connected populations.

There may also be extreme price changes—either to zero as existing export trades are destroyed, or to infinity if imports disappear. These drastic changes can cause dramatic losses of income, which may be very painful but nonetheless illustrate the gains that emanated from trade in the first place.

A household's ability to adjust to a trade shock—say, by switching production toward goods whose prices have risen—clearly affects the size of any impact it suffers. For many of the poor, a major constraint on improving agricultural productivity following an external liberalization, by making such an adjustment, has been shown to be the absence of key productive assets (draft animals, implements), capital, credit, or information. These demonstrations again highlight the importance of complementary policies targeted at small farmers to enable them to benefit fully from new trading opportunities—for example, fostering asset accumulation, improving access to credit, and providing good-quality extension services.

Adjustment is also the mechanism by which shocks in one market spill over into another, as consumers substitute from expensive to cheaper goods and producers substitute from lower-priced to higher-priced goods. If these spillovers are concentrated onto just a few products or regions, they can be significant locally. A major attraction of liberalizing small-scale agriculture is, arguably, that the direct beneficiaries (farmers) spend much of their extra income on goods and services—such as construction, personal service, and simple manufactures—that are provided locally by other poor people.

Factor Markets

For the self-employed, the main determinant of income is the difference between the prices commanded by their output and those paid for their inputs, but for employees it is factor prices (wages) or employment opportunities. Obtaining employment is one of the surest ways out of poverty, while the loss of a job is probably the most common reason for the precipitate declines into poverty that attract most public attention. The structure of the labor market is critical to how trade liberalization gets translated into wage and employment changes. If wages rise, many wage-earners will typically benefit. If, on the other hand, wages are somehow fixed and adjustment occurs through employment, the smaller number of lucky individuals who get the new jobs created by a trade liberalization are likely to win big increases in income. Thus, who gets the jobs becomes an important issue. Sometimes the lucky ones will be the poor, but at other times the jobs go to additional workers from households that already hold formal employment or to more skilled workers.

Where unskilled labor is abundant, the goods it produces will be plentiful and hence relatively cheap in the absence of international trade. But these are the goods that will be exported when trade is opened up, and hence trade liberalization will generally relieve poverty. However, not all developing countries fall into this class. For example, many Latin American and African countries enjoy very strong endowments of natural resources, and so liberalization will stimulate these sectors rather than labor-intensive ones. In these cases, an active redistribution policy—including helping the poor to obtain access to land, skills, markets, and so on—may be required to spread the benefits of openness.

One of the features of the past twenty years has been the growing skills gap—the excess of skilled wages over unskilled wages—even in developing countries. This effect is unexpected, given the analysis of the previous paragraph, but some authors attribute the widening gap to openness. Various reasons are given for this surprising development.

- The arrival of China on the world scene may have fixed the level of unskilled wages very low.

- When countries liberalize, they import new capital equipment, which tends to need more skilled than unskilled labor to work.

- The business of exporting requires skilled labor or calls for quality that only skilled workers can provide.

- The tasks that relocate from developed to developing countries as trade opens up are unskilled in the former but skilled relative to existing jobs in the latter—hence their transfer raises the relative demand for skills.

The increasing skill gap generally raises inequality.

The arguments in this section are almost bound to vary a good deal from case to case. Detailed research has not thrown up any universal regularities for these direct effects of trade on poverty or inequality. It has, on the other hand, shown that, with sufficient information, we can predict some of the effects—which is useful for designing policies to support a trade liberalization. It has also shown that the key issue to consider is how trade (or any other) reform affects the way people earn their living. This consideration is not just a matter of looking at the labor market, however, because the poor are frequently self-employed. Instead, it arises because while most households consume large number of goods and services, and in fairly similar proportions, they have very many different and much more specialized ways of earning their incomes. Thus, for identifying differences across households (inequalities), we need to focus on the income-generating component.

CONCLUSION

The conclusion of this survey is simultaneously simple and complex. Simply, the evidence suggests strongly that openness to trade tends to boost average incomes over the medium term. This growth has relatively little systematic effect on inequality, and so liberalizing trade tends to be poverty-reducing over- all. There will be some exceptions, but the broad tendencies are well-established.

At a more complex level, the direct effects of liberalizing international trade on the real incomes of households will often be small and, where they are not, may be either positive or negative. It is often possible to predict these effects when the household's characteristics are known, but in the absence of detailed information, no general tendencies or results can be relied upon. Thus, while the "average" trade liberalization may well hurt some households, its growth effects are very likely to reduce overall poverty significantly.

NO: Kate Vyborny and Nancy Birdsall, *Center for Global Development*

Free trade has increased global income as well as the total income of coun- tries that have opened up to it. However, when trade opens up, different groups within countries see differential increases in their income, and some groups may lose income in absolute terms. In the past in some countries—such as those for which trade leads to big increases in agricultural exports—the poor have, initially, gained more than the rich. But over the past three decades, the tendency in most countries has been in the other direction. The globalization of markets for goods and services has tended to benefit the relatively rich more, and so has tended to increase income inequality.

Because trade is beneficial in itself as well as a catalyst for other changes that are needed for countries to grow and reduce poverty, efforts to block trade and globalization have almost always ended with countries losing out. Instead of closing off borders to trade, therefore, the best solution is to find fair, sustain- able ways to compensate the losses and ease the transition of those who lose out from major economic shifts such as trade liberalization, and to open up opportunities for the poor and middle classes to take advantage of new eco- nomic opportunities. These policies are important for maintaining political support for trade liberalization, as well as for protecting the losers from disas- trous declines in consumption. Such policies are needed at both the national and international levels.

FREE TRADE INCREASES INCOME

We know that trade allows countries to specialize in what they produce most efficiently, increasing global income, and then exchange it for the products of others, making all countries better off—even those that are not "best" at producing anything, where producers can compete only by paying lower wages. The basic insight of David Ricardo into how trade can unlock a country's comparative advantage is well summarized in Paul Krugman and Maurice Obstfeld's textbook (1999), which offers the example of two countries, Home and Foreign. Home produces cheese at the rate of one hour of labor per pound, while Foreign produces cheese at six hours per pound; Home produces wine at two hours of labor per gallon, while Foreign produces wine at three hours of labor per gallon. In other words, *Home has higher labor productivity in both industries.* But, as Krugman and Obstfeld note,

> [A]n hour of Home labor produces only 1/2 gallon of wine. The same hour could be used to produce 1 pound of cheese, which can then be traded for 1 gallon of wine. Clearly, Home does gain from trade. Similarly, Foreign could use 1 hour of labor to produce 1/6 pound of cheese; if, however, it uses the hour to produce 1/3 gallon of wine it could then trade the 1/3 gallon of wine for 1/3 pound of cheese. This is twice as much as the 1/6 pound of cheese it gets using the hour to produce the cheese directly. In this example, each country can use labor twice as efficiently to trade for what it needs instead of producing its imports for itself … " (1999, 4–21).

Trade also stimulates investment. For example, when clothing can be exported with lower tariffs from a country, more foreign companies invest in clothing factories there. Open trade can also encourage the transfer of technology to developing countries—a U.S.-based company is more likely to invest and share technology with overseas suppliers in order to increase the quality and reliability of its own goods, and this enhanced technical capability may eventually spill over to the suppliers' domestic industries (see Saggi 2002).

Of course, the real world is more complicated than these examples may suggest. But the basic principle that trade increases the income of trading countries is one of the best verified findings in economics (Sachs and Warner 1995; Edwards 1993). (There are two exceptions to this principle, which we discuss later.)

THE ROLE OF RELATIVE INEQUALITY

So we know that trade increases total income. But does it matter how trade affects the distribution of income? Does inequality matter, too?

A thought experiment: if you could choose to make one change to your society, which of the following options would you choose?

1. Everyone has at least a minimum standard level of income, but the richest 5 percent have one thousand times that standard.

2. The poorest 5 percent have at least one-tenth the income of the richest 5 percent.

If you considered option 2, why did you do so? What is the inherent virtue of a more equal society? While absolute income is clearly important, it turns out that relative income is also important for a number of reasons.

First, relative income plays a major role in how content we are. Adam Smith, the first economist, noted that in one society a man may need enough income to buy a linen shirt in order to retain his dignity, while in another that expenditure may be seen as a luxury (Hirschman 1973). Surveys of people's relative happiness reveal that individuals report being happier when their own absolute income is higher, but also when their income is higher than that of others in their reference group (Easterlin 1995). This concern for relative well-being becomes important only above a low threshold—in abject poverty, people are primarily concerned about meeting their basic needs (Ravallion and Lokshin 2005). (As globalization has broadened people's access to information about the broader world, they may be comparing their income to a broader reference group as well—see Box 1).

Second, inequality may actually affect economic growth, the driver of any improvements in absolute income. Attempting to force perfect equality is counterproductive, for some level of inequality provides an incentive for people to work hard and innovate. But beyond that level, inequality can also become counterproductive. Such "destructive inequality" reflects inefficient privileges for the rich, a kind of social and economic discrimination that reduces incentives for effort, investment, and innovation, and in general cuts the potential for productive contributions by the poor (see Birdsall 2007b). This destructive potential is more of a problem in poor countries, where, for example, capital markets are less developed, and so those without collateral have little access to credit. Evidence suggests that growth has been lower in the past several decades than would have been expected in countries below a certain income level (about US$3,200), where income inequality is relatively high (described by a Gini coefficient higher than .45—see Box 2).[1]

Third, high levels of inequality can have a range of negative social and political effects. Because the size and economic power of the middle class, in particular, is thought to play a major role in democratic accountability, the "missing

Box 1

Inequality among Whom?

In the thought experiment just introduced, what did you have in mind when asked which change you would rather make to your society? Was it your neighborhood, your city, your state, country, or the whole world?

One effect of globalization has been to expand people's frame of reference, as travel becomes more accessible and mass communication expands. People living not just in Johannesburg or Phnom Penh, but even in rural villages in South Africa or Cambodia are now more likely to be able to compare their lifestyle with that of Americans or Europeans as shown on television shows or described by migrant relatives. This expanded perspective has an effect on how people perceive their relative income. So globalization has made global inequality more relevant for people's lives.

Besides measuring and considering the inequality within a single country, there are three ways to consider global inequality. The first is to compare average incomes country by country. But this method effectively weights the well-being of a citizen of Palau in the South Pacific (population 20,000) as 65,000 times more important than that of a citizen of China (population 1.3 billion). Alternatively, we can weight the incomes by population. But that method still completely ignores the inequality within countries. A third measure of global inequality is to compare all individuals globally as if we were measuring the inequality in a single country, thus taking into account inequality both within and between countries (Milanovic 2005). The sole disadvantage of this method is that it abstracts from the inequality within a country.

As globalization progresses, these measures become more important. We touch on the effects of trade on these global measures of inequality in this chapter, but we are dealing primarily with inequality within countries—which people care about because it is most immediate, and which affects country politics and policy.

middle" may be one of the reasons some states have such weak institutions and poor public services: the poor have too little clout and access to information and are too consumed with the day-to-day challenges of survival to exert much pressure on the government, and the rich are able to compensate for the poor quality of government services by using connections, offering bribes, or just paying for private schools or clinics instead (see Birdsall 2005, 2008).

So, if inequality is important in and of itself, how does free trade affect it? The real world is, of course, much more complex than the basic examples just discussed. As it turns out, opening up to trade affects different people's incomes in different ways. The losers—even when they lose only relatively to others—are often more vocal than the winners in this process, and they are

Box 2

How Do We Measure Inequality?

How does the income of the richest 1 percent of Americans compare to that of the other 99 percent? The income of the top 20 percent to that of the bottom 80 percent? Or is it more important to pay attention to the position of the bottom 10 or 20 percent?

These comparisons differ in the picture they draw. If the richest man in the country doubled his income this year, and everyone else's income stayed the same, that disparity would be much more noticeable in the first measure.

One measure of inequality along the entire income distribution is the Gini coefficient. To calculate the Gini coefficient, we draw a graph with a "Lorenz curve" that shows for each segment of the population what portion of total income that group commands. (The same measure can be applied to total income, disposable income, wealth, and so on.)

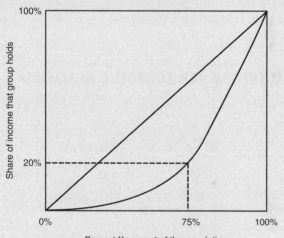

Poorest X percent of the population

In this graph, the poorest 75 percent of the population receives only 20 percent of the income—and so the top 25 percent receives the other 80 percent of the income. Each point on the curve represents such a ratio. The 45-degree diagonal line represents perfect equality, because 20 percent of the people have 20 percent of the income, and so on. The Gini coefficient measures the area between the straight line and the curved line.

So the higher the Gini, the more unequal the society. A society where everyone has exactly the same income would have a Gini coefficient of zero. A society where one person has all the income and the others have no income would have a Gini coefficient of one. The United States has a Gini coefficient of income inequality about .45 (UN WIDER 2008). Northern European countries such as Sweden, on the other hand, have Gini coefficients around .30. Brazil is consistently among the most unequal countries in the world by this measure, with a Gini around .55.

more likely to attribute the change to trade than are the winners. As one manufacturer says, "When NAFTA came into force, we closed a factory in Canada, where four hundred people lost their jobs, and replaced it by opening another one in South Carolina, where we hired eight hundred people. Now the four hundred in Canada hate free trade, and the eight hundred in South Carolina think they got the job because they are qualified, and don't care about free trade."

The gains also tend to be spread out—cheaper clothes, food, and appliances affect everyone's budgets, especially those of the poor, but people tend not to be aware of these benefits as the result of free trade, and they are unlikely to lobby for free trade because of them. And where the (potential) losers are well-organized, wealthy, or influential, their voices are heard more loudly—as with some wealthy farmers in rich countries who reap millions of dollars in agricultural subsidies at the expense of the poor abroad who could otherwise export crops such as sugar (Elliott 2005). So we must take reports of losses from trade in context.

ECONOMIC THEORY AND ECONOMIC REALITIES

Let us take a closer look at the theory and evidence of the effects of trade liberalization on inequality across and within countries.

Economic theory suggests that developing countries entering the global trading system in the most recent, post–World War II period of globalization were likely to gain more from this liberalization than richer countries because they were less integrated into the global economy at the start and so had more to gain—and because, from a lower initial income, those income gains could be more rapid (Lindert and Williamson 2001). (Of course, to the extent that some have liberalized less than industrialized countries, they should, in theory, have gained less, and so would not have converged or caught up with richer countries.)

What about inequality within countries? Economic theory predicts that freer trade will redistribute income in a country away from the factors of production (land, capital, skilled or unskilled labor) that are scarce and toward those that are more abundant, compared to the proportions available in the world as a whole.[2] Thus, in rich, industrialized countries, which have an abundance of capital and skilled labor, the wages of unskilled labor should go down, while in poor countries, which have an abundance of unskilled labor, those wages should go up.

So, what has actually happened? First, has free trade reduced inequality across countries?

Across developing countries, trade should, theoretically, increase the income of all those that participate, and especially of those that begin more closed and so can more fully exploit an opening. In reality, however, some—such as China—have grown rapidly while trading more, closing the income gap with the rich world, but many others—particularly in Africa and Latin America—have not. There seem to be two exceptions to the expected income benefits of trade for developing countries.

The first exception is where there are unusual pre-existing trade distortions benefiting some countries over others, such as free trade areas (such as NAFTA) or preferential trade agreements (that is, special trade privileges for the poorest countries, such as the Africa Growth and Opportunity Act). When other countries then open up, this special access gives the previous beneficiaries less of an edge, and they can lose income (see Vyborny 2005). In this case, compensation may be required to ease the transition—these proposed transfers of "aid for trade" for the poorest countries were the subject of much discussion in the (now dormant) Doha Round of global trade negotiations.

The second and more important exception is that in a global market, countries producing goods, such as primary commodities, may lack the people, financing, or access to broader markets that would encourage diversification, especially into manufacturing or new services—the kinds of production that would drive the development of technology and change the countries' comparative advantage over time. This inability to diversify tends to reduce economic growth in the long run (Lindert and Williamson 2001). Concern about this possibility has led many countries to try to nurture "infant industries" by closing themselves off to trade. But this approach has consistently failed, as trying to opt out of globalization has led to those countries' losing out. This pattern leaves countries with a strong comparative advantage in production of primary commodities in a bind—how best to develop a manufacturing base? It seems that many ingredients are needed: investing in education and health to develop a productive workforce, improving infrastructure, reducing corruption and streamlining regulatory processes to reduce costs to businesses, ensuring a functioning justice system that businesses can rely on to resolve disputes, and maintaining a stable macroeconomic environment. As it turns out, some have done better than others in managing these other factors and in diversifying their production to include manufacturing and services as well as primary commodities. Those countries have grown more rapidly and reduced the gap between their average income and the average income in rich countries (Birdsall 2007a).

What about inequality within countries: has trade increased inequality in rich countries and reduced it in poor countries, as theory predicted?

It is critical to understand that trade is not always the key factor—and it is never the sole factor—in bringing about changes in the economy, including those affecting inequality. And it is particularly difficult to tease out the effects that trade liberalization has had; while a country liberalizes, many other changes may be occurring, so simply looking at the changes in the level of inequality over that time is not enough to establish a relationship. For instance, technological change, which affects the types of jobs that are available, is a major driver of inequality—and it has tended to accompany trade liberalization. Also, some studies have found that the proportion of young people in a society is a major determinant of overall inequality, so a baby boom might affect income distribution independent of changes in trade (Higgins and Williamson 1999).

Countries that are more open to free trade are likely to share many other characteristics in addition, so simply comparing income distribution between countries that have and have not opened up is insufficient as well. This is part of the reason that any single study is insufficient to prove the answer one way or another. To establish a causal link requires careful quantitative analysis controlling for these other factors. The evidence that trade increases overall income is well established; but its effects on inequality have been less fully explored. Later, we sometimes refer simply to changes in trade coinciding with changes in inequality, without implying any necessary causal link.

In today's rich countries, as expected, there has been an increase in inequality coinciding with broad-based trade liberalization since the 1980s (Lindert and Williamson 2001). In fact, only a relatively small part of this increase is due to trade; the evidence suggests that at least half has been driven by other factors—most importantly, improvements in technology (see Lawrence and Slaughter 1993; Sachs and Shatz 1994; Wood 1994, 1995). More sophisticated equipment and computing power have made many jobs obsolete, reducing demand for unskilled labor, and so wages for unskilled labor have gone down relative to those for skilled labor.

But in some poor countries—in particular, those in Latin America—free trade has not brought the expected declines in inequality.[3] Why not?

Some of the increases in inequality in liberalizing developing countries have likely occurred because of other factors occurring at the same time as liberalization. The liberalization of Latin American countries in the 1970s and 1980s coincided with the entry into the world market of more competitive countries, including China and other Asian exporters (Lindert and Williamson 2001). Mexico was a higher-wage country than its new competitors—in this case Mexico was the richer country in the dynamics of trade liberalization described earlier, and so we would expect its inequality to increase.

Liberalization in some countries, including Chile and Mexico, coincided with removal of policies that had favored less skilled workers, such as powerful unions in Chile and protection of low-wage industries in Mexico. So unskilled, low-wage workers saw their relative wages fall compared to their more skilled counterparts.

But some of the increases in inequality have happened because the world differs from the simplifying assumptions of the textbook. For example, in the real world, there are more than two countries and two goods. In the real world, a worker who has completed high school—and so is considered "skilled" in Bangladesh—is counted as comparatively "unskilled" in the United States (without a college degree or English language skills). Let us now consider in detail some of the ways in which the real world becomes more complicated than the theory, allowing free trade to have some disequalizing effects.

Adjustment Costs

First, there are short-term costs of adjustment to changed patterns of production—for example, low-skilled jobs in garment factories may be lost, while low-skilled jobs in toy factories are generated. The same individuals may move from the garment to the toy factories, but they incur costs in searching for and training for their new jobs. These costs are difficult to measure, but are likely regressive, simply because hurdles such as searching for employment are more costly for the poor (Fernandez de Cordoba, Laird, and Serena). And the effects of unemployment and bankruptcy may be permanent for the poor, so repeated shocks can increase inequality (Diwan 2001). During periods without work, the poor may be forced to sell off productive assets (such as farm equipment, a milk cow, or a sewing machine); their children may drop out of school and never return (Székely 1999).

Advantages for Countries with Most Productive Assets

The inequality implications of trade theory outlined earlier build on the assumption that the main difference between countries in determining what they produce and trade is the difference between their endowments—one country may have more unskilled labor and land, the other more skilled labor and capital. But this assumption leaves out the major productivity differences between countries—producing the same good or service may require more of the total inputs in developing countries than in developed countries (Easterly 2004). In other words, everything else being equal, a hundred workers may be able to produce more widgets per hour in the United States than in Nigeria—

because of frequent power cuts in the Nigerian widget plant, higher costs to ship widget inputs and the finished widgets to and from the factory because of poor roads, higher operating costs from licenses and export procedures with a less efficient or corrupt government, and so on. Such differences in productivity help to explain why 80 percent of all foreign investment occurs among the industrialized countries, while just 0.1 percent of U.S. foreign investment goes to sub-Saharan Africa (UNCTAD 2001).

Recall that the gains from trade by Home and Foreign (discussed at the beginning of this chapter) demonstrated that lower- and higher-productivity coutries still gain from trade in aggregate income, even when a country can compete only by offering lower wages. But what do these differences mean for inequality? For inequality within countries, Easterly argues that these productivity differences effectively make skilled labor and capital more scarce in higher-productivity rich countries, so they would benefit more from trade liberalization. But the effect on intercountry inequality also depends on how freer trade affects productivity differences. Trade can lead to technology transfer, which increases productivity. So the effects of trade may depend on the extent of this effect. And if trade increases investment, that may also change factor endowments by making labor more scarce compared to capital. For inequality between countries might suggest that industrialized, higher productivity countries could experience a greater benefit than lower productivity countries because a larger share of the investment that trade helps to stimulate would flow to them.

In addition to these productivity differences, the change in global demand for goods and services has increased the demand for skilled labor, due to technological change and the resulting global growth in sectors with more complex inputs. Demand for skills has risen faster than the supply of skilled workers everywhere, despite the fact that more and more people are going to university, including across the developing world (Levy 1999; Duryea and Székely 1998; Terrell 2000). The earnings of those with a higher education relative to those without have therefore continued to rise. Because in many countries education is reinforcing initial advantages instead of compensating for initial handicaps, the resulting tendency is growing income inequality.[4]

Costs of Market Failures on the Poor

The classic example of a market failure is that of pollution, as the polluter captures the benefits of polluting without paying the full costs. Because free trade makes global production chains possible—allowing firms to shift production or switch suppliers between countries—the costs of market failures such as pollution often shift to the poor citizens of poor countries with the weakest institutions to control them. And global integration allows firms to shift greenhouse gas–generating production to countries with the weakest controls, making it harder to combat climate change, which disproportionately affects the poor (Cline 2007).

Bias against the Poor in Global Economic Rules

It is better to have a rules-based system—such as the World Trade Organization—than no system at all; such a system helps to level the playing field compared to the default to anarchy in international affairs, in which the most powerful countries simply determine the outcome. But the richer and more powerful countries are also able to influence the design and implementation of global rules to their own advantage, at the expense of the developing countries. And within those developing countries, the rules are slanted in particular against the poor, who have little voice in their government and even less voice at the negotiating table with trading partners.

The effort to reduce rich country agricultural subsidies and tariffs that discriminate against poor countries is a good example. Domestic agricultural lobbies in industrialized countries matter more at the negotiating table than unequal opportunities for cotton farmers in West Africa do. Developing countries are at a disadvantage in global trade and other negotiations, and the smallest and poorest countries need transfers of aid from rich countries simply to participate effectively—to command the legal and economic expertise to negotiate and analyze the potential effects for them of different outcomes of the negotiations. For example, about one-half of legal cases brought in the WTO against the trade violation known as "dumping" are initiated against developing country producers, who account for 8 percent of all exports (Birdsall 2005).

SOLUTION: COMPLEMENTARY "FAIR GROWTH" POLICIES

Despite the disequalizing tendencies they can have, trying to block trade and globalization has almost without exception caused whole countries to lose out economically (Lindert and Williamson 2001). As we stressed at the beginning of the chapter, the benefits of trade are significant, and staying on the sidelines is not the answer.

Instead, the best solution is to find fair, sustainable ways to compensate the losses and ease the transition of those who lose out from trade liberalization and other major economic shifts, as well as to open up opportunities for the poor and middle classes to become upwardly mobile by taking advantage of new economic opportunities. These policies are important to maintain political support for trade liberalization, as well as for equity where the losers from trade are poor.

Even where trade makes some people worse off and so increases inequality, it is still possible—and desirable—for everyone to gain if the "winners" from trade compensate the "losers" with a portion of their increased income. Since total income in a country will increase with trade liberalization, such partial transfers would still leave everyone better off than they started (Dixit and Norman 1980; Corden 1974). This sort of compensation is particularly important for poor people in poor countries, because they have the fewest assets to fall back on and less access to information about opportunities in other sectors (for example) and so are the least well-equipped to deal with the transitions that trade can bring (Bannister and Thugge 2001). The less diversified economies in many low-income countries also mean that a larger proportion of workers may lose their livelihoods at once, making it more difficult for all of them to find new sources of income.

But it turns out in practice that such compensatory policies often do not come through for these people, for a number of reasons. First, there is a strategic problem—governments and voters do not usually face a choice of a package of free trade plus compensation, so it is difficult for the poor to demand that trade liberalization take place if and only if they are adequately compensated. Government revenue also takes a hit when tariffs are cut, particularly in some of the poorest countries which rely heavily on tariffs for revenue, making boosting transfer programs unattractive. Finally, because the poor tend to be less organized and less politically effective, redistributive programs may never take place, and when they do, they often respond to more vocal entrenched interests, transforming these initiatives into a regressive tax rather than a safety net. For example, Senegal's program to cushion the effects of its economic reforms channeled state money to privileged groups within the system (civil servants and university graduates), while doing nothing to protect the urban and rural poor from rising consumer prices and unemployment. Often, even those subsidies originally meant for the poor are quickly captured by the middle class and the rich.

It is also logistically difficult for governments to make lump-sum transfers to the "losers" from trade, for there is a major challenge in identifying who has lost from trade, especially in poor countries where large segments of the population work in agriculture or the informal sector (Bannister and Thugge 2001; Winters 2000; Ravallion 1999). It is also difficult to justify paying those who have lost because of trade and not because of other economic shifts such as advancing technology making their jobs obsolete. (This identification problem has been an issue with the U.S. federal program to assist those who have lost jobs because of trade—the Trade Adjustment Assistance, or TAA program [GAO 2007].)

So what can be done to compensate the losers? Strengthening general social safety net policies such as food vouchers and adult job training programs is likely the fairest and most sustainable way to compensate the losers. The design and implementation of these programs still requires attention to ensure that they reach those who need them most. A broader set of "fair growth" policies that will empower the poor and the middle class to take advantage of new and existing economic opportunities—such as social investments in education and health, and fairer application of tax systems and regulatory changes to help small businesses formalize and grow—is also needed.[5]

A GLOBAL SOCIAL CONTRACT

Some policies to address the equity effects of trade, such as strong social safety net programs, can be made at the national level. But because of the political and economic challenges just outlined, the only way they are likely to become a reality is with at least some international support. The (now dormant) Doha Round of international trade negotiations has incorporated discussions on "aid for trade," including funds to compensate countries for adjustment costs to liberalization and/or to help countries better take advantage of new trading opportunities (Hoekman and Prowse 2005). But so far, these commitments have been problematic because they may not be binding and the aid may not be additional. And there has been almost no discussion of funding to ease the adjustment costs of the poor within countries, or to underwrite what may be a longer-term need for support for social safety net programs. These transfer payments are in the interest of rich as well as poor countries: fairer compensation can help to build broader support for trade liberalization that allows economic expansion and opportunity in the industrialized world as well.

There is also a need for compensatory policies that fall into the global arena, which cannot be addressed on the national level. Global regulatory arrangements and rules are needed to manage global market failures, such as climate change, and to discourage corruption and other anticompetitive processes (a global antitrust agency, for example).[6] These global programs are particularly important for the poor, but they would benefit everyone in both rich and poor countries. In principle, they could be financed internationally by some mechanism that mimics taxes within national economies, such as a levy on international aviation or on carbon emissions.

Free trade does not always—and cannot by itself—increase economic equality at the national or global levels. But in combination with these proposed policies at country and international levels, it can be a powerful instrument to increase wealth and welfare equitably.

3

poverty

Can Foreign Aid Reduce Poverty?

YES: Jeffrey Sachs, *The Earth Institute at Columbia University*
NO: George B. N. Ayittey, *American University*

More than 3 billion people—nearly half the world—live on less than $2 per day. Tens of thousands of children die every day from conditions associated with poverty, more than 1 million each year from diarrhea alone. Millions lack access to lifesaving immunizations that are routine in the West. More than 1 billion lack access to adequate water supplies. Figure 1 details the geographic distribution of the poor worldwide, indicating that while progress was made in most of the world—including significant improvements made in East Asia—over a recent twenty-year period, the percentage of those living in extreme poverty increased in sub-Saharan Africa. Statistics such as these are both appalling and overwhelming: how can material excess and deprivation exist side-by-side in our "globalized" world, and how can the relatively privileged provide assistance to the "bottom billion"?

The United Nations Development Programme (the principal development network within the UN), the World Bank (International Bank for Reconstruction and Development), and the International Monetary Fund (IMF) are the principal multilateral institutions for economic development and debt relief. After the Marshall Plan of 1947 helped to rebuild nations in Europe following World War II, President Harry Truman instituted bilateral foreign aid as a feature of U.S. foreign policy. In the 1960s, President John F. Kennedy established the U.S. Agency for International Development (USAID)—which provides development assistance as well as humanitarian aid—and the Peace Corps—which sends people to live and serve in developing nations. The Camp David accords of 1979 catapulted Israel and Egypt to the top of nations receiving U.S. foreign aid, although recently they have been supplanted by development assistance to Iraq. The 1980s and 1990s saw reductions in U.S. foreign aid, but in the

Figure 1

Percentage of Total Population Living on Less than $1.08/day, 1981–2001

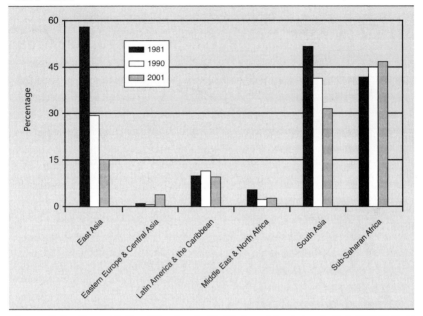

Source: M. Ravallion and S. Chen, "How Have the World's Poorest Fared since the Early 1980s?" *World Bank Research Observer* 19, no. 2 (Fall 2004): 152.
Note: $1.08/day and $2.15/day are international poverty lines expressed in 1993 PPP.

wake of the terrorist attacks on September 11, 2001, aid began to be seen as a potential impediment to terrorism, and it has increased since then, particularly in Iraq and Afghanistan. Figure 2 shows substantial increases in foreign aid contributions by the OECD's Development Assistance Committee (DAC) since 1960.

In response to extreme world poverty, the United Nations, in its Millennium Summit in 2000, agreed upon a set of Millennium Development Goals (MDGs) to be reached by year 2015 as a way of guiding future efforts to address poverty. (See table 1 in Jeffrey Sachs's contribution for a brief listing of these goals.) One of the important commitments required to meet the MDGs was for wealthy nations to increase their aid to 0.7 percent of gross national income, a target that had been in place since the mid-1960s. However, most of these nations remain far short of that goal. The United States contributes more than any other nation in raw figures—more than $21 billion in 2007—yet it sits at the

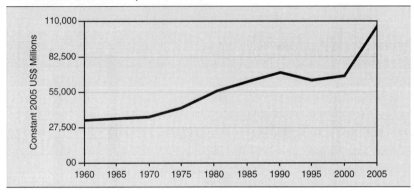

Figure 2

Net Official Development Assistance Disbursed by OECD Development Assistance Committee, 1960–2005

Source: OECD-DAC, online database (accessed February 16, 2008).
Note: Aid includes total assistance disbursed by all members of the OECD Development Assistance Committee (DAC).

bottom of the list in terms of its aid donations as a proportion of gross national income (GNI), of which it gives just 0.16 percent. Only five nations—Norway, Sweden, Luxembourg, Denmark, and Netherlands—have reached the UN target of 0.7 percent of GNI, and the average for the OECD's Development Assistance Committee is just 0.28 percent.

Some forms of "aid" are motivated more by internal politics and support for strong domestic constituencies in the developed nations than by recognition of the need for improving conditions elsewhere, and they may in turn harm developing nations. For example, food aid in the form of export subsidies in developed nations and delivery of heavily-subsidized or free food to developing nations is often a political effort to support domestic farmers (either in the United States or in Europe), and may serve to artificially depress food export prices and, therefore, extinguish food production possibilities in developing nations. Furthermore, the farm policies of the developed world all serve to stimulate production, thereby further depressing world food prices and stunting farm production in the developing world.

Three principal disagreements shape debates about foreign aid: (1) the extent to which it is simply an instrument of foreign policy, and therefore not intended to actually improve the lives of those most in need; (2) which types of foreign aid are most beneficial in combating poverty, regardless of the motivation; and (3) the relative importance of foreign aid compared with other forms of economic activity—such as international trade—in raising living standards. The two articles that follow present varying perspectives on the prospects for foreign aid influencing international development by reducing poverty. Dr. George Ayittey argues that a free press and independent judiciary are important ingredients to development, while Jeffery Sachs advocates large increases in development aid along the lines of the Marshall Plan.

Discussion Questions

1. Do wealthy nations have an obligation to provide aid to poor nations? In what ways can foreign aid be used as a foreign policy tool by wealthy nations? Does it matter what donor nations' motives are when they provide aid? Why or why not?

2. The Monterrey Consensus is an agreement among the world's wealthy nations that recognizes the importance of trade in reducing poverty in poor nations. It affirms the "aid for trade" concept whereby foreign aid is given to poor nations in order to improve the infrastructure needed for trade. Do you agree with this concept? Is this the best way to reduce poverty? In what other ways can foreign aid be used?

3. What recommendations does Jeffrey Sachs make for combating poverty? What justifications does he cite? Do you agree with his proposals?

4. What does George Ayittey cite as the biggest reason for foreign aid's failure to reduce poverty in Africa? He proposes "smart aid" as an alternative. What is "smart aid"? What are its key components?

YES: Jeffrey D. Sachs, *The Earth Institute at Columbia University*

In the broadest terms, national and international efforts to promote economic development around the world during the past fifty years have been
highly successful, with the notable exception of large parts of sub-Saharan
Africa, which remain trapped in extreme poverty. The biggest development
successes have come in Asia, a vast region with more than half the world's population. Economic growth in China, India, Korea, and many other countries—
along with public investments in health, education, and infrastructure—have
powered the most rapid improvement in living standards in world history. Aid
has played an enormous role in those gains. The fact that Asia can feed itself is
due in no small part to the Green Revolution that began in the 1960s, heavily
supported by the U.S. public and philanthropic sectors. The fact that disease
burdens have come down sharply is due in important part to global aid successes such as smallpox eradication, widespread immunization coverage,
malaria control (outside of Africa), and the uptake of oral rehydration to fight
death from diarrhea. The fact that population growth has slowed markedly is
a success of aid-supported family planning efforts, which the United States has
helped to initiate since the 1960s. The fact that countries such as Korea,
Malaysia, and Thailand became manufacturing successes grew out of U.S. and
Japanese aid for core infrastructure and technological upgrading.

DEVELOPMENT ASSISTANCE AS A TOOL IN PROMOTING ECONOMIC DEVELOPMENT

There are now sixty years of experience in deploying development assistance as
a tool in promoting economic development in low-income settings. Development aid has long been a mix of public and private contributions. When aid is
from the public sector, it is known as Official Development Assistance (ODA).
Both ODA and private assistance have played an important and successful role
in development. Many of the greatest successes in development assistance in
the past six decades have come through Public-Private Partnerships (PPPs),
which typically link ODA with private-sector and philanthropic leadership of

This article, which is based on excerpts from the HELP Commission Minority Report, "Revamping
U.S. Foreign Assistance," by Jeffrey Sachs, Leo Hindery Jr., and Gayle E. Smith (2007), was prepared in
August 2008 and does not take into account developments since the 2008 U.S. presidential election.

various kinds. The Green Revolution in India was spurred by such a partner-ship. The campaign against polio, which is on the verge of eradicating that dread disease, is a partnership of several public and private institutions, includ-ing the World Health Organization and Rotary International.

Of course, aid has worked in conjunction with powerful market forces, most importantly international trade and investment—the forces of globalization have helped to spread the benefits of advanced technologies to all corners of the world. Aid should certainly be seen not as a substitute for market-led devel-opment, but rather as a complementary component of market forces, espe-cially for impoverished countries that lack sufficient infrastructure, income, and creditworthiness to mobilize needed investments on their own behalf via market forces and domestic budget revenues.

The special role for ODA as one of several complementary forces of eco-nomic development was well described in the Monterrey Consensus, a 2002 agreement among the world's nations, which the United States strongly sup-ports and repeatedly backs. That agreement is notable in recognizing the inter-connections among private capital flows, international trade, and ODA—all of which are vital to economic development of the poor countries. Rather than pitting trade against aid, the Monterrey Consensus explains why they are both vital and complementary, and, indeed, why aid is vital to supporting trade competitiveness of the poorest countries. The Monterrey Consensus has there-fore contributed to the new concept of "aid for trade," in which ODA is used to help poor countries to improve their international trade, mainly by building the infrastructure (roads, ports, power) needed to support trade.

U.S. Commitments to Economic Development and Poverty Reduction

The United States has long recognized that it cannot and should not carry the world's development financing burden on its own. Support for economic development in the poorest countries must be a shared global effort, based on agreed targets. The United States and partner countries have therefore pursued shared global goals for several decades, achieving great successes in disease control, increased food production, the spread of literacy and numeracy, increased school enrollments, improved infrastructure, and many other core development objectives. By far the most important of the shared development objectives today are the Millennium Development Goals (see Table 1) adopted by all nations in the Millennium Declaration of the year 2000 and reconfirmed regularly since then, including at the G8 summits.

The Millennium Development Goals (MDGs) constitute a very important instrument for effective U.S. development assistance for the following reasons:

Table 1

The Millennium Development Goals

Goal 1: Eradicate extreme poverty and hunger	Target 1: Halve, between 1990 and 2015, the proportion of people whose income is less than $1 per day
	Target 2: Halve, between 1990 and 2015, the proportion of people who suffer from hunger
Goal 2: Achieve universal primary education	Target 3: Ensure that, by 2015, children everywhere, boys and girls alike, will be able to complete a full course of primary schooling
Goal 3: Promote gender equality and empower women	Target 4: Eliminate gender disparity in primary and secondary education, preferably by 2005, and in all levels of education by 2015
Goal 4: Reduce child mortality	Target 5: Reduce by two-thirds, between 1990 and 2015, the under-five mortality rate
Goal 5: Improve maternal health	Target 6: Reduce by three-quarters, between 1990 and 2015, the maternal mortality ratio
Goal 6: Combat HIV/AIDS, malaria, and other diseases	Target 7: Have halted by 2015 and begun to reverse the spread of HIV/AIDS
	Target 8: Have halted by 2015 and begun to reverse the incidence of malaria and other major diseases
Goal 7: Ensure environmental sustainability	Target 9: Integrate the principles of sustainable development into country policies and programs, and reverse the loss of environmental resources
	Target 10: Halve, by 2015, the proportion of people without sustainable access to safe drinking water and basic sanitation
	Target 11: By 2020, to have achieved a significant improvement in the lives of at least 100 million slum-dwellers
Goal 8: Develop a global partnership for development	Target 12: Develop further an open, rule-based, predictable, non-discriminatory trading (includes a commitment to good governance, development, and poverty reduction—both nationally and internationally)
	Target 13: Address the special needs of the Least Developed Countries (includes tariff- and quota-free access for their exports; enhanced program of debt relief for heavily indebted poor countries [HIPC]; and cancellation of official bilateral debt; and more generous official development assistance for countries committed to poverty reduction
	Target 14: Address the special needs of landlocked developing countries and small island developing states
	Target 15: Deal comprehensively with the debt problems of developing countries through national and international measures in order to make debt sustainable in the long term
	Target 16: In cooperation with pharmaceutical companies, provide access to affordable drugs in developing countries
	Target 17: In cooperation with the private sector, make available the benefits of new technologies, especially information and communications technologies

- The world has agreed to the goals and reconfirmed that support each year since 2000.

- The world has agreed to a trade and financing framework in the Monterrey Consensus.

- The MDGs address extreme poverty in all its interconnected dimensions: income, hunger, disease, deprivation.

- The MDGs promote long-term economic growth and wealth creation by encouraging countries to focus on productive investments to end the poverty trap.

- The MDGs are ambitious and yet achievable.

- The MDGs are quantitative and time-bound, therefore offering objective indicators of success and accountability.

Current Levels of U.S. Official Development Assistance in Comparative Perspective

Although development, defense, and diplomacy are the three pillars of U.S. national security, the current investments in national security are almost entirely in the direction of defense spending. In 2007 defense spending was $611 billion, while spending for diplomacy could be estimated at around $9 billion and that for development assistance at $22.7 billion. The allocation of official development assistance is equally important. U.S. aid is divided between "bilateral" aid, given by the U.S. government directly to other countries, and multilateral aid, given by the U.S. government to international organizations such as the World Bank, the African Development Bank, and the Global Fund to Fight AIDS, TB, and Malaria. Distressingly, only around one-quarter of overall bilateral aid is spent on development directed at long-term poverty reduction and disease control. The vast bulk of aid is devoted to emergencies and U.S. political aims, rather than to the objectives that are most effectively served by official development assistance: long-term economic development.

The United States is the largest aid donor in terms of absolute amount, as shown in Figure 1a, but this fact is hardly surprising since it is also by far the most populous donor country, with a 2006 population of 299 million, compared with 128 million in Japan, 83 million in Germany, 60 million in the United Kingdom, 63 million in France, 9 million in Sweden, and 5 million in Norway. In per capita terms, however, Norwegians average $629 per person in aid, while Americans average only $76 per person. As a share of national

Figure 1a

Net ODA in 2007—amounts

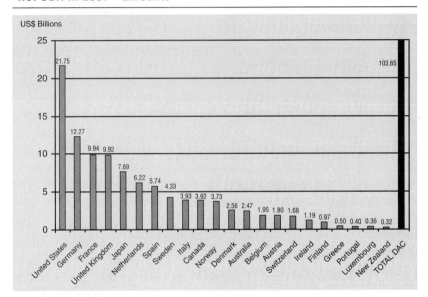

US$ Billions

Figure 1b

Net ODA in 2007—as a percentage of GNI

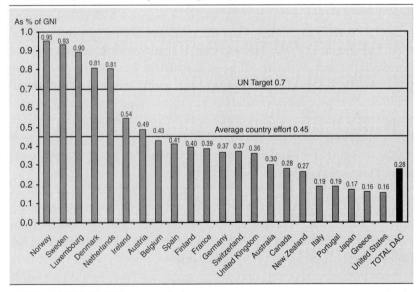

As % of GNI

Source: OECD, April 4, 2008.

income, U.S. aid is actually the lowest among donor countries, as shown in Figure 1b.

Since 1970, most donor countries have pledged to achieve the target of 0.7 percent of GNP as ODA (following a recommendation of an International Commission headed by Lester Pearson), and reiterated that pledge many times, most recently in the Monterrey Consensus.[1] Only five countries—Denmark, Luxembourg, the Netherlands, Norway, and Sweden—have consistently achieved or exceeded that goal. All of the other seventeen donors in the OECD's Development Assistance Committee (DAC) have fallen short, despite their adoption of the target.

Following the 2002 Monterrey Conference, most donor countries set a specific timetable to achieve the 0.7 percent target. Donors in the (pre-enlargement) European Union agreed to contribute at least 0.51 percent of GNP as ODA by 2010, and 0.7 percent by 2015. The United States, despite its strong and repeated support for the Monterrey Consensus, has not yet made concrete efforts to achieve the target of 0.7 percent of GNP. The current U.S. level of ODA, alas, remains stuck at 0.16 percent of GNP (2007)—the lowest level among all twenty-two donors in the Development Assistance Committee. Unlike the European Union, the United States has established no timetable or political consensus to reach that goal, despite its pledge at Monterrey to make concrete efforts to do so.

Private Development Assistance

During the 1960s, the idea took hold in various forums that the rich countries should support the poor countries with an annual transfer of 1 percent of national income. This transfer, in turn, was to be divided between ODA, targeted at 0.7 percent, and aid from private donors, targeted at 0.3 percent. While a few donor governments have achieved the 0.7 target, however, no donor country's private sector has come close to reaching the 0.3 percent of GNP target for private development assistance.

Meanwhile, it is often said that development assistance is passé, since private financial flows of all kinds (development assistance, foreign direct investment, foreign portfolio investments, and so on) now swamp official flows. Still, this fact does not make ODA obsolete, because the private capital flows are heavily concentrated in middle-income countries and in low-income countries with high-value natural resources such as hydrocarbons, minerals, or precious metals. Private capital flows bypass the world's poorest countries, which lack the basic infrastructure—roads, power, ports, clinics, and schools—that is needed to attract private investments in the first place. ODA is complementary to private capital flows, and it must generally *precede* private flows into impoverished regions. We should therefore think about using ODA to create the base—in infrastructure, health, skills, and other necessary conditions—to attract private capital.

Similar points can be made about trade. An open trading system is essential for economic development, including among the poorest countries. Developing countries need to import technology from abroad and must pay for that technology through their own exports. For this basic reason, export-led growth has been vital for economic success in recent decades. To achieve export-led growth, poor countries need to maintain relatively open trading systems (featuring low to moderate tariffs and convertible currencies), while rich countries, including the United States, have to keep their own borders open to the exports of the poor countries. However, even trade reforms such as these cannot substitute for official development aid.

WHAT WORKS AND WHAT DOESN'T WORK WITH ODA

The discussion on aid effectiveness is clouded by confusions, prejudices, and simple misunderstandings. Many studies try to find a correlation between overall aid and economic growth; when they find little positive correlation, they declare aid to be a failure. But the low correlation does not prove that aid is failing, since much of the aid is directed to countries in violence, famine, or deep economic crisis. It ought not to be a surprise, therefore, that aid often correlates with "economic failure"—not because aid has caused the failure, but rather because aid has responded to it.

There has been vast development success internationally, including stunning increases in average incomes, life expectancy, child survival, literacy, school completion rates, and other gains, in most parts of the world. When we look at ODA success stories, however, we find that aid is most successful when it is indeed used for development assistance. In other words, the ODA tool truly is a *development* tool.

Here are several great success stories of development assistance:

- **The Asian Green Revolution.** During the 1950s and 1960s, the Rockefeller Foundation and other donors spurred the development of high-yield seed varieties and new techniques for modernized farming. The U.S. Agency for International Development (USAID) helped to finance the rapid uptake of these new technologies, including the improved seeds, fertilizer, and irrigation. Dramatic successes were achieved in the 1960s in India and Pakistan, and later in China, Southeast Asia, and other parts of the developing world.

- **Smallpox Eradication.** In 1967 the World Health Organization (WHO) established the Smallpox Eradication Unit and launched a donor-supported worldwide campaign to eradicate the disease. By 1980, WHO was able to declare the world free of smallpox.

- **Family Planning.** During the 1960s, the U.S. government and various organizations (including the Ford Foundation and the Population Council) launched a global effort to spread access to modern contraception, based on individual voluntary choices. The uptake of these contraceptive methods, supported by international and U.S. funding, has been widespread (though still largely bypassing sub-Saharan Africa). As a result of these actions, together with declining child mortality rates, spreading literacy, and broader economic trends, fertility rates and population growth rates have declined sharply throughout most of the developing world.

- **The Campaign for Child Survival.** In 1982 UNICEF launched a campaign to promote child survival, based on the powerful combination known as GOBI: growth monitoring of children, oral rehydration therapy, breastfeeding for nutrition and immunity to infectious diseases, and immunizations against childhood killers. Backed by development assistance, the package enjoyed a remarkably rapid uptake, enabling many of the poorest countries to reach at least 80 percent immunization coverage.

- **Treatment for AIDS, TB, and Malaria.** After years of international neglect and underfinancing, international donors agreed to step up their actions to fight three killer pandemic diseases: AIDS, tuberculosis (TB), and malaria. At the urging of the then UN secretary-general Kofi Annan, they formed a new Global Fund to Fight AIDS, TB, and Malaria, as a means to pool their resources and invite countries to formulate national strategies that would be backed by development aid. In a period of only five years, the Global Fund successfully financed the access of more than 1 million HIV-infected individuals to antiretroviral medicines; the distribution of more than 30 million bed nets (protective against mosquitoes), mainly in Africa; and the treatment of more than 2 million individuals for TB. At the same time, the United States launched the PEPFAR (President's Emergency Plan for AIDS Relief) program to extend AIDS prevention and treatment programs in low-income countries.

There are six crucial lessons in these development success stories:

- First, the interventions are based on a powerful, low-cost technology. Given that the main underlying force of economic development is technological advance, it is not surprising that successful development assistance typically involves the diffusion of a powerful technology, such as high-yield seeds, immunizations, modern contraception, or Internet connectivity.

- Second, the interventions are relatively easy to deliver, based on standardized protocols and local ownership. Modern technologies are embodied in systems. Vaccinations, for example, are delivered on a specific timetable for young children, and high-yielding seeds are deployed in specific packages of farm inputs (such as combinations of seed, fertilizer, irrigation, and agricultural extension). The key to success is to deploy the technology in a system that is evidence-based, scientifically sound, administratively feasible, and tailored to local conditions.

- Third, the interventions are applied at the scale needed to solve the underlying problem. The key to success in the examples cited earlier was not the demonstration of the underlying technology, but rather the deployment of the technology at a scale in which it could make a difference. Typically, once the technology is known, and once the expert system has been identified, rapid scale-up is possible, building on global strategies and local adaptation and support.

- Fourth, the interventions are reliably funded. All of the success stories involve budget outlays over a period of many years, so that participating countries can be confident of sustained financing, and therefore can establish institutional systems and provide training and capacity-building.

- Fifth, the interventions are multilateral, drawing support from many governments and international agencies. The greatest development challenges—extreme poverty, hunger, disease, lack of infrastructure—are beyond the financing capacity of any single donor country. Moreover, a unified effort is more efficient than a congeries of small and disparate projects, at least once the technologies and delivery mechanisms have been developed.

- Sixth, the interventions have specific inputs, goals, and strategies, so that success rates can be assessed. All of the success stories involve clear strategies, such as coverage rates of immunizations, hectares planted with high-yield seeds, and timely isolation of smallpox outbreaks. They do not directly aim for excessively broad and overarching goals—such as "economic growth," or "rule of law," or "democracy," or "end of terror"— though broad goals such as these were among the indirect and long-term objectives that motivated the programs in the first place. Instead, the programs work on much more specific objectives, which can be measured, audited, evaluated, and reassessed as needed.

These six specific points all come down to one overarching lesson: be practical when deploying development aid—understand the targeted inputs, the outputs, the financing, and the objectives.

MODERNIZING U.S. DEVELOPMENT ASSISTANCE IN THE TWENTY-FIRST CENTURY

Development goals must be made clear and appropriate, the technologies must be identified, the systems for delivery must be assessed, and the multilateral financing must be assured. In this section, I consider each of these aspects of U.S. governmental efforts to provide Official Development Assistance.

The Goals

The priorities for U.S. development assistance should be based mainly on the development commitments that the United States and the rest of the world have made in recent years, after considerable diplomatic and scientific discussions and negotiations. At the core of the effort should be the Millennium Development Goals, which are already the central organizing tool for most development agencies and multilateral development institutions around the world. The MDGs have the profound advantage not only of specifying explicit and quantitative targets, but also of automatically aligning U.S. efforts with those of partner countries, thereby massively leveraging American resources and expertise. The focus of the development challenge is in those regions still trapped in extreme poverty, or those places suffering extremely high burdens of hunger, disease, or lack of infrastructure. This means that U.S. efforts should be mainly directed toward sub-Saharan Africa, Central Asia, the Andean region, Haiti, and the remaining pockets of extreme poverty in South Asia. Development aid for middle-income countries (such as China, Brazil, and Mexico) should be scaled back accordingly, since these regions can generally finance their own investment needs.

The Technologies

For each of the MDGs, there is a set of core interventions, based on proven low-cost technologies that can spur rapid advances toward the goals. The UN Millennium Project, among other studies, has identified the powerful tools at our disposal in each of the key areas of need. While much can be said about each area, the following recommended interventions should be noted:

- **Income poverty:** microfinance; electricity generation (off-grid and on-grid); all-weather roads; access to cell phones and Internet; improved population health (see below)

- **Hunger:** improved food production through the extension of "Green Revolution" technologies (high-yield seeds, fertilizer, small-scale irrigation, agricultural extension services); micronutrient supplementation for Vitamin A, iodine, zinc, and iron; nutrition interventions for low-weight children; school feeding programs, with take-home rations for pre-school-aged children

- **Universal school completion:** construction of schools; training of teachers; wireless Internet connectivity for (solar-charged) computers at schools; separate hygienic facilities for girls and boys; mid-day feeding programs

- **Gender equality:** time-saving infrastructure for rural women (water, power, mills, and clinics, within reach of villages); micro-finance for women's groups; improved inheritance and property rights

- **Reduced maternal mortality:** emergency obstetrical theatres in all sub-district hospitals; training of assistant medical officers (AMOs) to perform emergency procedures; use of wireless phone systems to create emergency-response units for ambulance services

- **Reduced child mortality:** integrated management of childhood illnesses (IMCI), including diarrhea, malaria, acute lower respiratory infection (ALRI), vaccine-preventable diseases, parasitic infections (worms), micronutrient deficiencies, and expert systems for neonatal care; increased use of community health workers, supported by mobile phone and Internet connectivity

- **Control of AIDS, TB, and malaria:** packages of preventative and curative health services, such as access to medicines and universal protection by insecticide-treated bed nets in the case of malaria

- **Universal access to family planning and contraceptive services:** logistics and supply chain management for contraceptive availability; community-worker outreach to ensure access to family planning services and contraception on a voluntary basis

- **Safe drinking water and sanitation:** application of modern hydrological tools to identify sustainable water sources, based on seasonal and annual runoff, rainwater harvesting, sustainable use of groundwater, and improved year-round water storage; investments in sanitation systems, including septic tanks and recycling of human and animal wastes in rural areas, and piped wastewater treatment in urban areas

While there is much debate about "development assistance" in the abstract, there is near consensus on the use of aid to expand access of the poor to vital and proven technologies. Aid-skeptic William Easterly, for example, endorses this approach:

> Put the focus back where it belongs: get the poorest people in the world such obvious goods as the vaccines, the antibiotics, the food supplements, the improved seeds, the fertilizer, the roads, the boreholes, the water pipes, the textbooks, and the nurses. This is not making the poor dependent on handouts; it is giving the poorest people the health, nutrition, education, and other inputs that raise the payoff to their own efforts to better their lives.[2]

The Delivery Systems

Much is made of the difficulty of delivering such technologies to the poor—focusing on perceived high risks of corruption, mismanagement, and other delivery failures. Yet such fears have been shown time and again to be misplaced as long as the aid is practical, subject to monitoring, adapted to local circumstances, endorsed by local communities, and embedded in a sensible delivery system with audits and evaluation. In recent years, enormous successes have been achieved in the mass distribution of anti-malaria bed nets, the mass scale-up of new vaccines (through the Global Alliance for Vaccines and Immunizations), the mass treatment of children for worm infections, the mass increase in primary-school enrollments and completion rates by eliminating school fees, and the mass access of farmers to high-yield inputs through voucher systems. In all of these cases, success has resulted from transparency, specificity, accountability, and auditing of delivery systems.

The Financing

The basic principles of financing are clear. First, donor aid should be directed at communities and regions that cannot fund their own development efforts. As the Monterrey Consensus rightly noted, this means an emphasis on the least developed countries, particularly on sub-Saharan Africa as a major focus for financing. Second, aid should avoid program designs that aim to have the poorest of the poor pay for vital services. Attempts to sell bed nets or health insurance or medicines to the poor have inevitably led to the exclusion of large parts of the population (especially in rural areas) from coverage. Third, donor aid should be a mix of bilateral and multilateral initiatives, divided roughly half-and-half. The United States will not, and should not, aim to fund the delivery of services on its own; such efforts should reflect a pooling of bilateral (that is, governmental) donors, international organizations, the private sector, and private philanthropy (including foundations and individuals). In some cases, such financing mechanisms already exist, but in other cases they need to be created. Here is a quick rundown.

- **Health financing.** The Global Fund to Fight AIDS, TB, and Malaria (GFATM) has become the most effective instrument for multilateral financing. The United States should increase its contributions to the GFATM, in conjunction with increases by other donor partners. There are currently three "windows" at the Global Fund (for the three diseases). At least two new funding windows should be opened: one for "health systems" (nurses, community health workers, clinic construction and facilities) and one for other readily controllable "neglected tropical diseases" (soil-transmitted helminthes, lymphatic filariasis, trachoma, onchocerciasis, and schistosomiasis).

- **Education financing.** The Education-for-All (EFA) initiative of the Millennium Development Goals is backed by a Fast Track Initiative (FTI) that is largely funded by the United Kingdom. The United States should join the U.K. and other donors in ensuring full financing for EFA-FTI.

- **Agriculture financing.** There is an urgent need for increased multilateral financing for improved agricultural productivity and food production of smallholder subsistence farmers in sub-Saharan Africa and other hunger hotspots. The Gates and Rockefeller Foundations have recently established an Alliance for a Green Revolution in Africa (AGRA), with initial financing of $500 million. The World Bank and the International Fund for African Development (IFAD) are prepared to channel increased assistance to smallholder agriculture, but so far they lack the requisite backing of donors to do so at the needed scale.

- **Infrastructure financing.** Some infrastructure, notably telecommunications and Internet connectivity, is being expanded rapidly on the basis of private-sector investments. Other infrastructure, including roads, power, ports, and large-scale urban water and sanitation systems, will require very substantial public financing. Currently, infrastructure financing is provided in a somewhat haphazard way by a variety of donors, including bilateral donors, the concessionary financing window of the World Bank (the International Development Association, IDA), the regional development banks, the European Investment Bank, and others. There is no overall coordination to ensure that total financing is in line with total needs. What is needed, therefore, is a new pooled financing system for critical infrastructure, especially for sub-Saharan Africa—and the United States should play an important role in developing that system.

THE STRUCTURE OF U.S. DEVELOPMENT ASSISTANCE

There is a strong case for moving U.S. development assistance to a new, separate, cabinet-level Department for International Sustainable Development (DfISD). The new department would house the existing USAID, PEPFAR, the President's Malaria Initiative, the Millennium Challenge Corporation, and emerging initiatives in climate change, especially vis-à-vis the developing countries. The case for a separate department rests on the following principles:

- The need to upgrade U.S. development assistance as a pillar of U.S. national security.

- The need to improve U.S. government management and expertise in public health, climate change, agronomy, demography, environmental engineering, and economic development.

- The need to work effectively with similar cabinet-level departments and ministries in partner countries.

- The need to depoliticize development assistance, so that it can be directed at the long-term investments that are critical in the fight against poverty, hunger, disease, and deprivation.

- The need for coherence of U.S. policies that impact international sustainable development, including ODA, trade relations with low-income countries, efforts on climate-change adaptation and mitigation, and efforts on global public health and disease control.

The current system, in which USAID is a part of the Department of State, is failing. U.S. aid is excessively politicized by connecting aid with short-term foreign policy exigencies (such as the war in Iraq and the Israel-Palestine crisis). It would be very useful to *insulate* development aid from such short-term diplomatic pressures. Moreover, USAID has been gutted of much key talent and staffing, and the U.S. government is currently unable to attract the best young experts in development fields—and it will remain unable to do so until the status of sustainable development within the government is improved. The organizational upgrade in the United Kingdom from a mere subcabinet development agency (the Overseas Development Administration) to a cabinet-level department (the Department for International Development, DfID) has dramatically increased that nation's standing, reputation, and expertise in the area of international development. DfID is far ahead of USAID as a global thought-leader in development policy, and DfID's departmental rank is playing a key role in that success.

The new U.S. cabinet-level department would have several specific tasks in its start-up years, in addition to the development challenges already described. DfISD would bring together countless aid programs now strewn in a disconnected way across the U.S. government. It would bolster technical competence (in health, agronomy, engineering, climate, hydrology, finance, and other areas related to sustainable development), and it would fix the procurement and contracting systems, widely regarded to be broken. It would promote results-based aid delivery, with monitoring, accountability, and audits. DfISD would be much better placed than USAID to work with counterpart Ministries of International Development and to coordinate multilateral efforts. DfISD would promote partnerships with civil society and the private sector. Businesses, especially, would be encouraged to utilize their technologies (in sectors such as health, agriculture, energy, logistics, finance, and ICT) in partnership with the U.S. government and multilateral agencies.

THE FINANCING OF U.S. DEVELOPMENT ASSISTANCE IN THE NEXT ADMINISTRATION

The current level of worldwide official development assistance—roughly $100 billion per year, of which roughly $25 billion is directed to sub-Saharan Africa—is widely and repeatedly acknowledged—by the United Nations, the G8, and the donor countries in the OECD Development Assistance Committee—to be inadequate to support the achievement of the Millennium Development Goals. This is a very important point for U.S. political leaders and the broader public to recognize. The global community, including the U.S. and other governments, have repeatedly acknowledged the need for much more aid and promised significant increases. Yet the administration and Congress have not yet delivered on those promises, most importantly the commitments made in Monterrey, Mexico, in 2002 to support the MDGs:

> We recognize that a substantial increase in ODA and other resources will be required if developing countries are to achieve the internationally agreed development goals and objectives, including those contained in the Millennium Declaration.[3]

It was in that context that the countries agreed to make concrete efforts to meet the 0.7 percent target. The recognition that much more aid is needed has since been reiterated on several occasions—at the G8 summits, the UN World Summit in September 2005, and several follow-up UN General Assembly sessions and special meetings on the MDGs. Many significant studies, including those of the UN Millennium Project and the Africa Commission (launched by Britain's then prime minister Tony Blair), outlined bottom-up estimates of the costs of achieving the MDGs. The UN Millennium Project found that the OECD-DAC donors would need to contribute around 0.54 percent of GNP as of 2015 in order to co-finance the MDGs on a global basis. Since ODA will be needed for other purposes as well—such as disaster relief or post-reconstruction financing—the UN Millennium Project recommended that donor countries honor their commitment of 0.7 percent of GNP, in order both to enable success in the MDGs and to meet other challenges that will surely arise.

The overwhelming problem is that, until now, these repeated pledges have not been fulfilled. Real cash flows of ODA have hardly risen since 2004, especially taking into account global inflation and exchange-rate movements. While President George W. Bush promised in 2002 that the Millennium Challenge Account would be funded at the level of $5 billion per year by fiscal year 2006, in fact the funding has been under $2 billion per year. Poor countries, unsure whether the promises will ever be fulfilled, are therefore not able to plan for the future, and they are certainly not able to rely on pledges to make multiyear investment decisions, including investments in capacity and training.

The United States should now join the European Union in setting a specific timetable for increasing aid through the period to 2015. The United States should commit to reach 0.5 percent of GNP no later than 2012, and 0.7 percent of GNP by the year 2015. Such a guaranteed schedule of aid would underpin global success in achieving the Millennium Development Goals by 2015, and would put the world on a trajectory to achieve the end of extreme poverty by the year 2025 (as I have described in *The End of Poverty*[4]). Of the total aid package, roughly half the U.S. aid should be allocated through multilateral channels (such as IDA; the Global Fund to Fight AIDS, TB, and Malaria; and a new Global Fund for African Agriculture), and roughly half should be allocated through U.S. bilateral initiatives (such as PEPFAR, the President's Malaria Initiative, and other effective programs).

In closing, it is well to remember the words of General George Marshall in 1947 in launching the concepts of the world-changing Marshall Plan—words that can help us to find a way to a renewed motivation and success in U.S. foreign policy. The rationale of the Marshall Plan, one of the most successful U.S. foreign policy initiatives in history, resonates today:

It is logical that the United States should do whatever it is able to do to assist in the return of normal economic health in the world, without which there can be no political stability and no assured peace. Our policy is directed not against any country or doctrine but against hunger, poverty, desperation and chaos. Its purpose should be the revival of a working economy in the world so as to permit the emergence of political and social conditions in which free institutions can exist. Such assistance, I am convinced, must not be on a piecemeal basis as various crises develop. Any assistance that this Government may render in the future should provide a cure rather than a mere palliative.[5]

NO: George B. N. Ayittey, *American University*

Africa remains a paradox: immense economic potential and, yet, faltering economic progress. Despite signs of recent progress, Africa's development prospects remain bleak. Former UN Secretary-General Kofi Annan warned at the January 2005 African Union summit in Abuja, Nigeria, that Africa was failing to meet its Millennium Development Goals (MDGs). This warning was echoed two years later by the United Nations' African Development director, Gilbert Houngbo, in Congo-Brazzaville: "The [African] continent will fail to reach the goal of slashing poverty in half by 2015."[1] In recent years, however, the international community has mobilized to come to Africa's aid.

In a 2005 meeting in Gleneagles, Scotland, G8 leaders pledged to write off $40 billion of poor nations' debts and to double aid to Africa (to $50 billion) by 2010. Two years later, at the G8 summit in Heiligendamm, Germany, Chancellor Angela Merkel again placed debt relief and more aid to Africa at the top of the agenda. Elsewhere, a cacophonous galaxy of rock stars, antipoverty activists, and African heads of state are demanding more: total cancellation of Africa's crippling $350 billion foreign debt and fulfillment of the promises made in Gleneagles to double aid to Africa. (By June 2007, only 10 percent of those promises had been realized.) Also, China declared 2007 to be the "year for Africa."

A cynic might note that all this concern for Africa's plight appears to follow a ten-year attention-deficit cycle. Every decade or so, rock concerts are held to whip up international compassion for Africa's woes (starvation, war, refugees, and disease); mega-plans are drawn up, but acrimonious wrangling over financing modalities ensues; years slip by, and the campaign fizzles. A decade later, another grand Africa initiative is unveiled. Back in 1985, there was "Live Aid" and a "Special Session on Africa" held by the United Nations to boost aid to Africa. Then, in March 1996, the UN launched a $25 billion "Special Initiative for Africa." With clockwork precision, the plight of Africa again took center stage at a UN conference in September 2005. Expect another major initiative in 2015.

The "more-aid for Africa" campaign has become so steeped in emotionalism, overt racial sensitivity, and guilt (over colonial iniquities) that pragmatism, rationality, and efficiency have been sacrificed. So many Western governments, development agencies, and individuals have tried to help a continent and its people that they do not understand. More than $450 billion in foreign aid—the equivalent of six Marshall Plans—has been pumped into Africa since 1960, with negligible results. Helping Africa is a noble exercise that has become a theater of the absurd, in which the blind are leading the clueless.

It may sound uncaring, but the truth is that Africa really doesn't need foreign aid. In fact, the resources it desperately needs can be found in Africa itself. Providing more aid to Africa is akin to pouring more water into a bucket that leaks horribly—obviously, plugging the leaks ought to be the first order of business. But even then, the provision of more foreign aid will make little difference unless it is coupled with meaningful reform. So far, African leaders have shown little interest in reforming their abominable political and economic systems.

AFRICA'S LEAKY BEGGING BOWL

Africa has the resources it needs to launch self-sustaining growth and prosperity. Unfortunately, the problem has been a leadership that is programmed to look only outside Africa —principally to the West—for such resources. The result has been hopeless dependency on foreign aid. When the African Union unveiled the New Economic Partnership for African Development (NEPAD) in 2000, it was trumpeted as "Africa's own initiative," "Africa's Plan," "African-crafted," and, therefore, "African-owned." NEPAD talked of "self-reliance" and argued forcefully that Africans must be "masters of their own destiny." Still, it sought $64 billion in investments from the West. The partnership's fate was sealed when, seven years after its launch, Senegalese President Abdoulaye Wade—one of the architects of NEPAD—dismissed it as "a waste of time of money which had failed to produce concrete results."[2]

At a workshop organized for the Parliamentary Sub-Committee on Foreign Affairs at Ho, Ghana, Dr. Yaw Dzobe Gebe, a fellow at the Legon Center for International Affairs at the University of Ghana, stressed the need for the African Union to look within the continent for capital formation to build a viable continental union with less dependency on foreign aid: "With an accumulated foreign debt of nearly $350 billion and estimated capital requirement of more than $50 billion annually for capacity building, it is time Africa begins to look within for capital formation. Experience in the last 40 years or more of independence and association with Europe and America should alert African leaders of the fact that there are very limited benefits to be derived from benevolence of the development partners."[3]

An irate Namibian, Alexactus T. Kaure, weighed in:

> What I want to talk about is the uncritical belief—especially by African leaders—that somehow Africa's salvation and development will come from outside. This state of affairs has in turn led to the development of a number of industries in Europe and North America to reinforce and sustain that belief. ... You would always hear of a conference on Africa, for Africans *but not by Africans*, to discuss this or that issue, being held in places like Paris, London, Stockholm, Washington, Toronto and, of course, Brussels. And as you are reading this piece now, there is one going on in Brussels—termed EU-Africa Week. This conference will discuss a range of issues such as (good) governance, social rights, corruption, inequalities and vulnerable groups and the role of the media in development among others.
>
> Now most of these issues don't need a rocket scientist to actualize them and thus there is no need for these endless conferences. To make things even worse, the very same people who are supposed to implement most of the good practices in their countries and who are either unable or unwilling to, are the ones frequenting these conference halls. For them, of course, it's just another short holiday and opportunity for shopping and a bit of extra cash through S&T (per diem).[4]

Africa's investment process may be compared to that leaky bucket. The level of the water therein—GNP per capita—is determined by inflows of foreign aid, investment, and export earnings relative to outflows or leakages of imports (food, luxury consumer items), corruption, and civil wars. In 2005 Africa's balance of payment situation showed a payment deficit of $21.7 billion. This deficit had to be financed by new borrowing, which would increase Africa's foreign debt, or by the use of reserves, which were nonexistent for most African countries. This number, however, does not tell the full story. Hidden from view was a much grimmer story—the other, more serious leakages.

According to one UN estimate, "$200 billion or 90 percent of the sub-Saharan part of the continent's gross domestic product (much of it illicitly earned), was shipped to foreign banks in 1991 alone."[5] Capital flight out of Africa is at least $20 billion annually. Part of this capital flight represents wealth created legitimately by business owners who have little faith in keeping it in Africa. The rest represents loot stolen by corrupt African leaders and politicians. Former Nigerian President Olusegun Obasanjo charged that corrupt African leaders have stolen at least $140 billion (£95 billion) from their people in the decades since independence.[6]

Foreign aid has not been spared, either. Said *The Economist*: "For every dollar that foolish northerners lent Africa between 1970 and 1996, 80 cents flowed out as capital flight in the same year, typically into Swiss bank accounts or to buy mansions on the Cote d'Azur."[7] At the Commonwealth Summit in Abuja, Nigeria, on December 3, 2003, former British secretary of state for international development, Rt. Hon. Lynda Chalker, revealed that 40 percent of wealth created in Africa is invested outside the continent. Chalker said African economies would have fared better if the wealth created on the continent were retained within: "If you can get your kith and kin to bring the funds back and have it invested in infrastructure, the economies of African countries would be much better than what there are today," she said.[8]

On October 13, 2003, Laolu Akande, a veteran Nigerian freelance journalist, wrote:

> Nigeria's foreign debt profile is now in the region of $25–$30 billion, but the president of the Institute of Chartered Accountants of Nigeria, ICAN, Chief Jaiye K. Randle, himself an eminent accountant and social commentator, has now revealed that individual Nigerians are currently lodging far more than Nigeria owes in foreign banks. With an estimate he put at $170 billion it becomes immediately clear why the quest for debt forgiveness would remain a far-fetched dream.[9]

In August 2004, an African Union report claimed that Africa loses an estimated $148 billion annually to corrupt practices—a figure that represents 25 percent of the continent's Gross Domestic Product (GDP). "Mr. Babatunde Olugboji, Chairman, Independent Advocacy Project, made this revelation in Lagos while addressing the press on the survey scheduled to be embarked upon by the body to determine the level of corruption in the country even though Transparency International has rated Nigeria as the second most corrupt nation in the world."[10] The pillage in Nigeria has been massive.

Mallam Nuhu Ribadu, the chairman of the Economic and Financial Crimes Commission, set up three years ago, said that £220 billion ($412 billion) was "squandered" between independence from Britain in 1960 and the return of civilian rule in 1999. "We cannot be accurate down to the last figure but that is our projection," said Osita Nwajah, a commission spokesman.[11] The stolen fortune tallies almost exactly with the £220 billion of Western aid given to Africa between 1960 and 1997—a sum that amounted to six times the U.S. help given to postwar Europe under the Marshall Plan.

To be fair, upon assuming office, former President Obasanjo vowed to recover the funding looted by former head of state, General Sani Abacha. Obasanjo established the Corruption Practices and Other Related Offences Commission, and much public fanfare accompanied the announcement that the sum of about $709 million and another $144 million had been recovered from the late Abacha's family and his henchmen. But, apparently, this recovered loot was itself quickly relooted, for the Senate Public Accounts Committee found only $6.8 million and $2.8 million of the recovered booty in the Central Bank of Nigeria (CBN).[12] Uti Akpan, a textiles trader in Lagos was not impressed: "What baffles me is that even the money recovered from Abacha has been stolen. If you recover money from a thief and you go back and steal the money, it means you are worse than the thief."[13]

Back in the late 1980s, Sammy Kum Buo, director of the UN Center for Peace and Disarmament, lamented that "Africa spends about $12 billion a year on the purchase of arms and the maintenance of the armed forces, an amount which is equal to what Africa was requesting in financial aid over the next 5 years."[14] Since then, this amount has increased for all of Africa: "Excluding South Africa, spending on arms in sub-Saharan Africa totaled nearly $11 billion in 1998, if military assistance and funding of opposition groups and mercenaries are taken into account. This was an annual increase of about 14 percent at a time when the region's economic growth rose by less than 1 percent in real terms."[15] Total expenditures on arms and militaries exceed $15 billion annually.

Civil wars continue to wreak devastation on African economies. They cost Africa at least $15 billion annually in lost output, wreckage of infrastructure, and refugee crises. The crisis in Zimbabwe, for example, has cost Africa dearly. Foreign investors have fled the region and the South African *rand* has lost 25 percent of its value since 2000. More than 4 million Zimbabwean refugees have fled to settle in South Africa and the neighboring countries, and the South African government is preparing a military base at Messina to house as many as 70,000 refugees. Since 2000, almost 60,000 physicians and other professionals have left Zimbabwe.[16] According to the *London Observer*, Zimbabwe's economic collapse caused $37 billion worth of damage to South Africa and other neighboring countries.[17] South Africa has been worst affected, while Botswana, Malawi, Mozambique, and Zambia have also suffered severely.

Finally, the neglect of peasant agriculture, the uprooting of farmers by civil wars, devastated infrastructure, and misguided agricultural policies have made it difficult for Africa to feed itself. Therefore, Africa must resort to food imports, spending $15 billion in 1998. By 2000, food imports had reached $18.7 billion, slightly more than donor assistance of $18.6 billion to Africa in 2000.[18]

Table 1 offers a breakdown of how Africa loses money (and how much). As the table shows, the amount of leakage grossly overshadows the $64 billion NEPAD sought in investments from the West. It is apparent that if Africa could feed itself, if the senseless wars raging on the continent would cease, if the elites would invest their wealth—legitimate or ill-gotten—in Africa, and if expenditures on arms and the military were reduced, Africa could find within itself the resources it needs for investment. In fact, more resources could be found if corrupt leaders would disgorge the loot they have stashed abroad. This dual perspective suggests a new way to approach the investment issue: plug the leakages and repatriate the booty that has been hoarded abroad.

MONUMENTAL LEADERSHIP FAILURE

The entire foreign aid business has become a massive fraud, a huge scandal, and a charade. The donors are being duped—and, in many instances, they know it. As Patricia Adams of Probe International, a Toronto-based environmental group, charged, "In most cases, Western governments knew that substantial portions of their loans, up to 30 percent, says the World Bank, went directly into the pockets of corrupt officials for their personal use."[19] Donors pretend that they are helping Africa in order to atone for the sins of colonialism and soothe their own conscience, and African leaders pretend that they are helping the people.

Monumental leadership failure remains the primary obstacle to Africa's development. After independence in the 1960s, the leadership, with few exceptions, established defective economic and political systems that set the stage for the ruination of postcolonial Africa. The economic system of statism (or *dirigisme*), with its plethora of state controls, created chronic commodity shortages and black markets and spawned a culture of bribery and corruption,

Table 1	

Causes of Africa's Loss of Money

Cause	Amount
Corruption	$148 billion
Capital flight	$20 billion
Food imports	$18 billion
Expenditures on arms and the military	$15 billion
Civil war damage	$15 billion
Total other leakages	$216 billion

Source: George B. N. Ayittey, *Africa Unchained* (New York: Palgrave/Macmillan, 2005), 326.

virtually destroying Africa's productive base. The political system of one-party states and military dictatorships degenerated into tyranny, as these systems, concentrating enormous economic and political power in the state, evolved into "vampire states." Government, thus, has ceased to exist as an institution—its power having been hijacked instead by a phalanx of unrepentant bandits and thugs, who use the state machinery to enrich themselves, their cronies, and their tribes. Those who do not belong to this charmed circle of relatives, cronies or tribesmen are excluded from the gravy train. The richest persons in Africa are heads of state and their ministers, and, quite often, the chief bandit is the head of state himself.

Eventually the "vampire state" metastasizes into what Africans call a "coconut republic" and implodes when politically-excluded groups rise up in rebellion: Somalia (1993), Rwanda (1994), Burundi (1995), Zaire (1996), Sierra Leone (1998), Liberia (1999), Ivory Coast (2000), and Togo (2005). Only reform—intellectual, economic, political, and institutional—will save Africa, but the leadership is not interested.

In 2005 Africa's case for more aid and debt relief was not helped by President Obasanjo of Nigeria, which has, arguably, the most mismanaged economy in Africa. Even as he was pleading for more aid at the World Economic Forum in Davos, Switzerland, in February 2005, four of his state governors were being probed by London police for money laundering. The most galling case was that of the Plateau State governor, Chief Joshua Dariye, who was accused of diverting N1.1 billion (over $90 million) into his private bank accounts. Dariye was dragged to the Federal High Court in Kaduna by the Economic and Financial Crimes Commission (EFCC), but Justice Abdullahi Liman ruled on December 16, 2004, that although Dariye was a principal actor in the case, Section 308 of the Nigerian Constitution protected sitting governors from criminal prosecution. Imagine.

And would the police apprehend such a thief if he had no "constitutional immunity"? In February 2005, Nigeria's police chief himself, Inspector General Tafa Balogun, was forced into early retirement—after being on the job for only two years—when investigators probing money-laundering allegations found $52 million hidden in a network of fifteen bank accounts. Balogun was eventually prosecuted and sentenced to a mere six-month jail term—a slap on the wrist.

The Governor of the oil-rich Nigerian state of Bayelsa, Chief Diepreye Alamieseigha, was arrested at London Heathrow Airport on September 15, 2005, for money laundering in Britain. Appearing in a UK court a few days later, he was charged with laundering £1.8 million ($3.2 million) found in cash and in bank accounts. Seven London bank accounts have been traced to him.

Nigeria's Economic and Financial Crimes Commission has overwhelming evidence on most of the alleged corrupt government officials—especially state governors. The commission's chairman, Mallam Nuhu Ribadu, has described the case the Bayelsa State governor as just the tip of the iceberg. In fact, an allegation of corruption has been leveled against President Olusegun Obasanjo himself by the governor of Abia State, Orji Uzor Kalu.

Many Nigerians scoffed at Obasanjo's anticorruption campaign as an elaborate form of public relations to win concessions from lenders and burnish the president's reputation as a world leader. Critics noted that he waited so long—over four years—before cracking down on corruption, and even then, no major figures were brought to justice and few went to jail. One such figure, General Ibrahim Babangida, an ex-military dictator, thumbs his nose at his people by refusing even to testify before the anticorruption commission. When senior government officials are caught, punishment often amounts to a mere dismissal.

ACROBATICS ON REFORM

Efforts to stem corruption in Nigeria began making headlines in August 2004, when Nasir Ahmad el-Rufa'i, who had just been named to a ministerial post overseeing the Abuja capital region, announced that two senators had asked him for bribes to facilitate his confirmation. El-Rufa'i estimated that at least three out of every four lawmakers, and more than half of the nation's governors and many of its civil servants, are corrupt. "If a few more ministers go to jail, if a few more members of the National Assembly go to jail, believe me, people will line up and do the right thing," el-Rufa'i said.[20]

Until then, outright debt relief and massive inflow of aid without any conditions, safeguards, or monitoring mechanisms—as well as substantial reform—would be absurd. Budgets have careened out of control in Africa. Dysfunctional state bureaucracies, riddled with inefficiency and graft, have swollen, packed with political supporters. Corruption is rampant. Without reform, new debts will simply replace canceled old debts. But, with few exceptions, the leadership is just not interested in reform, period.

Ask these leaders to develop their countries, and they will develop their pockets. Ask them to seek foreign investment, and they will seek a foreign country in which to invest their booty. Ask them to cut bloated state bureaucracies or government spending, and they will set up a "Ministry of Less Government Spending." Ask them to establish better systems of governance, and they will set up a "Ministry of Good Governance" (Tanzania). Ask them to curb corruption, and they will set up an "Anti-Corruption Commission" with no teeth and then sack the commissioner if he gets too close to the fat cats (Kenya). Ask them to establish democracy, and they will impanel a coterie of fawning sycophants to write the electoral rules, hold fraudulent elections while opposition leaders are either disqualified or in jail, and return themselves to power (Ivory Coast, Rwanda).

Ask them to privatize inefficient state-owned enterprises, and they will sell them off at fire-sale prices to their cronies. In 1992, in accordance with World Bank loan conditions, the Government of Uganda began a privatization effort to sell off 142 of its state-owned enterprises. In 1998, however, the process was halted twice by Uganda's own parliament because, according to the chair of a parliamentary select committee, Tom Omongole, it had been "derailed by corruption," implicating three senior ministers who had "political responsibility."[21] The sale of these 142 enterprises was initially projected to generate 900 billion Ugandan shillings or $500 million. However, by the autumn of 1999, the revenue balance was only 3.7 billion Ushs.

The reform process has stalled through vexatious chicanery, willful deception, and vaunted acrobatics—all sound and fury but no action. Only sixteen of the fifty-four African countries are democratic; fewer than eight are "economic success stories"; and only eight have free and independent media. Without genuine political reform, more African countries will implode. The continent is stuck in a political cul-de-sac.

BETTER WAYS OF HELPING AFRICA

Smart aid would be that which empowers African civil society and community-based groups to monitor aid money and to instigate reform from within. Empowerment requires arming these entities with information and with the freedom and the institutional means to unchain themselves from the vicious grip of repression, corruption, and poverty. The true agents of reform are found outside government, not in "reformist partnerships" with crooked governments.

Africa already has its own Charter of Human and Peoples' Rights (the 1981 Banjul Charter), which recognizes each individual's right to liberty and to the security of his person (Article 6); to receive information, to express and disseminate his opinions (Article 9); to free association (Article 10); and to assemble freely with others (Article 11). Though the Charter enjoins African governments to recognize these rights, few do.

The institutional tools the African people need are these: free and independent media (to ensure free flow of information); an independent judiciary (for the rule of law); an independent electoral commission; an independent central bank (to assure monetary stability and stanch capital flight); an efficient, professional civil service; and a neutral, professional armed security force. Events in Ukraine, Ghana, Zimbabwe, Lebanon, and Togo in 2004 and 2005 unerringly underscore the critical importance of these institutions. Elections alone do not make a country democratic; nor are democracies nurtured in a vacuum. What is needed is a "political space" in which the people can air their opinions, petition their government without being fired on by security forces, and choose who should rule them in elections that are not rigged by electoral commissions packed with government cronies. This "space" does not exist in much of Africa.

The institutions just listed could help to create this political space, and their establishment would solve the majority of Africa's woes. For example, the two effective antidotes to corruption are independent media and an independent judiciary. But only eight African countries have free media in 2003, according to Freedom House. These institutions cannot be established by the leaders or the ruling elites (because of conflict of interest); they must be established by the civil society. Each professional body has a "code of ethics," which should be rewritten by the members themselves to eschew politics and uphold professionalism. Start with the "military code," and then the legal code," the "civil service code," and so on. The military code should debar soldiers from intervening in politics, mandating that they be court-marshaled for doing so. The legal code should decertify corrupt judges who do not uphold the rule of law, and the civil service code should sack public servants who do not uphold professionalism. Assistance to the Bar Association or the Civil Service Association to enforce their respective codes would be useful.

On May 13, 2006, thousands of Egyptian judges, frustrated by government control over the judiciary, threatened to thwart their country's September presidential elections by refusing to oversee polling unless they were granted full independence from the executive in their oversight of the process. "The institutions are presenting Mr. Mubarak with an unexpected challenge from within, one that will be difficult to dismiss. The fact is, major changes in this country are going to come out of those institutions, not from the streets," said Abdel Monem Said, director of the Ahram Center for Strategic Studies, a government-backed research and policy organization.[22] Government-backed newspapers, long the official mouthpiece, have lately published articles deemed unfavorable to the government, says Hussein Amin, professor of journalism and mass communications at the American University in Cairo.

The seeming mutiny by the Egyptian judges presents an altogether different and, in many ways, more serious challenge to a corrupt status quo than does the opposition movement. This is where smart aid would put its money. The situation is dicey, however, as direct assistance to Egyptian judges may constitute an "interference in the internal affairs of a sovereign nation." Funneling aid through Western-based NGOs is an option—about 36 percent of Canadian aid is so channeled—but those organizations can be expelled if they incur the displeasure of an African government. They can be accused of "spying" or engaging in subversive activities—charges that were leveled by Russia against Freedom House, a human rights group, in Ukraine and Kyrgyzstan.

But if, alas, direct assistance to Egyptian judges proves impossible, both third and fourth alternatives exist: the Bar Association in Egypt can be a conduit, or, if that is not feasible, Egyptians or Africans residing abroad could be the next best alternative. Many Africans in the diaspora are professionals, human rights activists, and reformers in exile. They understand conditions in their home countries better than do the Western-based NGOs. Funneling covert aid through their organizations may yield great results. After all, such was the case with Soviet dissidents during the Cold War.

The distinction between African governments and the people is important. Naïve EU officials think handing aid money to governments in Africa necessarily helps the people—a model they did not follow when dealing with the former Soviet Union. There the West did not hand over money to communist regimes, nor simply cajole them to reform. Instead, assistance to such groups as Solidarity in Poland and the establishment of Radio Free Europe accelerated the demise of the former Soviet Union. Why treat Africa differently? And how about Radio Free Africa?

The entire Western foreign aid program needs to be critically evaluated—not by Western or African government officials, but by people outside government—before more money is wasted.

emerging technology and political institutions

Is the Precautionary Principle an Effective Tool for Policymakers to Use in Regulating Emerging Technologies?

YES: Indur M. Goklany, *U.S. Department of the Interior*[a]

NO: John D. Graham, *Indiana University, and*
Sarah Olmstead, *Pardee RAND Graduate School*

Globalization has brought not only technological innovation but closer physical and electronic connections as well. Such forces lead to the rapid dissemination of knowledge and new technologies, but may also result in the global distribution of potentially harmful and catastrophic technologies, products, germs, and so on. The challenge for managing new technologies is determining how societies should manage emerging technologies that hold both promise and fear, for their own use and for trade abroad, as well as how much risk is tolerable for new and untested technologies.

The so-called precautionary principle is one approach that attempts to stipulate a broad framework for considering how society should handle the onset of new technological risks. One version of the precautionary principle—it is something of a misnomer because there are competing views on what it means—essentially stipulates that in the absence of solid scientific information indicating that a new product or technology is safe, society should err on the side of caution and prevent its introduction. The burden of proof, in short, is on

---

[a]Views expressed here do not necessarily reflect those of the U.S. Department of the Interior.

those who would introduce the new technology to show definitively that it is safe to the general public.

Evolving from the German socio-legal tradition of the 1930s, the precautionary principle is not simply an academic exercise in stipulating conditions for the introduction of new technologies. It has been explicitly endorsed internationally in the 1992 Rio Declaration on Environment and Development, and it has found wide support in the European Union—not only in policy involving technology and the environment but in the introduction of new foods, consumer protection, and so on. It has found fewer applications in the United States, although the City of San Francisco is an exception, having passed a purchasing ordinance requiring it to weigh environmental costs. The precautionary principle should be understood as a political principle as much as a technological one, for its underlying philosophy guides the actions of many environmental, consumer-safety, and other interests in the United States and internationally. The National Environmental Protection Act, which is widely emulated abroad, establishes institutional mechanisms by which the precautionary principle may be applied—by, for instance, requiring environmental impact assessments before public projects can begin, and establishing a legal procedure by which inadequate assessments may be challenged in courts.

Varying perceptions of risk exist at the individual level as well. Prospect theory—developed by Nobel laureate Daniel Kahneman and Amos Tversky as an alternative to "expected utility theory," which suggests that people make rational decisions based on expected returns—indicates that individuals' views of risk have systematic biases that color their assessments of potential future risks.[1] One is "status quo bias," which means that individuals are willing to take bigger risks to maintain the status quo than to attain it in the first place. Other such biases are "anchoring" (over-influence by unknowledgeable others), framing (the way issues are framed affects individual perceptions of their suitability), the use of heuristics (where discrete events are treated as part of a pattern), and so on. In each of these cases, individuals systematically behave differently from what expected utility theory (or benefit-cost analysis) would suggest is most appropriate. If individuals and (presumably) policymaking institutions do not behave in a "rational" (risk-neutral) manner in the face of future risks, then the precautionary principle suggests that the burden of proof should be on promoters of new technologies to indicate that they are safe, not on opponents to prove their riskiness.

While relatively simple in concept—who opposes safe technologies?— the application of the precautionary principle is politically difficult and conceptually ambiguous in practice. First, there is the question of safety to whom? Certain subpopulations (the elderly, children, the infirm) may be particularly sensitive to new products. Do they require a wider "margin of error" to protect them, or is it acceptable to entirely exclude at-risk populations from access to the new technologies? Second, why should this stricter standard apply only to new technologies? Should older products and technologies not be evaluated according to the same criteria? Would cell phones, for example, pass the precautionary principle test? Third, and perhaps most fundamentally, ought not, as some argue, both the costs and the benefits of new products be evaluated, rather than simply rejecting technologies because they impose *some* risks?

The answer would be far simpler if we had complete information about potential future risks and benefits, but this is rarely the case. And the uncertainty is compounded by vastly different regulatory styles across nations. The combination of imperfect information, competing interests, and different regulatory styles has produced varied reactions cross-nationally to the prospect of new technologies. Genetically-modified crops have been a case in point, as the U.S. government has permitted their introduction while the European Union, believing there to be insufficient information indicating their safety, has limited or prohibited their introduction, leading to significant trans-Atlantic trade disputes.

More recently, these contrasting regulatory styles rendered different perspectives on meat and milk from cloned animals—the U.S. Food and Drug Administration concluded that the products were safe, but the EU has taken a far more cautious approach. Cloning is, of course, a new technology whose implications are not yet fully understood; the potential benefits include production of animals that are more resistant to disease and meatier, while the risks are less specific, arising from a relatively small number of studies and uncertainties in the risk assessments and, perhaps, fear of the unknown. An EU body concluded that it did "not see convincing arguments to justify the production of food from clones and their offspring."[2]

These contrasting regulatory styles produce conflicting interpretations of the suitability of various new technologies, such as pesticides—which in turn lead to trade disputes. Globalization in the face of contrasting national views on managing risks means that trade disputes may be inevitable. The precautionary principle is an expression of national interests as much as a rule that guides public policy. It is also something of a luxury that the world's poor are unlikely to be able to afford, unless they are willing to forgo the potential for economic growth in exchange for environmental safety. The two articles that follow favor different approaches to governing the use of new technologies. Indur Goklany argues that the precautionary principle can be an effective tool as long as it includes comparative risk assessments to ensure that environmental and health risks do not increase. John Graham and Sarah Olmstead argue that there are logical problems with the precautionary principle—such as its inability to recommend a policy alternative in the face of two risky situations—and urge a more balanced approach to regulating new technologies, including benefit-cost analysis, continued review of scientific evidence, and proportionality in decision making.

Discussion Questions

1. Do regulations on new technologies impede innovation and development? Do innovation and development advance human well-being and reduce risks?
2. Can a technology ever truly be safe? How do you know when it is safe? Who decides? How safe should it be?
3. There are already regulations to protect the environment, health and safety. Do you think these regulations are sufficient? If so, is the precautionary principle necessary?
4. The authors of both essays describe two different formulations of the precautionary principle: weak versus strong. Is either one the right approach? In what situations is one a more appropriate response than the other? How should societies decide?

YES: Indur M. Goklany, *U.S. Department of the Interior*[a]

TECHNOLOGY AND RISK REDUCTION IN THE TWENTIETH CENTURY

In the past two centuries, despite—or is it because of?—economic growth and technological change, life-threatening risks have, one-by-one, been reduced or eliminated in the world's richer nations (Goklany 2007). The twentieth century saw the population of the United States multiply by 4, its income by 7, its carbon dioxide emissions by 9, its material use by 27, and its chemical use by more than 100. Yet people are living longer, and healthier. Over that same period, life expectancy increased from 47 years to 77 years. The disability rate for seniors declined 28 percent between 1982 and 2004/2005 (Manton et al. 2006) and, despite quantum improvements in diagnostic tools, major diseases (such as cancer and heart and respiratory diseases) now occur eight to eleven years later than a century ago (Fogel 2003).

Such improvements are a global phenomenon. Worldwide, life expectancy has more than doubled—from 31 years in 1900 to 67 years today. The developing world's population suffering from chronic hunger declined from 37 percent to 17 percent between 1970 and 2001, despite an 83 percent increase in population. That, supplemented by wider knowledge about basic hygiene, greater access to safe water, sanitation, vaccines, antibiotics, pasteurization, basic health services and new medicines, helped to push average global life expectancy from 47 years in the early 1950s to 67 years today.

Regarding the environment, death and disease from various water-related ailments were reduced dramatically. During the twentieth century, partly due to chlorination, the cumulative death rate from typhoid, paratyphoid, dysentery, and various gastrointestinal diseases dropped 99.5 percent. Deaths from malaria dropped 99 percent partly because of DDT-spraying, better nutrition, and draining of wetlands. Similarly, air quality in richer countries has improved steadily. Outdoor particulate matter and sulfur dioxide concentrations in U.S. urban areas peaked in the 1960s or earlier, while indoor concentrations—more relevant from the public health perspective because people spend most of their time indoors—have been improving since the 1940s.

In developing countries, although many environmental indicators are deteriorating, they are ahead of developed countries at equivalent levels of devel-

---

[a]Views expressed here do not necessarily reflect those of the U.S. Department of the Interior.

opment because of the diffusion of technology and knowledge. Average U.S. income in 1913 was $5,300 (in constant 1990 dollars, adjusted for purchasing power), infant mortality was about 100 per 1,000 live births, and life expectancy was 52 years, whereas China in 1998 had an average income of $3,200, infant mortality was 31 per 1,000 live births, and life expectancy was 70 years.

The worldwide reductions in deaths and disease since 1900 despite increased population, energy, and material and chemical use are due to broad dissemination—through education, public health systems, trade and commerce—of numerous new and improved technologies in agriculture, health, and medicine, supplemented by various ingenious advances in communications, information technology, and other energy-powered technologies. While these technologies may have created new risks or exacerbated some existing risks, the above evidence shows that they reduced overall risks by a greater amount.

Yet, even as major risks to health and well-being were being reduced, expectations rose even faster; the safer we have become, the more we worry about the remaining risks, and despite the improvements from technology, many people are deeply suspicious of technology. But, as larger and more obvious risks are reduced, it becomes harder to identify the causes of remaining risks and to establish cause-and-effect relationships, especially at the lower levels at which many contaminants are currently found in the environment. Consequently, the public policy arena is riddled with conflicts over minutiae of risk analyses, such as whether or at what levels Alar on apples, arsenic in water, or acrylonotrile in food are safe for consumption. The need to resolve such conflicts and surrounding issues powered a vast expansion of the "regulatory state" during the past few decades, largely to manage health and welfare risks from technology. Such concerns also spawned the "precautionary principle."

The precautionary principle is a modern day articulation of the old saying, "Better safe than sorry." Depending on its precise wording, the principle may allow for—or, alternatively, require—regulation of an activity or technology that might create serious or irreversible environmental, health, or safety threats, even if the existence (and magnitude) of these new risks is scientific-ally uncertain. Some version of this principle is enshrined in at least fourteen international agreements, including the United Nations Framework Convention on Climate Change, the Rio Declaration, and the Convention on Biological Diversity.

Although there are many versions of the precautionary principle, all are premised on the notion of reducing, if not eliminating, risks to health, safety, and/or the environment. Therefore, I will interpret the question posed in this chapter's title as asking whether the principle is an effective tool *to reduce overall risks* from emerging technologies, rather than an effective tool to merely regulate emerging technologies.

To appreciate the distinction between the two questions, consider the European Union's experience with genetically modified (GM) crops. The EU's approach, which embodies a "strong" version of the principle, has ensured low rates of adoption of GM crops within Europe, but it does not follow that this approach has reduced overall environmental or health risks—the very reason for the precautionary principle. But the U.S. approach, which incorporates a moderate version of the principle (requiring governmental approval prior to commercial cultivation), has led to rapid adoption of GM crops and brought significant environmental benefits (relative to conventional crops). These benefits include higher yields (which reduces habitat lost to agriculture, the most important threat to biodiversity), lower pesticide usage, increased no-till cultivation (which reduces soil erosion, water pollution, and carbon emissions), and increases in biodiversity (Marvier et al. 2007). Thus, while the EU's version of the precautionary principle has effectively limited GM crops, by prolonging riskier practices, it has been environmentally counterproductive.

In the following sections, I will address the arguments for and against the precautionary principle and its various versions; compare the cost-benefit analysis (CBA) and precautionary principle–based approaches to managing technological risks; and offer a practical set of guidelines combining the precautionary principle and elements of CBA to ensure that risk-management decisions do, indeed, reduce overall risks to human and environmental well-being in ambiguous or uncertain situations where policies or actions might increase some risks while reducing others.

WEAK, STRONG, OR NO PRECAUTIONARY PRINCIPLE?

Both proponents and opponents of the precautionary principle have often argued that it substitutes for cost-benefit analysis or its subset, risk analysis. Its proponents view this substitution as one of its most attractive features. The *New York Times'* review of the best ideas of 2001 hailed the precautionary principle as "revolutionary" and superior to the risk-analysis paradigm employed by U.S. society and the World Trade Organization for managing technological risks. But opposition to the principle has coalesced around precisely the point that it seemingly rejects risk analysis and CBA.

Weak forms of the precautionary principle allow for regulating technology where "full scientific certainty" of harm from that technology is lacking. But since decisions are routinely made in both the public and private spheres despite the lack of "full scientific certainty," such formulations are uncontroversial, which accounts for the broad acceptance of the weak versions (Mandel and Gathii 2006).

Strong versions of the principle mandate regulation, if not an outright ban of the technology under consideration, unless it is proven "safe." These versions require proponents of the technology to bear the burden of proof demonstrating its safety. But how safe is safe enough?

Consider that no activity is completely risk-free. Whether one, for instance, merely stands on the curb waiting for the light to change or steps off to cross a street, there is a finite probability of getting hit by a passing vehicle. Second, as noted, historical experience suggests that even where technologies introduce new risks, they frequently reduce, or even eliminate, existing risks of greater magnitude (which is why we generally live longer and healthier than previous generations). For example, the indoor spraying of DDT to reduce malaria might also reduce populations of bald eagles, ospreys, and other species (Goklany 2001). Similarly, genetically modified crops, on the one hand, could reduce the environmental impacts of conventional agriculture and advance public health by enhancing the quantity and nutritional quality of food. But, on the other hand, they could increase the possibility of gene escape into the wider environment, with potentially adverse environmental consequences. For example, if the engineered gene is designed to be resistant to a pesticide, it could potentially create "superweeds."

The Burden of Proof

In light of such competing and plausible sets of risks, should the burden of proof be shouldered by the proponents of the new technology or by the defenders of the status quo? By the regulators or the regulated entity? Does the precautionary principle require action to regulate the new technology or inaction, thereby effectively endorsing existing technology, despite its risks?

Unfortunately, the various versions of the precautionary principle do not provide any practical guidance on how to minimize overall risks and avoid counterproductive outcomes. Consider, for instance, that although the strong version was invoked by environmental groups to support a global ban on DDT because of its environmental impacts, it could also be used to encourage DDT use because of its global public health benefits, including significant reductions in the 300–500 million incidences and the million deaths associated with malaria annually, mainly in Africa.

Because such contradictions are inherent in the strong versions, prominent legal scholar Cass Sunstein (2005) rejects the strong version as "paralyzing." Instead, he would manage risks based on three elements. First, he would use CBA to evaluate all relevant risks resulting from all options, including both action and inaction. Second, he would invoke an Anti-Catastrophe Principle—

which would essentially allow the use of the precautionary principle in cases in which one faced "truly catastrophic" risks but to which probabilities could not be assigned—although he would limit its reach if the costs of reducing harm were excessive or if scarce resources would be diverted from more pressing tasks (because expensive regulation can actually drive up risks to life and health). Third, he would employ "libertarian paternalism" to direct people's choices toward welfare-promoting activities while preserving freedom of choice.

Many analysts who are otherwise favorably inclined toward the strong version apparently recognize the force of these arguments, and so they espouse moderate versions of the principle. They would, accordingly, temper their support of the precautionary principle by requiring regulatory stringency to be proportional to the magnitude and nature of threat, sensitive to costs, and changeable in light of new information (Dickson 2005; Mandel and Gathii 2006).

Some analysts also argue that shifting the burden of proof to proponents of new technologies might freeze the status quo and stifle technological innovation, which has historically been instrumental in reducing existing risks to public health and the environment. The EU experience with GM crops lends credence to such fears.

Moreover, the standing of the precautionary principle as a legitimate risk-regulation tool has been hurt by the claim once advanced by environmental groups that it justified a global ban on DDT despite that pesticide's demonstrated effectiveness in reducing malaria. This claim, based on concentrating on DDT's environmental costs while downplaying its public health benefits, fuels suspicion that the principle can be used (or abused) to cherry-pick which risks to focus on during regulatory inquiry and regulation.

In today's world, unless the technology produces a novel product with hitherto unknown physical and chemical properties, it is likely that, in rich countries at least, approval must be obtained from one or another government agency under pre-existing environmental, health, and safety regulations. GM crops, for example, have to win approval prior to testing and commercial cultivation. By default, therefore, the burden of proof is on the proponent of the technology, and, given the political economy of the regulatory state, this burden is unlikely to shift in the future.

This state of affairs is further reinforced by the tendency of companies to protect themselves from liability and lawsuits by seeking some level of governmental approval, bolstered by the desire to avoid unfavorable publicity. Second, larger companies, in particular, actively court regulation, because it predictably leads to higher barriers to entry into the market for smaller, possibly more innovative upstarts. Third, government agencies and their officers often seek to expand their power, and enhance future employment possibilities, by filling regulatory vacuums. Thus any shift in the burden of proof to the regulator is unlikely, and debate over that possibility is mainly academic.

THE ROLE OF COST-BENEFIT ANALYSIS IN RISK REGULATION

The annual cost to the United States of regulating environmental and workplace risks has been estimated at $300 billion annually (excluding benefits and voluntary private expenditures)—or about 40 percent of Canada's gross economic product (Crews 2004).

Is the public being shortchanged? Clearly, it gets less risk reduction than it pays for. Some argue that society's resources would be better utilized if cost-benefit analysis (CBA) were used to discipline regulations of risks, noting that CBA also helps to answer a critical risk-management question—namely, how safe is safe enough? However, if CBA is legally precluded—as it is, for example, in the development of National Ambient Air Quality Standards—those critics would accept cost-effectiveness analysis as the next best solution, although it would not answer the question of what is safe enough.

Cost benefit analysis of a policy involves estimating its negative and positive social, economic, and environmental consequences—that is, its costs and benefits—in order to evaluate whether the policy's benefits would exceed its costs. If it would, then the policy should advance society's overall well-being.

If costs and benefits are to be compared on an equal footing, ideally both should be expressed quantitatively using a common measure, such as economic impact as measured by monetary value. However, in many instances, some of the significant consequences cannot be valued easily or accurately in monetary terms. Such consequences may include certain effects on public health (such as pain and suffering) or environmental quality (such as effects on species). In such instances, cost-benefit analysis may by default be reduced to a semi-quantitative (or qualitative) exercise (as we discuss later).

Whereas CBA is designed to determine whether a policy would produce a net benefit for society, cost effectiveness analysis (CEA) bypasses this threshold issue. Either the threshold is ignored, or the policy is taken for granted, perhaps because the policy has been promulgated by the legislature or, as in the case of the National Ambient Air Quality Standards, by the courts. Instead, CEA is used to figure out how one might implement the policy in the least costly or most effective manner. Thus, while CBA may be part of an inquiry as to whether society's well-being would be advanced—for instance, by reducing greenhouse-gas emissions by 50 percent by 2050—CEA would assume that such a reduction makes sense and would focus instead on identifying the mix of specific measures necessary to meet the emissions-reduction target and timetable most economically.

Sunstein argues that a fundamental problem with the current state of risk regulation is the public itself, and its inevitable influence on decision making in a democratic society. Members of the general public—by definition, non-specialists in toxicology and risk analysis—rely on "intuitive toxicology" to shape their attitudes and responses toward chemical and environmental risks. But intuitive toxicology is frequently based on misconceptions (such as the belief that animal carcinogens are necessarily human carcinogens, and the idea that there is no safe level of exposure to "cancer-causing" agents—the "no-threshold" model of carcinogenesis); wishful thinking (such as the notions that natural chemicals are more benign than synthetic chemicals, that zero risk is a practicable goal, and that reducing one set of risks would not increase other risks); and even erroneous information (including the conviction that our air, land, and water are more polluted now than ever before). Moreover, members of the general public frequently subscribe to dubious propositions, such as the idea that conservatism in risk analysis necessarily saves lives rather than diverting scarce resources from other, more worthwhile, risks or other gainful uses.

Compounding matters, nonspecialists rely on error-prone "mental short-cuts," such as assigning higher probabilities to types of hazards they can readily recognize—as in believing that nuclear plants are more hazardous because they remember Chernobyl—and an emotionally-driven tendency toward adopting the more alarming of competing narratives regarding a hazard ("alarmist bias"). Moreover, today's technology frequently detects chemicals down to levels at which health impacts cannot be reliably replicated—that is, dioxins may be detected down to 0.1 part per trillion (the equivalent of one penny in \$100 billion)—but, since absence of future harm is unprovable, these nonspecialists resort to their mental shortcuts to interpret the significance of such low dioxin levels.

Well-organized and, frequently, well-funded groups ranging from self-described "public interest" groups to those backed by industry itself attempt to exploit—sometimes, as in the Alar case, with brilliant success—the general public's false premises and cognitive failings in order to create "informational cascades" that are designed to bolster public demand for their policy agendas, which democratic governments and institutions are conditioned to heed. Thus, governments devote resources to small, rather than large, problems. Sometimes they react to short-term public outcries. Sometimes, being unaware of the harmful, unintended side-effects of regulation, they make matters worse. Consequently, the regulatory state could unwittingly be sacrificing tens of thousands of lives prematurely each year (equivalent to hundreds of thousands of life-years) that could otherwise be saved without increasing the total costs of risk-reduction activities (Sunstein 2002).

Establishing the primacy of CBA would, Sunstein argues, buffer overly-responsive governments from the forces that special-interest groups can generate and mobilize to skew society's risk-reduction priorities and thereby misdirect scarce resources. CBA, if undertaken by scientifically literate practitioners using peer-reviewed science, could, by providing a full quantitative rendering of both the good and bad consequences of risk-reduction proposals, diminish the likelihood of unintended consequences.

Although some proponents of the precautionary principle recognize that costs should play a role, that the regulation should be proportional to the nature and severity of potential risk, and that choices must occasionally be made between competing risks (Dickson 2005), many remain unconvinced about CBA (Ackerman and Heinzerling 2002; Mandel and Gathii 2006; Arcuri 2007). They argue that cost-benefit analysis requires certainty in order, first, to quantify costs and benefits and then to convert them into monetary units, and that in the absence of certainty, cost-benefit analysis has to resort to subjective probabilities to estimate risk. They are also skeptical of efforts to convert all consequences—particularly environmental effects such as species extinction or damage to exceptional ecosystems (such as coral reefs)—into monetary terms.

Third, they argue that the use of discounting in CBA to account for future consequences of a technology "improperly trivializes future harms and the irreversibility of some environmental problems" (Ackerman and Heinzerling 2002). (Discounting is used to compare today's costs and benefits to those that would accrue in the future. Its rationale is rooted in the empirical observation that consumers prefer to enjoy benefits sooner rather than later, and to postpone costs. The adjustment is made via the "discount rate," which reduces the present-day value of future benefits and costs. Thus, using a discount rate of 4 percent, a benefit that will be worth $100 next year would be worth about $96 today.) In fact, some proponents of the precautionary principle would explicitly weight the scales in favor of the environment over development if, despite uncertainty, the environmental consequences could be irreversible (Arcuri 2007). Fourth, they note that an examination of all relevant risks and options might itself lead to "paralysis by analysis."

CBA advocates, however, recognize that some categories of costs and benefits cannot always be quantified or valued in monetary terms. Under these conditions, they would use *qualitative* CBA, which would be acceptable to the U.S. Office of Management and Budget (OMB), the agency that oversees CBA undertaken by federal agencies in support of their regulatory actions. Notably, if qualitative factors are included in CBA, the process more closely resembles multicriteria decision making, which some precautionary principle proponents have raised as a possibility. Also CBA advocates would, to the extent practicable, include consideration of all plausible direct and indirect (including ancillary) costs and benefits, thus precluding, at least in theory, the possibility of cherry-picking ancillary consequences, whether they are costs or benefits.

With these provisos, CBA is appropriately viewed as a methodology to inform, rather than to make, decisions. It can be used to ensure that risk regulation fulfills its purpose of reducing overall risks, and there is no reason why agencies should not have to show that the benefits of their regulations would exceed the costs (or explain why not) and to show, by analyzing risk–risk trade-offs, that those regulations would not create larger countervailing risks.

Moreover, in response to claims that CBA and risk analysis are undemocratic, since these processes rely on technocratic experts who have their own inherent biases, CBA advocates echo Jefferson's opinion that "without better [and more reliable] information, neither deliberation nor democracy is possible" (Sunstein 2002, 257).

Finally, CBA can serve not just as a foil to popular but ill-informed and poorly evaluated actions purporting to reduce risks, but as a prod to advance regulations if benefits outweigh costs. For example, based on CBA, OMB urged the Occupational Safety and Health Administration to consider promoting automatic defibrillators in the workplace to reduce deaths following cardiac arrest.

Many CBA skeptics question the ethics of discounting. However, given human preferences and behavior (Cropper and Portney 1992), discounting is a necessary evil. It allows costs and benefits incurred at different times to be compared on the same basis. The only question—and it is a hotly debated one—is the magnitude of the discount rate, an issue that is beyond the scope of this essay.

ENSURING THAT THE PRECAUTIONARY PRINCIPLE REDUCES OVERALL RISKS

If the precautionary principle is to deliver on the promise implied by its name, any policy, regulation, or action (or "policy," for brevity's sake) predicated on the principle should not increase overall environmental and public health risks. In fact, the principle should favor those policies that would reduce overall risks the most.

That objective is easily met if a policy only reduces risks and is cost-free. Clearly, we should adopt that policy. Similarly, if a policy only increases risks, the decision is equally simple: avoid that policy. But policy options frequently reduce some risks while increasing or prolonging others—for example, global bans on GM crops or DDT. What do we do in such ambiguous situations?

To ensure that a policy is truly precautionary, we should compare the risks of adopting the policy to the risks of not adopting it (or of the default policy). This process inevitably requires comparative risk analysis, or risk–risk analysis. Thus, notwithstanding claims that risk analysis and the precautionary principle are different or incompatible, the latter requires risk–risk assessment to ensure that risks are indeed reduced (Goklany 2001).

Moreover, so that society gets as much risk reduction as it pays for, such risk–risk analysis should be embedded within a broader CBA. Risk–risk analysis itself, like CBA, can be qualitative or quantitative, depending on the available information and associated uncertainties.

The following set of commonsensical and ethical criteria have been proposed for use in conjunction with the precautionary principle to ensure that the principle actually reduces overall risks in cases where policies may lead to ambiguous and uncertain outcomes (Goklany 2002, 2007):

- **Human mortality criterion**. The threat of death to any human being—no matter how lowly that individual—outweighs similar threats to members of other species—no matter how magnificent that species.

- **Human morbidity criterion**. Nonmortal threats to human health should generally take precedence over threats to the environment, although there may be exceptions based on the nature, severity, and extent of the threat. (The first two criteria may be combined into an anthropocentric *public health criterion*.)

- **Immediacy criterion**. All else being equal, more immediate threats should be given priority over threats that could occur later. This priority can be justified by the fact that people tend to partially discount lives that might be lost in the distant future (Cropper and Portney 1992). It may also be justified on the grounds that the longer one lives, the greater the likelihood of discovering technologies that will enable one to live longer and healthier (Manton et al. 2006).

- **Uncertainty criterion**. Threats of harm that are more certain should take precedence over less certain harms, all else being equal.

- **Expectation value criterion**. An action resulting in fewer expected deaths should be preferred over one resulting in more expected deaths, ceteris paribus. Similarly, actions posing lower risk to biodiversity ought to be favored.

- **Adaptation criterion**. Impacts can be discounted to the extent that they can be reduced or nullified by coping or adaptive technologies.

- **Irreversibility criterion**. Greater priority should be given to outcomes that are adverse and irreversible, or likely to be more persistent.

Notably, very similar criteria have been proposed for identifying key vulnerabilities to climate change (Intergovernmental Panel on Climate Change 2007, 785).

Ideally, each criterion should be applied, one at a time, to the various sets of public health and environmental consequences of the action under review. But since the various factors are rarely equal, the net effects (on each of the sets of consequences) usually have to be evaluated by applying several of the criteria simultaneously. Then, if the results are equivocal with respect to the different sets of consequences, one should apply the human mortality and morbidity criteria. Thus, if the action, for example, might directly or indirectly increase net human mortality but improve the environment by, for instance, increasing the recreational potential of a water body, then that action ought to be rejected.

Of course, there will be instances where no cut-and-dried answer will emerge readily—for example, if an action might reduce cases of a nonlethal human disease while at the same time potentially killing a large number of animals. In such cases, in addition to considering factors such as the nature, severity, and curability of the disease, the cost of the disease and/or treatment, and the numbers of human and other species affected (factors subsumed in the previously specified criteria, namely, the adaptation, irreversibility, and expectation value criteria), the decision should also consider factors such as the abundance of the species, whether it is threatened or endangered, and so on.

Let's apply these criteria to the issue of whether there ought to be a global ban on genetically modified crops, as a case example. In 2000, 850 million people worldwide suffered from hunger and undernourishment and over 2 billion from malnutrition, resulting in more than 6 million deaths annually. Poor nutritional habits also contribute significantly to so-called diseases of affluence—heart disease, strokes, cancers—killing 23 million more. To reduce the future toll of hunger, malnutrition, and poor nutritional habits (despite the almost inevitable future increase in human population), the quantity and nutritional quality of food must be enhanced. The faster this enhancement occurs—with greater certainty—the fewer the expected casualties. And GM crops should help to increase the quantity and nutritional quality of food supplies faster and more surely than conventional crops can do. Given the magnitude of annual deaths involved, even a minor reduction in the 29 million deaths from hunger and poor nutrition will represent a significant benefit.

Therefore, a GM crop ban is more likely to increase deaths due to hunger, malnutrition, and diseases of affluence (Goklany 2007, chap. 9).

Moreover, considering that GM crops have been part of the U.S. diet since 1996 with no proven adverse cases, future adverse health effects of ingesting GM crops are neither certain nor comparable in magnitude to the global toll from hunger and malnutrition. Therefore, a global GM crop ban will likely increase net harm to public health, condemning large numbers to premature death.

As for the environmental risk, conventional agriculture, with its appetite for land, water, pesticides, and fertilizers, is the major stress on global biodiversity, as well as a significant source of greenhouse gases. These environmental pressures can be reduced or contained more rapidly (and more certainly) with GM crops because, relative to conventional crops, they are likely to increase agricultural productivity faster and with fewer land, water, and chemical inputs. Current evidence from the United States, China, and South Africa shows that GM crops reduce net environmental risks (Goklany 2007; Marvier et al. 2007). Thus, in aggregate, a GM crop ban would more likely than not increase risks to both global public health and environment. Consequently, such a ban would be poor public policy.

The above criteria have also been used to evaluate precautionary policies such as a global ban on DDT, the implementation of the Kyoto Protocol, and regulation of the blood transfusion risk associated with variant Creutzfeld-Jakob disease (Goklany 2001; Wilson and Ricketts 2004). In the first two cases, it was concluded that, contrary to conventional environmental wisdom, those specific policies would in fact increase overall health and environmental risks, thereby violating their fundamental premise—namely, that they are precautionary. The third case found that the regulations were justified.

CONCLUSION

The precautionary principle can be an effective tool for policymakers in regulating emerging technologies, provided that it is coupled with comparative risk analysis to ensure that overall risks do not increase inadvertently. Such analysis should employ criteria to help prioritize and compare countervailing risks based on their nature, severity, magnitude, certainty, irreversibility, and other characteristics. Moreover, since society's resources are scarce while its needs are numerous, such risk–risk analysis should ideally be part of broader quantitative or qualitative cost-benefit analysis or, failing that, cost-effectiveness analysis. In addition, there ought to be a mechanism for revisiting past decisions in light of new information.

With these embellishments, the precautionary principle can not only effectively manage risks from emerging technologies but can reduce overall risks and advance environmental and human well-being even as population and consumption of materials, minerals, and energy inevitably continue to increase. Failing that, the principle can be an equal-opportunity barrier to the dissemination, if not creation, of new technologies, whether they increase or decrease overall risks or provide net benefits to society.

Finally, the foregoing discussion suggests an alternative formulation for the principle—namely, "Risk management policies should attempt to minimize net risks to public health, safety, and the environment based on the best available scientific information and their net anticipated costs to society." Or, more succinctly: "All things considered, thou shalt attempt to minimize net risks at the least cost to society."

NO: John D. Graham, *University of Indiana,* and Sarah Olmstead, *Pardee RAND Graduate School*

Scientific inquiry has revealed that modern technologies pose a wide range of potentially adverse effects on human health, safety, and the environment. Saturated and trans fats are linked to heart disease; gasoline-powered cars contribute to global warming; and the electric and magnetic fields from power lines and cell phones may be related to brain cancer. As claims of technological risk have become pervasive in society, lawmakers constantly confront decisions about whether to regulate or restrict technologies based on limited evidence of risk, or whether they should await more definitive scientific indications of risk before issuing protective policies.

A concept called the precautionary principle (PP) was developed in Europe to help guide decisions about uncertain man-made risks, especially those that impose serious and irreversible impacts on public health and the environment. Although precaution is well-defined in the dictionary ("taking care beforehand") and is practiced widely by everyone from investors to physicians, there is considerable confusion about what the PP is and how it can be used wisely by policymakers.

In this article, we trace the evolution of the precautionary principle, focusing on why it has been suggested, why it is logically incomplete in a policy setting, and why its simplistic use can be detrimental. An important argument in favor of precaution is that technological risks often prove to be more serious than scientists originally anticipate. Moreover, the statistical standards of proof typically used in science may not be appropriate for use by policymakers charged with implementing precautionary policies toward uncertain risks. But we also point to a logical conundrum that occurs when a well-intended precautionary action can create unwanted effects on human health, safety, or the environment. We also explain that the PP is an incomplete guide for policymakers because it does not prescribe which precautionary measures should be implemented, or how the risks, costs, and benefits of alternative precautionary actions should be weighed by policymakers. In the future, we anticipate that the desire for precaution toward technological risks will be combined with formal decision-analytic tools, including hedging strategies, to ensure that wise decisions about technological risks are made over time.

WHAT IS THE PRECAUTIONARY PRINCIPLE?

There is no such thing as *the* precautionary principle, for the basic concept has been specified in many different ways by different declarations, treaties, and authors. In its most intuitive form, it requires a "better safe than sorry" approach to managing technological risk. It is intended to counteract the human tendency to ignore a problem until harm actually manifests itself, which is problematic for many reasons, not the least of which is that damage to human health and the environment can often be irreversible (such as the adverse effects of smoking tobacco).

The history of asbestos makes it clear how precaution might be needed to encourage regulatory action. The first evidence of the dangerous health effects of asbestos among miners and manufacturers came in 1898, nineteen years after mining began in Canada. However, the extent of the problem was unknown, and these warnings were not followed up by government officials. In 1931, after mounting evidence of the danger of working with asbestos—including 66 percent of asbestos workers in U.K. factories being diagnosed with the disease asbestosis—regulations were passed in the United Kingdom specifying dust-control measures in asbestos manufacturing and compensation for victims of asbestosis. But even then, these regulations were poorly enforced, and cases of asbestosis and lung cancer continued to appear throughout the world (Gee and Greenberg, in Harremoes et al. 2002).

In the 1960s, more evidence came to light in the rising number of cases of mesothelioma (lung cancer caused mainly by asbestos) among individuals employed in mining and manufacturing operations, as well as the neighbors and relatives of those workers. Nevertheless, experts continued to debate the precise risks of asbestos and its carcinogenicity into the 1990s (Brody et al. 1990). It was not until 1999, after hundreds of thousands of cases of asbestosis and mesothelioma had been diagnosed, and hundreds of millions of dollars had been paid in compensation, that the EU and France prohibited all asbestos products (Gee and Greenberg, in Harremoes et al. 2002). Had those and other governments been operating on a precautionary basis, much of this harm and cost could have been avoided.

Some observers break the principle into two formulations: "weak" vs. "strong" (Morris 2000), or "argumentative" vs. "prescriptive" (Sandin et al. 2002, 289). A strong, or prescriptive, PP generally states that government bodies should prohibit technology until the inventor of the technology proves that it is harmless to society; a weak, or argumentative, PP holds that lack of full certainty of harm is not a justification for preventing reasonable measures to avoid possible damage. These classifications of the precautionary principle could be rephrased as follows: uncertainty requires action versus uncertainty does not necessarily justify inaction (Wiener and Rogers 2002, 320). Within both the weak and the strong versions of PP, there is also a consideration of where to place the burden of proof—the strong version placing it on innovators of risky technologies, and the weak placing it on regulators. This breakdown is not a universal rule, however, and a more important issue might be the *standard* of proof, rather than the burden, as we discuss later.

Although Europe is traditionally considered to be a stronger proponent of the precautionary principle, U.S. law and regulation embody a variety of precautionary approaches. The Clean Air Act and the Clean Water Act, for example, have numerous precautionary provisions. Moreover, the United States had a significant role in shaping the wording of the 1992 Rio Declaration on Environment and Development, which states: "Where there are threats of serious or irreversible damage, lack of full scientific certainty shall not be used as a reason for postponing cost-effective measures to prevent environmental degradation" (*Rio Declaration* 1992), which is almost word-for-word the language used in the UN's Framework Convention on Climate Change, developed the same year (*United Nations* 1992). In the United States, the President's Council on Sustainable Development argued in 1999 that "even in the face of scientific uncertainty, society should take reasonable actions to avert risks where the potential harm to human health or the environment is thought to be serious or irreparable" (President's Council 1999). The Cartagena Protocol on Biosafety, the Maastricht treaty of the European Union, and other international bodies' pronouncements echo these sentiments. All are examples of the weak precautionary principle, for they specify that hazards should be "serious or irreparable" and that actions taken to avert danger should be "reasonable" or "cost-effective."

On the other hand, the 1998 Wingspread Statement, drafted by a group of scientists and activists at a conference aimed at defining the precautionary principle, propounds a stronger version, demanding that "when an activity raises threats of harm to human health or the environment, precautionary measures should be taken even if some cause and effect relationships are not fully established scientifically." This formulation specifies not that threats must be serious or irreversible, but that there has to be *any* threat of harm. Neither does it specify what measures should be taken, or whether they should be reasonable or cost-effective.

Even at the Wingspread conference, there was discussion of cost and proportionality of response as important characteristics of the PP (Jordan and O'Riordan 1998), though these considerations did not make it into the final statement. Strident opponents of the precautionary principle have complained about the sweeping and nonspecific nature of the strong PP, without really acknowledging the necessity for precaution. What is necessary now is more exploration of the analytics of precaution, including ways that courts and other bodies should interpret precaution to aid decision making (Sandin et al. 2002; Pittinger and Bishop 1999; O'Riordan and Cameron 1994).

THE CASE FOR MORE PRECAUTION

A common complaint about the precautionary principle is that it encourages viewing everything as a risk, leading to too many false-positive errors (deeming something a risk that is not). However, one recent report examining eighty-eight claims of regulatory false positives found little evidence of this phenomenon: only four of them were actually false positives—Swine Flu, Food Irradiation, Saccharine, and the Southern Corn Leaf Blight (Hansen et al. 2007). The authors of this report also point to the numerous false negatives (assuming that something is not a risk that is) that have had serious consequences on human health and the environment but were overlooked—including asbestos, Bovine Spongiform Encephalopathy ("mad cow disease"), and MTBE in gasoline, among others (Harremoes et al. 2002).

Rather than crying wolf, it appears that precautionary advocates *have* often been justified in their demands for regulation and, if anything, have not pressed the issue enough. We can see from the many late lessons that precaution is often warranted when there are fears for safety, and that policymakers and regulators need assessments that are interdisciplinary, independent, and accompanied by diligent monitoring for signs of danger. Since plausible threats often become actual threats, a precautionary view of possible hazards is both justified and useful.

Another issue is that scientific standards of proof are not necessarily relevant for precautionary decision makers. Much like the "CSI effect"—whereby juries, presumably influenced by a popular television series featuring the crime-solving prowess of forensic experts, now expect there to be DNA and other convincing forensic evidence in every case—lawmakers may expect that science can provide conclusive proof of safety or harm. Scientists employ statistical evidence, such as a 95 percent confidence interval (to indicate the plausible bounds for their estimates), but regulators need to look for broad consensus among qualified scientists, even when there are prominent and well-respected critics of that consensus.

Consider, for example, the geological concept of tectonic plates and the shifting of the continents (see Oreskes 2004). The theory of plate tectonics was developed in the 1920s, but it was mired in much controversy throughout the 1940s as scientists tried unsuccessfully to prove it. Although it remained unproven, by the 1960s, continental drift was accepted as fact by a majority of geologists and earth scientists. Nevertheless, some quite renowned experts still did not believe this theory, and they spoke vociferously against it. Eventually, measurements in the early 1980s proved, rather anticlimactically, that the continents were moving. This is a policy-irrelevant example, but it illustrates well the problem with scientific "proof." Just as many geologists of the 1960s did not wait for the conclusive measurements to decide what they believed was true, a decision maker challenged to make policy based on the incomplete body of evidence about a potentially risky technology might well choose to act on an educated guess about its likely effects.

As stated earlier, there is a tendency to defer regulatory action until further studies are done to "prove" harm or safety. Using the timeline of the continental drift example, though, that would have meant waiting over fifty years to regulate a possibly dangerous technology. If it proved that this was actually the case, fifty years of harm would have been allowed to pass. Thus, the formulation of the precautionary principle that says "uncertainty is not an excuse for inaction" would be very relevant here in preventing harm even in the absence of absolute proof.

LOGICAL PROBLEMS WITH THE PRECAUTIONARY PRINCIPLE

One of the most persuasive arguments against the precautionary principle is its failure as a decision tool—it is not always clear what the principle demands to be done about a possible hazard. If it is evident that the status quo situation presents an unacceptable risk but the solution may also be risky, the PP gives no clear guidance. There is a substantial literature suggesting that such "risk-

risk tradeoffs" are the norm rather than the exception (Graham and Wiener 1995). Tools such as risk analysis, decision analysis, and benefit-cost calculations offer ways to compare the costs from action and inaction and come to a conclusion; the PP, however, does not. In order to be useful as a decision-making tool, the precautionary principle must be combined with some kind of decision-analytic framework that removes the paralysis caused by competing risks and uncertainties.

One example in which a precautionary stance may have caused more problems than it prevented is the U.S. response to the risks of nuclear power. After the near-meltdown at the Three Mile Island reactor in Pennsylvania and the full meltdown at the Chernobyl reactor in the Soviet Union, the American public and decision makers began to move away from nuclear power as too risky. By taking such a precautionary stance, the United States effectively committed its energy sector to the use of fossil fuels, which currently produce nearly 70 percent of the electrical energy consumed in the country (nuclear power produces around 20 percent; Energy Information Administration 2007). U.S. reliance on fossil fuels has caused or exacerbated many other risks, including global warming, pollution, and political instability (due to our reliance on energy imported from various unsavory totalitarian regimes).

Maybe the precautionary principle would counsel us to choose neither fossil fuels nor nuclear power, but rather to look for safer alternatives, such as renewable energies. But even these options pose uncertain risks: environmentalists often express concerns about the placement of wind turbines in birds' flight paths; some solar photovoltaics contain toxic heavy metals, such as arsenic, cadmium, and lead that could be dangerous to human health; and even hydropower is known to be problematic for fish populations and other parts of the riparian ecosystem. Thus, there is no obvious alternative to nuclear power that does not pose some environmental risk. It is evident that precautionary policymakers need some way to balance all of these competing risks—a way to integrate precaution into practical decision analysis.

Many different decision-analytic refinements to the PP have been suggested, such as a *de minimis* rule (Sandin et al. 2002) or value-of-information analysis (Graham 2001). Even some of the precautionary principle's proponents agree that some decision-analytic element must be added to the PP to make it useful as a decision tool.

LEARNING AND HEDGING

In the face of uncertainty, the best strategy for dealing with an uncertain technological risk is unknown. Depending on what happens in the "actualized

future," the benefits and costs could end up being quite different than originally imagined. Due to differing interests that are innate to every decision,
an environmentalist might place a much higher value on protecting environmental quality than would a technological innovator, who might favor nonreg-
ulation (Jordan and O'Riordan 1998). Some new tools—such as value-of-
information analysis—have been developed in business and engineering for
decision making under uncertainty, but they are not yet widely applied in public policy contexts. These optimization methods could be useful in the precautionary context, especially when scientific uncertainty is a factor.

Given that there are huge uncertainties in policymaking, as well as limits to
the surety with which safety and hazard can be determined, it makes sense that
a good decision maker will want to pursue precautionary "hedging" strategies,
which may entail careful trial and error. If a strong version of the PP is invoked,
it is not clear that there is room for the trial and error that may accompany
innovation; prohibiting an action until safety is proven absolutely may lead to
technological stagnation.

A weak version of PP, however, may allow for trial and error. Such a strategy
demands that, while we implement some level of precautionary regulation, we
can also implement the new technology. The key to preserving both precaution
and innovation is monitoring of hazards and identification of timely safeguards. Strategies that hedge against risks, allowing mid-course corrections, are
often crucial to successful precautionary policy.

A much discussed example of either the failure or the success of the PP—
depending on the author's perspective—is DDT, a synthetic pesticide that was
banned in much of the world in the early 1970s, though exceptions were made
in parts of the developing world where malaria was a significant killer of children. In the United States, many opponents of the ban lamented that it would
decrease food security and lead to an increase in disease (Oreskes 2004). Pro-
DDT scientists and policymakers point out that, in some cases, the risks from
DDT are worth the benefits, and the World Health Organization currently calls
for its use in the most high-risk areas, though for indoor use only.

Many complaints about the DDT ban center on the fact that it was banned
by the Environmental Protection Agency (EPA) because of "unacceptable risks
to the environment and potential harm to human health" (EPA 1972)—harm
to birds and the environment had been discovered, while the harm to humans
was only *potential.*

But now there *is* some evidence that DDT exposure does cause harm to
humans. DDT appears to exert a statistically significant impact on the length
of breastfeeding, which in turn has a significant effect on infant mortality
(Chen and Rogan 2003). DDT resistance has also been discovered among

certain mosquitos, leading many communities to seek substitute technologies, such as various biopesticides (Bell 2007) and even fish that feed on mosquito larvae (Ogodo 2007). Many of these alternate solutions are emerging from malaria-prone countries in the developing world that are most affected by mosquitoes and would otherwise seem to have most to gain from using DDT.

While a complete ban of DDT was possibly overkill, it did encourage innovation in the area of malaria control and subdued the overuse of the substance, which had been common in DDT's heyday. It is no longer used in agricultural settings, and is permitted only for indoor use. In this case, the world was allowed to learn from its mistakes, both from its overuse of DDT and from a complete ban.

Faced with the same evidence of hazard or safety, different countries may also end up making different decisions based on their specific circumstances and the level of precaution that they decide to employ. In the northern, swampy areas of South Africa, the government has reinstated indoor spraying of DDT in a limited context. Across the border in Mozambique, on the other hand, policymakers decided that it was not worth the risk, pointing to the fact that the area also experiences flooding, by which the chemical residue could be washed away into the environment (BBC 2001).

Another example of a precautionary hedging strategy is the case of Vioxx, a drug used to treat arthritis and acute pain conditions, and the COX-2 inhibitors that constitute its therapeutic potential. Although at least three such COX-2 drugs were released on the market after clinical testing, post-release studies showed elevated risk of myocardial infarction and stroke (Graham and Hu 2007). Merck, the drug's manufacturer, voluntarily withdrew Vioxx from the market, and, after performing a risk-benefit analysis, the FDA ordered the recall of Bextra as well. Currently, research is ongoing to better characterize the risks of these drugs; while Celebrex remains on the market, Vioxx and Bextra do not.

Again, this situation reflects the different levels of risk tolerance that different companies face. A joint advisory committee to the FDA suggested that Vioxx and Celebrex could remain on the market, from a risk-benefit point of view, but that Bextra was not worth the risk. The makers of Celebrex decided to keep their drug on the market, alerting consumers to the risks and letting people make their own decisions, while the makers of Vioxx decided to take it off. The continuous monitoring of patients for serious side effects and the review of the study findings by a regulatory body is an important hedging action that the drug makers took. The FDA approved the drugs for sale, but then, when they were later found to present a significant health risk, the agency took stricter regulatory action.

Precautionary regulation does not have to be the "all or nothing" measure that extreme proponents and opponents of PP make it out to be. Instead of looking for perfect safety or maximum innovation, we should be looking for robust strategies that do well whether there ends up being a real threat or not. This perspective calls for hedging strategies. Technologies are rolled out in such a way that, if their effects end up being different than we expected—say, a chemical proves more toxic than we expected it to be, or vice versa—then we are not stuck forever with the wrong decision.

For instance, in the early stages of a new drug's use, doctors may monitor the levels of certain biomarkers in the bloodstream daily, or even in real time, while the drug is being ingested. By this process, which is called biochemical monitoring, doctors can tell if chemical levels are getting too high, and whether ingestion of the drug should be for some reason discontinued or the dose reduced. Doctors thus hedge against serious problems by using thoughtful precautionary strategy—they don't just give the patient the full dose and hope for the best, but neither do they deny the treatment because they don't know how the patient will react. Instead, they ease into the treatment regimen, remaining alert and ready to pull back if things begin to go awry. Hedging against uncertainty is clearly an important quality for precautionary decision making.

CHANGING OPINIONS IN EUROPE

In 1999 and 2000, there was a dispute between France and the United Kingdom over imports of British beef, at the end of the mad cow disease scare in Europe. Despite a 1999 ruling by the EU that lifted the 1996 ban on the export of U.K. beef, France maintained its embargo on precautionary grounds, defying Brussels on the grounds that French beef might be safer than British beef (Vedrine 1999). This dispute led to a strain on trade relations between France and Britain, and worry within the broader European Community about differing uses of the precautionary principle. In January 2000, the Commission of the European Communities brought a case against France to the European Court of Justice, which Brussels finally won in 2001.

Partly spurred by this lawsuit, the European Commission in 2000 released an official communication on the PP and the nature of its use. The communication stated that the PP should be used not only in the case of possible environmental harm, but "where preliminary objective scientific evaluation indicates that there are reasonable grounds for concern that the potentially dangerous effects on the *environment, human, animal or plant health* may be inconsistent with the high level of protection chosen for the Community" (CEC 2000). It specified particularly that "the precautionary principle should be considered within a structured approach to the analysis of risk which comprises three elements: risk assessment, risk management, risk communication" (CEC 2000). The EC communication required proportionality and consistency of response, cost-benefit analysis over the short and long term, and review of decisions under a changing scientific body of evidence. Europe, the originator of the precautionary principle, was clearly moving toward a reasoned approach to policymaking under conditions of uncertainty that manages to combine precaution with decision-analytic tools.

terrorism and security

Is International Terrorism a Significant Challenge to National Security?

YES: Scott Atran, *University of Michigan*

NO: John Mueller, *Ohio State University*

Terrorism is the use of violence for political ends. Rather than seeking to directly control territory, for which they lack resources, terrorists seek to instill terror in the citizens of the target, hoping to destabilize the government or to undermine the society's willingness to conduct a sustained war. Terrorism stands in stark contrast to more traditional wars of territorial occupation, such as World War II.

Since the attacks of September 11, 2001, terrorism has attracted much more attention in the United States and elsewhere than it drew in the past. In response, the United States has focused part of its security strategy on al Qaeda and the "war on terror." This focus may make it seem that terrorism is a new, or renewed, security threat, but terrorism is not new. There is a long history of terrorist attacks across borders going back millennia, and many other terrorist organizations besides al Qaeda operate today. The United Kingdom has long faced terrorism from the Irish Republican Army, as Turkey has from separatist Kurds; Israel is a target of both Hamas and Hezbollah, and many attacks in Iraq occur between Sunnis and Shi'ites. In the 1970s and 1980s, the radical Red Army Faction operated in Western Europe, seeking to challenge the ability of elected governments to protect their citizenry and thus to undermine the democratic state and capitalism in Western Europe. Indeed, as Figure 1 makes clear, terrorist attacks are reasonably common.

However, what is distinctive about recent terrorism directed at the United States is that it occurs on multiple fronts: attacks on U.S. citizens, assets, and allies have occurred in Beirut (1991), Kenya (1998), Aden (2000), and the United States (2001)—and this list does not include the failed 1993 World Trade Center bombing. In addition, although the data reveal that there are far

Figure 1

Number of Terrorist Incidents throughout the Globe, 1968–2004

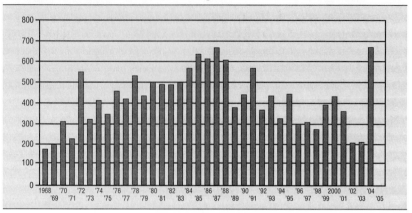

Source: Office of the Coordinator for Counter-Terrorism. U.S. Department of State; after 2003, National Counter-Terrorism Center (NCTC), www.the_counterterrorism.blog.

more terrorist incidents than those targeting only the United States, some terrorist activities on foreign soil are addressed at the United States through its allies, such as attacks in Spain (2004) and the United Kingdom (2005).

Hundreds of terrorist attacks are reported annually. Casualties from terrorism soared after the mid-1990s, although the majority of them resulted from sectarian violence within Iraq. The 9/11 bombings in the United States, while tragic, were only a small proportion of total terrorist attacks and casualties. Table 1 presents the regional distribution of terrorist attacks in 2005.

The policy challenge today is to understand the reasons for such attacks, to assess and respond proportionately to the terrorist threat to national security relative to other possible threats, and to appreciate the array of potential responses to punish terrorists and to deter future attacks.

Terrorists typically have a relatively small resource base. For example, they lack the ability for sustained traditional assaults as in conventional warfare. They do not have a lot of highly trained warriors—although the U.S. response to the ten-year Soviet occupation of Afghanistan led to the training of numerous potential terrorists for future engagements and to the circulation of missiles and explosives of use for terrorism. Thus the terrorists must rely on highly visible, possibly symbolic attacks that will undermine the will of the target population. Consequently, they typically focus on random bombings, or other attacks aimed at civilians.

The responses available to possible targets are limited. Nonstate terrorists cannot be deterred in the same way that states can—for instance, by threats of military and economic retaliation against specific states—which limits the

Table 1

The Most Frequent Geographical Targets of Terrorist Attacks, 2005

	Incidents	Injuries	Fatalities
Iraq	2336	9399	6234
West Bank/Gaza	479	302	74
Thailand	359	584	148
India (including Kashmir)	272	1051	398
Afghanistan	207	328	298
Pakistan	163	398	160
Russia (including Chechnya)	102	113	51
Colombia	101	208	112
Nepal	100	104	33

Source: Memorial Institute for the Prevention of Terrorism (MIPT),Terrorism Knowledge Base (TKB), Terrorism Trends 2005, http://www.pensitoreview.com/PDF/TKBPoster051506.pdf.

options available to countries for trying to deter terrorism. Close monitoring of movements of people and goods seems necessary, but the vast numbers of those entities moving through the world economy with globalization make such controls logistically daunting and would seriously slow the delivery of goods that are deemed necessary for national economies. Good military surveillance and policing is, of course, critical, requiring multiple sources and informants on the ground both in the United States and abroad. Thus, modern terrorism may be a security threat that is not easily addressed through traditional modes of military security policy, which relies on overwhelming material force.

Consequently, some argue that fighting terrorism requires proactive efforts. Yet such efforts in the United States have already entailed significant challenges to civil rights. If they are to be regarded as legitimate elsewhere in the international community, proactive efforts have to accurately target real threats without collateral civilian casualties—a very demanding standard when ambiguous intelligence is often involved. Finally, some authors say that the threats from terrorism may be overdrawn and are not worth the significant constraints on democratic societies that proactive efforts would require. The recent debates in the United States concerning the USA PATRIOT Act, and the debate in the international community about the legality of Guantanamo detentions, are clear examples of how some responses to fighting terrorism can infringe on civil liberties and human rights.

Recently, the defense community has begun to worry about threats from cyberterrorism. Rather than targeting civilians, terrorists may resort to hacking computer sites in order to destroy the virtual infrastructure of their targets. Such cyberterrorism requires an entirely new mode of response—one for which traditional military responses may be inappropriate, because they involve careful information collection and policing and coordination with foreign police forces (such as INTERPOL) to arrest possible terrorists based on good documentary evidence.

The authors of the two articles that follow address questions such as the degree to which fighting terrorism warrants overriding other foreign policy considerations, whether terrorism is a significant threat to national security, and what are the most effective means of combating terrorism. Although they agree that policies that exacerbate the fear of terrorism only fuel potential terrorists, the authors differ in their assessment of terrorism's place on the international agenda, and how terrorism can be combated most effectively. Scott Atran believes that the source of terrorism is to be found among the poor and increasingly marginalized in the Third World, and that U.S. and international policy should target the hearts and minds of those populations. John Mueller argues that the threats of terrorism are greatly exaggerated and that high-profile efforts to publicize or address them have the effect of creating the very threat that we fear.

Discussion Questions

1. What are the differences between state (or conventional) threats and nonstate threats? Do they require different policy approaches? What are they?
2. What are the root causes of terrorism? What policies would address these causes?
3. Has globalization changed the goals and means of terrorism? How?
4. What points does John Mueller make to refute the idea that terrorism is a major national security threat? What does he mean when he says that America "aids terrorists"? Do you agree with his assessment?
5. Scott Atran says that "publicity is the oxygen that fires modern terrorism." What does he mean? Would Mueller agree with that statement?

YES: Scott Atran, *Research Director, Anthropology, National Center for Scientific Research, Paris; Visiting Professor of Psychology and Public Policy, University of Michigan; Presidential Scholar, Sociology, John Jay College of Criminal Justice*

Is international terrorism a significant challenge to national security? The answer is both yes and no. By itself, contemporary terrorism cannot destroy our country, or our allies, or even seriously damage any of us. However, we can do grievous harm to ourselves by taking the terrorists' bait and reacting in ill-conceived, uninformed, and uncontrolled ways that inflate and so empower our enemies, alienate our friends, and frighten our own citizens into believing that they must give up basic liberties in order to survive. It is in this sense that terrorism does pose an existential threat: to our most sacred values of individual freedom and choice, to our sense of personal and collective security, and to any hope of peace of mind. Our fitful reaction to terrorism now risks further weakening and exposing less secure states, such as Iraq and Pakistan, to takeovers by extremist elements that could very well become a true strategic menace to national security.

EXAGGERATING THREATS

As matters now stand, material threats from nonstate terrorists in general, and religious terrorists in particular, are exaggerated. But it is precisely that exaggeration that makes the terrorist threat real.

A generation ago, at the height of the Cold War, the Soviet Union and the United States had tens of thousands of nuclear weapons that could annihilate much of the adversary's population in ninety minutes or so. Today's terrorists do not remotely pose such a threat. Even our darkest present fear, and the Department of Homeland Security's "worse case scenario"—the explosion of one or two 1–10 kiloton nuclear bombs by terrorists—pales by comparison.[1]

The 2007 *U.S. National Intelligence Estimate* focuses on "the rejuvenating effect the Iraq war has had on Al Qaeda."[2] But there is little evidence that Osama bin Laden or his close associates, who are thought to be holed up somewhere along the Afghan-Pakistani frontier, have much operational knowledge or control of what is happening in Iraq. There is undoubtedly resurgent jihadi activity and training along that frontier, especially in Waziristan, that involves remnants of al Qaeda, the Taliban, and volunteers from Pakistani and Central Asian jihadi groups. There is more money, more (small) camps, more communication, more interaction among the leaders; however, despite the hype,[3] this activity has apparently not extended much beyond the area.

There are attempts to enlist people with knowledge of the West, just as surely as would-be jihadis from Europe and elsewhere are trying to get to Iraq and Afghanistan. But the old al Qaeda, which actually had an infrastructure that might have assembled a weapon for massive destruction, is gone. The mostly Egyptian and Saudi hard core around bin Laden has not launched a successful operation in years, and its remainder does not know who most of the new would-be terrorists are—they are mostly self-starting groups of amateurs— and cannot reliably communicate with those they do know about. The viral influence of al Qaeda is diffuse and inspirational, not organized or operational. There are few, if any, al Qaeda "cells" with well-defined boundaries, organizations, or leaders—much less "sleeper cells."[4]

After some years of fact-finding, statistical analysis, and modeling by our team of researchers and consultants (including colleagues, post-graduate researchers and graduate students from the University of Michigan, the University of Washington, MIT, the City University of New York, and France's National Center for Scientific Research, as well as former intelligence operatives and members of jihadi terrorist groups), we think that the chief problem of terrorism is not a strong or resurgent al Qaeda organization directing global operations from Pakistan's Federally Administered Tribal Areas or anywhere else in particular. Instead, the chief problem is that terrorist dreams and actions today thrive mainly among the small groups and networks of youthful friends and their families in countless neighborhoods across the world, inspired by al Qaeda's heroic and viral ideology of uncompromising but equal justice before God. The exaggeration of the threat from an organized terrorist group directing global operations and the general ignorance of the real problem of terrorists thriving in small social networks poses a security threat.

PUBLICITY IS THE OXYGEN OF TERRORISM

Because terrorists thrive in small groups and among networks of family and friends, their threat is fueled beyond their actual strength by publicity.

In the past, spectacular killings were common both to small tribes and to great empires. Nearly three millennia ago, the ancient Hebrew tribes described in *Deuteronomy* were instructed by their no-name God not merely "to smite every male" in "the cities which the Lord thy God doth give thee for an inheritance," but to "save alive nothing that breatheth," be it "the women, the little ones, and the cattle." Recent archeological excavations in the southwest United States strongly indicate that a thousand years ago or so, competing Native American groups would feast on one another's men, women, and children when victorious, and then theatrically defecate on their remains for others to see. A few centuries later, the Mongols would routinely butcher all who resisted them, and stack the skulls of their victims in gruesome displays for other would-be resisters to witness. After the killing, for the great Genghis Khan, "the greatest pleasure is... to see their near and dear bathed in tears, to ride their horses and sleep on the bellies of their wives and daughters." The early Spanish conquistadores would slaughter Indian idolaters whenever they pleased, and savage the women to make them love Christ.

Today, whereas most nations tend to avoid publicizing their more wanton killings—including most killings that might be labeled "state terrorism"—publicity is the oxygen that fires modern terrorism.

Witness, for example, the reaction to the failed "doctor's plot" in the summer of 2007, when doctors who had recently immigrated to Britain and begun working for the National Health Service were arrested for packing gas canisters and nails into several cars and trying to blow up targets in London and Glasgow. The only real damage was the severe burning one of the car's drivers, an engineer who was a brother of one of the doctors and a cousin of another. Reaction from nearly all sectors of the British public to the actions of this so-called medical cell was almost indistinguishable in intensity from the reaction that had followed the successful London subway bombings two years before. Britain's new security minister grimly predicted that the country must be prepared to combat terrorism for the next "ten to fifteen years" and suggested that the "un-British" practice of informing on neighbors would have to be adopted to prevent the terrorists from "destroying our whole way of life."

In the United States, the media reported that "dozens of FBI agents have been given a two-week deadline to run down more than 700 leads on an FBI 'worry list,' developed in the wake of the failed attacks in London and Glasgow." The head of the U.S. Department of Homeland Security responded with a "gut feeling" that al Qaeda was planning a massive summer attack, but his warning was not based upon specific intelligence and was not serious enough to raise the alert level or to require any concrete action. The German interior minister reacted by proposing to scuttle his country's long-standing commitment to refrain from using military forces against people within the country and to consider a security policy that would allow the indefinite detention and "targeted killing" of terror suspects: "Let's say someone knew in which cave Osama bin Laden is sitting. Someone could then fire a guided missile to kill him. ... If for example potential terrorists—so-called sleepers—cannot be deported, what will we do then?"[5] No matter if bin Laden was really involved in setting up a "sleeper cell"—an unlikely prospect—or if this small Cambridge-based group of family and co-worker friends had self-radicalized. It's all "al Qaeda."

Terrorists are directly responsible for violent acts, but only indirectly for the reaction that follows. To terrorize and destabilize, terrorists need publicity and our complicity. And they have it. With publicity, even failed terrorist acts succeed in terrorizing; without publicity, terrorism would die down. The irony is that press and publicity are also the oxygen of an open society. But this ironic convergence does not require the equation of what is most scary and spectacular with what is really most threatening and politically important. By amplifying and connecting relatively sporadic terrorist acts into a generalized "war," our leaders have transformed the somewhat marginal phenomenon of terrorism into a primary preoccupation of our government and people. This transformation puts the lie to the constant refrain by those same leaders that "the terrorists will gain nothing."

Terrorism now tops the behavioral agendas of our political parties. This means that no matter what the outcome of our democratic elections, terrorists will continue to hold sway over our society in ways only the most audacious and outrageous among them ever imagined, at least in their thinking about the short-term product of their actions. In this sense, Osama bin Laden is already victorious beyond his wildest dreams and continues to be a constant threat—not because of anything he has done, but because of how we have reacted to his episodic success.

WHO BECOMES A TERRORIST AND WHY?

Terrorists' threats to security are amplified when policymakers are ill-informed or misled about where terrorists come from; thus their responses are misguided.

In his recent book, *What Makes a Terrorist*, Princeton economist Alan Krueger produces data for three general findings: (1) poverty and lack of education are uncorrelated, or slightly negatively correlated, with being a terrorist or support for terrorism; (2) most terrorists come from countries that are not poor but that restrict civil liberties; and (3) terrorism is mostly directed against democratic rather than authoritarian regimes.[6] Krueger then infers causes from these broad correlations: (a) poverty and poor education do not produce terrorism, but denial of political freedom does; and (b) terrorists target democratic regimes because terrorists seek publicity and widespread panic, and democracies are more responsive to public opinion. These conclusions echo political scientist Robert Pape's best-selling book, *Dying to Win.*[7]

A major problem with such works is the assumption that correlations with economic status, educational level, or degree of civil liberties usefully predict who or how people become terrorists. This mistaken premise misleads policy-makers and researchers. It is the *social networks* and *group dynamics* of these networks that are key to understanding how terrorist networks form and operate, not the demographic profiles of individuals and whole populations.

Let us consider Islamic terrorism, the main focus of Krueger's book. The extremely high correlation between the countries of origin of Islamic terrorists and countries that limit civil liberties is true but uninformative. The same correlation holds for a great many Muslim groups that have nothing to do with terrorism.

Only al Qaeda is interested in attacking the "far enemy"—that is, the United States and its allies. Isaac Ben Israel, an Israeli parliamentarian who currently heads his country's space agency, was former chief of air force operations and top military strategist in a successful campaign to stop suicide bombings orchestrated by Hamas. He told us that "al Qaeda is a very different problem and is not ours; our operational problems with Hezbollah and Hamas involve regional networks with regional aims, although we are ready to help the United States with its global al Qaeda problem whenever we can." Over 80 percent of those who have joined or expressed allegiance to al Qaeda have done so outside their country of origin; this, of course, is not the case with Hezbollah or Hamas. Whether one joins jihad in the diaspora or in one's native country— and not country of origin per se—is the key factor in determining how one is willing to use terrorism and against whom.

The correlation between terrorist acts and target countries—suggesting that democracies are victims more than autocracies—is spurious. Making such a correlation requires accepting that attacks on U.S occupation forces in Iraq and Afghanistan are attacks upon U.S. democracy. In fact, very few attacks have been carried out directly against Western democracies, and only three have produced significant casualties: United States, 9/11/01; Spain, 3/11/04; Britain, 7/7/05. There were no major attacks between the winter of 2006 and the fall of 2008 against the democracies of Israel (apart from a suicide bombing in February 2008 that killed one) or Indonesia, and only one major attack in India outside the disputed territory of Jammu-Kashmir (11/07/06 in Mumbai) before the massive Mumbai attack in November 2008. There have been 2,400 arrests related to jihadi terrorist activities in Europe, where civil liberties are guaranteed, and 3,000 arrests in Saudi Arabia, where civil liberties are restricted.

Only in Iraq and Afghanistan has there been a continuing high rate of attacks against U.S.-led coalition forces, which are increasingly perceived as occupation forces by large segments of the populations of these two countries. It is doubtful that reaction would be much different if invasion and occupation forces were those of a dictatorship, as with Soviet forces in Afghanistan in the 1980s. The world's newest and most active areas for suicide attacks are Pakistan and North Africa, where civil liberties are restricted. Over 200 people were killed in North Africa in 2007, mostly in Algeria. In Pakistan, nearly 500 were killed in suicide attacks between July and December 2007 (including former Prime Minister Benazir Bhutto)—more than have been killed in terrorist attacks in Europe in the past two decades. Local groups proclaiming allegiance or sympathy with al Qaeda have claimed responsibility, but that transnational organization has little if any operational command or control over these groups.

Consider, now, the relationship between socioeconomic status and terrorism. To independently confirm Krueger's findings on Hamas, we statistically regressed Palestinian support for suicide attacks against Israelis on education and income levels in three nationally representative surveys of Palestinians (West Bank and Gaza) from 1999, 2001, and 2005. We controlled for area of residence, refugee status, age, gender, and religion. Income and education levels were unrelated to support for suicide attacks ($P < 0.1$). When there was a relationship between support for suicide attacks and economic variables, we found, like Krueger, that income and education levels are modestly but *positively* correlated with support. In the 1999 survey, wealthier Palestinians expressed greater support for attacks,[8] while more educated Palestinians showed greater support for suicide attacks in the 2001[9] and 2005[10] surveys.

However, when we turned to al Qaeda's principal Southeast Asian ally, Jemaah Islamiyah (JI), we found something different. We analyzed every attack by this group between 1999 and the second Bali bombing of 2005 and entered demographic details on all known operatives. Of 180 people implicated in JI attacks, 78 percent worked in unskilled jobs, and only 23 percent had education beyond high school.

We also found that operational associations in JI are determined by these four variables:

1. being a member of the self-styled "Afghan Alumni"—that is, someone who went through training with the Indonesian volunteers in the Abu Sayyaf camp during the Soviet-Afghan War and its immediate aftermath,

2. continuing to work together (for example, on Abdullah Sungkar's chicken farm in Malaysia) or to play soccer together after demobilization from Afghanistan (and before JI was officially set up),

3. having studied or taught in at least one of the two religious schools established by JI's founders (Al Mukmin in Java and Lukman Al-Hakiem in Malaysia),

4. being related by kinship or marriage to someone else in the network (in fact, there are over thirty marriages woven through ten attacks).

SMALL SOCIAL NETWORKS, NOT LARGE ORGANIZATIONS

In contrast to the factors just noted, we find that the knowledge of JI's "official" organizational structure is practically worthless in helping us to understand the networks involved in JI attacks.

It is true that levels of education and skill are significantly higher for Hamas than for JI. Nevertheless, the main predictors for involvement in suicide attacks are, again, small-world aspects of social networks and local group dynamics rather than large-scale social, economic, and political indicators, such as education level and economic status. For example, Hamas's most sustained suicide bombing campaign (in 2003) involved seven members of the local soccer team of Hebron's Abu Katila neighborhood, four of whom belonged to one kinship group (the Kawasmeh clan). A closer look at actual bombings reveals that almost all are rooted in local networks of preexisting social relationships—the February 2008 suicide attack in Dimona, the first for which Hamas claimed responsibility since 2004, was also carried out by members of the same soccer team; Hamas leadership in Damascus only became aware of the attack after the fact.

The most complete data in Krueger's book concerns Hezbollah and Hamas; there is a secondary focus on al Qaeda. For all three cases, the data is old and of questionable relevance to global terrorism today. Hezbollah had ceased suicide bombings and attacks on civilians (outside of open war) by the 1990s, while Hamas stopped suicide attacks in 2004. Al Qaeda central—the command set up by Osama bin Laden in the summer of 1988, which was involved in the 9/11 attacks—has had no direct success in carrying out a terrorist operation since 2002 (the Djerba, Tunisia bombings), although it had a hand in prior financing of operations carried out later (the Istanbul bombings of 2003) and in training individuals who were implicated in subsequent attacks (about 50 suicide bombers involved in attacks in Saudi Arabia through April 2005).

The original al Qaeda group around bin Laden (mostly Egyptians) has been decimated, leaving its surviving remnants mostly concentrated in a handful of small mobile camps in Pakistan's Federally Administered Tribal Areas. The largest remaining al Qaeda camp in 2007—Mir Ali in North Waziristan—had a few dozen trainees under the tutelage of Abu Ubaydah Al-Masri. Al-Masri instructed those responsible for the summer 2006 suicide bombing plot to smuggle liquid explosives aboard twenty passenger jets, and he has likely been involved in a few other dangerous but (so far) unsuccessful plots.

For the most part, the "new wave" of terrorism that expresses allegiance to al Qaeda tends to be poorer, less educated, and more marginal than the old al Qaeda or its remnants. It relies to a greater extent for financing and personnel on preexisting petty criminal networks because large-scale financing is easily tracked—9/11 cost some $400,000, followed by the 2002 Bali and 2004 bombings at about $50,000 each; all others cost considerably less. The Saudi Ministry of Interior ran a study of 634 detainees through 2004 and is presently finishing a study of 3,000 more. The data from these studies indicate that the newer Saudi wave also tends to be younger, poorer, and less educated. Even in the older cohort, there was little traditional religious education; however, the newer cohort tends to be less ideologically sophisticated and especially motivated by desire to avenge perceived injustice in Iraq. This "new wave" pattern of increasingly marginality and "born-again" religion is reflected in European and North African groups that express allegiance to al Qaeda, as well as foreign fighters in Iraq (including 41 percent from Saudi Arabia and 39 percent from North Africa since August 2006).

Krueger and others repeatedly refer to predictive factors in "recruitment." It is important to understand, however, that there is not, and has never been, clear evidence of "recruitment" into al Qaeda. In its heyday, al Qaeda operated more as a funding agency than as a military organization. Individuals would come to al Qaeda with proposals for plots, of which the organization would accept some 10 to 20 percent. Even the 9/11 suicide pilots were not "recruited" into al Qaeda—they were Middle Eastern Arabs who lived in a middle-class German community (the Hamburg suburb of Harburg) and were seeking friendship and identity in an Islamic community that was mostly Moroccan. Our interviews with friends in their circle and with investigators reveal that the plotters met in the dorms and started hanging out together, going to mosque services and meeting in local restaurants. Three wound up living in the same apartment, where they self-radicalized. They thought of going, first, to Chechnya to engage in jihad (but getting there proved too difficult) and then to Kosovo (but the Albanian jihadis didn't want them); they eventually wound up in an al Qaeda training camp in Afghanistan as a distant third choice.

People go looking for al Qaeda, not the other way around. Because there is very little of the old al Qaeda left, many who go seeking it are caught. Those who seek out al Qaeda do so in small groups of friends, and occasionally through kin. Almost all are schoolmates or workmates, and soccer or camp buddies. Only a minority have gone beyond high school. Some have steady jobs and family, but many have only intermittent jobs and no families of their own. All have self-radicalized as friends before they go after al Qaeda, although an encounter with someone who has been to an al Qaeda training in camp in Afghanistan is occasionally an added stimulant. The overwhelming majority have not had sustained prior religious education but become "born again" into radical Islam in their late teens and early twenties. About 10 percent are Christian converts.

For example, in the wake of the U.S. invasion of Iraq in April 2003, a disciple of the radical Islamist preacher Sheikh Omar Bakri organized a barbecue in a London suburb for about 100 people, most from the immigrant Pakistani community. Guests were asked for donations to help in sending a few volunteers to Pakistan to train for jihad. Among those who used some of the 3,500 euros collected to pay their way to Pakistan were Mohammed Sidique Kahn, one of the four suicide bombers in the July 2005 London Underground attack, and Omar Khyam, one of the conspirators convicted in the 2005 "Crevice" plot to plant fertilizer bombs around London. Their original intention was to pursue jihad in Kashmir but, after a quick course in bomb-making, they were told to "go home" and do something there. Each joined up on his own with a few friends to concoct a plot. One of the four London suicide bombers was a Jamaican Christian convert and pin-ball buddy.

Another telling example is the Madrid train bombing in March 2004. Five of the seven plotters who blew themselves up when cornered by police had grown up within a few blocks of one another in the tumble-down neighborhood of Jemaa Mezuaq in Tetuan, Morocco. One, nicknamed "The Chinaman," had fled a murder charge in Morocco in 1993, to join his elder brother in Madrid in taking and dealing drugs. In 1995, with his teenage Christian girlfriend and fellow junkie five months pregnant, The Chinaman decided to kick his heroin habit. His wife says he did so cold turkey, with the help of the religious training he was getting in a local mosque. The Chinaman then turned around to preach reform to his drug-dealing associates, three brothers from the Mezuaq, convincing two of them to quit their habit. The two brothers became devoted to The Chinaman and were thereafter known in the barrio as his "bodyguards."

The fourth of Madrid's Moroccan suicide bombers was described by some of his friends as Mezuaq's first "Afghan" (a religious militant who grows a full beard who dresses with an Afghan hat, coarse knee-length tunic and sandals). He would preach jihad against "infidels" (*kuffar*) and Muslims who merit "excommunication" (*takfir*) because they refuse to follow "pure" (*salafi*) Islamic ways. The father and friends of the fifth suicide bomber, a young gay man in his early twenties known as "The Kid," told us that he had sold candies from a cart in Mezuaq until 2000. He did not care much for religion until he met up with The Afghan, who protected the delicate boy. By 2002, The Afghan and The Kid were in Madrid—the former employed as a part-time construction worker who dealt drugs with The Chinaman's "bodyguards," and the latter devoting himself to charity work, helping out other young immigrants.

A closer look at other terrorist groups reveals strikingly similar patterns of self-radicalization based on almost chance encounters within preexisting local circles of friends and kin. Former CIA case officer Marc Sageman analyzed Qaeda networks through 2003 and found that about 70 percent join with friends and 20 percent with kin. In his new book, *Leaderless Jihad*,[11] Sageman finds that more recent networks are also built up around friendship and kinship, but their members are more marginal relative to the surrounding society.

The boundaries of the newer-wave networks are very loose, and the Internet now allows anyone who wishes to become a terrorist to do so anywhere, anytime. For example, the "Al Ansar" chat-room network involved plotting in half a dozen countries—the United States, the United Kingdom, Canada, Sweden, Denmark, and Bosnia—by young men, many of whom had never actually met. They would hack into Western media sites to post jihadi videos—such as that of Zarqawi's beheading of Nicholas Berg—and recipes for making car bombs and suicide vests from scratch. From a basement apartment in Britain, a self-styled Irhabi 007 ("Terrorist 007") helped in his spare time to coordinate plots with some high school buddies in Toronto to blow up the Canadian parliament and with others to attack the U.S. embassy in Bosnia. (In the latter episode, three conspirators who did meet up physically in Bosnia were arrested with AK-47s, suicide belts, and thousands of rounds of ammunition).

LACK OF UNDERSTANDING

A main problem in terrorism studies is that most "experts" have little field experience (for understandable but not insurmountable reasons) and otherwise lack the required level of detail that statistical and trend analyses could then properly mine. There are many millions of people who express sympathy with al Qaeda or other forms of violent political expression that support terrorism. There are, however, only a few thousand who show willingness to actually commit violence, and they almost invariably go on to commit violent acts in small groups consisting mostly of friends and some kin.

Terrorist groups arise within specific "scenes": neighborhoods, schools (classes, dorms), workplaces, common leisure activities (soccer, mosque, barbershop café) and, increasingly, online chat rooms. The process of self-selection into terrorism occurs within these scenes. It is stimulated by a massive, media-driven, transnational political awakening in which jihad is represented as the only the way to permanently resolve glaring problems of global injustice. This media-hyped imagery incites moral outrage against perceived attacks upon Islam. If this outrage resonates with personal experience that reverberates among friends in a scene, and if aspects of the scene are already sufficiently action-oriented—such as a soccer team or study group—the willingness to go out and do violence together is much more probable.

Given these scenarios, it is critical to provide alternate local networks and chat rooms that are enticing for young people. This kind of constructive channeling of energy is what the Boy Scouts and high school football teams successfully offered to immigrants and potentially troublesome youth in the United States—it works. The greatest predictor of whether a sympathizer of violent jihad will actually commit violent acts himself is whether or not he and his buddies belong to an action-oriented group (often a soccer team) that may go on to violence as a group. There are no real lone wolves, although the emerging importance of the Internet is reflected in the fact that we are starting to see lone actors who belong to a virtual community.

In the long run, perhaps the most important counterterrorism measure of all is to provide alternative dreams that youth can connect with. It is faith in dreams and heroes—perhaps more than industry and power—that gives impetus to lives and civilizations.

CONCLUSION

Terrorism does pose a threat to national security today, though not because of the organization or strength of terrorist networks. Its major challenge to national security stems from the response that terrorists' threats receive— exaggerated, widely-publicized, and misguided.

Policymakers and researchers must understand that the threat of terrorism derives largely not from structured organizations with global operations and recruitment strategies, but rather from small groups of friends, families, and social networks of disaffected and self-radicalized individuals. The media and policymakers who fan the flames of terrorist threats by exaggerating their power and giving them much-wanted publicity are only helping the terrorists' cause and aims. Responses to terrorism—both politically and publicly—must be informed, measured, and proportional. Until then, terrorism will continue to pose an existential threat to our freedom and security.

NO: John Mueller, *Ohio State University*

In a 2008 interview, Homeland Security czar Michael Chertoff thundered that the "struggle" against terrorism is a "significant existential" one—thus carefully differentiating it, apparently, from all those insignificant existential struggles we have waged in the past.[1] At the same time, the *New York Times* was asserting that "the fight against al Qaeda is the central battle for this generation," and presidential candidate John McCain was more expansively labeling it the "transcendental challenge of the 21st century," while Democrats were routinely insisting that the terrorist menace has been energized and much embellished by the war in Iraq. But, in fact, international terrorism does not justify such extreme proclamations. It hardly represents an existential challenge—or even a very significant one—to just about any country's national security.

EVALUATING THE CHALLENGE

An excellent place to begin an assessment of the terrorist threat is with analyses provided by Marc Sageman in lectures and in a 2007 book, *Leaderless Jihad*. A former intelligence officer with experience in Afghanistan, Sageman carefully and systematically combs through both open and classified data on jihadists and would-be jihadists around the world, sorting the al Qaeda enemy—just about the only terrorists who seem to want to target the United States itself—into three groups.

First, there is a cluster left over from the struggles against the Soviets in Afghanistan in the 1980s. Currently they are huddled around, and hiding out with, Osama bin Laden somewhere in Afghanistan and/or Pakistan. This band, concludes Sageman, probably consists of a few dozen individuals. Joining them in the area are perhaps a hundred fighters left over from al Qaeda's golden days in Afghanistan in the 1990s.

These key portions of the enemy would total, then, less than 150 actual people. They may operate something resembling "training camps," but these camps appear to be quite minor affairs. They also assist with the far larger and very troublesome insurgency that is conducted by the Taliban.

Beyond this tiny band of holdovers from the last two decades of the twentieth century, concludes Sageman, the third group consists of thousands of sympathizers and would-be jihadists spread around the globe who mainly connect in Internet chat rooms, engage in radicalizing conversations, and variously dare each other actually to do something.

Of course, all of these rather hapless—perhaps even pathetic—individuals should be considered potentially dangerous. From time to time, they may be able to coalesce long enough to carry out acts of terrorist violence, and so policing efforts to stop them before they can do so are certainly justified. But the notion that they present an existential threat to just about anybody seems at least as fanciful as some of their schemes, and any idea that these characters could come up with nuclear weapons seems far-fetched in the extreme. The threat presented by these individuals is likely, concludes Sageman, to simply fade away in time. Unless, of course, the United States overreacts and does something to enhance their numbers, prestige, and determination—something that is, needless to say, entirely possible.

In general agreement is Fawaz Gerges, whose book, *The Far Enemy*, based on hundreds of interviews in the Middle East, parses the jihadist enterprise. As an additional concern, he suggests that Sageman's third group may also include a small, but possibly growing, underclass of disaffected and hopeless young men in the Middle East, many of them scarcely literate, who, outraged at Israel and at America's war in Iraq, may provide cannon fodder for the jihad. However, these radicalized individuals would mainly present problems in the Middle East (including in Iraq), not elsewhere.

Another way to evaluate the terrorist challenge is to focus on the actual amount of violence perpetrated outside of war zones around the world by Muslim extremists since 9/11. Included in the count would be terrorism of the much-publicized and fear-inducing sort that occurred in Bali in 2002; in Saudi Arabia, Morocco, and Turkey in 2003; in the Philippines, Madrid, and Egypt in 2004; and in London and Jordan in 2005.

Three think-tank publications have independently provided lists of such incidents. Although their tallies make for grim reading, the total number of people killed comes to some two or three hundred per year. That total, of course, is two or three hundred per year too many, but it hardly suggests that the perpetrators present a major threat, much less an existential one. By comparison: over the same period, far more people have drowned in bathtubs in the United States alone. In fact, until 2001, far fewer Americans were killed in any grouping of years by all forms of international terrorism than were killed by lightning. Moreover, except for 2001, virtually none of these terrorist deaths occurred within the United States itself. Indeed, outside of 2001, fewer people have died in the United States from international terrorism than have drowned in toilets.

Another assessment comes from astronomer Alan Harris. Using State Department figures, he assumes a worldwide death rate from international terrorism of 1,000 per year—that is, his estimate presumes another 9/11 somewhere in the world every several years. Over an eighty-year period under those conditions, some 80,000 deaths would occur—which would fix the lifetime probability that a resident of the globe who lives outside a war zone would die at the hands of international terrorists at about one in 75,000 (6 billion divided by 80,000). And if there were no repeats of 9/11, the lifetime probability of being killed by an international terrorist would be about one in 120,000—about the same as being killed by an ill-directed comet or meteor, notes Harris.

Not only has the number of individuals killed outside war zones been rather limited since September 11, 2001, but many of the attacks have been decidedly counterproductive.

To begin with, the 9/11 attacks themselves massively heightened concerns about terrorism around the world. Although some Arabs and Muslims may have taken a certain pleasure in the suffering inflicted on that day, the key result among jihadis and religious nationalists was a vehement rejection of al Qaeda's strategy and methods (Gerges 2005, 27, 228, 233; Sageman 2007, 138). Moreover, no matter how much they may disagree on other issues (most notably, perhaps, on the U.S. war on Iraq), there is a compelling incentive for states—including Arab and Muslim ones—to cooperate in dealing with any international terrorist threat emanating from groups and individuals connected to, or sympathetic with, al Qaeda.

This post–9/11 willingness of governments to take on terrorism has been much reinforced and amplified by subsequent, if sporadic, terrorist activity in such places as Pakistan, Saudi Arabia, Turkey, Indonesia, Egypt, Spain, Britain, Morocco, and Jordan. The terrorist bombing in Bali in 2002 galvanized the Indonesian government into action. Extensive arrests and convictions of those involved—including leaders who had previously enjoyed some degree of local fame and political popularity—seem to have severely degraded the capacity of the chief terrorist group there. When terrorists attacked Saudis in Saudi Arabia in 2003, that country seems, very much for self-interested reasons, to have become considerably more serious about dealing with internal terrorism, suddenly undertaking such efforts as clamping down on radical clerics (Gerges 2005, 249). Some rather inept terrorist bombings in Casablanca in 2003 inspired a similarly determined crackdown by Moroccan authorities. And when al Qaeda–linked suicide bombers killed sixty people in simultaneous explosions in three hotels in Jordan in 2005, the main result was to outrage Jordanians and other Arabs against the perpetrators: massive protests were held, and polls registered a plunge from 25 percent to less than 1 percent in the proportion of respondents expressing a lot of confidence in Osama bin Laden to "do the right thing."

Moreover, al Qaeda has continually expanded the list of enemies assailed in its declarations, so that, as Peter Bergen (2007) notes, that list has come to include "all Middle Eastern regimes; Muslims who don't share their views; most Western countries; Jews and Christians; the governments of India, Pakistan, Afghanistan, and Russia; most news organizations; the United Nations; and international NGOs." In sum, bin Laden and gang seem mainly to have succeeded in uniting the world, including its huge Muslim portion, against their violent global jihad.

Any "threat" appears, then, to derive principally from Sageman's leaderless jihadists: self-selected individuals, often isolated from each other, who fantasize about performing dire deeds. Despite post–9/11 estimates that there were thousands of al Qaeda operatives and supporters at loose in the United States, a secret 2005 FBI report acknowledged that it had been unable to uncover a single true al Qaeda sleeper cell anywhere in the country despite years of intense and very well-funded sleuthing.

Moreover, many of the people who have been picked up on terrorism charges within the United States do not seem likely, despite quite a bit of official hype publicized when they were arrested, to have presented much of a threat at all (Lustick 2006, chap. 3; Mueller 2006). There was, for example, the diabolical would-be bomber of a shopping mall in Rockford, Illinois, who, because he couldn't afford the asking price of $100, exchanged two used stereo speakers for a bogus handgun and four equally bogus hand grenades supplied by an FBI informant. Had the weapons been real, he might actually have managed to do some harm, but he clearly posed no threat that was existential—significantly or otherwise—to the United States, to Illinois, to Rockford, or, indeed, to the shopping mall.

If defending against enemies such as that hapless fellow is to be the "central battle" of our generation (or our century), we are likely to come out quite well.

WORST-CASE FANTASIES

In distinct contrast, what we mostly get from what might be called "the terrorism industry"—politicians, bureaucrats, journalists, and risk entrepreneurs who benefit in one way or another from exacerbating anxieties about terrorism—is fear-mongering and doom-saying, and much of it borders on hysteria. In particular, these purveyors of panic are truly virtuosic at pouring out, and poring over, worst-case scenarios, or "worst case fantasies."

In 2004, for example, former CIA analyst Michael Scheuer urgently argued that if the United States did not very significantly alter its policy in the Middle East, its very "survival" would be at risk. Two years later, there had been only a few sizable terrorist attacks outside of war zones around the world and none whatever within the United States (and no notable change in its Middle East policy), yet Scheuer remained comfortable in his gloom: "America faces an existential threat," he proclaimed, and, moreover, "time is short."

In fact, it has become fashionable in some extravagantly alarmist circles to denote the contest against Osama bin Laden and his sympathizers as (depending on how the Cold War is classified) World War III or World War IV. Even more grandly, General Richard Myers, then chairman of the Joint Chiefs of

Staff, once meticulously calculated that if terrorists were able kill 10,000 Americans in an attack, they would "do away with our way of life."

Columnist Charles Krauthammer claims that international terrorists threaten "civilization itself," and Michael Ignatieff warns that they imperil "the ascendancy of the modern state." Two counterterrorism officials from the Clinton administration contend that terrorists could precipitate America's decline or "trigger an existential crisis for the United States and its allies." And some academics maintain that terrorists could "destroy civilization as we know it" or "destroy our society" (Mueller 2006, 45).

THE PROSPECT OF A TERRORIST NUCLEAR BOMB

In order for any of the terrorism industry's dire scenarios—or fantasies—to become even remotely plausible, terrorists would have to become *vastly* more capable of inflicting damage. In fact, they would pretty much need to acquire an atomic arsenal and the capacity to deploy and detonate it. Nuclear weapons in the hands of a terrorist could kill tens of thousands of people or even, in exceptional circumstances, more.

Warnings about the possibility that small groups of terrorists or mafias could fabricate nuclear weapons have been issued repeatedly at least since 1946, when A-bomb maker J. Robert Oppenheimer agreed that "three or four men" could smuggle atomic weapons into New York and "blow up the whole city." Such assertions proliferated during the 1950s, when the "suitcase bomb" appeared to become a practical possibility, and with the stimulus of 9/11, dire warnings about nuclear terrorism have escalated—even though the terrorists in that case relied on weapons no more sophisticated than box cutters.

Obviously, these cries of alarm have so far proven to be off the mark, and it is essential to note that producing and deploying a nuclear weapon is an extraordinarily difficult task. As the Gilmore Commission (a special advisory panel to the president and Congress) stressed in 1999, building a nuclear device capable of producing mass destruction presents "Herculean challenges." The process requires obtaining enough fissile material, designing a weapon "that will bring that mass together in a tiny fraction of a second, before the heat from early fission blows the material apart," and figuring out some way to deliver the thing. And, the commission emphasized, these actions constitute only "the *minimum* requirements." If each requirement is not fully met, the result is not simply a less powerful weapon, but one that cannot produce any significant nuclear yield at all or cannot be delivered. After assessing this issue in detail, physicists Christoph Wirz and Emmanuel Egger (2005, 501) conclude that fabricating a nuclear weapon "could hardly be accomplished by a subnational group" because of "the difficulty of acquiring the necessary expertise, the technical requirements (which in several fields verge on the unfeasible), the lack of available materials and the lack of experience in working with these."

The task would also require the fabrication of a vast conspiracy, at once leak-proof and foolproof, that would necessarily include the subversion of a considerable array of criminals, corrupt officials, and opportunists, each of whom would have every incentive to push the price for cooperation as high as possible. And even at that, there would be a considerable risk that those so purchased would, at an exquisitely opportune moment of their choosing, decide to take the money and run—perhaps to the authorities representing desperate governments with essentially bottomless bankrolls and an overwhelming incentive to expend resources to foil the nuclear plot and to capture or kill the scheming perpetrators.

It also worth noting that, although nuclear weapons have been around now for well over half a century, no state has ever given another state—even a close ally, much less a terrorist group—a nuclear weapon (nor a chemical, biological, or radiological one either, for that matter) that the recipient could use independently. Donors understand that there is always the danger that the weapon could be traced to its origin, or that it could be used in a manner the donor would not approve or even, potentially, against the donor itself.

Nor is it likely that a working nuclear device could be stolen. "A theft," note Wirz and Egger, "would involve many risks and great efforts in terms of personnel, finances, and organization," while safety and security systems on the weapons "ensure that the successful use of a stolen weapon would be very unlikely" (502). Of particular concern in this regard are Russia's supposedly missing suitcase bombs. However, a careful assessment by the Center for Nonproliferation Studies (2002) has concluded that it is unlikely that any of these devices have indeed been lost and that, regardless, their effectiveness would be very low or even nonexistent because they require continual maintenance.

Moreover, no terrorist group, including al Qaeda, has shown anything resembling the technical expertise necessary to fabricate a bomb. In testimony before the Senate Select Committee on Intelligence on January 11, 2007, FBI director Robert Mueller, who had been highly alarmist about the terrorist potential in previous testimony, stressed that his chief concern within the United States was now homegrown groups, and that, while remaining concerned that things could change in the future, he now believed that "few if any terrorist groups" were likely to possess the required expertise to produce nuclear weapons—or, for that matter, biological or chemical ones.

Given the destructive capacity of nuclear weapons, it is sensible to expend some policy effort to increase the difficulties for any would-be nuclear terrorists, particularly by seeking to control the world's supply of fissile material. But the difficulties for the terrorists persist, and the likelihood of their acquiring such weaponry remains very low—even assuming that they try hard to do so.

THE CHALLENGE FROM WITHIN

Actually, the subtexts—and sometimes the texts—of the warnings issued by members of the terrorism industry often suggest that, insofar as international terrorism presents a significant threat to national security, this threat arises not so much from what the terrorists would do to us, but what we would do to ourselves in response.

Alarmist Ignatieff, who warns that "inexorably, terrorism, like war itself, is moving beyond the conventional to the apocalyptic," helpfully explains how the process would play itself out. Although Americans did graciously allow their leaders one fatal mistake in September 2001, they simply "will not forgive another one." In the case of several large-scale attacks, he confidently predicts, the trust that binds the people to its leadership and to each other would crumble, and the "cowed populace" would demand that tyranny be imposed upon it and quite possibly break itself into a collection of rampaging lynch mobs devoted to killing "former neighbors" and "onetime friends." Similarly, General Tommy Franks opined that a "massive casualty–producing event somewhere in the Western world" could cause the U.S. population "to question our own Constitution and to begin to militarize our country"—in the process losing "what it cherishes most, and that is freedom and liberty."

It seems, then, that it is not only the most feared terrorists who are suicidal. But we seem to need a reality check here. All societies are "vulnerable" to tiny bands of suicidal fanatics in the sense that it is impossible to prevent every terrorist act. But the United States is hardly "vulnerable" in the sense that it can be toppled by dramatic acts of terrorist destruction. In all probability, the country could readily, if grimly, absorb even extensive damage—just as it "absorbs" some 40,000 deaths each year from automobile accidents—without instantly becoming a fascist state. Israel, of course, has absorbed a great deal of sustained terrorism on its soil and still manages to have a functioning democracy.

General Myers' prediction that the sudden deaths from terrorism of 10,000 Americans would "do away with our way of life" might be assessed in this regard. It is easy to imagine scenarios in which 10,000 would have been killed on September 11—if the planes had hit the World Trade Center later in the day when more people were at work, for example. Any death is tragic, but it is not at all obvious that a substantially higher loss on 9/11 would have necessarily triggered societal suicide.

However, although the alarmists may exaggerate—a proclivity that is by nature (and definition) central to their basic makeup—the subtext of their message should perhaps be taken seriously: ultimately, the enemy, in fact, appears to be us. Thus far at least, terrorism is a rather rare and, appropriately considered, not generally a terribly destructive phenomenon. But there is a danger that the terrorism industry's congenital (if self-serving and profitable) hysteria could become at least somewhat self-fulfilling should extensive further terrorism be visited upon the Home of the Brave. As David Kilcullen, an Australian army officer who is an adviser to the U.S. State and Defense Departments, has put it, "It is not the people al Qaeda might kill that is the threat. *Our reaction* is what can cause the damage."

AIDING THE TERRORISTS

As military analyst William Arkin (2006) points out forcefully, although terrorists cannot destroy the United States, "every time we pretend we are fighting for our survival, we not only confer greater power and importance to terrorists than they deserve but we also at the same time act as their main recruiting agent by suggesting that they have the slightest potential for success." And two years before 9/11, the Gilmore Commission pressed a point it considered "self-evident," but one that nonetheless required reiteration because of the "rhetoric and hyperbole" surrounding the issue: although a terrorist attack with a weapon of mass destruction could be "serious and potentially catastrophic," it is "highly unlikely that it could ever completely undermine the national security, much less threaten the survival, of the United States." To hold otherwise "risks surrendering to the fear and intimidation that is precisely the terrorist's stock in trade." The fact that terrorists subsequently managed to ram airplanes into three buildings on a sunny September morning does not render this judgment less sound.

A key element in a policy toward terrorism, therefore, should be to control, to deal with, or at least productively to worry about the fear and overreaction that terrorism so routinely inspires. Policy approaches that exacerbate fears of terrorism not only very often do more harm than anything the terrorists have accomplished, but play into their hands.

6

nuclear weapons

Should the United States or the International Community Aggressively Pursue Nuclear Nonproliferation Policies?

YES: Scott D. Sagan and Josh A. Weddle, *Stanford University*

NO: Todd S. Sechser, *University of Virginia*

Nuclear nonproliferation is a recent world problem. Only since the 1950s have governments been able to destroy vast numbers of citizens of another country with a relatively small number of warheads and at such a distance. The increasing proliferation of nuclear weapons in succeeding decades is cause for increasing concern about national security.

Nuclear nonproliferation policies attempt to ensure that nuclear threats and exchanges—or worse, nuclear war—do not occur. Historically, only two nuclear weapons have been used: the United States dropped atomic bombs on Hiroshima and Nagasaki, Japan, on August 6th and 9th, 1945. Since then, the destructive power, numbers, and delivery systems of these weapons have grown extensively, making it far easier in principle to cause massive damage from great distances. Nuclear warheads can now be delivered not only by bombs carried on long-distance aircraft, but also by intercontinental land-based missiles and those launched from submarines, as well as by smaller tactical battlefield missiles and even bulky "suitcase" bombs.

A significant set of multilateral treaties has been introduced to try to contain nuclear proliferation. The International Atomic Energy Agency (IAEA) seeks to prevent the spread of "nuclear states" beyond the original five (the United States, the Soviet Union, the United Kingdom, France, and China) that had nuclear weapons at the time of its creation in 1970. The agency administers a large-scale bargain: in return for agreeing not to develop nuclear weapons, countries are given access to civilian nuclear power (for commercial energy generation). The IAEA also closely tracks the circulation of fissile materials. Its inspectors can visit power plants, and the Nuclear Suppliers Group keeps close tabs on who purchases fissile materials. In addition, countries that are seen to be violating IAEA rules face stiff economic sanctions.

The original nuclear states were the United States (1945), the USSR/Russia (1949), the United Kingdom (1952), France (1960), and China (1964). Subsequently, Israel (1979), India (1974), Pakistan (1998), and North Korea (2006) have developed nuclear arsenals of at least several warheads.

Table 1 shows the numbers of nuclear warheads existing in the 1990s, the current (as of 2008) arsenals, and projections of the estimated numbers in 2012.

But not all countries aspire to possession of a nuclear arsenal. Indeed, there are few good reasons for actually having one—it is extremely expensive to develop nuclear weapons, and the political costs of becoming a nuclear power are economically onerous, as the IAEA sanctions can be severe. Countries pursue nuclear weapons, nonetheless, as a possible deterrent against nuclear-armed adversaries (India, Pakistan, Iran), as status symbols (Libya, Pakistan), or as potential bargaining chips in international diplomacy (North Korea). There are also instances, however, of countries deciding that nuclear proliferation made no sense, and abandoning their programs. Brazil, Argentina, and Chile established a nuclear-free zone in the Southern Cone of South America in the 1980s. South Africa dismantled its few nuclear warheads in 1991. Libya finally halted its program in 2003, in the face of Western sanctions.

Table 1

Number of Warheads by Country, 1990s–2012

Country	Early 1990s	2008	2012
United States	9,680	3,575	1,700–2,200
Russia	10,996	3,340	1,700–2,200
United Kingdom	260	<160	<160
France	538	348	<300
China	100–200	<200	Replacing with more capable warheads
India	N.d.	50–60	Building more
Pakistan	N.d.	30–50	Likely to build more
Israel	100–200	100–200	100–200
Iran	None	Presumed to be 2–10 years from a nuclear capability	
North Korea	Possibly 1–2	<10	0
South Africa	6	0	0

Sources: *The Economist*, March 29, 2008, 80; *New York Times*, March 25, 1993, A1, A12.

A multitude of approaches have been devised in the attempt to promote nonproliferation. The centerpiece is the IAEA, verifying which states have nuclear capabilities and which do not, and administering sanctions for violators. During the Cold War, the United States and the Soviet Union signed a number of bilateral treaties that were intended to build mutual confidence so that a nuclear exchange could not occur accidentally (see the 1964 movie *Doctor Strangelove* for a satiric demonstration of this possibility) and to reciprocally reduce their arsenals.

Alternative approaches have stressed the role of deterrence in preventing the use of nuclear weapons. Kenneth Waltz, a major international relations scholar, famously argued that if everyone has a weapon, then no one will initiate out of fear of retribution.[1] Scott Sagan argues here that the most likely source of nuclear crisis is not bungled deterrence, but mishandled communications in case of a crisis. For Sagan, the focus of nonproliferation efforts should be on management and communication rather than on counting the number of warheads.

Recently, the spread of nonstate criminal groups, such as al Qaeda, has inspired a new fear of nonstate actors gaining access to nuclear weapons, either by building them or by stealing or buying them from a nuclear state. Few of the policies that have been developed to influence behavior by states would likely be effective for such nonstate actors, who are beyond the influence of many states and are not accountable to citizens, and thus would not suffer from sanctions.

The authors of the essays that follow discuss the principal reasons for nuclear proliferation, as well as alternative means for achieving nonproliferation. Todd Sechser argues that the case against deterrence may not stand up to close empirical scrutiny, and that deterrence may well limit states' willingness to pursue nuclear weapons. Scott Sagan and Josh Weddle elaborate on Sagan's opinion that the most serious threat of nuclear Armageddon may arise from mistakes and the mindless pursuit of organizational routines.

Discussion Questions

1. Why do countries decide to pursue nuclear weapons despite their considerable costs? Why do some countries decide against it?
2. Is it hypocritical for the United States to pursue nuclear nonproliferation policies when it currently possesses nuclear weapons? Why or why not?
3. What four requirements for stable nuclear deterrence do Scott Sagan and Josh Weddle lay out? What points do they make in

rejecting the likelihood that these requirements will be met? Do you agree with their position?

4. What questions does Todd Sechser raise in making his argument on nuclear proliferation and U.S. foreign policy? What policies does he recommend to address these questions? Do you agree with him?

5. Both authors recognize the dangers of a nuclear North Korea or a nuclear Iran. They also describe the dangers of a terrorist group acquiring nuclear weapons. Which situation presents the bigger threat? What policies should be put in place to prevent these parties from acquiring nuclear weapons? Are the same policies appropriate for both kinds of adversaries?

YES: Scott D. Sagan and Josh A. Weddle,
Stanford University

Should the United States pursue nuclear nonproliferation as a national security objective? The answer to this question should encompass two considerations. First, what would be the likely consequences of the further spread of nuclear weapons? Experts disagree over whether proliferation would reduce the risks of war by producing stable mutual deterrence relationships (in which both sides avoid nuclear conflict, knowing that retaliation would be catastrophic) or increase the danger of nuclear war and nuclear terrorism (by making the means to wage either kind of aggression more widely available). Second, can nonproliferation policies succeed? Setbacks to nonproliferation efforts over the past two decades have led some observers to conclude that a state determined to build nuclear weapons cannot be stopped. If this is true, then governments should allocate their limited national security resources to more achievable objectives.

A prominent group of scholars known as "proliferation optimists" argues that the spread of nuclear weapons promotes peace and stability by raising the costs of war to an unacceptable level. Following the logic of rational deterrence theory, optimists contend that statesmen know that a nuclear exchange would be catastrophic for their states and will thus be deterred from starting any military conflict that could escalate to nuclear war. These scholars point to the Cold War as evidence for their claims: despite deep political animosity, numerous crises, and a massive arms race, they argue, the superpowers avoided nuclear war. Why should we expect the experience of future nuclear powers to be any different?

Meanwhile, a growing sense of fatalism has also crept into the debate over the nuclear future. The view that further proliferation is inevitable now dominates U.S. public opinion: in a 2007 poll, 91 percent of Americans predicted that there would be more nuclear-armed states fifty years from now then there are today.[1] Such fatalism also influences policymakers: in March 2006, a U.S. official in the executive branch told the *New York Times* that nonproliferation strategies aimed at Iran were unlikely to succeed in the long run, stating, "The reality is that most of us think the Iranians are probably going to get a weapon, or the technology to make one, sooner or later."[2]

These opposing strains of widespread fatalism and proliferation optimism interact to produce a dangerous, mutually reinforcing complacency. If proliferation is seen as inevitable, it becomes tempting to downplay the consequences; and if deterrence is seen as foolproof, then costly and inconvenient nonproliferation policies become easy to dismiss.

The optimistic and the fatalistic views of proliferation are both deeply flawed, however, for each draws its evidence from a misreading of history. We present here both theoretical and empirical reasons to believe that the spread of nuclear weapons will increase the likelihood of crises, accidents, and nuclear war. We also show that the historical record suggests that the further spread of nuclear weapons can be constrained and even reversed if nonproliferation policies are constructed appropriately and pursued aggressively. In short, the United States should pursue nonproliferation as a high-priority goal and can succeed in its efforts.

THE SPREAD OF NUCLEAR WEAPONS: WHY WORRY?

Scholars who claim that nuclear proliferation begets stability ground their arguments in rational deterrence theory, which assumes that nuclear weapons are controlled by rational leaders who make careful decisions based on expected costs and benefits. While it is true that no rational statesman would launch an attack that would likely result in the destruction of his or her own nation's cities in retaliation, nuclear weapons are not controlled by perfectly rational statesmen. They are controlled by complex military organizations and civilian bureaucracies—imperfect, normal organizations composed of imperfect, normal human beings. An alternative theory that focuses on the workings of complex organizations—known as organization theory—should therefore be used to understand the problem and predict the consequences of nuclear proliferation.

There are four logical requirements for stable nuclear deterrence: avoiding preventive war during transition periods when one state has a temporary advantage over its rival; developing nuclear forces that can survive a first strike and be used to respond in kind; avoiding accidental nuclear war; and preventing terrorist theft of nuclear weapons. Rational deterrence theorists claim that meeting these objectives is relatively easy.[3] Insights from organization theory, however, suggest that military organizations will often behave in ways that undermine the ability of states to meet these requirements, leading to deliberate or accidental nuclear war.

Historical evidence supports the pessimistic view of organization theorists. Organizational proclivities sparked numerous near-catastrophes during the Cold War despite the strong mechanisms of civilian control that both superpowers developed. The danger of such incidents is likely to be even greater in future nuclear-armed states because many current and emerging proliferators have either military-run or weak civilian-led governments that lack the checks and balances necessary to buffer inordinate military influence on national policy. Moreover, the small size and primitive technology of new nuclear states increases the security and safety risks associated with their arsenals. Finally, the spread of nuclear weapons into regions that have both unstable governments and Islamic radical terrorist organizations creates especially frightening prospects.

The Problem of Preventive War

Organization theory posits that military officers are more likely to favor preventive war—deliberate attack during a period when one side has a temporary advantage—than are civilian authorities, for several reasons. First, military officers are more likely than civilians to believe that war is inevitable in the long term, a belief that stems from both their self-selection into the profession and their training once they enlist. The belief that war is inevitable in the long run makes preventive war a more appealing option than it might otherwise be, since the question becomes not whether to go to war, but whether to do so before or after the adversary has had time to strengthen its retaliatory capabilities. Military officers also prefer offensive doctrines that enable them to seize the initiative and implement their own war plans instead of reacting to enemy operations. Finally, military officers are less likely than civilians to focus on domestic or international political disincentives against preventive war.[4]

Considerable evidence from U.S. history during the Cold War period supports these theoretical predictions. The Truman administration discussed the possibility of preventive nuclear war after the 1949 Soviet atomic bomb test, but rejected the idea in April 1950. Nevertheless, many senior U.S. military officers continued to advocate preventive war against the Soviet Union well into the mid-1950s. In the most dramatic case, in 1954 Air Force chief of staff General Nathan Twining recommended a preventive attack on the Russians before they could develop larger nuclear forces, telling his fellow members of the Joint Chiefs of Staff: "We must recognize this time of decision, or we will continue blindly down a suicidal path and arrive at a situation in which we will have entrusted our survival to the whims of a small group of proven barbarians." President Dwight D. Eisenhower rejected these recommendations; he was not convinced that war with the Russians was inevitable, given U.S. deterrent capabilities and the possibility that containment would eventually lead the Soviet Union to collapse from within.

The danger of preventive war is raised anew each time an emerging nuclear state is considered threatening by its neighbors. For example, evidence suggests that South Asia came dangerously close to a preventive war of its own in 1986–1987. Then–chief of staff of the Indian army, General Krishnaswami Sundarji, designed a massive military exercise, code-named "Brasstacks," in hopes of creating fears that would provoke Islamabad and thereby enable Indian forces to destroy Pakistan's nuclear facilities under the pretense of retaliation. The Pakistani military initially took the bait, alerted its forces, and began its own military mobilization, which led Sundarji to recommend what he called a preemptive strike against Pakistan. Indian Prime Minister Rajiv Gandhi, fortunately, rejected this request.

Military biases can produce dangerously aggressive behavior outside the preventive war context as well. In 1999, for example, the Pakistan Army sent soldiers disguised as Islamic guerillas into Indian-controlled territory in the Kargil district of Kashmir, sparking a conflict in which over one thousand Indian and Pakistani soldiers were killed. Pakistan Army officers apparently believed that Pakistan's nuclear arsenal provided a shield of nuclear deterrence that permitted low-level aggression. Evidence suggests, however, that the civilian leadership in Islamabad did not share this belief. Eyewitnesses at the meetings where army officers claim to have briefed Prime Minister Nawaz Sharif on the planned incursions report that there was no mention of Pakistani troops crossing into Indian territory and that Sharif only approved general plans to "increase the heat" in Kashmir. Sharif's public statements during the conflict suggest that he did not share the military's confidence that escalation was unlikely, as he declared that he was "trying to avoid nuclear war" and feared that "India was getting ready to launch a full-scale military operation against Pakistan."

Similar problems of preventive war and biased decision making in crises are likely to occur elsewhere if many new states acquire nuclear weapons. There is no reason to believe that future potential proliferants—Iran, Syria, Burma, or Saudi Arabia—will be immune to the kinds of organizational pathologies that could lead to deterrence failure. Nuclear weapons make balanced civilian decision making essential, but they do not guarantee that it will occur.

Organizational Problems Compromising Survivability

Successful deterrence also depends on mutual fear of nuclear retaliation, a "balance of terror" that can only be maintained if the states involved develop survivable second-strike forces that are capable of enduring and responding to an enemy strike. Organization theory suggests, however, that military organizations will not take the necessary steps to ensure survivable second-strike forces without vigorous oversight from civilian authorities.

Even if military leaders do not make conscious decisions to oppose new systems and operations, organizational inertia can drive militaries to continue past behaviors and may lead them to maintain specific deployments that leave forces vulnerable to new threats from evolving adversaries. Organizational learning tends to occur only after failures: military organizations, like other organizations, have few incentives to review and adjust operations when they believe they are successful. At the same time, organizational routines often produce signatures that inadvertently reveal to enemy intelligence agencies secret information such as the location of otherwise hidden military forces.

Again, Cold War history offers substantial evidence to support these theoretical insights. On the U.S. side, air force leaders strongly supported the development of a more powerful intercontinental ballistic missile (ICBM) in the 1980s, but they showed little concern for whether it would be deployed in any of the expensive basing modes—such as mobile racetrack configurations, railway basing, and rotation between empty silos—that were under discussion to ensure survivability. Three decades earlier, the U.S. Navy leadership had opposed the creation of a ballistic missile submarine fleet because they preferred traditional (and more exciting) attack submarines. By emphasizing tradition over innovation, this policy delayed the development of what eventually became the most survivable leg of the U.S. strategic triad.

Organizational routines in the Soviet Union, meanwhile, often enabled the United States to recognize secret force deployments. U.S. observers discovered missile deployments in Cuba in 1962 by the Star of David pattern of air defense missile battery placements and the easily recognized slash marks on missile pads that characterized similar deployments in the USSR. American photointerpreters were also able to locate the secret ICBM silos of the Soviet Strategic Rocket Forces because of the triple security fences built around the silo buildings and the distinctive wide-radius curves in the entry roads designed to allow for transporting long missiles to the sites.

The recent experiences of new and emerging nuclear powers suggest that they, too, will struggle to produce survivable forces. In a striking parallel to Cold War history, Indian intelligence has been able to locate Pakistani M-11 missile deployments by recognizing communication terminals and wide-radius roads nearby. North Korea also inadvertently revealed its illicit nuclear weapons program to U.S. satellite surveillance in the early 1990s by building "secret" nuclear waste storage facilities from Soviet designs that U.S. observers had learned to recognize long ago. U.S. intelligence similarly discovered Iran's covert nuclear facilities near the end of 2001, and an Iranian dissident group publicly exposed the facilities' existence in August 2002. The same dynamics that have exposed these nuclear programs could well reveal deployment information should Tehran and Pyongyang eventually deploy nuclear arsenals.

The Risks of Accidental Nuclear War

If stable deterrence is to hold among nuclear powers, states also must be able to prevent the accidental or unauthorized use of the weapons that could inadvertently start a nuclear war. Maintaining a large nuclear arsenal with the necessary survivability measures in place, however, requires complex command-and-control systems that are inherently accident-prone. Social science research on safety in modern technological systems has shown that accidents are likely over time in systems that display two structural characteristics: high interactive complexity (numerous interrelated, but unintended, interactions that are not readily comprehensible) and tight coupling (highly time-dependent and invariant production sequences, with very little built-in slack).[5] Political factors such as conflicting objectives among actors within the organizations that manage hazardous technological systems can further heighten the danger of catastrophic accidents by inhibiting organizational learning about safety problems and placing other priorities such as production above safety concerns.[6]

Two organizational blunders during the most severe nuclear crisis the world has ever faced—the Cuban Missile Crisis of October 1962—powerfully illustrate the risks of accidental nuclear war. First, during the height of the crisis, the U.S. Air Force launched a test missile from Vandenberg Air Force Base in California after having taken crisis-alert measures that included arming many of the missiles at the base with nuclear warheads and aiming them at the Sino-Soviet bloc. No one considered the possibility that the nuclear alert might be detected by Soviet satellites and that the subsequent test launch might be misperceived by Moscow as a nuclear first strike. Then, just two days later, a technician at the special Cuban Missile Early Warning System set up by the United States during the crisis put a training tape into the online system showing what an attack would look like, leading confused radar operators to report that a Soviet missile had been launched from Cuba en route to Tampa, Florida.

These incidents demonstrate that there would be reason enough to worry about nuclear accidents in new proliferators even if their safety difficulties proved "only" as great as those the superpowers faced during the Cold War. For several reasons, however, new proliferators will face even more daunting challenges. First, some emergent nuclear powers may lack the organizational and financial resources to produce adequate mechanical safety devices and safe weapons design features. After the 1991 Persian Gulf War, for example, UN weapons inspectors found that the design for the nuclear weapons that Iraq was working to produce was highly unstable, leading one inspector to remark, "It could go off if a rifle bullet hit it," and then to add, "I wouldn't want to be around if it fell off the edge of this desk."

New nuclear states will also face greater tight-coupling problems than the superpowers did, since they are likely to lie in close proximity to their adversaries, as do India and Pakistan, Iran and Israel. From the very outset of nuclearization, new proliferators will thus face extremely short response times during which to determine whether warnings are real or false. New nuclear states may also have to develop their arsenals in secret in order to escape international condemnation. Such opaque efforts will be inherently less safe because the lack of public debate will reduce challenges to narrow bureaucratic and military interests, and tight compartmentalization will discourage safety monitoring efforts. Moreover, states with small nuclear arsenals have limited nuclear materials, and the resulting inability to conduct multiple nuclear weapons tests will hinder the development of safety designs.

Finally, history has shown that domestic political disputes and unrest can increase the risk of nuclear weapons accidents by encouraging unsafe transportation, exercises, or testing operations. Political instability prompted hasty transport of nuclear weapons out of peripheral regions during the collapse of the Soviet Union in 1991; French forces in Algeria tested the nuclear weapons in their possession in a rushed effort to prevent rebel units from seizing them in 1961; and, most dramatically, Marshal Nie Rongzhen ordered the launch of a test missile carrying a live nuclear warhead across China during the Cultural Revolution, in what he believed would serve as a public sign of success as part of his "strategy of siding with the radicals to fend off radical penetration of the program."

Political instability in recent and emerging proliferators could prompt similarly dangerous behaviors. The political situation in Pakistan has been one of near-perpetual crisis since the nuclear tests of 1998, with the coup against Prime Minister Nawaz Sharif in 1999, numerous assassination attempts against then-president Pervez Musharraf, the 2008 assassination of opposition leader and former prime minister Benazir Bhutto, and continuing al Qaeda and Taliban threats against the central government in Islamabad. And although North Korea and Iran have long eluded the political revolutions forecast by Western experts, neither Kim Jong-Il nor the clerics in Tehran have a firm enough grip on power to rule out the possibility of potentially dangerous unrest in the future. A revolution in either country could lead to nuclear weapons falling into the hands of rogue elements in the military or a terrorist organization.

Preventing Terrorist Acquisition

Proliferation optimists assume that the weapons and fissile material stockpiles of nuclear states will remain in the hands of the central governments that built them, but that assumption is not warranted. Several terrorist groups have tried to acquire nuclear weapons in the past, and the current surge of Islamic jihadi terrorism has increased the likelihood that nuclear weapons may be stolen or deliberately transferred to terrorist groups. Indeed, Osama bin Laden has declared the acquisition of nuclear weapons by Islamic radicals to be a "religious duty." Moreover, the consensus among nuclear weapons experts is that terrorist organizations would not face insurmountable obstacles to building a primitive nuclear bomb of their own if they could acquire the necessary fissile material, especially enriched uranium.[7] The difficulties of ongoing efforts to secure the world's existing fissile material stockpiles—in the former Soviet Union in particular—have been well-documented. The creation of new fissile material stockpiles by proliferating states will only worsen the problem.

If terrorists do acquire nuclear weapons, they are unlikely to be deterred from using them, for retaliation in kind would be exceedingly difficult against a covert network with no central locus of operations. The best way to prevent terrorists from ever using nuclear weapons is thus to prevent them from acquiring such weapons in the first place. Unfortunately, there are several reasons to believe that future nuclear-armed states will have difficulty protecting their arsenals and fissile materials from terrorist theft or deliberate transfer by sympathetic regime insiders. First, the governments of new nuclear-armed states are unlikely to give nuclear security measures the priority they deserve. Organization theory suggests that governments without strong civilian control of the military will demonstrate an over-reliance on the competence and loyalty of the professional military as guarantors of nuclear security instead of implementing other, more restrictive measures. They will be less likely to allocate resources to expensive technological safeguards such as Permissive Action Link locks (PALs) that prevent unauthorized use of weapons, and they will also be inclined to presume the loyalty and competence of military personnel instead of implementing personnel reliability programs with psychological stability testing and rigorous background checks. The threat of domestic instability that new proliferators are likely to face may also cause their military organizations to be "inward-looking"—that is, focusing more on regime stability and internal politics than on external security threats. Defense policy may thus be designed to protect the regime, not the nation's security, and military officers may be promoted based on loyalty rather than professional competence.

Pakistan's experience with nuclear weapons offers evidence for each of these expectations. Pakistani weapons lack PALs to prevent their use if stolen, and Islamabad had no dedicated personnel reliability program until at least 2001. When asked in that year to assess the likelihood, on a 1-to-100 scale, that Pakistani nuclear weapons would not fall into the hands of terrorists, President Musharraf replied alarmingly, "I would certainly give it over 90."

The case of Pakistan illustrates an alarming structural concern regarding the future of proliferation as well: many of the most likely proliferators in the medium term—Iran, Saudi Arabia, Syria, and Egypt—are states in the Islamic world. The spread of nuclear weapons to these states would put them closer to the hands of Islamic terrorists and their likely sympathizers. Pakistan's experience serves to highlight the potential for disaster that this situation would cause. After the 9/11 attacks, it came to light that senior Pakistani nuclear officials had met with Osama bin Laden in Afghanistan in August 2001 to discuss techniques for developing nuclear weapons and other weapons of mass destruction. Pakistani leaders also gave important custodial responsibilities to regime elements with terrorist ties, placing sensitive duties—such as approving which guards should have critical nuclear command-and-control responsibilities—in the trust of the notorious Inter-Services Intelligence (ISI), a group with intimate ties to the Taliban and to jihadi groups in Kashmir. According to the *Washington Post*, Pakistani military planners and the ISI even contacted Taliban officials in 1999 to discuss moving Pakistan's nuclear weapons to Afghanistan in order to hide them from a potential Indian attack.

Pakistani officials did not follow through on this proposition, but the incident highlights a vulnerability/invulnerability paradox that confronts leaders trying to ensure the safety, security, and survivability of their nuclear arsenals. To protect against terrorist theft and accidental or unauthorized use, states face an incentive to consolidate their nuclear weapons in a small number of secure locations and to keep them separated from delivery vehicles in an "unmated" state. In times of crisis, however, the threat of an enemy first strike can lead states to mate their nuclear weapons to delivery vehicles and to consider, as Pakistani officials did, moving them to remote locations so as to decrease their vulnerability. Such measures, which are intended to make nuclear weapons invulnerable to enemy attack, also increase their vulnerability to terrorist theft and accidental or unauthorized launch.

The opportunity to prevent emergence of a nuclear Pakistan has passed, but other states whose acquisition of nuclear arms would pose many of the same risks can still be constrained. The foremost case in point is Iran, which has, as far back as 1987, pursued covert nuclear activities in violation of its obligations under the Nuclear Nonproliferation Treaty (NPT). After these activities came to light in 2002, in fact, Iran began to accelerate its nuclear program in an apparent effort to develop at least the capability to build nuclear weapons. A nuclear Iran would drastically increase the risk of terrorists acquiring nuclear weapons, for Iran has a history of supporting terrorism, and an Iranian nuclear arsenal would likely be controlled by the Islamic Revolutionary Guards Corp (IRGC), the same military organization that manages Tehran's terrorist ties. Also, Iran has already dispersed its nuclear facilities throughout the countryside to reduce their vulnerability to preventive attack—a measure that decreases central control over the program and increases the likelihood that a future arsenal would be vulnerable to terrorist theft under precisely the paradoxical scenario just described. The widespread political instability and prevalence of Islamic terrorist groups throughout the Middle East makes the spread of nuclear weapons to Iran, and then to Arab rivals in the region, an especially harrowing prospect.

COMBATING PROLIFERATION FATALISM

The nuclear nonproliferation regime has suffered setbacks over the past two decades: India, Pakistan, and North Korea's emergence as nuclear powers; the operation of a clandestine nuclear proliferation network by Pakistani scientist A.Q. Khan; Iran's noncompliance with its NPT obligations; and backsliding by the United States on its disarmament commitments, among others. In the face of these obstacles, it is all too easy to dismiss the regime as a failure and succumb to the view that states determined to get the bomb cannot be stopped. With the diffusion of nuclear technology and know-how and the right of parties in good standing under the Nuclear Nonproliferation Treaty to enrich uranium and separate plutonium, this argument goes, little can be done to prevent a government that is willing to bear heavy costs from developing nuclear weapons.

Such fatalism, however, overlooks the impressive track record of nonproliferation policies since the signing of the NPT in 1968, during which time at least nineteen states that considered the nuclear option have chosen instead to forgo it, and four additional states—Belarus, Kazakhstan, Ukraine, and South Africa—have surrendered or destroyed the nuclear weapons in their possession (see Table 1).[8] Many other countries that have the technical capability to develop nuclear weapons have, at least for now, decided not to pursue that option.

A variety of policies tailored to the particulars of each case led to these successes. South Korea and Taiwan ended suspected military-related nuclear programs in the 1970s and 1980s, respectively, after the United States threatened to withdraw its security assistance. A mix of limited security assurances and economic incentives convinced Belarus, Kazakhstan, and Ukraine to return the nuclear weapons they had inherited after the collapse of the Soviet Union in 1991, and a similar mix of economic and security incentives led to North Korea's nuclear freeze under the Agreed Framework from 1994 to 2002. Punitive sanctions were particularly effective in convincing Libya that its nuclear program, which was not moving forward effectively anyway, was too costly to continue.

Table 1

Cases of Nuclear Reversal and Hedging since 1945

Never Tried (Nuclear Abstinence)	Tried (Nuclear Hedging/ Reversal)	Attained but Gave Up	Still Trying	Attained and Maintained
All (?) other states	Argentina	Belarus	Algeria	China
	Australia	Kazakhstan	Iran	France
	Brazil	South Africa	Syria	Great Britain
	Canada	Ukraine		India
	Egypt			Israel
	Germany			North Korea
	Indonesia			(2002–2008)
	Iraq			Pakistan
	Italy			Soviet Union/
	Japan			Russia
	Libya			United States
	Netherlands			
	North Korea (pre–2002)			
	Norway			
	Romania			
	South Korea			
	Sweden			
	Switzerland			
	Taiwan			
	Yugoslavia			

In all of these cases, nonproliferation policies succeeded by altering the incentives behind the states' demand for nuclear weapons. Supply-side approaches can work as well, and they are particularly important where nuclear terrorism is concerned. Export controls have long been instrumental in hindering covert nuclear weapons programs, and new measures—such as UN Security Council Resolution 1540 (requiring all states to take effective measures to prevent proliferation of weapons of mass destruction) and the Proliferation Security Initiative (a U.S.–led international effort to interdict shipments of weapons of mass destruction and related goods)—are promising steps toward more rigorous enforcement of supply-side controls. But recent history shows that supply-side measures alone are unlikely to succeed if concurrent policies do not address the reasons why states want the bomb. The Agreed Framework induced North Korea to freeze its nuclear programs for eight years, in large part because it provided Pyongyang with assurances against U.S. attack, assuaging the security concerns behind its nuclear drive. North Korea ended its nuclear restraint, however, after the George W. Bush administration drastically altered Pyongyang's security calculus by declaring a policy of regime change and labeling North Korea part of an "axis of evil." Similar security concerns appear to be driving Iran's nuclear pursuits, and the unwillingness of the United States and its negotiating partners to address that country's security issues has played a large part in the failure of nonproliferation efforts aimed at Tehran thus far.

Finally, the United States and the other nuclear weapons states that are party to the Nuclear Nonproliferation Treaty need to renew their pledges under the treaty to "work in good faith" toward eventual nuclear disarmament—and then take more serious incremental steps toward that goal. Increased movement toward nuclear disarmament may not directly influence decisions by highly motivated proliferators, but such efforts will create more nonproliferation cooperation by critical nonaligned states that are currently disenchanted with the nuclear powers' backsliding on disarmament and arms control. The United States will be better able to build coalitions to enforce and enhance the nuclear nonproliferation regime if it is seen to be living up to its own commitments.

CONCLUSION

That the Cold War passed without the use of nuclear weapons is cause for wonder and celebration, not an excuse for casting nonproliferation policies aside as unnecessary. An organization-theory approach to proliferation demonstrates that the further spread of nuclear weapons increases the chances that they will be used. The track record of nonproliferation policies, meanwhile, demonstrates that proliferation can be prevented.

The continued spread of nuclear technology and know-how should not be seen as a harbinger of widespread nuclear proliferation to come. Not all regimes with such potential will want to develop nuclear weapons, and history shows that at least some who do can be convinced otherwise. The long-standing dilemma for policymakers moving forward will be how to keep latent nuclear states in the closet. Success will require a consistent and dedicated effort to devalue nuclear weapons as guarantors of security.

For long-term success, a larger dose of intellectual persuasion about the dangers of nuclear weapons must be brought to complement existing supply- and demand-side policy initiatives. Government leaders and the organizations and citizens under them will need to be convinced that developing nuclear weapons will make them less secure in the long run by raising the risks of preventive attack, accidental or unauthorized use, nuclear terrorism, and outright nuclear war. In short, now is a time for creative and aggressive nonproliferation policies, not for accepting the future spread of nuclear weapons as an inevitable or desirable outcome.

NO: Todd S. Sechser, *University of Virginia*

Should the United States try to prevent the spread of nuclear weapons to states that do not already have them? At first glance, this appears to be a fairly uncontroversial proposition. After all, nuclear weapons are the most horrific and destructive weapons ever invented—how could the world possibly be better off with more fingers on the nuclear trigger? Indeed, for decades, official U.S. national security policy has embraced the doctrine of universal nonproliferation codified by the 1968 Non-Proliferation Treaty (NPT), aiming to prevent friends and enemies alike from acquiring nuclear weapons.

The idea that the United States should aggressively pursue nuclear nonproliferation rests in part on a widespread belief that the spread of nuclear weapons would destabilize international relations. But this pessimistic view confronts one incontrovertible fact: nuclear weapons proliferated to thirteen states[1] during the six decades since the dawn of the nuclear age, yet the world has not witnessed a single preventive or preemptive nuclear war, accidental nuclear attack, or instance of nuclear terrorism. Motivated by this striking observation, scholars known as "proliferation optimists" have suggested that nuclear proliferation may, in fact, exert a stabilizing force on international politics. They argue that nuclear states new and old will be highly motivated to avoid taking actions that might risk nuclear conflict.

The core of the optimists' position is that the cost of a nuclear war would be so grave that even the world's most risk-prone leaders will find themselves reluctant to risk fighting one. As Kenneth N. Waltz, perhaps the most prominent proliferation optimist, has argued, nuclear states quickly recognize that engaging in aggressive or risky behavior that could prompt nuclear retaliation is "obvious folly" (Sagan and Waltz 2003, 154). Because a nuclear conflict could place a state's very survival at risk, national leaders have powerful incentives to manage their arsenals with care and caution. Moreover, according to this view, even a few nuclear weapons constitute such a powerful deterrent to aggression that they obviate the need for high levels of spending on conventional arms. According to the optimists, then, the spread of nuclear weapons is likely to deter large-scale wars, restrain conventional-arms races, and produce greater international stability.

Here I contend that the historical record supports this optimistic position. I divide my argument into three parts. First, I present empirical data suggesting that nuclear proliferation is unlikely to destabilize international politics, and may in fact be stabilizing. Second, I evaluate the body of evidence cited by more pessimistic scholars and conclude that it is insufficient to bear out their skepticism. Finally, I consider the implications of my argument for U.S. foreign policy. In the end, I conclude that further nuclear proliferation would probably bolster—not undermine—international stability. If the lessons of the nuclear age are to be believed, a world with more nuclear states is likely to be, on balance, a more stable, peaceful, and secure world than one without.

PROLIFERATION AND THE HISTORICAL RECORD

Will additional nuclear proliferation stabilize world politics, or will it worsen the problem of interstate conflict? We cannot answer this question with certainty, of course, since we cannot collect data about the future. We can, however, learn from events that have already happened. Imagine that, at the advent of the nuclear age in 1945, today's proliferation optimists and pessimists had put forth their competing predictions about the likely consequences of the spread of nuclear weapons. Whose predictions would be borne out? In this section I argue that historical data confirm the predictions of proliferation optimism, while offering little corroboration for rival perspectives.

Scholars who take the view that proliferation bolsters global stability argue that the spread of nuclear weapons produces three observable effects.[2] First, by deterring aggression, nuclear weapons reduce the *frequency* with which wars occur. Second, nuclear weapons induce caution among leaders in crises and during wartime, thereby mitigating the *intensity* of wars. Third, nuclear weapons defuse arms races and obviate the need for high levels of *conventional-arms spending*. Let us now consider each claim with respect to five proliferators: China, Israel, India, South Africa, and Pakistan. These five states provide a useful laboratory for examining the behavior of proliferators because they more closely resemble the types of states most likely to proliferate today. The United States, the Soviet Union, Great Britain, and France were all major industrialized powers when they acquired nuclear weapons, but these five proliferators were weaker, poorer, and less internally stable—much as today's proliferators are likely to be.

The Frequency of Armed Conflict

The optimist camp's first and most important claim is that the presence of nuclear weapons suppresses international conflicts. Nuclear weapons, in this view, differ from conventional military tools in two central ways. First, nuclear weapons carry enormous destructive power. Whereas the targets of conventional weapons necessarily tend to be small in size (for instance, an airfield, communications center, or ammunition depot), the most powerful nuclear weapons can place entire cities at risk. The use of even a few nuclear weapons could destroy hundreds of thousands (if not millions) of human lives in a short span of time. Second, defenders have little control over the level of destruction they endure during a nuclear conflict. Without a reliable means to destroy incoming ballistic missiles or to shield cities from nuclear attack—neither of which exists today—nuclear combatants must rely on an enemy's restraint to limit the amount of damage they suffer. These two characteristics—colossal destructive capacity and the lack of an effective defense—combine to induce caution among leaders facing nuclear-armed adversaries. Leaders will behave less aggressively and will more eagerly seek peaceful solutions to crises, the logic goes, since they do not want to endure even a small risk that a conventional war might become nuclear.

These propositions can be evaluated empirically by comparing the rates at which proliferators have participated in interstate conflicts both before and after their acquisition of nuclear weapons. If the optimists are correct, nuclear states should experience fewer conflicts after they acquire nuclear weapons. One way to measure the turbulence of a state's foreign affairs is to calculate its participation in *militarized interstate disputes*, defined here as conflicts involving at least one military fatality. Figure 1 considers five proliferators and charts how much their involvement in military conflicts changed after they became nuclear states. Israel, for instance, participated in an average of 1.21 conflicts per year as a nonnuclear state, but entered into only 0.33 conflicts per year after becoming a nuclear state in 1972, so its bar in Figure 1 drops below zero to illustrate that Israel has been involved in fewer interstate conflicts since acquiring nuclear weapons.

Optimists predict that states will participate in fewer conflicts after going nuclear, since they expect nuclear weapons to deter aggression and dissuade opposing leaders from escalating crises. And indeed, four of the five states examined here participated in fewer interstate conflicts, on average, once they became nuclear states. For example, Israel fought four interstate wars against its neighbors before acquiring nuclear weapons, but just two afterward. India and Pakistan have gone to war against one another four times since achieving independence, but only one of those wars occurred after the two rivals acquired nuclear weapons. Indeed, India and Pakistan saw the average incidence of militarized disputes between them decline by half (from 0.55 disputes per year to 0.27) once both states had acquired nuclear weapons. Only South Africa experienced an increase in its conflict participation rate after achieving nuclear status, although the magnitude of this change (+0.06) was the smallest of the five proliferators considered here.

These data tell us that proliferation optimists are right to expect a decline in the frequency of interstate wars as more states acquire nuclear weapons.

Changes in Average Interstate Dispute Rates after Acquiring Nuclear Weapons

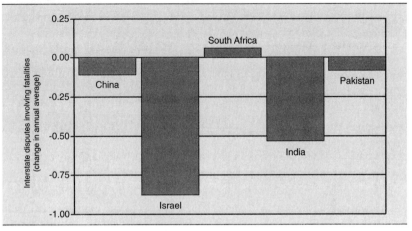

Source: Militarized Interstate Dispute dataset, http://cow2.la.psu.edu.

Admittedly, this analysis cannot demonstrate that these declines were caused entirely by nuclear weapons, but the strength of the correlation cannot be ignored. At a minimum, the data cast considerable doubt on the argument that nuclear weapons undermine conventional military stability.

The Intensity of Military Conflict

What about conflicts which, despite the shadow of nuclear weapons, nevertheless occur? Proliferation optimists argue that even if nuclear-armed states fight one another, their wars will not be intense: leaders will prevent such conflicts from escalating to avoid the risk that nuclear weapons might be used. As Waltz writes, "Everyone knows that if force gets out of hand all the parties to a conflict face catastrophe. With conventional weapons, the crystal ball is clouded. With nuclear weapons, it is perfectly clear" (Sagan and Waltz 2003, 114).

This reasoning was borne out clearly by the 1999 Kargil War between India and Pakistan—the only war ever to occur between two nuclear states. The episode is instructive because the war entailed far fewer causalities than any of the prior wars between India and Pakistan (see Table 1), owing in part to the restraint of the Indian military in expelling Pakistani insurgents from the Kargil region. The Indian military could have reduced its own losses and ended the war more quickly by attacking critical communication and supply lines in

Table 1

Wars between India and Pakistan

War	Year	Fatalities
Kashmir I	1948–1949	7,500
Kashmir II	1965	6,000
Bangladesh/East Pakistan	1971	11,223
Kargil	1999	1,200

Note: Military fatalities only. Battle deaths data available from the Peace Research Institute, Oslo.

Pakistani-controlled Kashmir, yet because crossing into Pakistani territory might have widened the war and risked provoking a Pakistani nuclear threat, Indian leaders instead opted for caution.

It is not hard to find other military crises in which the risk of nuclear escalation induced restraint. In March 1969, Chinese forces ambushed Russian troops along the Ussuri River in northwest China, prompting a Soviet counterattack. But one important reason we do not read about the catastrophic Sino-Soviet War of 1969 is that a Soviet threat to launch preventive strikes against Chinese nuclear targets induced Chinese leaders to de-escalate the crisis. Despite having initiated the challenge, China backed down rather than risk letting events get out of hand. The Soviet Union, of course, had itself recently backed down from a crisis it precipitated when Nikita Khrushchev agreed in 1962 to remove Soviet missile bases from Cuba rather than risk a potentially nuclear conflict with the United States.

These examples make clear that nuclear weapons cannot prevent all conflicts: indeed, the Cuban Missile Crisis, the Ussuri River crisis, and the Kargil War all came about because one nuclear power was bold enough to challenge another. But in a world without nuclear weapons, these clashes might have escalated to large-scale conventional wars. Instead, in each case the shadow of nuclear weapons helped to cool tempers and contain the crisis: retaliation remained limited, escalatory options were rejected, and eventually the challenger backed down.

Conventional-Arms Spending

A final question asks whether possession of nuclear weapons encourages states to restrain their spending on conventional arms and avoid arms races. Optimists argue that even a few nuclear weapons will provide adequate deterrence and security for new proliferators. As a result, those states will not need to remain as carefully attuned to the balance of forces as they would in a purely conventional world. Moreover, since nuclear weapons negate the offensive advantages of conventional forces, nonnuclear-arms racing among rivals will become both unnecessary and unlikely.

Does the evidence bear out this prediction? The charts in Figure 2 provide a tentative answer by tracking the proportion of gross domestic product (GDP) that China, Israel, South Africa, India, and Pakistan each devoted to military spending from 1960 to 2000. If the optimistic view is correct, these states should exhibit general declines in military expenditures following the acquisition of nuclear weapons. Indeed, this prediction is largely vindicated: all five of these states spent a smaller share of their GDP on defense in 2000 than in the year they first acquired nuclear weapons. To be sure, military spending did not immediately decline in all cases. But the acquisition of nuclear weapons appears to be associated with long-run declines in conventional military spending. Indeed, none of these states has exhibited any inclination to participate in the sort of tit-for-tat nuclear arms competition that characterized U.S.–Soviet relations during the Cold War. Even China, the only major power in this group, has remained content for decades with the security provided by its small strategic nuclear force (Lewis 2007).

DO NEAR-MISSES COUNT?

The evidence in the previous section tells against the view that the spread of nuclear weapons engenders instability. Yet proliferation pessimists nonetheless point to a very large body of empirical support for their arguments. Through years of painstaking archival research, scholars such as Bruce G. Blair (1994), Peter D. Feaver (1997), and especially Scott D. Sagan (1993) have amassed an extraordinary collection of "near-catastrophes"—incidents that almost resulted in nuclear accidents or outright nuclear war—that occurred in the United States, China, India, Pakistan, and elsewhere during the Cold War and afterward. Sagan and Josh Weddle, for instance, write of military officers who sought to provoke war with aspiring nuclear rivals, organizational missteps that inadvertently left nuclear forces vulnerable to attack, and blunders that nearly led to accidental nuclear detonations or launches.[3]

While doubtless worrisome, nuclear near-misses are insufficient to corroborate proliferation pessimism because they provide no information about the risk of *actual* accidents. Consider the following analogy. Imagine that an insurance company official is assigned to evaluate the accident risk for cars that use a particular brand of tires. After interviewing customers who have used these tires for many years, she writes a report concluding that clients using the tires

Figure 2

Military Spending as a Share of Gross Domestic Product, 1960–2000

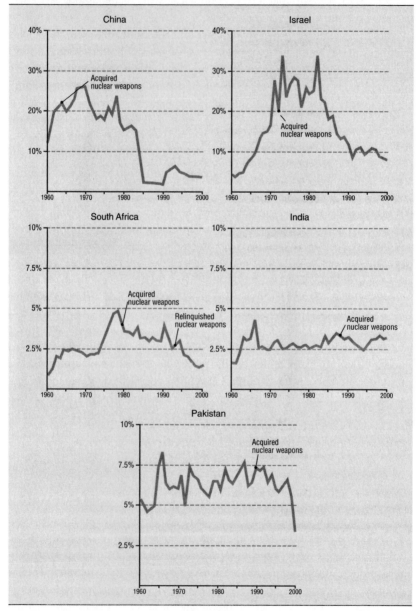

Sources: Nuclear acquisition data are from Sonali Singh and Christopher R. Way, 2004. "The Correlates of Nuclear Proliferation: A Quantitative Test." *Journal of Conflict Resolution* 48(6): 859–885. Military spending data are from the Correlates of War Project (http://www.correlatesofwar.org).

in the future will suffer a high risk of accidents. She bases her conclusion on reports that customers' cars sometimes skidded while taking tight turns or when stopping rapidly, although none of the customers in her study ever experienced an actual crash.

Would the researcher's conclusion be a reasonable inference from her data? It would not. The reason is that in the researcher's sample, experiencing skidding—that is, a "near-accident"—was not in fact associated with a higher likelihood of an actual accident. Cars that skidded had exactly the same likelihood of being involved in a crash—zero—as those that did not skid. Without having studied any actual crashes, the researcher can draw no inferences about the relationship between skidding and accidents. It may seem like common sense to assume that skidding cars have a greater likelihood of crashing, but intuition is no substitute for empirical data. Indeed, just the opposite might be true: perhaps skidding provides such a jolt to drivers that they become more cautious and attuned to road conditions as a result of the skid, thereby making a subsequent crash *less* likely.

So it is with the study of nuclear proliferation. Since none of the close calls in the sample collected by proliferation pessimists led to an actual nuclear detonation, it is inappropriate to infer that close calls raise the likelihood of nuclear accidents.[4] The only conclusion supported by such data is that states possessing nuclear weapons have a greater likelihood of *near-misses* than nonnuclear states. But near-misses, while dramatic and unnerving, are ultimately of little consequence if they never escalate to outright catastrophes.

A common response to this criticism holds that even a tiny risk of nuclear catastrophe is sufficient to justify a policy of universal nonproliferation. This is a staggering burden of proof, and it is flawed for two reasons. One reason is that scholars have not actually demonstrated that the risk of nuclear accidents or inadvertent nuclear war in a proliferated world is greater than zero. Of course, the absence of nuclear catastrophe in the past does not assure its absence in the future. But theories ultimately aim to predict real-world outcomes, and despite unearthing a valuable trove of nuclear near-misses, the theory of proliferation pessimism has not succeeded in accomplishing this task. To be sure, existing research has shown that the theory's predicted *causal mechanisms*—that is, organizational biases and mishaps—have appeared in organizations that handle nuclear weapons, but these mechanisms, thankfully, have never produced the theory's predicted *outcomes*. Safeguards and cooler heads have always prevailed—albeit sometimes at the last minute.

Second, the appropriate question is not whether the spread of nuclear weapons would result in *any* nuclear disasters, but whether a world with proliferation would *on balance* be more peaceful and more stable than a world without it. In other words, we must ask: will the gains outweigh the costs? Even if one of the terrible events feared by proliferation pessimists does occur at some point in the future (as indeed it may), this outcome will not necessarily imply that the costs of proliferation outweigh the benefits. If the spread of nuclear weapons also would prevent numerous conventional wars, then it may be entirely reasonable to conclude that the net overall benefit justifies a more relaxed nonproliferation policy. In deciding whether nuclear proliferation would be stabilizing or destabilizing for international politics, it is not enough to merely point out that risks exist—one must weigh those risks against potential rewards.

Another objection to my critique holds that the nuclear age has not yet provided enough data to test theories of proliferation. In other words, it is simply too early to evaluate the theories' predictions (see Sagan 1993, 12). This argument is unpersuasive. The nuclear age is now more than sixty years old, and more than a dozen nations have possessed nuclear weapons at one time or another. If we imagine that every operational nuclear warhead in existence provides, say, one "disaster opportunity" per year, then since 1945 there have been nearly *two million* opportunities for an accidental explosion, preemptive nuclear strike, nuclear terrorist attack, or preventive war against an emerging proliferator. At the very least, the fact that none of these scenarios has yet occurred should suggest that the risk is low enough to warrant a plausible cost-benefit case against universal nonproliferation.

Of course, the absence of a nuclear catastrophe to date does not "prove" that proliferation pessimism is wrong. But it is important that we recognize the sharp limits to the inferential leverage that near-misses provide. Each year that passes without a preemptive nuclear attack, preventive war against an aspiring nuclear power, nuclear accident, or act of nuclear terrorism must cast additional doubt on the theory. Ultimately, proliferation pessimism remains burdened by the contrast between the ubiquity of organizational pathologies and the absence of the disastrous nuclear outcomes it expects them to cause.

NUCLEAR PROLIFERATION AND U.S. FOREIGN POLICY

What are the implications of the preceding argument for U.S. foreign policy? There are two separate policy questions to consider: first, whether the United States should try to prevent its adversaries from acquiring nuclear weapons; and second, whether it should continue to adhere to a doctrine of universal nonproliferation.

The answer to the first question is unequivocally affirmative. The arguments in this chapter do not imply that the United States should stop trying to prevent its adversaries from acquiring nuclear weapons. Even if nuclear weapons are stabilizing overall, they could nevertheless permit hostile states to counter the power and influence of the United States, potentially threatening U.S. interests. A nuclear Iran, for example, might seek to deter, resist, or blackmail the United States. Stopping proliferation to U.S. adversaries will therefore remain an essential pillar of U.S. foreign policy even if the proliferation optimists are correct. On this, the optimists and pessimists can probably agree.

But a second—and distinct—question is whether the United States should maintain its commitment to preventing proliferation not only to its adversaries but to *all* states. The answer is significant because it carries implications for how the United States should treat new members of the nuclear club—in particular, whether the United States should assist new nuclear states in making their arsenals safe, secure, and reliable. Scholars in the pessimist tradition have noted that new nuclear nations may lack the resources and knowledge necessary to equip their nuclear arsenals with safety devices, survivability measures, and adequate command-and-control arrangements. Timely assistance from the United States could help to secure and protect nascent nuclear arsenals, thereby mitigating these problems.[5] But one barrier to a policy of direct technical assistance to new or aspiring proliferators has been a concern that it would violate the NPT's requirement that states not "assist, encourage, or induce any non-nuclear-weapon State to manufacture or otherwise acquire nuclear weapons." Providing technical assistance, the logic goes, could undermine the international nonproliferation regime.

For this reason, proliferation pessimists have been hesitant to advocate a policy of nuclear safety assistance, reasoning that it would further encourage the spread of nuclear weapons. In contrast, proliferation optimism suggests that we should consider replacing the doctrine of universal nonproliferation with a more nuanced approach that is designed to safely *manage* proliferation when it occurs.[6] If the spread of nuclear weapons would not necessarily be destabilizing, after all, then preventing proliferation to all states (rather than only to U.S. adversaries) is unnecessary; instead, U.S. foreign policy should focus on containing its risks.[7]

CONCLUSION

The historical data presented here suggest that nuclear weapons have had a sobering effect on international politics. They have bolstered stability by quelling conventional-arms races and by making wars less intense and less frequent. Although it is impossible to know what a world without nuclear weapons would have looked like in the decades following World War II, it is reasonable to conclude from these data that the existence of nuclear weapons has restrained some international conflicts and prevented others from igniting altogether. In contrast, despite a sizable number of "close calls" experienced by the United States and other nations, the absence of preventive, preemptive, and accidental nuclear attacks casts doubt on gloomy predictions about the consequences of proliferation.

The spread of nuclear weapons undoubtedly entails extraordinary risks. Nuclear weapons are the most horrific weapons humanity has ever known, and one of the foremost priorities of the United States should be to prevent them from ever being detonated by accident or in anger. But an accurate assessment of the risks of further proliferation requires that we acknowledge that nuclear weapons carry both costs and benefits to international stability. Weighing these costs and benefits, in turn, demands a sound empirical basis for evaluating the effects of nuclear weapons. If we are to make informed predictions about the nuclear future, we must first acknowledge the lessons of the past.

military intervention and human rights

Is Foreign Military Intervention Justified by Widespread Human Rights Abuses?

YES: Jack Donnelly, *University of Denver*

NO: Simon Chesterman, *New York University School of Law*

The issue of legitimizing military intervention has bedeviled the United Nations since its founding. Clear justification is required for the UN Security Council to authorize military intervention in a sovereign country. When the UN does attempt to provide legitimacy to an intervention in a member government's territory, however, it suffers both from the political difficulty of achieving consensus within the constraints of veto powers wielded by the P5 (the five permanent members of the Security Council: the United States, Russia, France, China, and the United Kingdom) and from the lack of a standing army. Instead, it has to rely on contributions of troops and finances from member states. Over the past sixty years and more, Security Council principles for military intervention have been selectively applied, and the justification for intervention has evolved to fit the current political climate.

During the Cold War, interventions were undertaken primarily to resolve civil wars or to impose cease-fires under the overall rubric of "peacekeeping." Most interventions in those years came at the request of states, and many either were vetoed or never came to a vote, because the United States and the Soviet Union both regarded them in light of support for their proxies in the Third World. Secretaries-general of the United Nations initiated interventions in Korea (1950–1953) and the Congo (1960–1964). Since the end of the Cold War, emphasis has shifted to two possible justifications for intervention: to offer humanitarian protection or to manage failed states.

Along with the war in the Balkans (1991–1995), the Rwandan genocide of 1994—and the UN's limited and delayed response to it—catalyzed the development of new norms for humanitarian intervention. The UN's 1992 *Agenda for Peace* tried to expand the definition of intervention and the conditions under which it was warranted to include failed states. The 2005 World Summit, enabled by UNSC Resolution 1674 of April 28, 2006, asserted the responsibility to protect populations from "genocide, war crimes, ethnic cleansing and crimes against humanity." There are strong legal norms in the UN Charter and in human rights treaties banning genocide and holding political leaders individually responsible for genocide. But the rules adopted so far have been aimed at enforcement after the fact, putting such criminals before tribunals or the International Criminal Court. As experience with humanitarian interventions grew over the 1990s, the UN learned that effective and lasting humanitarian protection required not just interventions to separate the parties and punish the guilty, but also to transform the underlying conditions that caused distress (peacemaking). These policy lessons led to more complex peace-keeping missions, as well as to greater reluctance on the part of many Security Council members to commit resources to interventions that were now understood to require lengthy and complex operations.

Recently, attention has shifted to failed states—cases of domestic collapse, wherein no one with authority can invite assistance or intervention. Failed states create political problems within the country, which collapses into a state of anarchy and civil warlordism, as well as problems for neighboring states, which have to face the prospects of receiving large numbers of refugees or repelling rebel forces that may seek to establish safe enclaves outside the failed state from which to launch their campaigns. In such instances, there is no legal authority able to ask for intervention, so the UN Security Council or the secretary-general must impose it. The first failed state to attract the UN's attention was Somalia (1991–1995, following the U.S. involvement there from 1988 to 1991). In 2008 *Foreign Policy* magazine estimated that there were sixty potential failed states— largely countries located in Africa, but also including Colombia, Haiti, the Dominican Republic, Iraq, Afghanistan, Bangladesh, and North Korea.[1]

Dealing with failed states involves a daunting array of responsibilities: recreating a working economy; combating poverty; disarming militias; providing food, education, and shelter; and hosting elections. In addition, intervention in such cases creates an ethical conundrum for the international community: how to protect the rights of individuals in a failed state without violating the legal integrity of national sovereignty? Some scholars have argued that foreign intervention to deal with failed states or to punish genocidal leaders is a new stage of imperialism, while others suggest that failed states carry no legal or moral authority, and that individual rights trump sovereignty.

Still other observers have worried that humanitarian intervention can lead to a slippery slope of justifiable interventions. If it is acceptable to intervene to protect human rights and save lives, is it also permissible to invade a state to prevent or mitigate famine? How about to provide humanitarian assistance after a natural disaster, when the state's government lacks the resources to do so? Intricate considerations such as these have made *ex ante* actions before intervention difficult to legitimize without a clear framework for intervention.

The following essays address this complex question, addressing international norms, international law, and questions of morality and ethics in their responses. Simon Chesterman points to the hypocrisy of selective humanitarian intervention by the United Nations and the industrialized countries, noting that the response resonates with the colonialism and imperialism of earlier epochs—thus rendering it illegitimate in the eyes of the developing world—and that it threatens to undermine the effectiveness of multilateral diplomacy more generally. Conversely, Jack Donnelly offers a highly nuanced argument that, when the interventions are reserved for the purpose of addressing abuses banned by UN treaties, humanitarian intervention is consistent with broad international norms on human rights. He also points out the pragmatic justification for intervention: that political order is preferable to conditions of anarchy and civil war, such as those that now persist in Somalia and the Congo.

Discussion Questions

1. Most would agree that human rights violations do cause moral concern. Given that general consensus, why do you think nations do not intervene to stop such violations more often? Are there situations that would justify nonintervention? What are they?

2. The United Nations recognizes state sovereignty but also authorizes state interventions in some cases of humanitarian violations. Are these positions contradictory? Why or why not?

3. Are principles of nonintervention universal? What are some of the country-specific considerations that might shape the decision to intervene or not?

4. Jack Donnelly says, "Good things done for the wrong reasons may not be as justified as good things done for the right reasons." What does he mean? How does he explain this judgment? Do you agree?

5. What are the four standards that Donnelly says must be considered in regard to humanitarian intervention? Which does he think is most important? Do you agree?

6. Does Simon Chesterman argue that humanitarian intervention is allowed by international law? What evidence does he give to prove his point?

YES: Jack Donnelly, *Joseph Korbel School of International Studies, University of Denver*

Justification of any aggressive action is a complex and multifaceted exercise. At least four standards of evaluation are relevant to humanitarian military intervention: "morality" or "justice" (I will use these terms interchangeably), law, order, and politics.

The moral justification for *concern* over widespread and severe human rights violations is uncontroversial. More contentious is a moral argument for the use of remedial military force. Even in the face of massive suffering, a potential intervener may lack the (moral) authority to use force. In addition, we must determine whether the proposed intervention has reasonable prospects for success, at acceptable cost, using permissible means.

Let us begin, though, by focusing on "just cause"—that is, whether violations are, in principle, sufficient to merit a military response. There is little disagreement that at least some massive human rights violations—such as the genocide in Rwanda and the massive political killings in Cambodia under the Khmer Rouge—provide a just moral cause for military intervention. Morality is not, however, the only relevant standard of justification.

International society has a body of law that governs the behavior of states and other international actors. Particularly relevant is the principle of territorial state sovereignty: each state has exclusive jurisdiction over its territory and the activities that take place there. Massive human rights violations, which characteristically involve a state mistreating its own citizens on its own territory, seem on their face to be protected exercises of sovereignty.

Exclusive jurisdiction, however, is only international law's theoretical starting point. States regularly exercise their sovereignty to create legal obligations in order to better realize their interests. For example, a military alliance may restrict a state's right to choose when, where, and for what purposes it will fight. An alliance, however, is an exercise of sovereignty, not a restriction of it. States, through alliances, limit their freedom of action in order to increase their security.

An extensive body of international human rights law, rooted in the 1948 Universal Declaration of Human Rights, is widely acknowledged to be part of customary international law. These norms have been given binding legal form in two International Human Rights Covenants, adopted in 1966, and in a number of single-issue treaties (most notably on racial discrimination, women's rights, torture, and rights of the child). States, by becoming parties to these treaties, accept obligations to protect and implement an extensive range of internationally recognized human rights. Today, on average, over 85 percent of the world's states are parties to these six treaties.[1]

Although the widespread acceptance of these norms establishes a legal right of the international community and its members to be concerned with the human rights practices of states, state sovereignty remains a powerful bar to action—especially military action—to implement and enforce those rights. Instead, international human rights law establishes international monitoring of state human rights practices, typically through periodic reports submitted by states to committees of experts. (Nongovernmental organizations and foreign states also engage in extensive monitoring.) In a few instances, supervisory committees may receive and pass judgment on complaints of violations from individual citizens. Such judgments, however, are not legally binding. We thus are left with a system of national implementation of international human rights norms.[2] States have retained for themselves sovereign authority to implement and enforce internationally recognized human rights within their own territories.

Later I will argue that a genocide exception was created in the 1990s. The legal bar to the use of foreign military force to implement internationally recognized human rights, however, is very high indeed. And considerations of order and politics suggest keeping the bar high.

International relations is a domain of "anarchy," in the literal sense of absence of hierarchical rule or a ruler. (The United Nations, for example, is not a world government but an organization whose members are sovereign states.) Armed states thus regularly face potentially hostile neighbors, as well as distant great powers, some of which have the interest and capability to intervene. Exclusive territorial jurisdiction is a powerful principle of order: it helps to keep states out of each others' way in the absence of international government.

Order, we must remember, is a value, no less than (although different from) the values of morality and legality. The absence of higher ruling authority makes order an especially pressing concern in international relations. This absence creates a characteristic tension between the values of order and justice, and international law usually leans more toward order.

In the case of armed humanitarian interventions, pursuing the just moral cause of intervening often would undermine the ordering (and legal) principles of sovereignty and nonintervention. (Consider, for example, how the U.S. invasion of Iraq made it easier to justify Russia's intervention in Georgia.) In addition, both increased international disorder and disrespect for international law are likely to have serious antihumanitarian consequences. Thus states— which, in any case, ordinarily are more interested in order than in justice—

tend to put law and order over morality in their decision making. So do multilateral actors, such as the United Nations, which are international legal creatures of the desires of states to foster order and cooperation (and, at best secondarily, some elements of international justice).

Morality, law, and order, as I have presented them here, operate at the level of the international system; they are practices of the society of states or the international community. States, however, also face national evaluation according to standards that I will call political. (We have no need here to consider the national dimensions of law, order, and morality.)

The leaders of states, by the nature of their office, are charged primarily with pursuing the *national* interest. States may define their national interests to include alleviating international suffering, as many states have indeed done, especially in the past two decades. But when faced with a conflict between these broader humanitarian interests and more particularistic national (especially security and economic) interests, national leaders typically do choose these narrower, more particularistic national interests—and are usually expected by their citizens to do so.

States, in other words, frequently have not merely good but compelling foreign policy reasons not to intervene against gross and persistent systematic human rights violations—or even to intervene in ways that harm human rights. As a result, a surplus of politically motivated *anti*humanitarian interventions has been at least as serious a moral problem as the shortage of genuinely humanitarian interventions. (The Cold War era was full of examples, including actions taken by foreign powers in such countries as Hungary, Czechoslovakia, Guatemala, and Nicaragua. More recently, the Great Lakes region of Africa has been repeatedly wracked by various interventions that have fostered ongoing humanitarian disasters.) A strong principle of nonintervention, in addition to contributing to international order, can help to protect not only states but also foreign citizens from self-interested intervention by the powerful.

States sometimes seek to hide their selfish national interests behind appeals to broader international values. Such partisan abuse of international norms, however, should not be confused with appropriate use of the national interest as a standard of international action. There is nothing necessarily sinister or even inappropriate about states pursuing their national interests. Quite the contrary—that is what national leaders usually are supposed to do. This political logic of the national interest, however, regularly conflicts with the logics of international law and order. And when national interests are pursued with antihumanitarian intentions or consequences, the logic of national self-interest conflicts with the moral logic of just cause as well.

Considering all these conflicting standards, it is easy to see how the international community has come down generally on the side of nonintervention. Although neither uncontroversial nor unproblematic, an extremely strong principle of nonintervention is almost universally endorsed by states, for reasons of both national interest and international order. And even many (most?) individuals and nonstate groups agree that this principle is the least unappealing compromise: an unfortunate sacrifice of humanitarian ideals to protect states and people against the more pressing dangers of armed states following a political logic of the national interest in the absence of international government.

THE GENOCIDE EXCEPTION

So far, we have not considered international rules on the use of force. The two central rules, laid out in the United Nations Charter, are these: only states (and the UN Security Council) may use force internationally, and such force may be used only in self-defense. These authoritative international restrictions on the use of force pose substantial additional constraints on armed humanitarian intervention.

The principle of state monopoly on the use of force is relatively uncontroversial. Most people agree that allowing multinational corporations, other private groups, or individuals to use force would be a recipe not only for disorder but for disaster. For example, much of the strength of the international reaction against terrorism depends on the breach, by its perpetrators, of the monopoly of states (and the Security Council) on the legitimate use of force.

Restricting the legitimate use of force to self-defense, in addition to its intrinsic attractions, strongly supports the principle of nonintervention, both as a legal norm and as a principle of order. It is also a powerful and important constraint on self-interested political action.

In the past two decades, however, we have seen substantial movement toward legal recognition of a limited humanitarian exception. The moral basis for this exception is clear. The idea that force can be used only in *self*-defense is deeply problematic. For example, it requires interested and capable actors to stand idly by while foreigners suffer at the hands of their own government or an occupying power. Restricting force solely to self-defense also, dubiously, suggests that force can be legitimately used only against force. (For example, if armed force could, at modest cost, eliminate poverty or gender discrimination, it certainly is not morally obvious that force should not be used. In the right circumstances, most people would agree that, considering only morality or justice, some things in addition to self-defense are worth fighting for.)

In the 1990s, faced with a number of prominent instances of genocidal ethnic conflicts in Europe, Africa, and Asia, a growing number of states and citizens, in both the Western and the non-Western worlds, became increasingly sympathetic to a limited legal exception allowing armed humanitarian intervention against genocide. In Somalia and Bosnia, international military action produced significant (if limited) humanitarian benefits. The absence of international action in Rwanda came quickly to be understood as a tragic failure of both the great powers and the international community. Then, in 1999, ethnic cleansing in Kosovo and genocidal violence in East Timor were met with armed humanitarian action.

The Kosovo intervention was certainly problematic, as we will see later. There was little international disagreement, however, that the Security Council acted within its legitimate authority in authorizing armed force to stop the violence in East Timor and to manage its transition to independence. Both in theory and in practice, an exception was carved out to the principles of nonintervention and the restriction of the legitimate use of force to self-defense.

This exception, however, applies only to genocide—which is defined in Article 2 of the 1948 Genocide Convention as actions "committed with intent to destroy, in whole or in part, a national, ethnical, racial or religious group, as such"—and comparable mass killing. There is no evidence of widespread support for military action against other kinds of human rights violations. Even massive repression does *not* (legally) justify international military action. (Consider, for example, Robert Mugabe's Zimbabwe.) Only the unusual death of a large number of people in a small place over a short period of time is widely accepted as legally justifying armed humanitarian action.

A limited genocide exception causes few problems of order. It may even increase order, as genocide typically leads to a disorderly flow of refugees across state borders, risking the spread of violence. A limited genocide exception also is relatively immune to partisan abuse. And it has few if any undesirable spillover effects on the basic principles of sovereignty and nonintervention.

Morally, of course, prioritizing genocide over other forms of suffering seems problematic. (Consider the fact that malnutrition is a far more serious threat to the lives of many more people than famine, but the international community today responds relatively effectively to famine while doing a rather poor job of combating malnutrition.) But there is even a moral argument for a narrow genocide exception.

Self-determination can be seen as providing the moral basis for the rights of sovereignty and the correlative duties of nonintervention. It is impossible to imagine, however, that any free people would freely consent to a government that practices genocide. Genocide thus strips away the underlying moral basis of nonintervention.

Some other practices—slavery and imperialism come immediately to mind—may fall into this category. Most injustices, however, do not involve such an uncontroversial denial of the principle of self-determination. Therefore, there is a moral case—a controversial case to be sure, but a (not im-)plausible one—to be made for something similar to the narrow genocide exception.

All things considered, then, a narrow genocide exception to the principles of nonintervention and restriction of the use of force to self-defense has come to seem a reasonable way to balance the competing standards of justification. And powerful concerns about disorder and partisan abuse suggest that any additional exceptions should also be narrowly drawn.

AUTHORITY, INTENTIONS, CONSEQUENCES, AND MEANS

So far, we have considered only whether genocide is, in principle, an appropriate occasion for armed international action. Having a just cause, however, is not enough to act justifiably, all things considered, whether that cause is moral, legal, order-based, or political. A fully justified military action must also be undertaken by those with the authority to use force—domestically, the police may employ different means than ordinary citizens—and the means used must be appropriate in both quantity and kind.

There is little controversy today that humanitarian military action by the UN Security Council is properly authorized. There is heated disagreement, however, about genuinely humanitarian action in the absence of Security Council authorization. Assessing such interventions requires drawing further distinctions concerning justification.

Most legal experts today agree that armed humanitarian action that is not authorized by the United Nations is illegal on its face. Nonetheless, there is a widespread belief (which I share) that an unauthorized intervention may be excusable—(not un-)justified, all things considered—if it is based on a just cause and carried out justly. (Consider the analogy of a poor person stealing only what is necessary to feed her family.)

Many observers saw the NATO intervention in Kosovo in these terms. For example, the Independent International Commission on Kosovo described it as "illegal but legitimate."[3] And many had responded similarly two decades earlier when Tanzania invaded Uganda to depose Idi Amin (and then quickly withdrew). The underlying presumption is that good intentions, in certain stringently defined circumstances, constitute a valid excuse for actions that *prima facie* (that is, on their face) are impermissible.

The two-step nature of this evaluation process, however, must be emphasized. Armed humanitarian intervention not authorized by the Security Council is illegal and thus, on its face and by this standard of evaluation, unjustified. The intervener, however, ought to be given the opportunity to rebut this judgment through appeals to other relevant standards. Although the burden of proof lies with the one who commits a *prima facie* illegal act, even in domestic courts, illegal behavior may be excusable.

We also need to recognize the possibility of an international equivalent to "jury nullification"—a situation in which the interests of justice lead to setting aside an otherwise unquestioned legal rule. For example, many critics of international inaction in response to the genocide in Rwanda argued that, when hundreds of thousands of lives could be saved by the judicious application of modest international force, "the law be damned." And when faced with what they saw as imminent genocide in Kosovo just five years later, the leaders of the United States and Britain, the principal proponents of NATO intervention, seem to have acted, at least in part, on the basis of this understanding.

Humanitarian interests and motivations were clearly predominant in the decisions to intervene in Kosovo and East Timor. In the latter case, the international community backed a small, poor, strategically insignificant former Portuguese colony against large, oil-rich, strategically significant Indonesia. Often, humanitarian interventions involve more mixed motives. But even where self-interested motives prevail, considerations of potentially dire consequences can establish a certain kind of justifiability.

I label such interventions (merely) tolerable. Consider, for example, India's intervention in East Pakistan in 1971, which helped to create Bangladesh. Although its action effectively halted genocidal violence against Bengalis, which had forced some 10 million people to flee, India seemed much more concerned with weakening Pakistan, its principal enemy. Similarly, Vietnam's invasion of Cambodia in 1979, ending the Khmer Rouge's four-year reign of terror, seems to have been largely a geopolitical move with a very thin, and not very consistently pursued, humanitarian veneer.

Good things done for the wrong reasons may not be as just as good things done for the right reasons. Improper motives alone, however, do not make an action simply or completely unjustified, particularly when tens or hundreds of thousands of lives are saved. Intentions, consequences, authority, and just cause all need to be factored into a final judgment of justifiability.

Finally, fully "justified" action must be carried out by proper means. More particularly, the means used must be proportional to the ends pursued. Prohibited means must not be used. And the special immunities of civilians (noncombatants) must be respected.

A justified intervention must not cause more suffering than it alleviates. More precisely, there must be a reasonable prospect that, with the actual means used, more suffering is likely to be eliminated than caused. Interveners are responsible for the predictable consequences of their actions, both negative and positive.

Where proportionality focuses on the consequences of the means used, the prohibition of the use of certain means reflects a categorical substantive ("deontological") judgment. Poison gas, for example, cannot legitimately be used, period. Soldiers who surrender must be treated according to the laws of war.

Noncombatant immunity is also a substantive principle of justice in war. Military action must minimize damage to or suffering imposed on civilians. Soldiers, because they are soldiers, are required to take some additional risks in order to minimize certain unintended but predictable injury to civilians. During the Kosovo campaign, for example, bombing was carried out at an altitude above the reach of Serbian anti-aircraft weapons, in order to minimize NATO casualties (and the consequent danger of losing public support). This military strategy led in at least one instance to the destruction of a civilian train on a targeted bridge. Had the plane in question been flying lower, it is likely that the pilot could have identified, and avoided destroying, the train. Most observers agree that this strategic choice involved giving insufficient weight to the principle of noncombatant immunity.

JUSTIFYING ARMED HUMANITARIAN INTERVENTION

The more one considers the issue of justification, the more complicated it becomes. At least four substantive standards—morality, law, order, and justice—are relevant in the case of military intervention on humanitarian grounds. In addition, considerations of authority and means are essential to judgments of justification. Intentions and consequences also may matter. Few actual interventions are unproblematic under all of these standards. And there simply is no agreement about which standard is most important. Neither the law, nor the national interest, nor any other single consideration is *the* essential element of justifiability.

It would be unreasonable, however, to say that only interventions that fully meet all relevant standards of justification are justified. We live in a world of multiple competing values and standards that can be resolved only through acts of judgment, not by appeal to lists of rules. I have argued for a position that gives special weight to considerations of order and law. Creating disorder may, all things considered, be worse than tolerating injustice. Disorder is itself often a cause of injustice. And justice that undermines order is rarely good in the long run for justice, unless that order is very deeply and systematically unjust.

In some severe cases, however, law and even order appropriately give way to the demands of justice. A limited humanitarian intervention exception for genocide allows us to respond to a severe injustice that undermines the moral rationale for sovereignty. It also is unlikely to increase—and may actually decrease—disorder. Thus, I would suggest, it is not surprising that such an exception has become fairly well-established in contemporary international law.

The special priority accorded to order arises from the absence of international government. The special priority accorded to law arises in part from its consensual nature. With few exceptions, international law binds only those who have consented to it—either directly, through a treaty, or indirectly, through the process of customary norm formation. Consensus (especially when it is a "lowest common denominator" consensus) hardly guarantees justice, but it is an important protection against certain kinds of injustice rooted in partisan interests.

Law also merits special weight because of its close association with order— as reflected in the common language of "law and order"—and because it is a domain where considerations of order, justice, power, and interest can be authoritatively adjudicated. Law frequently diverges from justice, but rarely as much as partisan political self-interest does. And when law and order are not equally distant from justice, law is more frequently the closer of the two.

Nonetheless, as I suggested above, sometimes the right course of action, all things considered, is "law be damned"—especially when a major injustice can be prevented at little cost to order. And it must be emphasized that partial justification—excusable or tolerable intervention—is justification (of a sort). Partially justified actions are precisely that: partially justified, not unjustified. And, often, the most appropriate evaluation of armed humanitarian intervention, as with many other kinds of international acts, is that, all things considered, it is (not un-)justified.

THE RESPONSIBILITY TO PROTECT

My argument for a limited right to intervene militarily against genocide and comparable humanitarian crises is a *long* way from supporting a so-called responsibility to protect. This idea has become a common theme in discussions of "armed humanitarianism" since the 2001 report by that name issued by the International Commission on Intervention and State Sovereignty.[4] I want to conclude by arguing that a responsibility to protect can be justified only as an aspirational moral principle.

A responsibility to protect is just that: a responsibility, an obligation, a duty. There is no evidence, however, that states do, in fact, acknowledge such a duty as a matter of either domestic or international law. Likewise, the practice of the UN Security Council shows no support for an obligation to protect the victims of genocide—as the continued suffering in Darfur tragically illustrates. A true responsibility to protect would also raise serious order problems, especially should the victims reside in states that are not failed or failing.

Further difficulties are posed by the idea of protection. Protection against what? A narrow response raises serious problems of morally inappropriate selectivity, while a broad response poses serious conflicts with other, no less important values. What does protection require? Stopping the killing? Establishing a rights-protective regime? Both answers seem both right and wrong. There are also serious issues of cost.

A *right* to military intervention carries with it no obligation. Except in the rarest of circumstances, right-holders are free to choose not to exercise their rights. If one chooses to act, the right provides justification. A right to intervene, however, does not impose a duty to intervene.

Nonetheless, advocacy of a *moral* responsibility to protect—understood as one set of claims that need to be balanced against competing moral, legal, order, and political claims—does push the Security Council and states (appropriately, in my view) toward exercising their right to humanitarian intervention more frequently than they might otherwise choose to do. Such a moral responsibility may even be seen as implicit in the basic framework of international human rights law.

As I noted above, states have created a system of national implementation of international human rights: citizens are presumed to receive their rights from "their own" government. This foundational legal fiction, however, becomes hopelessly implausible in the case of genocide. When this exceptional injustice occurs, the international community arguably has a residual moral responsibility to protect.

Consider the analogy of refugee law. Individuals with a well-founded fear of persecution have a right to asylum. More precisely, they have a right not to be returned to "their own" country (*non-refoulement*). In other words, when the assumption of state provision of human rights becomes perversely implausible, refugees have a claim—in this case, a legal claim—on other states and the international community.

Why not, then, recognize a legal right of victims of genocide to international protection? The principal reason against adopting this legal principle on a larger scale is the much higher costs it would entail. Few refugees with a well-founded fear of persecution are able to get to any particular asylum country and accommodating them usually imposes mostly financial costs that are generally modest. In particular, receiving states are not required to risk the lives of their own citizens or to bear the other costs of war. Furthermore, asylum in no way infringes sovereignty, and any impact on order tends to be positive rather than negative.

Genocide thus poses a true dilemma. Given not only the imperfections of the world of practice but also the competing values of justice, law, order, and politics, intervening on behalf of victims of genocide is almost always likely to be in some ways problematic. But so is *not* intervening.

Why, then, don't we pose the question as "Is failure to intervene militarily against widespread human rights abuses justified?" Because, for better or worse, sovereignty, nonintervention, and the restriction of force to self-defense have been accepted in international law and political practice as a baseline and starting point for discussion. The burden of proof lies with those who would infringe sovereignty, practice military intervention, or use force for reasons other than self-defense. As we have seen, however, this burden can sometimes be met, even in cases of unauthorized intervention by individual states or groups of states.

All things considered, I have argued, a limited right to humanitarian intervention against genocide is a good thing. So is a more frequent and forceful exercise of that right, especially by the UN Security Council. We must be careful, however, not to confuse the exception with the rule. And while lamenting the injustices that are tolerated out of considerations of law, order, and politics, we must remember that these values, too, are important and deserving of respect.[5]

NO: Simon Chesterman: *New York University School of Law Singapore Programme*

Three months after NATO concluded its seventy-eight-day campaign over Kosovo in 1999, Secretary-General Kofi Annan presented his annual report to the United Nations General Assembly.[1] In it, he presented in stark terms the dilemma confronting those who privileged international law over the need to respond to gross and systematic violations of human rights:

> To those for whom the greatest threat to the future of international order is the use of force in the absence of a Security Council mandate, one might ask—not in the context of Kosovo—but in the context of Rwanda: If, in those dark days and hours leading up to the genocide, a coalition of States had been prepared to act in defense of the Tutsi population, but did not receive prompt Council authorization, should such a coalition have stood aside and allowed the horror to unfold?[2]

The hypothetical neatly captured the ethical dilemma as many of the acting states sought to present it. Could international law truly prevent such "humanitarian" intervention?

The problem, however, is that this was not the dilemma faced in the context of Rwanda. Rather than international law restraining a state from acting in defense of the Tutsi population, the problem in 1994 was that no state wanted to intervene at all. When France, hardly a disinterested actor, did decide to intervene, its decision was swiftly approved in a Council resolution (though reference to "impartiality," a two-month time limit, and five abstentions suggested wariness about France's motivation).

The capriciousness of state interest is a theme that runs throughout the troubled history of humanitarian intervention. While much ink has been spilt on the question of the legality of using military force to defend human rights, it is difficult to point to actual cases that demonstrate the significance of international law on this issue. States do not appear to have refrained from acting in situations such as Rwanda (or Kosovo) simply from fear of legal sanction. Nor do any of the incidents frequently touted as examples of "genuine" humanitarian intervention correspond with the principled articulation of such a doctrine by legal scholars.

What, then, is the relevance of international law here? I will attempt to answer this question here by examining the legal status of humanitarian intervention. First, I consider "traditional" international law and arguments that it might entertain a right of humanitarian intervention. Then, I proceed to an examination of how states dealt with the apparent contravention of such traditional norms in relation to Kosovo and the impact this episode has had on subsequent military actions in East Timor and Afghanistan.

Of particular interest here is the relative importance of ethics and international law in the actual decision-making process of states. From a legal perspective, the question of whether the law may be violated is not itself susceptible to legal regulation. For the ethicist, running beneath this discussion is the basic question of whether international law itself demands obedience. If international law per se is suspect, states (or other actors) may be justified in disregarding it, or at least its more offensive provisions. A problem confronting one who would argue such a position is the absence of any situations in which the dilemma has been posed in these terms. It is difficult to point to a case in which international law alone has prevented a state from otherwise acting to protect a foreign population at risk. And, in those incidents usually marshaled as "best cases," factors other than concern for the population were paramount. (An important—but discrete—area of ethical inquiry is whether states and other actors have an *obligation* to act to protect populations at risk. Such action could, of course, take many forms other than military intervention.)[3]

Can ethical demands trump such legal structures? The answer, however unsatisfactory, will be that the question is so unlikely to arise in practice as to be of questionable value for probing in theory.

HUMANITARIAN INTERVENTION AND INTERNATIONAL LAW

The status of humanitarian intervention in international law is, on the face of it, quite simple. The United Nations Charter clearly prohibits the use of force. The renunciation of war must be counted among the greatest achievements of international law in the twentieth century; that the twentieth century was also the bloodiest in history is a sober warning as to the limits of law's power to constrain the behavior of states.

The passage agreed to by states at the San Francisco conference of 1945 was broad in its scope:

> All Members shall refrain in their international relations from the threat or use of force against the territorial integrity or political independence of any state, or in any other manner inconsistent with the Purposes of the United Nations.[4]

This prohibition was tempered by only two exceptions. First, the UN Charter preserved the "inherent right of individual or collective self-defense."[5] Second, the newly established Security Council was granted the power to authorize enforcement actions under Chapter VII. Although this latter species of military action is sometimes considered in the same breath as unilateral humanitarian intervention, Security Council authorization changes the legal questions to which such action gives rise.

Both exceptions provide examples of the inexorable expansion of certain legal rights. Self-defense, for example, has been invoked in ever-wider circumstances to justify actions such as a preemptive strike against a country's nuclear program and the military "response" to a failed assassination attempt in a foreign country. It also provided the initial basis for the extensive U.S. military actions in Afghanistan in late 2001. Security Council–authorized actions have expanded even further, encompassing interventions in Somalia and Haiti in the 1990s that would never have been contemplated by the founders of the United Nations in 1945. Nevertheless, neither exception encompasses humanitarian intervention—meaning the threat or use of armed force in the absence of a Security Council authorization or an invitation from the recognized government, with the object of protecting human rights.

A possible third exception concerns the role of the General Assembly. Interestingly, this possibility first arose at a time when it was feared that a Russian veto would block a resolution authorizing intervention. For some months in 1950, the representative of the USSR boycotted the Security Council in protest against the UN's continuing recognition of the recently defeated Kuomintang regime in China. In his absence, three resolutions were passed that in effect authorized the United States to lead a military operation against North Korea under the UN flag. The return of the Soviet delegate precluded any further Council involvement.

Three months later, at the initiative of Western states, the General Assembly adopted the *Uniting for Peace* resolution, providing that the Assembly would meet to recommend collective measures in situations where the veto prevented the Council from fulfilling its primary responsibility for the maintenance of international peace and security. In the case of a breach of the peace or act of aggression, the measures available were said to include the use of armed force.[6] The legal capacity of the General Assembly to do more than authorize peacekeeping is dubious, but a resolution was passed recommending that all states lend every assistance to the UN action in Korea, and similar measures were adopted again in relation to the Suez crisis in 1956 and in the Congo in 1960. The procedure has subsequently fallen into disuse, however. In particular, such authorization appears not to have been seriously contemplated during the Kosovo crisis—reportedly due to fears that NATO would have been unable to muster the necessary two-thirds majority support of the member states.

At first glance, then, traditional international law does not allow for humanitarian intervention. There have, however, been many attempts to bring such action within the remit of this body of law. These efforts have tended to follow two strategies: either limiting the scope of the prohibition of the use of force, or arguing that a new customary norm has created an additional exception to the prohibition.

The UN Charter prohibits the use of force "against the territorial integrity or political independence of any state, or in any other manner inconsistent with the Purposes of the United Nations." It has sometimes been suggested that certain uses of force might not contravene this provision. For example, one scholar has argued that the U.S. invasion of Panama in 1989 was consistent with the UN Charter because "the United States did not intend to, and has not, colonialized, annexed or incorporated Panama."[7] Such claims had earlier been rejected by another U.S. scholar as requiring an Orwellian construction of the terms "territorial integrity" and "political independence."[8] They also run counter to various statements by the General Assembly and the International Court of Justice concerning the meaning of nonintervention, as well as to the practice of the Security Council, which has condemned and declared illegal unauthorized uses of force even when such action is "temporary." This unconditional stance is consistent with the drafting history of the provision, which— as the U.S. delegate to the San Francisco conference (among others) emphasized—left "no loopholes."

Is it possible, however, that a new norm might have developed to create a separate right of humanitarian intervention? Customary international law allows for the creation of such norms through the evolution of consistent and widespread state practice when accompanied by the necessary *opinio juris*—the belief that a practice is legally obligatory. Some writers have argued that there is evidence of such state practice and *opinio juris*, typically pointing to the Indian action to stop the slaughter in East Pakistan in 1971, Tanzania's actions against Idi Amin in neighboring Uganda in 1978–1979, and Vietnam's intervention in Kampuchea in 1978–1979. In none of these cases, however, were humanitarian concerns invoked as a justification for the use of force. Instead, self-defense was the primary justification offered in each case, while humanitarian (and other) justifications were, at best, secondary considerations.

Such secondary justifications are important, as they may provide evidence of change in the law. As the International Court of Justice has observed:

> The significance for the Court of cases of State conduct *prima facie* inconsistent with the principle of non-intervention lies in the nature of the ground offered as justification. Reliance by a State on a novel right or an unprecedented exception to the principle might, if shared in principle by other States, tend towards a modification of customary international law.[9]

However, the fact that states continued to rely on traditional justifications—most notably self-defense—undermines arguments that the law has changed.

The international response to each of the incidents usually cited is also instructive. In relation to India's action (which led to the creation of Bangladesh), a Soviet veto prevented a U.S.-sponsored resolution calling for a cease-fire and the immediate withdrawal of armed forces. Tanzania's actions were broadly tolerated, and the new regime in Kampala was swiftly recognized, but states that voiced support for the action typically confined their comments to the question of self-defense. Vietnam's successful ouster of the murderous regime of Pol Pot, by contrast, was met with outright hostility. France's representative, for example, stated that

> the notion that because a régime is detestable foreign intervention is justified and forcible overthrow is legitimate is extremely dangerous. That could ultimately jeopardize the very maintenance of international law and order and make the continued existence of various régimes dependent on the judgement of their neighbours.[10]

Similar statements were made by the United Kingdom and Portugal, among others. Once again, only a Soviet veto prevented a resolution calling upon the foreign troops to withdraw; Pol Pot's delegate continued to be recognized as the legitimate representative of Kampuchea (later Cambodia) at the United Nations until 1990. Even if one includes these three "best cases" as evidence of state practice, the absence of accompanying *opinio juris* fatally undermines claims that they marked a change in the law.

More recent examples of allegedly humanitarian intervention without explicit Security Council authorization—such as the no-fly zones in protection of the Kurds in northern Iraq and NATO's intervention in Kosovo—raise slightly different questions. Acting states have often claimed that their actions were undertaken "in support of" Security Council resolutions, though in each case it is clear that the Council did not decide to authorize the use of force. Indeed, it is ironic that states began to claim the need to act when the Security Council faltered in precisely the same decade (the 1990s) that the Council's activities expanded so greatly. In the 1980s, when there was a far stronger argument that paralysis of the UN system demanded self-help, the International Court of Justice considered and rejected arguments that "present defects in international organization" could justify an independent right of intervention.[11]

Interestingly, despite the efforts by some legal scholars to argue for the existence of a right of humanitarian intervention, states themselves have continued to prove very reluctant to embrace such a right—even in defense of their own actions. This hesitancy, which was particularly evident in the case of NATO's intervention in Kosovo, appears to stem in part from a recognition of the dubiousness of the legal argument, but also from a sense that if any such right were embraced, it might well be used by other states in other situations.

Unusually among the NATO states, in October 1998 Germany referred to NATO's threats against the Federal Republic of Yugoslavia as an instance of "humanitarian intervention." The Bundestag affirmed its support for NATO's action—provided that it was made clear that this intervention would not be a precedent for further action.[12] This desire to avoid setting a precedent was reflected in subsequent statements by NATO officials. U.S. Secretary of State Madeleine Albright later stressed that the air strikes were a "unique situation *sui generis* in the region of the Balkans," concluding that it was important "not to overdraw the various lessons that come out of it."[13] British Prime Minister Tony Blair, who had earlier suggested that such interventions might become more routine, subsequently retreated from this position, emphasizing the exceptional nature of the air campaign. This emphasis was consistent with the more sophisticated U.K. statements on the legal issues.

This cautionary trend continued in the proceedings brought by Yugoslavia against ten NATO members before the International Court of Justice. In hearings on provisional measures, Belgium presented the most elaborate legal justification for the action, relying variously on Security Council resolutions, a doctrine of humanitarian intervention (as compatible with Article 2(4) of the UN Charter or based on historical precedent), and the argument of necessity. The United States also emphasized the importance of Security Council resolutions, and, together with four other delegations (Germany, the Netherlands, Spain, and the United Kingdom) made reference to the existence of a "humanitarian catastrophe." This phrase recalled the doctrine of humanitarian intervention, but some care appears to have been taken to avoid invoking the doctrine by name. (The formulation was first used by the United Kingdom as one of a number of justifications for the no-fly zones over Iraq, but no legal pedigree had been established beyond this instance.) In the International Court hearings, four delegations (Canada, France, Italy, and Portugal) did not offer any clear legal justification for intervening, and the court ultimately ruled against Yugoslavia for technical reasons concerning its jurisdiction, never discussing the merits of the case.

Such reticence to embrace a clear legal position was repeated in two major commissions that investigated the question of humanitarian intervention. The Kosovo Commission concluded somewhat confusingly (from an international legal perspective) that NATO's Kosovo intervention was "illegal but legitimate."[14] The International Commission on Intervention and State Sovereignty (ICISS) acknowledged that, as a matter of "political reality," it would be impossible to find consensus on any set of proposals for military intervention that acknowledged the validity of any intervention not authorized by the Security Council or the General Assembly:

> But that may still leave circumstances when the Security Council fails to discharge what this Commission would regard as its responsibility to protect, in a conscience-shocking situation crying out for action. It is a real question in these circumstances where lies the most harm: in the damage to international order if the Security Council is bypassed or in the damage to that order if human beings are slaughtered while the Security Council stands by.[15]

Key elements of the ICISS report, *The Responsibility to Protect*, were adopted by the UN World Summit in 2005, which acknowledged that a state's unwillingness or inability to protect its own population from genocide, war crimes, ethnic cleansing, or crimes against humanity may give rise to an international "responsibility to protect." This responsibility was limited to peaceful means, however, except in extreme circumstances where the provisions of Chapter VII of the UN Charter may be invoked.[16] The report and the UN were carefully silent about what happens if the Council doesn't agree.

What is a lawyer to make of all this? It seems fairly clear that there is no positive right of humanitarian intervention without authorization by the Security Council. Nor does it appear that a coherent principle is emerging to create such a right. Instead, the arguments as presented tend to focus on the nonapplication of international law to particular incidents. Next, let us explore the implications of such an approach to international law, and where it might lead.

THE EXCEPTION AND THE RULE

A State Department official who later became a journalist provides a graphic illustration of the debates between NATO capitals on the question of the legality of the Kosovo intervention:

> There was a series of strained telephone calls between [Secretary of State Madeleine] Albright and [British foreign secretary Robin] Cook, in which he cited problems "with our lawyers" over using force in the absence of UN endorsement. "Get new lawyers," she suggested. But with a push from Prime Minister Tony Blair, the British finally agreed that UN Security Council approval was not legally required.[17]

Such equivocation about the role of international law in decision-making processes is hardly new; the history of international law is to some extent a struggle to raise law above the status of merely one foreign policy justification among others. As indicated earlier, however, most of the acting states appear to have taken some care to present the Kosovo intervention as an exception rather than a rule.

This approach to humanitarian intervention is not uncommon. Various writers have attempted to explain the apparent inconsistency by reference to national legal systems. One scholar likens this approach to the manner in which some legal systems deal with the question of euthanasia:

> [I]n such a case the possibility of abuse is recognized by the legal policy (that the activity is classified as unlawful) but ... in very clear cases the law allows mitigation. The father who smothers his severely abnormal child after several years of devoted attention may not be sent to prison, but he is not immune from prosecution and punishment. In international relations a difficulty arises in that "a discretion not to prosecute" is exercisable by States collectively and by organs of the United Nations, and in the context of *practice* of States, mitigation and acceptance in principle are not always easy to distinguish. However, the euthanasia parallel is useful since it indicates that moderation is allowed for in social systems even when the principle remains firm. Moderation in application does not display a legislative intent to cancel the principle so applied.[18]

Obviously, as the demand for any such violation of an established norm increases, so the need for legal regulation of the "exception" becomes more important. This heightened concern seems to be occurring in the case of euthanasia, as medical advances have increased the discretion of doctors in making end-of-life decisions. In many jurisdictions, continued reliance on the possibility of a homicide charge is now seen as an inadequate legal response to the ethical challenges posed by euthanasia. In relation to humanitarian intervention, however, such demand remains low and it is widely recognized that legal regulation of any exception is unlikely in the short term.

For this reason, an alternative analogy is sometimes used: that of a person acting to prevent domestic violence in circumstances where the police are unwilling or unable to act. This analogy is appealing, as it appears to capture the moral dilemma facing an intervener, but it is of limited value because such acts are typically regulated by reference to the existing authority structures. Under most legal systems, an individual may defend another person against attack and, in certain circumstances, may exercise a limited power of arrest. In the context of humanitarian intervention, this analogy merely begs the question of its legality.

The better view, then, appears to be that humanitarian intervention is illegal but that the international community may, on a case-by-case basis, tolerate the wrong. In such a situation, claims that an intervention was "humanitarian" should be seen not as a legal justification but as a plea in mitigation. This approach has the merit of a basis in international law. In the *Corfu Channel* case after World War II, Britain claimed that an intervention in Albanian territorial waters was justified on the basis that nobody else was prepared to deal with the threat of mines planted in an international strait. The International Court of Justice rejected this argument in unequivocal terms, but held that a declaration of illegality was itself a sufficient remedy for the wrong.[19]

Similarly, after Israel abducted Adolf Eichmann from Argentina to face criminal charges for his role in the Nazi Holocaust, Argentina lodged a complaint with the Security Council, which passed a resolution stating that the sovereignty of Argentina had been infringed and requesting Israel to make "appropriate reparation." Nevertheless, "mindful" of the concern that Eichmann be brought to justice, the Security Council clearly implied that "appropriate reparation" would not involve his physical return to Argentina.[20] The governments of Israel and Argentina subsequently issued a joint communiqué resolving to "view as settled the incident which was caused in the wake of the action of citizens of Israel which violated the basic rights of the State of Argentina."[21]

This approach is also, broadly, consistent with current state practice. During the Kosovo intervention, some critics suggested that the action threatened the stability of the international order—in particular, the relevance of the Security Council as the Charter body with primary responsibility for international peace and security. In fact, the Security Council became integral to resolution of the dispute (despite the bombing of the embassy of one permanent member by another). In resolution 1244 (1999), the Council, acting under Chapter VII, welcomed Yugoslavia's acceptance of the principles set out in the May 6 meeting of G8 foreign ministers and authorized member states and "relevant international organizations" (in other words, NATO) to establish an international security presence in Kosovo. The resolution was passed within hours of the suspension of bombing, and it was prefaced with a half-hearted endorsement of the role of the Council:

> *Bearing in mind* the purposes and principles of the Charter of the United Nations, and the primary responsibility of the Security Council for the maintenance of international peace and security ... [22]

More importantly, resolution 1244 reaffirmed the commitment "of all Member States to the sovereignty and territorial integrity of the Federal Republic of Yugoslavia," even as it called for "substantial autonomy" for Kosovo. The tension between these provisions has left the province in a legal limbo ever since, and continues to complicate the independence it declared in early 2008.

Later in 1999, military action in East Timor affirmed more clearly the continued role of the Security Council, as its authorization was a prerequisite for the Australian-led INTERFET action. (This authorization, in turn, depended on Indonesia's consent to the operation.) Though it was presented at the time as evidence that the international community was prepared to engage in Kosovo-style interventions outside Europe, the political and legal conditions in which this intervention took place were utterly different. The view that the two situations were comparable reflected the troubling assumption that a humanitarian crisis with a military dimension poses a stark choice between doing something and doing nothing—and that "something" means the application of military force.

This narrow view was challenged by UN Secretary-General Kofi Annan, who stressed that "it is important to define intervention as broadly as possible, to include actions along a wide continuum from the most pacific to the most coercive." [23] Similarly, the International Commission on Intervention and State Sovereignty has sought to turn this policy question on its head. Rather than examining at length the right to intervene, it focuses on the responsibility of states to protect vulnerable populations at risk from civil wars, insurgencies, state repression, and state collapse. [24]

Implicit in many arguments for a right of humanitarian intervention is the suggestion that international law currently prevents interventions that should take place. This is simply not true—interventions do not take place because states choose not to undertake them. On the contrary, states have frequently intervened for a great many reasons, some of them more humanitarian than others. For those who seek to establish a law or a general ethical principle to govern humanitarian intervention, a central question must be whether it could work in practice. Do any of the incidents commonly marshaled as examples of humanitarian intervention provide a model that should be followed in future? Should Kosovo, for example, be a model for future negotiations with brutal regimes? If so, why were the terms presented to Serbia prior to the conflict more onerous than those offered after a seventy-eight-day bombing campaign?

Returning to Kofi Annan's challenge to the General Assembly (quoted at the beginning of this essay), the typical problem confronting human rights today is not Kosovo but Rwanda. Put differently, the problem is not the legitimacy of humanitarian intervention, but the overwhelming prevalence of inhumanitarian nonintervention.

CONCLUSION

Following the September 11, 2001, terrorist attacks on New York and Washington, D.C., the United States swiftly sought and received Security Council endorsement of its position that these acts constituted an attack on the United States and that action taken in self-defense against "those responsible for aiding, supporting or harboring the perpetrators, organizers and sponsors of these acts" was justified.[25] Self-defense does not require any form of authorization (though measures taken should be "immediately reported" to the Council), but the fact that the United Nations was involved so quickly in a crisis was widely seen as a welcome counterpoint to the unilateralist impulses of the Bush administration.

Nevertheless, the decision to seek Security Council approval also reflected a troubling trend through the 1990s. Military action under its auspices has taken place only when circumstances coincided with the national interests of a state that was prepared to act, thus placing the Council in danger of becoming a kind of "law-laundering service."[26] Such a position downgrades the importance of Security Council authorization to the point that it may be seen as a policy justification rather than a matter of legal significance. A consequence of this diminished role is that, when authorization is not forthcoming, a state or group of states will feel less restrained from acting unilaterally. And this possibility represents a fundamental challenge to the international order established at the conclusion of World War II, in which the interests of the powerful would be balanced through the exercise (real or threatened) of the Council veto.

In the context of humanitarian intervention, it was widely hoped that such a departure from traditional conceptions of sovereignty and international law would privilege ethics over states rights. In fact, as we have seen, humanitarian intervention has long had a troubled relationship to the question of national interest. Many attempts by scholars to formulate a doctrine of humanitarian intervention require that an acting state be disinterested (or "relatively disinterested"). By contrast, in one of the few articulations of such a doctrine by a political leader, Prime Minister Blair proposed his own criteria—one of which was whether "we" had national interests involved.[27]

The war on terror has reduced the probability of humanitarian interventions in the short term, but it has also raised the troubling prospect of more extensive military adventures being undertaken without clear legal justification. In particular, President Bush's 2002 State of the Union speech, in which he referred to an "axis of evil," suggested a preparedness to use ethical arguments (and absolute ethical statements) as a substitute for legal—or, it might be argued, rational—justification.

All such developments should be treated with great caution. A right of humanitarian intervention depends on one's acceptance of the proposition that humanitarian ends justify military means. As the history of this doctrine shows, the ends are never so clear and the means are rarely so closely bound to them. In such a situation where there is no ideal, where Kosovo presents the imperfect model (and lingers today as a testament to NATO's imperfect victory), it is better to hold that humanitarian intervention remains both illegal and morally suspect, but that arguments can be made on a case-by-case basis that, in an imperfect world, international order may yet survive the wrong.

climate change and the environment

Can International Regimes Be Effective Means to Restrain Carbon Emissions?

YES: Ruth Greenspan Bell, *World Resources Institute*
NO: Samuel Thernstrom, *American Enterprise Institute*

It may come as a surprise that it has been only twenty years since the prospect of climate change—now widely acknowledged both as a global problem and as one that is caused largely by the recent, and increasing, impact of human activity—was first popularized in the U.S. media and brought to the broader public's attention. James Hansen, a NASA scientist testifying before Congress during the very hot summer of 1988—and in a deliberately overheated hearing room—presented data showing the relationship between "greenhouse gases" and increasing global temperatures, as well as projections indicating that further increases could lead to substantial "global warming," with significant ecological impacts.

While scientific data supporting these claims were at least eighty years old, media coverage of climate change began to increase significantly only after this startling exposure. Since then, a steadily building scientific consensus maintains that humans—through greenhouse gas emissions as well as deforestation and other land-use changes—have caused increasing global temperatures and that unabated fossil-fuel consumption will have profound environmental impacts across the globe in the future. The most recent manifestation is the Intergovernmental Panel on Climate Change (IPCC) report that termed anthropogenic climate change unequivocal. Indeed, the issue of climate change has so increased in prominence worldwide that, in November 2007, UN Secretary-General Ban Ki-moon called it "the defining challenge of our age."

The belated recognition of climate change heralded both a new and important environmental problem and one that is qualitatively different from others: the fact that humans could alter the entire earth's climate was far different from pollutant-specific contaminants that had constituted most environmental perils to date. But, although recognition of a problem may be a necessary condition for arousing concern, it is far from sufficient as a spur to action. Part of the problem of generating a more appropriate response to this looming disaster stems from the paradox known as the "tragedy of the commons": when costs are spread widely and benefits concentrated locally, the incentive of individuals (or nations) is to continue to overproduce/-pollute. In terms of global warming, each rational-actor individual nation seeks to encourage all other nations to restrict their total greenhouse-gas emissions—to the benefit of all—while it continues to enjoy the economic advantages (and only a fraction of the costs) of its own unabated emissions. Thus, in the absence of a concerted effort of some kind, individual incentives lead to ruinous collective behavior.

A further difficulty inhibiting effective management of climate change stems from the current and future distribution of carbon emissions. As Figure 1 indicates, total carbon emissions are highest in OECD nations, while Figure 2 shows that although the United States continues to be the leading producer of CO_2, China is quickly catching up and many nations in the developing world are expanding their output considerably. This two-sided dynamic presents twin problems. First, the high-producers have economies that heavily depend on fossil-fuel consumption, so change will be costly. Second, developing nations resent pressures placed on them to restrict carbon emissions by the wealthy West, in full recognition that those older economies were built and enriched by burning petroleum, coal, and other fossil fuels.

Yet another driving force behind global warming is the worldwide growth not only in economic output but in population as well—almost all of it emerging in the developing world. Thus, the twin impacts of rising populations and quickly growing economies produce strong incentives to continue to produce greenhouse gases. These are powerful incentives to overcome, and international institutions lack the enforcement capabilities to compel behavioral changes. While OECD nations' share of world CO_2 emissions fell in the decades since 1990, emissions shares in East and South Asia are rising quickly. To make things worse, much of the current population growth is occurring among the middle classes of India and China, many of whom aspire to consumer lifestyles akin to those in the United States.

International institutions have enjoyed some success in addressing environmental problems, by adopting initiatives such as the Montreal Protocol limiting ozone-producing gases. But the stakes in climate change are considerably

Figure 1

Total Carbon Dioxide Emissions by Region, 1990 and 2004

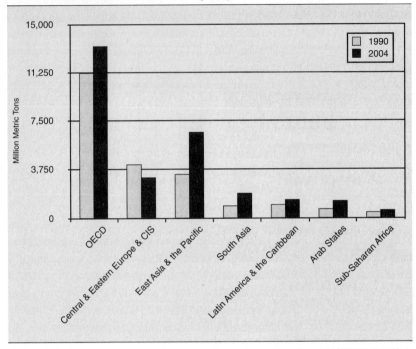

Source: United Nations Development Programme, *Human Development Report 2007/2008* (New York: Oxford University Press, 2007), 69.

higher and the number of producers far greater than can be addressed by such narrow-focused efforts, while the variety of sources—both natural and man-made—greatly complicates efforts to address the fundamental causes of global climate change. There are many possible technical paths to improving matters—from carbon sequestration to nuclear power to alternative vehicle fuels—yet the challenges are not simply technical; they involve requiring a sufficient number of nations to reduce carbon emissions to a significant degree in a verifiable manner.

The two articles that follow provide differing perspectives on the likelihood of achieving meaningful results through international institutions. Ruth Greenspan Bell argues that international institutions can be effective only if they recognize the specific cultural, political, and institutional adjustments that nations will be required to make to adapt to emissions changes. Samuel Thernstrom also emphasizes national differences that must be considered in implement-

Figure 2

Top Twenty Carbon Dioxide Emitters, 1990 and 2004

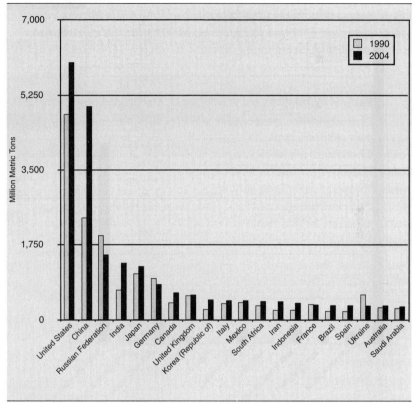

Source: United Nations Development Programme, *Human Development Report 2007/2008* (New York: Oxford University Press, 2007), 69.

ing climate-change policy; because some nations stand to lose (or even gain) from climate change, and because compliance with any international agreement is voluntary, climate-change policy must respect national differences if it is to be effective.

Discussion Questions

1. Is climate change a problem that is best addressed on a global, national, or subnational level? Why?

2. What policies can governments implement to address climate change? How will these policies impact different stakeholders? What are the obstacles to implementing these policies?
3. Who is responsible for climate change? Who bears the responsibility to stop it? What role should industrial nations have? What about developing nations?
4. What does Ruth Greenspan Bell propose as a new and complementary approach to ensuring the effectiveness of international regimes for curbing greenhouse-gas emissions? What are the characteristics of her proposal? Do you agree with her approach?
5. What reasons does Samuel Thernstrom cite to explain why past international efforts to curb carbon emissions, particularly the Kyoto Protocol, have failed? What does he propose for the future?

YES: Ruth Greenspan Bell, *World Resources Institute*

> Those who hope to persuade a nation to exert itself need to
> remind their country of what it can take pride
> in as well as what it should be ashamed of.
>
> Richard Rorty, *Achieving Our Country* (1998)

Elaborate negotiations to date in the climate world have hammered out the architecture of emissions reductions: the Kyoto Protocol sets emissions caps for developed countries and allows those countries to invest in, and get credit for, emissions reductions in the developing world to achieve the overall levels of reductions required by the caps. Future UN climate negotiations will attempt to put into place the much deeper cuts needed to address what the EU's environment commissioner has characterized as the "alarming" global warming projections of the Intergovernmental Panel on Climate Change.

The challenges are to establish rules and processes that can work in the multiple sources at play and, most important, to achieve genuine carbon reductions. A global process typically seeks to establish one set of rules for all or at least for substantial groupings of countries. In reality, however, differences between various countries' willingness and capacity to make reductions are unavoidable. The United States and Western Europe, as long-standing carbon emitters and fully developed economies, stand in a different position than, for example, India and China, whose emissions are rising sharply but whose economies are, relatively, just starting to take off. The potential for paralysis becomes painfully evident when some in the United States argue that this country should not enact legislation or reduce its emissions until it has assurances that China and India have acted, while China and India argue that the United States must act first, in view of its historical contribution.

Any effective global scheme must reconcile the wide variety of national interests and claims in order to produce a set of undertakings that are adequate to address the problem. And further, it must reflect differences in national cultures and institutional capacities for implementing these undertakings. Although the issue of emissions reduction is commonly formulated as a debate over whether it is fair to essentially hold all countries to the same mitigation goals and standards, the real problem is the varied willingness and capacity of countries to adopt and implement climate change measures. One size does not fit all in the global regulatory situation.

The limited efficacy of the Kyoto Protocol, added to the diversity of interests and the lack of a mechanism whereby a reluctant nation can be coerced into an arrangement over its objection, puts the success of future efforts in doubt. This uncertainty is particularly poignant in the context of the rapidly moving climate science, which argues for emissions reductions sooner rather than later.

The urgency of finding new directions suggests the need for a second, complementary enterprise—what might be called a "ground-up" effort. This attempt to develop new policy options would be conducted by an interdisciplinary team or teams that include specialists with deep knowledge of the traditions and cultures—that is, the beliefs, practices, and institutions that condition collective decisions and actions in a society—of the key countries, as well as their vulnerability to climate change. Instead of assuming that effective incentives and policy instruments are identical in all cultures, this effort would try to formulate a different kind of vocabulary to engage the handful of growing greenhouse-gas emitters, such as India and China, as well as countries that contribute to climate change through deforestation, such as Indonesia and Brazil. This effort would focus on tailoring appeals to national and local interests, country-by-country, and on harnessing existing cultural values and institutions in the handful of key countries that must rise to the climate challenge, if global solutions are to be reached. The inquiry would proceed on two levels: (1) tailored approaches to bring key developing nations to participate meaningfully in climate-change mitigation; and (2) options for effective implementation of policy goals within each of these nations. (I will refer to these as level-1 and level-2 inquiries, respectively.)

Although at this stage I cannot say what the results of this inquiry would be, I can discuss why such a rethinking is necessary, as well as describing the theory behind this venture and the process that I believe would be necessary to advance it.

THE THEORY AND PRACTICE OF THE CURRENT FRAMEWORK FOR GLOBAL EMISSIONS REDUCTION

Current proposals for curbing carbon dioxide emissions start with the reasonable assumption that the first step toward fighting climate change is to make the issue a global priority. This is the achievement of the UN Framework Convention on Climate Change, which was instituted in 1994, and its controversial Kyoto Protocol, which took effect after Russia ratified it in 2005. In the protocol, most industrialized nations agreed to strive between 2008 and 2012 to reduce greenhouse-gas emissions to levels below those of 1990.[1] Although the Kyoto signatories have just entered the 2008–2012 "commitment" period, it is not clear whether their commitments will yield significant results.

Having agreed to mandatory emissions reductions, each participating developed country is required, under the existing plan, to "implement domestic policies and measures in accordance with its national circumstances." However, the protocol gives each country broad discretion in how it achieves its assigned reduction.[2] Countries with reduction commitments may "participate in emissions trading for purposes of fulfilling their commitments," but emissions trading is to be "supplemental to domestic actions."

The protocol authorizes trading generally among participating industrialized countries (Article 17) and also a form of project-by-project trading in Joint Implementation (Article 6), which allows "donor" countries to invest in pollution-abatement measures in "host" countries in return for "credits" they can use to meet their own pollution-abatement targets. The protocol's Clean Development Mechanism (CDM; Article 12) facilitates trading with the developing world. This process works in the same way as the Joint Implementation mechanism, except that the trade is between an industrialized country with a reduction target and a developing country that has no target. Article 12 of the protocol further requires that the CDM's project-based credit-generating reductions "are additional to any that would occur in the absence of the ... project activity."

These trading mechanisms reflect a strong desire to reduce the costs of achieving reductions within and among industrialized (Annex I) nations (on the assumption that reductions are cheaper in the developing world) and to provide participation inducements to developing nations. These mechanisms are also intended to incentivize climate-friendly technological change and to aid in the transfer of technological capacity from developed to developing countries. But, as I will explore later, there are serious questions about whether the CDM is adequate to further the protocol's objectives. From a theoretical perspective, even proponents of market-based solutions to climate change have expressed doubts about the CDM's ability to assure net emissions reductions in the absence of total emissions caps for the host country; they cite concerns over "cross-project leakage" and the perverse effects of subsidies for abatement.[3]

The early experience with CDM confirms questions about its integrity and effectiveness. In addition, even among developed nations that are subject to emissions caps agreed to under the Kyoto Protocol, trading to date has surfaced a number of problems, including overly generous allocations of credits to greenhouse-gas emitters and price volatility in emissions credits.

Market-based systems for emissions control have some precedent in domestic programs within the United States, most notably the cap-and-trade system for sulfur dioxide emissions that was established under the 1990 amendments to the U.S. Clean Air Act; ramping this experience up to global proportions and applying it outside the U.S. context was a Kyoto innovation. Looking forward, some commentators have argued for cap-and-trade as the universal instrument of choice for implementation of climate-change policy, but others have questioned the viability of a global cap-and-trade system of the scale and complexity required to address climate change.[4]

As the future of the Kyoto Protocol is debated, it becomes necessary to ask, if the CDM is not the most effective way to secure the participation and enhance the capacity of developing nations, how shall we go about developing alternative means for this purpose? Second, as future iterations of the Kyoto Protocol are developed—and, hopefully, are extended to developing nations—how can we expand the inventory of implementing mechanisms to include tools more closely tailored to the cultures and institutional capacities of the new participants?

On the second question (a level-2 inquiry), U.S.-style environmental trading is not common outside the United States, and evidence suggests that it faces particular difficulties in developing countries. Independent of the Kyoto Protocol, there have been numerous efforts to stimulate domestic trading experiments in countries such as China and India, but these efforts, at best, achieved only a handful of administratively orchestrated domestic transactions between carefully selected polluters. Few of these countries have the proven experience and skills to deliver the goods—to actually cap pollution so that emissions credits can function, as intended, as part of a system of controls.[5] And some, especially economies transitioning into a freer role for markets, lack the legal and bureaucratic institutions to manage or enforce exchanges of complex intangible property rights such as polluted air escaping from a factory. The lack of well-developed regulatory and enforcement capacity in these countries limits their ability to implement cap-and-trade or other sophisticated regulatory schemes, or, indeed, more traditional means of controlling pollution.[6] These limitations are essential to consider in devising international environmental agreements, where compliance and enforceability, even among developed nations, has long been the Achilles' heel.

On the first question (a level-1 inquiry), one might expect that enforcement concerns would be less intense for multiparty CDM projects, which require involvement by a developed as well as a developing country and are approved and overseen by a committee representing the parties to the protocol. Despite safeguards, however, recent reports cast doubt on the integrity of some of these projects. Moreover, it is not clear that CDM is accomplishing its core purpose of engaging developing countries in the enterprise of controlling climate change and providing the capacity and the incentives for more robust involvement in future iterations of the Kyoto agreement. Financial inducements flowing from developed nations may be necessary to engage developing countries, but the particular form and content of those inducements are likely to be critical to their effectiveness. It is not clear that the payments being made under CDM are sending effective signals.

LIMITATIONS OF CDM TO OBTAIN MEANINGFUL REDUCTIONS IN DEVELOPING NATIONS

As noted, the Kyoto Protocol's CDM embodies the idea that the promise of profits and funding—the opportunity to earn money for reducing carbon emissions—is the single most important incentive to stimulate emissions reductions in developing nations. Its prominence in this role raises several questions. Does a single incentive work the same in each country, and do incentives—especially those that involve considerable amounts of money—operate independent of policing institutions and infrastructure? What about the possibility of corruption, accounting failures, or strategic behavior not consistent with policy goals, and how those lapses might affect the actual reductions achieved? And most critically, from my point of view, what other incentives or approaches exist, country-by-country, that might better achieve the goals of reducing greenhouse-gas emissions?

Now, a series of reports examining specific transactions are questioning the fundamental arrangement. An early report from India's Center for Science and the Environment (CSE) examined two transactions pursuant to the CDM that involved Indian companies and European governments. The CSE report cast serious doubt on the efficacy and integrity of the transactions. It concluded that certain conditions for the transactions had not been met, despite being specified in the transactions' design document; that it was impossible to determine whether the transactions met other standards, because their terms were not transparent; and that Indian authorities seemed to have approved the projects not on their merit, but on the basis of the prestige of the consultant who validated them. The CSE questioned whether these transactions could honestly be said to achieve either the CDM objectives or India's pollution-reduction goals.[7]

Stanford Law School professor Michael Wara examined CDM projects in China, finding that CDM has led to "widespread strategic behavior" in implementation.[8] One group of CDM projects that Wara studied involved incineration of HFC-23, a greenhouse gas produced during the manufacture of the refrigerant HFC-22, which is used in the growing Chinese market for air-conditioning. Wara found that these purchased reductions came at a huge cost—approximately forty times the actual cost of eliminating the emissions. Moreover, he found evidence that the excessive payments for these reductions stimulated increased production by HFC-22 plants that stood to gain from

CDM funding. In another group of CDM projects, involving construction of relatively efficient gas-fired electricity-generating facilities, Wara found a risk that credits would be issued and sold for facilities that would have occurred anyway. Project proponents have strong incentives to game the system, and international regulators, reviewing projects on a case-by-case basis, have difficulty in effectively policing it. The result is excessive payments for reductions that may represent little or no net progress toward achieving climate-change policy goals.

ARE THERE ALTERNATIVES THAT MIGHT IMPROVE THE EFFECTIVENESS OF DEVELOPING NATION PARTICIPATION?

CDM projects are concentrated in developing countries, whose effective participation will be crucial to reducing greenhouse-gas emissions. China, India, Brazil, and South Korea together currently collect four-fifths of the payments under CDM, and China alone collects almost half. These CDM projects, however, have not effectively engaged these countries in pursuit of meaningful climate-change goals and strategies. Much of the discussion about the future of a global response to climate change to date has centered on how to refine and make more effective the existing trading mechanisms, on the assumption that the fault is in the design rather than in the selection of the instrument. But I have considerable doubts about whether refining the existing Kyoto mechanisms, including CDM and interparty trading, should be the sole focus of future activities. In view of the evidence to date, I believe that trading can work in some circumstances and in some countries but not necessarily in all circumstances and in all countries. The same might be said of other instruments (such as a carbon tax) that have been advanced as global measures, as well as of conventional regulatory measures. These instruments are all designed to provide incentives for desired behavior. But their effectiveness will depend on the strength of different incentives in different countries and the effective communication of those incentives through existing institutions.

How do we determine what kind of program can actually work and where? Since the groundbreaking United Nations Stockholm Conference on the Human Environment in 1972 put environmental protection on the global agenda, countries around the world have tried numerous approaches to managing pollution and conserving natural resources, largely inspired by the latest developments in the West, only the latest of which have been market-based instruments and emissions trading.

Inspired by developments in the United States in the late 1960s, and particularly the National Environmental Policy Act (NEPA) of 1970,[9] there was an intense period of law-drafting and creation of formal institutions in developing countries to combat pollution. Few of these efforts have borne much tangible fruit. We now know that writing laws is, at best, a first step. Many of the countries who did so do not come from a tradition of resolving societal challenges through law or may have traditions of rule by law rather than rule of law.[10] Similarly, many of the formal institutions that were created—for example, environment ministries that would manage pollution-control efforts or advocate for the environmental perspective within their governments—have proven to be paper tigers, wielding little power even within their own governments, much less when faced with the challenge of taming domestic industry. Finally, starting in the early 1990s, there were substantial efforts toward instituting emissions-trading programs, but none of these efforts have resulted in much more than carefully orchestrated demonstration projects.[11]

If experience with previous pollution-control efforts and the Kyoto trading regime suggest that we do not yet have in hand all the tools we need, where should we be placing our efforts? Some clues, arguably, may be found in a handful of unique programs or efforts that have been effective in specific countries.

One of the most interesting examples involving pollution control is the Supreme Court of India's supervised transition that moved highly polluting industries in Delhi out of the center city and required commercial vehicles to power their vehicles with compressed natural gas (CNG). Although the process, which was initiated by a "public interest" lawsuit somewhat modeled on similar litigation in the United States, took almost twenty years, it resulted in measurably cleaner air in Delhi, one of the most polluted cities on the globe, and one where formal environmental institutions and law have been weak.[12]

I do not suggest that India has solved the puzzle of environmental protection in the developing world. Not many countries could replicate the factors at play—including a high degree of NGO involvement, public concern stoked from time to time by those NGOs, and the concentrated attention of a few dedicated justices of the court. The Delhi success, also, cannot be separated from institutional conditions in India—particularly, a lively and free press and the relative independence of and respect paid to the Supreme Court. These same factors, moreover, have not proved adequate to deal with other massive problems, such as delivering clean water to the residents of Delhi.

The point I take is that the Delhi results came about through a process of essentially local trial and error, built on a foundation of local institutions, practices, and knowledge, and pushed along at critical times by a domestic institution (the Supreme Court). While unique to India in ways already suggested, this example suggests the potential importance of local and national institutions, practices, and knowledge in managing climate change.

The Delhi case involved a matter of mostly local environmental significance, but other examples suggest the usefulness of engaging local institutions in addressing issues of global significance, such as biodiversity. Daniel Janzen, an ecologist from the United States, worked with the government of Costa Rica and with the local communities that would be affected by biodiversity protection to make the Guanacaste National Park (part of Guanacaste Conservation Area), a collaborative enterprise that offered training and employment to local residents as park police or parataxonomists and, more generally, engaged local stakeholders to help shape the project. By engaging directly with the aspirations and values of these residents, Janzen was able to turn potential local resistance into support and thus to greatly improve the likelihood that the park would succeed and thrive in the future.[13]

Again, this experience is indicative, not a template. The Guanacaste Park experience turned significantly on the experience and skill of one individual, was focused on a particular natural resource around which national and local support could be galvanized, and took place in a stable, largely rule of law–driven country. The more diffuse causes and effects of climate change may make this approach an unlikely precedent. But Janzen's willingness to work with national and local groups in the developing nation—to provide status, economic advancement, and other benefits in terms meaningful to them— could offer clues to more tailored strategies both for getting the buy-in of developing nations to mitigate climate change and for ensuring that that buy-in will produce results on a sustainable basis.

How does this evidence help us in the case of climate change, where the world is struggling to establish an architecture within which all countries can work and then, through it, to stimulate on-the-ground actions to reduce greenhouse-gas emissions in some of the most challenging parts of the globe?

It would be well for policymakers to consider how the specific societies in question solve problems within their own traditions and cultures, using the tools available to them today, not years in the future. This inquiry would be grounded in the principle that climate change is quintessentially a global problem whose solution must be effective globally, but that a solution may be made possible only by significantly tailoring its components to the circumstances of the key participants. Instead of offering inducements and ways of doing business that are closely associated with how business culture works in the United States and Western Europe, and with the institutions that support those approaches (particularly governance and oversight bodies), the approach I propose would seek to understand local interests and ways of doing business and of problem-solving and policy development, and to develop a wide range or menu of climate-control strategies customized to the needs, traditions, and institutional resources of the governments that must adopt and implement them.

To meet this challenge in very practical ways, it is useful to borrow from political scientist Charles Lindblom's theory of "muddling through," with a close eye to the effectiveness of the muddling.[14] Lindblom spoke of *incrementalism*— the recognition that, under most circumstances, policy change is evolutionary rather than revolutionary. *Adaptive management* refines that approach in the management of complex human-natural systems, such as the climate system, and features a process of learning-while-doing based on trial, monitoring, and feedback. *Historical ecology* examines the relationship between particular societies and their natural environments, with the understanding these connections and the local characteristics that have adapted to inevitable changes carry information about workable solutions to environmental uncertainty and to sustainability. It could be useful, as well, to consider other values— perhaps religious or cultural—or regional ecosystem management approaches that might motivate and shape local or regional solutions to reducing carbon emissions.

The approach I suggest would be pragmatic, looking for what might work in place, and pluralistic, entertaining diverse disciplinary and theoretical perspectives. It would document options with relevant data, and it would subject options to critical analysis from multiple perspectives to assess their likely effectiveness.

To date, climate policy has been largely devised by lawyers, economists, policy experts, and skilled diplomats. The skills of all of those experts will continue to be important, but in order to gain the unique insights necessary to find a path forward for greenhouse-gas reductions, I propose to add specialists who have spent their careers developing a deep understanding of specific cultures and traditions. These specialists include cultural anthropologists, social psychologists, political scientists, and internationalists who bring evidence of how societies respond when confronted with serious challenges. Climatologists and ecologists could help to interpret and translate information on the effects of climate change on nations or regions.

The approach I suggest is consistent with past and current thinking in such practical venues as the U.S. Department of Defense. The Pentagon historically has sought advice from outside the defense community in devising policies to manage conflict and to design territorial occupations—for example, consulting prominent anthropologists and sociologists to develop a plan for the occupation of Japan following World War II—and it is reported to have renewed this recognition of the importance of understanding how societies actually function in developing strategies for current conflict and counterinsurgency, following the Iraqi experience.[15] The challenge is to learn how these principles can be used in a climate or environmental context.

Obviously, this is a novel and untested approach in the climate policy world. In part because of this, and in part because at this stage, only a few countries are essential for reducing greenhouse-gas emissions, it would be strategically wise to focus only on the handful of countries that are contributing the largest growth in greenhouse-gas emissions—most likely India, China, Indonesia, and Brazil. A research team would likely be formed around each key country— including, critically, in-country partners in each of the key countries for which specific policies were to be developed.

Several closely intertwined questions must be sorted out. First, what kinds of information, appeals, or inducements might be particularly effective to get each of these nations "on board"? Although one might expect that each nation's decision on whether and at what level to participate in efforts to address climate change would turn on its own interest, we should remember that how that interest is defined or understood is culturally related. For example, the negative net benefits of the Kyoto Protocol indicated by some cost-benefit studies might suggest that it was not in the interests of developed nations to join the protocol.[16] But many of these nations did join; assuming that they did not act blindly, their participation may simply have evidenced an assessment of national interest that was not limited to cost-benefit justification. Concern for future generations, fairness to those less well-off, or other social values may have played a role.

A second, two-part question, closely related to the first, is what goals would it be reasonable and fair to encourage these nations to adopt, and could those goals be set without immediately jumping again into the virtually unsolvable problems of relative contribution? This difficulty would argue for developing notions of fairness from the ground up, so to speak, rather than trying to craft one notion from the top down.

Finally, what instruments or institutional arrangements would likely be effective in moving toward those goals? Analysts have identified a range of policy instruments for addressing environmental issues—including taxes and subsidies, cap-and-trade, traditional regulation, and information and social influence. In the climate-change context, the consideration of instruments takes place on at least two levels: (1) what instruments might be best at a global level to achieve cost-effective reductions in greenhouse-gas emissions and to induce participation by developing nations, and (2) what instruments might be best within individual nations to ensure that targets are met? Most of the debate has been, and will likely continue to be, focused on the first level. But research should also attend to the relatively neglected second level in order to understand, given the institutions and other cultural resources of each of the key nations, how climate goals can best be realized.

These two inquiries are closely related. As the Costa Rica example suggests, a plan for carrying out environmental goals that is consistent with a country's institutions and the interests and values of its citizens can also make that country more likely to adopt those goals in the first place. Understanding how climate-change goals might be successfully implemented in a country could help to structure incentives for the country's participation and establish the terms of that participation.

WHAT IS THE ENDPOINT OF THIS EFFORT?

My answer to the question, "Can international regimes be effective means to restrain carbon emissions," is yes. But that yes carries the important qualification that, if they are to be effective across the wide range of institutional settings in countries around the globe, those regimes must be responsive to differing local and national conditions.

This requirement suggests efforts to complement the ongoing UN climate-change initiative. Coordination and institution-building at the global level are essential to a stable and effective response to climate change over the long term. If fruitful, the additional effort recommended here will help to integrate negotiations and oversight at the global level with national participation and implementation. It will provide a wider range of policy options to engage the key countries of the developing world than is currently the case. And it will address the difficult issues of institutional capacity and enforcement, which have largely escaped notice yet are essential to constructive participation.

This effort, whether located within a revitalized U.S. government committed to climate goals under new leadership, or generated from a combination of nongovernmental and university efforts, can contribute to several tracks rather than one track in international negotiations, or alongside international negotiations, as well as bilateral and regional efforts. In the end, the matter of whether it is fair to essentially hold all countries globally to the same mitigation goals and standards is an unsolvable problem, undue attention to which can only delay the achievement of actual reductions in all places contributing to the climate crisis. Parallel or complementary negotiations are consistent with the objective of capturing notions of fairness and participation from the ground up, as well as the increasing need to speed the global negotiating process.

NO: Samuel Thernstrom, *American Enterprise Institute*

We stand at an unusual junction in climate policy. New national and international climate policies are widely expected. Congress is likely to enact some national limit on greenhouse-gas emissions in 2009 or 2010; international negotiators are intent on completing work in 2009 on a successor to the Kyoto Protocol, which is due to expire in 2012. Among environmental advocates, there is a sense that action is at hand at last. Momentum toward more ambitious national and international action has never been higher—yet success seems as far from our grasp as ever.

Policymakers have struggled to find ways to curtail greenhouse-gas emissions for twenty years, with little to show for their efforts. The Kyoto Protocol has had a negligible effect on global emissions—its targets were unpalatable for the United States, undemanding for energy-inefficient Russia, and impractical for the many countries that are missing them, while also being far too modest to have a meaningful effect on warming—yet the world seems more intent on replicating Kyoto's failures than on learning from them. Policymakers are eager to take more aggressive action to cut emissions, but there is as much reason as ever to doubt the prospects for success, given the scale and speed of the reductions that would be needed, according to many scientists, to prevent significant warming.

Despite two decades of debate, the core questions of climate policy remain unresolved: How much, and how quickly, should each nation cut its emissions if we are to prevent significant warming? Is there a fair and feasible way of allocating emissions-reduction obligations among all nations—and enforcing those terms? Can differing national interests be harmonized in a single global system? These critical questions were answered unsatisfactorily in Kyoto, as evidenced by the poor results, and yet there is relatively little evidence of substantially different thinking in the current negotiations for a successor treaty.

Casual observers of the issue might well assume that the basic direction of U.S. and international policy is very clear, given how single-minded the public debate has been. Attention is almost exclusively focused on consideration of various "cap-and-trade" proposals modeled on the Kyoto approach. Under such a system, countries commit to reducing emissions to a certain level over a period of time, and they are given flexibility in how those reductions are achieved.[1] In theory, this is an economically efficient method of achieving emissions reductions; in practice, the Kyoto experience with emissions trading has been an abysmal failure so far. Its failure has done little to lessen policy-makers' enthusiasm for this approach, however, since it allows governments to distribute billions of dollars worth of permits to favored constituencies while concealing from voters the total cost of compliance.

Environmental activists, European governments, and most members of the Democratic majority in Congress would like to extend the Kyoto Protocol in the next commitment period to include additional countries—chiefly, of course, the United States, which declined to ratify it. The United States has consistently favored including more countries in any agreement—in particular, major devel-oping world economies such as China and India—and that is not likely to change in the Obama administration. But whether those countries can be persuaded to participate—and under what terms—we can only imagine; whether the Senate will ratify a treaty that does not include them is even more uncertain.

How far to extend the reach of the treaty, and on what terms, remain highly contentious questions. While some would be satisfied with a treaty that included all major global economies, others argue for a more radical goal: universal—and, ideally, equal—participation in emissions reductions. Climate change is a global problem, the reasoning goes, so each country should contribute equally to solving it. Any country that avoids emissions-reduction obligations could potentially become a haven for energy-intensive industries seeking to circum-vent emissions limits. Countries could benefit economically by eschewing emissions limits while enjoying the benefits of the sacrifice of others—the clas-sic "free rider" problem. An equal standard for all countries would, therefore, be the fairest and most effective approach.

In fact, universal participation in any emissions-reduction effort is critical to its success. As William Nordhaus, one of the leading economists studying cli-mate change, has written,

> Our modeling results point to the importance of near-universal participa-tion programs to reduce greenhouse gases. Because of the structure of the costs of abatement, with marginal costs being very low for the initial reductions but rising sharply for higher reductions, there are substantial excess costs if the preponderance of sectors and countries are not fully included. We preliminarily estimate that a participation rate of 50 percent, as compared with 100 percent, will impose an abatement-cost penalty of 250 percent. Even with the participation of the top 15 countries and regions, consisting of three-quarters of world emissions, we estimate that the cost penalty is about 70 percent.[2]

While the argument in favor of universal participation in emissions limits has a theoretical logic and a certain emotional appeal, it would be a poor basis for negotiating a meaningful climate treaty that all nations might actually accept and implement. There is no way to compel participation—or adherence to—such a treaty; each nation must choose to join voluntarily. Countries have widely differing national interests, abilities, and preferences when it comes to the broad range of issues related to climate policy. While climate change is, indeed, a global concern, it does not have equal implications for all countries. Some countries stand to lose much more than others; some countries, such as China and Russia, might even benefit from a warming climate.[3] This differential impact has profound implications for the prospects of any future global agreement: countries that have different material interests at stake are unlikely to agree to make identical efforts to address the problem. There is a wealth of data to illustrate this point, but to pick just one key metric, consider the differences in the amount of economic damage that the countries and regions listed in Table 1 expect to suffer, as indicated by expected impact on gross domestic product (GDP).

Table 1

Projected Damages from 2.5°C Warming, as a percentage of GDP

India	4.93
Africa	3.91
OECD Europe	2.83
High-income OPEC	1.95
Eastern Europe	0.71
Japan	0.50
United States	**0.45**
China	**0.22**
Russia	**−0.65**

Source: Cass R. Sunstein, *The Complex Climate Change Incentives of China and the United States*, Working Paper 07-14 (Washington, D.C.: AEI-Brookings Joint Center for Regulatory Studies, August 2007), 11, table 3.

Just looking at those numbers, it is not hard to conclude that China and Russia are unlikely to accept significant emissions limitations at any time in the foreseeable future, or to bear the cost of mitigation if they do. The United States may be a somewhat different story, due to its political system and current preferences—but only somewhat. It seems implausible that, over the long run, the three countries that stand to lose the least from climate change will be as eager to bear the cost of mitigation as other countries with different national interests. These differences in national interests will inevitably limit the potential for a harmonized international climate treaty. As Harvard Law School professor Cass Sunstein observed,

> An agreement that is in the interest of the world as a whole is unlikely to
> be in the interest of China and the United States, the world's leading con-
> tributors. It is increasingly clear that the costs and benefits of emissions
> reductions are highly variable across nations. On prominent projections,
> neither China nor the United States is anticipated to be among the prin-
> cipal victims of climate change. The circumstances for an international
> agreement are distinctly unpromising if the leading emitters do not per-
> ceive themselves as likely to gain a great deal from emissions reductions.[4]

Furthermore, there is no way to compel participation—or adherence to—
such an agreement; each nation must choose to join voluntarily.[5] Kyoto was
essentially toothless in that it had no meaningful enforcement mechanism for
countries that missed their targets; it seems unlikely that future treaties will
provide for much stronger enforcement—doing so would only make it less
likely that developing countries would choose to ratify the treaty.

In the face of these fundamental political obstacles, the challenge for policymakers is to be realistic about crafting policies that will attract some form of
participation by the broadest range of nations, recognizing that each will necessarily prefer to respond differently to climate change. Emissions limits are
naturally the primary focus of a sound climate policy—but not the only one.

Some nations may want to focus nearly exclusively on one approach—
adaptation to the effects of rising temperatures, for instance—while others may
choose to combine different elements of these strategies. As it would be difficult,
if not impossible, to measure accurately the comparative value of different
approaches, each nation would necessarily make different judgments about what
policies would be the most cost-effective and appropriate for its circumstances.

Proponents of the one-size-fits-all approach to emissions reductions have
no solution to the participation problem, beyond hoping that it will improve
in time. Some imagine that a major developing nation such as China might be
induced to join an international emissions regime within the next twenty-five
years. The possibility cannot be dismissed, but there is little reason to expect it.

Kyoto's exemption of the entire developing world from any emissions obligations is the most conspicuous example of how fundamentally flawed the
protocol's structure is. But Kyoto's problems hardly stop there: even among the
countries that did choose to ratify it, many are missing their (quite modest)
emissions-reduction targets. This experience suggests that nations' willingness
to accept targets may well exceed their ability to meet them—which bodes ill
for the effectiveness of future agreements.

Even if the United States were to rejoin the Kyoto regime in 2009, and all
countries set stricter targets for the next commitment period and (truly wishful thinking) actually met them, the growth in emissions from the developing

world, if left unchecked, would mean that total global emissions will continue to rise for decades to come. China has at last overtaken the United States as the world's leading emitter of greenhouse gases—a symbolic turning point that policymakers cannot ignore—and is on pace to increase its emissions by 13 percent a year in this decade, far more than had been expected.[6] Given the persistence of greenhouse gases in the atmosphere (carbon dioxide can last for at least a century, and often much more), the continued rise in emissions that is expected in the coming decades will commit the planet to a century or more of warming. Americans are concerned about "the China problem"—how to make a treaty work without China's participation; in Europe, they talk of "the American problem." The American problem may well resolve itself, at least in some form, in the next few years—but the China problem will not.

THE FUTILITY OF EQUITY ARGUMENTS

Faced with the participation problem, many advocates turn to exhortations, often framed in terms of moral obligations rooted in a sense of fairness. These arguments are primarily directed at the United States, the most conspicuous holdout from the Kyoto regime. But their lasting strength and effectiveness will depend more upon their applicability to the China problem—and there they seem weakest.

Even though China has taken over as the world's leading emitter of greenhouse gases, the United States, we are often reminded, long held that position, and remains by far the leading emitter on a per-capita basis. It is easy—and politically popular in the international community—to argue that the United States has a unique obligation to lead the effort in reducing emissions. Former UN secretary-general Kofi Annan, for instance, has called for "climate justice"—that is, requiring reductions from the countries most responsible for past emissions, rather than those whose emissions are growing fastest now. "We must recognize," says Annan, "that the polluter must pay, and not the poor and vulnerable."[7]

Certainly this was the logic, if not the effect, of the Kyoto Protocol. And in the near future, it does seem likely that Americans will, indeed, undertake more aggressive measures to reduce their emissions; federal limits of some sort seem likely. But if "climate justice" means repeating Kyoto's errors in emissions allocations, particularly its exemption of the developing world, then we can be certain that global emissions will continue to rise. And if climate change is truly a moral issue, the obligation to act against it must fall on all shoulders, regardless of economic circumstances, since inclusion is the key to effectiveness.

Some believe that U.S. leadership will inspire China, India, and other major developing countries to accept emissions limits, as well. If we give any credence to the historical record and the current position of those governments, however, we must conclude that, if anything, unilateral acceptance of emissions limits by the United States is just as likely to reinforce China and India's incentives to reject limits of their own. The more inclusive and stringent the Kyoto regime becomes, the stronger the incentive for energy-intensive industries to relocate to developing nations that have no emissions limits—and, consequently, the higher the cost to those nations of joining the Kyoto regime. Further financial incentives to refuse emissions caps are provided by Kyoto's Clean Development Mechanism (CDM), which generates emissions-reduction credits by funding projects in the developing world.[8] Unfortunately, the CDM actually creates perverse incentives for developing countries: the less initiative a country takes to cut its own emissions voluntarily, the more it can earn from the CDM.

Advocates argue that, in time, rising standards of living in the developing world and growing evidence of the effects of climate change will persuade at least the major developing economies to accept emissions caps. One can never know what the future will bring, but it seems unlikely that such a transformation will occur quickly. But the possibility itself does raise again the question: Even if all nations agree that action of some sort is desirable, what principles can guide us to a fair and practical international agreement?

Equity, while naturally appealing to a simplistic sense of fairness, seems particularly ill-suited to the multifaceted challenges of global climate policy. There are both practical and conceptual problems with using equity—or any of the common alternatives, such as Annan's fairness argument—as a guide to allocating international obligations for climate policy.

The simplest application of the equity argument, for instance, is the idea that all nations should cut their emissions of greenhouse gases by equal amounts. Poorer and more populous countries, however, argue that emissions should be equalized on a per-capita basis. Surely an Indian is entitled to emit as many greenhouse gases as an American? The industrialized world is largely responsible for the man-made greenhouse gases currently in the atmosphere; shouldn't it be responsible for solving the problem?

There is certainly a logic in these countries' perspective—but as a practical matter, if we accept that claim, we accept a future of virtually unlimited global emissions. Until we invent technologies that can remove greenhouse gases from the atmosphere, there is no way to undo historical emissions; we can only seek to prevent future emissions, the majority of which will come from developing countries such as India.[9] There is no end to the fairness arguments, but as a practical matter they are irrelevant: it will be impossible to stabilize global atmospheric concentrations of greenhouse gases without significant emissions limits in the developing world.

One recent study projects that, absent an agreement to limit its emissions, China's greenhouse-gas emissions in 2030 will be equal to the entire world's current emissions.[10] This staggering fact underscores the fundamental reality: without a means of controlling emissions from China, India, and other major developing economies, efforts to halt warming through emissions reductions are doomed to failure. The Kyoto Protocol's exemption of China and other developing countries from any emissions-reduction obligations may well prove to be the single most damaging precedent in climate policy; the prospects for reversing it in future negotiations seem poor.

On the other side of the fairness argument, some (most notably to date, the Bush administration) have argued that it would be both unfair and unrealistic not to recognize differences in the size of national economies when calculating environmental obligations. Yes, the United States has been the leading global emitter—but it is also the largest economy in the world. In fact, not surprisingly, its share of the global economy corresponds precisely to its share of global emissions. Separating those trend lines is the goal of climate policies, but progress has been slow.

In February 2002, President Bush proposed reducing the greenhouse-gas "intensity" of the U.S. economy—that is, the amount of emissions per unit of GDP.[11] This metric has a logical appeal as well—it recognizes the fundamental fact that economic activity inevitably generates greenhouse-gas emissions, and that, consequently, emissions targets should reflect differences in the size and nature of each nation's economy. But, as with the per-capita approach, this metric can also be used to justify continued emissions, rather than curtailing them. Developing nations may object that this concept constitutes "carbon colonialism," reinforcing existing differences in global economic status through an economically controlling emissions regime.

In sum, accepting existing differences in economic growth and associated emissions levels would disadvantage less-developed countries, discouraging them from accepting emissions limits; allocating emissions obligations on an equal per-capita basis would sanction decades of additional growth in the developing world's—and, hence, global—emissions.

The obstacles to a "fair" allocation of emissions burdens do not end there, however. Some countries (Japan, for example) have highly energy-efficient economies, with far fewer opportunities for cost-effective emissions reductions. Should Japan be punished for its progress by asking it to cut its emissions as much as a country with an aging, highly inefficient industrial infrastructure?

There are nearly endless variations on this theme. The United States has enjoyed stronger economic and population growth than other countries. Shouldn't we expect its emissions to grow? France happens to have the benefit of a strong nuclear power sector; Britain shifted away from coal in favor of natural gas for reasons unrelated to climate change. Should those countries be given credit for those facts—or should they be expected to expend an equivalent effort at reducing emissions in other areas of their economies?

On the other side of the coin, Russia, of course, only ratified the Kyoto Protocol because it was bribed with generous credits based on its Soviet-era emissions levels. Russia's participation in Kyoto, in other words, was purchased at the price of granting it the right to emissions far in excess of its current level. The leading proposals to entice China into a new global agreement tend to replicate that example, although they obviously sacrifice effectiveness for the sake of achieving nominal participation. But without such favorable terms, countries such as China and Russia are unlikely to accept any emissions limits—and, from their perspective, why should they? Clearly, fairness is in the eye of the beholder when it comes to these issues.

The ultimate futility of the equity argument becomes even clearer when one considers the impossibility of accurately measuring the merit of each nation's investments in climate protection. Even if nations were simply to agree that each should make an equivalent effort at combating warming, a meaningful measure of a nation's effort would have to be far more complex than merely totaling annual emissions levels. It is a grave mistake to treat climate change as a single problem with a single solution; in fact, it is a much more complex and multifaceted group of issues requiring a much more complex policy response.

DIFFERING INTERESTS, ABILITIES, AND APPROACHES TO CLIMATE POLICY

Agreeing on what level of comparable effort might be a fair distribution of burdens among nations—and finding a way to measure that effort—is hard enough, but the task becomes impossible if there is also no way to measure progress objectively in the short term. Different nations would be wise to choose a variety of different climate policies, depending on their interests and abilities—some emphasizing adaptation to warming more than mitigation, and some vice versa. Some countries might favor aggressive action to reduce emissions quickly, while others might prefer investing in research efforts that could have an equal or greater effect in the long run. Each nation would have countless different decisions to make in crafting its policies. Determining what mix of actions is "fair" would involve an endless array of subjective, uncertain calculations—and what country would accept the judgment of others in that assessment?

Some countries have greater opportunities than others to reduce their emissions at relatively modest cost. Others may have different visions for achieving the same goals. How should we value differing national investments in emissions reductions, scientific and technological research and development, and adaptation measures to protect public health? Many countries, particularly in the developing world, would find that it makes most sense to invest their resources in programs to protect their citizens from the effects of climate change. Foremost on that agenda for many nations would be economic growth, which would raise living standards and protect citizens from the effects of climate change—while necessarily contributing to ever-rising global emissions.

Even within the industrialized world, different countries, depending on their interests and abilities, would rationally prefer different approaches to climate change that might be equally valid. If a wealthy, innovative country, for instance, were to invest heavily in an intensive research-and-development program for climate-related technologies that would make massive emissions reductions cost-effective in the long run—while eschewing ambitious emissions reductions in the short term—the long-term benefits of that approach could be far greater than another country's comparably costly effort to cut emissions as quickly as possible.[12] But there is no way to predict reliably which of these efforts would be more effective.

Since the key question is not necessarily how *quickly* we reduce global emissions but rather how *much* they can be reduced over the course of the remainder of this century, nations could reasonably choose different emissions-control pathways that might ultimately have equivalent effect—or might not, if unexpected obstacles should arise along one of the chosen routes. Measuring progress toward a hundred-year target in annual increments can easily give a distorted picture—but that is how political institutions tend to see these questions.

Ultimately, each country will have to make its own judgments. Purists may call for universal participation in an emissions-control regime, but there is no way around the fact that each country has different interests, abilities, and agendas. When it comes to designing an architecture and agenda for a global climate policy, it is not clear that uniformity or equality should be primary concerns. Each country should seek to make realistic commitments to a sustainable climate policy that is appropriate for its national interests and abilities.

THE QUEST FOR A COMPREHENSIVE INTERNATIONAL CLIMATE POLICY

The global population is expected to grow by 2.5 billion by mid-century.[13] Energy use is expected to increase by 57 percent by 2030. Within countries outside the Organization for Economic Cooperation and Development (OECD), that figure is 85 percent.[14] Despite two decades of effort to constrain them, global emissions continue to rise inexorably, and fundamental differences in the ability and motivation of countries to reduce emissions continue to undermine the level of consensus needed for effective global action.

Given those facts, it is far from clear that it is even possible to craft a truly effective international climate treaty, so vast is the scale of economic, social, and technological transformation that would be necessary and so fundamental the political and economic obstacles to success. If there is any hope of making such a treaty broadly attractive to a wide range of countries, it cannot be rigidly committed to universal and equal targets. Widely varying national circumstances should determine the nature of each nation's climate policies. It would be madness, for instance, for Bangladesh to focus its resources on emissions reductions—its environmental conditions dictate that adaptation to warming is the only rational priority for its government. Even if it were possible to force the world into a uniform emissions-reduction scheme, therefore, it is far from clear that it would be desirable.

The Kyoto Protocol was intended to be the first step in constructing a single, harmonized emissions-limitation regime. Although it was understood that its initial scope would be limited, advocates imagined that it could be slowly expanded and refined until it became complete. But since this goal remains elusive, perhaps a better approach would be to stop trying so hard. A growing number of scholars recognize that a single, harmonized approach to climate policy might not be preferable, even if it were feasible. William Pizer of Resources for the Future has noted three lessons we can take from our experience with Kyoto and other national efforts at emissions reductions:

> First, a binding international agreement is neither necessary nor sufficient for domestic actions. ... Second, whatever action a country takes, the form of that action is likely to be dictated by domestic features and forces. ... Third, even without formal mechanisms to equalize marginal costs across countries—e.g., international trading or a single, agreed upon tax rate—various forces seem to keep those costs in line.[15]

Pizer suggests that we set aside the quest for a single, all-encompassing structure for an international emissions-limitation regime and focus instead on encouraging countries to take action in whatever form seems most appropriate and most effective, given their national circumstances. "We need to recognize," he explains,

> that domestic circumstances and opportunities [for action on climate] differ; that, at least right now, at the beginning of a perhaps century-long global effort to address climate change, binding emission limits, prices, or

standards are unlikely to be helpful; and that formal mechanisms to equalize marginal costs (at this initial phase) are less important for efficiency than suggested in the literature. Instead, we should encourage countries to make some commitment to mandatory action, and focus our energy on a clear commitment to evaluate what actually happens.[16]

Gwyn Prins and Steve Rayner, two British scholars of climate policy, have made similar recommendations, offering seven key principles by which a new approach to climate policy might be guided. The first of these principles is to use a "silver buckshot" approach—that is, to adopt "a wide variety of climate policies—silver buckshot—and non-climate policies with climate effects. Each would have the potential to tackle some part of the overall problem, although it would not be clear which would be the most successful."[17]

Prins and Rayner suggest abandoning the pursuit of a universal treaty in favor of a focus on the major emitters, with more emphasis on state and regional initiatives, more research and development, and greater investment in adaptation. Freed from the strictures of an international treaty, nations could learn from their experiences and adjust their policies accordingly. "Sometimes the best line of approach," they conclude, "is not head-on, if one seeks long-lasting impact."

In an ideal world, a single, unified emissions-reduction regime might be the most effective and efficient approach to the climate problem—but given the fundamental political and economic factors at work in our less-than-ideal world today, a less coordinated and more creative approach may be our only hope of success. There is little prospect for successfully cutting global emissions dramatically in the near term, so long-term success must depend upon our ability to learn from our successes and failures and respond to changing conditions over the course of the century. Flexibility and innovation, not equity and arbitrary standards, should be our watchwords in designing national and international climate policies.

the future of energy

Should Governments Encourage the Development of Alternative Energy Sources to Help Reduce Dependence on Fossil Fuels?

YES: Christopher Flavin, *Worldwatch Institute*

NO: Michael Lynch, *Strategic Energy & Economic Research, Inc.*

The twin problems of high (and potentially rising) energy prices and climate change present an enormous challenge: how can countries find and use sustainable sources of economically efficient energy without releasing environmentally destructive greenhouse gases? And the challenge is exacerbated by other conditions that should ideally attend these changes: absence of significant risks, ease of transition from petroleum-based transportation to alternatives, ensuring that adjustment costs are not unequally distributed, and so on. Meeting future energy needs will be a formidable task; Figure 1 shows how significantly total world energy demands have increased and are expected to continue to increase over time. Taken together, energy consumption and climate change are technical as well as political challenges that confront the so-called developed and developing nations alike.

Expected growth in energy demand stems from rising world populations—mostly in the developing world—and from increasing wealth, which is strongly correlated with greater energy use. Figure 2 shows past energy use for several large nations, and it reflects particularly high energy growth in China. Even more alarming for those who seek to limit fossil-fuel use is the projected future consumption of coal, oil, and gas, which constitute the vast majority of energy resources tapped for current and future needs. Therefore, reducing dependence on fossil fuels will necessitate reversing long-standing trends, which will likely require significant economic and political dislocations.

Figure 1

Total World Primary Energy Demand, 1971–2030

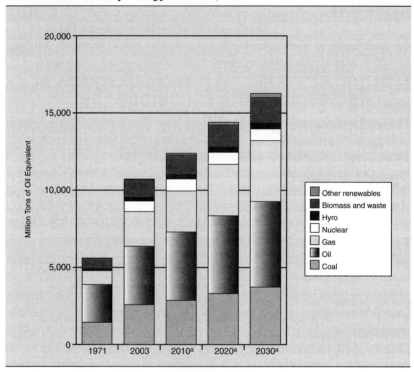

Source: International Energy Agency, World Energy Outlook 2005, Paris, 2005, 82.
[a]Predicted Values.

   While the problems of increasing energy use are clear, choosing between
solutions presents challenges. Increasing energy use is not inherently problematic, but continued burning of fossil fuels contributes to climate change as
well as to the realization that fossil-fuel reserves, while abundant, are subject
to eventual exhaustion. Means to address these problems tend to fall into one
of two broad categories. The first is market-driven: it essentially relies on rising energy prices to force technological and behavioral changes in energy
production and consumption. Of course, such changes also produce economic dislocations and disparities, as the poor suffer disproportionately from
sudden increases in prices. Relying on energy costs to encourage shifts to
alternative fuels also introduces a certain irony, as low fuel costs, which are
politically attractive to most citizens, inhibit longer-term investment in alternative fuels.

Figure 2

Percent Change in Energy Consumption, 1994–2004

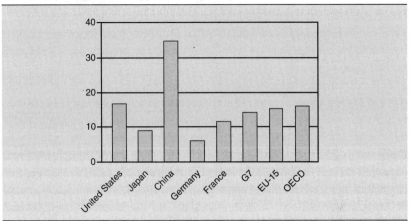

Source: *The OECD in Figures, 2006–2007*, 30–31.

Nonetheless, the market-driven model is a powerful argument because increases in prices are quickly distributed throughout the economy, creating immediate incentives to drill for more oil and to explore for alternatives, and because the incentives to change rely on producers wanting to make money and consumers looking to purchase energy at the lowest possible prices. Supporters claim that there is no fear of "running out" of fossil fuels (or any other type of fuel) since scarce supplies will drive prices so high as to restrict consumption and spur innovation in recovery techniques for fuels that are commercially attractive only at high prices. Therefore, by allowing higher prices to stimulate attempts to produce economically viable alternative energy sources, the market approach is said to stimulate innovation most effectively. Other related approaches recognize that greenhouse-gas (GHG) intensities vary with different fuels, and that policies can discriminate (for example, through taxes) based on the GHG intensity of various fuels.

One problem with the market model is that, in many instances, energy prices fail to reflect the full social costs of energy production and consumption. In the absence of significant taxes or other policies to discourage certain types of energy use, the burning of fossil fuels is typically underpriced. In other words, when individuals or institutions purchase energy, they are rarely, if ever, paying the full social cost of its consumption. For example, driving your gasoline-powered car costs you money for upkeep and gasoline, but you do not pay (and therefore do not fully account for) the social costs of pollutants. Under these circumstances, reliance on markets to produce innovation actually leads to overconsumption of energy because it is priced too low in relation to its full social costs. Furthermore, allowing market prices to regulate consumption produces economic and political dislocations, as the poor—whether measured as individuals or as nations—tend to bear the brunt of the reduced consumption.

Some observers have called instead for significant governmental intervention into energy markets, to spur the sort of innovation that they believe the markets alone will never produce. Pointing both to successes of some government-led innovations (such as the Internet) and to the myopia of markets (as well as their heavy discounting of social costs and benefits), supporters of a stronger industrial policy suggest government involvement as a superior means of delivering on important social priorities such as abundant and clean energy sources. Others ridicule this kind of industrial policy as forcing governments to "pick winners"—which, they argue, is a politically disputatious enterprise, based on developments that are difficult to foresee—and increasing the potential for political manipulation.

The two articles that follow outline different approaches to improving our production and use of energy. Christopher Flavin argues that markets are crucial to energy development, but he favors public-private partnerships as the most effective way to address the severe energy needs facing the global economy. Michael Lynch argues that many renewable energy sources are poor substitutes for oil in addressing future energy needs. Promoting technologies that are not economically viable wastes scarce resources, which, in his view, are better expended on improved battery technology and other innovations that will assist a broad range of energy sources.

Discussion Questions

1. What are the consequences of a dependence on fossil fuels? Consider the potential effects on the environment, the economy, public health, and national security.
2. Who should lead the initiative for reducing dependence on fossil fuels? The government? The market? The private sector? The consumer? Why?
3. To help reduce the U.S. dependence on foreign sources of fossil fuels, some advocate increased off-shore drilling and drilling in the Arctic National Wildlife Refuge (ANWR). Are there benefits to this

strategy? Drawbacks? As a policymaker, what stakeholders would you have to consider or consult when making your decision?

4. What does Christopher Flavin say are the three elements of an effective climate strategy? In what ways does he think government can help to implement this strategy? Do you agree with his approach?

5. What four general arguments does Michael Lynch describe as often being made by those who promote alternative energies? What evidence does he give for rejecting each of these arguments? Do you agree with his assessment?

YES: Christopher Flavin, *Worldwatch Institute*

The world is entering uncharted territory.

Fossil fuels made the modern economy and all of its material accomplishments possible. But soaring energy prices, concern about climate change, and an expected decline in production of crude oil in the next few decades makes the building of a low-carbon economy the central challenge of our age. Meeting that challenge will require that governments encourage the development of alternative energy sources and the restructuring of the global energy industry through technological, economic, and policy innovations that are as unprecedented as the climate change they must address.

Driven by the perfect storm of soaring energy prices and concern about climate change, companies around the world are now investing tens of billions of dollars in a wide array of clean-energy technologies with the potential to reduce dependence on fossil fuels. Solar energy, wind power, green buildings, and electric cars are among the pivotal technologies now entering the global marketplace on a grand scale. A combination of private-sector innovation and proactive government policies are making this new energy revolution possible: from the Federal Republic of Germany to the State of Texas and the People's Republic of China, government policies are being implemented that allow new energy technologies to overcome the head start that a century of public support has provided for fossil fuels.

The sheer magnitude of the transformation ahead requires bold action. Across the political spectrum, respected voices are calling for the United States to undertake a national commitment to reducing dependence on oil and coal—replacing it with indigenous energy sources such as solar and wind power and biofuels. Real change hinges on government policies that will stimulate production, increase efficiency, and reward investment in renewable energy.

AVOIDING CATASTROPHE

Only recently have scientists understood that changes in the concentration of carbon dioxide, methane, and other less common gases could trigger an ecological catastrophe of staggering proportions. Past climate changes have been caused by tiny alterations in Earth's orbit and orientation to the sun—providing, for example, just enough added energy to warm the planet over thousands of years, increasing the concentration of carbon dioxide in the atmosphere, and in turn triggering even larger changes in the temperature. Today's massive release of CO_2 and other greenhouse gases is leading to far greater changes to the atmosphere in a period of decades.[1]

Scientists now project that within the decades immediately ahead, the capacity of land and ocean to absorb carbon emissions will decline, while vast changes in the Arctic may further accelerate warming. Melting tundra will release millions of tons of methane, a greenhouse gas that is more powerful than CO_2. And as the Arctic ice pack recedes each summer—nearly half is already gone—it will be like removing a large air conditioner from the Northern Hemisphere. This effect will further warm the climate and could mean the end of the million-year-old Greenland ice sheet—which by itself contains enough water to raise worldwide sea levels by more than seven meters.[2]

When the world will reach such a tipping point remains uncertain. But it is already clear that ecological change of this magnitude would lead to unprecedented disruptions to the world's economies. A groundbreaking 2006 study led by former World Bank chief economist Nicholas Stern concluded that climate change could cut global economic output by between 5 and 20 percent. In his 2007 book, *The Age of Turbulence*, Alan Greenspan, the leading free-market economist of the day, included climate change as one of five forces that could derail the U.S. economy in the twenty-first century.

In 2006 the combustion of fossil fuels released 8 billion tons of carbon to the atmosphere—nearly a million tons every hour—of which coal and oil contributed roughly 40 percent each, while natural gas accounted for the rest. Global fossil-fuel carbon emissions have increased fivefold since 1950; they are up 30 percent just since 1990. Today, fossil fuels provide four-fifths of the energy that powers the global economy.[3]

Burning fossil fuels on this scale is a vast and risky experiment with Earth's biosphere. Scientists are still not sure when our environment will cross an invisible but catastrophic threshold of no return, but growing evidence suggests that it may be close. James Hansen, director of the NASA Goddard Institute of Space Studies, is among a growing group of climate scientists who believe that the world should make every effort to avoid pushing the atmospheric concentration of CO_2 beyond 450 parts per million and the effective concentration (including methane and trace gases) beyond 500 parts per million. This restraint would limit the increase in the average global temperature to 2.4–2.8 degrees Celsius above pre-industrial levels. The increase so far is just under 0.8 degrees Celsius.[4]

At the July 2008 G8 summit in Japan, the world's leading industrial nations called for a 50 percent cut in global emissions of greenhouse gases by 2050. This is an ambitious goal—achieving it will require reversing the upward trend in emissions that has been under way for a century and a half. The G8 statement marked a growing political consensus that the fossil-fuel economy will have to be substantially restructured in the decades ahead.

Providing energy services for the much larger global economy of 2050 while reducing emissions to 4 billion tons of carbon will require an energy system that is very different from today's. If the world as a whole is to cut emissions in half by 2050, today's industrial countries will need to cut theirs by more than 80 percent. Getting there depends on three elements in a climate strategy: capturing and storing the carbon contained in fossil fuels, reducing energy consumption through new technologies and lifestyles, and shifting to carbon-free energy technologies. This strategy will not be successful if left strictly to the market; a combination of government initiative and market demand are required.

Phasing out oil, the most important fossil fuel today, may turn out to be the easiest part of the problem. Production of conventional crude oil is expected to peak and begin declining within the next decade or two. By 2050, output could be a third or more below the current level. Reliance on natural gas, which has not been as heavily exploited as oil, and which releases half as much carbon per unit of energy as coal, is meanwhile likely to grow.

But the slowdown in the rate of discovery of oil and gas is pushing world energy markets toward dirtier, more carbon-intensive fossil fuels. The greatest problems for the world's climate are coal, which is both more abundant and more carbon-intensive than oil, and "unconventional" energy sources such as tar sands and oil shale, which, given current oil prices, have become economically accessible.

The central role of coal in the world's climate dilemma has led policymakers and industrialists to focus on so-called carbon capture and storage (CCS). Although this process is likely to be feasible only for large, centralized uses of fossil fuels, many energy planners are counting on it. They hope to build a new generation of power plants equipped with devices that capture carbon either before or after the combustion of fossil fuels and then pipe the CO_2 into underground geological reservoirs or into the deep ocean, where it could, in principle, remain for millions of years.

Expert opinion on the eventual commercial viability of carbon capture and storage is severely divided, but one thing is certain: it won't happen soon. In light of the lead times required for technology development and demonstration, it will be the 2020s at the earliest before significant numbers of carbon-neutral coal plants come online. That means that during the critical next decade, when emissions growth must turn downward in industrial countries—and begin to level off in developing countries—CCS will not be able to help. In the meantime, a growing number of climate experts are calling for a moratorium on building new coal-fired power plants unless or until CCS becomes available.

THE CONVENIENT TRUTH

Many energy industry executives argue that reducing carbon emissions as rapidly as scientists now urge would risk an economic collapse. According to conventional wisdom, the available alternatives are just too small, unreliable, or expensive to do the job. In 2001, for example, Vice President Dick Cheney described saving energy as a moral virtue but not important enough to play a major role in the national energy policy proposals he was developing at the time. The World Energy Council, which represents the large energy companies that dominate today's energy economy, declared in 2007 that renewable energy has "enormous practical challenges. It is unlikely to deliver a significant decarbonisation of electricity quickly enough to meet the climate challenge."[5]

However, a thorough review of studies that assess the potential contribution of new energy options, as well as the rapid pace of technological and policy innovation now under way, points to the opposite conclusion. Improved energy productivity and renewable energy are both available in abundance—and new policies and technologies are rapidly making them more economically competitive with fossil fuels. In combination, these energy options represent the most robust alternative to the current energy system, capable of providing the diverse array of energy services that a modern economy requires.

The first step in establishing the viability of a climate-safe energy strategy is assessing the available resources and the potential role they might play. Surveys show that the resource base is indeed ample; the main factors limiting the pace of change are the economic challenge of accelerating investment in new energy options and the political challenge of overcoming the institutional barriers to change.

ENERGY PRODUCTIVITY AND SUPPLY

Energy productivity measures an economy's ability to extract useful services from the energy that is harnessed. From the earliest stages of the Industrial Revolution, energy productivity has steadily advanced. In the United States, the economy has grown by 160 percent since 1973, while energy use has increased by 31 percent, allowing the nation's energy productivity to double during the period; Germany and Japan, starting with higher productivity levels, have achieved comparable increases. But even today, despite these advances, well over half the energy harnessed throughout the world is converted to waste heat rather than being used to meet energy needs.[6]

This vast inefficiency suggests enormous potential to improve energy productivity in the decades ahead. Light bulbs, electric motors, air conditioners, automobiles, power plants, computers, aircraft, and buildings are among the hundreds of systems and technologies that can be made far more efficient, in many cases just by using already available technologies more widely—such as compact fluorescent light bulbs and hybrid electric vehicles. Further gains can be made by altering the design of cities—increasing the role of public transport, walking, and cycling, while reducing dependence on automobiles.

The greatest potential turns out to lie in the most basic element of the energy economy—buildings—which could be equipped with better insulation, more efficient lighting, and better appliances, at costs that would be more than paid for by lower energy bills. With technologies available today, such as ground-source heat pumps that reduce the energy needed for heating and cooling by 70 percent, it is possible to construct zero-net-energy buildings, which do not require fossil fuels at all. All countries have this untapped potential to increase energy productivity, but the largest opportunities are found in the developing nations, where current energy productivity tends to be lower. Enchancing that productivity will not only reduce consumption of fossil fuels but will make it easier and more affordable to rapidly increase the use of carbon-free energy sources.[7]

On the supply side, renewable energy relies on two primary energy sources—sunlight and the heat stored below ground—that are available in vast abundance. The sunlight alone that strikes Earth's land surface in two hours is equivalent to total human energy use in a year. While much of that sunlight becomes heat, solar energy is also responsible for the power embodied in wind, hydro, wave, and biomass sources, each with the potential to be harnessed for human use. Only a small portion of that enormous daily, renewable flux of energy will ever be needed by humanity.[8]

Several studies have assessed the scale of the major renewable resources and estimated what their practical contribution to the energy economy might one day be. One study by the National Renewable Energy Laboratory in the United States, for example, concluded that solar thermal power plants built in seven states in the U.S. Southwest could provide nearly seven times the nation's existing electric capacity from all sources. And mounting solar electric generators on just half of the suitable rooftop area could provide 25 percent of U.S. electricity. In the case of wind power, the Pacific Northwest Laboratory found that the land-based wind resources of Kansas, North Dakota, and Texas could meet all the nation's electricity needs, even with large areas excluded for environmental reasons.

These reports demonstrate that resource availability will not be a limiting factor as the world seeks to replace fossil fuels. With improved technologies, greater efficiency, and lower costs, renewable energy could one day replace virtually all the carbon-based fuels that are so vital to today's economy.

MAKING ENERGY MARKETS WORK THROUGH GOVERNMENT

Although consumers should in theory be interested in making investments in energy efficiency whenever it is economical, they face many obstacles, including a lack of capital to invest in conservation and a lack of information about which investments make sense. Perceiving the lack of demand, potential manufacturers and installers of energy-efficient equipment have little incentive to scale up production or build businesses that would facilitate efficiency improvements. This lack of impetus is where government becomes important in this issue.

One of the easiest ways to overcome these kinds of market barriers is government mandates. Since the 1970s, many governments have required that home appliances, motor vehicles, and buildings meet minimum efficiency standards in order to be sold, and these standards have been gradually ratcheted up over time. Additional tightening is now in order, and many governments are moving quickly in that direction. Average auto efficiency standards, for example, will soon move to 47 miles per gallon in Japan and 49 miles per gallon in Europe, and in 2007 Congress raised the U.S. standard, which had remained at 27.5 miles per gallon for over two decades. Another approach to requiring efficiency can be seen in the law recently passed in Australia to phase out the use of most incandescent light bulbs, which can be replaced by compact fluorescent bulbs that are four times as efficient.

Government mandates are also being used to compel the construction of more energy-efficient buildings and to require the introduction of renewable energy into electricity grids as well as the markets for liquid fuels. Several national governments and twenty-four U.S. states now have binding "renewable portfolio standards" requiring that specified amounts of renewable electricity be added to their grids. In Spain, a recent update of building codes requires all new buildings to incorporate solar water heaters. As of April 2008, the state government of Baden-Wurttemberg, Germany, began requiring that 20 percent of new buildings' heating requirements be met with renewable energy. Brazil, the United States, and the European Union are among the jurisdictions mandating that a minimum proportion of biofuels be blended with gasoline and diesel fuel, spurring growth in their use.

Mandates such as these are a useful backstop to ensure that minimal rates of change occur and to remove the very worst technologies from the market.

However, it is also essential that markets reward innovation and investment that strive for the best possible performance. To achieve this goal, some regulation is needed. One important step in this direction is to decouple electric utilities' profits from the amount of power they sell by introducing a regulatory formula that instead rewards utilities for providing the best service at the least cost. California regulators have already made this change; as a result of this and other policies, Californians use less than half as much electricity per person as other Americans do.

Governments outside the United States have successfully promoted investment in renewable energy. Beginning in the early 1980s, Denmark decided to reduce its dependence on oil-fired generation by encouraging its agricultural industry to enter the power business by selling wind- and biomass-based electricity to the utilities at prices set by government. This government intervention stopped the utilities from thwarting potential competitors, and over two decades it reduced Denmark's dependence on fossil fuels and made it a leading generator of renewable power.[9]

Germany and Spain adopted similar market access laws in the 1990s, and they too moved quickly into the leading ranks of renewable energy development. Over time, the prices governments set have been adjusted downward as the cost of renewable technologies has fallen. As a result of this law, Germany now holds the inside track in solar photovoltaics and wind-generating capacity—despite the fact that it has modest resources of sun and wind.[10]

THE FINAL TIPPING POINT

There are good reasons to think that the world may be on the verge of a major transformation of energy markets. The powerful interaction of advancing technology, private investment, and policy reform have led to a pace of change unseen since pioneers such as Thomas Edison and Henry Ford created the last great energy revolution a century ago. But is it enough? Will the coming years bring the accelerated change and level of capital that are needed to reverse the tide of climate change?

The answer to that question will likely be found not in the messy world of economics but in the even messier world of politics. But time is growing short: in the United States alone, 121 new coal-fired power plants have been proposed; if built, they could produce 30 billion tons of carbon dioxide over their sixty-year lives. And China is building that many plants every year.[11] However, in 2007 there were growing signs that the years of political paralysis on climate change may be coming to an end, spurred by the warnings of scientists and the concerns of citizens. One sign of the changing times is that many of the planned coal plants are under attack by local and national environmentalists, and some have already been scrapped. Germany recently announced that its centuries-old hard coal industry will be closed by 2018. Several other potentially game-changing political developments are worth noting:

- Twenty-seven major U.S. companies—from Alcoa and Dow Chemical to Duke Energy, General Motors, and Xerox—announced support for national regulation of CO_2 emissions. Meanwhile, seventeen U.S. states moved toward adopting regulations on CO_2 emissions, thereby increasing pressure on Congress, which was considering national legislation.

- The European Union committed to reducing its CO_2 emissions to 20 percent below 1990 levels by 2020, and member states are ramping up their energy-efficiency and renewable-energy programs in order to achieve these goals.

- China announced its first national climate policy, pledging to step up its energy-efficiency and renewable-energy programs and acknowledging that earlier policies were not sufficient.

- Brazil recognized the threat that climate change poses to the country's economically crucial agriculture and forestry industries and signaled a new commitment to strengthening international climate agreements.[12]

CONCLUSION

As negotiations begin on the international climate agreement that will supplant the Kyoto Protocol after 2012, the world's political will to tackle climate change will be put to an early test. The politics of climate change are advancing more rapidly than could have been imagined a few years ago. But the world has not yet reached the political tipping point that would ensure the kind of economic transformation that is required. And the divide between industrial and developing countries over how to share the burden of action must still be resolved.

As people around the world come to understand that a low-carbon economy could one day be more effective than today's energy mix at meeting human needs, support for the needed transformation is bound to grow. Urgency and vision are the twin pillars on which humanity's hope now hangs.

NO: Michael Lynch, *Strategic Energy & Economic Research, Inc.*

> … we shall answer their demands for a gold standard by saying to them,
> you shall not press down upon the brow of labor this crown of thorns.
> You shall not crucify mankind upon a cross of gold.
>
> William Jennings Bryan, July 9, 1896

In recent years, a combination of high energy prices and concerns about global warming has led to calls for an array of new energy sources from across the political spectrum. Ralph Nader, John McCain, and both T. Boone Pickens, the Texas oilman, and Al Gore, the environmentalist, have announced plans involving a heavy emphasis on renewable energies such as solar and wind power. Even the Bush administration called for an end to our "addiction" to foreign oil.

It is a real oddity of the current craze for renewable energies that petroleum was originally considered a "green" fuel that reduced coal-based pollution in the United Kingdom. In fact, oil got its start by replacing biofuels—primarily whale oil used in lamps. Presumably, no one would now suggest replacing electric lighting with whale oil, but other examples, not as absurd, abound. In a more modern example, Haitians suffering from deforestation undoubtedly envy their neighbors in the Dominican Republic, who have access to propane for cooking.

While renewable energy sources have an important role to play in energy supply, the reality is that they are all too often given a free pass, analytically. Many proposals that would not stand the laugh test if made by large private companies are embraced by a variety of activists and politicians without serious thought as to their costs or benefits. I reject the notion that encouraging alternative energy sources is always positive. Instead, I want to emphasize here the need for economic efficiency when it comes to energy.

FINITE RESOURCES: MALTHUS REDUX

The renewable nature of wind, solar, and biomass power sources is often cited as a prime factor in making them desirable. But simply being renewable is a poor argument. Whale oil, after all, was a renewable resource, and, in fact, there are a lot more cases of scarcity among renewable resources than among nonrenewable ones, whether the resource in question be tuna or polar bears.

The best example of the irrelevance of the finite nature of nonrenewable resources is probably copper: the Bronze Age began about 5,000 years ago, and during the Trojan War, if Homer is to be believed, men would fight and die to retrieve valuable bronze armor. Today, most Americans would not stoop to pick up a copper penny.

In recent times, many have seized on the so-called peak oil theories—which maintain that oil production has already peaked and is currently in decline— to justify the desperate need to switch away from finite fossil fuels. But those arguments are based on simplistic analysis that is demonstrably false (Lynch 2003). The petroleum resource base is approximately 8 to 10 trillion barrels of conventional oil (that found in liquid oil fields), of which 1 trillion has been used in 150 years. Another 2.5 trillion barrels of the remaining resource are recoverable (from tar sands and shale oil) with current technology. The amount of the resource that is recoverable will easily increase, perhaps adding another 3 trillion barrels, even without considering the 10 or 15 trillion barrels of shale oil that is technically but (apparently) not economically recoverable.

The 2008 collapse of the financial industry was one more reminder that the finite resource most constraining the global economy is the lack of suffi-cient money to do everything we need to do, let alone everything we would like to do. The world faces enormous social, economic, and environmental problems—far beyond what can be resolved with existing government finances. Thus, it behooves us not to waste money on inefficient energy policies.

BENEFITS: GREEN PIE IN THE SKY?

The general arguments put forth by the great majority of proponents of alter-native energies are these:

- Most alternative energies are environmentally beneficial because they are approximately carbon-neutral and therefore lessen global warming.

- High energy prices are here to stay; therefore renewable energy will be economically more attractive in the future than in the past.

- Because they are largely produced domestically, alternative energies improve the energy security of the United States.

- Renewable energy improves American economic competitiveness and provides jobs.

Though renewable energy and other new fuels certainly have a role to play, these strong assertions deserve critical scrutiny.

Pollution Reduction

While there is no doubt that many new energy sources reduce pollution, the issues are, first, whether the pollutants they reduce are the most needful of reduction, and, second, whether the benefits are the best that can be achieved for the expenditure involved. Not all pollution does the same level of environmental harm, and different fuels and technologies obviously deliver different amounts of benefits. Simply stating that any approach that reduces any pollution should be pursued is wildly inefficient; comparisons of the relative costs and benefits will allow for much more efficient use of our scarce financial resources.

Bjorn Lomborg's "Copenhagen Consensus" is one laudable attempt to develop such broad social priorities. Given our finite budget, and the advances in our understanding of environmental—and social—challenges since the first Earth Day in 1969, this type of consideration should be applied to our energy policymaking.

Unfortunately, those developing new energy sources are unlikely to recommend diverting resources to health care, clean water supplies, and so forth—nor are proponents of these causes likely to defer to the renewable energy imperative. Such narrow-focused advocacy is simply human nature. But it doesn't mean that the proposals of new-energy promoters should be blindly accepted.

High Prices: Déjà Vu All Over Again

> The energy crisis has not yet overwhelmed us, but it will if we do not act quickly. … The most important thing about these proposals is that the alternative may be a national catastrophe. Further delay can affect our strength and our power as a nation.
>
> President Jimmy Carter

We have been here before. On April 18, 1977, President Jimmy Carter made his famous speech declaring the energy crisis to be the moral equivalent of war and proposing various measures in response, including setting up the Synthetic Fuels Corporation to promote alternative energies (primarily shale oil and coal gasification), while subsidies for solar and wind energy were implemented. Carter also encouraged conservation and more coal use. Solar thermal panels sprouted across the nation, even on the White House roof. Oil companies developed (or bought) solar power divisions. Windmills were erected in many places, and research into a variety of exotic energy sources was funded. The electric car was described as just around the corner, and Chrysler, for one, abandoned its large car line.

Most of these responses proved unwise, to put it mildly. All the computer models, all the economists and consultants, government organizations, and oil companies, turned out to be wrong about ever-rising prices and scarce resources. The belief that markets were myopic in not raising prices high enough to make crucially needed synthetic fuels viable turned out to be hubris on the part of the many experts.

The Synthetic Fuel Corporation was a bust; solar thermal panels and wind-mills had numerous technical problems; and Americans returned to their love of large vehicles, rewarding Ford and GM for their "prescience" (and punish-ing Chrysler). Meanwhile, electric cars are still "just around the corner." Some high-priced alternatives were later attacked by consumer advocates, who objected to the above-market prices being paid for them.

Has anything changed? Just go back to Christopher Flavin's 1979 "The Future of the Automobile in an Oil Short World"—its arguments are nearly identical to those still being heard today. Everyone at that time, including the oil industry, was sold on the notion of ever-rising prices and projects such as extraction of shale oil were thought not only wise but essential.

Jobs

> A century ago, the story goes, a construction foreman was approached
> by a union representative who demanded that he not use a steam
> shovel, but instead, a hundred men with shovels. He responded, "Why
> not a thousand men with teaspoons?"

Following the 2008 presidential election and in face of our current economic problems (the perfect recipe for policy disaster), the jobs-creating properties of renewable energies such as wind and solar power are being heavily touted. But if these energy technologies are not self-supporting economically without sig-nificant subsidies, their job-creating properties should not be sufficient cause to pour billions of dollars of new subsidies into them.

In fact, since the days of the Great Depression and the Public Works Administration, it has been common practice among conservatives to decry "ditch-digging"—hiring the unemployed for meaningless tasks, just to give them a paycheck—as a prime example of government waste. Yet the sugges-tion that money should be provided for renewable energy is only sinning to a lesser degree. Why not dig a massive ditch and pour water down it to gener-ate hydroelectric power? (And it could be dug with teaspoons to generate even more jobs.) Because it would be wasteful. How is buying jobs with federal subsidies for inefficient and economically unsustainable energy sources any better than ditch-digging jobs? The losses may be smaller, but they are not inconsequential.

Energy Security

The talk of energy independence by the 2008 candidates represents the triumph of rhetoric over reality. The likelihood that the United States could reduce its oil imports by 12 million barrels per day—which is what energy independence would look like—without doing major economic damage is fanciful, as is the expectation that renewable energy would be the primary reason for such a reduction. President Nixon's 1973 Project Independence report sensibly noted that becoming energy independent not only would be prohibitively expensive but would not eliminate our need to protect global energy supplies, given our interdependent economy and many alliance commitments. Only countries such as Albania under Communism and North Korea have developed autarky to that degree, and their examples are hardly to be emulated.

More poignantly, recalling that President George W. Bush, a Texas oilman and friend of the Saudi royal family, embraced Ariel Sharon as a great friend, it is all but impossible to see where our energy dependence has constrained our foreign policy significantly. Fears about resource wars are similarly overblown: international markets are so well-developed that "access" merely requires payment. The belief in scarcity of mineral resources, including energy, is based on simplistic analysis. In fact, fears about resource scarcity are not new, and they have been proven wrong repeatedly.

COMING DOWN TO EARTH

> In the 1960s, it was considered unacceptable to criticize labor, but that changed by the 1980s. Could the same thing happen to environmentalism?
>
> Denny Ellerman, MIT

Zealotry is the negative side of public policy, as racism is the negative side of nationalism. Given the obvious benefits of pollution reduction, it cannot be surprising that many environmentalists take on the role of crusaders. However, this role inflation has caused them not only to adopt a moralistic tone, but also to yield to the temptation to overstate their case.

Probably the most extreme case is pundit/activist Jeremy Rifkin's advocacy of the hydrogen economy—he argues that since we built the Internet, we can build a hydrogen economy (Rifkin 2003). The comparison is meaningless, implying that building a hydrogen economy, which would require vast investments of money and manpower, would be trivial.

Rationalizing the shortcomings of new energy sources has a long history. The extremely poor performance of electric cars has long been overlooked by their proponents. Yet it is hard to think of other products that are considered desirable despite similar limitations: a television that worked only sixteen hours a day? Or could operate for only three hours before shutting down for eight?

An article in *The Economist* ("Electrifying," December 18, 1997) described the situation clearly:

> Only two years ago, electric vehicles (EVs) seemed the answer to worries about the noise, pollution and environmental destruction that the internal-combustion engine leaves in its wake. California had plans to require the car industry to build and sell tens of thousands of EVs a year in the Golden State. Then, regulators reluctantly accepted that drivers would revolt if they were forced to drive cars powered by expensive batteries that had a range of less than 100 miles and took up to eight hours to recharge.
>
> Now, EVs are back in fashion. The biggest change in their prospects has come from the sudden emergence of affordable fuel-cell technology ... the new consortium hopes to produce an initial 10,000–50,000 cars a year powered by fuel cells, starting commercially in 2004.

Amazingly, a technology as incredibly complex and expensive as hydrogen-fuel-cell cars was seen as on the verge of being ready for the marketplace in 1997, although hydrogen production was not yet economical, a distribution system for hydrogen fuel was not in place, fuel-cell technology was still prohibitively expensive, and storage systems remained bulky and inefficient.

A typical response to the charge that these shortcomings make the electric car impractical for now is that technologies that are not currently attractive should be mandated or subsidized to allow them to achieve economies of scale and thus lower costs. However, this argument appears to be overselling. Nearly all consumer products achieve acceptance without mandates, and the fact that some technologies are said to need mandates implies that the industry does not believe that the economies of scale will lower costs enough to make them attractive; otherwise, they would undertake to do so themselves.

ECONOMICS: NOT THE ONLY THING, BUT AT LEAST SOMETHING

While conservatives are inclined to focus entirely on the relative costs of various energy sources, proponents of alternative energies take a different tack. They usually assert that (a) economics isn't very important; (b) the technologies are roughly economically viable already (or can be made so through government policy); or (c) intangible benefits outweigh the poor economics.

Engineers tend to adopt the first approach, especially academics. Renowned conservation proponent Amory Lovins often argues for technologies that are technically viable but far too expensive, which is why his predictions of huge efficiency increases in recent years have proved invalid.

But the debate should not be over straight cost and benefits, but over relative costs and benefits. The United States has many opportunities to reduce energy consumption, carbon emissions, and/or oil imports, and its budget is finite. Therefore, careful judgments will be required to produce the most efficient expenditure of funds, assuming that it is necessary to provide taxpayer or consumer dollars to accomplish these goals.

As Table 1 shows, the cost of wind power is nearly competitive with that of other sources, while photovoltaics are still far too expensive to be competitive outside of niche uses, such as generating energy for farms or towns that are distant from power lines. The government subsidies for both new sources are huge despite the fact that wind power doesn't require them and photovoltaics are simply not ready to make a significant contribution to our energy needs.

Yet many, such as Representative Bernie Sanders of Vermont, argue that renewable energy is the answer to the problem of high energy costs, which is rather like Marie Antoinette suggesting that peasants who don't have bread should eat cake.

Table 1

Costs and Subsidies for Electricity Generation

	Cents per Kilowatt-Hour	
	Generation cost	Federal subsidies
Pulverized Coal	4.3	0.044
Geothermal	4.4	0.092
Natural Gas Combined-Cycle	4.7	0.025
Wind	4.8	2.337
Open-Loop Biomass	5.1	
Nuclear	6	0.159
Solar-Thermal	12.6	
Photovoltaic	21	2.434
U.S. wholesale electricity price in 2006	5.9	

Source: Howard Greuenspecht, Statement Before the Subcommittee on Select Revenue Measures, Committee on Ways and Means, U.S. House of Representatives, May 24, 2005.
Note: Nuclear costs are for a plant entering service in 2013; all others are for 2010.

OTHER SHORTCOMINGS

It is rare to hear the admission that renewable energy sources have shortcomings, except from contrarians. Unfortunately, there are a variety of problems with renewable energy sources that are usually ignored, including the large land requirements, competition with food inputs, intermittency, and pollutants.

One example is ethanol. While ethanol may offer a net environmental benefit, it does impose a variety of negative consequences, including high energy needs for fertilizer, processing, and transportation, although these consequences are often exaggerated. The recent rise in global food prices has been partly driven by biofuel production, although that effect should be mitigated over the long term. Another example is gasoline with ethanol, which is associated with a variety of pollutants—not only higher levels of acetaldehyde and formaldehyde compared to regular gasoline, but also higher volatile organic compounds (VOCs) compared to gasoline with the additive MTBE.

Furthermore, photovoltaic cells can contain hazardous materials that can be released by accident, while solar concentration plants typically use oil or molten salts, and nearly all wind power installations require substances such as lubricants and hydraulic fluids.

CONCLUSION

Promoting technologies that are not yet ready for the marketplace will only waste money and damage their reputation with consumers. Our finite budget resources should be redirected, leaving sharply lower subsidies for wind power (which doesn't need them) and photovoltaics (which are not broadly viable). The money saved should be spent on research to reduce the costs of photovoltaics and to improve battery technologies, which would make a variety of energy sources and uses more attractive. But, especially, it must be recognized that it is a given energy technology's economic viability that results in widespread adoption by consumers, accomplishing far more than government mandates. Otherwise, consumers and taxpayers will simply be crucified on a cross of biomass.

hiv/aids

Should the Wealthy Nations Promote Anti-HIV/AIDS Efforts in Poor Nations?

YES: Kammerle Schneider and Laurie Garrett, *Council on Foreign Relations*

NO: Mark Heywood, *AIDS Law Project*

The worldwide devastation from AIDS is staggering—the World Health Organization estimates that more than 25 million people have died of AIDS since the early 1980s. Currently, more than 33 million men, women, and children are infected with HIV (see Figure 1); over 2 million individuals die annually of the disease (see Figure 2), and even more contract it every year (see Figure 3). There has been a steady increase in those living with HIV worldwide, rising from approximately 8 million in 1990 to more than four times that number in less than twenty years.

HIV/AIDS is thus a global killer whose effects are so overwhelming as to have had substantial impacts on the overall demographic profiles of some nations. For example, Swaziland—where the prevalence rate is 26 percent—has the largest percentage of its population living with HIV, followed by Botswana, where nearly one-fourth are infected. The average life expectancy in Swaziland has dropped from fifty-seven to thirty-one years; in Botswana, life expectancy fell from sixty-five to forty years in a single decade.

Yet the devastation is not spread equally around the world, as is indicated in Figure 4. More than two-thirds of those living with HIV reside in sub-Saharan Africa, where adult prevalence rates are 5 percent of the entire adult population. (This figure compares with prevalence rates of 0.6 percent in the United States, 0.3 percent in Europe, 0.1 percent in East Asia, and 0.8 percent worldwide.)

The impacts on nations such as Botswana and Swaziland extend far beyond the individuals infected; they also contribute to social disturbances and threats to government effectiveness. Family members forsake work to

Figure 1

Estimated Numbers of Adults and Children Living with HIV Globally in 2007

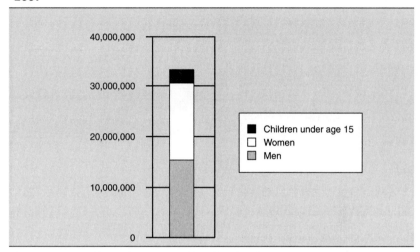

Source: Joint United Nations Programme on HIV/AIDS (UNAIDS) and World Health Organization (WHO), "AIDS Epidemic Update: December 2007," 1.

Figure 2

Estimated Numbers of Adult and Child Deaths Due to AIDS Globally in 2007

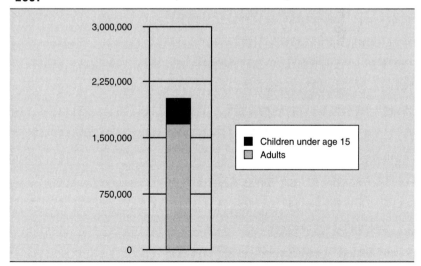

Source: Joint United Nations Programme on HIV/AIDS (UNAIDS) and World Health Organization (WHO), "AIDS Epidemic Update: December 2007," 1.

Figure 3

Estimated Numbers of Adults and Children Newly Infected with HIV Globally in 2007

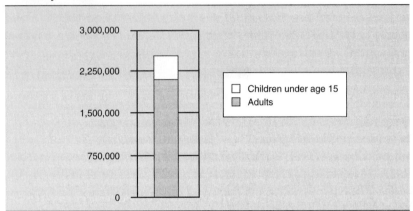

Source: Joint United Nations Programme on HIV/AIDS (UNAIDS) and World Health Organization (WHO), "AIDS Epidemic Update: December 2007," 1.

tend to the sick, children are orphaned—Swaziland alone has tens of thousands of orphaned children, many left to fend for themselves—and governments struggle to cope with providing health care and other social services. Hospitals are overrun with patients suffering from HIV-related diseases, and, as a consequence, hospital workers, including mid-wives, are particularly susceptible to infection.

In the United States in 2006, 49 percent of diagnosed AIDS cases were found among African Americans (a group that makes up just 12 percent of the population), 19 percent among Hispanics (who comprise 15 percent of the population), and 30 percent among white, non-Hispanic residents (who comprise two-thirds of the population). And higher concentrations of the disease are found in large states (California, Texas, Florida, New York), while more rural states have lower rates. A recent CDC study suggests that AIDS cases are substantially underreported in the United States.

To date, most of the immediate effects of AIDS have occurred nationally, because few people with AIDS travel abroad. Consequently, efforts have focused on treating patients and on containing the spread of the disease within countries, rather than across borders. A major problem—particularly in Africa—is the lack of administrative and financial resources by the national govern-ments. Foreign aid—from governments, international organizations, and private foundations—has been solicited as a way to fill the void.

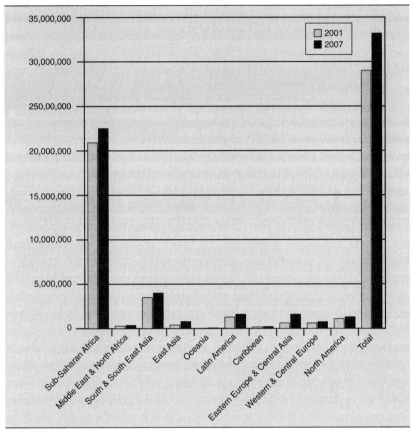

Figure 4

Estimated Number of Adults and Children Living with HIV, 2001 and 2007

Source: Joint United Nations Programme on HIV/AIDS (UNAIDS) and World Health Organization (WHO), "AIDS Epidemic Update: December 2007," 7.

Multiple strategies have been proposed and adopted for coping with the disease and preventing its expansion. These approaches range from condom distribution (which sometimes faces obstacles of local practice and custom); to widespread HIV testing; to government-sponsored efforts that target highly mobile populations, attempt to modify behavior, and provide anti-retroviral drugs. The impact of these strategies has been mixed, and their reach has been limited by the high costs of drug treatment.

Yet, for all the recognition of its horrible impact around the world (and particularly in sub-Saharan Africa), AIDS is not the only deadly disease threatening populations globally. Another is tobacco use, which the World Health Organization characterizes as the most preventable cause of death worldwide. The basic provision of clean water would save millions of lives per year in developing nations, and even modest immunization efforts would make significant public health inroads. Therefore, the articles that follow do not suggest that HIV/AIDS is unimportant, but their authors take different sides on the relative importance of narrowly focusing public health efforts on this one disease rather than adopting a more diversified approach. Kammerle Schneider and Laurie Garrett argue that the current foreign aid approach to AIDS is insufficient and urge a long-term global focus that recognizes needs "on the ground" and aims to prevent new cases—that is, there is too much attention to treatment and managing crises, while too little attention is paid to halting new cases. Mark Heywood argues that Western attempts to address the problem have been sorely inadequate and may eventually do more harm than good.

Discussion Questions

1. Should funding for anti-HIV/AIDS efforts be directed toward prevention or toward treatment? What are the risks of inadequately funding one or the other?

2. The world is faced with many public health issues and diseases—from HIV/AIDS to tuberculosis to malnutrition to unsanitary drinking water—and finite resources to address them. As a policymaker, how would you decide where to allocate resources? What criteria should be used?

3. Are wealthy nations responsible for alleviating suffering due to poor health in developing nations? Are there moral arguments for or against? What about economic arguments? What role does politics play?

4. What is the distinction, made in both essays, between global health and international health? Do the authors think a global health approach or an international health approach is the best way to fight the spread of HIV/AIDS?

5. Kammerle Schneider and Laurie Garrett argue that the global response to the HIV/AIDS pandemic has been inadequate, and they call for a new global strategy. What are the five key components of their strategy? What other additional components might you add?

6. Mark Heywood makes a direct link between health and the economy and health and politics. How does he see the economy and politics influencing public health?

YES: Kammerle Schneider and Laurie Garrett,
Council on Foreign Relations

The velocity at which HIV/AIDS has spread to every social stratum in every country in the world is a testament to globalization and the increasing interconnectedness of humankind. Over 11,000 people are infected with HIV/AIDS each day, yet the only means of passing the virus are sexual contact, needle-sharing, blood transfusions, and in utero transmission by an infected mother. In no other period in history would it have been possible for an infectious disease so comparatively difficult to transmit from person to person to spread to more than 70 million people in a little over a quarter of a century. The only disease comparable in magnitude to AIDS is the plague that ravaged many parts of the world in the early fourteenth century—at a time when it took over 365 days to circumnavigate the globe. Today, disease-infected goods, animals, and people can be transported to nearly any location on the planet in less than thirty-six hours, placing every nation at risk of the rapid spread of infectious disease.

Much like the fourteenth-century plague, HIV/AIDS is a disease that flourishes among the poor; 95 percent of new HIV infections occur in low- and middle-income countries.[1] AIDS most severely affects regions already crippled by other diseases, failing health systems, and political instability. The pandemic is lowering child survival rates, significantly reducing life expectancy, debilitating already overburdened health care systems, breaking down family structures, and destroying a generation in the most productive years of their lives. Poverty begets disease and disease begets poverty. Countries heavily burdened by infectious disease are often those least able to fight back. Poor countries are stranded in a deadly cycle, and it is the responsibility of the international community to help them to break this cycle—by providing resources to treat and care for those already infected, and to prevent the transmission of millions of new infections.

Over the past decade, the magnitude of the AIDS pandemic in poor countries has slowly captured the attention of leaders in the wealthy world who now recognize that, beyond the humanitarian imperative, pandemic disease, wherever it occurs, is a threat to their own security and to their economic and political stability. We are only as strong as our weakest link, and diseases know no borders. The debate today centers not on whether the wealthy world *should* promote anti-AIDS efforts in poor countries—but on *how* to best use funds to maximize efforts to curb the spread of the disease.

In recent years we have seen an unprecedented change in the global health landscape, which has been transformed by a sixfold increase in foreign aid spending and private giving for global health.[2] Far and away the largest proportion of this windfall has been committed to the struggle against a single disease, HIV/AIDS, transforming what was once a paltry million-dollar effort into a billion-dollar enterprise. With investment come expectations: political leaders devise strategies so that quantifiable progress can be reported to constituents before the next elections, religious leaders promote messages that keep their congregations filling donation baskets, and members of the general public in wealthy countries buy (Product) Red iPods to show their solidarity with those inflicted with the disease. Such increased funding, advocacy, and support can make a tremendous difference—as long as the political interests and religious ideologies of the wealthy world do not trump the implementation of strategies that are based on scientific evidence and designed to meet the needs of the people most at risk of infection.

Despite the expenditure of US$31 billion since 2003, HIV infection rates continue to rise, in part because political agendas are tragically undermining sound science.[3] We are now at a critical moment in global health history: we have the resources and the political support to make huge strides in the fight against AIDS, but, if we continue down the same path, we face donor fatigue, wasted resources, and millions of lives lost to preventable disease. Failure to curb HIV infection rates, extend life spans, and alleviate poverty in poor countries can no longer be blamed simply on a lack of funding or political interest.

KICK-STARTING THE FIGHT AGAINST AIDS

Throughout the 1980s and early 1990s, the global response to HIV was characterized by apathy and inaction. During that time, the developed world spent less than $300 million annually on AIDS-related activities in developing countries.[4] AIDS was essentially a death sentence, since the medical community had no arsenal to treat those already infected with the virus. In 1996, however, this dire prognosis changed when researchers discovered a triple cocktail of anti-retroviral therapy drugs (ARVs) that could slow the progression of the virus in infected individuals. Although it was not a cure, this treatment, taken daily, proved to significantly prolong the lives of HIV patients. At the International AIDS Conference in Vancouver that year, Dr. Emilio Emini of Merck Pharmaceuticals announced spectacular discoveries by a vast consortium of public- and private-sector scientists. As the conference participants rejoiced, a Zambian mother dying of AIDS took the stage and asked the question that would frame the

HIV/AIDS discussion for the next decade: "What does this mean for me?" The wealthy world had yet to consider what ARVs—carrying a price tag of $16,000 per year for the drugs alone—would mean for the world's poor, among whom the lion's share of new infections were taking hold.

Virtually overnight, HIV-positive individuals in wealthy countries started using the new drug treatments, and by mid-1997 many of the visible horrors of AIDS had disappeared from the United States and Europe. Yet treatment remained out of reach for the majority of the world's AIDS population. Such clear inequities sparked vocal outrage from individuals around the world, attracting the attention—and opening the pocketbooks—of many in the wealthy world to the need to address the injustices of global health.

In June 2001, at the urging of United Nations Secretary-General Kofi Annan and U.S. ambassador to the UN Richard Holbrooke, the UN General Assembly Special Session on HIV/AIDS unanimously endorsed the concept of a Global Fund to buy drugs at cost and make them available to the poorest people in the poorest countries. The Global Fund to Fight AIDS, Tuberculosis and Malaria operates as a financial instrument, not an implementing agency, with the goal of attracting, managing, and disbursing resources to fight those three deadly diseases.[5]

Meanwhile, in the United States, an unlikely alliance was being formed to push for a response to the pandemic. U2's Bono, leaders from the Evangelical community, and ultra-conservative Senator Jesse Helms advised the Bush administration that the United States had a moral imperative to stop the spread of AIDS. In his State of the Union address in January 2003, President Bush announced the largest financial commitment to a single disease in the history of the world. The President's Emergency Plan for AIDS Relief (PEPFAR) initially consisted of a five-year, $15 billion global initiative to provide treatment, prevention, care, and support to HIV-infected individuals and AIDS orphans in fifteen focus countries.[6] As a result of PEPFAR, the United States became the largest single contributor to the international HIV/AIDS pandemic, contributing 47 percent of the $5.6 billion global total spent on the disease in 2006.[7] In August 2008, Congress reauthorized the program for five years and increased its funding to $48 billion.

The combination of funding from multilateral and bilateral organizations—including the Global Fund, PEPFAR, UNAIDS, the World Bank, the United Kingdom's Department for International Development (DFID); private enterprise; and new foundations—has put the fight against AIDS into another league. The question now is how to curtail infection rates before the end of project or funding cycles.

LOSING THE NUMBERS GAME

"We have emerged from the Age of Inaction to the Age of Ineffective Action," wrote economist William Easterly. "In Africa, AIDS is now a multibillion-dollar industry … Unfortunately, these well-meaning efforts are badly weakened by political agenda, misdirected priorities, ignorance, and plain incompetence."[8]

Today, we have the money, political will, and public support, yet more than twenty-five years into the fight we are still losing the numbers game. HIV continues to grow, as does the number of deaths due to AIDS. A total of 39.5 million people were living with HIV in 2006—2.6 million more than in 2004.[9] Young people (fifteen to twenty-four years of age) accounted for 40 percent of new HIV infections in 2006.[10] Every year, over 4.3 million more people are newly infected with HIV, and more than 3 million people die of the disease.[11] If current trends continue, it is estimated that 60 million more HIV infections will occur by 2015, and the annual number of new HIV infections will increase by 20 percent or more by 2012.[12] Unless we devise strategies to sharply reduce the number of new infections, global efforts to makes AIDS treatment universally available will become prohibitively expensive, and millions more people will die as a result of preventable HIV infections.

HIV/AIDS may be the most formidable virus ever encountered. It is the ultimate chameleon: it reproduces at a rate of 10 billion copies per day and mutates rapidly as it reproduces. There are multiple strains of HIV globally, within countries, and even within an individual. Within days of infection, HIV begins to destroy critical immune cells, rendering the body powerless to fight off infection. Finally, HIV inserts itself into the DNA of human cells, where it can remain undetected indefinitely by the body's immune system. Even with extended drug therapy that reduces viral loads (measured as the quantity of viruses found in a milliliter of blood) to undetectable levels, HIV is never completely eradicated from the body. Although extensive research has not given us a "magic bullet" vaccine to end the pandemic, it has equipped us with a toolbox of effective prevention strategies that can slow the spread of the virus. Still, proven prevention strategies such as condom distribution, needle exchanges, and basic education about the disease reach less than 15 percent of the population.[13]

MEDICALIZATION VERSUS PUBLIC HEALTH

Since we have become better at treating the virus, a new temptation has emerged to dwell on qualitative aspects of HIV management and complex algorithms of anti-retroviral therapy that are labor-intensive and require substantial amounts of money and donors' time. The wealthy world has dedicated its resources and energies to treatment and has left prevention efforts, comparatively, by the wayside in pursuit of quick fixes and easily measurable treatment outcomes. With increased funding and commitment, the world has made progress toward the goal of universal access to treatment, as the number of people on ARVs has increased from 2 percent to 28 percent from 2003 to 2007.[14]

But treatment does not come without a cost. Treating AIDS requires the daily delivery of medications as well as the clinical management of patients—for the rest of their lives. If treatment is effective, those lives will be extended for decades to come. Anti-retroviral medications can help to control the disease, but they do not cure it, and treatment roll-out can never meet the pace of new infections—for every one person who goes on treatment, six more contract the virus.[15] More problematic yet, stopping treatment once started promotes the emergence of resistant strains of the virus, making halfway programs hazardous to public health. The sheer volume of health workers needed to tackle HIV disease—and of the health systems to support their work—is off the scale of any previous public health campaign. For international donors, making a commitment to provide treatment comes with a great deal of responsibility and a huge price tag.

Further exacerbating the difficulties of treating HIV and scaling up prevention efforts is the current state of health systems and capacity in the countries hardest hit by the pandemic. Decades of neglect have rendered hospitals, clinics, laboratories, and health care staffs dangerously deficient. Worse yet, local doctors and nurses often grow so exasperated by their dysfunctional health care systems that they apply for higher paying jobs abroad, thus accelerating a "brain drain" at home. There is also an internal brain drain within countries, as local doctors and nurses leave public hospitals and health centers for more lucrative jobs in clinics run by foreign NGOs, bilateral donors, and faith-based organizations.

According to the World Health Organization's World Health Report 2006, there is a shortage of more than 4 million health care workers in fifty-seven developing countries. One-quarter of physicians and one-in-twenty nurses trained in Africa currently work in thirty industrialized countries that are members the Organization for Economic Cooperation and Development (OECD). Although sub-Saharan Africa carries 24 percent of the global disease burden, it has only 3 percent of the worldwide health care workforce and accounts for less than 1 percent of global health care spending. By comparison, the Americas shoulder 10 percent of the global disease burden but attract 37 percent of the health care workforce, and more than half of global health care spending. Many experts identify a shortage of health care workers in the developing countries that are most affected by HIV/AIDS as the biggest challenge facing efforts to combat the disease.[16]

FAILURE TO FOLLOW THE EVIDENCE

HIV/AIDS was, and continues to be, an intensely hot-button issue in countries throughout the world. The basic ways in which it spreads from one person to another force societies to confront the most uncomfortable issues: unprotected sex and illicit drug use. The individuals with the highest risk of contracting HIV are unfortunately those with the least access to basic prevention tools because these populations are often invisible, even to HIV prevention planners.[17] Because of its means of transmission, HIV/AIDS has not been treated like other infectious disease agents, such as measles, to which governments and multilateral agencies respond in an evidenced-based manner. Instead, the response to AIDS has been characterized by a mixture of political interests, ideologies, and (only thirdly) science in the search to find a way to combat the disease. Despite their promise and evidenced-based success rates, prevention efforts have received short shrift in the global response to HIV. The same religious and moral ideologies that contributed to galvanizing funds to fight AIDS are ever-present in the design of anti-AIDS programming.

Abstinence-until-Marriage

The United States often describes its global HIV-prevention strategy with the acronym ABC, which stands for Abstain until marriage, Be faithful, and, when these fail, use Condoms. Prevention programs are designed for specific groups: Abstinence is for unmarried young people, Being faithful for married people, and Condoms for high-risk persons such as sex workers and people living with AIDS. In 2003 Congress authorized PEPFAR spending, but mandated that 33 percent of all money allotted to prevention activities must be spent on abstinence-only programs that encourage teenagers to delay their sexual debut and not have multiple partners after they begin sexual activity.[18]

In 2006 the U.S. General Accounting Office, an independent agency that audits U.S. government programs, released a stinging indictment of U.S. prevention policies that prioritize sexual abstinence and being faithful to an HIV-negative partner over scientifically proven methods of reducing the tide of infections. The GAO report charged that legislative earmarks for abstinence-only programming were impeding the ability of PEPFAR country teams to devise prevention programs that meet national needs.[19] The Institute of Medicine, a nonprofit organization that provides U.S. government agencies with scientifically informed analysis to improve health programs, stated in its 2007 report on PEPFAR that is was "unable to find evidence for the position that abstinence can stand alone (as a prevention message)," yet in fiscal year

2006, 11 million of the people reached by PEPFAR's prevention programs received only abstinence information, and an additional 29 million received only abstinence and be-faithful information.[20]

Such policies have a dramatic effect on countries receiving U.S. foreign aid to fight AIDS. For example, in Uganda, a country that has high HIV/AIDS prevalence rates and is a major recipient of PEPFAR funding, the abstinence approach has had a detrimental effect on prevention efforts among teenagers. More than 50 percent of Ugandan girls have sex by the age of seventeen, usually with older men, yet "abstinence only" programming does not teach Ugandan teens about how to use condoms, nor are condoms made readily available for their use. Unfortunately, abstinence is simply not an option for many girls who live in poverty and have little control over their own bodies or sexual decision making. Continued spending on prevention strategies that have been scientifically proven to be ineffective not only wastes precious resources but also costs lives: each day 6,000 young people between the ages of fifteen and twenty-four will become infected with HIV.[21]

Sex Workers

Preventing infections among marginalized populations such as women and men involved in prostitution can play a significant role in stemming the spread of HIV. Sex workers have some of the highest HIV infection rates in the world—50 percent prevalence in South Africa, 27 percent in Guyana, 33 percent in St. Petersburg (Russia), and 73 percent in urban areas of Ethiopia—yet fewer than 20 percent of sex workers globally had access to HIV prevention services in 2005.[22] Not only are sex workers and their clients at high risk of secondary HIV infection, but their clients' spouses and/or future partners are at increased risk as well.

Current U.S. law requires that any organization receiving U.S. government funding prohibit the use of funds for promoting, supporting, or advocating the legalization or practice of prostitution. This policy runs contrary to best practices in public health and undermines efforts to stem the spread of HIV and human trafficking. For example, the Sonagachi Project in Calcutta, India, has reached more than 30,000 people working in the commercial sex trade who are at risk of HIV. Sonagachi's peer educators work to stop the spread of HIV among women and men in prostitution by offering programs designed to earn their trust, reduce their social isolation, increase their participation in public life, and confront stigma and discrimination.[23] Sonagachi's work has received strong positive evaluations from both UNAIDS and the World Bank, and the project has been cited by UNAIDS as a "best-practice" model of working with women and men in prostitution.[24] Although these initiatives focus on protecting the fundamental human rights and health of sex workers, they do not equate to the promotion of prostitution. Yet valuable programs such as those run by Sonagachi, and organizations like it, are exactly the ones threatened by current U.S. laws and policies.

Injection Drug Users

Injection drug use is a highly efficient route for HIV infection because of the practice of sharing needles, and it accounts for one-third of new infections outside of sub-Saharan Africa.[25] Individuals infected in this way may then, in turn, infect their sexual partners. Despite the fact that the World Health Organization holds needle exchange to be a public health best practice for HIV prevention among injection drug users, only 8 percent of such users have access to HIV prevention services, including access to clean needles and condoms.[26] Instead of pursuing public health approaches for drug users, many countries have chosen a criminal justice approach. Where needle possession is against the law, individuals run the risk of arrest merely by participating in a needle-exchange project. Expansion of prevention services for drug users is particularly needed in Eastern Europe and Central Asia, where over 80 percent of new HIV infections are the result of needle-sharing.[27]

In the mid-1980s, HIV was spreading rapidly among drug addicts in cities throughout the United Kingdom, where in less than eighteen months the prevalence rate among this group jumped from 0 to 56 percent. In 1986 Health Minister Sir Norman Fowler convinced the government to authorize needle-exchange programs. Today, clean needles are distributed throughout the UK, where, by late 2007, transmission from injection drug use accounted for only 5.2 percent of HIV infections.[28] By contrast, in the United States, where federal funding for needle-exchange programs is prohibited, injection drug use was responsible for 25 percent of new infections in 2005. The U.S government continues to prohibit the use of foreign spending for needle exchange, embracing an ideological rather than an evidenced-based approach to the spread of HIV through injection drug use.

Our failure to fund and implement evidenced-based programs to combat the spread of HIV/AIDS among all groups at risk drains critical resources, exhausts donor support when results are not achieved, and put the lives of millions of people in peril.

FAILURE IN FOREIGN AID ARCHITECTURE

According to public health epidemiologist James Chin, "In recent years, a distinction has been made between global versus international heath.

International health focuses on providing aid to countries, while global health relates to health issues that transcend national borders. A global approach is needed to respond to the AIDS pandemic, but we have primarily an international response."[29] The response to the HIV/AIDS pandemic thus far has been an extension of short-term, results-oriented, unsustainable foreign aid giving that reflects the wealthy world's values and priorities, rather than a much-needed global strategy based on the situation on the ground combined with a long-term focus on preventing the occurrence of new infections.

Short-Term and Disease-Specific Commitments

Investment in strong health care systems is the key to curtailing the spread of infectious disease in any country. Success is measured by the number of infections prevented and the number of lives saved. Because these preventative effects are difficult for donors to quantify and report to constituents, there has been a focus, instead, on targeting foreign aid to fund easily measurable advances in specific attention-grabbing diseases, such as the number of people provided with AIDS treatment. The difficulty of HIV prevention is that it forces political leaders to think in the long term, not in relation to their own personal term limits.

There are great dangers in funding only disease-specific initiatives and not integrating them into wider-ranging programs to meet the public health needs on the ground. For example, Rwanda is a country with a relatively low rate of HIV/AIDS (about 3.1 percent) but with high infant- and child-mortality rates. Yet, in 2005 almost three-quarters of all donor assistance for health care in Rwanda was reserved for HIV/AIDS, while only 2 percent of the aid was dedicated to health care services for child illness; also, more than half of the donor-funded health projects there are financed for less than twelve months.[30] Child-mortality rates are now increasing in many countries, as highly coveted health care funding is dedicated to HIV/AIDS, regardless of epidemiological data. Providing treatment for specific diseases without corresponding investments in access to clean water, waste disposal, and health facilities is like putting a Band-aid on a gaping wound.

Donor Priorities vs. Needs-based Measures

Foreign aid spending tends to reflect the priorities of the donors' country. On a global basis, recent estimates reveal that AIDS accounts for less than 4 percent of the deaths of children up to fourteen years of age, while diarrheal diseases, malaria, measles, whooping cough, and tetanus account for close to 60 percent of deaths in that age group.[31] Effective and relatively inexpensive

preventive measures and/or treatments are available for these infectious diseases. But the decision to provide funding to save children suffering from
whooping cough rather than providing treatment for someone dying of AIDS
should not be an either/or proposition. Rich countries have enough money to
fund both efforts—what is required now is political commitment and prioritization so that the aid dollars committed can be spent most efficiently to
upgrade the *overall* health and well-being of societies.

GLOBAL SOLUTIONS

The excitement, energy, and resources now mobilized in the wealthy world to
address the problem of HIV/AIDS in the poorer world is historic in scale; it
may well represent the single greatest achievement to date in the Age of
Globalization. But as grand as it is, throwing money at the HIV pandemic—
particularly without effectively slowing spread of the virus—is simply not sufficient. We must take a deep breath, rethink both strategy and tactics, and
imagine a new world.

Targeted, Evidenced-based Interventions

Prevention measures that are already in existence could significantly slow, and
perhaps reverse, the dire projections for the worsening of the HIV epidemic.[32]
HIV/AIDS programs need to develop specific public health interventions for
each means of infection, based on local surveillance of the patterns and prevalence of these risk factors and risk behaviors.[33] By appropriately allocating prevention measures to those who need it, we could prevent half of the infections
projected for 2015.[34] This effect would then begin to snowball, resulting in 4
million fewer infections each year thereafter.[35]

   Existing successful models (Brazil, Thailand, and Uganda) all exhibit the following traits: sufficient funds; political support; evidence-informed action;
media coverage and other methods of raising awareness of HIV/AIDS and sex-
ually transmitted infections (STI); promotion of prevention technologies such
as condoms; community involvement; and anti-stigma efforts.[36] Each prevented infection not only saves the life of the protected individual but also has
positive benefits for the entire society. For example, every dollar invested in
Thailand's HIV prevention program saved $43 in future treatment costs.[37]

Mitigation of Gender Inequities

In sub-Saharan Africa, women are disproportionately affected by HIV/AIDS.
For every ten adult males living with HIV, fourteen adult women are infected.

In South Africa, women fifteen to twenty-four years of age are four times as likely as men of the same age to become infected.[38] The "feminization" of AIDS is a stark reminder that gender inequity and violence against women fuel the epidemic in much of the world. Life-saving drugs that prevent mother-to-child-transmission of the disease have been available to only 11 percent of pregnant women in low- and middle-income countries.[39] "If we're serious about saving lives, we need to face the realities and meet people with options that are realistic for their life circumstances," commented Dr. Helene Gayle, executive director of CARE.[40]

We must focus on strategies that mitigate gender inequities and increase women's access to health services, education, and economic livelihoods. In many countries, micro-credit programs—which offer poor women small loans for self-employment projects that generate income—are touted as an effective means of raising women out of extreme poverty and empowering them with a sense of self-worth that helps to combat the underlying power inequities that can make women more vulnerable to sexual violence or necessitate exchanges of sexual favors for food or shelter. Investing in women has also proven to be one of the surest ways to ensure the health of the family. An educated woman, for instance, is 50 percent more likely than an uneducated one to have her children immunized.[41]

Sustained Investment in Health Care Systems

Strengthening health care systems and management capacity requires a sustained, long-term investment. Innovative solutions are needed to solve the shortages of health care workers. Some promising partnerships do exist to increase the number of trained health care workers in developing countries. For example, in Bangladesh, BRAC University's new School of Public Health aims to train experts from the developing world for service in the developing world, while drawing upon the expertise of wealthy-world institutions such as Harvard's School of Public Health and Sweden's Karolinska School. The crucial element for the success of such initiatives is that wealthy countries support measures to limit the poaching of foreign-trained doctors to fill their own shortages of medical professionals.

Integrated Approach

AIDS treatment and prevention activities cannot be pursued in a vacuum: they have to be integrated into a larger functioning public health system in order to destigmatize the disease and create sustainable structures. This integration is of growing importance with the advent of extremely drug resistant tuberculosis and other opportunistic infectious diseases that take advantage of the weakened immune system of HIV/AIDS patients. HIV/AIDS services must also be merged with reproductive and maternal health services so that women are more readily diagnosed and treated, and mother-to-child transmission of the disease is prevented.

Expanded Research

The only way to curb the rate of infection and seal the bottomless pit of spending is by developing and implementing new prevention technologies, such as microbicides, male circumcision, post-exposure prophylaxis, and HIV vaccines. Beyond the humanitarian imperative, better prevention technologies such as these are critical to capping costs. A safe, effective, globally accessible, inexpensive HIV vaccine remains our best hope to control and, ultimately, end the pandemic. In addition to basic clinical, prevention, social, and policy research, we must identify which approaches are effective in the field, which are not, and why.

"We can't win anymore. There's no way we can win. The death toll is already at a high. But what we can do is we can mitigate the disaster because through mitigating the disaster, we can show our humanity. Beating HIV? HIV's going to be with us for a generation or more," commented Zachie Achmat, South African activist and founder and chairman of Treatment Action Campaign (TAC).

THE NEW WAY

Despite massive advocacy efforts, reenergized political will and significant increases in financial support, the global response to the AIDS epidemic has been sorely inadequate, focusing more on treatment and crisis management than on the prevention of new infections. Health care economist Mead Over warns that U.S. global AIDS spending, now largely considered a foreign policy and humanitarian success, "contains the seeds of a future crisis." He continues:

> Life-long treatment costs are increasing as those on treatment live longer, and the number of new HIV infections continues to outpace the number of people receiving treatment. Escalating treatment costs coupled with neglected prevention measures threaten to squeeze out U.S. spending on other global health needs, even to the point of consuming half of the entire U.S. foreign assistance budget by 2016.[42]

We are at a historic moment in the battle against HIV—we have both the will to fight and the armory to do so. Unless we come together as a global community to support evidenced-based treatment and prevention strategies, however, we risk losing hard-won momentum, and we face global resignation to the preventable deaths of millions of people.

NO: Mark Heywood, *AIDS Law Project*

Wealthy nations do have a legal and moral responsibility to promote anti-AIDS efforts in poor countries. However, arguments touting these moral and legal responsibilities often have fatal flaws: they overlook the role of AIDS activists in bringing about a truly global response to the problem and the role they must continue to play, and they pay insufficient attention to the politics of health in developing countries and therefore to the reasons for the evolution of what is frequently called a "vertical" response—one that channels resources directly to the problem, in this case HIV, rather than through the expansion and strengthening of existing health systems. Finally, they oversimplify the reasons why HIV treatment programs have been able to deliver more tangible benefits than HIV prevention.

My argument, therefore, focuses on what "promoting anti-AIDS efforts" actually entails, as well as how. Schneider and Garrett see the "excitement, energy, and dollars" mobilized in the wealthy world to address HIV/AIDS as "possibly the single greatest achievement to date in the Age of Globalization." But the reality is that the wealthy world's response to HIV has been *ad hoc*, prescriptive, paternalistic, and, at times, contradictory. If this approach continues, it may ultimately do more harm than good.

IS THERE A NEW COMMITMENT TO GLOBAL HEALTH?

Something is happening around the issue of health care, but is it froth or something more fundamental? Since the late 1980s, the HIV/AIDS epidemic has forced Third World health back onto global political agendas. The death of millions of poor people, mostly in Africa, is seen as a morally repugnant blight that, in the words of a former UN Special Envoy for AIDS in Africa, Stephen Lewis, "shames and diminishes us all."[1]

Initially in the United States, and later within the UN, AIDS activists have pressured politicians to open up new resources and commitments for tackling neglected diseases, including malaria and tuberculosis, around which there had been decades of fatalistic resignation and inertia. Significantly, the demands of AIDS activism evolved from advocacy for equal rights and nondiscrimination for people in the United States with HIV in the 1980s and 1990s to calling for action on social and economic rights for people in the Third World. At the beginning of the new century, activist campaigns were mainly about the right of access to affordable medicines. But, increasingly, they demand investment in health systems and health workers. It was a direct result of these campaigns that anti-retroviral (ARV) drug prices were made affordable to developing countries, and that bodies such as the Global Fund on AIDS, TB and Malaria (GFATM) were established.

Activist pressure also re-ignited debates about health governance. The 2002 appointment, by the UN Commission on Human Rights, of a Special Rapporteur on the right of everyone to the highest attainable standard of physical and mental health, and the establishment in 2005 of the Commission on the Social Determinants of Health (CSDH) were positive signals. So, too, are signs that a number of developing-country governments have begun to accept and assert their duty to protect and fulfill the human right to health, particularly when it comes to the clash between intellectual property law and the affordability of essential medicines.

Those wanting to claim that there is a commitment to global health will also point to a number of bi- and multi-lateral governmental initiatives around the issue of health. For example, in March 2007, the governments of Brazil, France, Indonesia, Norway, Senegal, South Africa, and Thailand issued a statement describing health as "one of the most important, yet still broadly neglected, long-term foreign policy issues of our time," and promising henceforth "to make impact on health a point of departure and a defining lens that each of our countries will use to examine key elements of foreign policy and development strategies."[2]

Another feature of the past decade has been the emergence of a range of governance institutions and vertical health programs that aim to staunch aspects of the health hemorrhage. Mechanisms such as the GFATM and the U.S. President's Emergency Program for AIDS Relief (PEPFAR) have stepped into the breach created by state and multilateral failures around issues of health. On July 30, 2008, President Bush signed a congressional authorization of $48 billion for PEPFAR.[3] Side-by-side with these mechanisms are the global health programs of late-in-the-day philanthropists such as Bill and Melinda Gates and Bill Clinton.

These initiatives have a positive impact on millions of lives, but they entail risks. By tacitly accepting developing-state failure in relation to health, they fragment and further weaken national health systems. In some cases, they even compound the crisis by sucking scarce health workers out of public health systems—an effect that was contemplated in a recent article analyzing PEPFAR: "The effect on the wider health care system of funding a disease-specific programme is harder to quantify."[4] This mixed result is why global and national health programs must be judged not by surface impressions or wishful thinking but by critical analysis.

These developments beg some questions. Why, despite the centrality of health to the Millennium Development Goals (MDGs), and the flurry of new health initiatives, is health aid declining?[5] Why are African governments not meeting their own pledges to increase spending on health as a percentage of total expenditures?[6] Why are First World governments not fixing their own health systems, given that the doctor/nurse shortage in poor countries is directly linked to their diversion to rich countries that are not training enough of their own health care workers?

These questions force us to face a sober reality: much as we may be inclined to misty-eyed approval of the contributions wealthy nations and wealthy individuals make to the fight against HIV/AIDS, we must ask (a) whether those contributions are sustainable for the millions of people whose lives now depend on them, and (b) whether they will bring about any change in the ability of governments to promote and protect health at a national level—or in citizens' power to demand the right to health and health care services. The answer to the first question is uncertain, particularly in the context of a global financial crisis. The answer to the second is "maybe—maybe not."

Morally and legally, wealthy nations do have a duty in relation to HIV/AIDS. But realpolitik and the future of public health require that we do more to ascertain the political and economic factors that are determining of health. In this way we may begin to shape a global response to health care issues, including better guidance to maximize the potential outcomes from the giving habits of wealthy nations.

FROM STATE TO NONSTATE

Health care has made itself global because disease has gone global, as evidenced by HIV. But this situation in itself is not new. Throughout history, economic expansion has spread disease; indeed, the notion of public health arose from the need of the state to prevent and treat this phenomenon. Protecting armies, navies, settler populations, and the aristocracy from being wiped out by "foreign" diseases about which there was no knowledge—or for which people had no immunity—was a necessity both for the "progress" of colonialism and for the expansion of national economies. Over time, this necessity led to vaccination campaigns, investment in water and sewerage systems, public health legislation, and the creation of rudimentary public health services. Growing state involvement with health led to declines in mortality.

But if such engagement was once the case, it is so no longer. Something has changed. Today, there is a deficit of coordination, investment, and planning in health care. Ironically, however (as we see later), the explanation for this health care deficit may still rest in the relationship between national governments and economic expansion. Many governments now neglect key functions of the state, such as health care and education—as is illustrated by the changing pattern of research and development of new medicines. At the start of the twentieth century, governments of industrialized countries—particularly those in Europe—invested heavily in research, which contributed significantly to such medical breakthroughs as the treatment of TB. However, since the early 1990s, there has been a dramatic decline in medical innovation that has been attributed, at least in part, to declining investments by European governments in pharmaceutical research, development, and application.[7]

Except in times of crisis or threat, the dominant politics of health care today seems to be one in which responsibility for the protection, maintenance, and improvement of public health is being separated from the state. In the so-called First World, this privatization movement is driven by a complacent assumption that infectious disease has largely been conquered.

GLOBAL DISEASE THREATS: SELF-INTEREST FIRST

Following upon the advent of neoliberal economic policies in the 1980s, wealthy countries underwent a transition away from proactive, state-driven strategies in public health, adopting instead a largely passive and technical approach that aims to manage the maintenance of health systems and infrastructure, while avoiding periodic disease outbreaks. The consensus is that, as long as major public health threats are held at bay or contained in developing countries, the *actual* health of their citizens—who are getting less healthy, but no longer primarily as a result of communicable disease—is of less concern to the state.

Thus, within developed countries, but to significantly varying degrees, the state supports health systems that maintain a high standard of health care "at home," such as the National Health System (NHS) in England or Medicaid in the United States. Compared with health systems in the Third World, these systems offer an undreamt-of standard of care. However, they, too, have been subject to attacks by government that have reduced the quality of care and, in countries such as the United States, have left millions of people uninsured and grossly disadvantaged in access to decent health services.

But even the praiseworthy parts of these state-run health systems overlook how infectious and communicable diseases take advantage of the explosion of inter- and intra-national travel to move pathogens swiftly, from causing local-ized to generating globalized epidemics. Most wealthy governments seem to believe that their duty to provide health care and their budgetary responsibili-ties and health policies end abruptly at national boundaries. What happens on the other side of these porous borders is not the responsibility of health depart-ments but of "development aid."

The health services of wealthy nations are not linked to an integrated global strategy that recognizes the transnational nature of both good and bad health. Although the world has acknowledged the impact of health on development—and vice versa—there is still no globally agreed *political* strategy on states' duty to tackle health care issues or the interventions and standards that will be required to achieve the MDGs. Thus, although funding for health programs, including the prevention and treatment of HIV/AIDS, represents a growing portion of devel-opment aid, such efforts continue to be implemented through vertical programs that often ignore or work around the larger political paralysis on health care.

Consequently, foreign assistance for health is rarely driven by precisely iden-tified and quantified local needs, but is instead determined by what wealthy nations consider those needs to be. New imbalances and inequalities arise because donor funds end up being transferred only to those organizations in recipient countries that have the capacity to design and (usually) implement these programs. This situation leads to further distortions and imbalances between urban and rural areas or between developing countries. A symptom of the want of coordination in the financing of health care is the lack of funding for TB, which derives from the fact that HIV may have initially squeezed out this less prominent disease in the "competition" for donor funds.[8] Given that TB is now the primary cause of death in people with HIV in developing coun-tries, this distortion is particularly grotesque.

The wheel has come full circle. A century ago, the state actively intervened to improve public health. Today, in both the industrialized and the developing worlds, it is the lack of action that influences patterns of disease. This is the politics that needs to be addressed both in relation to funding from wealthy nations and to the legitimate expectations of developing country governments by their citizens.

DEVELOPING COUNTRIES: HEALTH AT THE MARGINS

Schneider and Garrett call for "investment in strong health systems" and for a stepping-up of "targeted evidence-based" prevention interventions to replace the "religious and moral ideologies ... that are ever-present on the design of anti-AIDS programming." They are right to make these demands. But they overlook the lassitude of the governments of developing countries toward health and HIV, as well as the realities of what has happened to our health care systems over the past few decades.

In this context, it is unfortunate but relevant that the largely laissez-faire approach to health care adopted by industrialized-country governments has been mimicked by the governments of most developing countries. The rot started under the old policies of the International Monetary Fund and the World Bank, which in the 1980s and 1990s required cuts in social investment and in public goods, including health care. But today, the neglect of health takes place not under the whip of international financial institutions but as a voluntary policy of government. Many developing countries replicate the First World approach to health care policy by attempting to maintain expensive but still underfunded tertiary-care systems in urban centers (which are wrongly considered to be the template of a health care system), while throwing in an ingredient of what some describe as "selective primary health care" in rural and peri-urban districts.[9] In the spaces that public health should occupy, there have arisen large and profitable private health care sectors that cater to the health needs of the wealthy and the employed.

It is an unpalatable fact that public health is rarely regarded as a political priority by developing-country governments. Planning to improve health is not integrated into development or economic planning, or vice versa. For example, in South Africa, the media statements that are released after government cabinet meetings reveal no record of discussions of health broadly. Although there are discussions about HIV/AIDS, generally they have taken place only in response to activists' criticism of the country's response to that particular problem. Despite a burgeoning AIDS epidemic, former South African President Mbeki's annual State of the Nation speech to Parliament, given in February each year, often barely touched on health. Indeed, in 2004 and 2005, the issue of health occupied only a fraction of the time given to matters of economy, international affairs, and poverty.

This low prioritization of public health issues is borne out by the way in which, in many countries, poor performance and corruption are tolerated from health ministers and their departments. As a rule, developing-country governments approach health reactively rather than proactively. Their passive attitude is evidenced by the almost complete dependence of many African governments on wealthy nations for health investment; the absence of serious and consistently driven public health strategies; the acceptance of very high rates of maternal mortality; the neglect of primary health care; and the failure to control infectious diseases. The failure therefore is not limited to the "foreign aid architecture" around health funding that is referred to by Schneider and

Garrett, but is also found in the domestic architecture. The two constitute a vicious and mutually reinforcing circle.

HEALTH AND UNDERDEVELOPMENT: GLOBALIZATION AND ITS CONSEQUENCE FOR PUBLIC HEALTH

Developing-country governments cannot feign ignorance about the linkages between politics, health, and development. A succession of commissions—notably, the WHO's Commission on Macro Economics and Health (CMEH 2002) and its Commission on Social Determinants of Health (CSDH 2008), as well as the United Kingdom–sponsored Commission on Africa (2005)—has drawn attention to the linkages. For example, the report of the CMEH offers the following warning:

> As with the economic well-being of individual households, good popula-
> tion health is a critical input into poverty reduction, economic growth, and
> long-term economic development at the scale of whole societies. This point
> is widely acknowledged by analysts and policy makers, but is greatly under-
> estimated in its qualitative and quantitative significance, and in the invest-
> ment allocations of many developing country and donor governments.[10]

Why then, in the face of this repeatedly restated evidence, is health care failing so signally in so many countries? Why are U.S. donor dollars—which by March 2008 claimed to be keeping alive 1.7 million people with HIV—not altering the underlying determinants of health? Is there an explanation other than the wiles of politicians? Why has a period in history that has seen the advance of democracy been accompanied by declines in health? Why have the citizens of the new democracies not forced health issues into greater focus?

Modern health care, or the want of it, is rooted in economy and politics, as is population vulnerability to disease. Since the late 1980s, there have been rapid and important changes in economy and society. Improvements in technology and communications have been the primary drivers of a new phase of economic globalization and integration. What Karl Marx called "the means of production" (factories and technology) have become more and more capital-intensive—and less and less dependent on labor. Linked to this evolution—and enabled by it—were profound political developments, notably the end of the so-called cold war and the collapse of "communism," which opened new markets for economic expansion, especially in Asia. New technologies have been introduced to new and old markets, creating new consumption "needs." These new commodities depend less on the labor of human beings to produce them—making them cheaper. Yet they can be enormously profitable, by virtue of new economies of scale unleashed by the global economy.

How does this economic revolution relate to health? It has diminished the relative importance of human labor (and thus humans) to the production of wealth: more profit can now be made by fewer and fewer workers. In many emerging markets—including India, China, and South Africa—this devaluation of the human factor has left an enormous surplus population, who have little prospect of ever getting gainful employment. These people have no role in the formal economy. In South Africa, for example, despite a decade of rapid economic growth, unemployment remains at 40 percent. High and permanent unemployment will be a feature of the twenty-first-century economy. Thus, inadvertently perhaps, it is the health of the few—those who produce wealth—that matters in the modern economy, rather than the health of the population as a whole.

Because the health of poor people has been delinked from productivity and profit, developing-country governments behave as if they no longer have an economic interest in using the state's resources and power to improve public health. Investments in AIDS prevention and treatment have rarely been voluntary decisions of government—generally, they have been decisions taken under the pressure of local and international activists. Countries such as Botswana and Uganda, where political leadership has been more far-sighted, are the exception, not the rule. And even in these countries, AIDS programs and public health continue to exhibit enormous deficiencies and inequalities.

The past two decades have taught governments and capitalists that it is possible to sustain economic growth while generally ignoring general population health—a lesson in neglect that is also applicable in education and other areas of social welfare. This sorry spectacle seems to confirm the arguments of those political economists who claim that capitalism "generates economic growth, prosperity, employment as side-effects. It also causes much misery and destruction in its tendency towards incessant change."[11]

Thus, the same economic logic that discourages private investment in the research and development of new medicines for the poor because their sale will yield no profitable return works to deny public investment in population health—which is also thought to have no direct benefit to the state or the economy. Health may be a social necessity, but it is not necessarily an economic one.

IS INVESTING IN HEALTH AN ECONOMIC NECESSITY?

Failure to recognize the reality of governmental neglect may be the fatal flaw in the recommendations of commissions such as the CMEH and the CSDH, which may be astute and accurate but do not take sufficient account of, or speak honestly about, how national politics and economics influence health. In its executive summary, for example, the CMEH relays this finding:

> We estimate that approximately 330 million DALYs [disability adjusted life years] would be saved for each of the 8 million deaths averted. Assuming, conservatively, that each DALY saved gives an economic benefit of 1 year's per capita income of a projected $563 in 2015, the direct economic benefit of saving 330 million DALYs would be $186 billion per year, and plausibly several times that.[12]

This perceived benefit would seem to provide a huge incentive for governments to invest in health care. The problem is that it does not, because most of those ill or at risk of illness are outside the modern economy. Influenced by economists such as Amartya Sen, the CMEH's recommendations assume that governments attach an economic value to sick people who could be healthy, and that most of the people who are healthy but poor will be able to find a place in the modern economy. Neither assumption may prove true. If economic growth can be achieved by relatively small segments of the population utilizing increasingly capital-intensive technologies for ever-larger markets, then these assumptions are mistaken.

Crudely put, illnesses such as those caused by the HIV/AIDS epidemic, while causing widespread suffering and social dislocation, do nothing to further economically disable those segments of the population that are already socially disabled by the fact that there is no place in the modern economy for them.

The lack of a purely economic motive for investment in health care is further compounded by the fact that in many developing countries the financial cost to the state of treating illness is avoided because the collapse of health services means that most people die at home—burdening their families, but not necessarily requiring public expenditure. In South Africa, for example, as illustrated by Table 1, there has been a dramatic rise in mortality, most of it caused by HIV/AIDS and TB.[13] But despite this trend, as seen in Table 2, there was an overall decline in hospital admissions between 2001 and 2007.

This discrepancy suggests several things: that hospitals are saturated; that people are being admitted for longer periods (because they are sicker); and that many people are bypassing the lower rungs of the health system in order to access tertiary care. However, the net effect is that a large portion of the growing burden of disease is displaced onto the families of poor people—reports show that nearly 50 percent of deaths occur at home. This pattern probably exists in many other developing countries with high HIV prevalence.

Table 1

Mortality Trends in South Africa, 1997–2005

Year	Deaths	Deaths as % of total population	Deaths as % of uninsured population
1997	316,507	0,8%	0,9%
1998	365,053	0,9%	1,0%
1999	380,982	0,9%	1,1%
2000	414,531	1,0%	1,2%
2001	453,404	1,0%	1,2%
2002	499,925	1,1%	1,3%
2003	553,718	1,2%	1,4%
2004	572,350	1,2%	1,4%
2005	591,213	1,3%	1,5%

Source: *Statistics South Africa*

Table 2

Hospital Admissions in South Africa, 2000–2007

	2000/01	2001/02	2002/03	2003/04	2004/05	2005/06	2006/07
District	1,624,425	1,593,010	1,524,585	1,513,924	1,529,946	1,600,115	1,439,544
Regional	1,388,042	1,545,566	1,487,031	1,518,548	1,463,930	1,507,511	1,327,711
Central and tertiary	568,585	603,677	612,556	599,796	610,344	572,943	698,518
Total	3,581,052	3,742,253	3,624,172	3,632,268	3,604,220	3,680,569	3,465,773

Note: Reclassification in Eastern Cape for 2006/07 accounts for changes between regional and central.

HEALTH IS A HUMAN RIGHT AND A LEGAL ENTITLEMENT

I have drawn a rather pessimistic and tragic picture in response to Garrett and Schneider's affirmation that wealthy nations should promote anti-AIDS efforts in developing countries. I have done so because, while there must be no doubt that wealthy nations have a moral and legal duty to promote such efforts, more is required than just throwing money or medicines at the problem. It is incumbent on wealthy nations to take steps and adopt policies that aim to resuscitate global health.

The vertical response to HIV and treatment for AIDS, which is criticized by Garrett and Schneider as the "pursuit of quick fixes and easily measurable treatment outcomes," was necessary initially because AIDS presented the global system with a disease emergency that was unprecedented in modern times. HIV arrived at a time when the health systems of poor countries were dilapidated and without capacity to generate their own effective response. An externally driven, vertical response was necessary to save lives.

But developing countries are now in a catch-22 situation. Donor funding remains necessary to save millions of lives, but it fuels a vicious circle: because of the collapse of "horizontal" health systems, there is often no alternative other than the vertical funding streams. But funding health in this way further weakens the local base of health systems.

Reviving the world's failing health systems will require that health care reform and investment be demanded and driven by a recognition of legal duties that arise from the international human rights framework. Such an understanding should form the foundation of the efforts of wealthy nations to address the problem of HIV/AIDS.

In this respect, it is worth drawing attention to a proposal made by health law scholar Larry Gostin, who has argued for a Framework Convention on Global Health, which would set global norms and standards of health, as well as seeking to calculate the investment that is necessary for both health systems and priority-disease programs.[14] It is necessary to recognize in practice (and not just in prayers) the interconnectedness of developing- and developed-country health—a lesson that the AIDS epidemic has made glaringly apparent.

gender

Should the United States Aggressively Promote Women's Rights in Developing Nations?

YES: Isobel Coleman, *Council on Foreign Relations*

NO: Marcia E. Greenberg, *Cornell Law School*

Women have suffered from numerous forms of discrimination through the ages. While some inroads have been made in recent years in terms of political enfranchisement and entry into the workforce, widespread disparities persist between women's and men's wages and between the social status accorded to women and men in most societies. As of 2008, only 18 percent of legislators in the world's parliaments were women.[1] Also, in most countries, girls receive less education than boys (see Table 1) and are viewed as subservient in many ways.

From the 1970s on, international attention has become focused on women's rights and the need to achieve women's equality. Activist NGOs at UN conferences on population (1974, 1984, 1994) and women (1975, 1980, 1985, 1995) generated global publicity and national campaigns. Globalization has contributed to the rapid and universal spread of these ideas, as well as facilitating the creation of formal networks of activists to promote the ideas and coordinate their activities.

The 1994 Cairo Conference on Population and Development marked a sea change in attitudes about women's rights. The resulting Cairo Declaration maintained that women's equality was a necessary condition for economic development as well as for reducing population growth rates. In order to limit population growth rates, particularly in developing countries, women had to be empowered to play an equal role in family-planning choices. In addition, the new policy consensus held that women's equality was necessary for eco-

Table 1

Primary School–age Girls Not Enrolled in School in Developing Countries

	2002	(millions) Goal by 2015	Shortfall
Sub-Saharan Africa	23.8	9.6	3.8
Arab States	5.0	3.5	0.5
East Asia & the Pacific	4.9	7.1	0.7
South Asia	23.6	9.6	0.0
Latin America & the Caribbean	1.5	1.1	1.1
All developing countries	58.8	30.9	6.0

Source: UNDP, *Human Development Report 2005* (New York: Oxford University Press, 2005), 45.
Note: The shortfall represents the predicted number of primary-school-age girls in each region by which the goal of full primary education enrollment will not be met if current trends continue.

nomic development; that in order to combat poverty, women's wages had to be equal to men's; and that women needed to play a more influential role in the economy.

Women's equality became enshrined as an international aspiration in the Millennium Development Goals of 2000—one of which calls for reducing gender inequality and empowering women for development. The main target is to eliminate gender disparity in primary and secondary education by 2005, and at all levels of education by 2015. Current studies indicate significant movement toward achieving these goals in most areas other than Africa.

Women's equality thus serves a dual purpose. In the West, where individual rights are dominant, it is seen as a principled goal in and of itself. But, more universally, it is now regarded as instrumentally desirable in order to promote economic development and limit population growth rates. Despite this consensus on the necessity of promoting gender equality, policy debates have ensued on how to achieve these goals, and many observers have lamented the limited financial resources that have been committed to the struggle.

Including women in actively shaping family-planning decisions—by providing relevant information and contraception—has been strongly opposed by the Republican right in the United States; social conservatives believe that foreign aid should not be spent on any activities that disseminate information about abortion. Therefore, even those pursuing women's literacy projects encounter questions about funding priorities, for it is now conventional wisdom among development economists that more literate women enjoy greater influence over family-planning decisions because they are able to earn more money and thus enjoy greater social status, as well as being able to read family-planning materials. Moreover, while empowering women in developing societies is now regarded as a desirable policy instrument and objective, it is extremely difficult in practice to reverse traditional social habits based on male supremacy.

Women's equality spans a wide array of issues, and it is difficult to separate them. For instance, does promoting women's rights require improved literacy, increased focus on women's health issues, greater political empowerment, higher wages, and more job opportunities? Do all of these goals have to be pursued in combination, or can they be disentangled?

Analysts ask about the appropriate political channels through which to promote women's equality. National governments control much of the money for such activities, yet the involvement of powerful foreign governments such as that of the United States is often met with resentment abroad. International organizations, such as the United Nations Population Fund (UNFPA), national foundations and networks of NGOs (such as Planned Parenthood) can provide lower-profile channels to provide resources directly to target groups in developing countries.

The matter of women's rights is a complex issue. The articles that follow take differing positions on whether the United States should aggressively pursue its various aspects in developing countries in light of the normative justification for such efforts, and the possible indirect and unanticipated political consequences of such policies.

Discussion Questions

1. Is it possible to promote women's rights in some countries yet still respect cultural and religious beliefs and practices?

2. Why are women's rights important? Are there reasons beyond a moral right to equality? Is there a reason to focus on women's rights rather than human rights more generally?

3. Is promoting women's rights a development objective or a foreign policy objective?

4. Besides supporting education for girls and women, what other ways of promoting women's rights does Isobel Coleman propose? What strategy does she suggest for accomplishing these goals? Do you agree?

5. Marcia Greenberg makes a distinction between "rights-based" and "rights-focused" initiatives. What are the differences? What reasons does she give to explain why "rights-focused" initiatives often fail? What does she propose as alternatives to women's rights initiatives?

YES: Isobel Coleman, *Council on Foreign Relations*

Should the United States move aggressively to promote women's rights and education in developing nations? On the surface, it seems almost odd to be asking this question. Women's rights are not distinct from human rights, and since 1948, when the United States led the international community in adopting the Universal Declaration of Human Rights, the promotion of human rights has been a core U.S. foreign policy value. This is not to say that the United States has consistently backed human rights. On countless occasions, Washington has prioritized other foreign policy objectives over the promotion of human rights—a "sell-out" cynics might say, or, from a realist perspective, the inevitable result of hard strategic choices. When it comes to women's issues, cultural and religious constraints add additional complexities. But this is no reason to shy away from the imperative of women's rights. In our increasingly global world, the empowerment of women is critical to addressing the most serious issues of our time: the rise of global extremism, the persistence of crushing poverty, the spread of deadly infectious diseases and environmental degradation.[1] So the question on women's empowerment is not "whether," but "how."

If we define women's empowerment as increasing women's access to quality education, opportunities to generate income, political voice and health, there are ample opportunities for the United States to promote the role of women in global society in ways that support its other foreign policy objectives. The word *aggressively* in the question posed is somewhat vexing. Promoting women's rights in traditional societies must be done with sensitivity and caution, given the highly controversial nature of women's issues. The United States cannot simply impose its own understanding of women's rights on developing countries. Instead, it should support existing local women's groups and work through multilateral organizations to foster change from within. Even in the most conservative societies, there are leaders working to improve the status and opportunities of women in their communities. The benefits of promoting women's rights, and especially of investing in women's education, are so clear that it behooves U.S. policymakers to support these efforts.

SUPPORT FOR GIRLS' EDUCATION: A FOREIGN POLICY "NO-BRAINER"

In the early 1990s, Lawrence Summers, then the chief economist of the World Bank, made the economic case that investing in girls' education was the "highest return investment available in the developing world."[2] Numerous studies before and since corroborate that assertion. The World Bank, for example, has shown through its research that women's education improves the health and survival of both the mother and child.[3] According to its *Engendering Development* report, "there is a strong negative association between mother's average schooling and child mortality."[4] The report goes on to explain that a woman's schooling specifically increases the likelihood that she will immunize her children and give them proper medical care. Educated mothers are certainly more likely than uneducated mothers—and even more likely than educated fathers—to ensure that all their children, both boys and girls, attend school.

As numerous studies also show, female education leads to a decrease in fertility rates. A woman who is educated is likely to marry later (and therefore have fewer childbearing years), to have the confidence to make her own reproductive decisions, and to take better care of the children she already has. Since high fertility often exacerbates the problems associated with poverty and strains already limited government resources, educating women and realizing lower fertility rates is an important step in ending the vicious cycle of poverty in the poorest countries of the world.

Female education is also critical for economic productivity and growth. Development economist Stephan Klasen's work shows that when girls do not attend school, a society loses the productive capacity of some of its most able and competent members. Klasen concludes that gender equality in education, specifically at higher levels, improves the overall quality of education in a society and eventually leads to significant economic growth.[5] Although some economists continue to challenge the link between girls' education and economic growth, several other studies support Klasen's research.[6] David Kucera, a labor economist at the International Labour Organization, has found that gender equality in education also positively impacts foreign direct investment (FDI) in developing countries.[7] Many of the light manufacturing and service-sector jobs created in developing countries through FDI tend to employ women. These jobs are often an extended family's ticket to the middle class.

Agnes Quisumbing, a researcher at the International Food Policy Research Institute, has published several studies on the connection between female literacy and agricultural productivity, an important driver of economic growth, given agriculture's central role in many developing countries. Quisumbing's research demonstrates that raising the educational level of female farmers—more so than that of male farmers—increases the probability that new technologies and methods will be adopted.[8]

Ultimately, educated women are more productive members of society who can better improve the health of their families, lower fertility rates, contribute to economic growth, improve agricultural productivity, and attract foreign direct investment. Even in the most conservative societies, if women are able to contribute to the economy and health of the community, their status undoubtedly improves. The more active they become in the public sphere, the more they are able to impact policies and issues facing women across the country. Education gives women the skills and confidence they need to become active agents of change in their own local communities.

Many developed countries and international organizations are finally recognizing the benefits of investing in education in the developing world, particularly for girls and women. Universal primary education is one of the UN's Millennium Development Goals, to be achieved by the year 2015. Representatives from 164 countries gathered in 2000 for the World Education Forum in Dakar, Senegal, where they announced a platform of action for expanding quality education worldwide. Education promotion is central to the World Bank's long-term development strategies. The various UN agencies are at the forefront of this struggle, promoting literacy and quality education. Supporting this effort, the Bush administration pledged $525 million over five years specifically to educate the poorest children of the world.

Still, the problem is large: 781 million adults in the world are illiterate, and more than two-thirds of them are women. While many countries have made great strides in closing their persistent gender gaps, there are still millions of fewer girls in school today than boys.[9] Even worse, of those girls who are lucky enough to attend school, one out of five does not complete her primary education. The majority of the children not in schools are from just three regions of the world: sub-Saharan Africa, South Asia, and the Middle East. Girls' education is particularly neglected in these regions.

The United States should increase funding for both boys' and girls' education, particularly in the three regions most in need. Policymakers seem to be waking up to the strategic benefits of supporting universal education: in May 2007 several congressmen introduced an "Education for All" bill that would increase U.S. funding for primary education in the developing world to $10 billion over the next five years.[10] This unprecedented move would undoubtedly lead global efforts to provide universal primary education. Interestingly, the arguments put forward by the bill's supporters included an explicit appeal to U.S. national security interests. As Democratic congresswoman Nita Lowey, one of the four legislators to push for the bill, put the case, "Unstable societies are a breeding ground for terrorists. In countries plagued by violence and strife, diseases like HIV/AIDS and malaria, and poverty, education is an equalizing force. Today more than ever, education is a national security issue. It is the key to turning back the spiraling tide against fanaticism."

Despite such national security arguments, the bill has not been passed, and might never be approved at such an ambitious level of funding. That the bill was introduced at all, however, reflects a growing recognition on the part of policymakers that educating the world's poorest inhabitants, including its girls, makes sense economically, politically, and strategically. The proposed bill would support activities to train teachers, build schools, develop effective curricula, increase access to school lunch and health programs, and increase parent and community involvement in schools—all critical components of a sound plan to achieve universal education.[11]

The good news is that when the international community finally is beginning to rally behind universal education, we have a much better understanding today of what works with respect to building sustainable education programs. There is also an emerging consensus that the unique physical and cultural obstacles facing girls must be explicitly addressed in any attempt to promote girls' education. For example, studies show that, both for security and economic reasons, girls are less likely to attend school if they must walk more than a few kilometers from home. Girls also need flexible schedules to boost their enrollment. The reality is that across developing countries, girls do much of the household work, including carrying water and firewood, caring for younger siblings, and tending farm animals. School schedules that allow them to finish their chores cater to this reality. Providing latrines with privacy is also important. Whereas boys can easily use the surrounding fields, girls are reluctant to do so, for reasons of hygiene, modesty, and personal safety. As girls reach adolescence and begin menstruating, private latrines become essential; without toilets, girls simply will not attend school during menses, which causes them to fall behind and increases female drop-out rates.

In some societies, cultural constraints require girls to attend school separately from boys, or at least at different times of day. Active community and, specifically, parent involvement in choosing teachers, determining schedules, and setting curriculum also improves female enrollment. So, too, does the availability of female teachers.[12] Most communities encourage girls to attend school when their safety and privacy concerns are met.

Promoting universal education, and specifically girls' education, is a win-win proposition for U.S. foreign policy. Strengthening education improves the economic trajectory of poor countries and provides a better opportunity for the next generation to pull themselves out of economic instability. Educated girls become educated mothers, who are more likely to lift their families out of poverty. They also become active female citizens and members of civil society, strengthening the foundations of democracy.

BEYOND EDUCATION: HEALTH AND JOBS

The United Nations Development Program provides an annual "Gender Empowerment Measure" (GEM) ranking for countries, which reflects women's economic and political participation and decision making and their power over economic resources.[13] Each year, sub-Saharan African countries have the lowest rankings, followed closely by South Asian and Middle Eastern countries. Violence against women is high in these regions, educational gender gaps are largest, economic participation is low, and political participation is only recently occurring with any critical mass. Maternal mortality in many of these countries is also shockingly high. A recent global report by the World Health Organization (WHO), UNICEF, and the United Nations Population Fund (UNFPA) shows that a woman in sub-Saharan Africa has a 1-in-16 risk of dying from maternal causes, compared with a 1-in-2,800 chance for a woman in a developed country and a 1-in-28,000 risk for Scandinavian women.[14] Getting pregnant in many of these countries is the most dangerous risk a woman can take, since childbirth is the No. 1 killer of women of child-bearing age.

Clearly, these three regions are not alone in their gender discrimination. Serious abuses are committed against women all over the world. Sex-trafficking, rape, and domestic violence affect hundreds of millions of women regardless of their country or culture.[15] However, specific forms of violence against women—including female genital mutilation (FGM), acid burning, and honor killings—are more prevalent in these regions, where they are often justified on religious and cultural grounds. In numerous countries, the official laws reflect the fact that women's lives are valued less than men's lives, since they impose weak punishments for men killing women. Also, parents perpetuate the cycle of denigrating female life. So strong is the desire for sons over daughters that the spread of inexpensive sonogram technology has led to millions of sex-selective abortions. Nobel Prize–winner Amartya Sen has drawn the world's attention to "100 million missing women," mainly in India and China, where strong cultural preferences for male children have led to the abuse and neglect of female children. Girls in these countries may be denied medical care, proper nutrition, and education. And while there are laws in most countries outlawing such violence and discrimination against women, enforcement is still a problem. Most governments have signed the Convention to Eliminate Discrimination against Women (CEDAW), the most comprehensive international treaty to promote women's rights, yet they continue to allow gross violations of CEDAW's basic precepts.

For U.S. policymakers, addressing many of these sensitive topics is certainly more complicated than supporting girls' education, especially when the promotion of women's rights treads on cultural or religious landmines. In many societies today, issues related to women's rights are particularly fraught for a number of reasons: colonial legacies, the rise of religious fundamentalism, and suspicion of anything Western, including ideas of Western feminism. Western criticisms of specific cultural practices such as FGM are denounced as neocultural imperialism. And any initiative related to women's health gets immediately caught up not only in conflict with local customs, but also in vitriolic domestic U.S. politics about women's sexual and reproductive rights. How can the United States most effectively promote women's rights in this highly charged context?

U.S. policymakers would be well-advised to adopt the foreign policy equivalent of the Hippocratic Oath: Do no harm. When American officials publicly condemn practices and traditions that are seen, often incorrectly, as being religiously rooted, their words can create a backlash effect. It did not help women in Egypt, for example, when Laura Bush publicly called for an end to the practice of FGM. Her condemnation was manipulated by local proponents of the practice to prove that indigenous forces working to end FGM are under foreign sway and that their efforts are therefore illegitimate. The 2005 Egypt Demographic and Health Survey shows that 96 percent of Egyptian women between 15 and 49 years of age have been circumcised—indicating little or no decline from a decade earlier, when ending FGM first became a cause for numerous international women's groups.[16] On such controversial issues, working discreetly with local NGOs usually leads to more productive outcomes. Indeed, more recently, the U.S. government has been quietly backing Egyptian NGOs dedicated to ending FGM. In the long term, this strategy will have much more of an impact than strident denunciations by foreign dignitaries.

Given the much-maligned position of the United States in the world today, working through multilateral institutions on such sensitive topics as violence against women, legal discrimination, and women's health promotion is often the best strategy. This approach requires providing more financial support for UN agencies, regional organizations, and international NGOs that can distribute money to local community groups. In order to achieve results, the promotion of women's rights should not be tied too closely to the politics of the U.S. government. By working with groups such as UNFPA and the United Nations Development Fund for Women (UNIFEM), U.S. policymakers can often have a greater impact than by supporting these efforts directly through U.S. embassies or USAID programs, which are often perceived with mistrust and cynicism by the local population.

However, the fact that the United States is one of only a handful of countries—along with pariah states such as Iran, Sudan, and Somalia—that have not ratified CEDAW, the most important international treaty for women, undercuts its role in multilateral institutions and hurts its international image. Since the treaty was drafted in 1979, opposition in the United States has been small but vociferous. Critics of the treaty argue that the United States already protects the rights of women sufficiently, and that ratifying the treaty would only undermine American sovereignty. President Carter signed CEDAW in 1980, but his unpopularity with the American public left him without the political weight needed to push the treaty through Congress. Since then, CEDAW has been brought before the Senate on several occasions but blocked each time by a conservative minority.

As in the case of other international treaties, conservative critics contend that CEDAW represents a liberal conspiracy to impose "world government." They also falsely argue that based on its implementation in other countries, the treaty would force governments to decriminalize prostitution, give money in support of abortion, and even do away with Mother's Day on the grounds that it reinforces stereotypes of women. Such unfounded allegations about CEDAW continue to circulate today. In 2002 the U.S. State Department notified the Senate Foreign Relations Committee that CEDAW is "generally desirable and should be ratified," but the Bush administration publicly refused to push for its ratification.

U.S. credibility in promoting women's rights was further undermined by the Bush administration's refusal to fund UNFPA, the agency dedicated to reproductive health and family planning, and other similar organizations focused on sexual and reproductive health. Beginning in 2002, officials in the administration withheld UNFPA funds that had been appropriated by Congress, basing their action on spurious claims that UNFPA supports coercive abortion in China. The U.S. State Department itself investigated these allegations and issued a report stating that "based on what we heard, saw and read, we find no evidence that UNFPA has knowingly supported or participated in the management of coercive abortion or involuntary sterilization in the PRC (People's Republic of China). Indeed, UNFPA has registered its strong opposition to such practices."[17] Nevertheless, kowtowing to domestic anti-abortion groups and conservative Republicans in Congress, the Bush administration continued to deny funding to UNFPA.

By linking sexual and reproductive health to their anti-abortion credo, such conservatives in the Bush administration and in Congress ignored a critical issue that needs more U.S. support: maternal health. More than 500,000 women worldwide die every year from problems related to pregnancy and childbirth—equating to the death of one woman every minute, every day. WHO estimates that in addition to these tragic deaths, nearly 10 million women are seriously injured or contract a debilitating infection during childbirth. Millions of children are orphaned as a result, and a high percentage of them die within two years of their mother's death.

Improving maternal health worldwide should be a bipartisan priority for moral, political, economic, and social reasons. Furthermore, this is an issue on which developed countries can provide meaningful assistance, since the majority of deaths and injuries caused by childbirth are preventable. In particular, the United States can help to train health professionals, provide money to build better and more accessible prenatal and natal centers for women, and distribute information on reproductive health. By addressing this critical problem, the United States could help to improve the status of women worldwide.

Another less controversial but very important way for the United States to promote women's rights would be to provide more economic opportunities for women in developing countries. International polls show that women themselves prioritize jobs and their ability to earn income above less tangible notions of women's rights. Making explicit efforts to create jobs for women would be smart public diplomacy for the United States. Moreover, the long-term impact of putting income in the hands of women is highly positive. Studies have shown that, like education, earning income greatly improves a woman's status within her community and family. Female access to money also has a positive effect on the well-being of society. According to the World Bank's *Engendering Development* report, "additional income in the hands of women enlarges the share of the household budget devoted to education, health, and nutrition-related expenditures."[18] Marginal income in the hands of a mother improves child survival twenty times more than in the hands of a father. Improving women's economic status can be a non-threatening way for the United States to further women's rights around the world.

One way to accomplish this goal would be to increase support for microfinance organizations, which extend credit primarily to women. Although microfinance has grown considerably in the past decade, there are still more than a billion people in the world with no access to credit. Supporting the growth of the microfinance industry by providing access to capital, subsidizing new technologies, and promoting a sound regulatory environment are all important activities for U.S. policymakers to undertake. Also, the United States should increase funding to those microfinance institutions that are committed to serving the poorest of the poor.

The U.S. private sector also has an important role to play in women's empowerment. Some of the most effective drivers of change are U.S.-based multinational companies, which quietly but firmly bring their workplace practices to local markets. In Saudi Arabia, for example, global companies such as Kimberly-Clark and McKinsey & Company hire, train, and promote female professionals, creating opportunities for women and leading by example. Microsoft recently started a training program in Egypt, which has trained over 100 women to become computer technicians.[19]

In 2002 Cisco Systems launched an innovative project designed to get more women into the IT sector in Jordan, a country where less than 15 percent of women were economically active. In conjunction with UNIFEM, Cisco established ten Networking Academies across the country to train women in computer technologies and connect graduates with the job market. The program's explicit goal is to give women an edge in Jordan's job market, where cultural barriers to women's advancement remain high. The U.S. government can encourage such efforts through public-private partnerships that support scholarships for women to receive higher education, targeted vocational training, and leadership programs for women. Ultimately, women's success in the workplace will be an important catalyst for long-term change.

CONCLUSION

Women's empowerment in the developing world is not only a moral imperative, but also a pressing economic, social, and political issue, and one that the United States should stand behind firmly. Undoubtedly, some components of such an agenda are controversial, and they may create backlash in regions of the world where the United States is already battling unprecedented levels of anti-Americanism. But there are ample opportunities to promote the status of women in ways that contribute positively to the U.S. image abroad: by supporting girls' education, maternal health, economic opportunities for women, and even political and civic training for women in countries that are already encouraging women's political participation.

Empowering women is clearly associated with alleviating poverty, with undermining the conditions that foster human-trafficking, with stemming the spread of AIDS, and even with cleaner, less corrupt government. And there is some evidence that women's empowerment is negatively correlated with authoritarian government and tempers extremism.[20] Given that the payoff from enhancing women's rights is so compelling, women's empowerment should be a consistent priority of U.S. foreign policy.

NO: Marcia E. Greenberg, *Cornell Law School*

This essay is predicated on the firm conviction that all countries, including the United States, should take purposeful action to improve the lives of women and girls around the world. It takes issue, however, with the notion that "aggressively promoting women's rights" is a prudent or effective means for achieving the ultimate goals of improving the lives of women and girls and of gender equality.

While this position is rights-*based*, it challenges approaches that are rights *focused*—that is, approaches for which legal rights become both the final objective and the programmatic focus. It is rights-based in a normative sense, in that the concern for women stems from a conviction that women should enjoy a complete range of rights as human beings, including any particular to their sex. It emanates from a natural law perspective on rights—that they are inherently and fundamentally the "right thing to do," anchored in morality—as well as a positive law perspective, recognizing international laws that include the Universal Declaration of Human Rights; the Covenant on Civil and Political Rights and Covenant on Social, Cultural and Economic Rights; the Convention on the Elimination of All Forms of Discrimination against Women (CEDAW);[1] and the Rome Statute.[2] It strongly recognizes the power and import of the Beijing Platform for Action,[3] backed by "17,000 participants, including 6,000 delegates from 189 countries, over 4000 representatives of accredited non-governmental organizations ... [and] more than 30,000 people" at the NGO Forum[4] and of the Millennium Development Goals.[5]

Yet, despite such rights foundations and global commitments, this essay is written at a time when there is increased resistance to women's rights—coming from "fundamentalist" factions of nearly every religion.[6] Women in Iraq have seen their rights and freedoms decrease, [7] women and men in Turkey face uncertainty about the future of women's rights, [8] women and men in India persist in aborting the girl-child,[9] and women in the United States suffer restrictions on their reproductive rights as laws increasingly constrain women's ability to control their health and destiny.[10] Consequently, while the United States should adopt and endorse the objective of improving the rights and well-being of girls and women around the world, it should not take the suggested rights-focused approach because this approach is not likely to achieve the objective—and worse, it may cause more losses for women than gains.

This essay addresses the key issues in six sections: (1) recognizing the fundamental importance of clearly and correctly framing the objective, (2) underscoring the need to take account of the contexts in which violations of women's rights are most severe, (3) challenging assumptions regarding the quality and meaning of legal systems that are expected to establish and protect women's rights, (4) recognizing the changing U.S. role in a global context of diminished credibility and leadership, (5) shifting approaches from women's rights to gender equality, and (6) suggesting that the United States might make real contributions to women's enjoyment of their rights by paying attention to U.S. policies and their impacts on women. This "No" position is predicated on the need to be clear about the objective, and to be thoughtful in developing appropriate and effective strategies for achieving it.

REFRAMING THE OBJECTIVE: FROM RIGHTS TO THE STATUS AND WELL-BEING OF GIRLS AND WOMEN

A first step is to reframe the objective: getting beyond the word *rights* to define what is actually sought. What does a goal of "women's rights" really mean? Short-term, it may mean improving the well-being of girls and women, as articulated in the Beijing Platform for Action. Some may suggest that the real objective is "empowerment" or girls' education—Isobel Coleman raises both topics in her "Yes" response to this question. Another way of recasting the objective is in terms of human capabilities, as suggested by political philosopher Martha Nussbaum in *Women and Human Development: The Capabilities Approach.*[11] Nussbaum's "core idea is that of the human being as a dignified free being who shapes his or her own life in cooperation and reciprocity with others, rather than being passively shaped or pushed around by the world in the manner of a 'flock' or 'herd' animal. A life that is really human is one that is shaped throughout by these human powers of practical reason and sociability."[12]

Long-term, a goal of "women's rights" may call for more than legal reforms to achieve cultures of gender equality and respect—such that men and women can relate to one another with mutual respect—and may collaborate for the greater well-being of families, enterprises, communities, and nations. Whatever the specifics of the goal, achievements should be sustainable. To be so, they should be "owned" not only by girls and women, but also by boys and men.

In any case, the objective is promoting not rights per se, but what those rights mean to girls, adolescent girls, women, and older women themselves—as well as to the boys and men in their families and communities.

DIFFERENT EFFORTS IN DIFFERENT CONTEXTS

There are arguably at least two major ways in which the United States may directly promote women's rights *in* developing countries: (1) through diplomatic contacts worldwide and (2) by means of development assistance.[13] (It may also support private investment and trade policies that may in turn create opportunities to support women's rights, particularly economic rights relating to employment.) In each case, however, the "developing countries" offer vastly different contexts—politically, economically, socially, and culturally. It is rarely possible to employ the same approach to achieve a global objective in different contexts. There are enormous variations among the key issues, challenges, and constraints for achieving women's rights in "developing countries" (as within "developed countries"): they range from issues of political rights and economic opportunity to the more basic issues of health, education, and to life-threatening or brutal practices such as honor killings, bride-burning, or forced sex-work.

In order to anticipate in which contexts the United States might be compelled to support women's well-being, one way to identify countries where violations of women's rights are most severe—and to see beyond the visible dimension of rights enjoyed by elite women to the day-to-day experiences of all women—is to reference United Nations measurements. The UN Development Program's Human Development Office maintains indices for Human Development (HDI), Human Poverty (HPI), Gender Disparities (GDI), and Gender Empowerment (GEM).[14] The two relating to gender are also indicators of where women suffer greatest from inequality or denial of their rights. The GDI is based on measures of life expectancy, adult literacy, education enrollment rates, and estimated earned income. The GEM reflects numbers of seats in parliament held by women; of female legislators, senior officials, and managers; of female professional and technical workers;[15] and the ratio of estimated female-to-male income. Table 1 shows the countries with the most gender-based disparities—as determined by comparing each country's HDI, which measures development for all, with its GDI, which measures gender-based development—according to the United Nations. Table 2 displays the countries with the lowest levels of gender empowerment. In examining these tables, it is noteworthy that apart from itself, Ireland, Luxembourg, Japan, and Austria, the other named countries are those where the United States may be most likely to "aggressively promote women's rights."[16] Yet, as is explained later, those are precisely the countries where a rights-focused approach is likely to be least effective.

RIGHTS-FOCUSED APPROACHES RELY ON INAPT ASSUMPTIONS

Beyond the need to be cognizant of local reactions to its interventions, the United States should not rely on a legalistic, primarily juridical, women's rights

Table 1

Countries with the Greatest Disparities between Human Development Index and Gender-Related Development Index Rankings

Country	Disparity between HDI and GDI
Oman	−13
Saudi Arabia	−13
Ireland	−10
Libyan Arab Jamahiriya	−9
Pakistan	−7
Japan	−5
Luxembourg	−5
United Arab Emirates	−5
United States	−4
Austria	−4
Nepal	−4

Source: United Nations Development Program, *Human Development Report 2007–2008*, Table 28, pp. 326–329.

Table 2

Countries with the Lowest Gender Empowerment Measure (GEM) Rankings

Country	GEM ranking
Yemen	93
Saudi Arabia	92
Egypt	91
Turkey	90
Kyrgyzstan	89
Morocco	88
Iran (Islamic Republic of)	87
Nepal	86
Sri Lanka	85
Qatar	84
Cambodia	83
Pakistan	82

Source: United Nations Development Program, *Human Development Report 2007–2008*, Table 29, pp. 330–333.

approach because both the concept and the protection of rights depend on legal systems that can recognize and defend them. Most efforts focus on drafting laws that recognize women's rights, removing laws that abrogate women's rights, strengthening judicial systems to interpret laws to protect women, and building more effective mechanisms for enforcement.[17] When these efforts fail, funders and implementers typically place the blame on weak enforcement, or the need to sensitize magistrates and judges.

In many countries where women's rights are denied and violated, the "legal system" may actually enforce laws that violate women's rights or authorize systems that violate rights, such as prohibiting women from traveling without obtaining their husband's permission or being accompanied by a male relative, or precluding women from owning real property, serving as guardians, or running for public office. The system may have institutions that are incapable of applying and enforcing the law—either because of a lack of resources (whether courts exist in rural areas, or whether rural or poor or illiterate populations have any possibility of gaining access to courts), or because the personnel in the institutions (judges, magistrates, police officers, and so on) are not committed to following or applying the law on women's behalf (such as judges who "exercise their discretion" to ignore legal remedies, instead sending home a woman who seeks protection from domestic violence because they deem it a "family matter" that should be resolved there).[18]

In fact, the legal systems themselves are often unable to support an effective "rights-focused" approach. Rights approaches presume legal systems that are consistent with a liberal legal paradigm, including a legal system of laws, institutions, and culture that are similar to, or building toward, those of the United States or Western Europe. This paradigm presumes six components, as flagged by David Trubek and Marc Galanter back in 1974:

1. That there are *intermediate groups* between a society of individuals and the state;

2. That the *state exercises control* over individuals through law—but according to rules by which the state itself is constrained;

3. That the *rules are intended* to achieve social purposes and principles;

4. That when applied, the rules are *enforced equally for all citizens*, and for the purposes for which they were designed;

5. That *courts are central* to functioning of the legal system; and

6. That social actors *tend to conform to those state-generated rules* (both leaders and people).[19]

All too often, however, the liberal legal paradigm fails: In many contexts where women's rights are not respected, the state does not exercise control over individuals by law; instead, religious institutions or customary law at a local level may play the primary role in regulating behaviors.[20] In many instances, the legal system serves those who live in capital cities, and who have education and wealth—but means little to girls and women in rural areas. In many countries, courts do not serve as primary institutions of dispute resolution, or they may focus more on commercial issues than on "family" or social issues. Once those components of the paradigm are in doubt, it is legitimate to question whether a "rights-focused approach" has the requisite institutional foundations to be meaningful.[21] All too often, U.S. policymakers (and others) invest expertise and resources in improving legal institutions that have little or no impact on most women's lives.

Yet, beyond institutions, there are often issues of legal culture.[22] Even where the laws and institutions do exist, women may not turn to state-sponsored courts to support them or recognize rights. Instead, they may find other ways to resolve issues, relying on religious institutions or on traditional community or family leaders. This practice may vary from whether women who are subjected to home-based violence or who have been raped would turn to courts, and whether women whose employers discriminate against them in terms of wages or benefits or even sexual harassment will sue them, to whether attitudes regarding women's participation in political life are molded by civil society organizations or religious organizations. Often, state-supported courts simply do not play a role in women's lives.

If those countries or communities where violations of women's rights are greatest—that is, where women's circumstances of exclusion and disempowerment are most severe—are also those where the liberal legal model does not exist, then investing in promoting women's rights is often an ineffective way to achieve the objective of improving women's lives. The concepts of rights and legal systems presume that the state plays a major role in peoples' lives. In many developing countries, however, the state can be irrelevant or dysfunctional, or it may pose more threat than protection.

For most women striving for greater opportunities, for education, for respect and dignity, the state's legal system does not offer any near-term or effective support. Rights and laws should be regarded as tools that are effective in some contexts and not in others: As those who own a hammer may wish to see everything as a nail, rights advocates ought not to regard all rights violations as legal challenges.[23]

U.S. PROMOTION MAY BE COUNTERPRODUCTIVE

Even if the liberal legal paradigm holds, and legal systems are functional and relevant, U.S. promotion may be counterproductive. Beyond the tool of rights-oriented language and legal mechanisms, the United States must consider the effectiveness of its proactive, visible—even if not fully "aggressive"—intervention. Beyond the local or national legal context, the global context is important, too. Though seeking to do good, U.S. policymakers must be cognizant of how other peoples regard their nation. In general, the U.S. way of doing things may be deemed "foreign," "Western," or simply "American"—and thus considered inappropriate. Oddly, McDonald's hamburgers or Levis jeans or popular music may be acceptable or even attractive—despite being foreign, Western, or American. While it may not seem logical, opponents of women's rights may be glad to accept such changes to their culture, but still readily apply the "foreign" label to generate hostility when they charge that outsiders should not meddle with their "culture" regarding women's roles. If the United States wants to improve women's lives, it must recognize and address this political context.

Furthermore—and unfortunately—in the current global context, the United States has lost respect and credibility as a leading proponent of human rights and rule of law. The lack of due process accorded prisoners held at Guantanamo Bay, the harsh treatment of prisoners in disregard of the Geneva Conventions, the practice of "extraordinary rendition," and the continuing U.S. refusal to ratify such international treaties as CEDAW, the Convention on the Rights of the Child, and the Rome Statute establishing the International Criminal Court, undermine the power and legitimacy of U.S. calls to respect women's rights.[24]

Consequently, in many countries where women's rights are most seriously neglected or violated, the more the United States is associated with efforts to change the treatment of women, the more strongly there is pushback. One key adage for humanitarian work is "Do no harm." Yet forceful U.S. intervention may backfire, hurting the national or local leaders and organizations that are striving to improve women's lives. In recent years, the promotion of women's needs and rights has spread throughout the world. As has been demonstrated by attendance at the International Conference on Population and Development (ICPD) in 1994, the Beijing Conference in 1995, and at their respective review meetings, women's organizations and women's rights advocates around the world are working to promote gender equality. They need to be able to promote change without being weakened by opponents' claims that they are doing the bidding of the United States or introducing culturally inappropriate change.

One alternative would be for U.S. policymakers to work more through multilateral organizations, be they regional or international, and to support the work of others. At the international level, concern for women's rights and for gender equality is now well-established in an international and multinational way. Beyond CEDAW, to which 185 countries are party,[25] there are the foundations of four World Conferences on Women (Mexico, Copenhagen, Nairobi, and Beijing)[26] along with the five- and ten-year reviews of implementation, and the 1994 International Conference on Population and Development

(ICPD) in Cairo.[27] In the United Nations system, there are the Commission on the Status of Women (CSW), the UN Women's Fund (UNIFEM), the United Nations Population Fund (UNFPA)—and a 1997 mandate of the UN's Economic and Social Council (ECOSOC) for gender mainstreaming in all UN agencies. Indeed, many advocates for women's rights and gender equality would question U.S. leadership on international aid in this issue area, where the preeminent supporters and donors are, instead, the Nordic countries, the Netherlands, Canada, and the United Kingdom.

Admittedly, there are direct tensions between making U.S. promotion of women's rights highly visible, and playing a behind-the-scenes role. For domestic political purposes, publicizing and touting rights-focused efforts may seem necessary to assure domestic constituencies, including women's rights advocates, that the U.S. government is taking action on behalf of women around the world. Yet at the international level, local advocates may prefer quiet support. In an age of global communications media, it can be difficult for US policymakers to satisfy both expectations.

ALTERNATIVES TO PROMOTING WOMEN'S RIGHTS

The promotion of gender equality may present an alternative. In 1997, after the Beijing Conference but consistent with commitments made there by states and donors, the UN Economic and Social Council passed a resolution calling for "gender mainstreaming" that includes the statement: "The ultimate goal is to achieve gender equality."[28] Since that time, the international system has focused on gender mainstreaming and on achieving gender equality. Gender mainstreaming has required a shift from women-focused programming to recognizing women's contributions to "mainstream" programming, regarding men and boys as allies for gender equality rather than enemies, and recognizing the win-win potential of social and economic units that engage the skills and perspectives of men and women. Such approaches have also increased attention to *relations* between women and men. This perspective opens opportunities to focus on improving relations between women and men—and not, therefore, only on "equality," which, for some, arouses concerns about making everyone "the same"— and to address women's needs where and when they are overlooked.

Rather than posing rights issues as women-versus-others, or encouraging movements only of women-for-women, gender equality initiatives may take place within the context of other social and economic initiatives—ranging from women and men working together as family farms in Macedonia, women and men leading super-cyclone drills in India, collaboration to protect natural resources, and fathers and mothers taking joint responsibility for the nutrition and well-being of their children. Rather than focusing on laws and state power, gender equality work may focus on women's power in relation to others—what some describe as "power over," "power with," "power to," and "power within." [29] This vastly different approach is more oriented toward human relations and "real life" than are rights and law-focused approaches. While the ultimate goal may still be women's rights, the approach is inclusive—and the objective is increasingly recognized as one that will benefit boys and men, along with girls and women.

A shift to gender equality offers the potential to work for changes in attitudes and behaviors in ways other than legal mandates and penalties. Opportunities to promote gender equality present themselves in many more arenas than legal systems and courts—including political agreements, businesses, schools, and development projects, among others.

Finally, the alternatives promise greater sustainability because rights-focused successes may be short-lived. Laws can be overturned, courts can be moribund or corrupt, and enforcement can be reluctant, lax, or even obstructionist. [30] All too often, "promoting women's rights" fails to achieve long-lasting and widely accepted change. In contrast, efforts to build cultures of gender respect and equality promote sustainable change.

RECOGNIZING U.S. MANAGEABLE INTERESTS AND TAKING RESPONSIBILITY FOR IMPACTS

Lastly, the United States has opportunities to support women's rights by looking to its own policies and practices rather than to those of other countries. The United States may "promote gender equality" by demonstrating its value and effectiveness at home. U.S. Fortune 500 companies benefiting from women CEOs and mixed leadership teams, U.S. states with women governors working side-by-side with both male and female advisers, and U.S. women athletes performing in the Olympics all model the benefits of women's leadership and women's contributions. Women ambassadors, women scientists at international conventions, and women specialists in international agencies all demonstrate the importance of girls' and women's education.

Yet U.S. policies also have impacts on women around the world as a result of what may be regarded as "gender neutral" initiatives, but which nevertheless have impacts on women. Trade policies that encourage free-trade zones but omit any labor standards may result in women working in conditions and earning wages that violate their rights. [31] A "gag rule" imposed by conservative opponents of abortion affects women and men when it causes the withholding of support from organizations that help men and women to understand and manage their reproductive health and decisions. Immigration policies that mandate strict quotas may keep husbands and wives, or mothers and children, apart. Agricultural policies that discourage competition by family farms in Africa—many of which are managed by husbands and wives and extended families working together—may drive the men to earn wages in urban areas, leaving women behind to fend for themselves and their children alone. There are many ways in which U.S. policymakers may promote women's rights and gender equality by assessing the true impacts of their own policies, rather than focusing on laws and policies abroad.

CONCLUDING THOUGHTS

For those who wish to improve the status, well-being, and opportunities of women around the world, there are some basic principles by which to ascertain the wisdom of an approach:

- In each case, the approach should be tailored rather than one-size-fits-all.

- Any initiative should begin with a complete understanding of culture and society—that is, a gender analysis.

- Work should begin by connecting with thoughtful partners in each country or region, and engaging in partnerships of equals to explore options and debate strategies.

- Approaches that focus on "rights" must anticipate that rights require legal systems to support them—and that, if such systems are weak or nonexistent, improving the situations of girls and women in the immediate term requires action in other arenas.

- All tactics should be reviewed for how they will be perceived—by identifying entry points where it is possible to teach, not preach, and through which attitudes and behaviors may change gradually, per the acceptance and wishes of some of the local population.

- Sustainability requires ownership and appropriateness. (Development practitioners have learned that modern technologies—which may be inappropriate when, for example, spare parts, electricity, educational levels, and cultural acceptance are lacking—may be discarded as soon as outside promoters depart. So, too, the success of gender equality initiatives depends on their being appropriate to their contexts and enjoying local support.)

- Initiatives should include men as well as women (and adolescent boys as well as adolescent girls).

- U.S. policymakers should assess their own laws and programs to see whether they may undermine women's rights—or whether modifications might support the rights and opportunities of women in developing countries.

Should the United States be committed to assisting women whose rights are being violated? Yes. But should the United States seek to help women by "aggressively promoting women's rights in developing countries"? No. The objective must be more than promoting the legal manifestations of rights; it should be to use the normative foundations of women's rights to compel actions to improve women's lives, and to achieve sustainable gender equality that will benefit future generation of boys and girls.

immigration

Should Countries Liberalize Immigration Policies?

YES: James F. Hollifield, *Southern Methodist University*
NO: Philip Martin, *University of California, Davis*

The vast majority of people live in the country in which they were born, but international migration has expanded considerably in recent decades (see Figure 1). Many in the United States focus on immigration to the U.S. and think of immigrants as mostly from Latin America. In fact, the majority of those who immigrate to the United States today do come from Latin America—it is expected that more than 40 million U.S. residents are foreign-born, including more than 9 million from Mexico, the largest source. (At the turn of the twentieth century, most immigrants were from northern and western Europe, with shifts early in the century to larger numbers from southern, eastern, and central Europe.) However, the Americas actually account for a relatively small portion of international migration today, as is evident in Figure 2. Some nations, such as Saudi Arabia and the United Arab Emirates, now have immigrant populations that comprise a quarter or more of their populations and are a critical source of labor.

Immigration and free trade are not often discussed simultaneously, but some of the same arguments can be marshaled to support and oppose each position, although the political fault lines are not typically consistent. The proposition that free trade brings prosperity can hold for immigration as well. While libertarians tend to support free movement of both capital and labor, political conservatives and liberals often disagree on issues of free trade (for which there is greater support among political conservatives) and free immigration (more support among political liberals). Nonetheless, many views of immigration policy stem from a pragmatic rather than a doctrinaire perspective, hinging, finally, on the perceived benefits and costs.

Figure 1

Number of International Migrants by Region, 1970–2000

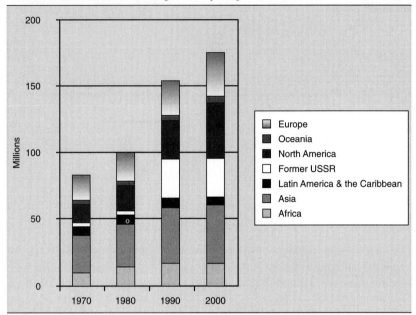

Source: UN Secretariat, *World Migration 2005: International Migration Data and Statistics* (New York: Department of Economic and Social Affairs, Population Division, 2005), 396.
Note: The numbers for Asia exclude Armenia, Azerbaijan, Georgia, Kazakhstan, Kyrgyzstan, Tajikistan, Turkmenistan, and Uzbekistan. Those for Europe exclude Belarus, Estonia, Latvia, Lithuania, the Republic of Moldova, the Russian Federation, and Ukraine.

The perceived benefits of immigration are considerable. Even setting aside the important cultural enrichment (food, language, historical perspectives, and so on) offered by a diverse population, immigrants provide substantial economic and demographic advantages to host nations. Immigrants tend to be younger than native populations—a substantial boon to the aging populations of the wealthy West—and they often work in fields that are unacceptable to many natives, such as domestic assistance, construction, agriculture, and food services. Some of this work (such as janitorial service) is immovable, while some (including low-skilled manufacturing or assembly jobs) might easily be exportable to other nations were it not for immigrants willing to fill these positions. Therefore, liberal immigration policies can inhibit outsourcing by retaining jobs within the host country.

Also, because immigrants are younger, they improve the demographic profile of host nations—an important consideration in terms of public health care

Figure 2

Distribution of International Migrants by Region, 1970 and 2000

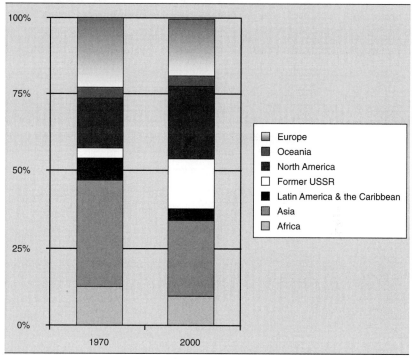

Source: UN Secretariat, *World Migration 2005: International Migration Data and Statistics* (New York: Department of Economic and Social Affairs, Population Division, 2005), 396.
Note: The numbers for Asia exclude Armenia, Azerbaijan, Georgia, Kazakhstan, Kyrgyzstan, Tajikistan, Turkmenistan, and Uzbekistan. Those for Europe exclude Belarus, Estonia, Latvia, Lithuania, the Republic of Moldova, the Russian Federation, and Ukraine.

and pensions. Indeed, to a considerable extent, the United States is far better positioned than much of Europe and Japan—whose populations are considerably older—largely due to the influx of immigrants. The replacement ratio (the number of workers per retiree) is a key factor in the political and economic support for public pensions, and those nations with aging populations face considerable hurdles in maintaining generous support systems for retirees. Finally, many migrants send payments, or remittances, back home, to the benefit of families left behind. For a number of developing countries, including the Philippines and Egypt, these remittances account for a significant proportion of their country's foreign exchange earnings.

On the other hand, immigration presents some serious challenges. In addition to the personal difficulties of mutual adjustment to new cultures, immigration is perceived to present economic, public health, and security challenges, as well as forcing the host nation to confront and potentially adjust its "national identity." Tensions arise when immigrants are perceived to "take" jobs from natives, often because of their willingness to work at lower pay, for longer hours, or in inferior conditions. However, most studies indicate that immigration, while it can sometimes cause economic dislocations, has a slightly positive or, at worst, a neutral impact on a host country's overall economic conditions.

The potential for exploitation—whether among Bangladeshi domestic servants in Saudi Arabia or among Mexican migrant farmers in the United States—is even more pronounced when migrants enter nations illegally. Furthermore, security considerations post–9/11 affect perceptions of immigration's impacts and drive policies that make residency and citizenship difficult for some subpopulations. Finally, there are impacts on the migrants' nations of origin, including concerns about a "brain drain" when highly educated emigrants leave developing nations for wealthy alternative destinations.

Immigration is inherently a political issue, as the movement of people becomes "immigration" only when it transcends a political boundary—that is, a national border. While Canada has the highest per capita net immigration in the world, the United States is the destination for the largest number of immigrants. One of the central immigration policy issues is how many immigrants a nation such as the United States should permit each year (recognizing the interrelationship between legal and illegal immigration). Another issue involves nations' policies for permitting entry and allowing foreigners to gain residency and citizenship. Countries such as Canada and Australia have used point systems based on potential economic contributions to their nations to assess potential immigrants, while the United States has made national origin and family ties the paramount considerations.

The impacts of immigrants (on both home and host countries) are considerable and complex, and, therefore, their political impacts are complicated. Liberalization of immigration policy produces costs and benefits—for host nations and for the migrants themselves—that defy easy political categorization. The articles that follow take alternating positions on the desirability of liberalizing immigration policies worldwide. James Hollifield argues that the manner in which immigration is managed by powerful liberal states will determine whether society benefits from or is harmed by increased migration, and he urges broader international frameworks for managing migration. Philip Martin argues that immigration has very small economic impacts, and that most immigrants earn higher wages abroad but cannot climb the economic ladder. Thus, he suggests that the costs of change may exceed the perceived benefits of expanding immigration for host states.

Discussion Questions

1. What motivates people to emigrate from their home countries? What impact has globalization had on their motivations? Is there a link between free trade and immigration?

2. Many immigrants strive to retain their cultural traditions and beliefs rather than integrating fully into their new country's culture. Does this tendency bring benefits or costs to the new country? What other benefits or costs do immigrants bring to a society?

3. Many countries would like to curb illegal immigration. What are the challenges to doing so? What policies should be adopted to meet this goal?

4. What is the "liberal paradox" as defined by James Hollifield? Is this something that states still struggle with or have they "escaped" from this dilemma? What policies or strategies have countries adopted to deal with the liberal paradox?

5. Philip Martin predicts that economically motivated migration is likely to increase in the future. What evidence does he cite to support his prediction? What impact does he say that immigrants have on the economy?

YES: James F. Hollifield, *Southern Methodist University*

Today tens of millions of people cross borders on a daily basis. International mobility is part of a broader trend of globalization, which includes trade in goods and services, investments and capital flows, greater ease of travel, and a veritable explosion of information. While trade and capital flows are seen as the twin pillars of globalization, migration often is overlooked, especially among scholars of international relations (Hollifield 2008). Yet migration is a defining feature of the global era in which we live. Although it is linked in many ways to trade and investment, it is profoundly different. Some clever person once observed that "people are not shirts," which is another way of saying that labor is not a pure commodity. Unlike goods and capital, individuals can become actors on the international stage, whether through peaceful transnational communities or in violent terrorist/criminal networks.

Migration and mobility can pose a threat to the security of states, as we have been reminded daily since the terrorist attacks of September 11, 2001; but migrants also are an asset. Immigrants bring human capital, as well as new ideas and cultures to their host societies, and they often come with a basic package of (human) rights that enables them to become members of society, if not citizens, of their adoptive countries. Conversely, they may return to their countries of origin, where they can have a dramatic effect on economic and political development (Hollifield et al. 2007).

And, lest we forget, not all migration is voluntary—in any given year, millions of people move to escape political violence, hunger, and deprivation, becoming refugees, asylum seekers, or internally displaced persons. In 2007 UN estimates put the global refugee population at 11.4 million—down considerably from the turbulent decade of the 1990s but trending upward. The total population of concern to the UN High Commission for Refugees, including Internally Displaced Persons, stands at almost 33 million. Because it is so complex and multifaceted, migration poses an enormous regulatory challenge for states and for the international community.

How can we explain the increase in immigration when governments in every region of the globe are under pressure to limit the influx and reverse the flows? It might be tempting to argue that international migration is simply a function of the inexorable process of globalization. Demand for labor—both skilled and unskilled—is high in the principal receiving countries of North America, Europe, and Australia, while the supply of workers from Asia, Latin America, and Africa who are willing to fill this demand is unlimited. Demand-pull and supply-push forces seem to account rather well for the surge in international migration.

Yet we know that individuals are risk-averse and that migration is fraught with risks—the transaction costs alone should be enough to deter most people from moving, and, indeed, this is the case. Two hundred million people live outside their country of birth, which represents less than 3 percent of the world's population. Nonetheless, despite efforts to restrict immigration, people are moving in increasing numbers, and in many receiving countries there is a sense of crisis and loss of control.

Sociologists and anthropologists have helped us to understand how individuals reduce the risks associated with migration (Massey et al. 2002). Individuals are more likely to migrate if they have friends or relatives in the destination country who are willing to ease the process of transition. Social networks lower the transaction costs associated with emigration, making it less risky while connecting supply and demand, like two poles of a battery.

Is this the end of the story? If so, there would appear to be no room for the state in managing migration. Policy, some say (Sassen 1996), may be irrelevant, playing at best only a marginal role in the migration process, and the institutions of sovereignty and citizenship are increasingly outdated (Soysal 1994). According to this logic, we are entering a postnational era and migration is redefining the international state system.

I shall argue, however, that it is a mistake to eliminate the state from our analysis. The necessary conditions for migration to occur may be social and economic, but the sufficient conditions are political and legal. States must be willing to open their borders to the movement of people, and, as people move, they can acquire rights. Immigration has profound political implications, and states are critical in shaping migration outcomes. I want to develop this argument in three steps: (1) we need to look at the causes and consequences of international migration, with an eye to understanding (2) how states have tried to manage migration and (3) the emergence of what I have termed the "migration state." First, let us put the contemporary migration crisis into historical perspective.

THE GLOBAL MIGRATION "CRISIS"

Migration, like globalization, is *not* a new phenomenon. Throughout history, the movement of populations has been the norm. Only with the advent of the nation-state in sixteenth- and seventeenth-century Europe did the notion of legally tying populations to territorial units (states) and to specific forms of government become commonplace. In the twentieth century, passport and visa systems developed and borders were increasingly closed to nonnationals (Torpey 1998). Almost every dimension of human existence—social-psychological, demographic, economic, and political—was reshaped to conform to the dictates of the nation-state. The migration "crises" of the late twentieth century pale by comparison with the upheavals associated with the Industrial Revolution, the two world wars, and decolonization, which resulted in genocide, irredentism (ethnonationalist movements to recapture lost territory), the displacement of massive numbers of people, and the radical redrawing of national boundaries, not only in Europe, but around the globe. This process was repeated at the end of the Cold War and the breakup of the Soviet empire.

Myron Weiner (1995) argues that the increase in international migration in the postwar period posed a threat to international stability and security, especially in those areas of the globe where nation-states are most fragile—the Balkans, Transcaucasia, the Middle East, the Great Lakes region of Africa, and Southern Africa. Weiner extends his argument to the Western democracies, pointing out that a rise in xenophobic and nationalist politics in Western Europe showed that even the most advanced and tolerant democracies risk being destabilized politically by an influx of unwanted immigrants. Weiner postulates that there are limits on how many foreigners a society can absorb. Samuel Huntington of "the clash of civilizations" fame has argued that failure to control American borders is the single biggest threat to the national security of the United States (Huntington 1996; 2004). Weiner and Huntington echo the sentiments of Arthur Schlesinger Jr. (1992) and others (Brimelow 1995), who fear that immigration and multiculturalism will lead to the "disuniting of America." According to this line of reasoning, nation-states are threatened both by globalization from above and by multiculturalism from below.

At the heart of the migration crisis are concerns about sovereignty, citizenship, national security, and identity. The ability or inability of a state to control its borders and hence its population is the sine qua non of sovereignty. With some notable exceptions—such as the international refugee regime created by the 1950 Geneva Convention in the aftermath of World War II—the right of a state to control entry and exit of persons to and from its territory is an undisputed principle of international law. But this political and legal principle immediately raises several questions: why are some states willing to accept rather high levels of immigration when it would seem not to be in their interest to do so (Hollifield 1992; Cornelius et al. 2004)? Does this influx pose a threat to the institutions of sovereignty and citizenship (Joppke 1998), and should we view migration primarily as an issue of sovereignty and national security (Rudolph 2006)?

A BRIEF HISTORY OF MIGRATION AND GLOBALIZATION

In international relations theory, states are defined primarily by their security, or military, function. The Westphalian state is above all else a *garrison state*. Realists and neorealists (Waltz 1979) view the state as a unitary rational actor, with the overriding responsibility to maximize power, protect its territory and people, and pursue its national interest. Since the beginning of the Industrial Revolution in Europe, however, the state has taken on an increasingly important economic function. Ensuring material wealth and power has required states to risk greater economic openness, and to pursue policies of free trade, giving rise to what Richard Rosecrance (1986) has called the *trading state*. As a result, states have been partially liberated from their dependence on control of territory and military might as sources of power. International relations theory has moved away from the narrow realist view of the state, recognizing that in an increasingly interdependent world, power is more diffuse (Keohane and Nye 1977). In this neoliberal view, states are linked together by international trade and finance, forcing them to alter their grand strategies and seek new ways to cooperate. I argue that migration and trade are inextricably linked—like two sides of the same coin (Hollifield 2000). Hence, the rise of the trading state necessarily entails the rise of the *migration state*, where considerations of power and interest are driven as much by migration (the movement of people, human capital, and manpower) as they are by commerce and finance.

For centuries, states have been in the business of organizing mass migrations for the purposes of colonization and economic development, and to gain a competitive edge in a globalizing economy. During the eighteenth and nineteenth centuries—a period of relatively free migration—many states with open frontiers, such as the United States and Russia, were happy to receive immigrants; whereas overpopulated societies, suffering from rural exodus and burgeoning cities, were happy to be rid of masses of unskilled and often illiterate peasants and workers.

By the early twentieth century, however, some of the traditional sending countries in Europe were well into the Industrial Revolution and entering a demographic transition that was characterized by falling birth rates and more stable populations. The great transatlantic migrations were drawing to a close (Nugent 1992), nationalism was on the rise, and it was increasingly important, in terms of military security, for states to be able to identify their citizens and to construct new demographic regimes (Koslowski 2000). The need to regulate national populations, for purposes of taxation and conscription, led to passport and visa systems and to the concomitant development of immigration and naturalization policies (Torpey 1998). Every individual was expected to have one and only one nationality; and nationality, as a legal institution, would provide the individual with a measure of protection in a hostile and anarchic world of nation-states. Countries of emigration, such as Germany, tended to opt for nationality laws based upon *jus sanguinis* (blood, kinship, or ethnicity), whereas countries of immigration, including the United States and France, developed a more expansive political citizenship based upon *jus soli* (soil or birthplace). Moreover, American immigration policy in the late nineteenth and early twentieth centuries evolved along racial lines, culminating in the Chinese Exclusion Act of 1882 and the National Origins Quota system, enacted in 1924 (Smith 1997; King 2000).

Until 1914, international migration was driven primarily by the dynamics of colonization and the push-pull of economic and demographic forces (Hatton and Williamson 1998), even though receiving countries such as the United States were struggling to establish regulatory schemes to manage immigration (Tichenor 2002). Illegal or unauthorized immigration was not recognized as a major policy issue, and there were virtually no provisions for political migration (involving refugees and asylum seekers). To a large extent, efforts to regulate immigration were rendered moot by the outbreak of war in Europe, which stopped economic migration in its tracks. However, the Great War fostered the rise of intense and virulent forms of nationalism—often with a strong ethnic dimension.

War in Europe sparked irredentism, and the redrawing of national boundaries, which in turn fostered new kinds of migration. Millions of displaced persons and refugees would cross national boundaries in the twentieth century to "escape from violence" (Zolberg, Suhrke, and Aguayo 1989). World War I marked a critical turning point in the history of migration and international relations. States would never return to the relatively open migration regimes of the eighteenth and nineteenth centuries, when markets (supply-push and demand-pull) were the driving force of international migration. Instead, the twentieth century world would be increasingly closed, and travel would require elaborate documentation. World War I also marked the beginning of the end of imperialism, as struggles for independence and decolonization began in Asia and Africa—movements that would eventually result in the displacement of more millions of people.

In the interwar years, the Westphalian system of nation-states hardened and became further institutionalized in the core countries of the Euro-Atlantic region, and it continued to spread around the globe with the creation of new states (or the reemergence of old ones) in Asia, Africa, and the Middle East. Old and new states guarded their sovereignty jealously, and peoples in every region gained a stronger sense of citizenship and national identity. Because of these developments, international migration took on a more political character, bringing diaspora and exile politics to the fore. Henceforth, crossing borders had the potential of being a political, as well as an economic act, and states reasserted their authority with a vengeance. The rise of antistate revolutionary movements, such as anarchism and communism, provoked harsh crackdowns on immigration, as well as a roll-back of civil rights and liberties, in the name of national security and identity (Smith 1997; King 2000).

The events of the 1930s and 1940s in Europe radically changed legal norms governing international migration. The Holocaust and World War II led to the creation of the United Nations and to a new body of refugee and human rights law. Although states retained sovereign control over their territory, and the principle of noninterference in the internal affairs of others still holds, the postwar international order created new legal spaces (rights) for individuals and groups. The 1951 Geneva Convention Relating to the Status of Refugees established the principle of asylum, whereby an individual with a "well-founded fear of persecution," once admitted to the territory of a safe state, cannot be arbitrarily expelled or sent back to the state of his or her nationality. Under international law, the individual is entitled to a legal hearing; but it is important to remember that no state is compelled to admit an asylum seeker. If, however, the state is a signatory of the Convention, the principle of *non-refoulement* holds that it cannot legally send an individual back to his or her country of origin, if he or she is threatened with persecution and violence.

The United Nations Charter as well as the Universal Declaration of Human Rights, which was adopted by the UN General Assembly in December 1948, reinforced the principle of the rights of individuals "across borders" (Jacobson 1996). Likewise, as a direct response to the Holocaust and other crimes against humanity, the international community in 1948 adopted and signed the Convention on the Prevention and Punishment of the Crime of Genocide. Alongside these developments in international law and politics, we can see a growing "rights-based liberalism" in the politics and jurisprudence of the most powerful liberal states in Europe and North America. These liberal developments in international and municipal law feed off one another, creating new rights (legal spaces) for migrants at the international and domestic level (Hollifield et al. 2008).

Why are these legal developments so important? Unlike trade and financial flows, which can be promoted and regulated through international institutions such as the World Trade Organization and the International Monetary Fund, the movement of individuals across borders requires a qualitatively different set of regulatory regimes—ones based squarely on the notion of rights. It is almost a truism to point out that individuals, unlike goods, services, or capital, have a will of their own and can become subjects of the law and members of the societies in which they reside (Hollifield 1992; Weiner 1995). They also can become citizens of the polity (Koslowski 2000). The resulting questions are these: how far are states willing to go in establishing an international regime for the orderly (legal) movement of people, and to what extent would such a regime rely upon municipal as opposed to international law (Hollifield 2000)?

MANAGING MIGRATION IN A NEW ERA OF GLOBALIZATION

The last half of the twentieth century marked an important new chapter in the history of globalization. Assisted by advances in travel and communications technology, migration accelerated, reaching levels not seen since the end of the nineteenth century. Because more than half the world's migrant population resides in the less developed countries (LDCs)—especially those rich in such natural resources as oil, gold, or diamonds—the biggest challenge confronts states such as South Africa and the United States, which share land borders with overpopulated and underdeveloped states. Supply-push forces remain strong, while the ease of communication and travel have reinforced migrant networks, making it easier than ever before for potential migrants to gather the information that they need in order to make a decision about whether or not to move.

To some extent, supply-push forces are constant or rising, and they have been so for many decades. Demand-pull forces are variable, however, both in the countries of the Organization for Economic Cooperation and Development (OECD) and in the wealthier LDCs, many of which suffer from a shortage of skilled and unskilled labor. The oil sheikdoms of the Persian Gulf are perhaps the best examples, but we have seen increasing labor shortages in the newly industrialized countries of East and Southeast Asia as well. Singapore, Malaysia, and Taiwan, for example, have become major importers of cheap labor from other LDCs in Southeast Asia, particularly the Philippines and Thailand.

With very few exceptions, however, these LDCs have not evolved elaborate laws or policies for managing migration. Wealthier LDCs have put in place contract or guest worker schemes, negotiated with the sending countries, and with no provisions for settlement or family reunification. These types of pure manpower policies leave migrants with few if any rights, making them vulnerable to abuse and arbitrary expulsion. The only protections they have are those afforded by the negotiating power of their home countries, which may choose to protest the treatment of their nationals. But, more often than not, the sending countries are unwilling to provoke a conflict over individual cases of abuse, for fear of losing access to remittances, which are one of the largest sources of foreign exchange for many LDCs (Hollifield et al. 2007). Hence, economics and demography (forces of supply-push and demand-pull) continue to govern much of international migration in the developing world. Summary deportations and mass expulsions are viable options for controlling immigration in these nonliberal states.

In the advanced industrial democracies, immigration has been trending upward over most of the post–World War II period, to the point that well over 40 percent of the world's migrant population resides in Europe and America, where roughly 10 percent of the population is foreign-born (Castles and Miller 1998). Postwar migration to the core industrial states of Europe and North America has gone through several distinct phases, which make these population movements quite different from the transatlantic migrations of the nineteenth century or economic migrations in the Third World today. The first wave of migration in the aftermath of World War II was intensely political, especially in Europe, where large populations were displaced as a result of the redrawing of national boundaries, irredentism, and ethnic cleansing. Much of the remaining Jewish population in Central Europe fled to the United States or Israel, whereas large ethnic German populations in East Central Europe flooded into the newly created Federal Republic of Germany. The partition of Germany, the Cold War, and the division of Europe contributed to the exodus of ethnic populations, seeking refuge in the democratic west. Until the construction of the Berlin Wall in 1961, twelve million German refugees arrived in West Germany.

Once this initial wave of refugee migration had exhausted itself and Europe began to settle into an uneasy peace that split the continent between the superpowers—thus cutting (West) Germany and other industrial states in Western Europe off from their traditional supplies of surplus labor in East Central Europe—new economic forms of migration began to emerge. The massive effort to reconstruct the war-ravaged economies of Western Europe in the 1950s quickly exhausted indigenous supplies of labor, especially in Germany and France. Like the United States, which launched a guest worker (*bracero*) program (1942–1964) during World War II to recruit Mexican agricultural workers (Calavita 1992), the industrial states of Northwest Europe concluded bilateral agreements with labor-rich countries in Southern Europe and Turkey, which allowed them to recruit millions of guest workers during the 1950s and 1960s (Hollifield 1992).

The guest worker phase ended in the United States with the winding down of the *bracero* program in the 1950s, whereas in Europe it continued until the first signs of economic slowdown in 1966. However, the big shift in migration policy in Western Europe came in 1973–1974, following the first major oil shock and recession, which rapidly spread around the globe. European governments abruptly suspended all foreign worker recruitment and took steps to encourage "guests" to return home. Policies were put in place to discourage or, wherever possible, prevent settlement and family reunification. The prevailing sentiment was that guest worker migrations were primarily economic in nature, and that these workers constituted a kind of economic shock absorber (*Konjunkturpuffer*). They were brought into the labor market during periods of high growth and low unemployment, and they should be sent home during periods of recession. In these circumstances of recession and rising unemployment, it seemed logical that guest workers—like all commodities—should behave according to the laws of supply and demand.

The difficulty of using guest workers for managing labor markets in Western Europe is a perfect illustration of what I call the "liberal paradox" (Hollifield 1992). States require labor for economic growth, hence the need for openness; but they also need to maintain a degree of closure to protect the social contract and the institutions of sovereignty and citizenship. Importing labor to sustain high levels of non-inflationary growth during the 1950s and 1960s was a logical move for states and employers. This move was in keeping with the growing trend toward internationalization of markets for capital, goods, services, and labor; and it was encouraged by international economic organizations, particularly the OECD. But, as the Swiss novelist, Max Frisch, pointed out at the time, the European governments had "asked for workers, but human beings came." Unlike goods or capital, migrants (qua human beings) can and do acquire rights, particularly under the aegis of the laws and constitutions of liberal states, which afford migrants a measure of due process and equal protection.

The settlement of large foreign populations transformed the politics of Western Europe, giving rise to new social movements and political parties demanding a halt to immigration (Givens 2005). Public opinion was largely hostile to immigration, and governments were unprepared to manage ethnic diversity (Lahav 2004; Messina 2007). Problems of integration began to dominate the public discourse, amid perceptions that Muslim immigrants in particular posed a threat to civil society and to the secular (republican) state. The fear was (and is) that dispossessed and disillusioned youth of the second generation would turn to radical Islam, rather than following the conventional, secular, and republican path to assimilation (Klausen 2005). European societies looked increasingly like the United States, where older, linear conceptions of assimilation had given way to multiculturalism and an increasingly uneven or segmented incorporation, whereby large segments of the second generation, particularly among the unskilled and uneducated, experienced significant downward mobility (Hollifield 1997; Portes and Rumbaut, 1996; Alba and Nee 2003; Messina 2007).

In spite of xenophobic pressures that were building in the last two decades of the twentieth century, European democracies maintained a relatively strong commitment to the international refugee and human rights regime; and in the 1980s and 1990s, asylum seeking became the principal avenue for entry into Western Europe, in the absence of full-fledged legal immigration policies and in the face of growing fears that large numbers of asylum seekers would undermine the refugee regime and destabilize European welfare states (Freeman 1986; Ireland 2004). In this atmosphere of crisis, control policies shifted in the 1990s to stepped-up external (border) control,—Operations Gatekeeper and Hold the Line on the U.S.-Mexican border and the Schengen system in Western Europe allowed states to turn away asylum seekers, if they had transited a "safe third country"—to internal regulation of labor markets (through employer sanctions and the like), and to integrating large, established foreign populations (Brochmann and Hammar 1999; Cornelius et al. 2004).

Controlling borders in Europe required a renewed emphasis on international cooperation, especially among the member states of the European Community (EC). The EC, soon to become the European Union (EU), was committed to building a border-free Europe, relaxing and eventually eliminating all *internal* borders, in order to complete the internal market. However, given the desire of member states to stop further immigration, creating a border-free Europe meant reinforcing external borders, building a "ring fence" around the common territory, and moving toward common asylum and visa policies.

A series of conventions dealing with migration and security issues were drafted to help construct a new European migration regime, including the Schengen Agreement of 1985, whereby EU governments committed themselves to eliminating internal border checks, in exchange for common visa requirements to control the movement of third-country nationals. In the same vein, the Dublin Convention of 1990 required asylum seekers to apply for asylum in the first "safe country" where they arrive. Schengen and Dublin helped to establish buffer states in the formerly communist countries of Central Europe, permitting EU member states to return asylum seekers to these now safe third countries, without violating the principle of *non-refoulement.* The Dublin and Schengen Conventions also were designed to eliminate "asylum shopping," by requiring signatory states to accept the asylum decision of other member states. Thus an asylum seeker is permitted to apply for asylum in only one state, assuming he or she did not transit a safe third country before arriving on the common territory.

Project 1992, together with the Maastricht process, launched the most ambitious program of regional integration and economic liberalization in European history. But just as this process was taking off in 1989–1990, the strategic situation in Europe was turned upside down by the end of the Cold War and the collapse of the USSR and its communist satellites in East Central Europe. This change in the international system, which began in the 1980s during the period of glasnost under Mikhail Gorbachev, made it easier for individuals wishing to emigrate from the East to leave and seek asylum in the West. The result was a dramatic increase in the number of asylum seekers in Western Europe, not just from Eastern Europe, but from all over the world.

International migration thus had entered a new phase in the 1980s and 1990s, as refugee migration and asylum seeking reached levels not seen since the period just after World War II. The situation in Europe was further complicated by a resurgence of ethnic nationalism, by war in the Balkans, and by a dramatic increase in the number of refugees from almost every region of the globe. By the mid-1990s, there were over 16 million refugees in the world, two-thirds of them in Africa and the Middle East. The UN system for managing refugee migration, which had been created during the Cold War—primarily to accommodate those fleeing persecution under communist rule—suddenly came under enormous pressure (Teitelbaum 1980; Gibney 2004). The United Nations High Commission for Refugees was thrust into the role of managing the new migration crisis, as the Western democracies struggled to contain a wave of asylum seeking. The claims of the vast majority of those seeking asylum in Western Europe and the United States would be rejected, leading Western governments (and their publics) to the conclusion that most asylum seekers were in fact economic refugees. By the same token, many human rights advocates feared that genuine refugees would be submerged in a tide of false asylum seeking.

Whatever conclusion one draws from the high rate of rejection of asylum claims, the fact is that refugee migration surged in the last two decades of the twentieth century, creating a new set of dilemmas for liberal states (Gibney 2004). A large percentage of those whose asylum claims were refused would remain in the host countries either legally—pending appeal of their cases—or illegally, simply going underground. With most of the European democracies attempting to slow or stop all forms of *legal* immigration, the number of *illegal* immigrants—many of whom are individuals who entered the country legally and overstayed their visas—has increased steadily. Closing off avenues for legal immigration in Western Europe led to a surge in illegal migration. But the perception among Western publics that immigration is raging out of control and the rise of right-wing and xenophobic political parties and movements, especially in Western Europe, has made governments extremely reluctant to create new programs for legal immigration, or to expand existing quotas.

Instead, the thrust of policy change in Western Europe and the United States has been in the direction of further restriction. For example, Germany in 1993 amended its constitution in order to eliminate the blanket right of asylum that was enshrined in Article 16 of the old Basic Law, while France in 1995–1996 enacted a series of laws (the Pasqua and Debré Laws) that were designed to roll back the rights of foreign residents and make it more difficult for immigrants to naturalize (Hollifield 1997; Brochmann and Hammar 1999). Also in 1996, the Republican-dominated U.S. Congress enacted the Illegal Immigration Reform and Immigrant Responsibility Act, which curtailed social or welfare rights for all immigrants (legal as well as illegal), and severely limited the due process rights of illegal immigrants and asylum seekers.

At the same time that Congress was acting to limit immigrant rights, it took steps to expand legal immigration, especially for certain categories of highly skilled immigrants. The H-1B program, which gave American businesses the right to recruit foreigners with skills that were in short supply among native workers, was expanded in the 1990s. In France in 1997 and in Germany in 1999, laws were passed to liberalize naturalization and citizenship policy (Hollifield 1997). Most European governments have accepted the reality of immigration, and, faced with stagnant or declining populations and a shortage of highly skilled workers, have enacted new recruitment programs, seeking to emulate some aspects of American and Canadian immigration policy and to make their economies more competitive in a rapidly globalizing world.

How can we make sense of these seemingly contradictory trends? Have states found ways of escaping from the liberal paradox, or are they still caught between economic forces that propel them toward greater openness (to maximize material wealth and economic security) and political forces that seek a higher degree of closure (to protect the demos, maintain the integrity of the community, and preserve the social contract)? Finding the appropriate "equilibrium" between openness and closure is a daunting task for states, which also face the very real threat of terrorism. The attacks of September 11, 2001, served as a reminder that the first responsibility of the state is to provide for the security of its territory and population.

THE EMERGING "MIGRATION STATE"

International migration is likely to increase in coming decades, unless there is some cataclysmic international event, such as war or economic depression.

Even the 9/11 terrorist attacks on the United States and the ensuing "war on terrorism" have not led to a radical closing of borders. Global economic inequalities mean that supply-push forces remain strong, while at the same time demand-pull forces are intensifying. The growing demand for highly skilled workers and the demographic decline in the industrial democracies create economic opportunities for migrants in those countries. Transnational networks have become more dense and efficient, linking the sending and receiving societies, helping to lower the costs and the risks of migration, and making it easier for people to move across borders and over long distances. Moreover, when legal migration is not an option, migrants have increasingly turned to professional smugglers, and a global industry of migrant smuggling—often with the involvement of organized crime—has sprung up. Hardly a week passes without some news of a tragic loss of life associated with migrant smuggling (Kyle and Koslowski 2001).

Regulating international migration requires liberal states to be attentive to the (human or civil) rights of the individual. If rights are ignored or trampled upon, the liberal state risks undermining its own legitimacy and raison d'être. As international migration and transnationalism increase, pressures build upon liberal states to find new and creative ways to cooperate, in order to manage cross-border flows. The definition of the national interest and *raison d'Etat* have to take this reality into account, as rights become a central feature of domestic and foreign policy. New international migration regimes will be necessary if states are to risk more openness, and rights-based (international) politics will be the order of the day.

Some politicians and policymakers, as well as international organizations, continue to hope for market-based/economic solutions to the problem of regulating international migration. Trade and foreign direct investment—bringing capital and jobs to people, either through private investment or official development assistance—it is hoped, will substitute for migration, alleviating both supply-push and demand-pull factors. Even though trade can lead to factor-price equalization in the long term, as we have seen in the case of the European Union (Straubhaar 1988), in the short and medium term exposing LDCs to market forces often results in increased (rather than decreased) migration, as is evident with NAFTA and the U.S.-Mexican relationship (Martin 1993; Massey et al. 2002; Hollifield and Osang 2005). Likewise, trade in services can stimulate more "high end" migration, because these types of products often cannot be produced or sold without the movement of the individuals who make and market them (Bhagwati 1998; Ghosh 1997).

In short, the global integration of markets for goods, services, and capital entails higher levels of international migration; therefore, if states want to promote freer trade and investment, they must be prepared to manage higher levels of migration. Many states (including Canada, Australia, and Germany) are willing, if not eager, to sponsor high-end migration, because the numbers are manageable, and there is likely to be less political resistance to the importation of highly skilled individuals. However, mass migration of unskilled and less educated workers is likely to meet with greater political resistance, even in situations and in sectors such as construction or health care, where there is high demand for this type of labor. In these instances, the tendency is for governments to go back to the old guest worker models, in hopes of bringing in just enough temporary workers to fill gaps in the labor market, but with strict contracts between foreign workers and their employers that limit the length of stay and prohibit settlement or family reunification. The alternative is illegal immigration and a growing black market for labor—a Hobson's choice.

As mentioned earlier, the nineteenth and twentieth centuries saw the rise of the trading state (Rosecrance 1986), while the latter half of the twentieth century gave rise to the migration state. In fact, from a strategic, economic and demographic standpoint, trade and migration go hand in hand; because the wealth, power and stability of the state is now more than ever dependent on its willingness to risk both trade and migration (Hollifield 2004). In launching a new "blue card" program to attractive highly skilled foreign workers, the European Union is clearly seeking to emulate the United States and Canada, on the premise that global competitiveness, power, and economic security are closely related to a willingness to accept immigrants.

Now more than ever, international security and stability are dependent on the capacity of states to manage migration. It is extremely difficult, if not impossible, for them to do so either unilaterally or bilaterally. Some type of multilateral/regional regime is required, similar to what the EU has constructed for nationals of its member states. The EU model points the way to future migration regimes, because it is not based purely on *homo economicus* but incorporates rights for individual migrants and even a rudimentary citizenship, which continues to evolve. The problem, of course, in this type of regional migration regime is how to deal with third-country nationals.

In the end, the EU, by creating a regional migration regime and a kind of supranational authority to deal with migration and refugee issues, allows the member states to finesse, if not escape, the liberal paradox (Geddes 2003). Playing the good cop/bad cop routine and using symbolic politics and policies to maintain the illusion of border control can help governments to fend off the forces of closure, at least in the short run (Rudolph 2006). In the end, however, it is the nature of the liberal state itself and the degree to which openness is institutionalized and (constitutionally) protected from the "majority of the moment," that will determine whether states will continue to risk trade and migration (Hollifield 2008; Hollifield et al. 2007).

Regional integration reinforces the trading state and acts as a mid-wife for the migration state, and it blurs the lines of territoriality, lessening problems of integration and national identity. The fact that there is an increasing disjuncture between people and place—which in the past might have provoked a crisis of national identity and undermined the legitimacy of the nation-state—is less of a problem when the state is tied to a regional regime like the EU. This does not mean, of course, that there will be no resistance to freer trade and migration. Protests against globalization and nativist or xenophobic reactions against immigration have been on the rise throughout the OECD world. Nonetheless, regional integration—especially when it has a long history and is deeply institutionalized as it is in Europe—makes it easier for states to risk trade and migration and for governments to construct the kinds of political coalitions that will be necessary to support and institutionalize greater openness.

Mexican leaders, such as former Presidents Raul Salinas de Gortari and Vicente Fox, looked to Europe as a model for how to solve problems of regional integration, especially the very delicate political issue of illegal Mexican immigration to the United States. Their argument is that freer migration and a more open (normalized) border are logical extensions of the North American Free Trade Agreement (NAFTA). But the United States has been reluctant to move so fast with economic and political integration, especially after the 9/11 attacks, preferring instead to create new guest worker programs, or to continue with the current system, which tolerates high levels of unauthorized migration from Mexico (Massey et al. 2002). Clearly, however, North America is the region that is closest to taking steps toward an EU-style regional migration regime, and the U.S. is facing the prospect of another amnesty comparable to the one carried out as part of the 1986 Immigration Reform and Control Act. In the long run, it is difficult for liberal states, such as the United States, to sustain a large, illegal population. For this reason, amnesties, legalizations, or regularizations have become a common feature of the migration state.

Even though there are large numbers of economic migrants in Asia, this region remains divided into relatively closed and often authoritarian societies, with little prospect of granting rights to migrants and guest workers. The more liberal and democratic states—Japan, Taiwan, and South Korea—are the exceptions; but they have only just begun to grapple with the problem of immigration, on a relatively small scale (Cornelius et al. 2004). In much of Africa and the Middle East, which have high numbers of migrants and refugees, there is a great deal of instability, and states are fluid, with little institutional or legal capacity for dealing with international migration.

In conclusion, we can see that migration is both a cause and a consequence of globalization. International migration, like trade, is a fundamental feature of the postwar liberal order. But as states and societies become more open, migration has increased. Will this increase create a virtuous or a vicious cycle? Will it be destabilizing, leading the international system into greater anarchy, disorder, and war; or will it lead to greater openness, wealth, and human development? Much will depend on how migration is managed by the more powerful liberal states, because they will set the trend for the rest of the globe.

To avoid a domestic political backlash against immigration, the rights of migrants must be respected and states must cooperate in building an international migration regime. I have argued that the first, halting steps toward such a regime have been taken in Europe, and that North America is likely to follow. As liberal states come together to manage this extraordinarily complex phenomenon, it may be possible to construct a truly international migration regime. But I am not sanguine about this opportunity in the short term, because the asymmetry of interests—particularly between the developed and the developing world—is too great to permit states to overcome problems of coordination and cooperation. Even as states become more dependent on trade and migration, they are likely to remain trapped in a liberal paradox, needing to be economically open and politically closed, for decades to come.

NO: Philip Martin, *University of California, Davis*

MIGRATION AND LABOR

International migrants, people who move from one country to another for a year or more, are the exception, not the rule. There are about 200 million international migrants, meaning that 3 percent of the world's people have left their country of birth or citizenship—a very inclusive definition that embraces naturalized citizens such as Henry Kissinger, legal immigrants, and long-term visitors such as foreign students and unauthorized migrants.[1] About 20 percent of the world's migrants, almost 40 million, are in the United States.

Most people never leave the country in which they were born. However, international migration for employment is increasing, as most migrant workers move from poorer developing countries to richer industrial countries.[2] Almost 20 percent, or 600 million, of the world's workers are in the industrial countries, leaving 2.5 billion in developing countries, where almost all labor-force growth occurs. The sheer force of numbers suggests that most new workers in developing countries will have to find jobs there. Between 2007 and 2020, industrial-country labor forces are expected to remain at about 600 million, while developing-country labor forces expand by 500 million—making the *growth* in developing-country work forces almost equal to the current industrial-country labor force.

Not all migrant workers settle in the country in which they work temporarily. For example, a million Filipinos a year leave for overseas jobs, but there are fewer than 3 million Filipino contract workers abroad, meaning that many return after two or three years abroad.

Here I will explore current global migration patterns and issues, explaining why economically motivated migration is likely to increase, examining the effects of migration on labor-sending and -receiving countries, and concluding that countries can adjust to the presence or absence of additional migrants. The most important policy challenge is to avoid allowing migration policy to shift from a national interest to a special interest, as occurred when the United States had been restricting imports of sugar from Caribbean islands since the 1950s and then allowed Florida sugarcane growers to import cane-cutters from Jamaica.[3] Finally, I will consider how these conclusions relate to the debate on liberalizing immigration policies. Advocates of liberalization argue that immigration speeds economic growth. More immigrants do produce a larger economy, but the net economic benefits of immigration are very small.

DIFFERENCES MOTIVATE MIGRATION

Migration—the movement of people from one place to another—is as old as humankind wandering in search of food, but international migration is a relatively recent development, since it was only in the early twentieth century that the system of nation-states, passports, and visas developed to regulate the flow of people over national borders.[4]

Again, international migration is the exception, not the rule. The No. 1 form of migration control is inertia—most people do not want to move away from family and friends. Second, governments have significant capacity to regulate migration—and they do so—with passports, visas, and border controls. One item considered by many governments when deciding whether to recognize a new entity that declares itself a nation-state is whether it is able to regulate who crosses and remains within its borders.

Nonetheless, international migration is likely to increase in the twenty-first century for reasons that range from persisting demographic and economic inequalities to communications and transportation revolutions that increase mobility. There are, also, more borders to cross. There were 193 generally recognized nation-states in 2000—four times more than the 43 that existed in 1900.[5] Each nation-state distinguishes citizens and foreigners, has border controls to inspect those seeking entry, and determines what foreigners can do while inside the country, whether they are tourists, students, guest workers, or immigrants.

Most countries discourage immigration, meaning that they do not anticipate the arrival of foreigners wanting to settle and become naturalized citizens. Some also discourage emigration, as when Communist nations tried to prevent their citizens from fleeing to the West during the Cold War—as symbolized by the Berlin Wall between 1961 and 1989—and the continuing effort of North Korea to keep its citizens from leaving.

Five countries plan for a significant annual inflow of immigrants: the United States (which accepted 1.2 million immigrants in 2006), Canada (250,000), Australia (125,000), New Zealand (50,000), and Israel (25,000). The number of newcomers arriving in industrial countries exceeds this planned total of 1.5 million a year, suggesting that many of these migrants are temporary visitors or unauthorized foreigners.

There are two extreme perspectives on the rising number of migrants in industrial countries. At one extreme, the *Wall Street Journal* advocates a five-word amendment to the U.S. Constitution: "There shall be open borders."[6] Organizations ranging from the Catholic Church to the World Bank have called for more migration, arguing that people should not be confined to their countries of birth by man-made national borders and that more migration would speed economic growth and development in both sending and receiving countries.

At the other extreme, virtually every industrial country has organizations such as the Federation for American Immigration Reform (FAIR), which calls for sharp reductions in immigration on the economic and social grounds that unskilled newcomers especially disadvantage low-skilled native workers, that increasing numbers of people have negative environmental effects, and that those from different cultures threaten established social norms. Many European countries have political parties that call for reducing immigration, such as the National Front in France, which, during the 1995 presidential campaign, proposed removing up to 3 million non-Europeans from France, mainly in order to reduce the number of Muslim residents.[7]

Amid regular reports of migrants dying in deserts and drowning at sea, some pundits see governments as powerless to manage international migration, for migrants seem determined to go over and under the walls that are meant to keep them out. The late President Boumedienne of Algeria appealed for more foreign aid on behalf of the Group of 77 developing countries, warning that if industrial countries did not respond, "no quantity of atomic bombs could stem the tide of billions … who will someday leave the poor southern part of the world to erupt into the relatively accessible spaces of the rich northern hemisphere looking for survival."[8]

Most people do not want to migrate to another country: international migrants make up 3 percent of the world's residents, not 30 percent. Furthermore, economic growth can turn emigration source nations into destinations for migrants within decades, as it has done in Ireland, Italy, and Korea. The challenge is to speed up such migration transitions, and to manage migration so as to reduce the differences that encourage people to cross borders over time. Planned immigration can produce socioeconomic dividends, but unplanned mass migration can be manipulated by special interests seeking cheap labor or more people from particular countries.

WHY PEOPLE MIGRATE

International migration is usually a carefully considered individual or family decision. The major reasons to migrate to another country can be grouped into two categories—economic and noneconomic—while the factors that encourage a migrant to actually move fall into three categories: demand-pull, supply-push, and networks. An economic migrant may be encouraged to move by employer recruitment of guest workers (a demand-pull factor), while migrants crossing borders for noneconomic reasons may be moving to escape unemployment or persecution (supply-push factors).

For example, a worker in rural Mexico may decide to migrate to the United States because a friend or relative tells him of a job, highlighting the availability of higher-wage jobs as a demand-pull factor encouraging a person to cross a national border. The worker may not have a regular job at home or may face debts from a family member's medical emergency, examples of supply-push factors that encourage emigration. Networks encompass everything from the moneylenders who provide the funds needed to pay a smuggler to cross the border to employers or friends and relatives at the destination who help migrants find jobs and places to live.

Demand-pull, supply-push, and network factors rarely have equal weight in an individual's decision to migrate, and their respective weights can change over time. Generally, demand-pull and supply-push factors are strongest at the beginning of a migration flow, while network factors become more important as migration streams mature.

The first migrant workers of a given migration stream are often recruited. For example, the U.S. government sent recruiters to rural Mexico in the 1940s to encourage Mexicans to move to the United States to fill jobs on U.S. farms. Many of these migrants then returned home with savings, encouraging more Mexicans to seek U.S. jobs and fueling unauthorized migration. Network factors ranging from settled friends and relatives to the expectation that young men in rural areas, in particular, should "go north for opportunity" sustained migration between rural Mexico and rural America after the Mexico-U.S. *bracero* program ended in 1964. A similar process played out in Western Europe, where governments stopped recruiting Turks and other southern European guest workers in 1973–1974, but others from those countries continued to arrive under family unification laws or came to France or Germany and asked not to be sent home to face persecution.

One of the most important noneconomic motivations for crossing national borders is family unification—such as the desire of a father settled abroad to have his wife and children join him. In such cases, the anchor immigrant is a demand-pull factor for family migration, and the immediate family may be followed by parents and brothers and sisters, creating a so-called chain migration.

Globalization has made people everywhere more aware of conditions and opportunities abroad. Tourism has become a major industry, as people cross national borders to experience new cultures, different weather, or the wonders of nature. Many young people find a period of foreign study or work experience enriching, and this initial exposure encourages them to migrate. In some cases, former colonies have become independent nations, but traditional migration patterns persist, as between India and Pakistan and the United Kingdom or between the Philippines and the United States.

Immigration policies aim to facilitate wanted migration, such as tourism, and deter unwanted migration, including those who arrive on tourist visas and do not depart as scheduled. However, it is often hard for inspectors at ports of entry to distinguish between legitimate and illegitimate migrants. Who is a legitimate tourist and who is a prospective unauthorized worker? Most countries require visas from foreigners wishing to enter and maintain consulates abroad to screen potential visitors to determine if they truly intend to return home. At many U.S. consulates around the world, most applicants for tourist visas are rejected.

DIFFERENCES AND LINKAGES

Globalization has increased linkages between countries, as evidenced by sharply rising flows of goods and capital over national borders and by the growth of international and regional bodies to set rules for such movements. However, although controlling the entry and sojourn of travelers is a core attribute of national sovereignty, flows of people are not governed by a comprehensive global migration regime. Most nation-states do not welcome newcomers as immigrants, but almost all of the industrial or high-income countries have guest-worker programs that allow local employers to recruit and employ temporary foreign workers. Many also have significant numbers of unauthorized or irregular migrant workers.

Most of the world's people—and most of its population growth—are to be found in developing countries. The world's population is growing by 1.3 percent, or 80 million a year, and 97 percent of that growth occurs in developing countries.[9] In the past, significant demographic differences between areas prompted large-scale migration. For example, as Table 1 shows, Europe had 21 percent of the world's almost one billion residents in 1800, and the Americas 4 percent. When there were five Europeans for every American, millions of Europeans emigrated to North and South America in search of economic opportunity as well as religious and political freedom.

Will history repeat itself? Africa and Europe have roughly equal populations today, but by 2050, Africa is projected to have nearly three times as many residents as Europe (see Table 1). If Africa remains poorer than Europe, the two continents' diverging demographic trajectories may propel young people to move from overcrowded cities such as Cairo and Lagos to Berlin and Rome, where there may be empty apartments.

The economic differences that encourage international migration have two dimensions, one fostered by inequality *between* countries and the other by inequality *within* countries. According to the World Bank, the world's almost 200 nation-states have per capita incomes that ranged from less than $250 per

Table 1

World Population by Continent, 1800–2050

	1800	1999	2050[a]
World (in millions)	978	5,978	8,909
Percentage shares:			
Africa	11	13	20
Asia	65	61	59
Europe	21	12	7
Latin America & Caribbean	3	9	9
North America	1	5	4
Oceania	0	1	1

Source: United Nations, "The World at Six Billion," 1999, Table 2, www.un.org/esa/population/publications/sixbillion/sixbillion.htm.
[a]projected

person per year to more than $50,000 in 2006—a difference that provides a significant incentive for young people, especially, to migrate in search of higher wages and more opportunities.[10]

The thirty high-income countries had one billion residents in 2006, or one-sixth of the world's population, while their gross national income was $36 trillion, which was 80 percent of the global total of $48 trillion.[11] The resulting average per capita income of $36,000 in high-income countries was 18 times the average $2,000 in low- and middle-income countries (see table 2). Despite rapid economic growth in some developing countries, including East Asian "Tigers" such as Korea and Thailand in the 1990s and China and India more recently, the per capita income ratio between high-income and other countries rose between 1975 and 2000, and it has shrunk only marginally since 2000. Average per capita incomes were sixty-one times higher in 2005 in high-income than in low-income countries, and thirteen times higher than in middle-income countries.

A second dimension to economic inequality between nation-states adds to international migration pressures. The world's labor force of 3.1 billion in 2005 included 600 million workers in the high-income countries and 2.5 billion in the lower-income countries. As figure 1 indicates, almost all growth in this area between 2005 and 2015 is projected to occur in lower-income countries, whose labor force is projected to increase by about 425 million, while the labor force in high-income countries is projected to remain stable at just over 600 million.

Table 2

Global Migrants and Per Capita Income Gaps, 1975–2005

	Migrants (millions)	World Pop. (billions)	Migrants World Pop.	Annual Mig. Increase (millions)	Countries grouped by per capita GDP ($) Low	Middle	High	Ratio High–Low	Ratio High–Mid
1975[a]	85	4.1	2.1%	1	150	750	6,200	41	8
1985	105	4.8	2.2%	2	270	1,290	11,810	44	9
1990[b]	154	5.3	2.9%	10	350	2,220	19,590	56	9
1995	164	5.7	2.9%	2	430	2,390	24,930	58	10
2000	175	6.1	2.9%	2	420	1,970	27,510	66	14
2005[c]	191	6.4	3.0%	3	580	2,640	35,131	61	13

Sources: UN Population Division and World Bank Development Indicators, www.un.org/esa/population/publications/publications.htm; http://go.worldbank.org/LOTTGBE9I0.
[a] 1975 income data are 1976.
[b] The 1990 migrant stock was raised from 120 million to 154 million because of the break-up of the USSR.
[c] 2005 data are gross national income.

In the lower-income countries, 40 percent of workers are employed in agriculture, a sector that is often taxed despite the fact that farmers and farm workers usually have lower-than-average incomes.[12] Because these taxes help to keep farm incomes lower than nonfarm incomes, there is often rural-urban migration—a major reason why the urban share of the world's population surpassed 50 percent for the first time in 2008.[13]

The United States and European countries had "Great Migrations" off the land in the 1950s and 1960s, providing workers for expanding factories and fueling population growth in cities. Similar Great Migrations are underway today from China to Mexico, and this rural-urban migration has three implications for international migration. First, ex-farmers and farm workers everywhere are most likely to accept so-called 3-D (dirty, dangerous, difficult) jobs, both inside their countries and abroad.[14] Second, rural-urban migrants often make physical as well as cultural transitions, and many find the transition as easy abroad as at home, as when Mexicans from rural areas find adapting to Los Angeles as easy as navigating Mexico City. Third, rural-urban migrants get one step closer to the country's exits by moving to cities, where it is usually easiest to obtain visas and documents for legal migration or to make arrangements for illegal migration.

Differences encourage migration, but it takes networks or links between areas to encourage people to move. Migration networks are a broad concept that has been shaped and strengthened by three revolutions of the past half-century: in communications, transportation, and rights.

Figure 1

Economically Active Populations (EAPs), 1980–2020

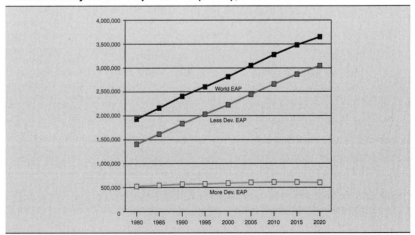

Source: ILO Laborsta, http://laborsta.ilo.org/.

The communications revolution helps potential migrants to learn about opportunities abroad. The best information comes from migrants who are already established abroad, since they can provide family and friends with information in an understandable context. Cheaper communications enable migrants to quickly transmit job information as well as advice on how to cross national borders to friends and relatives at home. For example, information about vacant California farm jobs may be received in rural Mexico, thousands of miles away, before it spreads to nearby cities that have unemployment rates of over 20 percent.[15] Meanwhile, films and television programs depicting life in high-income countries may encourage young people, especially, to assume that the grass is greener abroad, or that migration will lead to economic betterment.[16]

The transportation revolution accounts for the declining cost of travel. British migrants unable to pay one-way passage to North American colonies in the eighteenth century often indentured themselves, signing contracts that obliged them to work for three to six years for whoever met the ship and paid the captain. Transportation costs today are far lower—typically less than $2,500 to travel anywhere in the world legally, and $1,000 to $20,000 for unauthorized migration. Most studies also reflect faster payback times for migrants today, so that even migrants who have paid high smuggling fees can usually repay them within two or three years.

The communications and transportation revolutions help migrants to learn about opportunities and to cross national borders, while the rights revolution affects their ability to stay abroad. After World War II, most industrial countries strengthened the constitutional and political rights of residents to prevent a recurrence of fascism, and most did not distinguish between citizens and migrants when establishing social safety net programs.

As migration increased in the 1990s, policymakers began to roll back the socioeconomic rights of migrants in an effort to stem the influx of new residents. For example, many European governments, including Germany, had written liberal asylum provisions into their post–World War II constitutions so as to avoid repeating the situation in which refugees perished because other countries returned them to Nazi Germany. As a result, in the early 1990s, over 1,000 foreigners a day were applying for asylum in Germany, many from Turkey and other former guest-worker countries of origin. The German government distributed asylum seekers throughout the country and required local communities to provide them with housing and food. It was determined that over 90 percent of the foreigners applying for asylum were not actual refugees, and their false asylum claims contributed to a backlash that included "skinhead" attacks on foreigners.

The German and other European governments responded to this "asylum crisis" in three major ways.[17] First, nationals of the asylum seekers' major countries of origin (such as Turkey) had to obtain visas, which allowed the receiving governments to prescreen prospective foreign visitors and not issue visas to those who might request asylum. Second, airlines were fined heavily for transporting foreigners to France or Germany without visas and other documents, enlisting them in the quest to reduce the number of applicants. Third, European Union member countries agreed to make it difficult for foreigners from "safe" countries, and those who transited through safe countries, to apply for asylum in the EU—so that an Iraqi who traveled through Poland en route to Germany would be returned to Poland to apply for asylum. In this way, richer European countries maintained the constitutional protection of asylum while reducing the number of asylum applicants.

In the mid-1990s, the United States pursued a similar strategy of trying to manage migration by restricting the access of migrants to welfare assistance. When President Clinton pledged to "end welfare as we know it," migrants collecting welfare benefits became a target for those seeking to reduce the costs of the national welfare program. Illegal migration also influenced the debate, especially after the passage of NAFTA, which was expected to reduce unauthorized Mexico-U.S. migration but instead increased it during the worst recession in California in a half century.

In November 1994, a grassroots effort in California led voters to approve Proposition 187—which would have withheld social services, health care, and public education from illegal immigrants—despite the objections of almost all statewide political and opinion leaders.[18] In the ensuing national debate over immigrant numbers and rights, President Clinton argued that the number of needy migrants admitted to the United States should be reduced in order to maintain the access of legal immigrants (future Americans) to welfare benefits, while employers argued that the better solution was to allow the number of poor migrants arriving to remain at high levels, and to cut welfare costs by reducing immigrant access to social assistance.[19] Employers won the debate in Congress, and immigration was allowed to remain high, but those arriving after August 22, 1996, saw their access to means-tested benefits reduced.

Balancing migrant numbers and migrant rights is a major challenge.[20] Countries with the highest shares of migrants in their labor forces, such as the oil exporters of the Persian Gulf, extend few rights to migrants. There are no minimum wages in oil-exporting countries such as Saudi Arabia or the United Arab Emirates, which depend on millions of guest workers to build new cities and serve residents as domestic helpers, and migrant workers there are prohibited from forming unions or going on strike. Countries with fewer guest workers, such as Sweden and other Scandinavian countries, tend to grant them more rights, including equal wages and equal treatment under labor laws. Such policies make migrants as expensive to employ as local workers, and lead to the hiring of relatively few.

SHOULD COUNTRIES LIBERALIZE?

The numbers versus rights trade-off reflects the fact that the demand for labor is downward-sloping. As wages rise, economies adjust in ways that encourage the substitution of capital for labor, as when farmers use machines rather than workers to harvest crops. In some cases, rising wages prompt factories in the United States to close, and the production of toys and garments shifts to China and other lower-wage countries. There may be other adjustments to higher wages, such as self-service at gas stations. In industrial countries, wages and employment can rise together as the productivity of each employee increases.

There are millions of workers in developing countries who would like to move to industrial countries to earn in one hour what they earn in a day or a week at home. Should industrial countries open their doors wider to such low-wage workers? The World Bank and most international organizations promoting economic development say yes, pointing to the remittances that migrants send to their countries of origin to argue that migration can reduce poverty and speed development.[21] For example, one World Bank model estimated that increasing migration from developing to industrial countries would lift global economic output more than reducing trade barriers.[22] However, such models are based on many assumptions, including full employment, which assumes that all migrants find jobs and also that any local workers displaced by migrants find new jobs.

Unemployment in industrial countries fell between 2004 and 2007 despite high levels of migration, and most economic studies find little evidence of lower wages that can be attributed to migration. These studies are also based on assumptions, such as the idea that if the presence of immigrants depresses wages, cities with a higher share of immigrants in their labor forces should offer lower wages to U.S. workers with qualifications similar to those of the immigrants, such as high-school drop-outs. However, if natives move away from "migrant cities," or do not move to them, analysts can wrongly draw the conclusion that there is no migrant impact on wages.

Countries do not grow rich or poor because of immigration. An exhaustive study of the impact of immigrants on the U.S. economy by the National Research Council concluded that the United States obtained net economic benefits of $1 billion to $10 billion in the mid-1990s due to immigration.[23] Proponents of immigration stressed that the sign of the immigrant effect was positive; opponents argued that the impact of immigration was negligible because the then $8 trillion U.S. economy was expanding by 3 percent, growing by $240 billion a year—or $10 billion in two weeks.[24]

The United States is a nation of immigrants that first welcomed virtually all newcomers, later excluded certain types of foreigners, and since the 1920s has limited the number of immigrants by means of quotas. Immigrants and refugees arrive through America's front door, which was opened wider in 1990 to accommodate more relatives of U.S. residents and more workers desired by U.S. employers. But the fastest growth in migrant ingress has been through the side and back doors, as nonimmigrant tourists, foreign workers, and students—as well as unauthorized foreigners—arrive in ever-larger numbers.

Research on the economic, social, and political effects of immigration does not provide clear guidelines for policy. Overall, immigrants have minor effects—for better or worse—on the huge U.S. economy and labor market. Most immigrants are better off financially in the United States than they were at home, even though many arrive with little education and find it hard to climb the American job ladder.

Given the eagerness of migrants to cross borders and of employers to hire them, should industrial countries open their doors wider? There are no easy answers. Despite the World Bank's promotion of liberalization, more open borders do not necessarily mean less poverty. Since the effects of liberalization are not uniform across countries, the question of whether to liberalize is one that each country will have to consider and answer on its own. Immigration means change, much of which is hard to predict. Despite intentions to return, many migrants settle, and they and their children eventually gain a voice in the society and economy in which they live. Some residents welcome the changes that newcomers bring, while others fear them, which is why opening doors to newcomers has been and will continue to be controversial.

culture and diversity

Should Development Efforts Seek to Preserve Local Culture?

YES: Elsa Stamatopoulou, *United Nations*[a]

NO: Kwame Anthony Appiah, *Princeton University*

Culture is a difficult concept to pin down. It is the composite of language, food, history, and social relationships that help to define a national, subnational, or cross-national identity. Without cultures, individuals would lose the social contexts on which they rely to define their identities. Without varying cultures, the world would be a far less innovative, resilient, and interesting place.

Still, many traditional cultures are at risk. Small tribes in the tropics are dwindling because of low reproduction rates and emigration to the cities, where their people are rapidly assimilated or tempted to adopt more "modern" habits and attitudes. Many traditional languages are at risk of extinction as a result of globalization, as more people feel the need to speak the major languages of international commerce: Mandarin Chinese, Spanish, English, and Arabic. The Worldwatch Institute reports that over 50 percent of the 6,800 languages spoken worldwide are likely to become extinct by the end of this century. Some 4,000 to 9,000 languages disappeared over the past 500 years due to wars, genocide, legal restrictions, and the cultural assimilation of ethnic minorities. Table 1 shows just how tenuous is the existence of a number of languages, amid the dwindling numbers of their speakers.

Efforts are under way to preserve some cultures. Western anthropologists try to collect as much information as possible, and they even engage in educating younger generations in the traditions of their elders in hopes of restoring some cultures. Also, the United Nations Educational, Social and Cultural Organization (UNESCO) adopted a declaration in 2001 protecting national cultures and lin-

---

[a]The views expressed in this article do not necessarily represent those of the United Nations.

Table 1

The Status of the World's Languages, by Region

Region	Number of languages	Share of languages at risk[a]
Asia	2,197	53
Africa	2,058	33
Australia & Pacific Islands	1,311	93
The Americas	1,013	
North America		78
South America		77
Central America		36
Europe	230	30
World	6,809	59

Source: Payal Sampat, "World's Many Languages Disappearing," The Worldwatch Institute, *Vital Signs 2001*, http://macserv.murdoch.edu.au/N212/vital/lang.htm.
[a]Languages with fewer than 10,000 speakers.

guistic diversity. But there remain strong outside pressures operating on national cultures that bend them toward adjustment to external norms.

Preserving traditional cultures, or cultures of any sort, can be difficult. They are often social constructs, invoked to create a national identity for political purposes. Thus the articulation of culture can be politically molded and used for nationalistic and xenophobic ends. France argues that the French movie industry and French food are national cultural icons, and thus should be subsidized and protected from foreign competition, although these policies have been challenged by the World Trade Organization. Similarly, Japan has claimed that traditional modes of rice production are culturally grounded because of the distinctive type of rice that is grown locally and that Japanese consumers prefer. Thus the Japanese government uses a cultural argument to justify protection of a small, high-cost—but politically powerful—industry from foreign competition by means of import barriers that are counter to international trade law. Japan also argues that whaling is a Japanese cultural activity, and it is willing to face the wrath of international environmental groups to protect its small whaling industry.

Views on the acceptability of particular cultural expressions vary widely. Indeed, in one extreme example from the human rights domain, what is denounced as female genital mutilation in the West is regarded as a cultural tradition in some African societies. And Turkey is embroiled in a national debate about whether women should be allowed to wear the traditional Islamic headscarf, as a legitimate cultural artifact of the country's Ottoman (and Muslim) past, or whether its prohibition should be upheld as an articulation of the more secular culture imposed by Kemal Ataturk in 1924 (along with abolishing the fez for men) and perpetuated by the military and secular leaders since then.

Another question has to do with how static cultures actually are. Most current cultures are, in fact, robust, and most have adopted elements from other cultures. Globalization acts as a giant hothouse in which cultures selectively interact and borrow from one another. Traditionalists may find this give-and-take offensive, either because of beliefs about cultural purity or because their social status and influence thus become subject to question. The true policy challenge, however, is ensuring that traditional attitudes are not swamped by alien foreign views, but rather are able to meld the foreign ones into a comfortable blend that is amenable to local customs and beliefs.

The articles that follow offer different views as to whether preserving local culture should have a place in development efforts. Elsa Stamatopoulou believes that cultures, particularly traditional cultures, should be actively protected from globalization. Kwame Anthony Appiah is much more skeptical, believing that cultures follow their own organic evolution and should be allowed to develop independently of state protection.

Discussion Questions

1. Is it possible to preserve a local culture in the age of globalization—against influences such as the Internet, more global trade, and easier means of travel? How? Is it important to preserve local cultures? Why?
2. What is culture? How does it relate to identity?
3. In what ways can development efforts impact local cultures? Is this effect avoidable?
4. In the face of issues such as extreme poverty and poor health, should trying to preserve local culture be a priority in development efforts? Why or why not?
5. What does Elsa Stamatopoulou think are the merits of the UN Declaration on the Rights of Indigenous Peoples? What issues does this declaration address that past declarations have neglected? What does Stamatopoulou propose as a strategy for continued improvements in development and preserving culture?
6. Are all cultures worth protecting?
7. Why is Kwame Anthony Appiah opposed to adopting formal efforts to protect cultures? How does he think cultures develop and evolve? Should any cultures be preserved, according to him?

YES: Elsa Stamatopoulou, *Secretariat of the United Nations Permanent Forum on Indigenous Issues*

In 1923 Cayuga Chief Deskaheh, as the representative of the Six Nations of the Iroquois, traveled to Geneva to plead the cause of his people before the League of Nations. Despite one year of working for recognition by the League, he was not received, and so he returned to the United States. A few months before his death in 1925, Chief Deskaheh made a speech by radio from Rochester, New York. Here is an excerpt:

> This is the story of the Mohawks, the story of the Oneidas, of the Cayugas—I am a Cayuga—of the Onondagas, the Senecas, and the Tuscaroras. They are the Iroquois. Tell it to those who have not been listening. Maybe I will be stopped from telling it. But if I am prevented from telling it over, as I hope I do, the story will not be lost. ... I am the speaker of the Six Nations, the oldest League of Nations now existing. ... It is a League which is still alive and intends, as best it can, to defend the rights of the Iroquois to live under their own laws in their own little countries now left to them, to worship their Great Spirit in their own way, and to enjoy the rights which are as surely theirs as the white man's rights are his own.[1]

In 1925 Deskaheh did not mention "development" in conveying his vision of the future of his people, but today he might have done so. The verbs *to develop* and *to underdevelop* have sometimes been used to indicate top-down approaches to economic and social development, which sometimes lead to negative results. Indigenous leaders of today have also spoken of "development aggression" to indicate the imposition of the mainstream development paradigm on indigenous peoples—a paradigm that may be largely viewed as the promotion of industrialized societies and markets based on a continuously growing consumption of goods. Imposition of this paradigm has, more often than not, led to loss of indigenous peoples' lands, natural resources, and livelihoods; theft and patenting of their traditional knowledge; forced displacement of communities, often due to conflict; negation of benefit-sharing; forced assimilation, including loss of language and other aspects of culture; discrimination; marginalization; and extreme poverty.[2]

Often underlying the discussion about globalization and the expansion of free markets is a fear of the impact on local or national cultures. Some discussion—although not enough—has focused on this troubling issue at the intergovernmental level, where a few voices can be heard calling for more culturally sensitive development policies. The UN Scientific, Educational and Cultural

Organization (UNESCO), the UN Fund for Population Activities (UNFPA), and, especially, the UN Permanent Forum on Indigenous Issues (UNPFII) have been the most vocal actors, pointing out that culture is both the context for development as well as the missing factor in policies for development.[3]

Despite some progress at the international policy level, these steps are only initial moves at the normative level, while programs and other practices at the operational, country level demonstrate that there is still a lot to be done before the international community can justly claim that it supports cultural diversity in its development efforts. The parameters of this essay do not allow a full discussion of international practice, but research has demonstrated the inadequacy of current international practices.[4]

Any discussion in the public policy domain about globalization and local cultures begs a number of definitional clarifications, including the concept of development. This essay will thus start with conceptual issues. Given the existence of an organized indigenous movement and considerable international attention to indigenous peoples and their issues in the past thirty years, it will then bring into relief the subject of development and culture, using indigenous peoples' issues as a major focus. This approach will shed light on the overall challenges and opportunities of development with culture, an idea that is gaining increased visibility.

THE CONCEPT OF DEVELOPMENT WITHIN THE INTERNATIONAL NORMATIVE FRAMEWORK

Globalization is most often viewed as economic globalization of goods, services, and labor in accordance with the dominant development paradigm. In terms of international policy instruments and institutions, this paradigm is perceived as mostly expressed by international financial institutions such as the International Monetary Fund and the World Bank, as well as the World Trade Organization and relevant international agreements. However, these institutions and their policy instruments have not enjoyed the broad and democratic participation of governments and civil society, unlike the United Nations' global conferences of the 1990s, which have been reshaping the concept of development with the broad participation of the international community, both governments and civil society.[5]

What is still often forgotten in globalization debates is that, in addition to trade and other international financial agreements, international human rights treaties (which have received nearly universal acceptance by states) have for decades provided a comprehensive international legal framework of obligations by which states have voluntarily agreed to be bound and which provides the parameters of what governments may or may not do in the name of development. These human rights instruments, elaborated by the United Nations in the past five decades, include but are not limited to the following: the Convention on the Elimination of All Forms of Racial Discrimination; the International Covenant on Economic, Social and Cultural Rights; the International Covenant on Civil and Political Rights; the Convention on the Elimination of All Forms of Discrimination against Women; and the Convention on the Rights of the Child.[6] These treaties—and the international human rights treaty bodies[7] that monitor their implementation—have opened up considerable conceptual space in which to bring together human rights and development, creating what is now known as the human rights–based approach to development (HRBA), accepted since 2003 by the whole United Nations system in its development operations.

It is no exaggeration to say that the adoption of the HRBA as an international policy guideline put into sharper focus the increasing efforts to offset the macroeconomic approach to development, which has led to many failures around the world, and to redefine development as human development—combining social and economic development, placing the human being in the center, stressing participation, and requiring interventions targeted toward the most vulnerable. The HRBA was adopted by the UN Development Group (UNDG), which brings together all the UN development entities.

By stressing participation, the HRBA already prioritizes democratic principles and culture: if development is not a top-down but a bottom-up process, then peoples' wishes and expressions of their cultural particularities should find resonance in the development policies, programs, and budgets of their governments and those of international development actors. The common article 1 of both International Human Rights Covenants mentioned above recognizes that peoples have the right to self-determination and that, by virtue of this right, they freely pursue their economic, social, and cultural development.

Therefore, according to the international normative human rights framework, development is far from a single-model concept. If we accept peoples' human right to determine their fates, development should not be viewed as a linear concept, a mandatory recipe that will eventually turn all societies and economies into one homogeneous whole. Furthermore, the measure of democratic maturity of a state will be judged by how it treats its minorities, including how it factors in various visions of development.

Of course, the common perception of economic globalization would seem to counter such an understanding of democracy and human rights, including cultural rights. What we have noted in recent decades is that international trade negotiations have at times been conducted without attention to the already existing international human rights framework—sometimes forcing states, especially poor and powerless states, to accept trade agreements that would essentially weaken the human rights obligations they have undertaken toward their own populations under the human rights treaties. This contradiction has not escaped the attention of such human rights bodies as the Committee on Economic, Social and Cultural Rights.

THE CONCEPTS OF CULTURE AND OF PRESERVING CULTURES

There are numerous definitions of "culture." A definition or, more precisely, an understanding of culture that derives from the examination of literature and the work of the UN bodies and that is useful for examining development and cultural rights operates at three levels:

1. in its material sense, as product, *as the accumulated material heritage of mankind,* either as a whole or a part of particular human groups, including but not limited to monuments and artifacts;

2. *as a process of artistic or scientific creation*—the emphasis being placed on the process and on the creator(s) of culture; and

3. in its anthropological sense—that is, culture *as a way of life,* or, in UNESCO's words, the "set of distinctive spiritual, material, intellectual and emotional features of society or a social group"—which encompasses, "in addition to art and literature, lifestyles, ways of living together, value systems, traditions and beliefs."[8]

Culture is dynamic, ever-changing as it enters into contact with other cultures, especially in the increasingly interconnected world of today, where the "information society" spins the globe faster, bringing people into contact at an unprecedented pace.

Societies today are more and more culturally diverse. Minorities, indigenous peoples, and migrants, as well as other non-ethnically identifiable groups—such as persons with disabilities, gay people, and others—coexist and interface. How will a state formulate its development policies? Which voices will it listen to from within its own populations? What if different groups of the population advocate different types of development for themselves—indigenous peoples, for example? How will the state conform to its human rights obligations? How will it deal with its international trade engagements? What if human rights obligations and trade agreements lead to different responses?

Other questions that arise concern the very concept of preserving culture. Given the dynamic nature of culture and the context of globalization, what does it mean to preserve culture? Does it require protective measures on the part of the state that will "freeze" a culture at a specific moment in time? Can government action shield a culture from outside influences? Who should decide which influences are positive or negative, and how should such protections be achieved? To what extent are protection measures even possible in the current context of globalization and trade liberalization?

THE CONCEPT OF LOCAL CULTURE

The "local" is often juxtaposed to the global. But if we talk about human development and a human rights approach to development, local culture is about people and their ways of life. "Local" can mean national or subnational. In fact, we know that in today's world—even more than before—a state is composed of various cultures, given the diversity of its population. There is hardly a single culture that we can speak about in an absolute way in any given state. Indigenous peoples and minorities are realities in most states of the world.

It is significant that the 2004 Human Development Report of the UN Development Programme (UNDP) was devoted to "Cultural Liberty in Today's Diverse World." [9] The report gave figures that show the richness of the human tapestry—the human mobility but also the destructive trends around it. There are about 175 million migrants in the world, of which asylum seekers represent only 9 percent (16 million). The world's nearly 200 countries are home to some 5,000 ethnic groups. More than 150 countries have significant religious or ethnic minorities. Some 370 million indigenous peoples live in more than 90 countries, representing more than 4,000 languages. Of the estimated 6,000+ languages spoken today, 90 percent may have become extinct or face extinction in the next 100 years. (It is important to recognize what a great percentage of indigenous languages, and therefore of cultures, this loss may represent.) About 518 million people face restrictions on religion, language, ceremonies, and appearance. An example of the inadequate attention given to preserving this diversity is that in sub-Saharan Africa, only 13 percent of children in primary school receive instruction in their mother tongue.

It is known that linguistic diversity coincides with biodiversity on the world's map, and that most of the world's still-unexplored natural resources lie on indigenous peoples' traditional territories. We also know that the driving forces of the dominant development paradigm—states, a number of intergovernmental organizations, and private corporations—are actively and, at times, aggressively seeking those remaining unexplored resources.

Where is the voice of the local people in the state of the world as revealed by the statistics cited here? Any public policy debate, national or international, ought to be concrete in terms of putting a human face in its goals, targets, and indicators. To know, therefore, what the "local" is about, the state—which is the main responsible actor for the respect, protection, promotion, and fulfillment of human rights—has to create a public space for democratic dialogue—for full and effective participation of the people in the definition of what development should consist of—and to pursue a culturally sensitive program of development. The local, in other words, is given meaning through the democratic participation of people, as agents of development and not as passive recipients.[10]

INDIGENOUS PEOPLES AND INTERNATIONAL STANDARDS

The history of indigenous peoples knocking at the door of the institutions of the international community of "nations" is old. Indigenous peoples' sense of themselves as sovereign nations, in parity with the other nations of the world, has always been very strong. The fact that states, the colonizing powers, concluded treaties with many indigenous peoples is a testimony that indigenous peoples were viewed as sovereign by those who invented international law. There has been a vigorous and dynamic interface between indigenous peoples and the international community, especially through the United Nations—an interface that, difficult as it is, has produced at least three results: (1) a new awareness of indigenous concerns and indigenous rights; (2) recognition of indigenous peoples' invaluable contribution to humanity's cultural diversity and heritage, not least through their traditional knowledge; and (3) awareness of the need to address the problems of indigenous peoples through policies, laws, and budgets. Along with the decolonization, human rights, and the women's movements, the indigenous movement has been one of the four strongest civil-society interlocutors of the United Nations since 1945.

Human rights and dignity have a very concrete meaning when we speak of indigenous peoples. The ways in which our legal and economic systems manage to deal with bio-prospecting, the use of "killer-seeds," and other kinds of exploitation of indigenous traditional knowledge will reflect how we are able to protect together or ignore together a whole slew of issues involving justice, health, culture, or economic and social development. Whether we teach the mother tongue at school will show not whether we are ready to provide some luxury but whether or not we care about pushing kids out of school, whether or not we discriminate against indigenous peoples and their cultural rights.

Indigenous peoples make up about 5 percent of the world's population but 15 percent of the world's poor, according to the World Bank. In face of that disparity, what constitutes development? What is "human development" for indigenous peoples? What do they think? On the basis of what norms should we, the inhabitants of a globalized world, accept the definition of human happiness as a linear mono-model based on the overconsumption and overharvesting of natural resources that the globe cannot sustain? Must happiness be understood as a process that takes people from hunting and gathering, say, to having a plasma TV in every room of their house? These are some of the questions that indigenous peoples are raising and that have to do with everybody's survival and development. Perhaps not surprisingly, there are today indigenous peoples who live in voluntary isolation, because they wish to follow their own mode of development without being contacted by outsiders.[11]

The UN Permanent Forum on Indigenous Issues, the highest international body in this field, has in fact expressed concern that, unless indigenous peoples' visions of development are taken into account, the implementation of the Millennium Development Goals entails risks to indigenous peoples that include accelerated loss of lands and natural resources, displacement, forced assimilation, and further impoverishment, discrimination, and marginalization.[12] The challenges are enormous, although there are some promising examples of local and international campaigns that have brought the rights of indigenous peoples to the forefront.[13]

Contradictory visions of development that differ from the dominant development paradigm are not easy for the national policymaker to resolve, even in the case of a well-meaning state that wants to achieve equality and nondiscrimination, including cultural sensitivity. There are enormous international pressures on the state to conform to specific economic paths, which in turn impact both the human rights of the population and the local culture.

At the same time that economic globalization may have a negative impact on culture, it is certainly not oblivious to it. One example is traditional knowledge—in particular, indigenous peoples' traditional knowledge (ITK). The economic stakes of this phenomenon are enormous, and so some fifteen intergovernmental entities are dealing with the subject, including the World Intellectual Property Organization (WIPO), the World Bank, the Inter-American Development Bank, UNESCO, and others.

ITK, which is the creation of indigenous cultures over millennia, can yield important financial gains at a global level. The questions that arise are multiple: What is the concept and full spectrum of ITK? What are the appropriate protection and promotion measures to take vis-à-vis traditional knowledge? How do intellectual property regimes impact on ITK? What should be the role of traditional knowledge-holders? How should benefits be shared in case ITK-holders wish to commercialize their ITK heritage? How should indigenous customary law on ITK interface with national and international law on the matter? What kind of international *sui generis* regime should be put in place to protect ITK? The UN Permanent Forum on Indigenous Issues has been making efforts to map and coordinate the international policy scene on this complex matter.[14]

Should respect for culture in the context of development lead to protectionism, censorship of foreign cultural products, or limitation of international cooperation in the cultural domain? Obviously, part of the answer lies in governments' providing unhindered participation in cultural life nationally, including the freedom to create cultural products. A free and robust cultural life at the national level will be better equipped to engage in dialogue with other cultures, including the forces of the market, than a stifled cultural life. In the case of developing countries, governments may consider seeking international development assistance in order to better promote national culture—including, for example, the teaching of indigenous or minority languages.

The Vision of the Declaration on the Rights of Indigenous Peoples

After more than twenty years of negotiations, the United Nations General Assembly adopted the UN Declaration on the Rights of Indigenous Peoples in September 2007. The text has extraordinary resonance and already constitutes a body of customary law, not least because of the time devoted to its negotiation and the unprecedented and democratic participation of indigenous peoples together with states. The participation of indigenous peoples was direct and exemplary, and it not only led to the creation of a real charter of indigenous peoples' human rights, but also, in the process, crystallized an international indigenous peoples' movement, created dialogue and partnerships with states, forged cooperation with the UN system, and—last but not least—launched a global solidarity movement among indigenous peoples.

The Declaration on the Rights of Indigenous Peoples[15] emphasizes the rights of such peoples to maintain and strengthen their own institutions, cultures, and traditions and to pursue their development in keeping with their own needs and aspirations. The declaration addresses both individual and collective human rights, including cultural rights and identity, rights to education, health, employment, and so on. The text states that indigenous peoples and individuals are free and equal to all other peoples and individuals, and that they have the right to be free from any kind of discrimination in the exercise of their rights, in particular, those rights based on their indigenous origin and identity.

Nine preambular and fifteen operative paragraphs deal with consultation, partnership, and participation of indigenous peoples in a democratic polity.

Thus the text recognizes that indigenous peoples have the right to self-determination. By that right, they can freely determine their political status and pursue their economic, cultural, and social development. They have the right to maintain and strengthen their distinct political, legal, economic, social, and cultural institutions, while retaining their rights to participate fully, if they so choose, in the political, economic, social, and cultural life of the state.

Seventeen of the declaration's forty-six articles deal with indigenous cultures and how to protect and promote them, by respecting indigenous peoples' direct inputs in decision making and providing resources for education in indigenous languages and other areas.

The declaration recognizes subsistence rights and rights to land, territories, and resources, proclaiming that peoples deprived of their means of subsistence and development are entitled to just and fair redress.

Essentially, the declaration outlaws discrimination against indigenous peoples and promotes their full and effective participation in all matters that concern them, including the right to remain distinct and to pursue their own visions of economic and social development. The adoption of the declaration requires new approaches to global issues—such as development, diversity, pluricultural democracy, and peace—and encourages the building of genuine partnerships with indigenous peoples.

Although the declaration is not legally binding, it represents a dynamic development of legal norms and reflects the commitment of states to move in a pluralistic direction, abiding by principles that respect the human rights of indigenous peoples.

The Linkage of Indigenous Peoples' Cultural Rights to Development

The cultural rights of indigenous peoples in the context of development are protected and promoted by international legal standards that are found in international human rights instruments and further developed via the interpretation of international law by international courts and the international human rights bodies.[16] Those standards enforce the following precepts:

- The cultural rights of minorities and indigenous peoples consist of the right to education; the right to use their language in private life and various aspects of public life, such as before judicial authorities and to identify themselves as well as place names; the right to establish their own schools; access to mother tongue education to every extent feasible; access to the means of dissemination of culture, such as the media, museums, theatres, and so on, on the basis of nondiscrimination; the right to practice their religion; the freedom to maintain relations with their kin beyond national borders and the right to participate in decisions affecting them through their own institutions; and the preservation of sacred sites, works of art, scientific knowledge (especially knowledge about nature), oral tradition, and human remains, that is, both the tangible and the intangible objects that comprise indigenous cultural heritage. In the case of indigenous peoples, special cultural rights also include the right to continue certain economic activities linked to the traditional use of land and natural resources.

- The state and its agents have an obligation to respect the freedom of persons belonging to minorities and minority groups to freely participate in cultural life, to assert their cultural identity, and to express themselves culturally in the ways that they choose, unless those ways involve human rights violations. The state, as part of the regular discharge of its police and justice functions, must also protect minorities' right to participate in cultural life from infringement by third parties, whether they are individuals, groups, or corporations, domestic or foreign.

- International norms prohibit cultural practices that contravene internationally recognized human rights. Minority and indigenous rights are part of the human rights regime. States should thus adopt preventive and corrective policies and promote awareness of such problems so that such practices stop.

- Individuals living within groups are free to participate or not to participate in the cultural practices of the group, and no negative consequences may ensue because of their choice. In other words, the cultural autonomy of the individual is guaranteed.

- Minorities and indigenous peoples have the right to pursue their cultural development through their own institutions and, through those institutions, they have the right to participate fully and effectively in the definition, preparation, and implementation of cultural policies that concern them and development policies that affect their cultures. The state must consult the groups concerned via democratic and transparent processes.

CONCLUSION: DEVELOPMENT WITH CULTURE

The concept of development with culture is enshrined in international human rights standards that have been elaborated in the past five decades. Despite the pressures that globalization poses on governments to conform to the dominant development paradigm, it is important to recognize that the laws and ethics of development that the international community has passed on as part of our modern heritage are also part of the globalized world. They require that states respect their international human rights obligations, including the full and effective participation of people and groups in setting development policies and programs, even when those voices reflect alternative visions and cultural perspectives of human development.

One could summarize the way forward in this area as follows:

1. Governments must now translate the international normative framework into *concrete policies* for, by, and with local communities, especially indigenous peoples and minorities—that is, with their genuine participation in decision-making processes; with respect for their identities as groups, as communities with their histories, cultures, and aspirations; and with respect for their human dignity and for their human rights. Welfare approaches to development have failed, to a large extent because of the indigenous communities' poor or nonexistent participation. Thus the human-rights approach to development is particularly relevant because it places major emphasis on genuine participation, empowerment of those addressed by development programs, and respect for international human rights standards.

2. Policies must be matched by *national legislation and institutions* that will deal with major concerns, such as systemic discrimination, whether in the justice system, in health and education systems, or in the political system. Such legislation and institutions must also aim to correct these long-term injustices through positive measures.

3. Governments need to achieve *an equitable shift of resources* by designing targeted programs that will address discrimination and make a real difference to the disadvantaged members of local communities, including indigenous peoples.

4. International solidarity *needs to be mobilized at various levels*—economic, social, cultural, and political—for those who have been marginalized or excluded by globalization, so that they too may benefit from the implementation of human rights, democracy, and cultural pluralism.

NO: Kwame Anthony Appiah,
Princeton University

I'm seated on a palace veranda, cooled by a breeze from the royal garden. Before us, on a dais, is an empty throne, its arms and legs embossed with polished brass, the back and seat covered in black-and-gold silk. In front of the steps to the dais, there are two columns of people, mostly men, facing one another, seated on carved wooden stools, the cloths they wear wrapped around their chests, leaving their shoulders bare. There is a quiet buzz of conversation. Outside in the garden, peacocks screech. At last, the blowing of a ram's horn announces the arrival of the king of Asante, its tones sounding his honorific, *kotokohene*, "porcupine chief." (Each quill of the porcupine, according to custom, signifies a warrior ready to kill and to die for the kingdom.) Everyone stands until the king has settled on the throne. Then, when we sit, a chorus sings songs in praise of him, which are interspersed with the playing of a flute. It is a Wednesday festival day in Kumasi, the town in Ghana where I grew up.

Unless you're one of a few million Ghanaians, this will probably seem a relatively unfamiliar world, perhaps even an exotic one. You might suppose that this Wednesday festival belongs quaintly to an African past. But before the king arrived, people were taking calls on cell phones, and among those passing the time in quiet conversation were a dozen men in suits, representatives of an insurance company. And the meetings in the office next to the veranda are about contemporary issues: HIV/AIDS, the educational needs of twenty-first-century children, the teaching of science and technology at the local university. When my turn comes to be formally presented, the king asks me about Princeton, where I teach. I ask him when he'll next be in the States. In a few weeks, he says cheerfully. He's got a meeting with the head of the World Bank.

Anywhere you travel in the world today, you can find ceremonies like this one, many of them rooted in centuries-old traditions. But you will also find everywhere—and this is something new—many intimate connections with places far away: Washington, Moscow, Mexico City, Beijing. Across the street from us, when we were growing up, there was a large house occupied by a number of families, among them a vast family of boys; one, about my age, was a good friend. Today, he lives in London. His brother lives in Japan, where his

---

This piece has been adapted from *Cosmopolitanism: Ethics in a World of Strangers*, by Kwame Anthony Appiah (New York: W.W. Norton & Co., 2006). Reprinted with permission.

wife is from. They have another brother who has been in Spain for a while and a couple more brothers who, last I heard, were in the United States. Some of them still live in Kumasi, one or two in Accra, Ghana's capital.

When I was a child, we used to visit the previous king, my great-uncle by marriage, in a small building that the British had allowed his predecessor to build when he returned from exile in the Seychelles to a restored but diminished Asante kingship. That building is now a museum, dwarfed by the enormous house next door, where the current king lives. Next to it is the suite of offices abutting the veranda where we were sitting, recently finished by the present king. The British, my mother's people, conquered Asante at the turn of the twentieth century; now, at the turn of the twenty-first, the palace feels as it must have felt in the nineteenth century: a center of power. The president of Ghana comes from this world, too. He was born across the street from the palace to a member of the royal Oyoko clan. But he belongs to other worlds as well: he went to Oxford University; he's a member of one of the Inns of Court in London; he's a Catholic, with a picture of himself greeting the pope in his sitting room.

What are we to make of this? On Kumasi's Wednesday festival day, I've seen visitors from England and the United States wince at what they regard as the intrusion of modernity on timeless, traditional rituals—more evidence, they think, of a pressure in the modern world toward uniformity. They react like the assistant on the film set who's supposed to check that the extras in a sword-and-sandals movie aren't wearing wristwatches. And such purists are not alone. In the past couple of years, UNESCO's members have spent a great deal of time trying to hammer out a convention on the "protection and promotion" of cultural diversity. (It was finally approved at the UNESCO General Conference in October 2005.) The drafters worried that "the processes of globalization ... represent a challenge for cultural diversity, namely in view of risks of imbalances between rich and poor countries." The fear is that the values and images of Western mass culture, like some invasive weed, are threatening to choke out the world's native flora.

The contradictions in this argument aren't hard to find. This same UNESCO document is careful to affirm the importance of the free flow of ideas, the freedom of thought and expression and human rights—values that, we know, will become universal only if we make them so. What's really important, then—cultures or people? In a world where Kumasi and New York—and Cairo and Leeds and Istanbul—are being drawn ever closer together, an ethics of globalization has proved elusive.

The right approach, I think, starts by taking individuals—not nations, tribes, or "peoples"—as the proper object of moral concern. It doesn't much matter what we call such a creed, but in homage to Diogenes, the fourth-century Greek Cynic and the first philosopher to call himself a "citizen of the world," we could call it *cosmopolitanism*. Cosmopolitans take cultural difference seriously, because they take the choices individual people make seriously. But because cultural difference is not the only thing that concerns them, they suspect that many of globalization's cultural critics are aiming at the wrong targets.

COSMOPOLITANISM COMBATS HOMOGENEITY

Yes, globalization can produce homogeneity. But globalization is also a threat to homogeneity. You can see this as clearly in Kumasi as anywhere. One thing Kumasi isn't is homogeneous. English, German, Chinese, Syrian, Lebanese, Burkinabe, Ivorian, Nigerian, Indian: I can find you families of each description. I can find you Asante people, whose ancestors have lived in this town for centuries, but also Hausa households that have been around for centuries, too. There are people from every region of the country as well, speaking scores of languages.

But if you travel just a little way outside Kumasi, you won't have difficulty finding villages that are fairly monocultural. The people have mostly been to Kumasi and seen the big, polyglot, diverse world of the city. Where they live, though, there is one everyday language and an agrarian way of life based on some old crops, such as yams, and some newer ones, such as cocoa, which arrived in the late nineteenth century as a product for export. They may or may not have electricity. When people talk of the homogeneity produced by globalization, what they are talking about is this: Even here, the villagers will have radios; you will be able to get a discussion going about Ronaldo, Mike Tyson, or Tupac; and you will probably be able to find a bottle of Guinness or Coca-Cola. But has access to these things made the place more homogeneous or less? And what can you tell about people's souls from the fact that they drink Coca-Cola?

It's true that the enclaves of homogeneity you find these days—in Asante as in Pennsylvania—are less distinctive than they were a century ago, but mostly in good ways. More of them have access to effective medicines. More of them have access to clean drinking water, and more of them have schools. Where, as is still too common, they don't have these things, it's something not to celebrate but to deplore. And whatever loss of difference there has been, they are constantly inventing new forms of difference: new hairstyles, new slang, even, from time to time, new religions. No one could say that the world's villages are becoming anything like the same.

So why do people in these places sometimes feel that their identities are threatened? Because the world, their world, is changing, and some of them don't like it. The pull of the global economy—witness those cocoa trees, whose chocolate is eaten all around the world—created some of the life they now live. If chocolate prices were to collapse again, as they did in the early 1990s, Asante farmers might have to find new crops or new forms of livelihood. That prospect is unsettling for some people. Missionaries came a while ago, so many of these villagers will be Christian, even if they have also kept some of the rites from earlier days. But new Pentecostal messengers are challenging the churches they know and condemning the old rites as idolatrous.

Above all, relationships are changing. When my father was young, a man in a village would farm some land that a chief had granted him, and his maternal clan (including his younger brothers) would work it with him. When a new house needed building, he would organize it. He would also make sure his dependents were fed and clothed, the children educated, marriages and funerals arranged and paid for. He could expect to pass the farm and the responsibilities along to the next generation.

Nowadays, everything is different. Cocoa prices have not kept pace with the cost of living. Gas prices have made the transportation of the crop more expensive. And there are new possibilities for the young in the towns, in other parts of the country, and in other parts of the world. Once, perhaps, you could have commanded the young ones to stay. Now they have the right to leave—perhaps to seek work at one of the new data-processing centers down south in the nation's capital—and, anyway, you may not make enough to feed and clothe and educate them all. So the time of the successful farming family is passing, and those who were settled in that way of life are as sad to see it go as are American family farmers whose lands are accumulated by giant agribusinesses. We can sympathize with them. But we cannot force their children to stay in the name of protecting their authentic culture, and we cannot afford to subsidize indefinitely thousands of distinct islands of homogeneity that no longer make economic sense.

Nor should we want to. Human variety matters, cosmopolitans think, because people are entitled to options. What John Stuart Mill said more than a century ago in *On Liberty* about diversity within a society serves just as well as an argument for variety across the globe:

> If it were only that people have diversities of taste, that is reason enough for not attempting to shape them all after one model. But different persons also require different conditions for their spiritual development; and can no more exist healthily in the same moral, than all the variety of plants can exist in the same physical, atmosphere and climate. The same

things which are helps to one person towards the cultivation of his higher nature, are hindrances to another. . . . Unless there is a corresponding diversity in their modes of life, they neither obtain their fair share of happiness, nor grow up to the mental, moral, and aesthetic stature of which their nature is capable.

If we want to preserve a wide range of human conditions because it allows free people the best chance to make their own lives, we can't enforce diversity by trapping people within differences they long to escape.

THE AMBIGUITY OF AUTHENTICITY

Even if you grant that people shouldn't be compelled to sustain the older cultural practices, you might suppose that cosmopolitans should side with those who are busy around the world "preserving culture" and resisting "cultural imperialism." Yet behind these slogans you often find some curious assumptions. Take "preserving culture." It's one thing to help people sustain arts they want to sustain. I am all for festivals of Welsh bards in Llandudno financed by the Welsh arts council. Long live the Ghana National Cultural Center in Kumasi, where you can go and learn traditional Akan dancing and drumming. Restore the deteriorating film stock of early Hollywood movies; continue the preservation of Old Norse and early Chinese and Ethiopian manuscripts; record, transcribe, and analyze the oral narratives of Malay and Masai and Maori. All these are undeniably valuable.

But preserving culture—in the sense of such cultural artifacts—is different from preserving cultures. And the cultural preservationists often pursue the latter, trying to ensure that the Huli of Papua New Guinea maintain their "authentic" ways. What makes a cultural expression authentic, though? Are we to stop the importation of baseball caps into Vietnam so that the Zao will continue to wear their colorful red headdresses? Why not ask the Zao? Shouldn't the choice be theirs?

"They have no real choice," the cultural preservationists say. "We've dumped cheap Western clothes into their markets, and they can no longer afford the silk they used to wear. If they had what they really wanted, they'd still be dressed traditionally." But this is no longer an argument about authenticity. The claim is that they can't afford to do something that they'd really like to do, something that is expressive of an identity they care about and want to sustain. This is a genuine problem, one that afflicts people in many communities: they're too poor to live the life they want to lead. But if they do get richer, and they still run around in T-shirts, that's their choice. Talk of authenticity now just amounts to telling other people what they ought to value in their own traditions.

Besides, trying to find some primordially authentic culture can be like peeling an onion. The textiles most people think of as traditional West African cloths are known as Java prints; they arrived in the nineteenth century with the Javanese batiks sold, and often milled, by the Dutch. The traditional garb of Herero women in Namibia derives from the attire of nineteenth-century German missionaries, though it is still unmistakably Herero, not least because the fabrics used have a distinctly un-Lutheran range of colors. And so with our kente cloth: the silk was always imported, traded by Europeans, produced in Asia. This tradition was once an innovation. Should we reject it for that reason as untraditional? How far back must one go? Should we condemn the young men and women of the University of Science and Technology, a few miles outside Kumasi, who wear European-style gowns for graduation, lined with kente strips (as they do now at Howard and Morehouse, too)? Cultures are made of continuities and changes, and the identity of a society can survive through these changes. Societies without change aren't authentic; they're just dead.

ADAPTING AND INTERPRETING CULTURAL INFLUENCES

The preservationists often make their case by invoking the evil of "cultural imperialism." Their underlying picture, in broad strokes, is this: There is a world system of capitalism. It has a center and a periphery. At the center—in Europe and the United States—is a set of multinational corporations. Some of them are in the media business. The products they sell around the world promote the creation of desires that can be fulfilled only by the purchase and use of their products. They do so explicitly through advertising, but more insidiously, they also do so through the messages implicit in movies and in television drama.

That's the theory, anyway. But the evidence doesn't bear it out. Researchers have actually gone out into the world and explored the responses to the hit television series *Dallas* in Holland and among Israeli Arabs, Moroccan Jewish immigrants, kibbutzniks, and new Russian immigrants to Israel. They have examined the actual content of the television media in Australia, Brazil, Canada, India, and Mexico. They have looked at how American popular culture was taken up by the artists of Sophiatown, in South Africa. They have discussed *Days of Our Lives* and *The Bold and the Beautiful* with Zulu college students from traditional backgrounds.

And one thing they've found is that how people respond to these cultural imports depends on their existing cultural context. When the media scholar Larry Strelitz spoke to students from KwaZulu-Natal, he found that they were anything but passive vessels. One of them, Sipho—a self-described "very, very strong Zulu man"—reported that he had drawn lessons from watching the American soap opera *Days of Our Lives*, "especially relationship-wise." It fortified his view that "if a guy can tell a woman that he loves her, she should be able to do the same." What's more, after watching the show, Sipho "realized that I should be allowed to speak to my father. He should be my friend rather than just my father." It seems doubtful that that was the intended message of multinational capitalism's ruling sector.

But Sipho's response also confirmed that cultural consumers are not dupes. They can adapt products to suit their own needs, and they can decide for themselves what they do and do not approve of. Here's Sipho again:

> In terms of our culture, a girl is expected to enter into relationships when she is about 20. In the Western culture, a girl can be exposed to a relationship as early as 15 or 16. That one we shouldn't adopt in our culture. Another thing we shouldn't adopt from the Western culture has to do with the way they treat elderly people. I wouldn't like my family to be sent into an old-age home.

Dutch viewers of *Dallas* saw not the pleasures of conspicuous consumption among the superrich—the message that theorists of "cultural imperialism" find in every episode—but a reminder that money and power don't protect you from tragedy. Israeli Arabs saw a program that confirmed that women abused by their husbands should return to their fathers. Mexican telenovelas remind Ghanaian women that, where sex is at issue, men are not to be trusted.

Talk of cultural imperialism "structuring the consciousnesses" of those in the periphery treats people like Sipho as blank slates on which global capitalism's moving finger writes its message, leaving behind another cultural automaton as it moves on. It is deeply condescending. And it isn't true.

COSMOPOLITANISM VERSUS NEOFUNDAMENTALISM: TENSION BETWEEN LIBERTY AND DIVERSITY

Sometimes, though, people react to the incursions of the modern world not by appropriating the values espoused by the liberal democracies but by inverting them. One recent result has been a new worldwide fraternity that presents cosmopolitanism with something of a sinister mirror image. Indeed, you could think of its members as counter-cosmopolitans. They believe in human dignity across the nations, and they live their creed. They share these ideals with people in many countries, speaking many languages. As thoroughgoing globalists, they make full use of the World Wide Web. They resist the crass consumerism of modern Western society and deplore its influence in the rest of the world.

But they also resist the temptations of the narrow nationalisms of the countries where they were born, along with the humble allegiances of kith and kin. They resist such humdrum loyalties because they get in the way of the one thing that matters: building a community of enlightened men and women across the world. That is one reason they reject traditional religious authorities. Sometimes they agonize in their discussions about whether they can reverse the world's evils or whether their struggle is hopeless. But mostly they soldier on in their efforts to make the world a better place.

These are not the heirs of Diogenes the Cynic. The community these comrades are building is not a polis; it's what they call the *ummah*, the global community of Muslims, and it is open to all who share their faith. They are young, global Muslim fundamentalists. The ummah's new globalists consider that they have returned to the fundamentals of Islam; much of what passes for Islam in the world, much of what has passed as Islam for centuries, they think a sham. As the French scholar Olivier Roy has observed, these religionists—his term for them is "neofundamentalists"—wish to cleanse from Islam's pristine and universal message the contingencies of mere history, of local cultures. For them, Roy notes, "globalization is a good opportunity to dissociate Islam from any given culture and to provide a model that could work beyond any culture." They have taken a set of doctrines that once came with a form of life, in other words, and thrown away that form of life.

Now, the vast majority of these fundamentalists are not going to blow anybody up. So they should not be confused with those other Muslims—the "radical neofundamentalists," Roy calls them—who want to turn jihad, interpreted as literal warfare against the West, into the sixth pillar of Islam. Nonetheless, the neofundamentalists present a classic challenge to cosmopolitanism, because they, too, offer a moral and, in its way, inclusive universalism.

Unlike cosmopolitanism, of course, it is universalist without being tolerant, and such intolerant universalism has often led to murder. It underlay the French Wars of Religion that bloodied the four decades before the Edict of Nantes of 1598, in which Henri IV of France finally granted to the Protestants in his realm the right to practice their faith. In the Thirty Years' War, which ravaged central Europe until the Peace of Westphalia in 1648, Protestant and Catholic princes from Austria to Sweden struggled with one another, and hundreds of thousands of Germans died in battle. Millions starved or died of disease as roaming armies pillaged the countryside. The period of religious conflict in the British Isles, from the first Bishops' War of 1639 to the end of the English Civil War in 1651, which pitted Protestant armies against the forces of a Catholic king, resulted in the deaths of perhaps 10 percent of the population. All these conflicts involved issues beyond sectarian doctrine, of course. Still, many Enlightenment liberals drew the conclusion that enforcing one vision of universal truth could only lead the world back to the bloodbaths.

Yet tolerance by itself is not what distinguishes the cosmopolitan from the neofundamentalist. There are plenty of things that the heroes of radical Islam are happy to tolerate. They don't care if you eat kebabs or meatballs or kung pao chicken, as long as the meat is halal; your hijab can be silk or linen or viscose. At the same time, there are plenty of things that cosmopolitans will not tolerate. We sometimes want to intervene in other places because what is going on there violates our principles so deeply. We, too, can see moral error. And when it is serious enough, we will not stop with conversation. Toleration has its limits.

Nor can you tell us apart by saying that the neofundamentalists believe in universal truth. Cosmopolitans believe in universal truth, too, though we are less certain that we already have all of it. One tenet we hold to, however, is that every human being has obligations to every other. Everybody matters: that is our central idea. And again, it sharply limits the scope of our tolerance.

To say what, in principle, distinguishes the cosmopolitan from competing universalisms, we plainly need to go beyond talk of truth and tolerance. One distinctively cosmopolitan commitment is to pluralism. Cosmopolitans think that there are many values worth living by and that you cannot live by all of them. So we hope and expect that different people and different societies will embody different values. Another aspect of cosmopolitanism is what philosophers call fallibilism—the sense that our knowledge is imperfect, provisional, subject to revision in the face of new evidence.

The neofundamentalist conception of a global ummah, by contrast, admits of local variations—but only in matters that don't matter. These counter-cosmopolitans, like many Christian fundamentalists, do think that there is one right way for all human beings to live; that all the differences must be in the details. If what concerns you is global homogeneity, then this utopia, not the world that capitalism is producing, is the one you should worry about. Still, the universalisms in the name of religion are hardly the only ones that invert the cosmopolitan creed. In the name of universal humanity, you can be the kind of Marxist, such as Mao or Pol Pot, who wants to eradicate all religion, just as easily as you can be the Grand Inquisitor supervising an auto-da-fé. All of these men want everyone on their side, so we can share with them the vision in their mirror. Join us, the counter-cosmopolitans say, and we will all be sisters and brothers. But each of them plans to trample on our differences—to trample us to death, if necessary—if we will not join them.

That liberal pluralists are hostile to certain authoritarian ways of life—that they're intolerant of radical intolerance is sometimes seen as a kind of self-refutation. That's a mistake: you can care about individual freedom and still understand that the contours of that freedom will vary considerably from place to place. But we might as well admit that a concern for individual freedom isn't something that will appeal to every individual. In politics, including cultural politics, there are winners and losers—which is worth remembering when we think about international human rights treaties. When we seek to embody our concern for strangers in human rights law, and when we urge our governments to enforce it, we are seeking to change the world of law in every nation on the planet. We have declared slavery a violation of international law. And, in so doing, we have committed ourselves, at a minimum, to the desirability of its eradication everywhere. This is no longer controversial in the capitals of the world. No one defends enslavement. But international treaties define slavery in ways that arguably include debt bondage, and debt bondage is a significant economic institution in parts of South Asia. I hold no brief for debt bondage. Still, we shouldn't be surprised if people whose incomes and style of life depend upon it are angry.

It's the same with the international movements to promote women's equality. We know that many Islamists are deeply disturbed by the way Western men and women behave. We permit women to swim almost naked with strange men, which is our business, but it is hard to keep the news of these acts of immodesty from Muslim women and children or to protect Muslim men from the temptations they inevitably create. As the Internet extends its reach, it will get even harder, and their children, especially their girls, will be tempted to ask for these freedoms, too. Worse, they say, we are now trying to force our conception of how women and men should behave upon them. We speak of women's rights. We make treaties enshrining these rights. And then we want their governments to enforce them.

Like many people in every nation, I support those treaties; I believe that women, like men, should have the vote, should be entitled to work outside their homes, should be protected from the physical abuse of men, including their fathers, brothers, and husbands. But I also know that the changes these freedoms would bring will change the balance of power between men and women in everyday life. How do I know this? Because I have lived most of my adult life in the West as it has gone through just such a transition, and I know that the process is not yet complete.

So liberty and diversity may well be at odds, and the tensions between them aren't always easily resolved. But the rhetoric of cultural preservation isn't any help. Again, the contradictions are near to hand. Take another look at that UNESCO Convention. It affirms the "principle of equal dignity of and respect for all cultures." (What, all cultures—including those of the KKK and the

Taliban?) It also affirms "the importance of culture for social cohesion in general, and in particular its potential for the enhancement of the status and role of women in society." (But doesn't "cohesion" argue for uniformity? And wouldn't enhancing the status and role of women involve changing, rather than preserving, cultures?) In Saudi Arabia, people can watch *Will and Grace* on satellite TV—officially proscribed, but available all the same—knowing that, under Saudi law, Will could be beheaded in a public square. In northern Nigeria, mullahs inveigh against polio vaccination while sentencing adulteresses to death by stoning. In India, thousands of wives are burned to death each year for failing to make their dowry payments. Vive la différence? Please.

UNDERSTANDING, AND POSSIBLY (BUT NOT NECESSARILY) AGREEING

Living cultures do not, in any case, evolve from purity into contamination; change is more a gradual transformation from one mixture to a new mixture— a process that usually takes place at some distance from rules and rulers, in the conversations that occur across cultural boundaries. Such conversations are not so much about arguments and values as about the exchange of perspectives. I don't say that we can't change minds, but the reasons we offer in our conversation will seldom do much to persuade others who do not share our fundamental evaluative judgments already. When we make judgments, after all, it's rarely because we have applied well-thought-out principles to a set of facts and deduced an answer. Our efforts to justify what we have done are typically made up after the event, rationalizations of what we have decided intuitively to do. And a good deal of what we intuitively take to be right, we take to be right just because it is what we are used to. That does not mean, however, that we cannot become accustomed to doing things differently.

Consider the practice of foot binding in China, which persisted for a thousand years—and was largely eradicated within a generation. The anti-foot-binding campaign, in the first two decades of the twentieth century, did circulate facts about the disadvantages of bound feet, but those facts couldn't have come as news to most people. Perhaps more effective was the campaign's emphasis that no other country went in for the practice; in the world at large, then, China was "losing face" because of it. (To China's cultural preservationists, of course, the fact that the practice was peculiar to the region was entirely a mark in its favor.) Natural-foot societies were formed, their members forswearing the practice and further pledging that their sons would not marry women with bound feet. As the movement took hold, scorn was heaped on older women with bound feet, and they were forced to endure the agonies of unbinding. What had been beautiful became ugly; ornamentation became disfigurement. The appeal to reason can explain neither the custom nor its abolition.

So, too, with other social trends. Just a couple of generations ago, most people in most of the industrialized world thought that middle-class women would ideally be housewives and mothers. If they had time on their hands, they could engage in charitable work or entertain one another; a few of them might engage in the arts—writing novels, painting, or performing in music, theater, and dance. But there was little place for them in the "learned professions"—as lawyers or doctors, priests or rabbis; and if they were to be academics, they would teach young women and probably remain unmarried. They were not likely to make their way in politics, except perhaps at the local level. And they were not made welcome in science.

How much of the shift away from these assumptions is a result of arguments? Isn't a significant part of it just the consequence of our getting used to new ways of doing things? The arguments that kept the old pattern in place were not—to put it mildly—terribly good. If the reasons for the old sexist way of doing things had been the problem, the women's movement could have been done in a couple of weeks.

Consider another example: In much of Europe and North America, in places where a generation ago homosexuals were social outcasts and homosexual acts were illegal, lesbian and gay couples are increasingly being recognized by their families, by society, and by the law. This is true despite the continued opposition of major religious groups and a significant and persisting undercurrent of social disapproval. Both sides make arguments, some good, most bad. But if you ask the social scientists what has produced this change, they will rightly not start with a story about reasons. They will give you a historical account that concludes with a sort of perspectival shift. The increasing presence of "openly gay" people in social life and in the media has changed our habits. And over the past thirty years or so, instead of thinking about the private activity of gay sex, many Americans and Europeans started thinking about the public category of gay people.

One of the great savants of the postwar era, John von Neumann, liked to say, mischievously, that "in mathematics you don't understand things, you just get used to them." As in mathematical arguments, so in moral ones. Now, I don't deny that all the time, at every stage, people were talking, giving one another reasons to do things: accept their gay children, stop treating homosexuality as a medical disorder, disagree with their churches, come out. Still, the short version of the story is basically this: People got used to lesbians and gay men.

I am urging that we should learn about people in other places, take an interest in their civilizations, their arguments, their errors, their achievements, not because that will bring us to agreement but because it will help us get used to one another—something we have a powerful need to do in this globalized era. If that is the aim, then the fact that we have all these opportunities for disagreement about values need not put us off. Understanding one another may be hard; it can certainly be interesting. But it doesn't require that we come to agreement.

THE CASE FOR CONTAMINATION

The ideals of purity and preservation have licensed a great deal of mischief in the past century, but they have never had much to do with lived culture. Ours may be an era of mass migration, but the global spread and hybridization of culture—through travel, trade, or conquest—is hardly a recent development. Alexander's empire molded both the states and the sculpture of Egypt and North India; the Mongols and then the Mughals shaped great swaths of Asia; the Bantu migrations populated half the African continent. Islamic states stretch from Morocco to Indonesia; Christianity reached Africa, Europe, and Asia within a few centuries of the death of Jesus of Nazareth; Buddhism long ago migrated from India into much of East and Southeast Asia. Jews and people whose ancestors came from many parts of China have long lived in vast diasporas. The traders of the Silk Road changed the style of elite dress in Italy; someone buried Chinese pottery in fifteenth-century Swahili graves. I have heard it said that the bagpipes started out in Egypt and came to Scotland with the Roman infantry. None of this is modern.

Our guide to what is going on here might as well be a former African slave named Publius Terentius Afer, whom we know as Terence. Born in Carthage, Terence was taken to Rome in the early second century B.C., and his plays were widely admired among the city's literary elite. Terence's own mode of writing—which involved freely incorporating any number of earlier Greek plays into a single Latin one—was known to Roman littérateurs as "contamination."

It's an evocative term. When people speak for an ideal of cultural purity, sustaining the authentic culture of the Asante or the American family farm, I find myself drawn to contamination as the name for a counter-ideal. Terence had a notably firm grasp on the range of human variety: "So many men, so many opinions" was a line of his. And it's in his comedy, *The Self-Tormentor*, that you'll find what may be the golden rule of cosmopolitanism—*Homo sum: humani nil a me alienum puto*: "I am human: nothing human is alien to me." The context is illuminating. A busybody farmer named Chremes is told by his neighbor to mind his own affairs; the *homo sum* credo is Chremes's breezy rejoinder. It isn't meant to be an ordinance from on high; it's just the case for gossip.

The ideal of contamination has few exponents more eloquent than Salman Rushdie, who has insisted that the novel that occasioned his *fatwa* "celebrates hybridity, impurity, intermingling, the transformation that comes of new and unexpected combinations of human beings, cultures, ideas, politics, movies, songs. It rejoices in mongrelisation and fears the absolutism of the Pure. Mélange, hotch-potch, a bit of this and a bit of that is how newness enters the world." No doubt there can be an easy and spurious utopianism of "mixture," as there is of "purity," or "authenticity." And yet the larger human truth is on the side of contamination—that endless process of imitation and revision.

A tenable global ethics has to temper a respect for difference with a respect for the freedom of actual human beings to make their own choices. That's why cosmopolitans don't insist that everyone become cosmopolitan. They know they don't have all the answers. They're humble enough to think that they might learn from strangers; not too humble to think that strangers can't learn from them. Few remember what Chremes says after his "I am human" line, but it is equally suggestive: "If you're right, I'll do what you do. If you're wrong, I'll set you straight."

civil society

Do NGOs Wield Too Much Power?

YES: Kenneth Anderson, *American University*

NO: Marlies Glasius, *University of Amsterdam*

"Civil society" is an all-encompassing title for a host of nonstate, noncorporate actors that participate in various ways in global governance. This category includes individual NGOs, transnational action networks (collections of NGOs in different countries with a shared vision and tactics), and social movements. The presence of these representatives of civil society at international negotiations and conferences has become a common feature of international politics. Environmental NGOs were identified as important actors at the 1992 Earth Summit, where they were recognized as a "major group" in the conference documents. Starting with protests at the 1999 Seattle WTO meeting, large-scale public demonstrations against globalization have been widespread, and they commonly accompany meetings of major international organizations.

Given the large number of individual NGOs and the various types of actors, it is difficult to offer simple statements about civil society. It is equally unclear if any unifying political visions or beliefs exist within civil society. Many claim to act on behalf of the public good, although there are often variations between different actors' views of what constitutes the public good and how it is to be provided; some may have positive effects as a consequence of their global involvement by improving governments' accountability to their citizens and by directly delivering services to local communities.

A minimal definition of an NGO can be found in the list of required features that is used by the United Nations in granting recognition to these organizations: an established headquarters, an administration, authorized representatives, a policymaking body, and a presence in at least two countries. By conservative estimate, there were 37,281 international NGOs in 2000, which is 19 percent higher than the number from 1990. Table 1 shows the growth in number of international NGOs by purpose from 1990 to 2000.

Table 1

Growth in the Number of International NGOs by Purpose, 1990–2000

	1990	2000	Percentage change, 1990–2000
Social services	2,361	4,215	78.5
Health	1,357	2,036	50.0
Law, policy, and advocacy	2,712	3,864	42.5
Religion	1,407	1,869	32.8
Culture and recreation	2,169	2,733	26.0
Education	1,485	1,839	23.8
Environment	979	1,170	19.5
Research	7,675	8,467	10.3
Economic development	9,582	9,614	0.3
Politics	1,275	1,240	−2.7
Defense	244	234	−4.1
Total	**31,246**	**37,281**	**19.3**

Source: Helmut Anheier, Marlies Glasius, and Mary Kaldor, eds., *Global Civil Society 2001 (Oxford: Oxford University Press*, 2001), 300.

NGOs engage in activities targeted at a wide range of issues, as is reflected in the table. The largest numbers of NGOs are involved in matters of economic development, policy research, and social service provision.

NGOs also perform a wide array of functions. Activist NGOs contribute to international agenda-setting by publicizing new issues. Many engage in public education and consciousness-raising on the specific issues of importance to them. At international negotiations, NGOs lead lobbying efforts and provide valuable policy information to smaller delegations. NGOs contribute to the enforcement of international commitments, by identifying state and corporate violators and shaming them through public campaigns. Many NGOs conduct human rights verification studies, as well as monitoring compliance with various international agreements. For example, organized transnational NGO campaigns have led to the elimination of landmines and overturned an international treaty aimed at liberalizing international investment (the Multilateral Agreement on Investment).

Many NGOs also play key roles in delivering development services such as education, food and medicine, and job training in developing countries, as well as in administering governmental foreign aid. Governments channel assistance through NGOs, which conduct the training activities on the ground. The share of governmental aid actually flowing through NGOs varied from 5 to 12 percent between 1990 and 2006. Table 2 shows OECD development assistance as actually disbursed through NGOs, from 1990 to 2006. Many NGOs

Table 2

Net OECD Development Assistance Committee Grants Disbursed through NGOs, 1990–2006

	(constant 2005 US$ Millions)
1990–1991 average	6,943
1995–1996 average	6,624
2002	11,141
2003	11,419
2004	11,566
2005	14,712
2006	14,291

Source: OECD-DAC, *Statistical Annex of the 2007 Development Cooperation Report*, Table 2: Total net flows from DAC countries by type of flow, http://www.oecd.org/document/9/0,3343,en_2649_34447_1893129_1_1_1_1,00.html (accessed February 28, 2008).

based in developing countries engage in public education, research, lobbying, and the local delivery of services.

Civil society's ability to effectively perform this array of governance functions has been subject to much debate, in part because of the relative novelty of widespread involvement by nonstate networks at the international level. Civil society can be uncivil and unruly: the large public antiglobalization demonstrations since 1999 have often been disruptive of the routines of the host nations. In order to attract publicity for their activities, a small number of high-profile antiglobalization actors have engaged in property damage and ecoterrorism, such as the Sea Shepherd Society's ongoing antiwhaling campaigns and the French farmer José Bové's 1999 assault on a French McDonalds.

Some observers have suggested that NGO campaigns may be shaped by their need to attract publicity and funding. Consequently, they may choose topics by their potential to outrage, rather than by a calculation of needs; and they may abandon campaigns before having fully achieved their goals.

Unchecked NGO activism may have detrimental effects on local communities. The journalist Sebastian Mallaby found that a Ugandan dam project that was intended to cut by 40 percent the number of people living below the absolute poverty line was opposed by international NGOs because of their general antipathy to dams, regardless of the specific benefits of individual projects. Mallaby suggests that NGOs may disregard such mitigating factors in their determination to elevate their own political standing or to promote their universal mission.[1]

The operation of Western NGOs in the global South may also be seen by host governments as an infringement on their sovereignty. Vladimir Putin tried to limit their civil rights within Russia. Prominent U.S. political scientist Robert Keohane cautiously notes that these agents of civil society may be internationally destablizing, because they undercut the principle of national sovereignty on which international relations are grounded.[2] Thus states may be reluctant to actively involve civil society in global governance. Conversely, global governance catalyzed by civil society may lack legitimacy in the eyes of states.

Policy questions revolve around civil society's relationship with traditional authoritative actors. It is unclear to what extent NGOs are potentially coopted or diffused by having to deal with the extensive detailed procedural red tape that is associated with regular involvement with governments and international organizations, or to what extent NGOs may be subversive by means of their ability to educate governments and other major actors, as well as their impact in galvanizing local communities.

Many analysts and policymakers find civil society to be both analytically and normatively attractive as a liberal or cosmopolitan approach to world politics. Unlike international politics, which is usually understood as a hierarchical set of political relationships in which a few powerful states run things, NGOs operate more horizontally and in networks. Thus they provide a more attractive model of politics, which is potentially more egalitarian and efficient at diffusing information than the traditional hierarchical approach.

The following articles address the legitimacy of NGOs operating in the developing world, and their accountability. Kenneth Anderson questions the authority of NGOs, asking whose interests they, in fact, represent and to whom they are accountable. Thus he challenges the legitimacy of the political and policy agenda that NGOs advance. Marlies Glasius argues that NGOs contribute to transparency and thus make governments more accountable to their citizens as well as to the international community.

Discussion Questions

1. What is civil society? Who are its members? Where does their power derive from? Who are they accountable to?
2. In what way does civil society's involvement in governance benefit society? Who does it benefit most? Are there drawbacks to its involvement?
3. Some claim that NGOs help to make international governance and decision making more democratic. Others contend that NGOs only add to the democratic deficit in international bodies. Which position do you agree with? Why?

4. Kenneth Anderson says that NGOs seek too much influence depending on where they derive their power from and to what extent they seek to use their power. What does he mean? What examples does he give to make his argument? Do you agree with him?

5. What is the "ethical contribution" of NGOs as described by Marlies Glasius? What impact does she think this ethical contribution has on governments? Do you agree with her conclusion?

YES: Kenneth Anderson, *Washington College of Law, American University*

NGOs can claim excessive power depending on *where* the power they exercise, or hope to exercise, is supposed to come from and in what *capacity* they seek to use their power.

The Nobel Peace Prize Committee, in awarding the 1997 prize to Jody Williams and the International Committee to Ban Landmines, put forth the proposition that NGOs are full-fledged members of the global society, alongside states and public organizations:

> Public opinion must be formed and directed by the active involvement of individual members ... in society's manifold organizations or associations. These are the fundamental institutional elements of what we have learned to know as a civil society. ... [I]n the extensive cooperation ... between ... non-governmental organizations, ... national governments, and the international political system ... we may be seeing the outline of ... a global civil society.[1]

When international NGOs assume power and authority to join with international organizations such as the United Nations on the grounds that they represent what the UN Charter calls the "peoples of the world" and claim authority to act on their behalf, then indeed they have too much power—or, at least, they claim power on the basis of a false premise.

If, on the other hand, they simply seek to lobby international organizations and governments by speaking for themselves and not claiming to speak for anyone else, and if they make their advocacy claims based on accurate and demonstrated evidence of expertise and competence at what they do, then they merit close attention by actual decision makers in governments and international organizations. Their legitimate power depends on what NGOs claim as the reason why anyone should listen to them, and on whether they claim that their point of view should prevail simply because they are NGOs and somehow "represent" the peoples of the world—whether the peoples of the world know it or not.

NGOs that are competent, expert, and knowledgeable in the way that good advocates should be merit the not-insubstantial power that goes along with powerful advocacy—not as a matter of right, but as a matter of persuasiveness.

FROM "INTERNATIONAL NGOS" TO "GLOBAL CIVIL SOCIETY"

With the end of the cold war and the fall of the Soviet empire in 1989, the weight of bipolar superpower struggle ended. A broad but loose U.S. hegemony guaranteed the security of the world's industrialized democracies. The expanding NATO alliance and the demise of the Soviet Union and the Warsaw Pact meant that the United States had no external state enemies to speak of. Saddam Hussein's 1990 invasion and annexation of Kuwait, leading to the First Gulf War, raised hopes among many "liberal internationalists" that a new era could be ushered in—an era in which international law and institutions such as the UN could create "global governance" that would overcome the anarchy of states and their power struggles and establish some form, however loose, of binding law over states.

What did these geopolitical shifts among nation-states have to do with international NGOs? The end of the Cold War persuaded many NGOs, particularly in those focusing in the areas of human rights, the environment, and the women's movement, that the moment had come to claim their rightful part in globalization—and go global themselves. This prospect meant, first, expanding their activities, membership, and organizational structures across borders, so as to be genuinely cross-border organizations. But also, Western and northern-based NGOs that had not seen much point in engaging with the UN during the frozen decades of bipolar superpower struggle now came to see the UN as a fruitful—indeed, a *rightful*—place to lobby, advocate, and organize.

Throughout the decade that followed, international NGOs were taking part in, or else learning lessons from, the transformative experience of NGOs of the early 1990s. The most significant of these examples was the international campaign to ban antipersonnel landmines, begun in the 1980s initially as a grave concern of the International Committee of the Red Cross (ICRC), which saw firsthand the humanitarian damage of landmines, mostly in civil wars. This campaign took shape in the early 1990s as a loose coalition of leading international NGOs that crossed disciplinary lines—human rights, humanitarianism, medical relief, development, and others—and came together as the network of the International Campaign to Ban Landmines (ICBL). Along with its director, Jody Williams, the ICBL won the 1997 Nobel Peace Prize for the achievement of a comprehensive ban treaty, the Ottawa Convention, which has attained ratification by states worldwide.

The landmines ban campaign contains many lessons for international NGOs, but the one that concerns us here is perhaps the most abstract and most politically ambitious. It is the idea that international NGOs can be understood as more than simply skillful lobbyists and advocates for causes that concern their organizations and memberships. Instead, they can be perceived as advocating on behalf of the citizens of the world. Moreover, this lesson demonstrates that international NGOs should be regarded in the international community as a force for "democratizing" international politics by breaking down the state-centric nature of the international system and its core assumption that states deal only with one another or with the international organizations that states themselves create, such as the UN, and not with individuals or NGOs or citizens groups.

The landmines ban campaign, among its many other dimensions, challenged that state-centric model, asserting that the international system would henceforth have to deal, if not precisely with individuals, then with organizations that would advocate their interests before international bodies. International NGOs were to be understood as advocating on behalf of individuals and populations directly, as opposed to states advocating on behalf of their citizens. Hence, in virtue of this direct representation function, international NGOs must be accorded parallel status to states and international organizations in making decisions, creating treaties, and setting standards on issues ranging from human rights to international development to the content of international law. The landmines ban campaign had secured a place for NGOs alongside states in negotiating the Ottawa Convention; since the ICBL had been responsible for bringing the treaty about, it would have been unseemly, churlish even, for the negotiating states to exclude from their meetings its main promoter—and this recognition established a new precedent of international NGO participation as speaking on behalf of the world's peoples. No longer claiming merely to advise or advocate or lobby on the basis of their expertise and competence in a particular area, international NGOs now asserted a breathtakingly sweeping claim to a seat at the table of global governance on the basis of *speaking for* the "peoples of the world." Representation, in a word: international NGOs, rather than governments, would represent people.

The final version of the idea that emerged during the 1980s and 1990s was that civil society consisted of social and political activity that was neither part of the state, nor part of the market. Its locus was the space of social life, sometimes political and sometimes not, where human beings pursued interests that were ordered—and ordered about—by neither the state nor the market. Such social spaces made possible organized, civilized politics in a liberal sense because they allowed for organizing, for discussion, for mediation of social and political claims, outside the impositions of state authority but also outside the economic inequalities and hierarchies imposed by the market.

However, critical concerns were raised about the role of civil society in relation to domestic societies. The proposition that international NGOs should be conceived as a kind of global civil society was, in fact, a double assertion. First, the claim that this global civil society, analogous to domestic civil society, served as the organized response of citizens across the globe, as intermediaries on behalf of the world's peoples, and as representatives for their sakes, then, naturally, posed several questions: the organized response to whom, as intermediaries before whom, and representatives to whom?

Second, global civil society was claimed to act in those roles both "in front of" and "in partnership with" international organizations such as the UN. Regarding states, on the other hand, the relationship was always one of equality—as equal pretenders in addressing issues, on the one hand, and in addressing international organizations of global governance, on the other. Global civil society might work with states in "partnership," as representatives of the people of the world, or it might work against them, insofar as global civil society believed that states, or particular states, were not representing the interests of the world's peoples.

Theorists of global civil society took various positions on the exact relationships among global civil society, states, international organizations, and the "international community" generally. But the core point was that global civil society saw itself as at least as legitimate, if not more so, in proclaiming, advocating, and insisting that it was right in its representation and intermediation on behalf of the peoples of the world, as the states that otherwise purported to represent them. And if international organizations—such as the UN—wanted to have the legitimacy of a genuinely global constituency, they too would have to accept partnership with global civil society.

WHAT'S WRONG WITH THE CONVENTIONAL ACCOUNT OF GLOBAL CIVIL SOCIETY?

Given the undeniable attractions of greater transparency and visibility in the making of global policy—whether by states together or through the UN—what could possibly be wrong with this intellectual and ideological ratcheting up, in effect, of international NGOs from mere observers, advocates, and advisers to the status of representatives? What's not to like?

The most obvious problems are with the claims, made with greater and greater extravagance throughout the later 1990s, of the special status of global civil society as representatives and intermediaries. Policy analyst David Rieff put the matter bluntly in a sharp intellectual challenge in 1999, asking, "So who elected the NGOs?"[2] It was a question that increasing numbers of previously sympathetic observers began to ask following the antiglobalization riots in Seattle in December 1999, when violent protests succeeded in shutting down meetings of the World Trade Organization (WTO). Those disturbances were largely forgotten as the terrorist attacks of September 11, 2001, and the Iraq and Afghanistan wars took over the central attention of global elites, but they inaugurated a wave of skepticism about the inflation of ideological claims by international NGOs that still echoes today.

The Seattle riots, and the fact that so many supposedly "respectable" NGOs that had been considered to be desirable interlocutors of institutions such as the

World Bank and the UN stood aside from criticizing the violence in the streets, caused what might be called the "responsible global business community" to question their support and to wonder aloud just who and, indeed, how many, these organizations actually represented. Influential global establishment voices such as *The Economist* magazine and the *Financial Times* had been favorable throughout the 1990s to the landmines ban campaign. Indeed, they had generally favored the role played by NGOs and had, in effect, endorsed the idea that a maturing global capital system would have a global civil society—which is to say, they had accepted uncritically the idea that global civil society really was the analogue of civil society in a domestic democratic society. Following Seattle, however, they began to sharply question the issue of representativeness.

For instance, when Fareed Zakaria, then managing editor of *Foreign Affairs*, contacted ten NGOs after the Seattle riots, he found that "most consisted of 'three people and a fax.'" He expressed the concern, which was widely echoed among global elites outside the NGOs and the antiglobalization community, that the "rich world will listen too much to the loud minority" of First World activists and "neglect the fears of the silent majority" in the developing world who would benefit from activities not considered virtuous by the elites of the developed world.[3] *The Economist* ran a series of articles with titles such as "NGOs: Sins of the Secular Missionaries" and "Citizens Groups: The nongovernmental order: Will NGOs democratize, or merely disrupt, global governance?"[4]

These observers were not opposed ideologically to the idea of either international NGOs or global governance, but in their eyes, the claims of representativeness suddenly, after Seattle, appeared to be as dangerous as they were unfounded. Journalist Sebastian Mallaby, in a famous—or infamous—article in *Foreign Policy* and, later, in a section of his book on the World Bank, recounted his visit to an NGO in Uganda that had been widely touted by the International Rivers Network (an American NGO based in Berkeley, California), as representing local opposition to a dam project that promised to bring electricity to a vast number of people: he went to the Uganda offices and discovered, looking at the inscription record, that the NGO had a total of twenty-five members.[5]

Do NGOs wield too much power when they inflate themselves into global civil society, representing supposedly vast populations with which, in fact, they have no real contact at all? Yes. The claim of representation amounts to a claim of being the legitimate intermediaries for all these people, which in turn really amounts to a claim of knowing what they want and what is best for them. One is entitled to be skeptical of the power that NGOs claim. Can the world's peoples really set aside their governments so easily, and dismiss the complex trade-

offs that governments—even ones that are not especially transparent or democratic—have to make in governing? It is one thing to criticize these governments for not representing their citizens democratically—and fair enough. But
there is an immense gap between making that criticism and saying that international NGOs and their judgments should substitute for those governments
and *their* judgments. Whatever one might (correctly) think about those governments, assessing the legitimacy of NGOs is another matter entirely.

These nonstate actors' claims to representativeness and intermediation are
thus gravely suspect, and to the extent that international NGOs rely upon such
claims—rely upon them and so characterize themselves as global civil society—they exercise, or seek to exercise, too much power. Or, more precisely,
they seek to exercise power from a source to which they are not legitimately
entitled. And the path of NGOs today has been one of carefully hedged retreat,
at least in public, from these claims of representativeness. Thus, for example,
the head of Greenpeace UK, Peter Melchett, stated in an interview not long
after the Seattle riots what might seem to be the obvious view:

> Democratic governments are elected and have democratic legitimacy.
> Other organizations, such as Greenpeace, *The Spectator* and the *Guardian*,
> do not. We have the legitimacy of our market of who buys us or supports
> us. I don't claim any greater legitimacy than that, nor do I want it.[6]

The self-abnegation and self-effacement of this statement are admirable—if
only one could quite believe it. However, the general experience of negotiations, discussions, and drafting sessions at international organizations such as
the UN, the World Bank, the International Monetary Fund, the WTO, and so
on, is that global civil society does indeed expect to be invited in and have a seat
at the table. It really does believe that it is in partnership with democratic governments, or at least ought to be. This is what it learned from the landmines
campaign, after all.

The UN Charter recognizes a certain advisory and expert role for NGOs, but
what is sought and claimed here goes far beyond that status. To claim a role not
merely as an advocate representing one's own organizational point of view,
buttressed by expertise that is respected by others (or perhaps not), is really
only possible if NGOs believe, and expect others to believe, that they cannot be
kept out of the decision-making processes because they really *are*, even after all
the skepticism, truly "representative" of the peoples of the world in a way that
no one and nothing else is: not international organizations, and certainly not
states, not even democratic ones.

Moreover—and this is a point not sufficiently acknowledged in the debate—
to the extent that an NGO is granted access and status and legitimacy by virtue

of being "representative" of someone or something, its actual expertise, competence, and accomplishment become correspondingly less relevant. The right of access is granted on account of the claim of representation, not on the claim of relevant expertise. Such access dangerously undercuts the idea that NGOs ought to know whereof they speak—and, because it empowers the incompetent equally as the competent, makes it more difficult for the objectively and genuinely competent NGOs to make their voices heard.

YES, TOO POWERFUL IF . . .

Expertise and competence are not everything. In democratic societies, we elect people who may indeed lack expertise and competence; the consent of the governed, including faith in those who rule them, wisely or unwisely, belongs to those same governed. Nor, for that matter, would most of us want to be governed by technical experts alone; too many of the questions that make up a politics cannot be settled on technical grounds alone, but inevitably involve questions of values.

The problem is that even if governments lack all the legitimacy one might want—even if they lack democratic legitimacy—that is very, very far from justifying the argument that therefore global civil society can take over for them. And the case is the same for international organizations that lack any real basis in democratic legitimacy. Expertise and competence are not enough to give international NGOs the kind of authority within the international system that they plainly believe—still believe—they merit.

In that sense—the sense of their self-proclaimed role as global civil society—NGOs will wield too much power if given the opportunity, because that is the power they believe they merit. Eventually, the role of faux-representativeness undermines such competence and expertise as the NGOs have, because over the long term their incentives are changed. Yet this change cannot be good for them or for those whom, without claiming to represent them in the world, at their best they can and should serve. The unpleasant burden upon states and international organizations, therefore, is to tell the international NGOs "no" when they overreach from claims of expertise to claims—however covert, however much at odds with their public proclamations of modesty—of representation of the peoples of the world. NGOs do not represent the people; they represent themselves, and their power ought to be tied strictly to that condition.

NO: Marlies Glasius, *University of Amsterdam*

Over the past fifteen years, diplomats and officials of international organizations have been celebrating the advent of newcomers in their midst. In
1994 Boutros Boutros-Ghali addressed a gathering of NGO representatives as
follows: "I want you to consider this your home. Until recently, these words
might have caused astonishment. The United Nations was considered to be a
forum for sovereign states alone ... [NGOs] are now considered full participants in international life" (Boutros-Ghali 1994). According to Dutch diplomat
Adriaan Bos, chair of the negotiations on the International Criminal Court, the
presence of international NGOs "fills in gaps arising from a democratic deficit
in the international decision-making process" (Bos 1999, 44–45). Why are
these officials so pleased to be sharing the stage with new actors whose mandate to be part of the negotiations is much less obvious than their own? Should
we share their enthusiasm?

International decision making has not traditionally been a democratic
process. Yet there is an increasing sense among national and international
diplomats that, as more decisions have moved up to the international level,
international decision making, and international lawmaking in particular,
ought to be (more) democratic. This idea is related to a more general recognition by political thinkers that, while more states have been converted to parliamentary democracy, the onset of globalization has eroded the substance of
democratic participation and choice (see, for instance, Held 1995; McGrew
1997; Scholte 2001). The enthusiasm for NGOs, and the claim that they
make international decision making "more democratic" should be seen in this
context.

Assessing this claim requires, first of all, a brief enquiry into the meaning of
democracy. Its Greek root means simply "rule by the people," but in its modern
use, the term usually implies a system of governance whereby "the people"
periodically elect representatives, while key civil and political rights are
observed. It is difficult to make a direct link between either of these meanings
and the contribution of NGOs to international decision-making processes. In
fact, Kenneth Anderson's strong objection to the idea of a global civil society—
echoed in his essay in this book—is based precisely on what he believes to be a
conflation of the roles of elected representatives at the national level and of
NGOs at the global level. "But who elected the international NGOs?" he asks,
then going on to observe that most NGOs are "not very often connected, in any
direct way, to masses of 'people'" (Anderson 2000, 112–118).

This is true. But neither, many democratic theorists would point out, are political parties. Since the 1970s, there has been a severe drop in the number of party members, in the attendance at party conferences, and in voter turnout in most established democracies. Like the electorate at large, democratic theorists have become increasingly disillusioned with representative democracy, calling it "thin" or "procedural" democracy. While by and large continuing to advocate representation and civil and political rights as minimum conditions for democracy, they have explored forms that would make citizens participate more actively in politics, referring to such forms as "strong" (Barber 1984), "participatory" (Pateman 1970), and, especially, "deliberative" (Bessette 1980; Cohen and Rogers 1983; Gutmann and Thompson 1996) democracy.

It is on such notions of democracy, rather than on classic representation, that the argument is built that NGOs democratize international decision making—or "global governance," as its proponents tend to call it. They agree that such processes are not democratic in their present form, but contend that NGO participation makes them more so than they would otherwise be (Scholte 2001; Van Rooy 2004). NGOs, grandly renamed "global civil society actors," have been conceptualized as a "functional equivalent" (Rosenau, 1998, 40–41) or "alternative mechanism" (Scholte 2001, 15) to the multiparty representational system, for democratizing global governance.

Here I will first examine some of these supposed democratic functions of NGOs by considering their contribution to five generally accepted characteristics of democracy: transparency, equality, deliberation, representation, and participation. Subsequently, I will suggest that the tortured democracy question is not the only justification for NGO involvement in international politics. I will discuss the much-overlooked and by no means unproblematic "ethical contribution" of NGOs and then offer a qualified defense of more international law, with more NGO participation, on this basis.

TRANSPARENCY

Transparency or openness is a necessary condition of all forms of democracy. Whether in direct or in representative democracy, the process of deliberation and the eventual vote must take place openly. Even in experimental forms of democratic procedure that eschew the vote, public discussion is highly valued. Karl Popper (1952), the philosopher who profoundly influenced financier George Soros, considered "openness" the prime instrument to keep any form of government from usurping too much power. More recently, democratic theorists Amy Gutmann and Dennis Thompson have drawn on such different philosophers as Jeremy Bentham and Immanuel Kant to construct publicity as a necessary condition for deliberative democracy, while also insisting (in line with human rights law) that certain forms of regulated secrecy are necessary in a democratic society (Gutmann and Thompson 1996, 95–127).

Yet in international negotiations, secrecy has traditionally been the norm. All that became available to the public was the final product. This situation changed somewhat after the Second World War, with the advent of superpower summits and international UN conferences. Now, citizens would be informed via the media that negotiations were proceeding, politicians might make statements, and journalists would speculate about the outcome. Nonetheless, the substance of the negotiations would still take place behind closed doors.

NGO coalitions have really challenged this convention of secrecy, and the Coalition for an International Criminal Court (CICC) is a prime example. It tracked the state negotiations on the establishment of the International Criminal Court between 1995 and 1998, bringing 236 NGOs to the final leg of the negotiations in Rome. Its working methods included forming twelve shadow teams to monitor negotiations on different parts of the draft text, debriefing friendly state delegates after closed meetings, and keeping "virtual vote" tallies on crucial issues. These mechanisms made the official decision-making process more transparent: for its members, for journalists, and, through them, for a wider audience of interested parties and even for state delegates. The entire texts of interim proposals, with an analysis, were reprinted in special conference newspapers. Information was also sent to thousands of national activists and observers, by the Coalition itself, by some of its member NGOs, and by the press teams of two special news bulletins devoted to the conference's proceedings (Glasius 2005, 38–43).

More importantly perhaps, many state representatives found these channels of publicity useful, either to state their positions or to vent their frustrations with other states or with the process of negotiation, particularly when they believed that public opinion might be on their side. As the conference wore on, state delegates even began to complain in these media about a lack of transparency in the process itself ("Chairman Struggles" 1998; "Where Are Decision Being Made?" 1998). This was a significant development, because state delegates thus addressed the interested wider public by making an appeal to a norm of transparency that has no tradition in international negotiations.

Beyond direct coverage of international negotiations, NGOs play an important role in public education on global issues: with respect to rather esoteric topics such as global warming, Third World debt, or intellectual property rights, they open up more general debates, in which active citizens can inform themselves and take part. As in national democracies, certain discussions and negotiations will continue to take place behind closed doors, but NGOs have shifted the balance much further toward openness as the default setting in international negotiations.

EQUALITY

Another key condition of democracy, representative or deliberative, is equality. According to political theorist David Beetham, "a system of collective decision-making can be said to be democratic to the extent that it is subject to control by all members of the relevant association, or all those under its authority, considered as equals" (Beetham 1999, 5). Formally, there is such equality between the members of the association called the United Nations, at least in its General Assembly and its Economic and Social Council, if not in the Security Council. Formal equality is also much bruited about as one of the characteristics of the World Trade Organization (WTO).

However, in practice, some states are more equal than others. This inequality is not just a question of perceived power, but also of capacity to be involved in multiple complex negotiations. Regardless of whether or not one believes that citizens should somehow be able to have a direct involvement in global processes that affect them, levelling the playing field between the formally equal players—the states—would contribute to democratizing international decision making. And NGOs do, at times, play such a role. Most eye-catching has probably been the expert advice, and publicity, given to developing countries in the negotiations of the WTO in recent years (Said and Desai 2003, 80–82). The documents produced by NGOs helped to educate those countries' representatives with respect to the issues involved. The provision of interns and legal experts swelled their delegations in quality and quantity. The NGOs' monitoring of both public and, as far as possible, secret negotiations, has made the process more transparent and easier to follow for such states.

The NGO Coalition for an International Criminal Court made another interesting contribution to formal equality: it periodically recorded a "virtual vote" (discussed extensively in Glasius 2005) on different aspects of the negotiations. This tally of the preferences of each state, gleaned from their official statements, focused attention on absolute numbers of states supporting particular positions. Without this effort, the fact that, for instance, more than 80 percent of the states favored an independent prosecutor would simply have gone unrecorded. Through the virtual vote count, this democratic preference became a topic of debate and a counterweight to the inevitable spotlight on the position of "important" states such as the five permanent members of the Security Council. Thus, the formal equality of states was given a little more substance by at least polling and publicizing each state's views, although actual voting was avoided until the very end.

DELIBERATION

The idea of deliberative democracy is that proposals can be debated on their merits through rational arguments rather than solely on the basis of represen-tation of interests. (This aspect of democracy is therefore related to the ethical contribution discussed later in this essay.) Deliberative democracy entails giv-ing and demanding reasons for each position—reasons that would at least the-oretically be capable of swaying other participants in the debate. It also means participants should be prepared to be swayed to some extent by arguments that appear "reasonable." States' disposition to engage in such deliberations is fos-tered by their constant discussions with NGO representatives, who demand explanations for state policies, scrutinize them, and relay them to a wider audi-ence. The Bush administration's belated U-turn on climate change, while per-haps owing something to Al Gore's documentary, *An Inconvenient Truth*, might also be attributed to the drip-drip effect of years of NGO advocacy and ensu-ing public debate (Newell 2005).

On the matter of deliberation between NGOs, there is rather more doubt. NGOs are notoriously fractious. One of the most obvious differences between the functioning of NGOs at the international level and political parties at the national level is that one can have an infinite number of NGOs, each devoted to a single issue or representing a slightly different viewpoint on various issues, and so there is little incentive for either deliberation or compromise. On the contrary, NGOs depend on and compete for funding, and since funding is at least partly related to publicity, there is an incentive to shout each other down. However, Alison Van Rooy, who has written extensively on the role of NGOs in development, suggests that the lack of a united front detracts from the moral authority of NGOs: "The rule here suggests that if activists cannot agree on a united position, there are fewer reasons to listen to what they have to say" (Van Rooy 2004, 99).

Coalitions are sometimes held up as the solution. In its report, the Panel of Eminent Persons appointed by then UN Secretary-General Kofi Annan to make recommendations on United Nations–Civil Society Relations, expressed a desire for amalgamation of NGO views through "disciplined networking and peer review processes of the constituencies" ("We the Peoples," para. 26). But is such unity really the most desirable in terms of fostering deliberation? As the late political theorist Iris Marion Young put it, deliberative democracy should not be "a comfortable place of conversation among those who share language, assumptions, and ways of looking at issues" (Young 1997, 401). On the contrary, "confrontation with different perspectives, interests, and cultural meanings teaches individuals the partiality of their own, and reveals to them their own experience as perspectival" (403).

While precisely playing the role of bringing the experience of "others" to the attention of state representatives, NGO coalitions do often too much resemble a "comfortable place of conversation," and fall into the trap of providing a convenient single "NGO perspective" to the UN and state officials, instead of reflecting a sometimes confusing, sometimes confrontational plurality of voices.

On the other hand, global confrontations like that between women's groups and pro-family groups (Glasius 2004), or between anti-weapons activists and the fast globalizing pro-gun lobby (Bob 2007) do not meet the requirements of "deliberative democracy" either, for listening to one another and engaging in a rational set of arguments and counterarguments are also characteristics of the idea of deliberation, and there is certainly no such process of engagement between such opposing groups. Nonetheless, one could argue that the presence of both perspectives contributes to the deliberative process of the negotiations as a whole, even if the exchanges between NGOs are vitriolic.

If the UN is serious about the role of NGOs as fostering real deliberative processes, it should actively look for a *plurality* of views, including starkly opposing ones, instead of trying to weed out such controversy before allowing NGOs entry into its chambers. Networks are a powerful tool in strengthening the potential influence of NGOs on state negotiations, but they also tend to homogenize diverse views, to neglect minority views, and, of course, to exclude views that oppose their founding mission. Therefore, a heavy focus on networks is not conducive to the role of NGOs as fostering reasoned debate between different views.

REPRESENTATION

Representative democracy was invented because the decision-making constituencies, the *demos*, of nation-states were too large and too dispersed to allow every individual to take part in debates and voting. It is therefore natural that, when thinking about the possibility of a global democracy or of democratizing existing global institutions, representative mechanisms of democracy spring to mind. Some would assert that the UN General Assembly already functions as such: now that three-quarters of the world's states are at least formally democratic, one could argue that citizens elect their governments, which then represent them in the United Nations.

However, there are various problems with this line of thinking. For one, governments, unlike parliaments, are formed only out of the winning party or parties. The General Assembly is therefore not comparable to national parliaments, because only the national "winners" (the governments) are represented. Moreover, complex international issues are not usually an important element in election campaigns. We still elect national governments primarily to govern us, not to represent us at the international level. So, as is often remarked, the United Nations do not, in fact, represent "We the peoples," but "We the governments."

So, can NGOs represent "We the peoples" instead? The Panel on UN–Civil Society Relations certainly seems to suggest that such popular representation is possible, by calling its 2004 report "We the Peoples: the United Nations, Civil Society and Global Governance." But how does this representation work? Some organizations have a mass membership. Amnesty International is considered a very large NGO, with more than 2.2 million members from 150 countries (amnesty.org), but this is nothing compared to the 168 million combined membership of the International Trade Union Confederation (ituc-csi.org). Other influential organizations, such as Greenpeace, Oxfam, and the World Wide Fund for Nature, do not have members, but instead rely on financial "supporters"—although Greenpeace does claim to speak for its 2.8 million supporters (greenpeace.org). As Van Rooy (2004, 62–76) has pointed out, the geographical spread and depth of members' commitment differ vastly between organizations, as do procedures for internal democracy. There are also very small organizations, and, in fact, many NGOs do not claim to represent anyone but themselves.

It becomes obvious very quickly that conceptualizing NGOs as a global equivalent of political parties, organizing the global electorate into voting blocks whom they represent in international negotiations, is inaccurate and misleading. Having a large membership base may be a source of legitimacy and influence to particular organizations, but democratic representation in the traditional sense cannot be considered a functioning attribute of NGOs as a group.

But are there other forms of representation? And who or what ought to be represented? David Held (1995, 136) uses the phrase "overlapping communities of fate" to express the fact that those who are affected by certain decisions are, due to globalization, no longer always found neatly in a single political entity, controlled by a democratic process. NGOs can sometimes be a solution to such situations where the decision-making power is not located where the voting is, through an informal form of representation. One could argue, for instance, that NGOs represented people living with HIV/AIDS in developing countries by means of their advocacy for the production of generic drugs during the WTO negotiations on intellectual property. In the absence of any other form of representation, such non-state-based advocacy may be helpful to those affected—as it certainly was in this case.

But the fact that there is no agreed form for consulting those who are supposedly represented remains problematic. The resistance against the Narmada dam in India, which if built would displace thousands of villagers, is an oft-cited example of a civil society success: the villagers' international advocates succeeded in dissuading the World Bank from funding the project, and their influence has even been institutionalized in the form of a World Commission on Dams, which advises the World Bank on similar projects. But only those who stood to lose their homes and livelihood from the building of the dam were represented at the international level. The arguably much larger number of people who might have benefited from its hydroelectric power did not have such advocates.

And who would constitute the "community of fate" for climate change? It may affect all our futures, but it is impossible to pinpoint in advance exactly who will be most affected, and in what ways. Representation should therefore be conceptualized in a very different way in these situations. NGOs can still make claims "on behalf of," but those made on behalf of the environment, on behalf of future victims of human rights violations, or on behalf of the unborn child, have little or nothing to do with a parliamentarian's work on behalf of his constituency. On the one hand, consultation mechanisms are not a necessary part of such claims. On the other hand, no formal voting rights can or should be based on it. NGOs are not, and should not be, seen as a kind of global parliament. Indeed, as the eminent "reflective practitioner" Mike Edwards (2003) put it, civil society is "a voice not a vote."

PARTICIPATION

Another way of conceptualizing this democratic characteristic is to say that participation, not representation, is the point of NGOs. As the Panel on UN–Civil Society Relations puts it: "Citizens increasingly act politically by participating directly, through civil society mechanisms, in policy debates that particularly interest them. This constitutes a broadening from representative to participatory democracy" ("We the Peoples," Executive Summary, x). But whose voices are, and should be, heard under the banner of global civil society? Who gets to participate?

Some actors, it should be said, do not wish to participate, or at least not on the invitation and according to the rules of the decision makers. As Iris Marion Young puts it, they typically "make public noise outside while deliberation is supposedly taking place on the inside," although sometimes they "invade the houses of deliberation and disrupt their business" (Young 2001, 673).

The Madres (mothers) de la Plaza de Mayo and the Abuelas (grandmothers) de la Plaza de Mayo typify the differences between "outsider" and "insider" activism. Both groups emerged during the Argentinian military regime (1976–1983) when thousands of political opponents were "disappeared" by government forces—kidnapped, held in secret detention, and mostly killed—and, after the advent of democracy, both have continued to look for their lost family members. The Abuelas focus on finding their grandchildren born in custody, who were given up for adoption. They go through the courts in their efforts to find the children of their disappeared children and to see the perpetrators punished; as a result of their efforts, Argentinian junta leader Jorge Videla was reimprisoned in 1997. The Madres, on the other hand, "think that accepting financial compensation and exhumation of bodies are a 'betrayal' for their children—because this, in a legal sense, stops what had been an ongoing crime" (Kirk 1998). As Young (2001, 676) points out, such outsiders do in fact "aim to communicate specific ideas to a wide public," so they do participate in politics even though they reject formal participation.

But what of those who cannot participate? Deliberate efforts to block the activities of NGOs, which were particularly evident at the 1995 Beijing Conference on Women, have become rarer, as the furor they cause tends to result in negative publicity for the state and more publicity for the NGO and its cause than those activities might otherwise have received. Nonetheless, states still have the power to block accreditation of NGOs to the United Nations. During the Cold War, states would routinely deny accreditation to organizations they labelled either "communist" or "imperialist." While such practices receded in the 1990s, today they have found a new label: "terrorist."

Beyond deliberate obstruction by states, there is a wider problem with participation. The UN Panel describes participatory democracy as a process in which "anyone can enter the debates that most interest them, through advocacy, protest, and in other ways" ("We the Peoples," para. 13). But, a few pages later, it acknowledges that there are practical constraints: "if the United Nations brought everyone relevant into each debate, it would have endless meetings without conclusion" (para. 23).

Not only is participation limited—it is typically limited in ways that confirm existing power imbalances. As Young (2001, 680) puts it: "Under conditions of structural inequality, normal processes of deliberation often in practice restrict access to agents with greater resources, knowledge, or connections to those with greater control over the forum." Even at the very local level, Young sums up a number of barriers to participation by "anyone with an interest." These constraints are, of course, multiplied at the global level. Although they are meant to be conduits for the marginalized, NGOs thus can also become mechanisms of exclusion.

Discussions of these inequalities often focus rather crudely on geographical representation, but the imbalance is not simply a matter of North versus South. Almost without exception, the international NGO staff represented at an international forum belong to an English-speaking, university-educated, computer-literate middle class. Perhaps such elitism is inevitable, but it does not reflect the diversity of the world population, nor does it necessarily mirror the profile of future victims of poverty, violence, or environmental disaster.

If participation in global processes is necessarily selective on practical grounds, then a particular effort should be made, particularly by NGOs but also by global institutions, to include the voices of "experiential experts"—on human rights violations, on HIV/AIDS, on child soldiers—and not just technical ones. In some forums, NGOs and networks have engaged in "accompaniment": people who are affected by the issues discussed, but who would normally have neither the means nor the political consciousness to get involved are taken to the negotiations under the tutelage of seasoned activists. Some small farmers have, for instance, been present at WTO negotiations under such constructions (Edelman 2003, 210–211). Such practices can lead to the inclusion of "experiential experts," provided that they offer real participation, and not a symbolic trotting out of "the victim" to support the NGO's already formed position. Unfortunately, given the very small number of people who can be offered "accompaniment" in relation to the numbers affected by global negotiations, it seems doubtful that such inclusion can ever be much more than symbolic.

THE ETHICAL CONTRIBUTION

NGOs have greatly contributed to strengthening certain features that are commonly associated with democratic procedure—in particular, transparency, equality, and deliberation. They should not be seen as offering a form of representation of the global *demos*, however, or at least not representation in its traditional form. Their activism could be conceptualized as a form of participation, but in practice this participation is so limited and so uneven that international NGOs cannot entirely be considered an adequate "functional equivalent" or "alternative mechanism" to parliamentary democracy, operating at the global level. NGOs do contribute to making international decision-making processes more democratic than they might otherwise be, but a democratic deficit remains. Another contribution made by NGOs, however, has received much less attention than the democratizing aspect: that of moral values.

The hundreds of groups and individuals who engaged in the International Criminal Court negotiations—whether they were criminal law experts, pro-family groups, or world federalists—all became involved because of their belief in, or concerns about, a particular kind of Court. For some, such as the European Law Students Association, career considerations may have played something of a role. For some NGO professionals, it was "their job" to be there. But even the involvement of these professionals went far beyond that of an ordinary job. Often, they had had to convince their own organizations of the importance of being there. The overriding motivation for being involved was that of ethical conviction.

But what of the states' representatives—do they have ethical convictions? In international relations, there are two classic theories on foreign policy and ethics. The first, and certainly the most influential until the 1990s, is realism. Based on a particular reading of Machiavelli or, alternatively, on a transposition of Hobbes's "war of every man against every man" theory to the international plane (Walker 1993), realism teaches that international relations are an anarchical sphere, where each state pursues its national interest, and there is no place for ethics. Liberal or idealist theory, in contrast, teaches that there is a "society of states," where rules in the common interest of mankind are constructed, and for the most part, obeyed. According to the latter theory, there is a space for "ethics," or enlightened self-interest, in foreign policy. This theoretical bent also gives more space to the conceptualization of intergovernmental organizations, and sometimes even NGOs, as independent actors. But neither theory really understands the diplomats themselves as social actors who are subject to environmental influences (as the social constructivist school does; see, for instance, Onuf 1989; Walker 1993). Whether based on "national interest" or conceived on a more cooperative plane, the policies of states are conceptualized as holy writ, handed down from black-box foreign ministries. According to traditional IR theory, therefore, state representatives are not to have convictions, ethical or otherwise.

In reality, state representatives do, of course, have value dispositions of their own. Nor are state positions on issues such as the ICC, intellectual property rights, or climate change arrived at in isolation from those who negotiate on them. In fact, they are gradually formulated, informed by inside expertise and outside information, and constantly re-adjusted; even the atmosphere of the negotiations can influence the substance of the positions. As discussed earlier, NGOs have transformed that atmosphere in terms of transparency and deliberation. But another aspect of the sustained presence of NGOs is that they constantly invoke ethical considerations—claims about the needs of humankind.

International relations theories such as realism and idealism do not seek merely to explain state behavior—or as I would rather put it, the behavior of state representatives—they also end up informing such behavior. In domestic politics, it is not ethically acceptable for politicians to defend policies simply as being in the self-interest of a particular group: "This policy is good for the small businessmen, or for the Catholic minority, who vote for me." Instead, they need to present such policies as being for the common good: "Small businesses will kick-start the national economy," "Catholic emancipation will make our society more equitable." The dominance of realist theory made any such arguments for the general interest unnecessary in the international sphere—it even characterized them as foolish—by legitimizing the invocation of a (flexibly definable) "national interest" by diplomats as the sole motivation for this or that position.

International NGOs present themselves precisely as the champions of values beyond such state interests, working toward a global common good. But having a majority of such actors around is like being accompanied to a brothel by a delegation of priests—even without any formal status, they constrain behavior and change the terms of debate. Nowadays, forthright statements that "this is not in our nation's interest" can still be heard in international negotiations, but they jar in an environment where appeals to reason and to universal justice are increasingly common currency. States are thus more motivated to frame their proposals in terms of appropriateness and justice in the presence of NGOs.

If it is accepted that NGOs move states toward appreciating, or at least appearing to appreciate, "ethical" or "common good" arguments over national-interest arguments in international negotiations, the question remains which ethical projects make it to those forums and get taken up. Those who do not agree on the dominant projects will point to the democratic deficit—the lack of representation and limits to participation—and they are likely to point back to national democracy as the solution.

The existence of a democratic deficit at the global level, and the fact that NGOs cannot entirely fill it, should not be denied. But the number of victims created by states violating human rights over the past century is staggering. Some of these governments were flawed democracies, too. This is why it is worth giving up some national democratic supremacy in exchange for international law—first, to frame norms on human rights, disarmament, and the environment; and second, to actually enforce them. And NGOs should be there to help make these laws and get them enforced; to strengthen transparency, equality, and deliberation in international decision-making processes; and to help inch states from narrow interests toward global common interests. Those who think that this wider participatory process is not, in fact, in the interest of humanity, should come and join the debate with their own ethical projects— and, perhaps, found their own NGOs.

democracy

Should All Nations Be Encouraged to Promote Democratization?

YES: Francis Fukuyama, *Johns Hopkins University, and* Michael McFaul, *National Security Council*

NO: Edward D. Mansfield, *University of Pennsylvania, and* Jack Snyder, *Columbia University*

Since Woodrow Wilson's presidency, the United States has promoted democratization as a foreign policy goal. Democracy promotion or democratization has been particularly salient on the international agenda since the 1990s, when it informed the design of UN post-conflict peacemaking missions. Since the 1960s, the United States had replaced its historical penchant for armed intervention in Latin America with foreign aid as an instrument of building democracy.

In general, Western governments promote democratization for both principled and instrumental reasons. Sharing a set of liberal political values and experiences dating back to the Enlightenment, these countries value individual rights, including numerous social and political freedoms and liberties. Instrumentally, democratization has been put forward most forcefully in the so-called Democratic Peace formula, which posits that democracies are more peaceful—at least in their relations to other democracies—than are other political systems, because it is harder to mobilize a society to fight when citizens have a direct say over government policy. In particular, citizens in a democracy are believed to have an affinity for their counterparts in other democracies. Democracies may also be capable of more robust and sustainable economic development, because democratic institutions tend to reward technological innovation.

Since 1972, democratization has been spreading worldwide, and when the Cold War ended, the transition from authoritarian political structures to more democratic ones accelerated. Figure 1 presents these trends, showing that the number of countries ranked as "free" grew from forty-four in 1972 (forty-three, if South Africa under apartheid is regarded as only partly free)—or 29 percent of all the independent countries in the world—to ninety (47 percent) by 2007. Meanwhile, the number of partly free countries also increased slightly, from thirty-eight (25 percent of independent countries) in 1972 to sixty (31 percent) in 2007, and the number of not-free countries fell from sixty-nine (46 percent) to forty-three (22 percent) over the same period.

However, democratization is not a geographically universal trend. It has occurred primarily in Southern and Eastern Europe and Latin America. Following the collapse of the Soviet Union, many countries in Eastern Europe tried to emulate the West. In Latin America, democratization has occurred as a combination of blossoming organic processes, supported by initiatives from the United States and other Western nations.

Definitions of democracy vary, and the spread of democratization does not make for a standard that is universally understood. A minimalist sense of democracy is limited to holding multiparty elections in which the losing party voluntarily transfers power. A much more demanding vision of a fully democratic society is articulated by prominent Yale political scientist Robert Dahl, whose list of requirements entails inclusive participation; a one-vote, one-person equality; and informed consent by citizens about the agenda and platforms of candidates. Many of these more demanding definitional elements overlap with the human rights protected by the UN. Achieving such a vision in

Figure 1

Freedom in the World (Country Rankings), 1972–2007

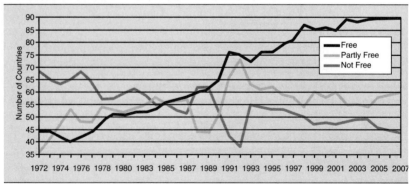

Source: Freedom House, *"Freedom in the World* Country Rankings," http://www.freedomhouse.org/uploads/fow08/CountryStatusAndRatingsOverview1973–2008.pdf.

practice calls for literacy, a free press, a multiparty political system, judicial independence, a trustworthy police force, and respect for individual rights.

Democracy creation is a long and difficult process. Even attempting to meet the weak definition requires assuring citizens that they will not be punished by other ethnic or political groups when power shifts. Consequently, provisions for dealing with prior human rights abuses, an independent judiciary and police force, and impartial elections are necessary. More demanding approaches to democratization may necessitate extensive social engineering in order to promote increased gender equality, respect for democratic values and institutions, literacy, and an independent media.

Not all countries or peoples share a commitment to the Western political values of open participation in political processes. Prime Ministers Mahathir Mohamed of Malaysia and Lee Kwan Yew of Singapore, for instance, claimed that Asian countries share a distinct political culture of "Asian values" that prefers autocratic systems because of habits of social deference and obligation. An important question is whether these systems are sustainable over time and across different rulers.

Democratization is beset with challenges, and it may not occur smoothly or easily. Transitional democracies are in a particularly delicate stage, for democratic openings offer opportunities for authoritarian and nationalistic groups to gain political power. If the economy does not flourish under the new democratic institutions, groups will fight to control the distribution of state resources, and the populace will lose confidence in democracy.

In addition, the ideal of democracy promotion may conflict with other policy goals. During transitional periods, trade-offs must often be made, as scarce state resources have to be allocated either to democracy-building or to economic development. Also, democratization often involves the redistribution of economic control away from a plutocracy or small number of firms that control domestic markets.

Trade-offs may also be needed between democratization and domestic political stability. This potential exchange of values is of particular concern in the Middle East, where, for security purposes, the United States supports many governments that are not democratic. In countries such as Pakistan, Kazakhstan, Saudi Arabia, Egypt, China, Armenia, Azerbaijan, and maybe even Russia, democracy promotion would undermine the government's domestic political support by creating the potential for alternative governing elites or coalitions. Promoting democracy forcefully in such situations could weaken potential allies during a period when the United States needs the full cooperation of states sympathetic to U.S. interests.

The writers in this chapter look at the ease with which democratization can be achieved, the attendant risks associated with promoting democracies, and the question of whether democratization should be promoted in all countries. They engage such issues as the background conditions for democratization, the relationship between foreign and domestic pressures for democratization, and the timing of the democratization process.

Discussion Questions

1. Can democracy be imposed on a country or encouraged from the outside? Or can it only develop within a country on its own? Explain.
2. Are democracy promotion and advocacy for human rights inextricably linked? Can you promote one and not the other?
3. What three reasons do Francis Fukuyama and Michael McFaul give to explain why the United States should promote democracy abroad? What new strategies or foreign policy approaches do they suggest as a way for U.S. policymakers to effectively promote democracy? Do you agree with their proposals?
4. What risks of indiscriminate democracy promotion do Edward D. Mansfield and Jack Snyder highlight? What are the steps in the sequencing strategy they propose for promoting democracy? Do you agree with their proposal?

YES: Francis Fukuyama, *Johns Hopkins University, and* Michael McFaul, *National Security Council*

In his second inaugural address on January 20, 2005, President George W. Bush used the word *freedom* twenty-five times, *liberty* twelve times, and *democracy* or *democratic* three times. Bush did not enter the White House with a mission to promote freedom around the world. Instead, as a presidential candidate, he had put forward a modest foreign policy agenda that eschewed nation-building. The events of September 11, 2001, however, radically jarred his thinking on the nature of international threats and triggered a fundamental reevaluation of his administration's national security policy that elevated democracy promotion as a central objective of his foreign policy agenda.

In the years since that September 11, though, the rhetorical attention devoted to the advance of freedom, liberty, and democracy has greatly outpaced any actual progress in expanding democracy. To date, democracy has failed to take hold in the two countries where Bush ordered the forcible ouster of autocratic regimes: Afghanistan and Iraq. Nor did the toppling of these dictatorships send liberty rippling through the greater Middle East, as some Bush officials and supporters had hoped. Instead, autocratic regimes in the region have used the excuse of terrorism (Egypt, Pakistan) or the alleged threat of U.S. invasion (Iran) to tighten their grip on power. Outside this region, some countries have made some progress toward developing democracy (Georgia, Ukraine), but just as many have moved toward greater autocracy. Freedom House concluded, "The year of 2006 saw the emergence of a series of worrisome trends that together present potentially serious threats to the stability of new democracies as well as obstacles to political reform in societies under authoritarian rule...the percentage of countries designated Free has failed to increase for nearly a decade. ..."[1]

Not surprisingly, many in Washington are pressing for a change in U.S. foreign policy objectives. Only those at the extremes on both ends of the political spectrum advocate the complete abandonment of democracy promotion as a U.S. foreign policy objective. Instead, skepticism is largely couched as "realism" and a "return" to a greater focus on "traditional" U.S. national security objectives.

Revised from Francis Fukuyama and Michael McFaul, "Should Democracy Be Promoted or Demoted?" in *Bridging the Foreign Policy Divide*, ed. Derek Chollet, Tod Lindberg, and David Shorr (New York: Routledge 2007), chap. 9.

From this perspective, democracy promotion should take a back seat to strategic aims such as securing U.S. access to energy resources, building military alliances to fight terrorist organizations, and fostering "stability" within states.

We do not reject the importance of focusing on more traditional goals of national security. However, we do reject the simple assumption that there is a zero-sum trade-off between these traditional security objectives and democracy promotion. We also share the negative assessments of the Bush administration's efforts to promote democracy. However, our response to this mixed record of achievement is not to downgrade or remove democracy promotion from U.S. foreign policy priorities. Instead, we analyze why the United States *should* promote democracy. First, we present the positive case for including democracy promotion as an important component of U.S. foreign policy. Then we present the counterarguments and our reasons for viewing these counterarguments as unpersuasive. Finally, we suggest new strategies and better modalities for promoting democracy.

THE CASE FOR DEMOCRACY PROMOTION

While we believe that the spread of democracy is a good thing in itself, no administration can sell democracy promotion to Congress or the American people unless it is linked to American interests. Fortunately, there are a number of ways in which democracy serves U.S. interests.

U.S. Interests

No country in the world has benefited more from the worldwide advance of democracy than the United States. Not all autocracies are or have been enemies of the United States, but every U.S. enemy has been an autocracy. The transformation of powerful autocracies into democracies has served U.S. national security interests. Most obviously, the end of dictatorship and the consolidation of democracy in Germany, Italy, and Japan after World War II made the United States safer.

During the Cold War, some viewed the Soviet threat as so paramount that all enemies of communism, including dictators, had to be embraced. They predicted that any political change to the status quo in autocratic societies would produce not democratic regimes and U.S. allies but communist regimes and U.S. enemies. There were enough examples of this trajectory—Cuba, Angola, and Nicaragua—to warrant worry. But these were failed cases of democratic transition. In contrast, successful democratic transitions did not undermine U.S. security interests. Transitions in Portugal, Spain, Taiwan, the Philippines,

South Korea, Chile, and South Africa helped to deepen American ties with these countries.[2]

The parallels to today's situation are obvious. Once again facing a new worldwide ideological threat in the form of radical Islamism, strategic thinkers both inside and outside the U.S. government worry that political change in autocratic U.S. allies will produce theocratic regimes hostile to U.S. interests. The concern is valid, but is often overplayed by the very same autocrats as they seek to retain power. So far, successful democratization has never brought to power a government that then directly threatened the national security interests of the United States or its allies.

The advance of democracy in Europe and Asia over the past century made the United States safer—giving reason to hope that democracy's advance in other regions of the world will also strengthen U.S. national security. In the long run, we expect that consolidation of democratic regimes in the greater Middle East would increase the legitimacy of those governments and thereby reduce the appeal of anti-systemic movements such as al Qaeda. In the shorter term, democratic government throughout the region would increase internal stability within states, since democracies have longer life spans than autocracies. If democratic regimes ruled all countries in the region, conflicts between states would be less likely, and, consequently, demand for weapons—including weapons of mass destruction—would decrease. Finally, a more secure and stable region would reduce the need for a U.S. military presence.

In the short run, however, there are potential risks for U.S. security associated with democratic development in the greater Middle East. Without question, the toppling of the Taliban regime in Afghanistan deprived al Qaeda of a base of operations that offered more assets than its current base in Pakistan. Yet this advantage for U.S. strategic interests was not a result of democratization. In fact, the difficult process of developing democratic institutions in Afghanistan has so far failed to produce stable government or a growing economy—a situation that has created an opening for the Taliban's resurgence. In Iraq, neither democratic government nor an effective state has taken root. To date, the American people are not safer as a result of regime change in Iraq. In both countries, U.S.-led invasions brought about regime change. But because these operations were neither launched to bring democracy nor followed through toward that end, the resulting new or resurgent threats to U.S. national security emanating from Afghanistan and Iraq cannot be blamed on democratization or U.S. democracy promotion.

We admit that we do not know whether the analogy between democratization in the wider Middle East and democratization in other regions will hold and yield the same benefits. The destruction of fascist and communist regimes and the emergence of more democratic regimes—first in Europe and Asia after World War II and more recently in Eastern Europe and the former Soviet Union—significantly enhanced U.S. national security. It is reasonable to expect a similar outcome in the wider Middle East; that is, the emergence of more democratic regimes in the most autocratic region of the world should also make the United States more secure.

American Values

Debates about democracy promotion cannot be couched solely as a balance sheet of material benefits and liabilities for the United States. American values must also enter the discussion. Since the beginning of the Republic, U.S. presidents have to varying degrees invoked America's unique, moral role in international affairs. Apart from serving U.S. strategic interests, democracy promotion is also the right thing to do.

First and foremost, democracy is the best system of government. It provides the best institutional form for holding rulers accountable to their people. If leaders must compete for popular support to obtain and retain power, they will be more responsive to the preferences of the people. The institutions of democracy also prevent abusive rule, constrain bad rule, and provide a mechanism for removing corrupt or ineffective rule. Furthermore, democracy provides the setting for political competition, which in turn is a driver of better governance. Like markets, political competition between contending leaders, ideas, and organizations produces better leaders, ideas, and organizations. The absence of political competition in autocracies produces complacency and corruption, and it offers no mechanism for producing new leaders.

Second, democracies provide more, or more stable, welfare for their people than do autocracies. Democracies avoid the worst threats to personal well-being, such as genocide and famine. Over the past several decades, democracies around the world have not produced higher economic growth rates than autocracies: "The net effect of more political freedom on growth is theoretically ambiguous."[3] Instead, autocracies produce both much higher and much lower rates of growth than democracies: for every China there is a Burma. Democracies tend to produce slower rates of growth than the best autocratic performers, but also steadier rates of economic development. The old conventional wisdom that dictators are better at economic modernization than their democratic counterparts is not supported by data.

Third, the demand for and appeal of democracy as a system of government are widespread, if not universal. Public opinion surveys conducted throughout the world show that majorities of people in most countries support democracy.[4] Ideological challengers remain, but compared to earlier historical periods, these opponents of democracy have never been weaker.

The United States, therefore, has a moral interest in promoting democracy. If democracy is the best system of government, demanded by the majority of people around the world, then the United States should help to promote its advance. Conversely, any U.S. involvement in sustaining autocracy is immoral. Obviously, American leaders constantly face situations in which immediate security interests require cooperation with autocratic regimes. But such policies should not be defended on moral or ethical grounds.

ENGAGING THE CASE AGAINST DEMOCRACY PROMOTION

Three arguments are generally offered for why the United States should not pursue democracy promotion. The first argument—that democracy is not a universally valid or desirable goal—has a number of proponents. Postmodernism and other relativist philosophies argue that there are no universally valid political or institutional orders because it is impossible to arrive at philosophical certainty per se. A more common assertion is that democracy is culturally rooted, and that societies with other cultural backgrounds may choose other forms of government as they wish. The late political scientist Samuel Huntington makes this kind of case.[5] According to him, liberal democracy is rooted in Western Christianity, which proclaimed the universal dignity of man made in God's image; thinkers from Tocqueville to Nietzsche have argued that modern democracy is simply a secularization of Western values. There is no particular reason why other civilizations based on other cultural preferences should prefer democratic governments. Former Singaporean prime minister Lee Kwan Yew and other proponents of "Asian values" have argued that, given the poor performance of many democratic regimes in non-Western settings, this form of government is distinctly less desirable than a growth-orientated authoritarian regime.

There are certainly serious philosophical and political cases to be made against a universality of liberal democratic values on a number of grounds. While acceptance of democratic norms and basic human rights has spread far and wide since the onset of the Third Wave democratization that began in the mid-1970s, there are still parts of the world where they are openly rejected on cultural grounds. The Chinese government, various East Asian leaders and thinkers, Islamists of assorted stripes, and many Russian nationalists are among those arguing that their cultures are inherently inimical to one or another aspect of liberal democracy.

We offer the following observations in contention. First, democracy promotion never implied *imposition* of either liberalism or democracy on a society that did not want it. By definition, this is impossible: democracy requires popular consensus, and it works only if the vast majority of a society's citizens believe it is legitimate. Democracy promotion is intended only to help to reveal public preferences in the society itself. Dictatorships often resort to violence, coercion, or fraud to prevent those preferences from carrying political weight; democracy promoters simply try to level the playing field by eliminating the authoritarians' unfair advantages.

A second counterargument that is somewhat more difficult to make is that human rights and the democratic institutions that spring from them are immanently universal. In keeping with the case made by Tocqueville in *Democracy in America*, the historical arc toward universal human equality has been spreading for the past 800 years. Not only has it now encompassed the Western, culturally Christian world, but it has spread and taken root in many other parts of the world as well. This wide-ranging acceptance suggests that democracy has spread not as a manifestation of a particular civilization's cultural preferences, but because it serves universal needs or performs functions that are universally necessary. One can argue that the procedural rule of liberal democracy guarantees that governments behave in a transparent, law-governed way and remain accountable to the people they serve. Even if a culture does not put a value on individual rights per se, liberal democracy is ultimately required for good governance and economic growth.

A second argument against democracy promotion is made by international relations "realists"—namely, that world order depends on states accepting the Westphalian consensus to respect each other's sovereignty and mutual agreement not to meddle in the internal character of each other's regimes. There are countless variants of realist theory today, united primarily in their opposition to democracy promotion as a component of foreign policy. Some argue not from a world-order point of view, but from the perspective of narrower American interests: the United States needs oil, security, trade, and other goods whose availability is compromised by an emphasis on human rights or democracy. These views have acquired particular resonance since the Iraq war, which was seen as being driven by a neoconservative agenda of democracy promotion and political transformation in the Middle East. These critics would argue that U.S. pressure for liberalization of political space and calls for elections have brought to power groups such as Hamas in Palestine, Hezbollah in Lebanon, and the Muslim Brotherhood in Egypt—all of which are illiberal and hostile to U.S. interests. There has been criticism, especially, of the Bush administration's use of coercive regime change as a means to spur the political transformation of the Middle East.

We make several arguments in response to the realists. The first has to do with prudence in means. To say that the United States should promote democracy in its foreign policy does not mean that it should put idealistic goals ahead of other types of national interests at all times and places—or that it should use military force in pursuit of these goals. Indeed, the United States has never made democracy promotion the overriding goal of its foreign policy. The Bush administration invaded Iraq primarily out of concern over weapons of mass destruction and terrorism; democracy promotion was a tertiary goal that received heavier emphasis only when the other justifications of the war proved hollow. The United States has promoted democracy in such places as Germany and Japan after World War II, but only in concert with its security goals. In these cases, transformation of two former enemies into democratic countries did indeed align with U.S. strategic interests, and few realists would argue that the United States would have been better served by an alternative policy.

The Bush administration made the general argument that the deep root cause of terrorism and Islamist radicalism is the Middle East's lack of democracy, and that promoting democracy is therefore one route to eradicating the terrorist threat. It is quite clear in retrospect that this reading of the sources of Arab radicalism was too simplistic. The deep sources of terrorism are much more complex than just the Middle East's democratic deficit. Many of the Iraqis who went to the polls in the various elections in 2005 were Shiites who wanted not liberal democracy but Shiite power, and who have subsequently worked to establish an Iranian-style Islamic republic in areas under their control. The winners of democratic elections elsewhere in the region tend to be profoundly illiberal Islamist groups, who are also more hostile to America's ally Israel than to the authoritarian governments they would like to displace. The political tide in the Middle East is not running in favor of pro-Western liberal opposition groups. The assertion in President Bush's second inaugural address that there is no necessary trade-off between U.S. security interests and its idealist goals would thus seem to be false.

In our view, the appropriate policy in response to this political landscape needs to be a calibrated one that takes account of particular circumstances. There are some countries, such as Saudi Arabia, where there is no realistic democratic alternative to the current authoritarian leadership, or where likely alternatives would clearly be worse from a strategic perspective. In these cases, authoritarian allies indeed represent the lesser of two evils. On the other hand, there are some countries, such as Pakistan, where there is hope for a democratic alternative.

The final argument against the current agenda of democracy promotion concerns the sequencing of democratic reforms. State-building, creation of a liberal rule of law, and democracy are conceptually different phases of political development, which in most European countries occurred in a sequence that was separated by decades, if not centuries. State-building and creation of a rule of law are more critical for economic development than democracy is. Political scientists Jack Snyder and Edward Mansfield have argued that democratization's early phases pose special dangers of promoting nationalism and illiberal politics.[6] Authors from Samuel Huntington to journalist Fareed Zakaria have consequently argued that U.S. policy ought to focus on a broad governance agenda and delay pushing for democracy until a higher level of economic development has been achieved.[7] This so-called "authoritarian transition" has been followed by a number of countries, such as South Korea, Taiwan, and Chile, and is often recommended as a model for U.S. policy in regions such as the Middle East.

There is no question that such liberal authoritarianism has worked quite successfully in places such as Singapore, and even less liberal variants, as in China, can boast impressive economic growth rates. If these countries eventually follow the Korean and Taiwanese paths toward a broadening of political participation, it is not obvious that an accelerated democratic transition would bring about a better long-term result. In addition, there are specific instances where outside pressure for early elections arguably resulted not in the emergence of democratic political parties but in the locking in place of the same groups responsible for the original conflict.

As the analyst of democracy promotion Thomas Carothers has pointed out, however, there are a number of problems with the sequencing strategy.[8] First, in most parts of the world it is very difficult to find liberal, developmentally minded authoritarians on whom such a strategy can be built. The more typical cases in Africa, the Middle East, and Latin America have been characterized by authoritarian governments that are corrupt, incompetent, or self-serving.

A further problem with the sequencing strategy is that it presumes that the United States and other foreign powers can somehow control democratic transitions, holding back pressure for democratic elections while pushing for rule of law and good governance. This assumption vastly overestimates the degree of control that outsiders have over democratic transitions. The toolbox for democracy promotion is more modest, a subject that we will consider next.

MODALITIES OF DEMOCRACY PROMOTION

To argue that the United States has strategic and moral interests in the spread of democracy does not mean that the United States *can* spread democracy. Domestic factors, not external forces, have driven the process of democratization in most countries. Consequently, and especially in light of the tragedy in Iraq, some have argued that the United States can best promote democracy abroad by simply watching it develop "naturally."

We disagree. While we recognize the limits of America's ability to promote democracy abroad, we also know that U.S. policies can be very important in helping to nurture democratic development. The war in Iraq has fostered the false impression that military force is the only instrument of regime change in the U.S. arsenal, when in fact it is the most rarely used and least effective way to promote democratic change abroad. A wiser, more effective, and more sustainable strategy must emphasize nonmilitary tools aimed at changing the balance of power between democratic forces and autocratic rulers and, only after there has been progress toward democracy, building liberal institutions.

Restoring the American Example

Inspiration for democrats struggling against autocracy and a model for leaders in new democracies are two U.S. exports that are now in short supply. Since the beginning of the Republic, the American experiment with democracy has provided hope, ideas, and technologies for others working to build democratic institutions. In the second half of the twentieth century, when the United States developed more intentional means for promoting democracy abroad, the preservation and advertisement of the American democratic model remained a core instrument.

Today, this instrument needs repair. The American model has been severely undermined by the methods that the Bush administration used to fight the so-called global war on terrorism. Irrespective of the legal particulars that may or may not justify the indefinite detention of combatants/terrorists at Guantánamo Bay in Cuba, opinion polls demonstrate overwhelmingly that most of the world views U.S. detention policies as illegitimate and undemocratic. Furthermore, the debate surrounding the unauthorized wiretappings of U.S. citizens helped to create an impression abroad that the U.S. government will sacrifice the civil liberties of individuals in the name of fighting terrorism—the very argument that autocrats across the world use to justify their repressive policies. Finally, the Bush administration's propensity for unilateralism, most centrally in its decision to invade Iraq, coupled with its general suspicion of international law and international institutions, has encouraged the perception that Americans do not believe in the rule of law. The merits of these claims about U.S. behavior are debatable. But it is indisputable that America's image abroad as a model for democracy has been tarnished.

Therefore, the first step toward becoming a more effective promoter of democracy abroad is to get our own house in order. To begin with, the political costs to America's credibility as a champion of democratic values and human rights outweigh the value of holding prisoners at Guantanamo indefinitely. The facility should be closed, and, in place of legalistic attempts to pretend that the United States does not engage in torture, a broader range of prohibited techniques should be explicitly defined and ruled out. More generally, the president of the United States must demonstrate a clear commitment to restoring and perfecting the U.S. democratic system of government.

In parallel, our efforts at public diplomacy have to improve.

The United States cannot hope to recruit people to the side of democratic values if it does not pay attention to what non-Americans say they want, rather than what we think they should want. In the Middle East, many Arabs have argued that the United States is disliked not for its basic values, but for its one-sidedness in the Palestinian-Israeli conflict. In Latin America, populist leaders such as Hugo Chavez and Evo Morales have gained enormous support by promoting social policies aimed at the poor—an issue that America's democratic friends in the region have largely ignored. The starting point for a better public diplomacy, therefore, is to stop talking so much about ourselves and start listening to other people.

Indeed, it may be better for the United States to dramatically tone down its public rhetoric about democracy promotion. The loudly proclaimed instrumentalization of democracy promotion in pursuit of U.S. national interests (such as the war on terrorism) taints democracy promotion and makes the United States seem hypocritical when security, economic, or other concerns trump our interests in democracy (as they inevitably will). Acting in concrete ways to support human rights and democratic groups around the world, while speaking more modestly about American goals, might serve both our interests and our ideals better.

The idealistic component of U.S. foreign policy has always been critical to maintaining a domestic American consensus in favor of a strongly internationalist stance, so we do not recommend permanently abandoning this rhetorical stance. We have to recognize, however, that the Iraq war and other events related to the war on terrorism have for the moment tainted such valid and important concepts as democracy promotion and democratic regime change.

Revitalizing Dual Track Diplomacy

It is naïve to believe that the United States should deal only with other democracies. After all, in our own history, the creation of the United States as an independent country required military assistance from France's absolute monarchy. The alliance with Stalin's Soviet Union was necessary for victory in World War II. Today, the wide range of U.S. security, economic, and environmental interests around the world necessitates diplomatic engagement with autocracies.

Nonetheless, American policymakers can conduct relations with their counterparts in autocratic regimes while simultaneously pursuing policies that may facilitate democratic development in these same countries. When it comes to autocratic regimes with which the United States is friendly, American leaders have real leverage to press for evolutionary change, especially over countries that are dependent on U.S. military protection or economic assistance. Rather than coercing them, U.S. officials must first try persuading our autocratic friends that they can ultimately best protect their material and security interests by proactively leading rather than reactively resisting a process of evolutionary change. American officials did exactly this when they helped to coax allies in South Korea, Chile, and South Africa toward embracing democratic change.

Paradoxically, the same logic of engagement applies when considering the promotion of democracy in dictatorships that are hostile to the United States. Attempts to isolate or sanction these regimes have rarely worked. Sanctions against the apartheid regime in South Africa succeeded only because the United States, Great Britain, and other European countries had developed deep economic ties beforehand. Because the United States does not have significant trade with or investments in Iran, Cuba, or Burma, sanctions against these autocracies do little to help the pro-democracy forces inside these countries. However, diplomatic relations with such regimes create a more hospitable environment for internal democratic development.[9] In the USSR, for instance, democratic forces gained strength in the late 1980s when U.S.-Soviet relations were improving, not earlier in the decade when tensions were high. With rare exception, policies that open societies and economies up to international influence have helped to spur democratic change, while policies that isolate societies impede such progress.

Reorganizing Democracy Assistance

For most of American history, U.S. foreign assistance did not explicitly aim to promote democracy. President Kennedy created the United States Agency for International Development (USAID) in 1961 to counter communism, but the agency's focus was economic development. Over time, however, the U.S. government has increasingly become a direct provider of democracy assistance. Ronald Reagan made democracy promotion a central objective when he worked with Democrats in Congress to create the National Endowment for Democracy (NED) in 1983. With the announcement of its "Democracy Initiative" in December 1990, USAID made democracy promotion a core focus and soon became the main source of funding for many nongovernmental organizations (NGOs) in the democracy promotion business.

After September 11, 2001, President Bush increased general foreign assistance funding, including support for democracy promotion. Within the State Department, the Bush administration established the Middle East Partnership Initiative, which became a new funding source for democracy assistance programs, among others. At State, the Bureau for Democracy, Human Rights, and Labor Affairs received major increases in its democracy assistance budget. To better coordinate civilian, military, and intelligence operations in post-conflict settings, the Bush administration established the Coordinator for Reconstruction and Stabilization, a new office within the State Department. Most dramatically, under Secretary of State Condoleezza Rice's transformational diplomacy initiative, the department tried to reform the way in which foreign assistance is funded and delivered.

This focus on how the government is organized to provide democracy assistance is badly needed. The reform ideas to date, however, have not been ambitious enough. Any strategy for more effective democracy promotion must include significantly greater resources as well as reorganization of all U.S. government bureaus and agencies that are tasked with providing democracy assistance.

Democracy promotion should also be placed in a broader context of promoting economic development, reducing poverty, and furthering good governance. The four objectives are interlinked in multiple ways: good governance is widely accepted as a requisite for economic growth; widespread poverty undermines democracy legitimacy; growth reduces poverty; democratic accountability is often required to combat corruption and poor governance; and growth creates a favorable climate for democracy consolidation. Good governance in recipient countries is also critical to maintaining congressional and popular support for assistance programs. Nothing undermines support as much as the perception that U.S. taxpayers' dollars are going into a proverbial Swiss bank account. The United States cannot limit itself to the promotion of democracy—it must also use its leverage to promote development and good governance. These connections need to be reflected in how policy is articulated as well. Senior foreign policy officials in the Bush administration rarely invoked values such as equality and justice; yet historically, American leaders have considered these ideas fundamental to shaping our own government.

Enhancing and Creating International Institutions for Democracy Promotion

After World War II, American internationalists spearheaded the creation of a military alliance—the North Atlantic Treaty Organization (NATO)—to contain the Soviet threat in Europe, and crafted bilateral security pacts with Japan and South Korea to thwart the communist menace in Asia. American leaders also launched the Bretton Woods system and its institutions, the International Monetary Fund (IMF) and the World Bank, as a strategy for maintaining an open, liberal capitalist order and avoiding a repeat of the protectionist-driven meltdown of the 1930s. Democracy promotion was not an explicit objective of either NATO or the IMF; member states in these institutions did not even have to be democracies. Nonetheless, NATO's security umbrella did help to prevent communist coups in Western Europe, to keep the peace between formerly hostile countries within the alliance, and to contain Soviet military expansion in Europe—all of which surely would have undermined democratic institutions.

The stable security environment was conducive to the deepening of democracy within member states and to increasing economic and political cooperation among those states, later culminating in the creation of the European Union. NATO expansion after the collapse of the Warsaw Pact offered Western multilateral connectivity to the new democracies in East Central Europe and served as a bridge as they prepared bids to join the European Union. The gravitational pull of the European Union may be the most powerful tool of democratic consolidation in the world today. The U.S. security umbrella in Asia provided a similar facilitating condition for democratic development first in Japan, then in South Korea, and eventually in Taiwan.

Given the success of these multilateral institutions in promoting democracy, it is striking how little effort President Bush devoted to creating new multilateral institutions or reforming existing ones to advance freedom. After September 11, 2001, not one new major international organization was formed to promote democratic reform. Nor did the Bush administration devote serious effort toward boosting existing international organizations' focus on democracy promotion. This neglect of multilateral institutions must end.

More than any other region in the world, the greater Middle East is devoid of multilateral security institutions. The United States, Canada, the European Union, and other consolidated democracies should partner with their Middle East counterparts to establish regional norms, confidence-building measures, and other forms of dialogue and political reassurance. The goal should be to establish a regional architecture that will affirm human rights and promote regional security.

The impetus for creating regional structures must come from within the region, but the initiative should also be supported from the outside. Such efforts can draw inspiration and lessons from past experiences in Europe, such as the Helsinki process in Eastern Europe, and elsewhere. At the heart of the Helsinki process was the recognition that true security depended not only on relations among states but also on the relationship between rulers and the ruled. Many Middle Eastern governments have signed statements committing themselves to democratic reform, yet the Middle East lacks a regime that can empower citizens to hold their rulers accountable to such pledges at home and in their relations with their neighbors.

The idea of a new multilateral organization committed to advancing democratic practices—be it a revamped Community of Democracies (the international grouping formed during the Clinton administration) or a new League of Democracies—is needed.[10] More boldly, American leaders must embrace new modalities of strengthening ties within the community of democratic states, whether through a new treaty or an alliance.[11]

Even the World Trade Organization (WTO) and other trade agreements must be viewed as levers that help to open up economies, which in turn fosters democratic development. Excluding countries such as Iran from the WTO only hurts the democratic forces inside Iran who favor more, not less, integration of their country into the world system. In some rare circumstances such as South Africa under apartheid, economic sanctions have effectively pressured autocratic regimes to liberalize. The list of failures—including decades-long sanctions against Cuba and Iran—is equally striking. As a rule of thumb, the world democratic community should take its cues about sanctions from the democratic opposition in the target country.

Strengthening International Norms

The collapse of communism ushered in a giddy era for democracy promotion. Because so many autocratic regimes disappeared at the same time, new postcommunist regimes welcomed Western democracy promoters into their countries with few restrictions. Today, however, the atmosphere for democracy promotion is markedly different. The allegedly easy cases for democratic transition in East Central Europe have consolidated and require no further assistance from democracy promoters. Autocratic regimes, at first weak after communism's collapse, have themselves consolidated and now have the means to push back. Finally, the war in Iraq has greatly tainted the idea of external regime change and put under suspicion all foreigners working to promote democratic change.

The new context requires a new strategy for bolstering the legitimacy of democracy promotion and the defense of human rights. Governments must come together to draft a code of conduct for democratic interventions in the same way that governments and the international human rights community have specified conditions in which external actors have the "responsibility to protect" threatened populations. A "right to help" doctrine is needed. A starting point for this new normative regime would be the "right" to free and fair elections, which in turn would legitimize international election monitors and international assistance targeted at electoral transparency. Once these rules of the road are codified, signatories to such a covenant would be obligated to respect them. And if they did not, the violation would serve as a license for further intrusive behavior from external actors.

The United States and other democracies will be effective in promoting freedom abroad only if we develop international institutions that enhance mutually beneficial cooperation, and then abide by the rule of these institutions in the conduct of our foreign policy.

In highlighting the moral and strategic imperatives for promoting democracy abroad, President Bush continued a long-standing tradition in U.S. foreign policy. Declaration of any important objective, however, must be accompanied by a realistic and comprehensive strategy for achieving it. Simply trumpeting the importance of the objective over and over again is not a substitute for a strategy. The tragic result of the gap between objectives and strategies is that many Americans are starting to view this goal as no longer desirable or attainable. A more effective strategy for promoting democracy and human rights is both needed and available.

NO: Edward D. Mansfield, *University of Pennsylvania, and* Jack Snyder, *Columbia University*

The Bush administration argued that promoting democracy in the Islamic world, rogue states, and China would enhance America's security, because tyranny breeds violence while democracies coexist in peace. But recent experience in Iraq and elsewhere shows that the early stages of transitions to electoral politics have often been rife with violence.[1]

Such episodes are not just a speed bump on the road to the Democratic Peace. Instead, they reflect a fundamental problem with the Bush administration's strategy of forced-pace democratization in countries that lack the political institutions to support this process.

It is true that mature, stable democracies do not fight each other and rarely become embroiled in civil and ethnic warfare. However, countries that are just starting down the path toward democracy are at high risk for war, especially if they are ill prepared for the journey. Pushing countries too soon into competitive electoral politics not only risks stoking war, sectarianism, and terrorism, but it also makes the future consolidation of democracy more difficult. Pressure to democratize, applied under the wrong conditions, is likely to be counterproductive and dangerous.

President Bush claimed that "it is the practice of democracy that makes a nation ready for democracy, and every nation can start on this path."[2] Perhaps, but for ill-prepared countries this initial practice means starting to build the governmental institutions that underpin democracy, not holding immediate elections. Without a coherent state grounded in a consensus on which people constitute the nation that will exercise self-determination, unfettered electoral politics often gives rise to nationalism and violence at home and abroad. Absent these preconditions, democracy is impossible, and such ill-founded transitions toward democracy usually revert to autocracy or to chaos.

THE DEMOCRATIC PEACE

One of the best-known findings in the field of international relations is that democracies rarely go to war with each other.[3] This finding has stimulated much of the recent interest in democracy promotion. Two principal reasons have been advanced for what is known as the Democratic Peace. The first explanation is that effective democratic institutions and elections render the government accountable to the people, who bear the costs and risks of war. The philosopher Immanuel Kant, who is often considered the intellectual architect of arguments about the Democratic Peace, grounded his claims in this institutional explanation. Monarchs could shift the costs of war to their subjects without fearing the loss of power, he argued, whereas elected heads of state would suffer at that ballot box if they become embroiled in bloody and expensive overseas conflicts. The electoral consequences of war, Kant predicted, would make democratic governments more prudent when deciding whether to resort to the sword. As a result of this prudence, democracies do not fight each other and are generally better than other regimes at avoiding unsuccessful, costly wars.

A second explanation for the Democratic Peace is that mature democracies do not fight each other because they share a liberal democratic identity and common norms governing appropriate political behavior. Advocates of this explanation hold that democracies have deeply ingrained civic norms, such as rule by consent of the governed, the right to free speech, due process of law, fair electoral competition, and the settlement of political disputes by peaceful procedures. A society that has internalized these norms will consider it illegitimate to use military force against another democratic country and will expect such a country to behave in an equally nonthreatening way. Consequently, relations between mature democracies are not characterized by security fears that can otherwise trigger conflict in the anarchic international system.

Although debates over which of these two explanations truly accounts for the Democratic Peace have yet to be resolved, it is widely acknowledged that mature democracies rarely come to blows with one another. Frequently, however, the process of becoming a democracy is anything but peaceful. The early stages of democratic transitions are often quite violent if the necessary institutional infrastructure to help manage regime change is lacking.

The Democratic Peace rests on the presence of coherent domestic institutions that regulate mass political participation, including the rule of law, civil rights, a free and effective press, and representative government. These institutions render foreign-policymakers accountable to society at large. Even those observers who argue that liberal norms underpin the Democratic Peace realize that these norms only operate in conjunction with coherent democratic institutions.[4]

In certain cases, demands for broader political participation that arise as an autocratic regime breaks down can be managed through institutions that either already exist or can be rapidly established. When this kind of managed transition occurs, democracy is usually consolidated relatively smoothly and peacefully. More commonly, however, demands for broader participation are voiced in countries where authoritarian rule has broken down but the institutional preconditions needed for democracy to function effectively are missing. The rule of law is poorly established, state officials are corrupt, elections can be rigged, militaries or warlords threaten to overturn electoral outcomes, and journalistic media are unprofessional and dependent on the state or economic elites. As political scientist Samuel Huntington has argued, when demands for greater mass political participation are made in the face of domestic institutions that are too weak to manage such political activity, the result is likely to be a chaotic situation in which key groups in society threaten to take unilateral actions to protect their parochial interests.[5] Governing in this setting requires an ideological basis for popular political support, since ideology can help to fill the gap between high levels of participation and weak political institutions. This ideology may appear in several forms, but it usually takes the form of some variety of nationalism.[6]

TRANSITIONS TO NATIONALISM AND WAR

From the French Revolution to contemporary Iraq, the beginning phase of democratization in unsettled circumstances has often spurred a rise in militant nationalism. Democracy means rule by the people, but when territorial control and popular loyalties are in flux, a prior question has to be settled: Which people will form the nation? Nationalist politicians vie for popular support to answer that question in a way that suits their purposes. When groups are at loggerheads and the rules of the game remain uncertain, the answer is more often based on a test of force and political manipulation than on democratic procedures.[7]

When authoritarian regimes collapse and countries begin the process of democratization, politicians of all stripes have an incentive to play the nationalist card. Holdovers from the old regime know that they need to recruit mass support if they are to survive in the new, more open political setting. For them, nationalism is attractive as a populist doctrine, promising rule for the people but not necessarily rule by the people. Slobodan Milosevic, for example, opportunistically misled Serbs about threats from ethnic Albanians in order to win votes in the elections after Tito's death. This hollow populist appeal is a tried-and-true strategy with a long, bloody pedigree. German Chancellor Otto von Bismarck and his successors between 1870 and 1914 used belligerent, divisive nationalism to maintain the authority of the monarchy and the aristocracy in the face of universal suffrage. Exaggerating foreign threats rallied middle-class and rural Germans to the regime, but it contributed to the onset of World War I as well.

Rising political figures also have incentives to tout nationalism in the early stages of a democratic transition. Nationalist rhetoric often involves criticism of monarchs, colonial overlords, dictators, and communist apparatchiks for ruling in their own interest, rather than in the interest of the people. Where ethnic or religious groups were oppressed under the old regime, the emergence of a new regime often emboldens them to demand a state of their own. This solution strikes these groups as safer than counting on the hypothetical success of ethnicity-blind liberal democracy.

Elections in many newly democratizing states have been an ethnic census, not a deliberation about public issues. Ethnic leaders can quickly mobilize nationalist mass movements based on crony and clan ties, common language, and cultural practices. It is harder for secular or "catch-all" leaders to forge new ties across groups. When Saddam Hussein's regime collapsed in Iraq, for example, Shi'a groups readily formed political parties and militias based on existing social networks and religious authority figures; Kurds did the same from their regional base; and Baathist remnants were able to mount a fierce insurgency among some elements of the divided but resentful Sunni. In contrast, secular leaders worked futilely against the grain of the existing social timber to construct an army and credible political parties.

The earlier the elections come during the process of democratization in deeply divided societies with weak political institutions, the worse this problem is. In Bosnia after the 1995 Dayton peace accord, early elections were won by nationalist parties representing the three major ethnic groups, because the power of ethnic factions was not yet broken. Ten years later, they remain locked into this pattern. Early elections likewise reinforced the divisions in Iraqi society, reflecting the party organizations that could be fashioned quickly rather than ones that might have fostered more effective governance but would have taken longer to forge. Even worse, the Iraqi electoral law, which was based on countrywide proportional representation rather than local districts, magnified the exclusion of the Sunni from the political process, since the insurgency kept a disproportional number of Sunni voters away from the polls.

The nationalist and ethnic politics that prevail in many newly democratizing states load the dice in favor of international and civil war. The decade following the end of the Cold War witnessed some peaceful transitions to democracy in parts of Eastern Europe and other countries where the preconditions for democracy were in place. Elsewhere, however, turbulent experiments with democratic politics led to bloody conflicts. In 1991 Yugoslavia broke up into separate warring nations within six months of elections in which ethnic nationalism was a powerful factor.[8] In the wake of the Soviet collapse, popular sentiment expressed in the streets and at the ballot box fueled warfare between Armenia and Azerbaijan over the disputed enclave of Nagorno-Karabakh.[9] As Peru and Ecuador democratized fitfully during the 1980s and 1990s, troubled elected governments gained popularity by provoking a series of armed clashes that culminated in a war in the upper Amazon in 1995.[10] Several years after the collapse of Ethiopia's Dergue dictatorship, the country's elected government fought a bloody border war from 1998 to 2000 with Eritrea, which had just adopted, though not yet implemented, a democratic constitution.[11]

In an especially worrisome case, the nuclear-armed, elected regimes of India and Pakistan fought the Kargil War in 1999. After the 1988 death of Pakistani military dictator Zia ul-Haq, a series of revolving-door elected civilian governments had presided over a rise in militant Islamic efforts to liberate majority-Muslim Kashmir from Indian control. In Kashmir itself, the restoration of elections after Indira Gandhi's period of "emergency" authoritarian rule (1975–1977) had polarized politics and led to violent conflict between Muslims and the state. These turbulent processes culminated in the 1999 war, when Pakistani forces infiltrated across the mountainous frontier in northern Kashmir. The war broke out as Pakistan was taking steps toward greater democratization, including constitutional changes in 1997 that were intended to strengthen the powers of elected civilian rulers.[12]

Democratization also played a catalytic role in the horrible slaughters that engulfed central Africa. The 1993 elections in Burundi—even though they were internationally mandated, free, and fair—intensified ethnic polarization between the Hutu and Tutsi ethnic groups, resulting in some 200,000 deaths. In neighboring Rwanda, an internationally orchestrated power-sharing accord intended to usher in more pluralistic and open politics instead created the conditions for the 1994 genocide that killed nearly a million Tutsi as well as some moderate Hutu.[13]

In East Timor, a favorable vote on independence from Indonesia in an internationally mandated 1999 referendum prompted a violent response by Indonesian-backed Timorese militias, creating an international refugee crisis. Newly democratizing Russia fought two wars against its breakaway province of Chechnya. Vladimir Putin won election in 2000 as Russia's president mainly on the popularity of his plan to invade Chechnya in order to clean out what was characterized as a lair of terrorists and brigands. In each of these varied settings, the turbulent beginning phase of democratization contributed to violence in states with weak political institutions.

War-prone transitions to democracy were not just an aberration of the 1990s. Since the origins of modern mass politics around the time of the French Revolution, virtually all of the great powers turned belligerent and fought popular wars during the early phases of their experiments with democracy. Indeed, democratizing countries of any size have been war-prone. Throughout the nineteenth and twentieth centuries, incomplete democratic transitions—those that get stalled between the breakdown of an autocratic regime and the emergence of full-fledged democracy—increased the likelihood of involvement in external war for countries that had weak governmental institutions at the outset of the transition. In such states, war was four to fifteen times more likely than in other countries, based on various measures of regime type.[14] In these wars, the democratizing country was usually the attacker. Seven percent of all international and colonial wars since 1816 are associated with incomplete democratic transitions. The pattern holds for civil wars in more recent decades, too. Statistical studies show that a country undergoing an incomplete democratic transition is more likely to experience civil war than either a pure autocracy or a fully consolidated democracy.[15] Democratic transition is only one of many causes of war, but it can be a potent one.

THE DAUNTING "TO DO" LIST OF DEMOCRATIZATION

There is little reason to believe that the long-standing link between democratization and nationalist war is weakening. Many of the countries that remained on the Bush administration's "to do" list of democracy promotion lack the institutional infrastructure needed to manage the early stages of a democratic transition. The "third wave" of democratization in the 1980s and 1990s consolidated democratic regimes mainly in the richer countries of Eastern Europe, Latin America, Southern Africa, and East Asia.[16] A fourth wave would involve more challenging cases: countries that are poorer, more ethnically divided, and ideologically more resistant to democracy, with more entrenched authoritarian elites and a much frailer base of governmental institutions and citizen-skills.[17]

Many Islamic countries that figured prominently in the Bush administration's efforts to promote democracy are particularly hard cases. Although democratization in the Islamic world might contribute to peace in the very long run, Islamic public opinion in the short run is generally hostile to the United States, ambivalent about terrorism, and unwilling to renounce the use of force to regain disputed territories. Although the belligerence of the Islamic public is partly fueled by resentment of the U.S.-backed authoritarian regimes under which many of them live, renouncing these authoritarians and pressing for a quick democratic opening is unlikely to lead to peaceful democratic consolidations.[18]

On the contrary, unleashing Islamic mass opinion through sudden democratization might well raise the likelihood of war. All of the risk factors are there: the media and civil society groups are inflammatory, as old elites and rising oppositions try to outbid each other for the mantle of Islamic or nationalist militancy.[19] The rule of law is weak, and existing corrupt bureaucracies cannot serve a democratic administration properly. The boundaries of states are mismatched with those of nations, making any push for national self-determination fraught with peril. Per capita incomes, literacy rates, and citizen-skills in most Muslim Middle Eastern states are below the levels normally needed to sustain democracy.[20] The richer states' economies are based on oil exports, which exacerbate corruption and insulate regimes from accountability to citizens.

In the Arab world, every state has at least one risk factor for failed, violent democratization: Algeria, Egypt, Jordan, Morocco, the Palestinian territories, Syria, and Yemen have annual per capita national incomes under $2,000. Algeria, Egypt, Iraq, Morocco, Oman, Saudi Arabia, Tunisia, the United Arab Emirates, and Yemen have rates of illiteracy above 20 percent among adults over the age of fifteen. The best bet for democratization by these indicators is Lebanon, a state that does not produce petroleum and where illiteracy stands at 13.5 percent and the average income is $4,040. However, Lebanon is deeply divided among distrustful, armed ethnic and religious groups. Its electoral power-sharing institutions provide a rigid system for managing these divisions that locks in ethnic identity as the political trump card and prevents the formation of groups based on nonethnic platforms.

Our argument is not that Islam is culturally unsuited for democracy. Public attitude surveys in Islamic states typically record large majorities that favor democracy of some kind, including a certain segment of society that favors secular democracy and another segment that prefers religious varieties of democracy. In several non-Arab, Muslim-majority states—most notably Turkey and Indonesia—moderate Muslim parties that seem committed to democratic processes vastly outpoll antidemocratic Islamicist parties.[21] The problem is not religion and culture per se, but rather the fact that the institutional preconditions needed for democracy to function effectively have not been met in most Islamic states. Consequently, sudden increases in mass political participation are likely to be dangerous.

The theocratic, illiberal semidemocracy established by the popular Iranian Revolution, for example, relentlessly pressed the offensive in a bloody war of attrition with Iraq and supported violent movements abroad. A quarter of a century later, Iranian electoral politics still bears the imprint of incomplete democratization. Because liberal democratic reformers were barred from running for office, Iranian voters looking for a more responsive government turned in the June 2005 presidential election to the religious fundamentalist, populist mayor of Tehran, Mahmud Ahmadinejad, a staunch proponent of the Iranian nuclear program. Appeals to popular nationalism thus remain common in electoral systems that rule out liberal alternatives.

Islamic democratization is hardly the only such danger on the horizon. A future democratic opening in China, though much hoped for by advocates of human rights and democratization, could produce a sobering outcome.[22] China's Communist rulers have presided over a commercial expansion that has generated wealth and a potentially powerful constituency for broader political participation. However, given the huge socioeconomic divide between the prosperous coastal areas and the vast, impoverished hinterlands, it seems unlikely that economic development will lead as smoothly to democratic consolidation in China as it has in Taiwan. China's leadership cracked down on student pressures for democratic liberalization at Tiananmen Square in 1989, but party elites know that they will need a stronger basis of popular legitimacy to survive the social and ideological changes that economic change has unleashed.

Nationalism is a key element in their strategy. China's demand to incorporate Taiwan in the People's Republic of China, its animosity toward Japan, and its public displays of resentment at U.S. slights are themes that resonate with the Chinese public and can be used to rally national solidarity behind the regime. At the same time, newly rising social forces see that China's leaders permit more latitude to expressions of nationalism than to liberalism. Thus, some of the same intellectuals who played a role in the Tiananmen prodemocracy protests turned up a few years later as authors of a nationalist text, *The China That Can Say No.*[23]

Like many other established elites who have made use of popular nationalist rhetoric, China's party leadership has walked a fine line, allowing only limited expressions of popular nationalist outrage after such perceived provocations as the U.S. bombing of the Chinese embassy in Belgrade in 1999, anti-Chinese pogroms in Jakarta in 1998, the U.S. spy plane incident of 2001, and the Japanese bid for a permanent seat on the UN Security Council in 2005. These leaders realize that criticism of external enemies can be quickly transformed into popular criticism of the government for not being sufficiently diligent in defense of Chinese national interests. It is doubtful that they could maintain such fine-tuned control over an aroused nationalist public opinion if an incompletely democratizing China should become embroiled in a future crisis with Taiwan.

THE OXYMORON OF IMPOSED DEMOCRACY

If a country lacks the preconditions for democracy, can this infrastructure be forcefully supplied by an external source? Few would argue in favor of conquering countries simply to make them democratic, but democratic great powers—particularly Great Britain and the United States—have sometimes conquered countries for other reasons and then struggled to remake them as friendly democracies before withdrawing. Those who are nostalgic for empire view this secondary democratization as a policy with a future. Indeed, if it were not for the establishment of courts, free press, and rational public administration in British colonies, democracy would probably be scarcer in the developing world today. Most of the postcolonial states that have remained almost continuously democratic since independence—such as India and some West Indian island states—are former British possessions. Still, many former British colonies have failed to achieve democratic stability: Pakistan and Nigeria oscillate between chaotic elected regimes and military dictatorships; Sri Lanka has held elections that stoked the fires of ethnic conflict; Malaysia has averted ethnic conflict only by limiting democracy. The list continues with even more parlous cases, from Burma to Zimbabwe.

In part, this mixed result reflects the difficulty of establishing democracy anywhere the preconditions are initially lacking. However, it also reflects the counterproductive expedients of imperial rule while the institutions of democracy are being built. Until that task is completed, the empire must often govern through local elites whose legitimacy or political support is based on traditional authority or ethnic sectarianism. To retain power without devoting massive resources to the military occupation of the country, the empire plays the game of divide-and-rule, favoring some groups who help it stay in power at a manageable cost. Such short-run expedients hinder the long-run transition to stable democracy by increasing ethnic polarization. Even if the empire does not take active steps to politicize ethnicity, the act of unleashing demands for mass political participation that nascent democratic institutions are not strong enough to manage is likely to increase the risk of a polarized, violent, unsuccessful transition. British imperialists repeatedly fell prey to these dilemmas between the 1920s and 1960s, even when their intentions were benign.[24]

The United States fell into the same trap as it tried to promote democracy in the wake of military interventions. In Iraq, the United States found that it had to rely on Shi'a clerics and Kurdish ethnic nationalists in trying to create political order. In Afghanistan, as a second cousin of President Hamid Karzai put it on the eve of the violence-marred September 2005 election, the newly elected Parliament "will have tribal leaders, warlords, drug lords, but also democratic new faces and policies."[25] And this is the view of an optimist.

When outside powers have succeeded in establishing democracy by military intervention, it has usually been in countries where favorable preconditions existed, and indeed where the countries had had a history of democracy.[26] Germany and Japan enjoyed many such preconditions before U.S. troops set foot on their soil: wealth, literacy, an effective state bureaucracy, and a historical legacy of well-developed political parties. Panama was a harder case, but it nonetheless had a democratic legacy to build on. Where those conditions do not exist, the occupying power usually must resort to heavy-handed methods or rule through ethnic elites in the short run, making it difficult to peacefully navigate the initial stages of democratization. Even in the tiny countries of Bosnia and Kosovo, peace through imposed democracy seems likely to last only as long as the presence of international military forces.

BEING PATIENT AND GETTING THE SEQUENCE RIGHT

Military occupation is a costly and risky method for promoting democratization, but other kinds of inducements and pressures can be helpful. The lure of potential membership in the European Union (EU), conditioned on democratic reform and respect for minority rights, has helped to realign incentives for several multiethnic states—such as Slovakia, Croatia, Romania, and some smaller Baltic countries—that might otherwise have turned down the path toward nationalism and violence. These same incentives helped to consolidate

Turkey's democracy and improve the position of its ethnic Kurds, notwithstanding the rise to power of an Islamic party. These achievements may or may not endure if the likelihood of EU membership fades.[27] Likewise, the U.S. military umbrella and its leadership in constructing an open, stable trading system permitted states such as West Germany, Taiwan, and South Korea to create the preconditions for stable democracy although their nations were divided by the Cold War.

International democracy promoters can also take some active steps to help put in place the preconditions of democracy, but these actions need to be undertaken in the right sequence. Generally, the starting point should consist of economic reform and the development of impartial state administration.[28] Taking these steps strengthens the rule of law and provides the state with effective administrative arms that will be capable of carrying out the edicts of a democratically elected government and independent courts when these institutions come to fruition. For the most part, this was the path followed by the former British colonies that democratized successfully; by Taiwan and South Korea; and by Chile, the Latin American country that had the most successful experience with democratization.

But even if an authoritarian regime undertakes these reforms to improve its own economic and administrative performance, why would it take the next step and allow broad political competition? Normally, this next step is prompted by more than international cajoling—there also needs to be a strong domestic constituency that favors taking it. A labor movement, civil society groups, or internationally oriented business groups typically need to organize to reinforce the pressure to liberalize.[29] Professionalized, objective journalists need the freedom to evaluate the regime's policies and rhetoric.

However, this phase of open contestation should come after institutional reform has been completed, especially in multiethnic societies. Otherwise, political rivalry is likely to degenerate into ethnicity-baiting, patronage-grabbing, and election-fixing. Sometimes these outcomes are unavoidable, but democracy-promotion strategies should be sequenced to try to prevent them. The danger is not just that the transition will be messier and more violent, but also that anti-democratic groups and ideas will be mobilized and will become a long-lasting fixture on the political scene. Out-of-sequence, incomplete democratization often creates an enduring template for illiberal, populist politics: the cycling between military dictatorship and illiberal democracy in Pakistan, the theocratic populism of Iran, and ethnic tyrannies of the majority in many transitional states. These political habits, once rooted in ideologies and institutions, are hard to break. It is preferable to wait and get the process right the first time.

IN THE MEANTIME, NORMAL DIPLOMACY

While conducting a patient strategy to promote a longer-term global Democratic Peace, the United States can use the tools of diplomacy to protect its security interests in a world where nondemocracies persist. President Bush had high praise for Natan Sharansky's book *The Case of Democracy*, which argues that the Israelis should not negotiate with the Palestinians until they are a full democracy of Sweden-like perfection.[30] This is poor advice.

Diplomacy works better between democracies, but it often works well enough between democracies and nondemocracies to head off tensions and forge peace. Israel's security was immeasurably enhanced by the Camp David Accord, concluded with the undemocratic Egyptian president Anwar Sadat. Normal diplomacy can often be effective in maintaining peace between democracies and nondemocratic states, not to mention gradually reforming states. More recently, diplomacy worked without regime change to neutralize the threats from undemocratic Libya.

Rarely are matters so desperate that there is no alternative to forced-pace democracy promotion at gunpoint. It is better to be patient and get the sequence right.

GLOSSARY

Amnesty International An NGO aimed at protecting human rights by raising awareness of human rights abuses.

Antiglobalization movement A radical protest movement—which started with the 1999 anti-WTO demonstrations in Seattle—that is generally opposed to globalization. Antiglobalization activists argue that globalization tends to disproportionately benefit multinational corporations and international financial institutions, and even may be promoted by them. While many different philosophies are associated with antiglobalization, supporters of the movement generally believe that governments are working to further the interests of corporations at the expense of citizens.

Asian Development Bank A regional development bank focused on Asia and the Pacific, with aims and methods that are similar to those of the World Bank. Its goals are reducing poverty and promoting development through loans and other assistance.

Autarchy An autocratic government or a state where the government retains absolute sovereignty.

Balance of payments An economic measure of the total capital of a country's international economic transactions. This measurement includes trade and monetary transfers to both non-residents within the country and residents abroad.

Barriers to trade Government policies that restrict international trade, such as the establishment of import or export quotas or tariffs.

Bilateral aid Assistance that is given directly by one country to another.

Brain drain The migration of trained professionals from poor to rich countries, leading to a shortage of skilled technical workers or adept bureaucrats in the sending countries.

Cairo Declaration A nonbinding declaration signed in 1943 by the victorious Allies, returning territories taken by the Japanese—including Taiwan—to China. It has become a point of contention in debates over Taiwan's independent status.

Camp David Accords Agreements signed in 1978 by the leaders of Israel and Egypt, facilitated by President Jimmy Carter at Camp David. The Accords led to the Israel-Egypt Peace Treaty in 1979.

Cap-and-trade system A pollution control technique used by governments to reduce emissions by placing a cap on overall emissions and then granting to each company that produces pollutants an allowance or credit to emit that amount. Companies can then trade credits in order to keep the aggregate emissions level at the cap.

Carbon Capture and Storage (CCS) A technique that involves capturing and storing carbon emissions before they are released into the atmosphere. While it is projected that this technology could significantly reduce emissions, there is still a debate surrounding the viability of long-term carbon storage.

Cartagena Protocol An international protocol on biosafety, stating that new products and technologies must abide by the precautionary principle, and placing particular concern on genetically modified species and their effects.

Center for Disease Control and Prevention (CDC) An agency of the U.S. government that is tasked with developing methods to combat disease and promote health. Its research is used by the United States and by other entities in setting policy and in evaluating threats to both national and global health.

Clean Air Act Legislation passed by Congress in 1967 and most recently amended in 1990 that aimed to reduce air pollution by setting limits on auto and other emissions. The most recent amendments included provisions for dealing with acid rain and proposed emissions-trading programs.

Clean Development Mechanism (CDM) A provision of the Kyoto Protocol that allows industrialized countries to fund emissions reductions in developing countries rather than in their own countries where it would be more expensive. In order to qualify under this provision, the emissions-reduction project must be unachievable without the aid or funding of the industrialized country.

Commission of the European Communities The executive branch of the European Union, now known as the European Commission.

Comparative advantage An economic theory holding that countries should devote their resources to only the outputs that they produce most efficiently and should gain all other products through trade. The theory states that if every country specializes, all countries will gain through trade.

Crimes against humanity Crimes committed systematically against a civilian population—including, but not limited to, murder, enslavement, and apartheid.

Cultural Revolution A period of power struggles within China from 1966 to the mid-1970s, during which a campaign to eliminate the "four olds"—old customs, old culture, old habits, and old ideas—led to gross violations of human rights, the death of many Chinese citizens (particularly intellectuals), and the destruction of many important artifacts of Chinese culture and history. The activity of the Revolution was mainly carried out by the Red Guards, groups of young Chinese who were told that it was their duty to combat the "four olds," but who ultimately ended up beyond of the control of the Communist Party.

Cyberterrorism An attack against a computer or network with the intent to cause harm, in order to achieve political or ideological ends.

De minimus rule A rule that determines whether something is to minimal to be worth notice. In legal terms, it refers to something not worth the concerns of the law.

Democratic peace The view that democracies are more peaceful than non-democracies, especially towards other democracies.

Direct Foreign Investment (DFI) Investment in one country's industries by a company that is based in another country.

Dirigisme An economy directed by the government or with heavy government participation. Such economies can be capitalist or socialist, and most modern economies contain some level of dirigisme.

Ecoterrorism The use or threat of violence to advance an environmental agenda, such as sinking whaling ships. As with more general types of terrorism, the exact definition of this phenomenon remains highly debated.

Emissions trading (see cap-and-trade system)

Enlightenment, the A new political ideology that emerged in Europe in the eighteenth century, based on the belief that human progress was possible through the systematic application of reason. Gaining credence during a time of optimism and concern for the rights of the individual, its principles heavily influenced the drafting of both the U.S. Constitution and the French Declaration of the Rights of Man and of the Citizen.

Environmental Protection Agency (EPA) A U.S. federal government agency that is charged with the protection of the environment and the nation's health. The EPA sets and enforces national environmental standards.

European Court of Justice The European Union's highest court.

Failed state A state where the central government no longer has effective control over the territory within its borders. The degree of control that must be retained by the government to avoid this status is highly debated.

Fossil fuels Fuels derived from hydrocarbons, often petroleum, coal, or natural gases. These fuels are a nonrenewable resource, and their use produces greenhouse gases.

Free trade A system of trade that is free from government-imposed barriers (see barriers to trade).

Gender Empowerment Measure (GEM) A scale for determining the level of inequality between men and women, using both economic and political factors.

General Agreement on Trade and Tariffs (GATT) The international organization for the regulation of trade policy from 1948 until it was replaced by the WTO in 1995.

Geneva Conventions A group of treaties drawn up in Geneva, Switzerland, all four of which address the rights of prisoners of war and noncombatants. The Conventions have been ratified by almost every nation.

Genocide Acts committed to intentionally eliminate an ethnic, religious, national, or racial group. This phenomenon was recognized internationally as a crime in 1948.

Gini coefficient A ratio used to measure inequality of income distribution between 0 and 1, where 0 is perfect equality and 1 is perfect inequality.

Greenhouse gases (GHG) Gases in the earth's atmosphere that cause the greenhouse effect, warming the earth's temperatures. Some of these gases—such as carbon dioxide—are naturally present in the atmosphere, but emissions from the use of fossil fuels have drastically increased their concentrations, causing global warming.

Greenpeace An NGO aimed at preventing environmental harm and promoting behaviors and technology to protect the Earth.

Green revolution The spread of advanced agricultural technologies from developed to developing countries, allowing many of those countries to become major agricultural exporters and increasing food security.

Gross Domestic Product (GDP) A measure of a country's output—or goods and services produced—within any given year. It is derived by adding the following components: consumption, investment, government spending, and the balance of trade. GDP is an important gauge of a country's standard of living and economic health.

Gross Fixed Capital Formation (GFC) A measure of a country's spending on physical infrastructure.

Gross National Product (GNP) A measure that includes the same components as GDP, but also adds income from citizens abroad and subtracts income from foreigners working within the country. GNP is also an indicator of economic health.

Group of 77 (G77) A group of developing nations formed in 1964 to advocate for the collective economic interests of its members. The group now includes 130 nations.

Group of 8 (G8) A group of 8 states—Canada, France, Germany, Italy, Japan, Russia, the United Kingdom, and the United States—and the EU whose annual summit is meant to serve as a forum for issues of global or mutual concern and as a way for its member countries to pool resources and share information.

Hegemony The domination or heavy influence of one country over others.

Heuristics Rule of thumb to guide decision making.

Humanitarian intervention The interference, usually militarily, by one or more states in another state, with the express purpose of ending a humanitarian crisis and aiding the civilian population of that state.

Import substitution A technique for reducing dependency on foreign goods, whereby the government promotes internal production of important goods rather than relying on imports.

Internally displaced person (IDP) An individual who has been forced from his/her home, but has remained within his/her country's borders, and therefore is not classified as a refugee.

International Atomic Energy Agency (IAEA) An independent international organization established in 1957 to promote the peaceful use of nuclear technology and end its use as a weapon. Though independent, the IAEA reports to both the UN General Assembly and the Security Council.

International Criminal Court (ICC) A tribunal established in 2002 as a forum to prosecute perpetrators of genocide and other crimes against humanity. A total of 108 countries have signed on to the Rome Statute establishing the ICC, though China, the United States, and India are among the prominent nations that have not signed.

International Criminal Police Organization (INTERPOL) An international agency founded to facilitate cooperation among national police agencies to combat international crime. INTERPOL remains politically neutral, only involving itself in crimes that concern two or more of its member countries and that do not have a political, military, religious, or racial nature.

International Monetary Fund (IMF) An international financial institution that, like the World Bank, offers loans and technical assistance. The IMF, however, focuses not only on development, but also on stable exchange markets and international monetary cooperation.

Intergovernmental Panel on Climate Change (IPCC) A panel established by the World Meteorological Organization and the United Nations Environmental Programme in order to provide policy-neutral scientific reports to aid governments in addressing climate change and to provide information for the United Nations Framework Convention on Climate Change.

Iranian Revolution The 1979 revolution that deposed the shah of Iran and instated Ayatollah Ruhollah Khomeini as the leader of Iran as an Islamic republic.

Joint Chiefs of Staff A group of the chiefs of each branch of the U.S. military—the army, navy, Marine Corps, and air force—that is tasked with unifying strategy and insuring integration of the branches, as well as advising the president in his role as commander-in-chief.

Joint United Nations Programme on HIV/AIDS A program started by the United Nations Economic and Social Council in 1996 to facilitate collaboration between governments and private entities in combating the AIDS epidemic.

Kant, Immanuel An 18th century philosopher, born in Germany, who tried to balance empiricism and rationalism in his work. He believed that constitutional republics were necessary to bring about world peace (see Democratic Peace).

Khmer Rouge The political party, led by Pol Pot, that ruled Cambodia from 1975 to 1979 and derived its philosophy from a number of nations' communist parties. It was responsible for the deaths of 1.5 million of its citizens.

Kyoto Protocol An agreement reached under the United Nations Framework Convention on Climate Change in which the signatories agreed to either reduce greenhouse-gas emissions or to practice emissions trading if they found themselves unable to do so on their own. The only industrialized country that did not ratify the protocol is the United States.

League of Nations An international organization replaced by the United Nations in 1946. As a significant component of U.S. President Woodrow Wilson's Fourteen Points for Peace, it was intended to prevent and resolve conflict by providing a forum for international negotiation.

Maastricht Treaty The treaty, signed in 1992, that created the European Union and laid the groundwork for the adoption of the euro.

Marshall Plan A plan created by the United States to provide financial aid to rebuild Europe following World War II.

Millennium Development Goals (MDGs) Eight objectives—covering issues such as eradicating poverty and promoting development, protecting the environment, promoting human rights and democracy, meeting the special needs of Africa, and strengthening the United Nations—that were developed at the Millennium Summit in 2000. The UN member nations have pledged to try to achieve these goals by 2015.

Molotov-Von Ribbentrop pact A treaty of nonaggression between Nazi Germany and the USSR signed in 1939. Germany invaded the Soviet Union in 1941, ending the pact.

Monterrey Consensus An agreement signed by numerous countries, as well as the heads of the UN, IMF, World Bank, and WTO, concerning international cooperation to promote development.

Montreal Protocol An international treaty, established in 1989, aimed at protecting the ozone layer by limiting the use and production of harmful substances such as chlorofluorocarbons (CFCs).

Multilateral aid Relief assistance from many countries or sources, usually distributed through an organization such as the World Bank or the IMF.

Multinational corporation A corporation that operates in numerous countries and often has significant economic influence.

Neoclassical economics A school of thought—focused on supply and demand as they affect prices and outputs—that influences most mainstream economics. Rational choice theory forms the basis of many of its models.

New Partnership for African Development (NEPAD) An African Union program that is aimed at facilitating economic cooperation between African countries, with the aim of promoting African development.

Nongovernmental organization (NGO) An organization that is legally independent from any government, although it can be a recipient of government funds. No government representative may be a member of an NGO.

Non-refoulement A principle of international law that protects refugees from being returned to a country where their lives would be in danger or their rights would be violated.

North American Free Trade Agreement (NAFTA) A trade bloc formed by Canada, Mexico, and the United States, allowing free trade between the three countries. It has been debated whether NAFTA has had an overall positive effect or if it has harmed the countries involved, particularly Mexico.

North Atlantic Treaty Organization (NATO) A military alliance formed in 1949 between Belgium, Canada, Denmark, France, Iceland, Italy, Luxembourg, the Netherlands, Norway, Portugal, the United Kingdom, and the United States in order to check the Soviet Union.

Nuclear Nonproliferation Treaty (NPT) A treaty signed in 1968 to limit the proliferation of nuclear weapons. It is considered to have three principles: non-proliferation, disarmament, and the right to peaceful use of nuclear technology.

Official Development Assistance (ODA) A type of development aid that is given to developing countries by OECD member states.

Organization for Economic Cooperation and Development (OECD) An international organization composed of the world's principal industrialized countries. It serves primarily as a policy think tank for these governments.

Outsourcing The practice of hiring an outside company to perform a function, such as manufacturing, that is traditionally performed by the original company. The second company is frequently based in another country and can perform the same tasks either more cheaply or more efficiently. Labor in the original country fears job loss from outsourcing.

Oxfam An NGO aimed at combating poverty and injustice. Originally, Oxfam was solely concerned with famine relief, but the organization has developed a much broader focus in order to deal with the root causes of famine.

P5 The five permanent members of the United Nations Security Council—China, France, Russia, the United Kingdom, and the United States—which are the only members to have veto powers.

Planned Parenthood An NGO, originally based in the United States, that has created an international network of NGOs tasked with providing reproductive health services and promoting reproductive rights.

Precautionary principle The rule that the burden of proof concerning the effects of a new technology falls upon those introducing it. In the absence of scientific proof that the technology will do no harm, the society should prevent its introduction.

President's Emergency Plan For AIDS Relief (PEPFAR) A U.S. federal government program initiated in 2003 to provide antiretroviral drugs to those infected with HIV/AIDS in fifteen countries with high rates of infection and limited resources. The program was designed to promote the ABC ideology (Abstain, Be faithful, and use Condoms), and to fund AIDS research. The focus on abstinence-only programs has been criticized as a moral choice rather than one that is crafted in the interests of public health.

Prima facie A term usually used in legal proceedings to refer to evidence that is sufficient to prove the fact or argument in question, barring rebuttal.

Protectionism A government policy aimed at protecting domestic industry by restricting imports by means of barriers such as tariffs or quotas or by providing subsidies.

Purchasing power parity A measure of how much can be bought with a particular currency.

Rio Declaration on Environment and Development A United Nations document outlining principles to inform future sustainable development. The twenty-seven principles include the eradication of poverty, priority for the least developed, the important role of indigenous peoples, the precautionary principle, and the right to state sovereignty concerning resources and national policy.

Rotary International The umbrella organization for various chapters known as Rotary Clubs, aimed at promoting humanitarianism and ethics among business and professional leaders.

Sovereignty The right, in international law, of a country's government to control its own domestic affairs without intervention or direct interference from other countries. This right, which is considered integral to many of the principles of international law, can also complicate international intervention in cases of failed states and/or humanitarian crisis.

Status quo bias The principle that an individual is predisposed to prefer the status quo and will work harder to keep it from changing.

Terrorism A concept whose definition is a controversial issue in international law. Generally, it is agreed that terrorism involves criminal acts intended to provoke fear and intimidate a population or government in order to achieve political ends. Whether a state can commit an act of terrorism is highly debated.

Trade deficit A negative balance of trade, produced when the net value of imports exceeds the net value of exports—the deficit country then owes the difference to the surplus country. A positive balance of trade is known as a trade surplus.

Trade liberalization The removal of trade barriers in order to move closer to free trade.

Tragedy of the commons A classic problem in game theory that is often used as a metaphor for the overexploitation of resources whose use is not regulated. The inherent conflict is between the common good and the motivation for each individual entity to take or use as much of the resource as possible without regard for the needs of others or the long-term sustainability of that resource.

Transnational Action Networks An international organization or coalition of independent NGOs that share a similar vision or goals.

UNAIDS (see Joint United Nations Programme on HIV/AIDS.)

United Nations Charter The 1945 treaty that established the United Nations and outlined the principles of the organization and powers given to it.

United Nations Children's Fund (UNICEF) An organization that provides assistance to children and mothers in developing countries. It is entirely funded by voluntary contributions from UN member nations and private donors.

United Nations Development Fund for Women (UNIFEM) A UN fund created to promote the human rights of women and gender equality.

United Nations Development Group (UNDG) A division of the UN created in 1997 to reform and improve the effectiveness of UN development programs. The UN's other development funds are members of the group.

United Nations Development Programme (UNDP) A UN organization that provides development assistance to developing nations in the form of grants, advice, and other assistance. The UNDP focuses on factors such as democratic governance and poverty reduction in promoting development.

United Nations Education, Scientific, and Cultural Organization (UNESCO) An agency of the UN that is aimed at promoting international cooperation in areas of education, science, and culture—reflecting a core belief that world peace can be fostered through education and cultural familiarity. UNESCO contributes to achieving the Millennium Development Goals.

United Nations Framework Convention on Climate Change (UNFCCC) An international treaty, which contains the provisions for the Kyoto Protocol, aimed at reducing emissions to stabilize greenhouse-gas levels.

United Nations High Commissioner for Refugees (UNHCR) A UN agency tasked with coordinating international efforts to protect refugees and ensuring that their rights are protected.

United Nations Population Fund (UNFPA) An international organization that provides funding for population and reproductive health programs and is particularly concerned with ending unwanted pregnancy, unsafe birth, and the spread of HIV/AIDS, as well as promoting the equality of and respect for women.

Universal Declaration of Human Rights (UDHR) A declaration passed by the UN General Assembly in 1948, detailing the human rights recognized in international law. Articles include the right to life, the right to be presumed innocent until proven guilty, and the right to freedom of movement within a nation's borders.

Veto powers The ability—given only to the five permanent members of the Security Council (see P5)—to prevent, by a single negative vote, the passage of a nonprocedural decision of the Security Council.

Von Bismarck, Otto The first chancellor of the second German Empire. Also known as the Iron Chancellor, he was largely responsible for the unification of Germany. Both his domestic and his foreign policy strategies have continued to inform international politics and theory since his death in 1898.

Warlordism A situation occurring in failed states where rival warlords, rather than the central government, have de facto control over various parts of the country.

Westphalian state A nation that retains its sovereignty based on the principles of territoriality and the governance of domestic affairs free from external actors. This concept of sovereignty is traced back to the Peace of Westphalia in 1648, but the term is currently used to describe the modern nation-state.

World Bank The International Bank for Reconstruction and Development and the International Development Association, created after World War II to provide financial and development assistance to developing countries.

World Health Organization (WHO) An agency of the United Nations that combats disease and promotes international health.

World Trade Organization (WTO) An international organization that succeeded the General Agreement on Tariffs and Trade (GATT) as the international body responsible for supervising and liberalizing international trade between its member nations.

Worldwide Fund for Nature (WWF) An NGO aimed at promoting conservation and protecting the environment. It mostly focuses on three types of habitats: forest, freshwater ecosystems, and oceans and coastal ecosystems.

Xenophobia The fear or distrust of that which is foreign. It is often coupled with a belief in the superiority of one's homeland over other cultures or countries.

NOTES

INTRODUCTION: Understanding Globalization

1. "Global Capital Flows," *Finance & Development*, March 2007, 14.
2. See http://www.uia.be/yearbook.
3. See also Held and McGrew 2007, 187–189.
4. See http://www.mdgmonitor.org/.
5. See http://hdr.undp.org/en/.
6. *The Economist*, June 30, 2007, 31.
7. *The Economist*, July 26, 2008, 34.

CHAPTER 1: Trade Liberalization and Economic Growth

YES

1. Views expressed are those of the author and do not necessarily represent official views of the World Bank.
2. It is difficult to take the survey-based estimates of poverty back before 1980. Bourguignon and Morrison (2002) combine what survey data are available with national accounts data to provide rough estimates of poverty back to 1820. The broad trend is clear: The number of poor in the world kept rising up to about 1980.

NO

1. I thank Diana Weinhold, Brian Hindley, Razeen Sally, and Manfred Bienefeld for good discussions.
2. Seminar at London School of Economics, April 30, 2008.
3. Jagdish Bhagwati, "Rethinking Trade Strategy," in *Development Strategies Reconsidered*, ed. J. Lewis and V. Kallab (New Brunswick, N.J.: Transaction Books), 93. In "The Free Trade Consensus Lives On" (*Financial Times*, October 10, 2007), Bhagwati recently reiterated the point: "Turn to the leading U.S. newspapers these days and you will read the ... 'loss of faith' in free trade by economists. ... The truth of the matter is that free trade is alive and well among economists."
4. Bruno Frey, W. Pommerehne, F. Schneider, and G. Gilbert, "Consensus and Dissensus among Economists: An Empirical Inquiry," *American Economic Review* 74 (1984): 986–994.

5. World Bank, "Strengthening Trade Policy Reform" (Washington, D.C.: World Bank, November 13, 1989).

6. Erik Reinert, "Globalisation in the Periphery as a Morgenthau Plan: The Underdevelopment of Mongolia in the 1990s," in *Globalization, Economic Development and Inequality: An Alternative Perspective*, ed. Erik Reinert (Cheltenham, U.K.: Edward Elgar, 2004).

7. From a participant who requested anonymity.

8. Martin Wolf, *Why Globalization Works* (New Haven, Conn.: Yale University Press, 2004), 4, emphasis added.

9. This essay is limited to the trade policy–production structure–economic prosperity links, with reference primarily to (a) national economies as the unit and (b) developing countries facing the challenge of catch-up growth. It does not go into the literature on the impact of trade on income and wealth distribution, or that on the impact of rich country trade policy on developing countries. The essay avoids the effects of trade liberalization on public revenues, as well as the contentious subject of exchange rate regimes and the absence of international coordination of exchange rates, even though exchange rates are directly relevant to trade policy and trade flows. For an idiosyncratic and entertaining discussion of some of these issues, see Edward Leamer, "A Flat World, a Level Playing Field, and Small World After All, or None of the Above? A Review of Thomas L. Friedman's *The World Is Flat*," *Journal of Economic Literature* 45 (March 2007): 83–126. For a World Bank argument substantially more nuanced than anything the Bank has said about trade policy for decades, see World Bank, *Economic Growth in the 1990s*, Washington, D.C., 2005, chap. 5.

10. *Financial Times*, "Free Trade's Best Defence is the Truth," editorial, July 25, 2006.

11. For example, I. Little et al., *Industry and Trade in Some Developing Countries* (London: Oxford University Press, 1970); A. Kreuger, *Foreign Trade Regimes and Economic Development: Liberalization Attempts and Consequences* (Cambridge: Ballinger, 1978); J. Bhagwati, *Foreign Trade Regimes and Economic Development: Anatomy and Consequences of Exchange Control Regimes* (Cambridge: Ballinger, 1978); B. Balassa and Associates, *Development Strategies in Semi Industrial Economies* (Baltimore: Johns Hopkins University Press, for the World Bank, 1982); World Bank, *World Development Report 1987* (Washington, D.C.: World Bank, 1987), chap. 5; Armeane Choksi, Michael Michaely, and Demetris Papageorgiou, *Liberalizing Foreign Trade* (Oxford: Blackwell, 1989), vols. 1 and 7; World Bank, *Best Practices in Trade Policy Reform* (New York: Oxford University Press, 1991); World Bank, *World Development Report 1991* (Washington, D.C.: World Bank, 1991), chap. 5; J. Sachs and A. Warner, "Economic Reforms and the Process of Global Integration," *Brookings Papers on Economic Activity* 1 (1995), 1–118, Brookings Institution; World Bank, *Building an Inclusive World Economy*, 2002.

12. World Bank, *Globalization, Growth, and Poverty*, 50.

13. See Ian Little, *Economic Development: Theory, Policy and International Relations* (New York: Basic Books, 1982). For counterarguments, see Robert Wade,

Governing the Market: Economic Theory and the Role of Government in East Asian Industrialization, chap. 12 (Princeton, N.J.: Princeton University Press, 2004).

14. See "Symposium on Infant Industries," contributions by Adrian Wood, John Roberts, Robert Wade, Sanjaya Lall, *Oxford Economic Papers* 31, no. 1 (2003): 3–20.

15. E. Helpman and P. Krugman, *Market Structure and Trade* (Cambridge, Mass.: MIT Press, 1985); G. Grossman and E. Helpman, *Innovation and Growth in the World Economy* (Cambridge, Mass.: MIT Press, 1991); P. Romer, "Endogenous Technological Change," *Journal of Political Economy* 98 (1990): 71–102.

16. M. Melitz, "The Impact of Trade on Intraindustry Reallocations and Aggregate Industry Productivity," *Econometrica* 71 (2003): 1695–1725; A. Bernard, J.B. Jensen, S. Redding, and P. Schott, "Firms in International Trade," *Journal of Economic Perspectives* 21, no. 3 (Summer 2007); R. Baldwin and F. Robert-Nicoud, "Trade and Growth with Heterogeneous Firms," CEP Discussion Paper 727, Centre for Economic Performance, London School of Economics, June 2006.

17. Paul Krugman, "Is Free Trade Passé?" *Journal of Economic Perspectives* 1 (1987): 143.

18. Alan Goodacre, "What Would Post-Autistic Trade Policy Be?" *Post-Autistic Economics Review* 41 (March 2007), 2–8; Thomas Palley, "Rethinking Trade and Trade Policy: Gomery, Baumol and Samuelson on Comparative Advantage," Levy Economics Institute, Public Policy Brief 86, 2006.

19. R. Gomery and W. Baumol, *Global Trade and Conflicting National Interests* (Cambridge, Mass.: MIT Press, 2000); P. Krugman and A. Venables, "Globalisation and the Inequality of Nations," *Quarterly Journal of Economics* 110 (1995): 857–880; A. Thrilwall and P. Pacheco-Lopez, *Trade Liberalisation and the Poverty of Nations* (Cheltenham, U.K.: Edward Elgar, 2008).

20. On Liechtenstein, see Eric Pfanner, "Liechtenstein Works to Move Beyond Tax Feud," *New York Times*, February 23, 2008.

21. For a non-technical discussion of this argument, see Ha-Joon Chang, *Bad Samaritans* (London: Random House, 2007), chap. 3.

22. Gregory Hook, "The Rise of the Pentagon and U.S. State Building: The Defense Program as Industrial Policy," *American Journal of Sociology* 96, no. 2 (1990): 358–404.

23. Robert Wade, "Goodbye Doha, Hello New Trade Round," *Challenge*, November–December 2006, 14–19.

24. Paul Samuelson, "Where Ricardo and Mill Rebut and Confirm Arguments of Mainstream Economists Supporting Globalization," *Journal of Economic Perspectives* 18 (2004).

25. Jennifer Mbabzi, Oliver Morissey, and Chris Milner, "The Fragility of Empirical Links between Inequality, Trade Liberalization, Growth and Poverty," in *Perspectives on Growth and Poverty*, ed. Rolph van der Hoeven and Anthony Shorrocks Tokyo: United Nations University Press, 2003), at 113 and 137.

26. Banerjee, Abhijit, Angus Deaton, Nora Lustig, and Ken Rogoff, "An Evaluation of World Bank Research, 1998-2005," World Bank, 2006, 53–56, www.tinyurl.com/yck7wc.

27. R. Hausmann, L. Pritchett, and D. Rodrik, "Growth Accelerations," *Journal of Economic Growth* 10 (2005): 303–329; Charles Sabel, "Bootstrapping Development: Rethinking the Role of Public Intervention in Promoting Growth," Columbia University Law School, November 2005.

28. J. Imbs and R. Wacziarg, "Stages of Diversification," *American Economic Review* 93, no. 1 (March 2003): 63–86, discussed in Dani Rodrik, "Industrial Policy for the Twenty-first Century," Kennedy School of Government, Harvard University, September 2004. See also Jane Jacobs, *Cities and the Wealth of Nations* (New York: Viking, 1984).

29. Robert Wade, "Industrial Policy in East Asia: Does It Lead or Follow the Market?" in *Manufacturing Miracles: Paths of Industrialization in Latin America and East Asia*, ed. Gary Gereffi and Donald Wyman (Princeton, N.J.: Princeton University Press, 1990).

30. Robert Wade, "Economic Liberalism and the 'Outward Alliance' of State, Finance and Big Companies: A Perspective from the United Kingdom," in *National Perspectives on Globalization*, ed. Paul Bowles et al., Basingstoke, UK: Palgrave, 2007), 154–173.

31. Paul Bairoch, *Economics and World History: Myths and Paradoxes* (Chicago: University of Chicago Press, 1993), 30. Also, Chang, *Bad Samaritans*.

32. Robert Wade, "Managing Trade," *Comparative Politics* 25, no. 2 (1993); Wade, *Governing the Market*, 2004, chap. 5; Alice Amsden, *Asia's Next Giant* (Oxford: Oxford University Press, 1989); Ha-Joon Chang, *Kicking Away the Ladder* (London: Anthem Press, 2002).

33. See Albert Fishlow, Catherine Gwin, Stephan Haggard, Dani Rodrik, and Robert Wade, *Miracle or Design? Lessons from the East Asian Experience* (Washington, D.C.: Overseas Development Council, 1994).

34. See further, UNDP, *Making Global Trade Work for People*, Earthscan, 2003; Amit Bhaduri, "Toward the Optimum Degree of Openness," in *Putting Development First*, ed. Kevin Gallagher (London: Zed, 2005).

35. On the economic institutions of primacy, see Robert Wade, "Globalization as the Institutionalization of Neoliberalism: Commodification, Financialization, and the Anchorless Economy," in *Institutions and Market Economies: The Political Economy of Growth and Development*, ed. William Garside, Basingstoke, UK: Palgrave, 2007); Wade, "The Invisible Hand of the American Empire," *Ethics and International Affairs* 17, no. 2 (2003).

36. The A/B comparison comes from Dani Rodrik, "The Global Governance of Trade as if Development Really Mattered," in *One Economics, Many Recipes* (Princeton, N.J.: Princeton University Press, 2007).

37. See Kuen Lee, John Mathews, and Robert Wade, "Rethinking Development Policy: From Washington Consensus to Beijing-Seoul-Tokyo Consensus," ft.com, October 19, 2007.

38. Wade, *Governing the Market*, chaps. 5, 6, 9; Richard Luedde-Neurath, *Import Controls and Export-oriented Development: A Reassessment of the South Korean Case* (Boulder, Colo.: Westview, 1986).

39. A recent World Bank report acknowledges that the Bank gave excessive emphasis to trade liberalization during the 1990s. World Bank, *Economic Growth in the 1990s: Learning from a Decade of Reform*, 2005.

CHAPTER 2: Trade and Equality

1. Nicholas D. Kristof, "In Praise of the Maligned Sweatshop," *New York Times*, June 6, 2006.

YES

1. For example, see McCulloch, Winters, and Cirera 2001; Winters 2002; and Winters, McCulloch, and McKay 2004, on all of which I draw freely. Winters 2006 offers an accessible account of the field, and Winters 2007 provides a collection of economic readings on the subject.
2. Milanovic also shows that our view of the degree of inequality and changes in it over time depend strongly on the following: the index of inequality that we use (that is, how we value one income against another); the prices we use to value different elements of consumption (haircuts and piano lessons are cheap in China but not in the United States); and the source of our income data—household surveys (Milanovic's preference) or national income accounts (as, for example, in Bhalla 2005). I shall not discuss these issues here, but when considering contributions to the debate, they must be taken into account.
3. A simple example helps. Two countries have incomes per head of $1,000 and $10,000, respectively, so that the max/min ratio (one measure of inequality) is 10. If both grow by 50 percent to $1,500 and $15,000, the ratio remains 10. Note, however, that the absolute gap has increased from $9,000 to $13,500. Such absolute inequality almost always increases with income growth, but it is not the concept we commonly use.
4. This question is often expressed as "Is openness good for growth?" but growth is the change in income, not the level. The evidence suggests that openness raises the level of income but does not boost growth permanently, although, of course, increasing openness (liberalization) will lead to increasing income (growth) as the economy converges to the higher level of income commensurate with its greater openness; see Winters 2004.
5. If income is very unequally distributed, there will be only a relatively small proportion of households whose income is, say, 5 percent below the poverty line. Thus, if growth increases everyone's income by 5 percent, only a relatively small number of these households are pulled up over the line. If, on the other hand, income distribution is very concentrated, but the average is still low enough to reflect significant poverty, a large share of households will be just below the line and thus will be pulled above it by an increase in all incomes. Imagine two economies, each with one hundred households whose incomes are spread evenly over a range. The unequal society might have a range of $50 to $150—basically one household for

every dollar of the distribution. If the poverty line is $100, there are only five households with incomes between $95 and $100, which would be pulled above $100 by 5 percent growth. The more equal society might have all its households in the range of $90 to $115—four households per dollar, or twenty in the range $95 to $100. Here, 5 percent growth will pull twenty households over the poverty line.

6. The informal sector is, loosely speaking, that part of the economy that is not registered, pays no tax, and provides no benefits for workers apart from wages. It is typically comprised of single-person or very small enterprises, such as selling cigarettes on the sidewalk.

NO

1. Barro 2000. Also, Cornia, Addison, and Kiistki (2004) report a positive effect on growth as the Gini coefficient increases from very low levels (from the .15 typical of subsistence economies and of the former socialist economies to .30) and a negative effect as the Gini coefficient rises from .45 (typical in Latin America and sub-Saharan Africa) to higher levels. The $3,200 is in purchasing power parity terms, in 2005.
2. This result is known as the Stolper-Samuelsen theorem.
3. Easterly 2004. Also see, among many others, Milanovic and Squire 2005; Lindert and Williamson 2001; Stiglitz 2002; and Wade 2004.
4. Cuba, China, and Kerala in India are exceptions; see Birdsall 2005.
5. For a menu of fair growth policies and their application in Latin America, see Birdsall, de la Torre, and Menezes 2007.
6. Birdsall (2005) refers to Bardhan 2004 on this idea.

CHAPTER 3: Poverty

YES

1. The Monterrey Consensus of the International Conference on Financing for Development, http://www.un.org/esa/sustdev/documents/Monterrey_Consensus.htm.
2. William Easterly, *The White Man's Burden* (New York: Penguin, 2006), 368–369.
3. Paragraph 41 in Monterrey Consensus.
4. Jeffrey Sachs, *The End of Poverty* (New York: Penguin, 2005).
5. General George Marshall, speech at Harvard University, June 5, 1947.

NO

1. *Washington Times,* April 26, 2007, A14.
2. *London Mail and Guardian,* June 29, 2007.
3. *Daily Graphic,* July 24, 2004, 16.
4. *The Namibian,* November 24, 2006; http://www.namibian.com.na.

5. *New York Times*, February 4, 1996, A4.

6. *London Independent*, June 14, 2002; www. independent.co.uk.

7. *The Economist*, survey, January 17, 2004, 12.

8. *This Day* [Lagos], December 4, 2003.

9. http://nigeriaworld.com/columnist/laoluakande/articles.html.

10. *Vanguard* [Lagos], August 6, 2004; www.allafrica.com.

11. *London Telegraph*, June 25, 2005.

12. *Post Express*, July 10, 2000.

13. *New York Times*, August 30, 2000, A10.

14. *West Africa*, May 11, 1987, 912.

15. *Washington Times*, November 8, 1999, A16.

16. *Washington Post*, March 3, 2002, A20.

17. *London Observer*, September 30, 2001.

18. *Africa Recovery*, January 2004, 16.

19. *Financial Post*, May 10, 1999.

20. *Washington Post*, May 1, 2005, A18.

21. *The East African*, June 14, 1999.

22. *Washington Post*, June 6, 2008, A20.

CHAPTER 4: Emerging Technology and Political Institutions

1. Daniel Kahneman and Amos Tversky, "Prospect Theory: An Analysis of Decisions under Risk," *Econometrica* 47 (1979): 313–327.

2. *New York Times*, July 25, 2008, C4.

CHAPTER 5: Terrorism and Security

YES

1. Such a "gun-type" device, weighing over 500 kg, consists of four elements: a "gun" that shoots a "uranium bullet" from one end of a "rail" to a "uranium target" at the other end. Neither the bullet nor the target has enough Uranium-235 to generate a chain reaction, but when they are slammed together, a "critical mass" is achieved that is sufficient for a nuclear explosion. According to physicist Richard Garwin, who built America's first hydrogen bomb, the minimum "fizzle bomb" needed to do serious damage is estimated to be about one kiloton, and it could be fabricated in a small apartment. The effective distances within which (roughly speaking) all the people die and all those outside survive are shown in the table on page 430.

   As Garwin notes: "Although a country would not be destroyed by such an explosion, it could ruin itself by its reaction." Richard Garwin, "Nuclear and Biological Megaterrorism," Report to the 27th Session of the International

Summary of ranges for significant effects (in meters).

Yield (kt)	(a)*	(b)*	(c)*	(d)*
1	275	610	790	5500
10	590	1800	1200	9600

a* Range for 50% mortality from air blast (m)
b* Range for 50% mortality from thermal burns (m)
c* Range for 4 Gy initial nuclear radiation (m)
d* Range for 4 Gy fallout in first hour after blast (m) (downwind)

　　Seminars on Planetary Emergencies, World Federation of Scientists, Erice, Italy, August 21, 2002, http://www.fas.org:rlg/020821-terrorism.htm; and personal communication, February 11, 2005.

2. The *National Intelligence Estimate*'s key judgments are available online at http://www.dni.gov/press_releases/20070717_release.pdf.

3. Katherine Shrader and Matthew Lee, "Al-Qaida Plots New Attacks on U.S. Soil," *Associated Press wire*, July 17, 2007, http://apnews.myway.com/article/20070717/D8QEKKBG1.html.

4. A "sleeper" is a planted agent who lives a normal life in the host country until activated years later. The only sleeper in America over the past century was Soviet Colonel Vilyam Fisher (aka Rudolf Abel) who was arrested in the late 1950s and exchanged in 1962 for CIA spy pilot Francis Gary Powers (shot down over the USSR and captured in May 1960). Former counterterrorism czar Richard Clarke (*Against All Enemies: Inside America's War* [New York: Free Press, 2004]) and former CIA director George Tenet (*At the Center of the Storm: My Years at the CIA* [New York: HarperCollins, 2007]) continue to claim that the U.S. is awash in sleeper cells—a sentiment that is widely echoed in the media: "The law of averages would indicate the near certainty of sleeper cells in the United States," according to Arnaud de Bourchave, "Terror Wars: The Missing Sleeper Cells," *United Press International* (online), May 3, 2007.

5. German Interior Minister Wolfgang Schaeuble in an interview with *Der Spiegel*, July 9, 2009, http://www.spiegel.de/international/germany/0,1518,493364,00.html.

6. Alan Krueger, *What Makes a Terrorist: Economics and the Roots of Terrorism* (Princeton, N.J.: Princeton University Press, 2007).

7. Robert Pape, *Dying to Win: The Strategic Logic of Suicide Terrorism* (Chicago: University of Chicago Press, 2005).

8. (B = .08, SE = .03, t = 2.69, P = .007).

9. (B = .06, SE = .02, t = 3.05, P = .002).

10. (B = .07, SE = .02, t = 3.25, P = .001).

11. Marc Sageman, *Leaderless Jihad* (Philadelphia: University of Pennsylvania Press, 2007).

NO

1. This article updates, develops, and draws upon material in Mueller 2006.

CHAPTER 6: Nuclear Weapons

1. Kenneth Waltz, "The Spread of Nuclear Weapons: More May Better," *Adelphi Papers* no. 171 (London: International Institute for Strategic Studies, 1981).

YES

1. Steven Kull, "Public Opinion in Iran and America on Key International Issues," WorldPublicOpinion.org, January 24, 2007.
2. David E. Sanger, "Suppose We Just Let Iran Have the Bomb," *New York Times*, March 19, 2006.
3. Kenneth N. Waltz, "More May Be Better," in Scott D. Sagan and Kenneth N. Waltz, *The Spread of Nuclear Weapons: A Debate Renewed* (New York: Norton, 2003), 3–45; Martin van Creveld, *Nuclear Proliferation and the Future of Conflict* (New York: Free Press, 1993), 122–124; Sumit Ganguly and Devin T. Hagerty, *Fearful Symmetry: India-Pakistan Crises in the Shadow of Nuclear Weapons* (Seattle: University of Washington Press, 2005), 192–200.
4. See Barry R. Posen, *The Sources of Military Doctrine* (Ithaca, N.Y.: Cornell University Press, 1984).
5. Charles Perrow, *Normal Accidents: Living with High-Risk Technologies* (New York: Basic Books, 1984).
6. Scott D. Sagan, *The Limits of Safety: Organizations, Accidents, and Nuclear Weapons* (Princeton, N.J.: Princeton University Press, 1993), 31–45.
7. Siegfried S. Hecker, "Toward a Comprehensive Safeguards System: Keeping Fissile Materials out of Terrorists' Hands," *Annals of the American Academy of Political and Social Sciences* 607 (Year): 121. See also Matthew Bunn, *Securing the Bomb 2007* (Cambridge, Mass.: Project on Managing the Atom, Harvard University and Nuclear Threat Initiative, 2007); Charles D. Ferguson and William C. Potter, *The Four Faces of Nuclear Terrorism* (Monterey, Calif.: Monterey Institute of International Studies, 2004).
8. For a comprehensive assessment of states that have abandoned prior nuclear weapons aspirations, see Ariel E. Levite, "Never Say Never Again: Nuclear Reversal Revisited," *International Security* 27, no. 3 (Winter 2002/2003). Table 1 is updated from this source.

NO

1. States currently possessing nuclear weapons include the United States, Russia, Great Britain, France, China, Israel, India, Pakistan, and North Korea. South Africa, Kazakhstan, Belarus, and Ukraine acquired and then relinquished them.
2. See Waltz's chapters in Sagan and Waltz 2003 for an in-depth discussion of these claims.
3. See Sagan and Weddle's chapter in this volume.
4. It should be noted that in his book, *The Limits of Safety* (1993, 11–13), Sagan quite explicitly acknowledges the difficulty of evaluating the risk of an event that has never happened.

5. Indeed, shortly after the September 11, 2001, terrorist attacks, the United States reportedly offered technical nuclear assistance to Pakistan in an effort to prevent its nuclear weapons from falling into terrorist hands (Sanger and Broad 2007).
6. Elsewhere I have argued for precisely such a policy (Sechser 1998).
7. Universal nonproliferation may still be preferable, of course, if one believes that permitting some states to have nuclear weapons would undermine efforts to prevent U.S. adversaries from acquiring them.

CHAPTER 7: Military Intervention and Human Rights

1. "The Failed States Index 2008," *Foreign Policy*, July–August 2008, http://www.foreignpolicy.com/story/cms.php?story_id=4350).

YES

1. These and other treaties can be found at http://www2.ohchr.org/english/law/. Up-to-date data on ratification can be found at http://www2.ohchr.org/english/bodies/ratification/index.htm.
2. For introductory overviews of the international human rights machinery, see David P. Forsythe, *Human Rights in International Relations*, 2nd ed. (Cambridge: Cambridge University Press: 2006), chaps. 3 and 5; and Jack Donnelly, *Universal Human Rights in Theory and Practice*, 2nd ed. (Ithaca, N.Y.: Cornell University Press, 2003), chap. 8.
3. http://www.reliefweb.int/library/documents/thekosovoreport.htm.
4. http://www.iciss.ca/pdf/Commission-Report.pdf.
5. Two good collections that provide additional representative views on the law, politics, and ethics of humanitarian intervention; see J. L. Holzgref and Robert O. Keohane, eds. *Humanitarian Intervention: Ethical, Legal, and Political Dilemmas* (Cambridge: Cambridge University Press, 2003); and Terry Nardin and Melissa S. Williams, eds., *Humanitarian Intervention* (New York: New York University Press, 2006).

NO

1. This chapter draws upon ideas explored at greater length in Simon Chesterman, *Just War or Just Peace? Humanitarian Intervention and International Law*, Oxford Monographs in International Law (Oxford: Oxford University Press, 2001); and Simon Chesterman, "Hard Cases Make Bad Law: Law, Ethics, and Politics in Humanitarian Intervention," in *Just Intervention*, ed. Anthony F. Lang Jr. (Washington, D.C.: Georgetown University Press, 2003), 46.
2. Kofi A. Annan, "Address to the General Assembly," United Nations Press Release SG/SM/7136, New York, September 20, 1999, http://www.un.org/news/Press/docs/1999/19990920.sgsm7136.html.

3. See, e.g., International Commission on Intervention and State Sovereignty (ICISS), *The Responsibility to Protect* (Ottawa: International Development Research Centre, December 2001), http://www.iciss.ca.

4. United Nations Charter, art. 2, sec. 4.

5. United Nations Charter, art. 51.

6. United Nations General Assembly Resolution 377A(V) (1950).

7. Anthony D'Amato, "The Invasion of Panama Was a Lawful Response to Tyranny," *American Journal of International Law* 84 (1990): 520.

8. Oscar Schachter, "The Legality of Pro-Democratic Invasion," *American Journal of International Law* 78 (1984): 649.

9. *Case Concerning the Military and Paramilitary Activities In and Against Nicaragua (Nicaragua v. United States of America) (Merits),* International Court of Justice, June 27, 1986, *ICJ Rep,* http://www.icj-cij.org, 109.

10. Verbatim record of the 2109th meeting of the UN Security Council, S/PV.2109 (1979) para 36 (France).

11. *Corfu Channel (United Kingdom v. Albania) (Merits),* 1986, *ICJ Rep* 4, http://www.icj-cij.org, 35.

12. Deutscher Bundestag, Plenarprotokoll 13/248, October 16, 1998, 23129, http://dip.bundestag.de/parfors/parfors.htm.

13. U.S. Secretary of State Madeleine Albright, Press Conference with Russian Foreign Minister Igor Ivanov, Singapore, July 26, 1999, http://secretary.state.gov/www/statements/1999/990726b.html.

14. Independent International Commission on Kosovo, *The Kosovo Report* (Oxford: Oxford University Press, 2000), 4.

15. ICISS, *Responsibility to Protect,* 54–55.

16. 2005 World Summit Outcome Document, UN Doc A/RES/60/1 (September 16, 2005), http://www.un.org/summit2005, paras. 138–139.

17. James Rubin, "Countdown to a Very Personal War," *Financial Times* (London), September 30, 2000.

18. Ian Brownlie, "Thoughts on Kind-Hearted Gunmen," in *Humanitarian Intervention and the United Nations,* ed. Richard B. Lillich (Charlottesville: University Press of Virginia, 1973), 146 (emphasis in original).

19. *Corfu Channel* case.

20. S/4349 (1960); SC Res 138 (1960).

21. Joint Communiqué of the Governments of Israel and Argentina, August 3, 1960, reprinted in 36 *ILR* 59.

22. SC Res 1244 (1999), preamble.

23. Annan, "Address to the General Assembly."

24. ICISS, *Responsibility to Protect.*

25. SC Res 1368 (2001).

26. Richard A. Falk, "The United Nations and the Rule of Law," *Transnational Law and Contemporary Problems* 4 (1994): 628.

27. Michael Evans, "Conflict Opens 'Way to New International Community': Blair's Mission," *The (London) Times*, April 23, 1999. The five criteria were: Are we sure of our case? Have we exhausted all diplomatic options? Are there military options we can sensibly and prudently undertake? Are we prepared for the long term? And do we have national interests involved?

CHAPTER 8: Climate Change and the Environment

YES

1. Kyoto Protocol, Annex 1; http://unfccc.int/kyoto_protocol/background/status_of_ratification/items/2613.php.
2. Kyoto Protocol Art. 2, Sec. 1(a).
3. Richard B. Stewart and Jonathan B. Wiener, *Reconstructing Climate Policy: Beyond Kyoto* (Washington, D.C.: American Enterprise Institute Press, 2003).
4. Compare ibid., at 54–82, with Ruth Greenspan Bell, "What To Do about Climate Change," *Foreign Affairs*, May/June 2006; "The Kyoto Placebo," *Issues in Science and Technology*, Winter 2006; "Market Failure," *Environmental Forum*, March/April 2006.
5. Ruth Greenspan Bell, "Choosing Environmental Policy Instruments in the Real World," OECD, http://www.oecd.org/dataoecd/11/9/2957706.pdf.
6. Ruth Greenspan Bell, "Monitoring International Greenhouse Gas Emissions Trading," *BNA Daily Environment Reporter*, Analysis & Perspective, August 2, 2002 (also available at *BNA International Environmental Reporter*, Analysis & Perspective, August 14, 2002); Elizabeth C. Economy, "The Great Leap Backwards? The Costs of China's Environmental Crisis," *Foreign Affairs*, September/October 2007.
7. "Newest Big Deal," *Down to Earth*, online publication of Center for Science and Environment (Delhi, India), http://www.downtoearth.org.in/cover.asp?foldername=20051115&filename=anal&sid=1&sec_id=7.
8. Michael Wara, "Measuring the Clean Development Mechanism's Performance and Potential," January 2008, http://ssrn.com/abstract=1086242.
9. 42 U.S.C. Secs. 4321-4370f.
10. Ruth Greenspan Bell, "Culture—and History—Count: Choosing Environmental Tools to Fit Available Institutions and Experience," *Indiana Law Review*, April 2005.
11. Ruth Greenspan Bell and Clifford Russell, "Ill-Considered Experiments: The Environmental Consensus and the Developing World," *Harvard International Review*, Winter 2003; Ruth Greenspan Bell and Clifford Russell, "Environmental Policy for Developing Countries," *Issues in Science and Technology* (Spring 2002), reprinted in electronic journal *Failsafe*, http://www.felsef.org/summer02.htm#4b (June 17, 2002); also reprinted in *The Theory and Practice of Command and Control in Environmental Policy*, ed. Gloria E. Helfand and Peter Berck

(Burlington, Vt.: International Library of Environmental Economics and Policy Series, Ashgate Publishing, 2003).

12. Ruth Greenspan Bell, Kuldeep Mathur, Urvashi Narain, and David Simpson, "Delhi respire mieux grâce aux gaz naturel," *LaRevueDurable*, Fevrier-Mars 2005; Ruth Greenspan Bell, Kuldeep Mathur, Urvashi Narain, and David Simpson, "Clearing the Air: How Delhi Broke the Logjam on Air Quality Reforms," *Environment Magazine*, April 2004; Urvashi Narain and Alan J. Krupnick, "The Impact of Delhi's CNG Program on Air Quality," RFF Discussion Paper 07-06 (February 2007).

13. William Allen, *Green Phoenix: Restoring the Tropical Forests of Guanacaste, Costa Rica* (New York: Oxford University Press, 2001).

14. Charles E. Lindblom, "The Science of 'Muddling Through,'" *Public Administration Review* 19 (1959): 79; on adaptive management, see C. S. Holling, *Adaptive Environmental Assessment and Management* (Caldwell, N.J.: Blackburn Press, 1978); and, on cultural and historical ecology, see Carole Crumley and others, e.g., http://www.triquete.org/.

15. See George Packer, "Knowing the Enemy; Can Social Scientists Redefine the 'War on Terror?'" *New Yorker*, December 18, 2006.

16. Cass R. Sunstein, "Of Montreal and Kyoto: A Tale of Two Protocols," *Harvard Environmental Law Review* 31, no. 1 (2007): 29–36.

NO

1. A "cap-and-trade" system is an innovative way of reducing pollution while providing companies the freedom to find the most cost-effective means of improving their environmental performance, offering incentives to exceed conventional emissions standards if there are cost-effective opportunities to do so. The idea was first adopted in the 1990 Clean Air Act amendments, and while it was highly controversial at the time, it has proven to be quite successful in that context, leading many people to assume—perhaps falsely—that it is the ideal mechanism for reducing greenhouse-gas emissions. The basic idea is simple: Set an overall emissions limit for a given pollutant and industry—say, the total amount of sulfur dioxide emissions that electric power plants on the East Coast can emit—and a target for how much that pollutant should be reduced in order to meet environmental standards. Distribute "emissions credits"—the right to emit a given amount of pollution—to each power plant, and then reduce the number of credits available to plants each year until the desired target is met. Plants that have affordable opportunities to reduce their emissions will do so, freeing up credits that can be sold to other power plants that cannot economically reduce their own emissions. The end result is that overall pollution targets are met while giving companies the flexibility to find the most cost-effective opportunities to cut their emissions. The Clean Air Act's emissions trading system has been effective at reducing the pollutants that cause smog; the analogous system established under the Kyoto Protocol by European nations has not been effective, for complicated

reasons having to do with the scale of the system, the technological and economic limitations on companies' ability to substantially reduce their greenhouse-gas emissions, the difficulty in allocating credits and verifying the value of projects certified to earn emissions-reduction credits, and the lack of meaningful enforcement mechanisms to ensure that countries meet their emissions targets.

2. William Nordhaus, *A Question of Balance* (New Haven, Conn.: Yale University Press, 2008), 19.

3. Richard B. Stewart and Jonathan Weiner, *Reconstructing Climate Policy: Beyond Kyoto* (Washington, D.C.: AEI Press, 2003), 15.

4. Ibid, 2.

5. Some people have advocated the use of trade sanctions as a means of compelling participation—by either the United States or China, for example—in an emissions-control regime. Such an approach would, of course, tread on dangerous ground. It is far from clear that such an effort would be legal under the terms of the World Trade Organization; even if the WTO did sanction carbon tariffs, the result could well be a "green trade war" that could do significant damage to free trade without producing the desired effect.

6. Roger Pielke Jr., Tom Wigley, and Christopher Green, "Dangerous Assumptions," *Nature* 452 (April 3, 2008): 531–532.

7. Associated Press, "Former UN Chief Calls for Climate Justice," *International Herald Tribune*, June 24, 2008, http://www.iht.com/bin/printfriendly .php?id=13961173.

8. The value of the CDM program itself has also been questioned, as there is evidence that many of the credits it issued were essentially fraudulent; see, for instance, Michael W. Wara and David G. Victor, *A Realistic Policy on International Carbon Offsets* (Working Paper #74, Program on Energy and Sustainable Development, Stanford University), http://pesd.stanford.edu.

9. It is actually possible to remove carbon dioxide from the atmosphere, a technique commonly referred to as "air capture"; Professor Klaus Lackner of Columbia University's Earth Engineering Center has built a prototype of a machine to do just that. This sort of technology may, however, be many decades from being economically feasible for application on a scale sufficient to significantly lower the level of greenhouse gases in the atmosphere.

10. Ning Zeng, Yihui Ding, Jiahua Pan, Huijun Wang, and Jay Gregg, "Climate Change—the Chinese Challenge," *Science* 319, no. 5864 (February 8, 2008): 730–731.

11. President George W. Bush, speech announcing Clear Skies and climate-change initiatives, February 14, 2002, available at: http://www.whitehouse.gov/news/ releases/2002/02/20020214-5.html, and supporting materials available at http://www.whitehouse.gov/news/releases/2002/02/clearskies.html.

12. Bjorn Lomborg's 2007 book, *Cool It: The Skeptical Environmentalist's Guide to Global Warming* (New York: Alfred A. Knopf, 2007), provides a detailed and approachable exposition of this argument. Lomborg calls for all nations to spend

0.05 percent of their GDP on research and development of carbon-free energy technologies. This would amount to $25 billion a year in funds for research—a vast increase in spending on this field, while still seven times cheaper than Kyoto, and vastly cheaper than Kyoto's likely successor.

13. Andrew C. Revkin, "Budgets Falling in Race to Fight Global Warming," *New York Times*, October 30, 2006.

14. Energy Information Administration, *International Energy Outlook 2008*, available at: http://www.eia.doe.gov/oiaf/ieo/highlights.html.

15. Joseph E. Aldy and Robert N. Stavins, eds., *Architectures for Agreement: Addressing Global Climate Change in the Post-Kyoto World* (Cambridge: Cambridge University Press, 2007) 302–303.

16. Ibid, 304.

17. Gwyn Prins and Steve Rayner, "The Wrong Trousers: Rethinking Climate Policy," James Martin Institute for Science and Civilization, Oxford University, and the MacKinder Centre for the Study of Long-Wave Events, London School of Economics, 26, http://www.martininstitute.ox.ac.uk/JMI/Library/James+Martin+Institute+Editorial/The+Wrong+Trousers+-+Radically+rethinking+climate+policy.htm. See also Gwyn Prins and Steve Rayner, "Time To Ditch Kyoto," *Nature* 449 (October 25, 2007): 973–975, http://www.nature.com/nature/journal/v449/n7165/full/449973a.html.

CHAPTER 9: The Future of Energy

YES

1. E. Jansen et al., "Palaeoclimate," in Intergovernmental Panel on Climate Change (IPCC), *Climate Change 2007: The Physical Science Basis* (New York: Cambridge University Press, 2007), p. 449.

2. IPCC, *Climate Change*, pp. 342, 350, 537, 543; M. Serreze et al., "Perspectives on the Arctic's Shrinking Sea-Ice Cover," *Science*, March 16, 2007, 1533–1536.

3. "Summary for Policymakers," in IPCC, *Climate Change*; International Energy Agency, *Key World Energy Statistics* (Paris: 2007), 6; recent carbon emissions cited by Worldwatch, based on G. Marland et al., "Global, Regional, and National Fossil Fuel CO_2 Emissions," in Carbon Dioxide Information Analysis Center (CDIAC), *Trends: A Compendium of Data on Global Change* (Oak Ridge, Tenn.: Oak Ridge National Laboratory, U.S. Department of Energy, 2007); BP, *Statistical Review of World Energy* (London: 2007).

4. J. Hansen et al., "Dangerous Human-made Interference with Climate: A GISS ModelE Study," *Atmospheric Chemistry and Physics* 7, no. 9 (2007): 2287–2312; 0.8 degrees Celsius is the midpoint of estimates of warming, as reported in IPCC, op. cit. note 1, p. 5.

5. Remarks by U.S. Vice President Cheney at the annual meeting of the Associated Press, Toronto, Canada, April 2001; World Energy Council, *Energy and Climate Change Executive Summary*, London, May 2007, 5.

6. U.S. Department of Energy, *Monthly Energy Review*, Washington, D.C., September 2007, 16; energy productivity based on data from International Monetary Fund (IMF), *World Economic Outlook* (Washington, D.C., April 2007); International Energy Agency, *Energy Technology Perspectives—Scenarios and Strategies to 2050* (Paris: 2006), pp. 48–57; U.S. Department of Energy, *International Energy Annual 2004*, Washington, D.C., 2006, Table E.1; BP, *Statistical Review of World Energy* (London: 2007); estimate of useful energy from G. Kaiper, *U.S. Energy Flow Trends–2002* (Livermore, Calif.: Lawrence Livermore National Laboratory, 2004).

7. B. Griffith et al., *Assessment of the Technical Potential for Achieving Zero-Energy Commercial Buildings* (Golden, Colo.: National Renewable Energy Laboratory, 2006); Bressand et al., *Curbing Global Energy Demand Growth: The Energy Productivity Opportunity* (McKinsey Global Institute, May 2007), 13.

8. S. Mufson, "U.S. Nuclear Power Revival Grows," *Washington Post*, September 2007.

9. J. Sawin, "The Role of Government in the Development and Diffusion of Renewable Energy Technologies: Wind Power in the United States, California, Denmark and Germany, 1970–2000" (PhD diss., The Fletcher School of Law and Diplomacy, Tufts University, Somerville, Mass., September 2001).

10. M. Ragwitz and C. Huber, *Feed-In Systems in Germany and Spain and a Comparison* (Karlsruhe, Germany: Fraunhofer Institut fr Systemtechnik und Innovationsforschung, 2005); ranking based on Travis Bradford, Prometheus Institute, emails to Janet Sawin, April 5–8, 2007.

11. E. Shuster, *Tracking New Coal-Fired Power Plants* (Washington, D.C.: National Energy Technology Laboratory, U.S. Department of Energy, October 2007).

12. "Germany to Close Its Coal Mines," *Spiegel Online*, January 30, 2007; United States Climate Action Partnership, "U.S. Climate Action Partnership Announces Its Fourth Membership Expansion," press release, Washington, D.C., September 2007; European Council, "The Spring European Council: Integrated Climate Protection and Energy Policy, Progress on the Lisbon Strategy," press release, Brussels, March 12, 2007; National Development and Reform Commission, *China's National Climate Change Programme*, (Beijing, June 2007); Pew Center on Global Climate Change, "Climate Change Initiatives and Programs in the States," press release, Arlington, Va., September 11, 2006; "Statement of H. E. Luiz Incio Lula da Silva, President of the Federative Republic of Brazil, at the general debate of the 62nd Session of the United Nations General," press release (New York: Ministry of External Relations, September 25, 2007).

CHAPTER 10: HIV/AIDS

YES

1. UNAIDS, "Report on the Global HIV/AIDS Epidemic," 2006.

2. National budget funding in 29 reporting countries reached over $750 million in 2006. Global funding grew by more than 2000 percent over a six-year period. UN

Secretary-General Ban Ki-moon, "Declaration of Commitment on HIV/AIDS and Political Declaration on HIV/AIDS: Focus on Progress over the Past 12 Months," United Nations General Assembly, 61st session, A/61/816, 2007.

3. John Norris, "It's Politics vs. Science in Global Health," *Campaign for Fighting Diseases Bulletin*, August 9, 2007.
4. P. Alagiri, C. Collins, T. Summers et al., "Global Spending on HIV/AIDS: Tracking Public and Private Investments in AIDS Prevention, Care, and Research," AIDS Research Institute, University of California, San Francisco, July 2001, ari.ucsf.edu/science/reports/global_spending.pdf.
5. To date, the Global Fund has committed US$7.7 billion in 136 countries to support aggressive interventions against all three diseases.
6. PEPFAR provides intensive support in 15 focus countries, mostly in Africa—Botswana, Côte d'Ivoire, Ethiopia, Guyana, Haiti, Kenya, Mozambique, Namibia, Nigeria, Rwanda, South Africa, Tanzania, Uganda, Vietnam, and Zambia—but also offers lower-level assistance in numerous other countries.
7. Mead Over, "Prevention Failure: The Ballooning Burden of U.S. Global AIDS Treatment Spending and What To Do about It," Center for Global Development Working Paper No. 144, April 2008.
8. William Easterly, "How, and How Not to Stop AIDS in Africa," *New York Review of Books* 54, no. 13 (August 16, 2007).
9. UNAIDS, "Global Facts and Figures, December 2006."
10. UNAIDS/WHO, "AIDS Epidemic Update, December 2006."
11. UNAIDS, "Global Facts and Figures, December 2006."
12. Global HIV Prevention Working Group, "Bringing HIV Prevention to Scale: An Urgent Global Priority," June 2007.
13. Ibid.
14. UNICEF, WHO, UNAIDS, "Towards Universal Access: Scaling Up Priority HIV/AIDS Interventions in the Health Sector: Progress Report, April 2007."
15. Ibid.; and UNAIDS, "AIDS Epidemic Update 2006."
16. World Health Organization, "The World Health Report 2006: Working Together on Health," http://www.who.int/whr/2006/en/index.html.
17. Global HIV Prevention Working Group, "Bringing HIV Prevention to Scale."
18. PEPFAR was authorized under the United States Leadership Against HIV/AIDS, Tuberculosis, and Malaria Act of 2003 (Public Law 108-25).
19. U.S. Government Accountability Office, *Global Health: Spending Requirements Presents Challenges for Allocating Prevention Funding under the President's Emergency Plan for AIDS Relief,* April 2006.
20. Institute of Medicine, *PEPFAR Implementation: Progress and Promise,* March 30, 2007; "First Lady Laura Bush Supports Waiver of Abstinence-Until-Marriage Earmark," press release, July 3, 2007.
21. United Nations Population Fund (UNFPA), http://www.unfpa.org/adolescents/facts.htm.

22. Ban Ki-moon, "Declaration of Commitment on HIV/AIDS and Political Declaration on HIV/AIDS: Focus on Progress over the Past 12 Months"; and UNAIDS, "Report on the Global HIV/AIDS Epidemic, 2006."
23. World Health Organization, *Toolkit for Targeted HIV/AIDS Prevention and Care in Sex Work*, 2004.
24. UNAIDS, "Female Sex Worker HIV Prevention Projects: Lessons Learnt from Papua New Guinea, India, and Bangladesh," UNAIDS Best Practice Collection, November 2000.
25. UNAIDS, "Report on the Global HIV/AIDS Epidemic, 2006."
26. Ibid.
27. Ibid.
28. PBS *Frontline:* "The Age of AIDS," transcript, 2006.
29. James Chin, *The AIDS Pandemic: The Collision of Epidemiology with Political Correctness* (Oxford: Radcliffe Publishing, 2007).
30. "Scaling Up to Achieve the Health MDGs in Rwanda: A Background Study for the High-Level Forum Meeting in Tunis, June 2006," Ministry of Economics and Ministry of Health, Rwanda, May 2006.
31. Disease Control Priorities Project, July 2006.
32. J. Wegbreit et al., "Effectiveness of HIV Prevention Strategies in Resource-Poor Countries," *AIDS* 20 (2006): 1217–1235.
33. Chin, *AIDS Pandemic.*
34. Futures Institute, data-based modeling undertaken at the request of Global HIV Prevention Working Group, 2007.
35. Ibid.
36. UNAIDS, "HIV Prevention Needs and Successes: A Tale of Three Countries—An Update on HIV Prevention Success in Senegal, Thailand and Uganda, 2001."
37. Mead Over et al., "The Economics of Effective AIDS Treatment in Thailand," *AIDS* 21, suppl. 4 (July 2007): S105–A116.
38. UNAIDS, "Report on the Global HIV/AIDS Epidemic, 2006."
39. UNICEF, WHO, UNAIDS, "Towards Universal Access."
40. PBS *Frontline,* "Age of AIDS."
41. DFID, "Girl's Education: Towards a Better Future for All," 2005.
42. Over, "Prevention Failure."

NO

1. S. Lewis, *Race against Time* (Toronto: Anansi, 2005).
2. The Oslo Ministerial Declaration, "Global Health: A Pressing Foreign Policy Issue of Our Time," www.thelancet.com, April 2, 2007.
3. See www.theglobalfund.org and www.pepfar.gov.
4. W. El Sadr and D. Hoos, "The President's Emergency Plan for AIDS Relief—Is the Emergency Over?" *New England Journal of Medicine* 359, no. 6 (August 7, 2008).
5. A recent report has pointed out that, within the European Union, funding for health dropped from 7 percent of Overseas Development Assistance in 1996 to

5 percent in 2005 and that "only one third of these commitments were actually disbursed." Action for Global Health, "An Unhealthy Prognosis: The EC's Development Funding for Health," May 2007.

6. See African Union, "Abuja Declaration on HIV/AIDS, Tuberculosis and Other Infectious Diseases, April 2001," which pledged to set a target of "at least 15% of our annual budgets to the improvement of the health sector."

7. R. Laing, *Priority Medicines for Europe and the World*, World Health Organization, November 2004.

8. S. Kaufmann and S. Parida, "Changing Funding Patterns in Tuberculosis," *Nature Medicine* 13 (2007).

9. D. Werner and D. Sanders, *Questioning the Solution: The Politics of Primary Health Care and Child Survival* (Palo Alto, Calif.: HealthWrights, 1997). The concept of primary health care, which originally rested in human rights, has been starved of imagination and funds. In South Africa, the concept has been perverted and now refers to "health centres" or "clinics" that are "close to the community" but under-funded, ill-equipped, understaffed, and rarely involved in community health pro-motion. Not surprisingly, a 2007 report by the South African Human Rights Commission (SAHRC) found that "many patients are by-passing clinics and going straight to hospitals. This seems to indicate that despite clinics being geo-graphically accessible, they are unable to meet patient needs."

10. WHO, "Report of the Commission on Macroeconomics and Health, Macroeconomics, and Health: Investing in Health for Economic Development, 2001," 21–22.

11. M. Desai, *Marx's Revenge: The Resurgence of Capitalism and the Death of Statist Socialism* (London and New York: Verso, 2002), 313.

12. Ibid., Executive Summary, 12–13.

13. Statistics South Africa, "Mortality and Causes of Death in South Africa, 2005: Findings from Death Notification," July 2007.

14. L. Gostin, "Meeting the Survival Needs of the World's Least Healthy People: A Proposed Model for Global Health Governance," *JAMA*, July 11, 2007, Vol. 289, 2, 225–228.

CHAPTER 11: Gender

1. "Women in National Parliaments (Situation as of 31 October 2008)," Inter-parliamentary Union, http://www.ipu.org/wmn-e/world.htm.

YES

1. Isobel Coleman, "The Pay-Off from Women's Rights," *Foreign Affairs* 83, no. 3 (May–June 2004).

2. L.H. Summers, "Investing in All the People: Educating Women in Developing Countries," EDI Seminar paper no. 45, World Bank, Washington, D.C., 1994, 1.

3. Elizabeth King and Andrew Mason, *Engendering Development* (Oxford: World Bank/Oxford University Press, 2001), 79.

4. Ibid.

5. Stephan Klausen, "Does Gender Inequality Reduce Growth and Development?" World Bank, 1999, 23, http://siteresources.worldbank.org/INTGENDER/Resources/wp7.pdf.

6. It should be noted, though, that the link between girls' education and economic growth has been challenged by some economists.

7. David Kucera, "The Effects of Core Workers Rights on Labour Costs and Foreign Direct Investment: Evaluating the 'Conventional Wisdom,'" International Institute for Labour Studies, 2001.

8. Agnes Quisumbing, "Gender Differences in Agricultural Productivity: A Study of Empirical Evidence," International Food Policy Research Institute, 52, http://www.ifpri.org/divs/fcnd/dp/papers/dp05.pdf.

9. UNICEF estimates that of the roughly 93 million children in the world who are not in school, the majority are girls. ("Basic Education and Gender Equality: The Big Picture," http://www.unicef.org/girlseducation/index_bigpicture.html.)

10. DATA Press Releases, "Bono Joins Lowey, Clinton, Smith and Bachus in Unveiling Education for All Act," May 1, 2007, http://www.data.org/news/press_20070501.html.

11. Ibid.

12. Gene Sperling and Barbara Herz, "What Works for Girls' Education," Council on Foreign Relations, 2004, 9–13, http://www.cfr.org/content/publications/attachments/Girls_Education_full.pdf.

13. UNDP, "Gender Empowerment Measure," 2003, http://hdr.undp.org/statistics/data/indic/indic_229_1_1.html.

14. Global Health Council, "Women's Health," www.globalhealth.org.

15. In the U.S. alone, an estimated 5.3 million women are abused each year; http://www.aidv-usa.com/Statistics.htm.

16. UNICEF, "Egypt FGM/C Country Profile," November 2005, http://www.childinfo.org/areas/fgmc/profiles/Egypt/Egypt%20FGC%20profile%20English.pdf.

17. "Report of the China UN Population Fund (UNFPA) Independent Assessment Team," U.S. State Department, http://www.state.gov/g/prm/rls/rpt/2002/12122.htm.

18. King and Mason, *Engendering Development*, 81.

19. Sarah El Sirgany, "Microsoft Opens Technology Center to Train Youth, Women," *Daily News of Egypt*, June 14, 2006, http://www.dailystaregypt.com/article.aspx?ArticleID=1882.

20. Steven Fish, "Islam and Authoritarianism," *World Politics* 55 (October 2002): 4–37.

NO

1. http://www.un.org/womenwatch/daw/cedaw/.

2. http://untreaty.un.org/cod/icc/index.html.

3. http://www.un.org/womenwatch/daw/beijing/platform/.

4. UN Secretary-General Boutros Boutros-Ghali, Introduction to the *Platform for Action and the Beijing Declaration* (New York: Department of Public Information, United Nations, 1996), 1.

5. MDG #3 is Promote Gender Equality and Empower Women, but all of the goals should benefit women and each goal should also benefit from women's contributions and from respectful gender relations. See http://www.unmillenniumproject.org.

6. Beyond attention commonly paid to Islam, there are fundamentalist threats to women's rights by other religions. See, for example, Susan Berns, "Women's Rights are in Jeopardy Maintains Israel's Top Feminist," *Jewish News Weekly*, April 4, 1997, http://www.jewishsf.com/ ; and Susan M. Shaw, "Gracious Submission: Southern Baptist Fundamentalists and Women," *NWSA Journal* 20, no.1 (Spring 2008): 51–77,
http://muse.jhu.edu/login?uri=/journals/nwsa_journal/v020/20.1.shaw.html.

7. "Saddam Hussein's Baath Party espoused a secular Arab nationalism that advocated women's full participation in society. But years of war changed that." See Nancy Trejos, "Women Lose Ground in the New Iraq," *Washington Post*, December 16, 2006.

8. "Secular opposition lawmakers voted against the change [lifting a ban on head scarves] …Crowds of secular Turks backed them on the streets of the capital, Ankara, chanting that secularism—and women's right to resist being forced to wear head scarves by an increasingly conservative society—was under threat." See Ilene Prusher, "Turks Tangled in Politics of Scarves," *Christian Science Monitor*, October 28, 2002; and Sabrina Tavernise, "Turkey's Parliament Lifts Scarf Ban," *New York Times*, February 10, 2008.

9. See, e.g., "Indians Crack Down on Gender Abortions," *Christian Science Monitor*, March 31, 2006, http://www.csmonitor.com/2006/0331/p07s02-wosc.html; Amartya Sen, "Missing Women," *British Medical Journal* 304 (1992): 586–587; and Amartya Sen, Editorial, *BMJ* 327 (December 6, 2003):1297–1298.

10. For discussions of religion, fundamentalisms, and women's rights, see Frances Raday, "Culture, Religion and Gender," Oxford University Press and NYU School of Law *I.CON* 1, no. 4 (2003): 663–715; Mahnaz Afkhami, "Gender Apartheid, Cultural Relativism, and Women's Human Rights in Muslim Societies," in Women, Gender, and Human Rights: A Global Perspective, ed. Marjorie Agosin (New Brunswick, N.J.: Rutgers University Press, 2001), 234–245; Martha C. Nussbaum, "The Role of Religion," in *Women and Human Development: The Capabilities Approach* (Cambridge: Cambridge University Press, 2000), chap. 3, pp. 167–197, 235–240; Jennifer Block, "Christian Soldiers on the March," *The Nation*, Feb. 3, 2003, reprinted in *Women's Rights*, ed. Jennifer Curry (New York: H.W. Wilson, 2005), 138–143; and Anthony Chase, "The Tail and the Dog: Constructing Islam and Human Rights in Political Context," in *Human Rights in the Arab World*, edited by Anthony Chase and Amr Hamzawy (Philadelphia: University of Pennsylvania Press, 2006), chap. 1, pp. 21–36.

11. Martha Nussbaum, *Women and Human Development: The Capabilities Approach* (Cambridge: Cambridge University Press, 2000).

12. She proposes the importance of ten "central human functional capabilities": (1) Life, being able to live to the end of a human life of normal length; (2) Bodily health, including nourishment, reproductive health and shelter; (3) Bodily integrity, including the ability to move freely from place to place and to be free from violence; (4) Senses, Imagination, and Thought, in ways informed and cultivated by adequate education; (5) Emotions, including not having one's emotional development blighted by overwhelming fear and anxiety, or by traumatic events or abuse or neglect; (6) Practical Reason; (7) Affiliation; (8) Other species (being able to live with concern for and in relation to animals, plants, and the world of nature); (9) Play, being able to laugh and enjoy recreation; and (10) Control over one's environment. Ibid., 72.

13. Two other ways for the United States to promote women's rights, though not "in" developing countries, but yet affecting developing countries, are (1) by example, and (2) by assessing its own policies and actions for their positive or negative impacts on women's lives—and both of these ways will be addressed later in this paper.

14. In 1995, the UNDP's Human Development Report launched "two new measures of human development that highlight the status of women." The Gender-related Development Index (GDI), measures achievement in the same basic capabilities as the Human Development Index, but accounts for disparities of achievement between women and men. The methodology penalizes a country for inequality so that the GDI falls when the disparity between men and women's achievements increases. The second measure, the Gender Empowerment Measure (GEM), focuses on agency—on women's standing in political and economic forums. It examines the extent to which women and men are able to actively participate in economic and political life and take part in decision making. While the GDI focuses on expansion of capabilities, the GEM is concerned with the use of those capabilities to take advantage of the opportunities of life. See http://hdr.undp.org/en/statistics/indices/gdi_gem/.

15. The first three factors are percentages of women from the total of male and female.

16. Note that neither Afghanistan nor Iraq is included for lack of reliable and complete data.

17. For a range of programs addressing women's rights, see, e.g., American Bar Association, Rule of Law Initiative Gender Issues Program, http://www.abanet.org/rol/programs/gender-issues.html; Global Rights, http://www.hrlawgroup.org/; Human Rights Watch, http://www.hrw.org/women/; and Open Society Institute's International Women's Program, http://www.soros.org/initiatives/women.

18. Akua Kuenyehia, "Legal Literacy and the Law Enforcement Agencies in Ghana," in *Legal Literacy: A Tool for Women's Empowerment*, ed. Margaret Schuler and Sakuntala Kadirgamar-Rajasingham (New York: UNIFEM, 1992), 301–312.

19. David Trubek and Marc Galanter, "Scholars in Self-Estrangement: Some Reflections on the Crisis in Law and Development Studies," *Wisconsin Law Review* (1974): 1062–1102. Note that in "Lessons Not Learned: Problems with Western Aid for Law Reform in Post-communist Countries," Wade Channell argues that the rule of law "industry" continues to rely on those assumptions and to follow the problematic paradigm. See Carnegie Papers #57, The Rule of Law Series, Democracy and Rule of Law Project, Carnegie Endowment for International Peace (May 2005).

20. And in some cases, the context is a "failed state" where there is little if any presence or power of a "state," and the situation is fundamentally "lawless" from a state-law perspective.

21. This brings to mind an analogy from Barbara Kingsolver's *Poisonwood Bible*: The missionary father, who is also a minister, seeks to plant in his garden in Africa seeds that had thrived in the U.S.—but the soil conditions are such that the seeds fail. So, too, planting "rights" in a legal system that lacks the fundamental conditions means that the rights culture and practices and protections are at risk of failing.

22. Lawrence M. Friedman and Stewart Macaulay, "Legal Culture and Social Development," in *Law and the Behavioral Sciences*, 2nd ed. (Indianapolis: Bobbs-Merrill, 1977): 1000–1017.

23. Where a nation's legal system may offer some meaningful recourse, however, there are two issues regarding relevance and effectiveness for women: First, do they reach demographic groups such as rural populations or women? If not, absent purposeful attention to issues of access, they will not protect women's rights. See Stephen Golub, "Beyond Rule of Law Orthodoxy: The Legal Empowerment Alternative," Rule of Law Series, Democracy and Rule of Law Project, Carnegie Endowment for International Peace, Number 41, October 2003. Second, in a world of limited resources, would resources focused on legal systems be more effective for women and girls if invested in different sorts of programs?

24. See also Adam Liptak, "U.S. Court, a Longtime Beacon, Is Now Guiding Fewer Nations," *New York Times*, September 18, 2008.

25. See http://www.un.org/womenwatch/daw/cedaw/states.htm—and, as of November 2007, 90 states were party to the Optional Protocol, http://www.un.org/womenwatch/daw/cedaw/protocol/sigop.htm.

26. For a history of the women's conferences, see *The Global Women's Movement: Origins, Issues and Strategies* by Peggy Antrobus, Zed Books (2004).

27. http://www.iisd.ca/Cairo.html

28. Agreed Conclusions 1997/2, 18 July 1997.

29. See Lisa VeneKlasen, Valerie Miller, Cindy Clark, and Molly Reilly, "Rights-Based Approaches and Beyond: Challenges of Linking Rights and Participation," IDS Working Paper 235, Institute of Development Studies, 2004, Appendix B: Power, 46–49; and "Power and Empowerment," in *A New Weave of Power, People & Politics: The Action Guide for Advocacy and Citizen Participation*, ed. Lisa

VeneKlasen with Valerie Miller (Oklahoma City: World Neighbors, 2002): 1–17.

30. One example of reversals and losses through politics and elections would be Poland—where hard-fought gains disappeared with an election.

31. For more information, see "African Women and Trade: Helping End Poverty in Africa" from the organization Women Thrive Worldwide, http://www.womensedge.org/index.php?option=com_content&task=view&id=391&Itemid=152.

CHAPTER 12: Immigration

NO

1. United Nations, "Report of the Secretary-General on International Migration" (A/60/871), May 2006, www.unmigration.org. Table available at www.un.org/esa/population/publications/2006Migration_Chart/2006IttMig_chart.htm.

2. The world's population was about 6.6 billion in 2007, including 4.8 billion of workforce age, defined as persons fifteen and older (http://laborsta.ilo.org). The world's workforce was 3.1 billion, including 2.9 billion employed and 200 million unemployed—an unemployment rate of 6.2 percent.

3. See chapter 5 of Philip Martin, *Importing Poverty? Immigration and the Changing Face of Rural America* (New Haven, Conn.: Yale University Press, 2009).

4. John Torpey, *The Invention of the Passport: Surveillance, Citizenship and the State* (Cambridge: Cambridge University Press, 1999).

5. Charles C. Lemert, *Social Things: An Introduction to the Sociological Life* (Lanham, Md.: Rowman & Littlefield, 2005), 176, says there were fewer than fifty nation-states in 1900.

6. An editorial on July 3, 1986, first made this proposal, which was repeated in an editorial on July 3, 1990.

7. The National Front candidate, Jean Marie Le Pen, received 15 percent of the vote in the first round of presidential voting in 1995; www.irr.org.uk/europebulletin/france/extreme_right_politics/1995/ak000006.html.

8. Quoted in Michael S. Teitelbaum, "Right versus Right: Immigration and Refugee Policy in the United States," *Foreign Affairs* 59, no. 1 (Fall 1980): 45–46.

9. The average woman in developing countries (excluding China) has 3.5 children, versus 1.5 children per woman in developed countries. According to the Population Reference Bureau (www.prb.org), the world's fastest-growing population is in Gaza, where the growth rate is 4.5 percent a year, and the fastest-shrinking population is in Russia, where the population is declining by 0.5 percent a year.

10. Young people are most likely to move over borders because they have the least invested in jobs and careers at home and the most time to recoup their "investment in migration" abroad.

11. Average per capita was $7,400 per person in 2006, according to the World Bank's *World Development Report 2008*, Selected Economic Indicators, http://go.world-

bank.org/LOTTGBE9I0. Per capita GDP ranged from $130 in Congo to $66,000 in Norway. At purchasing power parity, which takes into account national differences in the cost of living, the world's gross national income was $66 trillion or $10,200 per capita in 2006—$34,700 per capita in the high-income countries and $5,600 in low and middle-income countries.

12. Taxes are extracted from agriculture via monopoly input suppliers who sell seeds or fertilizers at high prices or via monopoly purchasers of farm commodities who buy from farmers at less-than-world prices and pocket the difference when the coffee or cocoa is exported. In the high-income countries, farmers' incomes are generally higher than those of non-farmers, in part because high-income countries transfer funds to producers of food and fiber.

13. United Nations Population Fund (UNFPA), *State of the World's Population, 2007*, www.unfpa.org/swp/2007/english/introduction.html.

14. This situation is evident in Chinese coastal cities, where internal rural-urban migrants fill 3-D jobs, and abroad, where Chinese migrants are employed in industries that range from services to sweatshops.

15. These farm-worker recruitment networks are examined in *Rural Migration News*, http://migration.ucdavis.edu/rmn/index.php.

16. Even if migrants know that movies and TV shows portray exaggerated lifestyles, those who find themselves in slave-like conditions abroad sometimes say that they did not believe that things in rich countries could be "that bad."

17. Philip Martin, "Germany: Managing Migration in the 21st Century," 221–252, in *Controlling Immigration: A Global Perspective*, ed. Wayne A. Cornelius, Takeyuki Tsuda, Philip L. Martin, and James F. Hollifield (Stanford, Calif.: Stanford University Press, 2004).

18. Proposition 187, approved by a 59–41 percent margin in November 1994, would have created a state-funded screening mechanism to ensure that unauthorized foreigners did not obtain state-funded services, including public school education. Its implementation was stopped by a federal judge, but some of its provisions were included in 1996 federal immigration reforms. See http://migration.ucdavis.edu/mn/more.php?id=492_0_2_0.

19. Details of the three U.S. laws enacted in 1996 are at *Migration News*, 1996, http://migration.ucdavis.edu/. One provision that was eventually dropped from the final bill would have made legal immigrants deportable if they received more than 12 months of welfare benefits. In the late 1990s, the access of some legal immigrant adults and children to some welfare benefits was restored.

20. Martin Ruhs and Philip Martin. "Numbers vs. Rights: Trade-offs and Guest Worker Programs," *International Migration Review* 42, no 1 (2008): 249–265.

21. World Bank, *Global Economic Prospects: The Economic Implications of Remittances and Migration*, 2005, www.worldbank.org/prospects/gep2006.

22. Chapter 2 of *Global Economic Prospects* uses a CGE model to estimate the impacts of increasing by 14 million the number of developing-country migrant workers in industrial countries. The increased economic output was $356 billion, or 0.6 per-

cent of global GDP, or more than the estimated gains from reducing trade restrictions.

23. James P. Smith and Barry Edmonston, eds., *The New Americans: Economic, Demographic, and Fiscal Effects of Immigration* (Washington, D.C.: National Academy Press, 1997).

24. The U.S. GDP in 2005 topped $12 trillion, suggesting that the net economic benefits were up to $15 billion; this larger economy, expanding by 3 percent, grows by $360 billion a year, or almost $15 billion in two weeks.

CHAPTER 13: Culture and Diversity

YES

1. See the Web site of the Secretariat of the UN Permanent Forum on Indigenous Issues, www.un.org/esa/socdev/unpfii.

2. The term "development aggression" is used frequently by Victoria Tauli-Corpuz, an Igorot indigenous leader from the Philippines and chair of the UN Permanent Forum on Indigenous Issues (2005   ). See her excellent piece, "Our Right to Remain Separate and Distinct," in *Paradigm Wars: Indigenous Peoples' Resistance to Economic Globalization*, A Special Report of the International Forum on Globalization Committee on Indigenous Peoples, ed. Jerry Mander and Victoria Tauli-Corpuz (San Francisco: International Forum on Globalization, 2005), 9–16.

3. See, for example, the report of the Fourth Session of the UNPFII, E/2005/23, wherein the Forum made comprehensive recommendations in the context of indigenous peoples and the Millennium Development Goal 1, which calls for the eradication of extreme poverty by the year 2015. See also UNESCO's Universal Declaration on Cultural Diversity, adopted at the 31st General Conference of UNESCO in October 2001, www.unesco.org.

4. For a comprehensive discussion, see Elsa Stamatopoulou, *Cultural Rights in International Law: Article 27 of the Universal Declaration of Human Rights and Beyond* (Leiden/Boston: Martinus Nijhoff , 2007), 83–96.

5. These global conferences include the Rio Conference on Environment and Development, the Copenhagen Social Summit, the Vienna World Conference on Human Rights, the Beijing Conference on Women, and the Cairo Conference on Population and Development.

6. The text of these human rights treaties may be found in *Human Rights: A Compilation of International Instruments*, vol. I (Pt. I and Pt. II) and vol. II, Sales No. E.97.XIV.1 and E.02.XIV.4.

7. Of special importance is the work of the Committee on Economic, Social and Cultural Rights, which monitors the implementation of the International Covenant on Economic, Social and Cultural Rights. For its documentation, see

the Web site of the Office of the UN High Commissioner for Human Rights, www.ohchr.ch.

8. Stamatopoulou, *Cultural Rights in International Law*, 108–109.

9. UNDP, *Human Development Report 2004: Cultural Liberty in Today's Diverse World*, http://hdr.undp.org/en/reports/global/hdr2004/.

10. In international forums, such as the World Intellectual Property Organization (WIPO) and the International Fund for Agricultural Development (IFAD), the term "local communities" almost always refers to indigenous peoples.

11. The UN Permanent Forum on Indigenous Issues and the Special Rapporteur on the human rights and fundamental freedoms of indigenous people of the UN Human Rights Council have expressed their concern about the situation of these peoples who are at times attacked by outsiders, including those prompted by mining or logging interests. An international UN expert workshop was organized in 2006 by the Office of the High Commissioner for Human Rights; for the comprehensive recommendations adopted at that workshop, see the report of the OHCHR to the Sixth (2007) Session of the UNPFII, www.un.org/esa/socdev/unpfii.

12. E/2005/23, also available at www.un.org/esa/socdev/unpfii.

13. It was, for example, reported in October 2006 in the *New York Times* that a Chinese oil company, SAPET, refused to drill on isolated indigenous peoples' land in the Peruvian Amazon. In November 2005 SAPET had been awarded a concession (known as Lot 113) that was superimposed over an existing reserve for indigenous peoples who are not in contact with the non-indigenous society. Responding to the advocacy of local indigenous organizations, SAPET asked for the boundary of Lot 113 to be modified to exclude the uncontacted indigenous peoples' reserve, and the Peruvian government has agreed to this request. This kind of action by an oil company, while still rare, would have been unthinkable even ten years ago; it shows how local and international campaigns have brought the rights of indigenous peoples to the forefront of multinational firms' thinking.

14. At the request of the UNPFII, an interagency workshop took place in 2005 to discuss the issue; for the report, see www.un.org/esa/socdev/unpfii. For a discussion of ITK within the context of cultural rights, see Stamatopoulou, *Cultural Rights in International Law*, 207–225.

15. For the text of the Declaration on the Rights of Indigenous Peoples, see www.un.org/esa/socdev/unpfii.

16. Ibid.; Stamatopoulou, *Cultural Rights in International Law*, 171–173.

CHAPTER 14: Civil Society

1. Sebastian Mallaby, "NGOs: Fighting Poverty, Hurting the Poor," *Foreign Policy* 144(2004): 50–59.

2. Robert O. Keohane, "Global Governance and Democratic Accountability," in *Taming Globalization*, ed. David Held and Mathias Koenig-Archibui (Oxford: Polity, 2003).

YES

1. Francis Sejersted, Nobel Prize Committee Chairman, Presentation Speech for Nobel Laureates ICBL and Jody Williams, December 10, 1997; this quotation borrows Roger Alford's useful interpolation in his "The Nobel Effect: Nobel Peace Prize Laureates as International Norm Entrepreneurs," *Virginia Journal of International Law* 49, no. 1 (2008): 61, 147.
2. David Rieff, "The False Dawn of Civil Society," *The Nation*, February 22, 1999.
3. Justin Marozzi, "Whose World Is It Anyway?" *The Spectator* (London), August 5, 2000.
4. *The Economist*, January 29, 2000; and December 11, 1999, respectively.
5. See Sebastian Mallaby, *The World's Banker: A Story of Failed States, Financial Crises, and the Wealth and Poverty of Nations* (New York: Penguin, 2004), 7–8. This incident has generated practically a whole industry in NGO responses, none of which I myself find very convincing. However, perhaps the best and most representative is that of the former director of International Rivers, Juliette Majot, "On Trying To Do Well: Practicing Participatory Democracy through International Advocacy Campaigns," in Lisa Jordan and Peter Van Tuijl, eds., *NGO Accountability: Politics, Principles, and Innovations* (London: Earthscan, 2006); and see my review of that book and article in Kenneth Anderson, "What NGO Accountability Does and Does Not Mean," *American Journal of International Law* (January 2009).
6. Marozzi, "Whose World Is It, Anyway?"

CHAPTER 15: Democracy

YES

1. *Freedom in the World 2007: Selected Data from the Freedom House Annual Global Survey of Political Rights and Civil Liberties* (Washington, D.C.: Freedom House, 2007), 1.
2. David Adesnik and Michael McFaul, "Engaging Autocratic Allies to Promote Democracy," *Washington Quarterly* 29, no. 2 (Spring 2006): 7–26.
3. Robert Barro, *Determinants of Economic Growth: A Cross Country Empirical Study* (Cambridge, Mass.: MIT Press, 1997), 58.
4. Ronald Inglehart, "The Worldviews of Islamic Publics in Global Perspective," in *Worldviews of Islamic Publics*, ed. Mansour Moaddell (New York: Palgrave, 2005), 16; James Zogby, *What Arabs Think; Values, Beliefs and Concerns* (Washington, D.C.: Zogby International, 2002); Mark Tessler, "Do Islamic Orientations

Influence Attitudes toward Democracy in the Arab World? Evidence from Egypt, Jordan, Morocco, and Algeria," *International Journal of Comparative Sociology* 43, nos. 3–5 (June 2002): 229–249; and the cluster of articles under the rubric "How People View Democracy" in *Journal of Democracy* 12, no. 1 (January 2001): 93–145.

5. Samuel Huntington, *The Clash of Civilizations and the Remaking of World Order* (New York: Simon and Schuster, 1996).

6. Jack Snyder, *From Voting to Violence: Democratization and Nationalist Conflict* (New York: Norton, 2000); and Jack Snyder and Edward D. Mansfield, *Electing to Fight: Why Emerging Democracies Go to War* (Cambridge, Mass.: MIT Press, 2007).

7. Samuel P. Huntington, *Political Order in Changing Societies* (New Haven, Conn.: Yale University Press, 1968); Fareed Zakaria, *The Future of Freedom: Illiberal Democracy at Home and Abroad* (New York: Norton, 2003).

8. Thomas Carothers, "The 'Sequencing' Fallacy," *Journal of Democracy* 18, no.1 (2007): 12–27.

9. Michael McFaul, Abbas Milani, and Larry Diamond, "A Win-Win U.S. Strategy for Dealing with Iran," *Washington Quarterly*, Winter 2006–2007.

10. Senator John McCain proposed the idea of a new league of democracies in a speech at the Hoover Institution on May 2, 2007.

11. On these other modalities, see Tod Lindberg, "The Treaty of the Democratic Peace," *Weekly Standard*, February 12, 2007, 19–24; and Ivo Daalder and James Lindsey, "Democracies of the World Unite," *The American Interest* 2, no.3 (January–February 2007): 5–19.

NO

1. This chapter is a revised version of Edward D. Mansfield and Jack Snyder, "Prone to Violence: The Paradox of the Democratic Peace," *The National Interest* 82 (Winter 2005–2006), 39–47.

2. George W. Bush, "Remarks by the President," November 6, 2003.

3. See Michael Doyle, "Liberalism and World Politics," *American Political Science Review* 80, no. 4 (1986): 1151–1169; and Bruce Russett, *Grasping the Democratic Peace: Principles for a Post-Cold War World* (Princeton, N.J.: Princeton University Press, 1993).

4. See, for example, John M. Owen, "Perceptions and the Limits of Liberal Peace: The Mexican-American and Spanish American Wars," in *Paths to Peace: Is Democracy the Answer?* ed. Miriam Fendius Elman (Cambridge, Mass.: MIT Press, 1997).

5. Samuel P. Huntington, *Political Order in Changing Societies* (New Haven, Conn.: Yale University Press, 1968).

6. Jack Snyder, *From Voting to Violence: Democratization and Nationalist Conflict* (New York: Norton, 2000).

7. This section is based on Edward D. Mansfield and Jack Snyder, *Electing to Fight: Why Emerging Democracies Go to War* (Cambridge, Mass.: MIT Press, 2005).

8. Susan Woodward, *Balkan Tragedy* (Washington, D.C.: Brookings Institution, 1995), 17.

9. Stuart Kaufman, *Modern Hatreds: The Symbolic Politics of Ethnic War* (Ithaca, N.Y.: Cornell University Press, 2001), chap. 3.

10. David R. Mares, *Violent Peace: Militarized Interstate Bargaining in Latin America* (New York: Columbia University Press, 2001), chap. 7.

11. Franklin Steves, "Regime Change and War: Domestic Politics and the Escalation of the Ethiopia-Eritrea Conflict," *Cambridge Review of International Affairs* 16, no.1 (2003): 119–133.

12. On India, see Ian Talbot, *India and Pakistan* (London: Arnold, 2000), 275; on Pakistan, see Hasan-Askari Rizvi, *Military, State and Society in Pakistan* (New York: St. Martin's, 2000), chap. 10. Bruce Russett and John Oneal, in *Triangulating Peace: Democracy, Interdependence, and International Organizations* (New York: Norton, 2001), 48, discuss whether the Kargil War should be counted as a war between democracies.

13. Gérard Prunier, *The Rwanda Crisis: History of a Genocide* (New York: Columbia University Press, 1995), chaps. 3 and 5.

14. See Mansfield and Snyder, *Electing to Fight*, chaps. 5 and 6.

15. James Fearon and David Laitin, "Ethnicity, Insurgency, and Civil War," *American Political Science Review* 97, no. 1 (2003): 91–106.

16. Larry Diamond, "Is the Third Wave Over?" *Journal of Democracy* 7, no. 3 (July 1996): 20–37.

17. Adrian Karatnycky, ed., *Freedom in the World: The Annual Survey of Political Rights and Civil Liberties, 2001–2002* (New York: Freedom House, 2002), 11–15, 20–34.

18. F. Gregory Gause, "Can Democracy Stop Terrorism?" *Foreign Affairs* 84, no. 5 (September–October 2005): 62.

19. Sheri Berman, in "Islamism, Revolution, and Civil Society," *Perspectives on Politics* 1, no. 2 (June 2003): 257–272, esp. 265, draws parallels to belligerent civil society in the flawed democracy of Weimar Germany and stresses the "Huntingtonian gap" between high demand for political participation and ineffective state institutions. See Huntington, *Political Order in Changing Societies*.

20. United Nations Development Programme, *Human Development Report 2004* (New York: Oxford University Press, 2004); Adam Przeworski et al., *Democracy and Development* (Cambridge: Cambridge University Press, 2000), 101; Council on Foreign Relations, *In Support of Arab Democracy: Why and How*, task force report 54 (New York: Council on Foreign Relations, 2005), 61–62; and Daniela Donno and Bruce Russett, "Islam, Authoritarianism, and Female Empowerment: What Are the Linkages?" *World Politics* 56, no. 4 (July 2004): 582–607.

21. Vali Nasr, "The Rise of 'Muslim Democracy,'" *Journal of Democracy* 16, no. 2 (April 2005): 13–27.

22. For a balanced view that discusses many of the following points, see David Bachman, "China's Democratization: What Difference Would It Make for U.S.-

China Relations," in *What If China Doesn't Democratize?* ed. Edward Friedman and Barrett McCormick (Armonk, N.Y.: M.E. Sharpe, 2000).

23. The authors are Song Qiang, Zhang Zangzang, and Qiao Bian.

24. Jack Snyder, "Empire: A Blunt Tool for Democratization," *Daedalus*, Spring 2005, Volume 134, no. 2: 58–71.

25. Carlotta Gall, "New Generation of Afghan Voters Is Finding Its Voice," *New York Times*, September 15, 2005, A3.

26. Mark Peceny, "Forcing Them to Be Free," *Political Science Quarterly* 52, no. 3 (September 1999): 549–582, esp. table 1, p. 564.

27. On the links between membership in regional organizations and democratization, see Jon Pevehouse, *Democracy from Above* (New York: Cambridge University Press, 2005).

28. For a balanced discussion, see Thomas Carothers, "Is Gradualism Possible? Choosing a Strategy for Promoting Democracy in the Middle East," chap. 18 in *Critical Mission: Essays on Democracy Promotion* (Washington, D.C.: Carnegie Endowment for International Peace, 2004).

29. Adrian Karatnycky and Peter Ackerman, *How Freedom Is Won: From Civic Resistance to Durable Democracy* (New York: Freedom House, 2005).

30. Natan Sharansky with Ron Dermer, *The Case for Democracy: The Power of Freedom to Overcome Tyranny and Terror* (New York: Public Affairs, 2004), 173.

REFERENCES

Introduction: Understanding Globalization

Beck, U. 1992. *Risk Society: Towards a New Modernity*. Newbury Park, Calif.: Sage.

Bello, Walden. 2004. *DeGlobalization: Ideas for a New World Economy*. London: Zed Books.

Bhagwati, J. 2008. "Globalization with a Human Face." In *The Future of Globalization*, edited by E. Zedillo. New York: Routledge.

Biersteker, T. 2000. "Globalization as a Mode of Thinking in Major Institutional Actors." *The Political Economy of Globalization*, edited by N. Woods. New York: St. Martin's.

Brzezinski, Z. 2007. *Second Chance*. New York: Basic Books.

Burman, Stephen. 2007. *The State of the American Empire: How the USA Shapes the World*. London: Earthscan.

Castells, Manuel. 2005. "Global Governance and Global Politics," *PS*, January, 9–16.

Cavanagh, J., Ed. 1995. *South-North: Citizen Strategies to Transform a Divided World*. San Francisco: International Forum on Globalization.

Chasek, Pam. 1995. "Environmental Organizations and Multilateral Diplomacy." In *Multilateral Diplomacy and the United Nations Today*, edited by James P. Muldoon Jr., 156–157. Boulder, Colo.: Westview.

Clark, W. C., and R.E. Munn, eds. 1986. *Sustainable Development of the Biosphere*. Cambridge: Cambridge University Press.

Crutzen, P.J. 2002. "Geology of Mankind—The Anthropocene." *Nature* 415: 23.

Fishman, C. 2006. *The Wal-Mart Effect*. New York, Penguin.

Frieden, Jeffry A. 2006. *Global Capitalism*. New York: Norton.

Friedman, Thomas L. 2000. *The Lexus and the Olive Tree*. New York: Anchor Books.

Giddens, Anthony. 2003. *Runaway World*. New York: Routledge.

Gilani, Ijaz. S. 2008. *Uncovering the Ethical: Recovering Meaning in International Relations Scholarship*. Conference Honoring the Memory of Hayward R. Alker, Watson Institute, Brown University.

Haq, M. ul. 1995. *Reflections on Human Development*. New York: Oxford University Press.

Held, D., and A. McGrew. 1999. "Globalization." *Global Governance* 5, no. 4: 483–496.
_____. 2007. *Globalization/Anti-Globalization*. 2nd ed. Cambridge: Polity.

Huntington, Samuel P. 1991. *The Third Wave: Democratization in the Late Twentieth Century*. Norman: University of Oklahoma Press.

Jervis, R. 1997. *System Effects: Complexity in Political and Social Life*. Princeton, N.J.: Princeton University Press.

Kates, R., B.L. Turner II, and William C. Clark. 1990. "The Great Transformation." In *The Earth as Transformed by Human Action*, edited by B.L. Turner II, R. Kates, J. Richards, J. Mathews, and W. Meyer. Cambridge: Cambridge University Press, 1–17.

Keck, Margaret E., and Kathryn Sikkink. 1998. *Activists beyond Borders*. Ithaca, N.Y.: Cornell University Press.

Keohane, Robert O., and Joseph S. Nye. 2000. "Globalization: What's New? What's Not? (And So What?)." *Foreign Policy*, Spring.

Khagram, Sanjeev, James V. Riker, and Kathryn Sikkink, eds. 2002. *Restructuring World Politics*. Minneapolis: University of Minnesota Press.

Khor, Martin. "Effects of Globalisation on Sustainable Development after UNCED," http://www.twnside.org/sg/title/rio-cn.htm.

Kissinger, Henry. 2001. *Does America Need a Foreign Policy?* New York: Simon & Schuster.

Klein, Naomi. 2002. *No Logo*. New York: Picador.

Knowlton, Brian. 2007. "Globalization, According to the World, Is a Good Thing. Sort Of." *New York Times*, October 5.

Krugman, Paul. 1994. *Peddling Prosperity*. New York: Norton.

La Porte, T. R., ed. 1975. *Organized Social Complexity: Challenge to Politics and Policy*. Princeton, N.J.: Princeton University Press.

Ling, C.Y., and M. Khor. 2001. *International Environmental Governance: Some Issues from a Developing Country Perspective*. Penang, Malaysia: Third World Network.

Maddison, A. 2007. *Contours of the World Economy, 1–2030 AD*. Oxford: Oxford University Press.

Muldoon, J. P. A., Jr., JoAnn Fagot, Richard Reitano, and Earl Sullivan, ed. 1999. *Multilateral Diplomacy and the United Nations Today*. Boulder, Colo.: Westview.

Nye, Joseph S. 2002. *The Paradox of American Power*. Oxford: Oxford University Press.

Perrow, C. 1999. *Normal Accidents: Living with High-Risk Technologies*. Princeton, N.J.: Princeton University Press.

Ponting, C. 1993. *A Green History of the World: The Environment and the Collapse of Great Civilizations*. New York: Penguin Books.

Rice, Condoleeza. 2000. "Promoting the National Interest." *Foreign Affairs*, February.

Rodrik, Dani. 2001. "The Global Governance of Trade as if Development Really Mattered." New York: United Nations Development Program.

Rosenau, J. N. 2003. *Distant Proximities*. Princeton, N.J.: Princeton University Press.

Roy, Arundhati. 2001. *Power Politics*. Boston: South End Press.

Ruggie, John Gerard. 1998. *Constructing the World Polity*. London: Routledge.

Schellnhuber, H. J., P. J. Crutzen et al., eds. 2004. *Earth System Analysis for Sustainability*. Cambridge, Mass.: MIT Press.

Scott, James. 1998. *Seeing Like a State*. New Haven, Conn.: Yale University Press.

Scholte, J. A. 2000. *Globalization: A Critical Introduction*. New York: St. Martin's.

Shiva, Vandana. 2005. *Earth Democracy*. London: Zed Books.

Simmons, Beth A., Frank Dobbin, and Geoffrey Garrett. 2006. "Introduction: The International Diffusion of Liberalism." *International Organization* 60, no. 4: 781–810.

Simon, H.A. 1981. "The Architecture of Complexity." *The Sciences of the Artificial,* ed. H.A. Simon. Cambridge, Mass.: MIT Press.

Slaughter, Anne-Marie. 2004. *A New World Order.* Princeton, N.J.: Princeton University Press.

Speth, J. G. 2008. *The Bridge at the Edge of the World.* New Haven, Conn.: Yale University Press.

Stiglitz, Joseph E., and Andrew Charlton. 2005. *Fair Trade for All.* Oxford: Oxford University Press.

Wolf, Martin. 2003. "The Morality of the Market." *Foreign Policy,* September/October.

_____. 2001. "Will the Nation-State Survive Globalization?" *Foreign Affairs* 80, no 1. (January–February).

World Bank. 2004. *Mini Atlas of Global Development.* Washington, D.C.: The World Bank.

Zedillo, E., ed. 2008. *The Future of Globalization.* New York: Routledge.

Chapter 1: Trade Liberalization and Economic Growth

YES

Bhagwati, J. 1992. *India's Economy: The Shackled Giant.* Oxford: Clarendon Press.

Bourguignon, F., and C. Morrisson. 2002. "Inequality among World Citizens: 1820–1992." *American Economic Review.*

Chen, S., and M. Ravallion. 2004. "How Did the World's Poorest Fare Since the Early 1980s?" World Bank mimeo.

Collier, P., and R. Reinikka. 2001. "Reconstruction and Liberalization: An Overview." In *Uganda's Recovery: The Role of Farms, Firms, and Government,* edited by R. Reinikka and P. Collier. Washington, D.C.: World Bank, Regional and Sectoral Studies.

Dollar, David, and Aart Kraay. 2002. "Institutions, Trade, and Growth." *Journal of Monetary Economics.*

Dollar, David, and Borje Ljunggren. 1997. "Going Global, Vietnam." In *Going Global: Transition from Plan to Market in the World Economy,* edited by Padma Desai, 439–471. Cambridge, Mass.: MIT Press.

Eckaus, R. 1997. "Going Global: China." In *Going Global: Transition from Plan to Market in the World Economy,* edited by Padma Desai, 415–437. Cambridge, Mass.: MIT Press.

Lindert, P., and J. Williamson. 2001. "Does Globalization Make the World More Unequal?" National Bureau of Economic Research Working Paper No. 8228. Cambridge, Mass.: National Bureau of Economic Research.

Romer, P. 1986. "Idea Gaps and Object Gaps in Economic Development." *Journal of Monetary Economics* 32.

Chapter 2: Trade and Equality

YES

Atkinson, A.B., and A. Brandolini. 2001. "Promise and Pitfalls in the Use of 'Secondary' Data-Sets: Income Inequality in OECD Countries as a Case Study." *Journal of Economic Literature* 39, no. 3: 771–800.

Bhalla, S. 2005. *Imagine There's No Country: Poverty, Inequality, and Growth in the Era of Globalization.* Washington, D.C.: Institute for International Economics.

Chang, R., L. Kaltani, and N. Loayze. 2005. "Openness Can be Good for Growth: The Role of Policy Complementarities." World Bank Policy Research Working Paper no. 3763.

Dollar, D., and A. Kraay. 2002. "Growth is Good for the Poor." *Journal of Economic Growth* 7, no. 3: 195–225.

Fields, G.S. 1989. "Changes in Poverty and Inequality in Developing Countries." *World Bank Research Observer* 4, no. 2: 167–185.

Kraay, A. 2006. "When Is Growth Pro-poor? Evidence from a Panel of Countries." *Journal of Development Economics* 80, no. 1: 198–227.

McCulloch, N., L.A. Winters, and X. Cirera. 2001. *Trade Liberalization and Poverty: A Handbook.* London: Center for Economic Policy Research.

Milanovic, B. 2005a. *Worlds Apart: Measuring International and Global Inequality.* Princeton, N.J.: Princeton University Press.

_____. 2005b. "Can We Discern the Effects of Globalisation on Income Distribution?" *World Bank Economic Review* 19, no. 1: 21–44.

Noguer, M., and M. Siscart. 2005. "Trade Raises Income: A Precise and Robust Result." *Journal of International Economics* 65, no. 2: 447–460.

Ravallion, M. 2001. "Growth, Inequality and Poverty: Looking Beyond Averages." *World Development* 29, no. 11: 1803–1815.

_____. 2005. "Globalization and Poor People: The Debate and Evidence." Max Corden Lecture, University of Melbourne.

Reinikka, R., and P. Collier, eds. 2001. *Uganda's Recovery—The Role of Farms, Firms, and Government.* Washington, D.C.: World Bank.

Rodriguez, F., and D. Rodrik. 2001. "Trade Policy and Economic Growth: A Skeptic's Guide to the Cross-national Evidence." *NBER Macroeconomics Annual 2000* 15: 261–325. Cambridge, Mass.: MIT Press.

Wacziarg, R.T., and N.H. Welch. 2005. "Trade Liberalization and Growth: New Evidence." NBER Working Paper no. 10152.

Winters, L.A. 2002. "Trade Liberalisation and Poverty: What Are the Links?" *The World Economy* 25, no. 9: 1339–1367.

_____. 2004. "Trade Liberalisation and Economic Performance: An Overview." *Economic Journal* 114, no. 493: F4–21.

_____. 2006. "International Trade and Poverty: Cause or Cure?" *Australian Economic Review* 39, no. 4: 347–358.

_____. 2008. "North-South Trade," in *Princeton Encyclopedia of the World Economy*. Princeton, N.J.: Princeton University Press.

Winters, L. A., ed. 2007. *Critical Perspectives on the World Trading System: The WTO and Poverty and Inequality*. Cheltenham, UK: Edward Elgar. 2 vol.

Winters, L. A., N. McCulloch, and A. McKay. 2004. "Trade Liberalization and Poverty: The Evidence So Far." *Journal of Economic Literature* 42 (March): 72–115.

NO

Atkinson, A. B., ed. 2004. *New Sources of Development Finance*. WIDER Studies in Development Economics. Oxford: Oxford University Press.

Bannister, Geoffrey, and Kamau Thugge. 2001. "International Trade and Poverty Alleviation." Washington, D.C.: International Monetary Fund Working Paper 01/54.

Bardhan, P. 2004. "The Impact of Globalization on the Poor," in *Globalization, Poverty, and Inequality*, edited by S. M. Collins and C. Graham. Brookings Trade Forum 2004. Washington, D.C.: Brookings Institution Press.

Barro, Robert. 2000. "Inequality and Growth in a Panel of Countries." *Journal of Economic Growth* 5, no. 1.

Birdsall, Nancy. 2005. "The World Is Not Flat: Inequality and Injustice in Our Global Economy." WIDER Annual Lecture 9, UNU-WIDER, Helsinki.

_____. 2007a. "Stormy Days on an Open Field: Asymmetries in the Global Economy." Working Paper Working Paper 81. Washington, D.C.: Center for Global Development.

_____. 2007b. "Income Distribution: Effects on Growth and Development." Working Paper 118. Washington, D.C.: Center for Global Development.

_____. 2008. "Reflections on the Macro-Foundations of the Middle Class." Policy Brief. Washington, D.C.: Center for Global Development and International Food Policy Research Institution.

Birdsall, Nancy, Augusto de la Torre, and Rachel Menezes. 2007. *Fair Growth: Economic Policies for the Poor and Middle-Income Majority*. Washington, D.C.: Center for Global Development.

Cline, William. 2007. "Global Warming and Agriculture: Impact Estimates by Country." Washington, D.C.: Center for Global Development.

Corden, W. M. 1974. *Trade Policy and Economic Welfare*. Oxford: Oxford University Press.

Cornia, Giovanni Andrea, Tony Addison, and Sampsa Kiiski. 2004. "Income Distribution Changes and Their Impact in the Post–Second World War Period." In *Inequality, Growth, and Poverty in an Era of Liberalization and Globalization*, edited by Giovanni Andrea Cornia. Oxford: Oxford University Press.

Dixit, Avinash, and Victor Norman. 1980. *Theory of International Trade*. Cambridge: Cambridge University Press.

Diwan, I. 2001. "Debt as Sweat: Labor, Financial Crisis, and the Globalization of Capital." Washington, D.C.: World Bank. Mimeo.

Duryea, S., and M. Székely. 1998. "Labor Markets in Latin America: A Supply-Side Story." IDB OCE Working Paper 374. Washington, D.C.: Inter-American Development Bank.

Easterlin, Richard A. 1995. "Will Raising the Incomes of All Increase the Happiness of All?" *Journal of Economic Behavior and Organization* 27, no. 1: 35–47.

Easterly, William. 2004. "Channels from Globalization to Inequality: Productivity World versus Factor World," in *Brookings Trade Forum 2004: Globalization, Poverty, and Inequality*, edited by S. M. Collins and C. Graham. Washington, D.C.: Brookings Institution Press.

Edwards, Sebastian. 1993. "Openness, Trade Liberalization, and Growth in Developing Countries." *Journal of Economic Literature* 31: 3.

Elliott, Kimberly. 2005. "Big Sugar and the Political Economy of U.S. Agricultural Policy." Washington, D.C.: Center for Global Development.

Fernandez de Cordoba, Santiago, Sam Laird, and Jose Maria Serena. Nd. "Trade Liberalization and Adjustment Costs." United Nations Conference on Trade and Development. http://r0.unctad.org/ditc/tab/events/nama/docs/Adjustment_Cost17Jan_v1.pdf.

Government Accountability Office. 2007. "Industry Certification Would Likely Make More Workers Eligible, but Design and Implementation Challenges Exist." Washington, D.C.: GAO Report 07-919.

Higgins, Matthew, and Jeffrey Williamson. 1999. "Explaining Inequality the World Round: Cohort Size, Kuznets Curves, and Openness." Boston: National Bureau of Economic Research Working Paper 7224.

Hirschman, Albert O. 1973) "The Changing Tolerance for Income Inequality in the Course of Economic Development, with a Mathematical Appendix by Michael Rothschild." *Quarterly Journal of Economics* 87: 544–566.

Hoekman, Bernard, and Susan Prowse. 2005. "Economic Policy Responses to Preference Erosion: From Trade as Aid to Aid for Trade." Washington, D.C.: World Bank Policy Research Working Paper No. 3721.

Krugman, Paul, and Maurice Obstfeld. 1999. *International Economics: Theory and Policy*. Reading, Mass.: Addison Wesley.

Lawrence, Robert, and M. Slaughter. 1993. "International Trade and American Wages in the 1980s: Giant Sucking Sound or Small Hiccup?" Brookings Papers on Economic Activity. Washington, D.C.: Brookings Institution Press.

Levy, F. 1999. *The New Dollars and Dreams: American Incomes and Economic Change*. New York: Russell Sage Foundation.

Lindert, Peter, and Jeffrey Williamson. 2001. "Does Globalization Make the World More Unequal?" Boston: NBER Working Paper 8228.

Milanovic, Branko. 2005. *Worlds Apart: Measuring International and Global Inequality*. Princeton, N.J.: Princeton University Press.

Milanovic, Branko, and Lyn Squire. 2005. "Does Tariff Liberalization Increase Wage Inequality? Some Empirical Evidence." Boston: NBER Working Paper 11046.

Ravallion, Martin. 1999. *Protecting the Poor in Crisis*. PREM Note No.12. Washington, D.C.: The World Bank.

Ravallion, Martin, and Michael Lokshin. 2005. "Who Cares about Relative Deprivation?" World Bank Policy Research Working Paper 3782. Washington, D.C.: The World Bank.

Sachs, Jeffrey D., and Andrew Warner. 1995. "Economic Reform and the Process of Global Integration." *Brookings Papers on Economic Activity* 1:1–118.

Sachs, Jeffrey, and H. J. Shatz. 1994. "Trade and Jobs in U.S. Manufacturing." *Brookings Papers on Economic Activity* 1: 1–84.

Saggi, Kamal. 2002. "Trade, Foreign Direct Investment, and International Technology Transfer: A Survey." *World Bank Research Observer* 17, no. 2: 191–235.

Stiglitz, J. 2002. *Globalization and Its Discontents.* New York: Norton.

Székely, M. 1999. "Volatility: Children Pay the Price." *Latin American Economic Policies* 8 (Third quarter): 3–4.

Terrell, K. 2000. "Worker Mobility and Transition to a Market Economy: Winners and Losers," in *New Markets, New Ideas: Economic and Social Mobility in a Changing World,* edited by N. Birdsall and C. Graham. Washington, D.C.: Brookings Institution and Carnegie Endowment for International Peace.

UN World Institute for Development Economics Research. 2008. World Income Inequality Database.

UNCTAD. 2001. *World Investment Report 2001: Promoting Linkages.* New York: United Nations Conference on Trade and Development.

Vyborny, Katherine. 2005. "What Could the Doha Round Mean for Africa?" Washington, D.C. Carnegie Endowment for International Peace.

Wade, Robert. 2004. "Is Globalization Reducing Poverty and Inequality?" *World Development* 32, no. 4: 567–589.

Winters, Alan. 2000. "Trade Liberalization and Poverty." Poverty Research Unit at Sussex Working Paper 7. University of Sussex.

Wood, Adrian. 1995. "How Trade Hurt Unskilled Workers." *Journal of Economic Perspectives* 9: 3.

_____. 1994. *North-South Trade, Employment and Inequality.* Oxford: Clarendon Press.

Chapter 4: Emerging Technology and Political Institutions

YES

Ackerman, F., and L. Heinzerling. 2002. "Pricing the Priceless: Cost-Benefit Analysis of Environmental Protection." *University of Pennsylvania Law Review* 150: 1553–1584.

Arcuri, A. 2007. "The Case for a Procedural Version of the Precautionary Principle Erring on the Side of Environmental Preservation." Global Law Working Paper No. 09/04, Social Sciences Research Network, http://ssrn.com/abstract=967779.

Crews, C. W. 2004. *Ten Thousand Commandments: An Annual Snapshot of the Federal Regulatory State.* Washington, D.C.: Competitive Enterprise Institute.

Cropper, M. L., and P. R. Portney. 1992. "Discounting Human Lives." *Resources* 108 (Summer 1992): 1–4.

Dickson, B., ed. 2005. *Biodiversity and the Precautionary Principle: Risk, Uncertainty and Practice in Conservation and Sustainable Use.* London: Earthscan.

Fogel R. W. 2003. *Changes in the Process of Aging during the Twentieth Century: Findings and Procedures of the Early Indicators Project.* National Bureau of Economic Research Working Paper 9941. Cambridge, Mass.: NBER.

Goklany, I. M. 2001. *The Precautionary Principle: A Critical Appraisal of Environmental Risk Assessment.* Washington, D.C.: Cato Institute.

_____. 2002. "From Precautionary Principle to Risk-Risk Analysis." *Nature Biotechnology* 20: 1075.

_____. 2007. *The Improving State of the World: Why We're Living Longer, Healthier, More Comfortable Lives on a Cleaner Planet.* Washington, D.C.: Cato Institute.

Intergovernmental Panel on Climate Change. 2007. *Climate Change 2007: Impacts, Adaptation and Vulnerability.* Contribution of Working Group II to the Fourth Assessment Report of the Intergovernmental Panel on Climate Change. Cambridge, U.K.: Cambridge University Press.

Mandel, G. N., and Gathii, J. T. 2006. "Cost-Benefit Analysis versus the Precautionary Principle: Beyond Cass Sunstein's Laws of Fear." http://ssrn.com/abstract= 822186.

Manton, K. G., X. L. Gu, and V. L. Lamb. 2006. "Change in Chronic Disability from 1982 to 2004/2005 as Measured by Long-term Changes in Function and Health in the U.S. Elderly Population." *Proceedings of the National Academy of Sciences* 103: 18374–18379.

Marvier, M., C. McCreedy, J. Regetz, and P. Kareiva. 2007. "A Meta-Analysis of Effects of Bt Cotton and Maize on Nontarget Invertebrates." *Science* 316: 1475–1477.

Pollan, M. 2001. "The Year in Ideas: A to Z; The Precautionary Principle." *New York Times Sunday Magazine,* December 9, 2001, 92, 94.

Sunstein, C. R. 2002. *Risk and Reason: Safety, Law and the Environment.* Cambridge, U.K.: Cambridge University Press.

_____. 2005. *Laws of Fear: Beyond the Precautionary Principle.* Cambridge, U.K.: Cambridge University Press.

Wilson, K., and M. N. Ricketts. 2004. "The Success of Precaution? Managing the Risk of Transfusion Transmission of Variant Creutzfeldt-Jakob Disease." *Transfusion* 44: 1475–1478.

NO

BBC. 2001. "DDT and Africa's War on Malaria." London: *BBC News.*

Bell, Bob W., Jr. 2007. "Combating Malaria and Poverty with Biopesticides." *Business Daily Africa.*

Brody, Arnold R., et al. 1990. "In Reply: Asbestos, Carcinogenicity, and Public Policy." *Science* 248, no. 4957: 795–802.

Bullard, Clark. "Letter to the Editor: Elizabeth Whelan Deserves a Response." 2005. *Rachel's Precaution Reporter,* http://www.precaution.org/lib/05/prn_response_to_ whelan.050919.htm (accessed August 18, 2007).

Chen, Aimin, and Walter J. Rogan. 2003. "Nonmalarial Infant Deaths and DDT Use for Malaria Control." *Emerging Infectious Diseases* 9, no. 8: 960–964.

Commission of the European Communities. 2000. "Communication from the Commission on the Precautionary Principle." Brussels: Commission of the European Communities.

Cranor, Carl. 2005. "Scientific Inference in the Laboratory and the Law." *American Journal of Public Health* 95: S121–S128.

DeKay, Michael L., et al. 2002. "Risk-Based Decision Analysis in Support of Precautionary Policies." *Journal of Risk Research* 5, no. 4: 28.

Energy Information Administration. 2007. *Annual Energy Review.* Report No. DOE/EIA-0384(2007), posted June 23, 2008, http://www.eia.doe.gov/emeu/aer/pdf/pages/sec8_3.pdf.

Environmental Protection Agency. "DDT Ban Takes Effect." 1972. http://www.epa.gov/history/topics/ddt/01.htm (accessed August 24, 2007).

European Court of Justice. 2001. "Commission of the European Communities V French Republic." Case C-1/00.

Government of Canada. 2003. "A Framework for the Application of Precaution in Science-Based Decision Making About Risk."

Graham, John D. 2001. "Decision-Analytic Refinements of the Precautionary Principle." *Journal of Risk Research* 4, no. 2: 14.

———. "A Future for the Precautionary Principle?" 2001. *Journal of Risk Research* 4, no. 2: 3.

———. "Perspectives on the Precautionary Principle." 2000. *Human and Ecological Risk* 6, no. 3: 3.

Graham, John D., and Susan Hsia. 2002. "Europe's Precautionary Principle: Promise and Pitfalls." *Journal of Risk Research* 5, no. 4: 19.

Graham, John D., and Jianhui Hu. 2007. "The Risk-Benefit Balance in the United States: Who Decides?" *Health Affairs* 26, no. 3: 11.

Graham, John D., and Jonathan B. Wiener. 1995. *Risk Versus Risk: Tradeoffs in Protecting Health and the Environment.* Boston: Harvard University Press.

Hansen, Steffen Foss, Martin P. Krayer von Krauss, and Joel Tickner. 2007. "Categorizing Mistaken False Positives in Regulation of Human and Environmental Health." *Risk Analysis* 27, no. 1: 15.

Harremoes, Poul, et al., eds. 2002. *The Precautionary Principle in the 20th Century: Late Lessons from Early Warnings.* London: Earthscan.

Jordan, Andrew, and Timothy O'Riordan. 1998. "The Precautionary Principle in Contemporary Environmental Policy and Politics." *Wingspread Conference on "Implementing the Precautionary Principle."* Racine, Wisconsin.

Kysar, Douglas. 2006. *It Might Have Been: Risk, Precaution, and Opportunity Costs.* Cornell Legal Studies Research Paper No. 06-023.

Lempert, Robert J., and Myles T. Collins. 2007. "Managing the Risk of Uncertain Threshold Responses: Comparison of Robust, Optimum, and Precautionary Approaches." *Risk Analysis* 27, no. 4.

Marchant, Gary E. 2003. "From General Policy to Legal Rule: Aspirations and Limitations of the Precautionary Principle." *Environmental Health Perspectives* 111, no. 14: 1799–1803.

Mayer, Brian, Phil Brown, and Meadow Linder. 2002. "Moving Further Upstream: From Toxics Reduction to the Precautionary Principle." *Public Health Reports* 117, no. 6: 12.

Morris, Julian, ed. 2000. *Rethinking Risk and the Precautionary Principle.* Boston: Butterworth-Heinemann.

Ogodo, Ochieng'. 2007. "Kenyan Fish Joins the Fight against Malaria." *SciDev.net.*

Oreskes, Naomi. 2004. "Science and Public Policy: What's Proof Got to Do With It?" *Environmental Science & Policy* 7, no. 5: 369–383.

O'Riordan, Timothy, and James Cameron, eds. 1994. *Interpreting the Precautionary Principle.* London: Earthscan.

Peterson, Martin. 2006. "The Precautionary Principle Is Incoherent." *Risk Analysis* 26, no. 3: 6.

Pittinger, Charles A., and William E. Bishop. 1999. "Unraveling the Chimera: A Corporate View of the Precautionary Principle." *Human and Ecological Risk* 5, no. 5: 12.

President's Council on Sustainable Development. 1999. *Towards a Sustainable America: Advancing Prosperity, Opportunity, and a Healthy Environment for the 21st Century.* Washington, D.C.

Raffensperger, Carolyn, and Joel Tickner, eds. 1999. *Protecting Public Health and the Environment: Implementing the Precautionary Principle.* Washington, D.C.: Island Press.

Rio Declaration on Environment and Development. 1992. UN Doc. A/CONF.151/26 (vol. I); 31 ILM 874.

Sandin, Per. 1999. "Dimensions of the Precautionary Principle." *Human and Ecological Risk* 5, no. 5: 20.

_____. 2004. "The Precautionary Principle and the Concept of Precaution." *Environmental Values* 13: 14.

Sandin, Per, et al. 2002. "Five Charges against the Precautionary Principle." *Journal of Risk Research* 5, no. 4: 12.

Sunstein, Cass. 2003. "Beyond the Precautionary Principle." *University of Pennsylvania Law Review* 151, no. 3: 55.

_____. 2005. *Laws of Fear: Beyond the Precautionary Principle.* New York: Cambridge University Press.

Tickner, Joel, ed. 2003. *Precaution, Environmental Science, and Preventive Public Policy.* Washington, D.C.: Island Press.

United Nations Framework Convention on Climate Change. 1992. UN Doc. A/AC.237/18 (Part II)/Add.1; 31 I.L.M. 849.

Vedrine, Hubert. 1999. "French Minister Defends Beef Ban." Transcript of radio broadcast. *BBC News*, London, December 9.

Wagner, Wendy. 2000. "The Precautionary Principle and Chemical Regulation in the U.S." *Human and Ecological Risk* 6, no. 3: 19.

Whelan, Elizabeth. 2000. "Can Too Much Safety Be Hazardous? A Critical Look at the 'Precautionary Principle.'" American Council on Science and Health. http://www.acsh.org/healthissues/newsID.236/healthissue_detail.asp (accessed August 18, 2007).

Wiener, Jonathan B., and Michael D. Rogers. 2002. "Comparing Precaution in the United States and Europe." *Journal of Risk Research* 5, no. 4: 44.

Chapter 5: Terrorism and Security

NO

Arkin, William M. 2006. "Goodbye War on Terrorism, Hello Long War," http://blogs.washingtonpost.com/earlywarning (26 January).

Bergen, Peter. 2007. "Where You Bin? The Return of Al Qaeda," *New Republic,* January 29.

Center for Nonproliferation Studies. 2002. "'Suitcase Nukes': A Reassessment." Monterey Institute of International Studies, Monterey, Calif., September 22, cns.miis.edu/pubs/week/020923.htm.

Gerges, Fawaz A. 2005. *The Far Enemy: Why Jihad Went Global.* New York: Cambridge University Press.

Lustick, Ian S. 2006. *Trapped in the War on Terror.* Philadelphia: University of Pennsylvania Press.

Mueller, John. 2006. *Overblown: How Politicians and the Terrorism Industry Inflate National Security Threats, and Why We Believe Them.* New York: Free Press.

Sageman, Marc. 2007. *Leaderless Jihad.* Philadelphia: University of Pennsylvania Press.

Wirz, Christoph, and Emmanuel Egger. 2005. "Use of Nuclear and Radiological Weapons by Terrorists?" *International Review of the Red Cross* 87, no. 859 (September): 497–510, http://www.icrc.org/Web/eng/siteeng0.nsf/htmlall/review-859-p497/$File/irrc_859_Egger_Wirz.pdf.

Chapter 6: Nuclear Weapons

NO

Blair, Bruce G. 1994. *The Logic of Accidental Nuclear War.* Washington, D.C.: Brookings Institution.

Feaver, Peter D. 1997. "Neooptimists and the Enduring Problem of Nuclear Proliferation." *Security Studies* 6, no. 4: 93–125.

Lewis, Jeffrey G. 2007. *The Minimum Means of Reprisal: China's Search for Security in the Nuclear Age.* Cambridge, Mass.: MIT Press.

Sagan, Scott D. 1993. *The Limits of Safety: Organizations, Accidents, and Nuclear Weapons.* Princeton, N.J.: Princeton University Press.

Sagan, Scott D., and Kenneth N. Waltz. 2003. *The Spread of Nuclear Weapons: A Debate Renewed.* New York: Norton.

Sanger, David E., and William J. Broad. 2007. "U.S. Secretly Aids Pakistan in Guarding Nuclear Arms." *New York Times*, November 17.

Sechser, Todd S. 1998. "How to Live with the Bomb." *Wall Street Journal*, September 1, A18.

Chapter 9: The Future of Energy

NO

Lynch, Michael C. 2003. "The New Pessimism about Petroleum Resources: Debunking the Hubbert Model (and Hubbert Modelers)." *Minerals and Energy* 18, no.1.

Rifkin, Jeremy. 2003. *The Hydrogen Economy.* New York: Penguin.

Chapter 12: Immigration

YES

Alba, Richard, and Victor Nee. 2003. *Remaking the American Mainstream: Assimilation and Contemporary Immigration.* Cambridge, Mass.: Harvard University Press.

Bhagwati, Jagdish. 1998. *A Stream of Windows: Unsettling Reflections on Trade, Immigration, and Democracy.* Cambridge, Mass.: MIT Press.

Brimelow, Peter. 1995. *Alien Nation: Common Sense about America's Immigration Disaster.* New York: Random House.

Brochmann, Grete, and Tomas Hammar, eds. 1999. *Mechanisms of Immigration Control: A Comparative Analysis of European Regulation Policies.* Oxford: Berg.

Brubaker, Rogers, ed. 1989. *Immigration and the Politics of Citizenship in Europe and North America.* Lanham, Md.: University Press of America.

_____. 1992. *Citizenship and Nationhood in France and Germany.* Cambridge, Mass.: Harvard University Press.

Calavita, Kitty. 1992. *Inside the State: The Bracero Program, Immigration and the INS.* New York: Routledge.

Castles, Stephen, and Mark Miller. 1998. *The Age of Migration: International Population Movements in the Modern World.* New York: Guilford.

Cornelius, Wayne A., Takeyuki Tsuda, Philip L. Martin, and James F. Hollifield, eds. 2004. *Controlling Immigration: A Global Perspective*, 2nd ed. Stanford, Calif: Stanford University Press.

Freeman, Gary. 1986. "Migration and the Political Economy of the Welfare State," *The Annals* 485 (May): 51–63.

Geddes, Andrew. 2003. *The Politics of Migration and Immigration in Europe.* London: Sage.

Ghosh, Bimal. 1997. *Gains from Global Linkages: Trade in Services and Movement of Persons.* London: Macmillan.

Gibney, Matthew J. 2004. *The Ethics and Politics of Asylum: Liberal Democracy and the Response to Refugees.* Cambridge: Cambridge University Press.

Givens, Terri E. 2005. *Voting Radical Right in Western Europe.* Cambridge: Cambridge University Press.

Hatton, Timothy J., and Jeffrey G. Williamson. 1998. *The Age of Mass Migration: Causes and Economic Impact.* New York: Oxford University Press.

Hollifield, James F. 2008. "The Politics of International Migration: How Can We 'Bring the State Back In?'" In *Migration Theory: Talking Across Disciplines,* edited by Caroline B. Brettell and James F. Hollifield. New York: Routledge.

_____. 2004. "The Emerging Migration State," *International Migration Review* 38: 885–912.

_____. 2000. "Migration and the 'New' International Order: The Missing Regime." In *Managing Migration: Time for a New International Regime,* edited by B. Ghosh. Oxford: Oxford University Press.

_____. 1997. "Immigration and Integration in Western Europe: A Comparative Analysis." In *Immigration into Western Societies: Problems and Policies,* edited by E. Uçarer and D. Puchala. London: Pinter.

_____. 1992. *Immigrants, Markets and States: The Political Economy of Postwar Europe.* Cambridge, Mass.: Harvard University Press.

Hollifield, James F., and Thomas Osang. 2005. "Trade and Migration in North America: The Role of NAFTA." *Law and Business Review of the Americas* 11, nos. 3 and 4: 327–360.

Hollifield, James F., Pia Orrenius, and Thomas Osang, eds. 2007. *Trade, Migration and Development.* Dallas: Federal Reserve Bank of Dallas.

Hollfield, James F., Valerie F. Hunt, and Daniel J. Tichenor. 2008. "The Liberal Paradox: Immigrants, Markets and Rights in the United States." *SMU Law Review* 16, no. 1: 67–98.

Huntington, Samuel P. 1996. "The West: Unique, Not Universal," *Foreign Affairs* 75, no. 6: 28–46.

_____. 2004. *Who Are We? The Challenges to America's Identity.* New York: Simon & Schuster.

Ireland, Patrick. 2004. *Becoming Europe: Immigration, Integration and the Welfare State.* Pittsburgh: University of Pittsburgh Press.

Jacobson, David. 1996. *Rights across Borders: Immigration and the Decline of Citizenship.* Baltimore, Md.: Johns Hopkins University Press.

Joppke, Christian, ed. 1998. *Challenge to the Nation-State: Immigration in Western Europe and the United States.* Oxford: Oxford University Press.

Keohane, Robert O., and Joseph S. Nye. 1977. *Power and Interdependence: World Politics in Transition.* Boston: Little, Brown.

Kettner, James H. 1978. *The Development of American Citizenship, 1608–1870.* Chapel Hill: University of North Carolina Press.

King, Desmond. 2000. *Making Americans: Immigration, Race and the Diverse Democracy.* Cambridge, Mass.: Harvard University Press.

Klausen, Jytte. 2005. *The Islamic Challenge: Politics and Religion in Western Europe.* New York: Oxford University Press.

Koslowski, Rey. 2000. *Migrants and Citizens: Demographic Change in the European System.* Ithaca, N.Y.: Cornell University Press.

Kyle, David, and Rey Koslowski. 2001. *Global Human Smuggling: Comparative Perspectives.* Baltimore, Md.: Johns Hopkins University Press.

Lahav, Gallya. 2004. *Immigration and Politics in the New Europe.* Cambridge: Cambridge University Press.

Martin, Philip L. 1993. *Trade and Migration: NAFTA and Agriculture.* Washington, D.C.: Institute for International Economics.

Massey, Douglas, et al. 2002. *Beyond Smoke and Mirrors: Mexican Immigration in an Era of Economic Integration.* New York: Russell Sage Foundation.

Messina, Anthony. 2007. *The Logics and Politics of Post–WWII Migration to Western Europe.* New York: Cambridge University Press.

Nugent, W. 1992. *Crossings: The Great Transatlantic Migrations, 1870–1914.* Bloomington: Indiana University Press.

Portes, Alejandro, and Ruben Rumbaut. 1996. *Immigrant America: A Portrait.* Berkeley and Los Angeles: University of California Press.

Rosecrance, Richard. 1986. *The Rise of the Trading State.* New York: Basic Books.

Rudolph, Christopher. 2006. *National Security and Immigration: Policy Development in the United States and Western Europe since 1945.* Stanford, Calif.: Stanford University Press.

Sassen, Saskia. 1996. *Losing Control? Sovereignty in an Age of Globalization.* New York: Columbia University Press.

Schlesinger, Arthur Jr. 1992. *The Disuniting of America.* New York: Norton.

Schuck, Peter H. 1998. *Citizens, Strangers and In-Betweens: Essays on Immigration and Citizenship.* Boulder, Colo.: Westview.

Smith, Rogers. 1997. *Civic Ideals: Conflicting Visions of Citizenship in U.S. History.* New Haven, Conn.: Yale University Press.

Soysal, Yasemin N. 1994. *Limits of Citizenship: Migrants and Postnational Membership in Europe.* Chicago: University of Chicago Press.

Straubhaar, Thomas. 1988. *On the Economics of International Labor Migration.* Bern: Haupt.

Teitelbaum, Michael S. 1980. "Right Versus Right: Immigration and Refugee Policy in the United States," *Foreign Affairs* 59, no. 1: 2–59.

Tichenor, Daniel J. 2002. *The Politics of Immigration Control in America.* Princeton, N.J.: Princeton University Press.

Torpey, John. 1998. "Coming and Going: On the State's Monopolization of the Legitimate 'Means of Movement,'" *Sociological Theory* 16, no. 3: 239–259.

Waltz, Kenneth N. 1979. *Theory of International Politics.* Reading, Mass.: Addison-Wesley.

Weiner, Myron. 1995. *The Global Migration Crisis: Challenge to States and to Human Rights.* New York: HarperCollins.

Zolberg, Aristide R., Astri Suhrke, and Sergio Aguayo. 1989. *Escape from Violence: Conflict and the Refugee Crisis in the Developing World*. New York: Oxford University Press.

Chapter 14: Civil Society

NO

Anderson, Kenneth. 2000. "The Ottawa Convention Banning Landmines, the Role of International Non-governmental Organizations and the Idea of International Civil Society." *European Journal of International Law* 11, no. 1: 91–120.

Barber, Benjamin. 1984. *Strong Democracy: Participatory Politics for a New Age.* Berkeley: University of California Press.

Beetham. David. 1999. *Democracy and Human Rights.* Cambridge: Polity Press.

Bessette, Joseph. 1980. "Deliberative Democracy: The Majority Principle in Republican Government." In *How Democratic is the Constitution?* edited by Robert A. Goldwin and William A. Schambra. Washington, D.C.: American Enterprise Institute.

Bob, Clifford. 2007. "Conservative Forces, Communications, and Global Civil Society: Toward Conflictive Democracy." In *Global Civil Society 2007/8*, edited by Martin Albrow, Helmut Anheier, Marlies Glasius, and Mary Kaldor, 198–201. London: Sage.

Bos, Adriaan. 1999. "The International Criminal Court: Recent Developments." In *Reflections on the International Criminal Court: Essays in Honour of Adriaan Bos,* ed. Herman A.M. von Hebel, Johan G. Lammers, and Jolien Schukking. The Hague: T.M.C. Asser Press.

Boutros-Ghali, Boutros. 1994. Speech to the 1994 DPI Annual Conference, United Nations, New York, September.

"Chairman Struggles to Define Compromise Package." 1998. *On the Record* 1, no. 14 (July 7).

Cohen, Joshua, and Joel Rogers. 1983. *On Democracy: Toward a Transformation of American Society.* Harmondsworth, U.K.: Penguin.

Edelman, Marc. 2003. "Transnational Peasant and Farmer Movements." In *Global Civil Society 2003*, edited by Mary Kaldor, Helmut Anheier, and Marlies Glasius. Oxford: Oxford University Press.

Edwards, Michael. 2003. "NGO Legitimacy: Voice or Vote?" *BOND Networker.* February.

Glasius, Marlies. 2004. "Who is the Real Civil Society? Women's Groups versus Pro-Family Groups at the International Criminal Court Negotiations." In *Gender and Civil Society*, edited by Jude Howell and Diane Mulligan. London: Routledge.

———. 2005. *The International Criminal Court: A Global Civil Society Achievement.* London: Routledge.

Gutmann, Amy, and Dennis Thompson. 1996. *Democracy and Disagreement.* Cambridge, Mass: Belknap Press.

Held, David. 1995. *Democracy and the Global Order: From the Modern State to Cosmopolitan Governance.* Cambridge: Polity Press.

Kirk, Alejandro. 1998. "Desaparecidos: A Festering Wound." *Terra Viva.* June 24.

McGrew, Anthony. 1997. *The Transformation of Democracy? Globalization and Territorial Democracy.* Cambridge: Polity Press.

Newell, Peter. 2005. "Climate for Change? Civil Society and the Politics of Global Warming." In *Global Civil Society 2005/6,* edited by Marlies Glasius, Mary Kaldor, and Helmut Anheier. London: Sage.

Onuf, Nicholas Greenwood. 1989. *World of Our Making: Rules and Rule in Social Theory and International Relations.* Columbia: University of South Carolina Press.

Pateman, Carole. 1970. *Participation and Democratic Theory.* London: Cambridge University Press.

Popper, Karl R. 1952. *The Open Society and Its Enemies.* 2nd ed. (revised). 2 vols. London: Routledge and Kegan Paul.

Rosenau, James. 1998. "Governance and Democracy in a Globalizing World." In *Re-Imagining Political Community: Studies in Cosmopolitan Democracy,* edited by Daniele Archibugi, David Held, and Martin Köhler. Stanford, Calif.: Stanford University Press.

Said, Yahia, and Meghnad Desai. 2003. "Trade and Global Civil Society: The Anti-Capitalist Movement Revisited." In *Global Civil Society 2003,* edited by Mary Kaldor, Helmut Anheier, and Marlies Glasius. Oxford: Oxford University Press.

Scholte, Jan Aart. 2001. *Civil Society and Democracy in Global Governance.* CSGR Working Paper No. 65/01, Centre for the Study of Globalisation and Regionalisation, Warwick University, U.K.

Van Rooy, Alison. 2004. *The Global Legitimacy Game: Civil Society, Globalization, and Protest.* Basingstoke, U.K.: Palgrave Macmillan.

Walker, Rob. 1993. *Inside/Outside: International Relations as Political Theory.* Cambridge: Cambridge University Press.

"We the Peoples: Civil Society, the United Nations and Global Governance." 2004. Report of the Panel of Eminent Persons on United Nations–Civil Society Relations. UN Doc. A/58/817, http://www.un-ngls.org/Final%20report%20-%20HLP.doc.

"Where Are Decisions Being Made?" 1998. *Terra Viva,* July 15.

Young, Iris Marion. 1997. "Difference as a Resource for Democratic Communication." In *Deliberative Democracy: Essays on Reason and Politics,* edited by James Bohman and William Rehg. Cambridge, Mass.: MIT Press.

_____. 2001. "Activist Challenges to Democracy." *Political Theory* 29, no. 5 (October).

INDEX